Change in
Contemporary South Africa

Perspectives on Southern Africa

Change in Contemporary South Africa

Edited by
Leonard Thompson
and
Jeffrey Butler

UNIVERSITY OF CALIFORNIA PRESS
BERKELEY AND LOS ANGELES

University of California Press
Berkeley and Los Angeles, California

Copyright © 1975, by
The Regents of the University of California

ISBN 0-520-02839-2
Library of Congress Catalog Card Number: 74-82851
Printed in the United States of America

Contents

TABLES

Acknowledgments

The starting point for this book was a conference held at Seven Springs Farm Center, Mount Kisco, New York, from 7 to 12 April 1974. We are indebted to the Ford Foundation for financial support—especially to Wayne Fredericks, David Smock, and William Herman. At Seven Springs, the director, Joseph Greene, Jr., with Mrs. Greene and their staff, created a marvellously congenial atmosphere for our debates. All the authors of the chapters in this book attended the conference, except Kogila Moodley, who was more productively engaged elsewhere, F. van Zyl Slabbert, who was a candidate in the general election and is now a member of the South African Parliament, and Tim J. Muil. Besides the authors, John Adams, Richard Boyd, Richard Elphick, William Foltz, Wayne Fredericks, Stanley Greenberg, Kenneth Heard, William Herman, Elizabeth Landis, William McClung, Ben Magubane, Richard Sklar, Newell Stultz, and Absolom Vilakazi participated in one or more sessions of the conference; and three Yale graduate students—Beverly Grier, John Hopper, and David Yudelman—assisted in various ways.

Subsequently, all authors have radically revised—in some cases virtually rewritten—the papers that were discussed at Seven Springs. Shelia Steinberg, as copy editor, had to reconcile a great range of styles and rules. We also gratefully acknowledge the vast amount of extra work put in by our secretaries—Rene Vroom at Rhodes, Dorothy Hay and Edna Haran at Wesleyan, and Cleo Thompson and Pamela Baldwin at Yale. And we thank the three institutions involved, Rhodes, Wesleyan, and Yale, for the facilities they provided and the hidden costs they met.

The editors alone are responsible for deciding who was invited to the conference, for arranging the agenda, and for seeing the book through the press. Other authors are responsible only for their individual chapters.

December 1974   **Leonard Thompson**   **Jeffrey Butler**

The Authors and Editors

Heribert Adam — Professor of Sociology and Political Science, Simon Fraser University

Jeffrey Butler — Professor of History, Wesleyan University

André du Toit — Senior Lecturer in Political Philosophy, Stellenbosch University

Sean Gervasi — Special Consultant, United Nations Special Committee on Decolonization

Philip Mayer — Professor of Social Anthropology, Rhodes University

J. Congress Mbata — Associate Professor of African Studies, Cornell University

Kogila A. Moodley — Graduate Student, University of British Columbia

Tim J. Muil — Senior journalist in Natal, specializing in African affairs.

Sam C. Nolutshungu — Lecturer in International Relations, University of Lancaster

Christian Potholm — Associate Professor of Government and Legal Studies, Bowdoin College

Albie Sachs — Lecturer in Law, University of Southhampton

Michael Savage — Senior Lecturer in Sociology, University of Cape Town

Lawrence Schlemmer — Director, Institute for Social Research, University of Natal, Durban, and member of the KwaZulu Planning Committee

F. van Zyl Slabbert — Member of the South African Parliament; formerly Professor of Sociology, University of the Witwatersrand

Leonard Thompson — Professor of History, Yale University

David Welsh — Senior Lecturer in African Government and Law, University of Cape Town

Francis Wilson — Senior Lecturer and Head of the Division of Research, School of Economics, University of Cape Town

Introduction*

LEONARD THOMPSON

The news about South Africa often seems contradictory. On the one hand, many items suggest that South Africa is an unstable country with a regime that is anathema to most of its inhabitants and condemned by the rest of the world. For example, during recent years there have been strikes of African workers in Durban, Johannesburg, and Namibia—events without precedent since African political organizations were banned and crushed in the early 1960s. There have also been disturbances in all the segregated universities that the government has created for African, Colored, and Asian students. Several of the African politicians who operate the institutions that the government has established in the "Bantu Homelands" have been demanding greater power for their administrations and also publicly articulating the grievances of the entire African population. South African athletes have been excluded from the Olympic Games and many other international sports competitions; and in 1974 a move to expel South Africa from the United Nations was stopped in the Security Council only by the vetoes of Britain, France, and the United States, and even so the South African delegation was then excluded from the proceedings of the General Assembly. Moreover, the guerrilla forces of the African liberation movements have been so successful in Portuguese territories that military officers seized power in Lisbon in April 1974 and began to decolonize Mozambique and Angola which, with Rhodesia, had previously functioned as buffers between the Republic and Black-controlled Africa.

On the other hand, other news items suggest that the South African regime is perfectly secure. For example, South Africa's gross national product has continued to soar; during 1974 the value of her principal export—gold—rocketed to $190 a fine ounce. European, American, and Japanese corporations have continued to increase their highly profitable participation in the South African economy by trade and investment and through their industrial subsidiaries. Moreover, although the government has been flexible in some respects (e.g., in not

---

*This Introduction has been revised in consultation with Jeffrey Butler and in the light also of comments by Richard Elphick, David Robinson, Newell Stultz, and Absolom Vilakazi.

preventing "homeland" leaders from speaking out), it has also been refining its extremely efficient apparatus of coercion. It has continued to eliminate potential leaders of resistance among the subject peoples by banning them, imprisoning them, or forcing them into exile. It has similarly been harassing White opponents. A commission has investigated the activities of the four White-controlled organizations that have been most critical of its racial policies—the University Christian Movement, the National Union of South African Students, the Christian Institute of South Africa, and the South African Institute of Race Relations—and parliament has passed legislation limiting access by "affected organizations" to funds from outside South Africa. And in a general election on 24 April 1974 the National party, which has held power without a break since 1948, was returned by the exclusively White electorate with an increased majority.

How do facts such as these fit together? Which of them reflect the dominant trends in South African society and point the way to the future: those that express the will and the power of the regime to maintain the essence of the present system, or those that foreshadow fundamental change? Are the White South Africans invincibly entrenched in their monopoly of real political power and their inordinate share of the wealth of the country? Or is White domination being undermined? Or are pressures building up that must eventually produce a cataclysm?

Obviously there are no simple answers to such questions. Despite some similarities with the American South as it was as recently as two decades ago, there has never been a society quite like modern South Africa, so not much is to be gained by extrapolating from other cases. A process model of the system would have to take account of continuous interactions across the major divide between White and Black, with Black as well as White initiatives and White as well as Black responses to initiatives from the other side. But if these were the only forces that the model included, it would be far from sufficient. It should also provide for interactions across the secondary divisions in South African society. Besides the numerous secondary ethnic divisions (Afrikaner-British; African-Colored-Asian; Xhosa-Zulu-Sotho-etc.) the entire ethnic spectrum is cut across by cultural, occupational, and regional groupings. Finally, a model of the dynamics of contemporary South Africa could not be complete without allowance for external forces, which are themselves varied and often ambiguous in purpose and effect.

One's capacity to assess the direction of change in any society, including contemporary South Africa, is also impeded by the problem of evaluating the relative significance of events that make newspaper headlines and trends that do not. The former may merely be expressions of the established forces (e.g., election results); the latter may be altering people's interests, perceptions, and behavior (e.g., the emerging class stratifications within the African, Colored, and Asian communities, as well as within the Afrikaner community).

This book grapples with these questions. The first two sections consider the processes of change that are taking place within the White and the African communities respectively. The third section examines the instruments of White domination, the role of an intermediate group (the Asians), and interactions among the races. The final section deals with the relationships between the Republic and the external world. Each section concludes with a chapter that seeks to draw the salient threads together and to establish the principal dynamics of the present time.

Nearly all the authors have had extensive experience of life in South Africa and many have a real stake in the country. They represent a variety of ethnic backgrounds, academic disciplines, and national, social, and professional affiliations. They also cover an ideological spectrum that, in other societies, would be regarded as extending from conservatives to socialists. However, supporters of the National party were not invited to contribute, so the reader will not find any overt defense of the government that has been in power since 1948.

Two questions lie at the heart of the book: what would constitute significant change in South Africa? And, to what extent is significant change made likely by contemporary trends and events? But a resolution of these questions is impeded by underlying problems of a general character: what measures of significance do we have? How do we assess the cumulative significance of trends and events?

The contributors are, we believe, agreed that by "significant change" we mean change in the structure of South African society, that is to say *radical redistribution of power and wealth*. This formulation recognizes that political and economic factors are inextricably involved; but it is open to different interpretations, especially as to the extent of redistribution that would constitute significant change in South Africa. All would agree that significant change would result in orders no longer being given exclusively in one direction—by Whites to Blacks; but most would go further and recognize that significant change will not have occurred unless all adult members of the population participate in the central political process ("majority rule") and there is also a substantial increase in the Black share of the resources and wealth of the country. A strong minority would go further still and specifically assert that in South Africa change would not be significant unless the outcome was a socialist order.

There are four main interpretations of the trends in contemporary South Africa. First, there is the possibility that the overriding trend is an accentuation of the authoritarian features that have been present in

South Africa since the nineteenth century. In support of this conclusion, there is a considerable body of evidence that the principal decision-makers in the ruling party are now concerned, above everything else, to maintain their power; that they have the will to adopt all measures that seem necessary for the purpose; and that they have the capacity to succeed for the foreseeable future. This conclusion follows from focusing on the power of the South African state: the laws in the statute-book; the bureaucratic structures that enforce the laws; the rapid identification and suppression of potential leaders of resistance and organizations that might foment resistance; and the build-up of advanced military and police technology. Within the White oligarchy, the reasoning continues, opposition to these trends is marginal; and, despite all their newsworthiness, the Bantustan politicians, the Black workers and peasants, the Black students, the new regimes in Angola and Mozambique, the South African guerrillas and exiled politicians, and the foreign critics do not have the capacity to overthrow the South African system. On the contrary, their main effect, in this interpretation, is to accentuate the authoritarian trend in South Africa by frightening the White population.

Secondly, there is the possibility that the dominant trend is what one contributor calls "reactionary reformism." By this he means that the government is indeed making "concessions" in response to internal and external pressures, but that these concessions are not promoting change in the basic structure of South African society. In support of this interpretation is the evidence that South African Blacks have recently been receiving increasing opportunities for political self-expression in the Bantustans and the Colored and Indian councils, and for material well-being in improved wages and fringe benefits. The government—this argument continues—has shrewdly drawn a distinction between those laws and practices that are essential for the maintenance of the overall system of White domination, which are being retained and enforced with the utmost rigor, and those that are not essential, which are being relaxed. In the former category are the White monopoly of the franchise for the central Parliament and White ownership of the bulk of the land, the natural resources, and the industries; in the latter, the so-called petty apartheid laws and regulations, such as those that segregate people by race in trains, buses, restaurants, hotels, libraries, and parks. It is compatible with this assessment that the Bantustans may become formally independent, that the wages of Black workers may rise appreciably, and that skilled Black workers and their families may acquire greater security of residence in the towns provided they abstain from founding organizations that could generate political power. But so long as the central government remains an exclusively White institution and Whites retain control of the bulk of the land and its resources, individual Africans will be utterly dependent on Whites for their livelihood, the Bantustans will be impoverished, neocolonial satellites of the Republic with scarcely any means for independent political action, and the new regimes in Mozambique and Angola, like those in Botswana, Lesotho, and Swaziland, will also be constrained to tolerate the *status quo* in the Republic. Skilfully applied, this policy is considered capable of defusing internal resistance, stabilizing South Africa's frontiers, disarming Western criticism, and creating ever-stronger ties between the Republic and Western political, commercial, industrial, and military interests.

The third interpretation is derived from highlighting much the same data as the second, but assessing them differently. According to this interpretation, whatever the intentions of White decision-makers may be, the Black peoples of South Africa are capable of turning the situation that now exists to their advantage, so that although current reforms may be reactionary in intent they will become revolutionary in effect. Some Black South Africans, the reasoning goes, are beginning to use the bargaining power that they have as indispensable workers in the modern industrial economy and as operators of the segregated political institutions that the government itself has created. Already they are influencing the central decision-making process and raising the political consciousness of the Black masses; and the consequence of these developments is that Blacks will inexorably generate enough power sooner or later to effect fundamental change.

Finally, there is the interpretation that the essential dynamics in REVOLUTION-ARY contemporary South Africa are a prelude to revolution. In this view, authoritarianism has been the central feature of South Africa throughout the twentieth century, and current developments are not beginning to rid South African society of its oppressive characteristics, but are merely seducing a few members of the Black population from loyalty to their race and class and substituting a particularly vicious form of neocolonialism for the earlier forms of oppression. However, after the interlude of relative impotence that followed the suppression of African political organizations in the early 1960s, the recent strikes in South Africa and guerrilla successes in neighboring territories show that the future lies with the Black liberation movement. Already a revolutionary consciousness is pervasive and it will generate overwhelming power once the Black peasants and townsmen are provided with guns, as they soon will be as a result of the liberation of Angola and Mozambique.

The logic of the fourth—the revolutionary—interpretation may not convince people who are impressed by the power of the South African state and the manipulative skills of the government. A skeptic may doubt whether the preconditions for guerrilla-led revolution exist in South Africa. What precedent is there for guerrilla forces overthrowing a modern industrialized State? In this vein, Heribert Adam concludes his chapter with the observation that "to take full account of a complex, contradictory reality distinguishes social science from wishful thinking." However, other contributors consider that no scholar is free from ideological assumptions that are derived from his class interests and that affect the questions he asks and the conclusions he reaches, and Albie Sachs reminds us that some visionaries, such as Rousseau, Lenin, Mao Tse-tung and Castro, have made more accurate predictions than social scientists. "All revolutions," writes Sachs, "are impossible to the social scientist until they happen; then they become inevitable."

These four interpretations of contemporary processes in South Africa are not fully spelled out in this book, which is structured along different lines. Nor, for the most part, do contributors associate themselves exclusively with any one assessment of the dominant trends. Indeed, it is the editors' impression that most contributors recognize that most if not all of the interpretations have some cogency. Moreover, they are not mutually exclusive, especially when they are related to each other over time. For example, authoritarianism accompanied by conservative-inspired reforms may in fact be the dominant processes at the present time; but the ground may simultaneously be being prepared for fundamental change, either through a gradual accretion of power in the hands of Blacks, or by outright revolution, or by some combination of both these processes.

The book pinpoints a series of major questions, the answers to which will probably determine the future of South Africa. Will such restraints as exist among White South Africans (for example, in the Progressive party and among the *verligte* Afrikaners) be overwhelmed by the authoritarian forces in White society? Will the African skilled workers and the Bantustan politicians and administrators become satisfied with the rewards available to them as a result of the modifications that are being made in the South African system, or will they associate themselves with the demands of the African masses? Will Colored and Asian South Africans identify with the Whites or the Africans? Will Western critics continue to exert pressure on the South African government and, if so, will their effect be blunted by the division between advocates of disengagement and advocates of radical reform? Will the South African guerrilla and political organizations in exile resolve their factional disputes and develop a coherent leadership and a realistic strategy for liberation? And, when the dust has settled on the decolonization of Angola and Mozambique, will the independent African states and the Communist powers provide more substantial support for the South African liberation movement than they have in the past?

There are still many gaps in our knowledge of crucial processes in contemporary South Africa. We know too little about how decisions are made within the White oligarchy. Political scientists have likened this problem to Kremlinology. We have still less knowledge, based on systematic research, about the inner dynamics of thought and behavior among the majority of Black South Africans. If we are better to comprehend the realities of this unique society, we need more thorough investigation of such factors; but, of course, it is not easy to conduct research on the most fundamental issues in so coercive and tense a society.

We realize that there are major omissions in this book, for no one book of reasonable length could deal in depth with all the factors related to change in so complex a situation. We had intended to include a chapter on the Colored people, but we were not successful. Moreover, there is not much analysis of South Africa's military strength, nor of the strategic significance of South Africa to the Great Powers, nor of the internal structures and tendencies in the neighboring territories. Nevertheless, we hope that the book does shed light on the most vital processes within contemporary South Africa and their relationship to external processes.

The book illuminates some of the remarkable complexities of contemporary South Africa and should assist readers in making their own assessments of events as they occur. Since the central issue in South Africa is racial inequality and oppression, the problems of the country are not likely to be ignored by the present generation of Americans and Europeans who claim to have renounced racism. Moreover, it is conceivable—and some contributors think it is likely—that southern Africa is a flashpoint, like Korea, Vietnam, and the Middle East, that may become the scene of a conflagration that would provoke serious tensions if not actual conflict among the Great Powers.

I
Changes within the
White Oligarchy

1
Afrikaner Nationalism, White Politics, and Political Change in South Africa

F. VAN ZYL SLABBERT

INTRODUCTION

South Africa is a political anachronism. Elsewhere there has been a radical redistribution of power in the last two centuries with the result that in most states the entire adult population can now participate in the political system. Furthermore, since World War II European states have dismantled their colonial empires; when Portugal has withdrawn from its remaining "overseas territories" this process will be nearly complete. However, decolonization has not always been accompanied by the elimination of racial stratification that was characteristic of many colonial societies. Britain transferred power to the white minority in South Africa, which has continued to resist the trend toward universal suffrage. Four million Whites in South Africa rule sixteen million Africans, two million Coloreds, and seven hundred thousand Asians.

The White minority has distinctive Afrikaans- and English-speaking sections. Although English-speaking Whites are not legally excluded from national politics, Afrikaners dominate the political system. In South Africa, therefore, if a change took place within the political system, another White party than the Afrikaner National party would gain control of decision-making; but if the political system itself were changed, Africans, Coloreds, and Asians might then become participants, as regards both electoral processes and decision-making.

3

The fundamental problem is essentially a Black-White problem. If Afrikaners lost control of decision-making to another White group, it would not necessarily lead to a major reduction of racial stratification in South Africa. The structural constraints are such that in the long run it may make no difference which White group is in control. Such a prediction would, however, rest on a priori assumptions that dispense with the need to examine carefully what takes place among the present holders of power.

This chapter presents old material in a new way. Its major theoretical point of departure can be found in treating the Afrikaner Nationalists as an independent variable in relation to political change and in arguing their strategic significance in terms of the following assumptions:

(a) The nature of present Afrikaner Nationalist control of political decision-making must be understood in terms of the development of Afrikaner bureaucracies in the period from 1910 to 1948.
(b) Political control achieved in 1948 resulted in the interlocking of Afrikaner bureaucracies and consolidated Afrikaner Nationalist unity.
(c) At present the quality of Afrikaner nationalism is changing away from political exclusivism, but political control is still entrenched in the same organizational structures. This broadens the base of political support, but does not significantly affect Afrikaner nationalist monopoly of political decision-making.
(d) Consequently an electoral change of government, particularly from "left" of the government, is extremely remote and poses the problem of the role of White electoral opposition in relation to the central problem of the devolution of political decision-making to Blacks.

Before elucidating these assumptions it should be made clear that in discussing Afrikaner nationalism the emphasis will not be on the ideological level (i.e., the major tenets or philosophical content of the belief system), but on the organizational conditions within which this ideology is reflected. These conditions provide basic indicators of the parameters within which a change in White political decision-making is possible.

THE BUREAUCRATIZATION OF AN ETHOS

One of the persistent myths of Afrikaner unity is the "all hearts beating as one" explanation. Frequently, Afrikaner Nationalist politicians and cultural leaders propagate the idea that every Afrikaner, even before the Great Trek, was part of a national movement that was the result of each Afrikaner individual's desire for freedom and independence, of his wish to maintain himself as part of an independent nation, and of his firm belief in the predestination of God. Largely, in the contemporary situation, this type of explanation becomes a self-fulfilling prophecy and, within certain spheres of Afrikaner cultural life, acts as a strong factor for political mobilization.

However, the mythical nature of this explanation becomes evident when events concerning White politics in general, and Afrikaner politics, in particular in the period from 1910 to 1948, are recalled. For example, an Afrikaner prime minister and general of the Boer War persecuting previous comrades in arms during the rebellion of 1914;[1] the political conflict between Smuts and Hertzog, both veterans of the war against British imperialism; an Afrikaner minister of religion, Malan, breaking away and attacking other Afrikaner leaders; Hertzog's rejection of the Broederbond and Malan's repudiation of the Ossewa Brandwag; the fact that the majority of the active servicemen during World War II were Afrikaners;[2] the uneasy truce between Malan, Havenga, and Strydom for the purposes of the general election that led to an Afrikaner victory in 1948.

These events illustrate the high degree of disunity and internal conflict within Afrikaner ranks, rather than the opposite. Yet, paradoxically, the groundwork for Afrikaner unity was also laid during this period. This came about because of the development of Afrikaner bureaucracies on diverse fronts and the role of elites within them.

Up to 1910 the majority of White people in South Africa lived in a rural society. One can safely assume that the 25 percent of the White population that lived in urban areas by 1910 consisted largely of non-Afrikaners.[3] Although Van Jaarsveld argues that Afrikaners had a collective consciousness by 1881, what he says about the early Dutch colonists largely remained true for the Afrikaners in the Republic and the Cape up to 1881, viz., that their unity was more a common response to environmental factors rather than a well-organized and articulated ideological movement.[4] Obviously a number of factors before 1910 were responsible for the Afrikaners developing some self-awareness, e.g., British occupation, territorial needs, and conflict with Blacks among others. Singer's concept of "ethnogenesis" is appropriate to developments within Afrikaner ranks during this period. This concept refers to a process whereby an ethnic group is formed and the final stage in this development depends on "the nature of the structures that

---

[1] D. Krüger, *The Making of a Nation* (Johannesburg, 1969), ch. 5.
[2] F. van Jaarsveld, *Van van Riebeeck tot Verwoerd: 'n Inleiding tot die Geskiedenis van die Republiek van Suid-Afrika* (Johannesburg, 1971), pp. 247, 250, 252.
[3] Ibid., p. 297.
[4] F. van Jaarsveld, *The Awakening of Afrikaner Nationalism* (Cape Town, 1961), p. 2.

develop the content of the group's self image and the shared conception of its destiny."[5]

The point is that these structures, as far as the Afrikaners were concerned, were either absent or had a very tenuous hold on them. The most important organizations were the churches and those organizations related to the language movement. The low level of Afrikaner urbanization at this stage, as well as poorly developed facilities for communication and transport, made regular meetings and reinforcement of common loyalties extremely difficult. The type of Afrikaner leadership during this stage is also characteristic. Most Afrikaner leaders either were charismatic personalities (Krüger, Steyn), or were prominent in the Afrikaner's military struggle (de Wet, de la Rey, Botha, Hertzog, and Smuts).

Thus one can argue that with the achievement of union in 1910 the Afrikaners might have shared a common awareness based on shared experiences, but they still did not have an organized unity of purpose. If there existed a collective ethos at this time it was not yet bureaucratized and there was no clear indication in which direction it would develop. This soon became apparent in the leadership struggles that developed among Botha, Smuts, Hertzog, and Malan. In fact the period between 1910 and 1948 was one characterized by factionalism, breakaways, redefinitions of loyalty, and the intermittent rejection of leaders, most of whom had been hailed as heroes a few years earlier. During this period there was not a single Afrikaner organization that seemed to enjoy the continued support and loyalty of the majority of Afrikaans-speaking people. One cannot take seriously the statement that it is a "traditional characteristic" of the Afrikaner that he has always been loyal to his church, political party, and organizations such as the FAK[6] especially if one remembers that in the election of 1943 Smuts had 650,000 votes in his favor against the 350,000 of the opposition.[7] To talk of a collective ethos as the main factor shaping the destiny of the Afrikaner during this period is a concession to ideology that distorts the truth.

And yet the process of bureaucratization of Afrikaner life, coinciding with the processes of urbanization and industrialization, provided the conditions for the development of such an ethos. If one could single out an outstanding feature reflecting the average Afrikaner's life during the period from 1910 to 1948, then it is the various processes by which the Afrikaner became an "organization man." On all

---

[5]L. Singer, "Ethnogenesis and Negro Americans To-day," in D. Wrong and H. Gracey, eds., *Readings in Introductory Sociology* (New York and London, 1967), pp. 436-7.

[6]D. Kotzé, *Positiewe Nasionalisme* (Cape Town, 1968), p. 55.

[7]van Jaarsveld, *Van Riebeeck tot Verwoerd*, p. 252.

fronts of Afrikaner life bureaucracies developed. On the economic front there were SANLAM, SANTAM, the Reddingsdaadbond, Federale Volksbelegging, Blanke Werkers Beskermingsbond, Ko-ordinerende Raad van Suid-Afrikaanse Vakbonde, Yskor, Foskor, and Evkom. In 1936 Dr. A. Hertzog formed a "reform league" to launch an attack on the leaders of trade unions with a large Afrikaner membership.[8] The cultural bureaucracies were the Akademie vir Taal, Lettere en Kuns, the Broederbond, the FAK, the Ossewa Brandwag, and SABRA. Political organizations included the South African National party (Botha); the National party (Hertzog); the United party (Hertzog and Smuts); the Purified National party (Malan); the New Order (Pirow); and the Afrikaner party (Havenga).

A common feature of all these bureaucracies is that the majority of people belonging to them spoke Afrikaans. Language was also one of the main issues in two other prominent Afrikaans bureaucracies, viz., the Afrikaans churches and educational institutions. The important point about these bureaucracies is that they originated in different spheres of activity often for diverse and even contradictory goals. However, in them elite groups could articulate the needs of their members as they conceived of them and interpret the events that the majority of Afrikaaners were experiencing. Above all, Afrikaner collective action could be mobilized on diverse fronts and the recruitment of regular leaders was made possible. The leaders encouraged, exhorted, and pleaded with Afrikaners to understand and to respond to the changes they were experiencing.

These changes were formidable and extensive. The two more important concerned the massive process of urbanization of Afrikaners and their economic position during a period of equally large-scale industrialization. An idea of the rate of urbanization can be gained if one remembers that in 1910 about 75 percent of Whites were rural inhabitants, whereas in 1961 only 16 percent of Whites still lived in rural areas. The dislocation brought about by such a migration as well as the economic position of the Afrikaner vis-à-vis non-Afrikaner Whites and Blacks was a common thread that linked various Afrikaner bureaucracies. Cultural, political, and economic organizations addressed themselves to this problem. Thus the Afrikaans churches held national conferences on the poverty of the Afrikaner in 1893, 1916, 1923 and 1934.[9] Hertzog used the state bureaucracy to introduce a "civilized labor" policy in 1924. The FAK, a cultural organization, organized a national conference in 1939 from which developed the Reddingsdaadbond—an organization specifically geared to the eco-

[8] M. Horrell, *South Africa's Workers: Their Organization and the Patterns of Employment* (Johannesburg, 1969), p. 10.
[9] van Jaarsveld, *Van Riebeeck tot Verwoerd*, p. 313.

nomic advancement of the Afrikaner. At the same time the Afrikaans language was both a symbol of this poverty and a strong unifying factor in education, literature, and religion.

Yet, despite all these changes and attempts to deal with them, political unity before 1948 remained an unattainable goal for Afrikaners. When it did happen it was brought about by events outside Afrikaner ranks. These events were symbolized by the vote in Parliament on September 4, 1939, when Smuts committed South Africa to World War II. This decision did not immediately lead to political unity but as Stultz argues persuasively, it lead to Hertzog's breaking away from Smuts and joining Malan in the Re-United National party.[10] Although Smuts won the election in 1943 with a handsome majority, his opposition consisted of all the realigned Afrikaner organizations. The average members may not have been as devoted and enthusiastic as their leaders, but the latter could negotiate and consolidate among themselves. They desperately needed political victory to consolidate the unity of Afrikaners. The declaration of peace and the immediate postwar situation favored this possibility. Malan and Strydom decided to forget their differences for the moment, but most important, Malan and Havenga decided to join forces for the 1948 election. On this agreement Stultz comments as follows:

> The importance to Malan of his alliance with Havenga became clear on the morning of May 28 when the final results of the general election were known. The Re-United National Party increased its representation in the House of Assembly by 22, from 48 to 70 members, but this total was still 7 seats short of an absolute majority. The Afrikaner Party however, won 9 of the 10 seats it had contested. For only the second time in the political history of the Union a government was turned out of office by voters.[11]

However, for the first time in the history of the Afrikaners, a fully fledged "organization man" was prime minister. He had been at various times a minster of religion, newspaper editor, and a party political leader. The "age of the generals" was past and Malan, in a sense, was a symbol of a collective ethos that had been bureaucratized. The victory of 1948 meant among other things that political power could now be used to give organizational consolidation to this ethos. Thus Krüger could write of the Afrikaners that only one year after political victory: "Afrikanerdom was closing its ranks, ignoring outside opinion and preparing to raise barriers to safeguard itself. The unveiling of the Voortrekker Monument on 10 December 1949 was a remarkable manifestation of this spirit."[12]

[10]N. Stultz, "South Africa's Apartheid Election of 1948 Reconsidered," *Plural Societies* (Autumn 1972), p. 26.
[11]Ibid., p. 32.
[12]Krüger, *Making of a Nation*, p. 250.

THE CONSOLIDATION OF AFRIKANER NATIONALISTS

It is generally agreed that the years immediately subsequent to 1948 was a period of consolidation.[13] This was mainly brought about by a process of Afrikaner organizations interlocking with one another at the top or elite level and clarifying the priorities for maintaining Afrikaner unity.[14] One clear priority that even today transcends whatever internal differences might exist among Afrikaner institutions is the necessity to maintain political control of South Africa. The almost hysterical reaction of the Afrikaner establishment to the breakaway of the HNP (a right-wing split from the National party) in 1969 under Dr. A. Hertzog gave evidence of how sensitive it was to any development threatening political unity. The time-worn bureaucratic slogan of "change from within" became the rallying cry against the HNP accusation that the National party was betraying the Afrikaner ethos for political pragmatism.

The interlocking of Afrikaner organizations has had a few important consequences for Afrikaners in South Africa. First, it has integrated leadership at the top of Afrikaner organizations. The trafficking of top personnel among these organizations (as in the case of Malan) has become a familiar occurrence: from professor-to-editor-to-prime minister (Verwoerd); from teacher-to-party organizer-to-cabinet minister (M. C. Botha); from minister of religion-to-editor-to-member of Parliament (A. Treurnicht); the list includes many of the best-known figures in Afrikaner public life.

Secondly, it has introduced a great deal of organizational independence into everyday Afrikaner life. A child born into an Afrikaans family could move from the cradle to the grave within the framework of Afrikaner organizations: Afrikaans nursery, primary, and high schools; in the place of Boy Scouts, the Voortrekkers; the equivalent of the Chamber of Commerce, the Afrikaanse Sakekamer; and then a variety of cultural organizations already mentioned, plus new ones that developed such as the Rapportryers and the Ruiterwag.

Thirdly, it has facilitated the formulation of collective goals for Afrikaner organizations and introduced a unity of purpose into corporate Afrikaner action (e.g., "the church" supports the government; "the universities" support "the church" and vice versa). This corporate support and interaction was in turn facilitated by the integrating role

[13] van Jaarsveld, *Van Riebeeck tot Verwoerd*, ch. 15; Krüger, *Making of a Nation*, chs. 15 and 16.

[14] For a behind-the-scenes look at how this was done, B. Schoeman's book, *Van Malan tot Verwoerd* (Cape Town, 1973), is as good as any in the field of political gossip.

performed by certain Afrikaner organizations with overlapping membership such as the FAK, National party, the churches, and the Broederbond. For example, according to H. Serfontein the FAK has affiliated to it more than 2,000 cultural, religious, and youth bodies to which it gives financial and organizational assistance. The Broederbond has in its membership: 24 principals of universities and teachers training colleges; 171 professors and 116 lecturers; 468 headmasters; 121 school inspectors; 647 teachers; 22 newspaper editors; 15 directors of the SABC; 59 secretaries of state departments, and 16 Judges.[15] Whether these figures are completely accurate is not as important as the underlying principle that such a voluntary organization performs an important integrating role with regard to other organizations. It is not so important within which particular Afrikaner organization a decision is eventually formalized as long as the taking of such a decision has the backing of other Afrikaner organizations with possible vested interests. It is this kind of information that can effectively be transmitted by an exclusive organization with extensive overlapping membership.

The fourth consequence of interlocking Afrikaner organizations has been to present the average Afrikaner with his own "establishment." If one could venture a generalization especially about the "white-collar" Afrikaans worker, it would be that he is an "organization man" with a well-developed awareness of "the establishment." Who exactly embodies the establishment can, of course, vary from one community to another, but for the average white-collar Afrikaner they are conceived of as having the power to ostracize him and to influence his career and general social acceptance.

These consequences are of course not unique to the case. Most cultural groups with a high degree of ethnocentricism have their own organizations and display a certain degree of exclusiveness. The distinctive feature of the Afrikaners as an ethnic group within the political context of South Africa is that through their control of political power, they not only govern themselves, but the whole country. This fact presents both advantages and liabilities.

The advantages for Afrikaner unity are almost self-evident. It seems highly unlikely that the Afrikaner government could mobilize support from all its adherents, be they Afrikaners or non-Afrikaners, on purely exclusive values or ideological grounds. Ideological appeals are usually more effective with culturally conscious Afrikaners in the fields of education, religion, agriculture, and some professional or semiprofessional occupations. The White "blue-collar" worker is far more

[15] *Sunday Times* (Johannesburg), 28 January 1973.

sensitive to issues that affect his immediate material interests. In this respect political power and the machinery of state become very effective instruments of manipulation.

The ratio between Afrikaners and non-Afrikaner Whites was already 1,790,000 to 1,150,000 in 1960, and 71 percent of the Whites employed by the state were Afrikaners.[16] Apart from Whites employed by the state it has become tradition in South Africa, since the implementation of Hertzog's "civilized labor" policy, that the government looks after the interests of the White worker. If it is taken into account that it is in any case the prerogative of the governing party in an electoral system to manipulate, within limits, wage increases and economic conditions to mobilize support, then it is clear that Afrikaner political control is reinforced not only by the "faithful," but by White workers who are more or less indifferent to higher ideals of Afrikaner Nationalism.

The picture that has been sketched of Afrikaner unity rests on two assumptions: that this unity could not have been consolidated without the use of political power; secondly, that political power alone could not have brought about this consolidation were it not for the existence of a variety of Afrikaner organizations within which elite groups could resolve differences and mobilize collective support. Thus, individually, political power and Afrikaner organizations were necessary but not sufficient conditions for unity; together they became sufficient and also interdependent.

Herein, then lies the strategic significance of Afrikaner Nationalists within the overall political context of South Africa. As a group they control political decision-making. This control is conceived by them as a precondition for their existence as a national group. This factor modifies a simplified collusion theory between Afrikaner political power and "English capital"; or a straightforward White-vs.-Black conspiratorial explanation; or the underlying assumption of Adam that the Nationalists are guided by a commitment to a new pragmatism.[17] What is true of all these types of explanations is the primary importance of the relative degree of affluence and economic security of the Afrikaners as a group. But so far this is mediated by the Afrikaners' control of the state and not so much of private capital. As the group in control, they have made and undoubtedly will make adjustments to the economy and to demands from the sociopolitical sphere, but the tempo of these adjustments has, no doubt for very different reasons, been a source of frustration for liberal economists and Black activists. The real source of this frustration could very well be the difference for

[16]van Jaarsveld, *van Riebeeck tot Verwoerd*, p. 275.
[17]H. Adam, *Modernizing Racial Domination* (Berkeley, Los Angeles, and London, 1971), pp. 169-83.

Afrikaner Nationalists between Afrikaner political control and White political control. Although a change of White government would not really mean a significant structural change vis-à-vis Blacks, there could be a difference between the approach to and tempo of adjustments of White government A (Afrikaner Nationalist) on the one hand, and White government B on the other.

The liabilities for Afrikaner unity revolve around the difficulty of coming to terms with societal issues in such a way that Afrikaner political support is not threatened. External to the Afrikaners, a major problem is that political decision-making does not only involve themselves. Internally, the dilemma is presented by the tension between maintaining an exclusive cultural identity and at the same time maintaining political control. To put it differently, Afrikaner Nationalists are making a cost benefit analysis of those "traditional characteristics" that are no longer regarded as necessary to maintain political control. It is not completely fortuitous that such an analysis can be afforded at a time when there is significant change in the economic position and degree of urban adjustment of Afrikaners generally. Some of the possible directions of this change can be evaluated within the framework of the preceding analysis.

THE POSSIBILITIES OF CHANGE

Recently, across the spectrum of "White politics" in South Africa, a great deal of attention has been given to changes within the Afrikaner ranks. A number of events have contributed to this interest: the rejection of HNP leaders by the Nationalist government and by the electorate; the ferment of discussion and questioning by Afrikaner intellectuals that sparked off the infatuation with the concept of *verligtheid* ("enlightenment"); and attitude surveys by Afrikaans newspapers and academics. For example *Rapport* (an Afrikaans Sunday newspaper) found that 75 percent of Afrikaners regarded themselves to be South Africans first and then Afrikaners; 69 percent of the supporters of the National party regarded themselves as *verlig*.[18] In five Dutch Reformed church congregations in Pretoria, 62.9 percent of the males and 52.2 percent of the females said it was not a sin to vote for a political party that did not explicitly maintain the Afrikaans language and traditions.[19] Afrikaner businessmen, academics, and editors have appealed for a more tolerant attitude on racial and economic matters. This tolerance as far as Afrikaner exclusivism is concerned is succinctly summarized by de Klerk (editor of *Die Transvaler*, an Afrikaans daily,

[18] *Rapport* (Johannesburg), 19 February 1972.
[19] C. Alant, *Navorsingsverslag oor Ondersoek na Vyf Gemeentes van die Nederduits Gereformeerde of Hervormde Kerk* (Pretoria, 1972), p. 47D.

and coiner of the term *verligtheid*). Under the significant caption of "Who are the Real Afrikaners" he pleads that "we should not disqualify Afrikaners who do not conform to our definition of what constitutes an Afrikaner. Today, being an Afrikaner has a much more heterogenous meaning. There are many kinds of Afrikaners but they are still Afrikaners."[20] He then goes on to state that one can find liberal, progressive, atheistic, and even Roman Catholic Afrikaners. Compared to the position adopted by D. J. Kotzé (professor of History at the University of Stellenbosch and chairman of the Rapportryers), in his book *Positiewe Nasionalisme*, de Klerk's plea is nothing less than cultural blasphemy.[21]

These events led to a rather widespread conclusion that Afrikaner Nationalists were becoming more enlightened, thus making a realignment of political affiliation in "White politics" possible, despite the fact that even at present no clarity exists as to what *verligtheid* is supposed to imply. The concept itself is fast losing any political significance due to the fact that political and quasi-political movements outside establishment Afrikaner ranks have appropriated it in order to draw support from Afrikaners. This is true of movements such as Verligte Action, the Progressive party, and the "Young Turks" of the United party. Within these movements the hope is cherished that somehow *verligte* Afrikaners will "save the situation." However if one confines the concept of *verligtheid* to the context within which it originated, viz., establishment Afrikanerdom, this enthusiasm appears to be somewhat misplaced.

Afrikaner *verligtheid* is not a movement. An Afrikaner *verligte* is an individual who experiences a conflict between the parochial demands of the particular organization within which he finds himself and the more universal demands of his occupation. Thus an Afrikaans minister of religion experiences a conflict between the demands made on him as a member of an Afrikaans church and as a member of the "Universal Christian church"; an Afrikaans businessman feels the tension between the demands of Afrikaner economic and political interests and the dictates of supply-and-demand economic rationality; an Afrikaner academic, especially in the humanities, has to come to terms with problems regarded as "controversial" within his own university and the predominant theories on those problems within the international academic community. Should such an individual make a public concession to these universal demands, he becomes a *verligte* Afrikaner. "Verligte Action" has thus far been individual action. The important point is that different Afrikaner *verligtes* respond to different and sometimes contradictory tensions. A minister of religion who

[20]*Die Transvaler* (Johannesburg), 21 December 1973.
[21]D. Kotzé, *Positiewe Nasionalisme*.

demands material sacrifice has something else in mind than the businessman who pleads for a high economic growth rate. This is an important reason why no unified *verligte* movement can develop. Different Afrikaners are simply *verlig* about different kinds of things.

The attention given to Afrikaner *verligtes*, especially by the English press, is due to the individually prominent Afrikaner *verligtes'* nuisance value to the establishment *within* the institutional boundaries of the Afrikaner organization in which he finds himself. The moment he moves outside these organizational boundaries the term *verligtheid* is no longer appropriate and he can be placed on the traditional liberal-conservative continuum of White politics. The dilemma of the Afrikaner *verligte* is precisely that what he has to say is regarded as far more important outside Afrikaner organizations than within them. At the same time he realizes that he can have a significant impact for change only if he can penetrate the oligarchy within his own organization. The price for this membership is conduct exactly contrary to what he is trying to do, viz., cautious conformity.

This brings the argument back to one of the central themes of the preceding analysis, viz., the power of Afrikaner Nationalist elites making up the establishment. Any fundamental split in Afrikaner unity will be manifested at the top, i.e., within the oligarchic ranks of Afrikaner organizations. Thus, for example if the synods of the major Afrikaans churches should consistently oppose the caucus of the National party, or vice versa, or if Afrikaans universities, in their corporate capacity through councils and senates, should denounce the caucus or synods, then significant threats to Afrikaner unity will arise. Up to now, the advantages brought about by political control have succeeded in transcending internal oligarchic dissension and maintaining a workable "elite consensus."[22]

It was indicated, however, that on this elite level the tensions between maintaining an exclusive cultural identity and political control are beginning to manifest themselves. It is against this background that de Klerk's statement can be understood. In the most general terms the implications for Afrikaner unity are that those organizations that give primacy to the rigid and exclusive cultural and moral values traditionally associated with Afrikaner Nationalists (for the sake of brevity they can be called cultural organizations), are beginning to lose influence in political decision-making, whereas those who can broaden the scope of political support are gaining in strength. In the latter category the Afrikaans press is definitely playing an important role much to the chagrin of Afrikaner cultural organizations such as the FAK, the Broederbond,

[22] Again Schoeman's book *Van Malan tot Verwoerd*, gives interesting insights into the personal infighting behind the scenes to reach such a consensus on a political level.

the churches, and the GHA (an organization whose goal is to promote the purity of the Afrikaans language).

These developments are symptomatic of the underlying structural changes that the Afrikaners have experienced, namely, adjustment to urban living and greater economic mobility. Because of this cultural organizations have a decreasing appeal for Afrikaners generally and consequently a concomitant loss of political influence. This is evident especially with regard to the more affluent upper-class Afrikaners who have become catholic in their tastes or generally bourgeois in their cultural pursuits, or both, and consequently, strongly hostile to Afrikaner traditionalism. Particularly interesting also is the antagonism between the "cultural purists" and the Afrikaner literary and artistic establishment. Afrikaans literature and poetry has up to the sixties always been a strong source of support for Afrikaner cultural organizations with its emphasis on "colloquial realism."[23] Since the sixties Afrikaans literature has revealed various phases of alienation from its own cultural background and is generally regarded with suspicion and sometimes openly rejected by Afrikaner cultural bodies.

Afrikaners lower down the economic scale are also becoming more indifferent to cultural organizations. Their concerns have always been immediate and material and their support could only be effectively consolidated after political victory had been achieved. Insofar as their political support entrenches their economic position, they are quite amenable to elite groups decorating it with ideological or cultural pretensions. To the extent that these cultural pretensions increasingly are no longer a precondition for political membership, the ranks of Afrikaner workers will be swelled by White workers generally, thus further decreasing the appeal of exclusive Afrikaner cultural organizations. It can be argued that the failure of the breakaway HNP to read these signs lent a particular pathos to their attempt to create a new political platform for the "true" Afrikaner Nationalist movement. On the one hand the Afrikaner worker had no major cause for dissatisfaction under the Nationalist government; on the other hand, the cultural organizations, without their alignment to political power, stood the chance of losing whatever remaining influence they had. From neither of these social groups was it realistic to expect a major defection to the HNP.

The conclusion to be reached from these changes is that a number of Afrikaner organizations that played a significant role in bringing about the political victory in 1948 are experiencing a form of goal displacement, i.e., they are still part of the machinery of political control, but not quite for the goals to which they pledged primary allegiance.

---

[23]N. Van Wyk Louw, *Vernuwing in Die Prosa* (Cape Town, 1970).

Although their allegiance is being compromised by the need to maintain political control, it does not seem in danger of being lost to the Nationalist government. Thus, Afrikaner political control in White politics seems to be ensured for the foreseeable future even though the quality of Afrikaner nationalism and unity is changing. This change away from cultural exclusivism will strengthen the appeal of the National party amongst the electorate making the maintenance of White privilege and prosperity the issue that will cut across the traditional (language) divisions in White electoral politics. Given the institutional support that the National party enjoys as the "political arm" of a Nationalist movement, the success it has in manipulating the issue of White prosperity and privilege will entrench its position even more within White politics.

So far, the analysis has focused almost exclusively on the "internal" dimension of Afrikaner politics. From this analysis three general inferences can be drawn:

(a) Given the historical development of Afrikaner political dominance, it is today quite clear that political decision-making is dominated by Afrikaner oligarchies.

(b) A decrease in cultural exclusivism in Afrikaner politics makes an increase in electoral support on grounds other than "tribal" or ethnic affiliation much easier.

(c) This has coincided with a greater emphasis on White rather than Afrikaner, privilege and prosperity as the predominant goal of political decision-making. The most important changes that made this possible were the urban adjustment of the Afrikaner and the drastic narrowing of the affluence gap between Afrikaners and other Whites since 1948.

However, when the analysis shifts to the "external" dimension of Afrikaner Nationalist control, i.e., in relation to the central political problem posed in the Introduction, namely, the devolution of effective political decision-making, these generalizations concerning developments within Afrikaner ranks, have to be modified in terms of their implications for White politics in particular and the problem of political change in general.

SOME IMPLICATIONS OF CHANGE

Insofar as one of the principal functions of political power is the redistribution of rewards and facilities, the Nationalist government finds itself subject to contradictory demands—the one electoral and the other not. The common denominator of White political contentment is the level of privilege and prosperity enjoyed. At the same time the lack of privilege and prosperity on the part of the Blacks is the most prevalent source of political discontent. The contradiction lies therein: the Nationalistic government or any White government under the present dispensation has to tread the path of White electoral politics to get into power and once there has to use its power to accommodate demands that do not exclusively originate from the electorate.

Within the framework of electoral politics, the government is vulnerable, i.e., removable, only from the Right (i.e., insofar as it can be outbid by an opposition party in maintaining or promoting White privilege or both). As has been pointed out, the possibility of this happening in the conventional electoral sense of the work seems remote at this stage. This was recently underlined by the defection of a prominent member of the United party (Marais Steyn) to the government. His considerable influence within the United party has been applied to recruiting the "grudge vote" in White politics. His defection coincided with internal and policy changes in the United party. The new emphasis on federalism and "shared power" (with Blacks), however ambiguously formulated, is easily exploitable by the Nationalist government as a "sell-out" to the Blacks—a point already repeatedly made in the Afrikaans press.

Within the framework of national (societal) politics, i.e., Blacks included, the government is under pressure from the Left (i.e., insofar as Black demands for improvement in material conditions can be effectively organized, articulated, and brought to bear on the government). To whatever extent this does happen, it immediately becomes an issue in White politics. This should not be understood in a simplified economic sense of what is given to the one (Blacks) is literally taken away from the other (Whites), but rather the point tries to indicate the political boundaries within which the problem of the devolution of power and consequently privilege and prosperity have to be evaluated. In terms of these boundaries, it is clear that the government will be extremely sensitive to the possibility of major fluctuations in the economy and other nonelectoral sources of pressure that cannot be readily translated for the voters.

Given these points, it follows that any White opposition political party left of the government will be forced into a reevaluation of its role as an opposition, as the option of getting into power becomes increasingly remote. With the decreasing importance of "White tribalism" as an issue in electoral politics a realignment of political affiliation on the liberal-conservative continuum seems plausible. In the general election held on April 24, 1974, conservatives in the official opposition, the United party, suffered a serious defeat at the hands of the Progressive party.

Given the relative security of the Nationalist government in the electoral sense, it is likely to become increasingly intolerant of any White forms of "liberal" nonparliamentary opposition. This was borne out in

1973 with regard to organizations such as the Christian Institute, SPROCAS, and NUSAS. It would appear that the major reason for this intolerance is the one given by the government when threatening to curb the English press in 1974, viz., that such forms of extraparliamentary opposition simply confuse and exacerbate the debate between White control and Black demands. The same intolerance has been evident with regard to nongovernment-sanctioned forms of Black opposition. The general pattern that seems to be emerging is that all forms of dissent or opposition, whether Black or White, will increasingly be forced into government-sanctioned organizations or institutions. This will ensure that the Afrikaner Nationalists will play a strategic role in whatever political change may come about.

2

Ideological Change, Afrikaner Nationalism and Pragmatic Racial Domination in South Africa

ANDRÉ DU TOIT

Ideological debates figure prominently in White South African politics. Political commentators tend to take ideological issues seriously and often attribute far-ranging implications for fundamental political change to some new trend or shift in the ideological climate. Thus, for example, the shift from *baasskap* apartheid to the rhetoric of "separate development" or the rise of the *verligte* Afrikaner Nationalists have been interpreted as indicative of major political realignments. Though tempting this is a more dubious enterprise than is often realized. It is highly problematic to what extent ideological changes can be used as a basis for making predictions about possible political change: the social functions and the political uses of ideology include the legitimation of the existing order, the *post hoc* justification of political policies and action, and the rationalization of sectional interests. Indeed, the issue of "false consciousness," i.e., the mystification of "real" interests or aims, is always relevant in ideological contexts. Still, ideologies may also have a strong prescriptive content, and even political myths or collective fictions may become potent forces for change when they are adopted as the unifying symbols and programs for action by important social groups. *Prima facie* that would certainly seem to be the case with Afrikaner nationalism.

Within the wider context of South Africa's racial oligarchy the hegemony of the Afrikaner section is a central feature. On any account this is a remarkable phenomenon. The White minority together do not constitute a full 20 percent of the total population; and though the Afrikaans speakers form a majority of the Whites, the active Afrikaner Nationalists are only a subsection of them, and at times very much of a minority group within Afrikanerdom. Moreover, the present century started with what seemed the total political defeat of the Afrikaner people at the hands of British imperialism, with the irrevocable loss of the republics. In the ensuing decades the breakdown of the traditional Afrikaner rural society in the wake of South Africa's progressive urbanization and industrialization became apparent, with the numbers of "poor Whites" in the towns increasing. From this condition of relative weakness and dispersion Afrikaner nationalism emerged at midcentury to gain the political ascendancy. The mobilization of a collective Afrikaner ethos played a crucial role in this process. And it has continued to remain important in the last twenty-five years, during which time the political hegemony of Afrikaner nationalism has not merely been maintained and consolidated, but its effective control of political decision-making has also been used to improve the social and economic position of the Afrikaners relative to the economically dominant English groups and to regulate race relations and the political economy of South Africa in unprecedented ways.

This chapter may be seen as companion piece to van Zyl Slabbert's assessment of the strategic significances of the Afrikaner Nationalists who are at present in power. It will not, like that chapter, be concerned with the organizational conditions of Afrikaner power, nor indeed with its material and social bases in general, but with the changing content of the Afrikaner ethos, and more particularly with the possible significance that such ideological change might have for general political change in South Africa. To obviate possible misunderstanding it must be stressed that this is an open-ended and indeed a skeptical inquiry. It will not be assumed, even implicitly, that ideological factors are, or can be, independent variables in political change. If ideological factors are relevant to political change in the required sense, even merely in affecting the manner in which the ruling group might come to terms with the problem of the devolution of political power to the Black groups (see Slabbert, p. 4), this needs to be demonstrated. In short, our investigation will have to raise such questions as the following: To what extent is Afrikaner nationalism an ideological movement? What are the functions and uses of the ideological component of the Afrikaner's collective ethos? Is there any reason why this ideological component would have a special relevance to fundamental political change? What ideological changes have taken place, why, and what are their implications?

Our approach will be analytical and critical. Rather than giving a direct survey of the data, we will primarily be concerned with the interpretive framework within which they might best be seen.[1] The argument will perforce be general and exploratory in nature, and at many crucial points it will become obvious how much further research is needed.

ATTITUDES, POLITICS AND IDEOLOGY

For the purposes of this inquiry it will be best to introduce a working definition of "ideology" as a comprehensive and articulated set of ideas and values held by a group or movement and to stress particularly its close relation to political action. Following Carl Friedrich we may thus define ideologies as "action-related systems of ideas," having the function of uniting a party or group for effective participation in political life, and consisting of a reasonably coherent body of ideas concerning both the rationale and the means for changing or maintaining a social and political order.[2] In this sense a political ideology is a more distinctive phenomenon than the general system of beliefs and values held in common by the members of a collectivity, however important the latter may be to general social theory. It also follows that nationalism, insofar as it primarily consists of a complex of political sentiments associated with the assertion of national identity, cannot without additional qualifications be considered as an ideology.[3] Given this definition, it will therefore not be a tautology to inquire whether Afrikaner nationalism is characterized by a specific ideological content. Granted that there is a nationalistic movement with a certain collective ethos we would like to know whether this also embraces a distinctive and coherent set of ideas about the kind of general social and political order that should be maintained or brought about. The central theme of this paper will be an investigation of the relation between Afrikaner nationalism, political ideology, ideological change, and general political change in South Africa. But first we must differentiate this from two other sets of considerations that are often used as springboards for predictions about political change, viz., changes in social

[1]We are particularly indebted to the invaluable fund of data contained in T. Dunbar Moodie's study *The Rise of Afrikaner Nationalism* (Berkeley, 1975), which we read in manuscript form. It would be impracticable to indicate this in every specific instance, or to show how and why our interpretation in some cases differs from his. We have also made extensive use of the material given in a number of papers by David Welsh, in particular "The Political Economy of Afrikaner Nationalism," in A. Leftwich, ed., *South Africa: Economic Growth and Political Change* (London, 1974), pp. 249-86.

[2]C. Friedrich, *Man and His Government* (New York, 1963), pp. 89-90.

[3]Ibid.

attitudes, and the consequences inherent in the processes of modernization.

A major purpose for taking ideology in this narrower sense is to differentiate a range of phenomena that may have a more direct bearing on political change. Thus it is common to attribute all sorts of political significance to persisting or changing patterns of social attitudes or racial prejudices among certain groups—the Afrikaners, in particular—but, generally speaking, both the theoretical and the empirical bases for this are very tenuous indeed. Since the pioneering studies by MacCrone there have been many South African attitude surveys, and in recent years considerable progress has been made both in the quantity and the quality of the data that have become available.[4] The significance of these findings for political change are, however, quite another matter. As the more sophisticated analyses of such surveys show the relation between, for example, racial prejudice and material interest is a close and complex one; and a strong case can be made for the thesis that the prevalent pattern of racial prejudice derives from the historical pattern of conquest and is reinforced by the structural conditions of the present conflict situation.[5] Similarly Orpen has argued that "authoritarianism" is much less useful as a possible explanatory factor for high levels of racial prejudice in a situation, like that of South African society, where discriminatory patterns are the norm.[6] In short, it is doubtful that authoritarianism, ethnocentric and particularistic attitudes, or racial prejudices can be viewed as independent variables in this context: they are effects and symptoms or at best intervening variables rather than the underlying causes of political change.

No doubt the existing patterns of prejudice and the prevalent set of social attitudes at any given time form an important constraint on the action that might be undertaken by political leaders, particularly with respect to specific issues or policy changes. We may also accept, in more general and theoretical terms, that the presence of a shared value system providing the binding force for a common society is a necessary

[4]A survey of the existing literature is given in J. Mann, "Attitudes towards Ethnic Groups," in H. Adam, ed., *South Africa: Sociological Perspectives* (London, 1971), pp. 50-72. Recent surveys include L. Schlemmer, *Privilege, Prejudice and Parties: A Study of Patterns of Political Motivation among White Voters in Durban* (Johannesburg, 1973); H. van der Merwe et al., *White South African Elites: A Study of Incumbents of Top Positions in the Republic of South Africa* (Cape Town, 1974); and regular opinion polls by Mark en Meningsopnames **(Pty) Ltd. for *Rapport* (Johannesburg) and by Market Research Africa Ltd.**

[5]Schlemmer, *Privilege, Prejudice and Parties*, pp. 51-4.

[6]C. Orpen, "The Effect of Cultural Factors on the Relationship between Prejudice and Personality," *Journal of Psychology*, 78 (1971): 73-9, and "Authoritarianism and Racial Attitudes among English-Speaking South Africans," *Journal of Social Psychology* 84 (1971): 301-2.

precondition for the development and stability of a democratic polity,[7] and that in this respect plural societies are structurally conducive to polarized conflict or coercive domination.[8] But in the latter case it is not so much the content or the development of the value system itself, but rather the underlying structure of the society, i.e., the pattern of cross-cutting memberships and multiple affiliations or of deep and mutually reinforcing cleavages, and the political procedures and institutions by means of which generalized conflict is managed that is of decisive import.[9] And in the former case the relation between a specific set of personal prejudices or attitudes and a given public policy need not be a direct one, but can take varied and complex forms. Thus it is quite possible that, despite the well-known disagreements on public policy between the Cape liberals and the northern segregationists, there was nevertheless at the beginning of the twentieth century a fundamental unity of white South African attitudes (see Welsh, p. 52) on race relations. The point is that, unlike their northern counterparts, the Cape politicians did not view their franchise policy or its social and political implications as an extension of their own private attitudes. John X. Merriman, in a letter to Smuts in 1906 could write, "*To me personally* the idea of a Native franchise is repellent but I am convinced that it is a safety-valve and the best safety-valve,"[10] and Onze Jan Hofmeyr in a similar vein declared, "*whatever my own prejudices of colour and race may be*...the political and social security of white South Africa would be none the worse for retaining the goodwill of the five million of coloured and aboriginal inhabitants...and for reconciling them with our political institutions."[11] In other words, personal values, attitudes, and prejudices need not necessarily be translated into equivalent public policies. The attempt to do this is the mark of a certain kind of politics that sets up essentially private virtues as political ideals and then "naturally" mobilizes and manipulates consonant feelings, attitudes, and prejudices among the general public in its cause. As against this it may well be argued, as Dahrendorf has done with reference to the German experience, that a sense of the common good and of public virtues is the hallmark of democratic politics: "The constitution of

[7]S. Cilliers, "A Sociological Perspective on the South African Situation" in his *Appeal to Reason* (Stellenbosch, 1971), pp. 2-4.

[8]L. Kuper, "Plural Societies: Perspectives and Problems," in L. Kuper and M. Smith, eds., *Pluralism in Africa* (Berkeley, 1969), pp. 10-16.

[9]This argument is developed in ch. 10 of P. Randall ed., *South Africa's Political Alternatives: Report of the SPROCAS Political Commission* (Johannesburg, 1973).

[10]Letter dated 19 July 1908, in W. Hancock and J. van der Poel, ed., *Selections from the Smuts Papers*, vol. 2:448. Italics mine.

[11]Quoted in E. Walker, *The Cape Native Franchise* (Cape Town, 1936), pp. 10-11. Italics mine.

liberty works, then, to the extent to which a society is dominated by public virtues (as opposed to private virtues)... A functioning liberal democracy does require...a sense of public life, of the market of men and its rules, which is lacking in those who have fallen in love with private virtues."[12] In this connection Lawrence Schlemmer has made some interesting comments on the significance, in a multiracial society, of the well-known stereotype concerning the Afrikaner's frank and forthright expression of his racial attitudes and prejudices in contrast with the more civil—or hypocritical—attitudes of the English.[13]

For our purposes the relevant point is, however, that the different links between private attitudes and public politics may, in part, be a matter of the operative political ideology as an intervening variable. A widely accepted ideology may, on the one hand, serve as a barrier against the introduction of certain kinds of social attitudes into the public domain, and, on the other hand, operate as both the conductor and the authorization of others.[14] In different ideological climates the same set of attitudes may thus remain private or gain public acceptability. Thus surveys in the Western liberal democracies have generally found a surprising prevalence of authoritariansim and illiberal attitudes among the rank and file, as opposed to the elite group's public commitment to democratic values.[15] Conversely, in the very different context of contemporary Afrikaner politics researchers have found evidence that members of the elite group might privately avow relatively liberal attitudes, but are severely inhibited from giving any public indication of this.[16] In the circumstances we can only conclude that the independent significance for political change of whatever changing or persisting patterns of attitudes might be found among

[12]R. Dahrendorf, *Society and Democracy in German* (London, 1967), pp. 30, 310.

[13]Schlemmer, *Privilege, Prejudice and Parties*, pp. 54-6; see *also* H. Adam, *Modernizing Racial Domination* (Berkeley, 1971), pp. 81f. and the implicit argument of O. Krause, "Trends in Afrikaner Race Attitudes," in N. Rhoodie, ed., *South African Dialogue* (Johannesburg, 1972), pp. 532-42.

[14]It is unnecessary and indeed it would be misleading, to restrict "ideological politics" to the mobilization of moral beliefs or personal attitudes and prejudices for political ends, and to maintain that the democratic politics of pragmatic bargaining and consensus is not "ideological." See ch. 6, "Status Politics and New Anxieties; On the Radical Right and Ideologies of the Fifties," in D. Bell, *The End of Ideology* (New York, 1962), pp. 120f. In terms of our working definition of ideology both kinds of politics may be considered as equally "ideological."

[15]*See* e.g., S. Lipset, *Political Man* (New York, 1960), ch. 4.

[16]H. van der Merwe and J. Potgieter, "Fundamentale Verandering Binne die Afrikaanse Strukturele Raamwerk?" (Paper given at the workshop on Die Afrikaner Vandag, Centre for Inter-Group Studies, Cape Town, March 1974, and published in part in *Deurbraak* [July 1974]).

various groups is highly doubtful. It may be more relevant to investigate those articulated and coherent sets of ideas and values bearing more directly upon political action—i.e., ideologies that may or may not be held by such groups, in our case by the Afrikaners.

MODERNIZATION AND AFRIKANER CULTURE

Another more general line of argument proceeds from the presumed effects of modernization and urbanization on the content and solidarity of Afrikaner nationalism. It is argued that the social forces to which the Afrikaners are increasingly being exposed in the secular and cosmopolitan urban environment, as well as the general requisites for participation in an industrial economy, must undermine the traditionalist values of Afrikaner society, reduce their sense of exclusiveness, and make them more amenable to political liberalization.

There can be no doubt about the urbanization of the Afrikaner. The structure and values of the traditional Afrikaner rural community or *Boeresamelewing* have been thoroughly transformed into the largely urban, more secular and diversified Afrikaner society of today.[17] But the implications for the politics of Afrikaner nationalism are by no means obvious, and speculations about its possible fusion into a wider (White) South African nationalism due to the "anglicization" of Afrikaner life-styles may be premature. It is not merely a matter of the anachronistic rhetoric of Nationalist cultural leaders who insist on the continuing significance of the traditional agrarian values for the urbanized Afrikaner.[18] The romantic stereotypes of the "true Afrikaner" can readily be recognized for the nostalgic and quasi-normative projections that they are.[19] The point is rather that, so far from being rendered obsolete by the modern urban world, Afrikaner nationalism as a political movement essentially is a modern and urban phenomenon.

It is precisely the central argument of van Zyl Slabbert's paper that the necessary precondition for the mobilization and consolidation of a unitary Afrikaner nationalism in power is to be found in the development and diversification of the organizational substructure—which coincided with the processes of Afrikaner urbanization and modernization. The social and cultural consequences were also profound. The Afrikaner was not simply exposed to and assimilated by an alien urban

[17]D. Welsh, "The Political Economy of Afrikaner Nationalism," in Leftwich, ed., *South Africa*; also "Urbanization and the Solidarity of Afrikaner Nationalism," *Journal of Modern African Studies* 7 (1969): 265-76.
[18]F. van Jaarsveld, *Afrikaner Quo Vadis?* (Johannesburg, 1971); also D. Kotzé, *Positiewe Nasionalisme* (Cape Town, 1968).
[19]*See* e.g., B. Booyens, "Die Wesenskenmerke van Ons Identiteit" (Paper given at the FAK Jaarvergadering, Bloemfontein, July 1970).

environment. The wide range of separate Afrikaner institutions and organizations largely succeeded in isolating the Afrikaner from other groups so that in the towns he tends to live in a predominantly Afrikaner environment. David Welsh has aptly termed this process the "encapsulating of the urban Afrikaner,"[20] and it might indeed be compared with the characteristic phenomenon of *verzuiling* in Dutch social and cultural life. If this strategy has, in a sense, prevented the threat of the "denationalizing" of the urban Afrikaner, it has also completely transformed his traditional collective ethos into something very different. Contemporary Afrikaner nationalism is quite simply a different kind of social and cultural phenomenon than the "natural" and spontaneous sense of solidarity and the cohesive integration of a number of central values that might have characterized the traditional Afrikaner community. In an incisive paper on "'Afrikaans' en 'Kultuur'" the philosopher D. C. S. Oosthuizen has accordingly argued that modern Afrikaner nationalism should be regarded as a form of neoconservatism. The very process of mobilizing Afrikaner cultural identity presupposes the breakdown of the traditional order and responds precisely to the needs and pressures of the urban context by propagating such an intensely conscious identification with "Afrikaner" values and symbols.[21]

It is in this light that one should see what appear at first sight to be rather surprising findings showing little or no correlation between the extent of urbanization of Hillbrow or Durban Afrikaners and their level of ethnic prejudice or the possible liberalization of their political and moral attitudes.[22] These and other surveys do show a positive correlation between higher income groups and an increasing degree of racial tolerance.[23] But characteristically it emerges that even for this group of *verligte* or "enlightened" Afrikaners "the sense of cultural identity is [still] a major determinant of their political attitudes.[24] Whatever the significance for political change of the *verligte* Afrikaners

[20]Welsh, "Political Economy of Afrikaner Nationalism," p. 266.

[21]D. Oosthuizen, "Analyses of Nationalism" (Occasional Papers of the Department of Philosophy, Rhodes University, vol. 1, no. 1 January 1965): 1-18. For an attempt by an Afrikaner intellectual to give a critical reinterpretation of nationalism and to find an alternative and more positive stance toward the modern secular world, *see*, J. Degenaar, *Op WegNa'n Nuwe Politieke Lewenshouding* (Cape Town, 1963) and "Nasionalisme," in J. Degenaar, W. A. de Klerk, M. Versfeld, eds., *Beweging Unitwaarts* (Cape Town, 1969).

[22]H. Lever and O. Wagner, "Urbanization and the Afrikaner," *Race* 11 (1969); Schlemmer, *Privilege, Prejudice and Parties*, p. 12.

[23]*See*, e.g., *Rapport*, 5 December 1971, for an opinion poll on White attitudes to the appointment of Black postmen; *also* Schlemmer, *Privilege, Prejudice and Parties*.

[24]Schlemmer, *Privilege, Prejudice and Parties*, p. 50; *see also* pp. 56-7.

might turn out to be, the mere fact that they are a modern and, indeed, a modernizing elite is highly ambivalent. In fact, they may well serve as a further instance of the general observation by Cynthia Enloe that the political development of an ethnic group need not necessarily terminate in the set of values that is usually associated with modernity.[25] She is of course dissenting here from the more orthodox view, which might be described as the modernization assumption. This is closely allied, in turn, to the so-called industrialization hypothesis, which maintains that the requirements of sustained economic growth and the logic of industrial development will eventually override the "irrational" features of racial discrimination. The industrialization hypothesis has been increasingly disputed, particularly following on Blumer's contrary contention that industry tends to adapt to the system of race relations.[26] The relevant point in the present context is that even in an urban and industrialized context the traditional self-definition of a group, or its conscious redefinition of its collective identity, may, in large part, continue to shape its members' perceptions of their values, needs, and interests. This self-definition may be vague and latent, largely a matter of sentiment, or it may take the form of an articulated and coherent ideology. Which is the case with Afrikaner nationalism?

AFRIKANER NATIONALISM AND IDEOLOGY

Notwithstanding reports to the contrary, Afrikaner nationalism in its historical development was not primarily an ideological movement. From the first stirrings of a wider group consciousness among the scattered rural population of the Cape Colony and the republics in the 1880's through the cultural and language movements of the early twentieth century to the collective political ethos of the modernizing Afrikaner elite that is now in power it has had a much more variegated career than it is usually credited with. Nor should this be surprising. The last 100 years have seen dynamic transformation of South Africa from an agrarian society to a modern industrial state; based on a minority group in a complex plural society the Afrikaner movement had to find its course amid changing patterns of new political and economic alignments. In the circumstances it is only to be expected that the Afrikaner's political history should not be a steady and unswerving progress toward some predefined goal, but rather constitutes a complex pattern of apparent demise, resurgent assertion, consolidation, fusion, and faction. At different times the activities of the Afrikaner

[25]C. Enloe, *Ethnic Conflict and Political Development* (Boston, 1973), pp. 8ff.
[26]H. Blumer, "Industrialisation and Race Relations," in G. Hunter, ed., Industrialisation and Race Relations (Oxford, 1965); *see also* F. Johnstone, "White Supremacy and White Prosperity," *African Affairs* 69 (1970): 124-40.

movement was centered mainly in the cultural and educational sphere, the political arena, or the socioeconomic front, with a markedly different *modus operandi* in each case. Different organizations—the church, the National party, the Broederbond, the Ossewa Brandwag—in turn acted or claimed to act as the main bearers of the Afrikaner idea, sometimes in a harmonious cooperation with a mutually agreed allotment of different spheres of interest, in other cases resulting in schismatic conflicts involving the very definition and direction of the Afrikaner movement itself. If there is an underlying continuity in the collective ethos that persisted throughout this whole period it can be found only in a diffuse set of sentiments associated with common language, history, and identity. Consider, for example, the following characteristic attempt by an Afrikaner leader to formulate the "Afrikaans Idea": "It is rather difficult to give a verbal definition of the 'Afrikaans Idea.' It is something that is more susceptible to intuition than to description. In general, the scope of the 'Afrikaans Idea' can be summarised as that which pertains to our ethnic identity ('*volkseie*') on each of the many terrains of our Afrikaner life ('*volkslewe*').[27]

That there is some common ideological core that persisted through all the successive transformations of the Afrikaner movement and that provided the basis for these developments, or a standard against which they can be measured is a fiction with little or no historical basis. Of course it is a central tenet of the Nationalist faith that there is but a single national ideal, and when in the later stages of Afrikaner nationalism, particularly in the thirties and forties, more explicit conceptualizations and ideological variants were beginning to be produced, these were quite naturally claimed by their exponent to be merely a statement of what had always been the Afrikaner position. A number of critical and polemical accounts of Afrikaner nationalism have similarly imputed a central ideological significance to one or other of the versions of Christian nationalism, or have used the National Socialist ideas entertained in certain Afrikaner groups in the later thirties and early forties as the key to all subsequent developments in Nationalist policy and politics.[28] In neither case will the claim to, or imputation of, ideological coherence bear a close examination of the actual historical career of Afrikaner politics and thought.

[27]T. Donges, *Die Afrikaanse Gedagte en die draers daarvan*, (Johannesburg, 1953).

[28]*See* e.g., B. Bunting, *The Rise of the South African Reich* (Harmondsworth, 1964); A. Hepple, *Verwoerd* (Harmondsworth, 1967); W. Vatcher *White Laager: The Rise of Afrikaner Nationalism* (New York, 1965). A more wide-ranging discussion of Afrikaner nationalism and ideology is given by D. Worrall, "Afrikaner Nationalism: A Contemporary Analysis," in C. Potholm and R. Dale, eds., *Southern Africa in Perspective* (New York, 1972), pp. 19-30.

Obviously a vast and complex subject, it also has clear relevance to our general theme. The possible significance of "ideological change" for the strategic position of the Afrikaners in the modern South African oligarchy, and hence for political change in the sense of a devolution or liberalization of the present political order, is closely bound up with the extent and degree to which Afrikaner nationalism is or is not a coherent ideological movement. If a specific ideological component is indeed central to Afrikaner solidarity and if it is indeed a major determinant of Nationalist policy and politics, then a change in the content of this ideology or a slackening of ideological control may conceivably have considerable consequences. But this involves a pretty big assumption, and a larger view of the history of the Afrikaner movement would require a careful reconsideration of the possible force and scope of such a hypothesis.

NONIDEOLOGICAL COMPONENTS OF THE AFRIKANER MOVEMENT

It will be argued that, particularly in the formative stages of its development, the crucial role in the articulation of the Afrikaners' collective ethos was not played by ideological factors, in the sense specified above. Obviously this cannot be adequately documented in the present context; we will merely give a brief survey of these various nonideological factors and indicate their contribution to the Afrikaner movement and collective consciousness.

It is common ground that the nascent Afrikaner group consciousness developed through a history of contact and clashes with such outgroups as the Africans and the English.[29] The movement that gave shape and content to this diffuse and unstructured self-definition of the Afrikaners as a distinctive ethnic group in the first two decades of the century was not primarily a political nationalism. It was the language and cultural movement. The sharpest spur was at first provided by the threat of Milner's anglicization policy immediately after the Anglo-Boer War, but increasingly education and language were perceived as general instruments for creating and preserving a separate social and cultural identity. This is clearly stated in Malan's address on the language issue in 1908:

> Give the young Afrikaner a written language which is easy and natural for him, and you will thereby have set up a bulwark against the anglicisation of our people.... Raise the Afrikaans language to a written language, make it the bearer of our culture, our history, our national ideals, and you

[29]See F. van Jaarsveld, *Die Ontwaking van die Afrikaanse Nasionale Bewussyn 1868-1881* (Johannesburg, 1959); H. Giliomee, "The Development of the Afrikaner's Idea of Himself," in H. W. van der Merwe, ed., *The Afrikaner Today* (forthcoming).

will thereby raise the people who speak this language.... The Afrikaans
Language Movement involves nothing less than the awakening among
our people of a feeling of self-respect and to the calling of taking a worth-
ier place in world civilisation.[30]

Education in the mother-tongue and the replacement of Dutch by the
erstwhile socially inferior patois of Afrikaans in school, church, press,
and university, as much as the creation of an original Afrikaans literature, these were the major landmarks for the cultural movement
leading to the recognition of Afrikaans as an official language in 1925.
In short, the issue of the Afrikaans language itself first served as a
shibboleth, and then as a major mobilizing factor for Afrikaners
during the early decades after union.

A crucial role in shaping the self-definition of the Afrikaners was also
played by the cultivation of a particular historical consciousness, a set of
ideas and feelings about the divine calling and special destiny of the
Afrikaner people as manifested in their history.[31] Conscious analogies
between Afrikaner history and that of Israel in the Old Testament
were already current in the nineteenth century, and this sense of being
a chosen people was later revived and codified in a particular interpretation of Afrikaner history, which centered on selected crucial events
like the Great Trek. Dunbar Moodie has analyzed this "sacred history"
of the Afrikaner from Slagtersnek to the death of Jopie Fourie in terms
of the concept of a "civil religion," a received faith implanted at school
and ritually celebrated on the Day of the Covenant (16 December) and
other *Volksfeeste* at the holy places or *Volksmonumente*. He perceptively
shows the significance of certain central themes such as the prominence given to a cycle of suffering and death rather than to the heroic
feats of national leaders, or the emotive image of the ever patient and
suffering, but strong, "Afrikaner Woman."[32] The development of this
special historical consciousness should itself be seen in its own historical
context. After long periods of disinterest it gained increasing momentum in the thirties—i.e., at the time of the Depression and the height of
the "poor White" problem—culminating in the massive mobilization of
popular sentiment and fervor with the centennial celebration of the
Great Trek in 1938. This had a decisive impact on the consolidation of
the now increasingly urbanized Afrikaner's group consciousness. In

---

[30]D. Malan, "Dit is ons Ernst," in S. W. Pienaar, ed., *Glo in U Volk:
Dr. D. F. Malan as Redenaar, 1908-1954* (Cape Town, 1964), p. 175. Freely
translated.

[31]*See* F. van Jaarsveld, "The Ideas of the Afrikaner on his Calling and
Mission," in *The Afrikaner's Interpretation of South African History* (Cape Town,
1964), pp. 1-32.

[32]Moodie, *Afrikaner Nationalism*, ch. 1.

Moodie's words, "for all that it may have been incoherently and graphically comprehended, there can be little doubt that by 1938 the ordinary Afrikaner had made the main themes of the civil religion part of his own emotional identity."[33] But what was the political content of this identity? The popular fervor resulting from the massive mobilization of the civil religion at most created a diffuse sentiment for *Volkseenheid* ("ethnic or national identity"—the term is characteristically ambiguous), which may or may not imply a special political unity. Likewise the idea of a special calling of the Afrikaner people tends to be quite unspecified or to become completely circular: Afrikaners received their identity in their divine calling and the divine calling was that they should have a special identity as Afrikaners.[34]

The specific political content of the Afrikaner movement was, of course, supposed to be provided by the republican ideal. The republican issue, however, hardly ever became a matter of practical politics, and its significance should be seen in a different light. Initially an active republicanism had fitfully been kept alive in the northern provinces by those who had not quite given up all hope for the restoration of the Boer republics. The political order of Kruger's republic was indeed of a very specific kind, and not merely in the special function of the presidency, but in the sovereignty given to the *Volkswil* ("will of the people"), amounting almost to a kind of direct democracy—within the very limited definition of the citizenry, of course—and a very flexible constitution.[35] Though "Krugerism," combining a sort of popular egalitarianism with strong executive power in contrast to the more "constitutionalist" outlook of the Cape, was for a time a distinctive strand in Afrikaner nationalism there has been little or no serious efforts to reestablish anything like this political order in place of the parliamentary democracy of White South Africa created at union. In fact, the republican ideal did not even appear in the first program of principles of the National party in 1914, nor did it figure in the earliest activities of the Afrikaner Broederbond from 1919. When the republican issue was reasserted it was mainly though perhaps never entirely—the Republican Draft Constitution is a case in point though its precise political significance is characteristically obscure and controversial—as a symbol of South African national sovereignty as against the constitutional connection with the British Crown. Together with the national

---

[33]Ibid., p. 21.
[34]*See* Ibid.,pp.163-164 with reference to P. Meyer, *Die Afrikaner* (Bloemfontein, 1941).
[35]W. Kleynhans, *Volksregering in die Z. A. Republiek: die Rol van Memories* (Pretoria, 1966); for a brief survey and discussion, *see* S. Patterson, *The Last Trek: A Study of the Boer People and the Afrikaner Nation* (London, 1957), pp. 74-8.

flag and anthem the republican ideal became one of the many symbolic
issues that absorbed much of the political attention of Nationalist politicians for several decades. The significance of such symbolic matters to
nationalist politics was well expressed by Malan when he introduced
the South African Nationality and Flag Bill in 1926:

> The Bill is certainly the most important Bill which has been introduced
> into the House for many a year.... The Bill has got nothing to do, at least it
> has got nothing directly to do, with the material welfare of the country. It
> has no direct connection with what is generally called "bread-and-butter-
> politics," important and necessary as "bread-and-butter-politics" may be
> in its place. On the other hand, it has to do with the nation itself.... It has to
> do with the unity of our national life and sentiment.... It has to do with
> what is more than material possessions, with what is, after all, even more
> than our fatherland; it has to do with the soul of our nation... with the
> establishment of an outward and visible symbol of our independent
> nationhood, and our national status.[36]

The creation of the Republic of South Africa in 1961 was the concluding symbolic event of this kind, a change in its formal constitutional
status, but not a new political order in any real sense.

More important for the emerging structure of modern South Africa's political economy was the increasing harnessing of forces for a
movement of social emancipation and economic advancement of Afrikaners as a group during the twenties and thirties. The "civilized labor"
policy of Hertzog's Pact government sought to safeguard the White
worker against direct competition from the African; the Carnegie
Report and the 1934 Volkskongres aimed at the social and economic
upliftment of poor Whites to forestall the development of class differences dividing Afrikaners as well as to prevent the creation of a multiracial urban proletariat; and the Ekonomiese Volkskongres of 1939
announced the intended entry of the Afrikaner into business and
finance. We are not concerned now with the manner in which this
social emancipation was realized, but rather with its crucial part in the
diversifying Afrikaner movement. The mobilization of Afrikaner
"identity" was, after all, not merely a cultural or symbolic matter. It is
rather an apt illustration of Heribert Adam's perceptive proposition:
"instead of reifying cultural heterogeneity as a quasi-natural state of
affairs, ethnic identifications should be seen as [in part] the result of
efforts by underprivileged groups to improve their lot through collective mobilization."[37]

[36]Quoted in D. Krüger, ed., *South African Parties and Policies, 1910-1960*
(Cape Town, 1960), p. 122; it is significant and characteristic that Kruger
should devote a major part of this source book (section 3 pp. 115-238) to
material dealing with "the development of constitutional independence and
the symbols of nationhood."
[37]Adam, *Modernizing Racial Domination*, p. 22. *See also F. van zyl Slabbert,*

Finally, within the arena of White politics the numerical majority of Afrikaans-speaking voters ensured that ethnic politics, either playing up an exclusive Afrikaner nationalist orientation, or playing it down and seeking a wider White consensus, would be a constant factor. In this connection there were major differences between such political leaders as Hertzog and Malan on the interpretation of "*volkseenheid*," i.e., whether the cultural and social encapsulation of the Afrikaner should also be reflected on the highest level of national politics. The isolationist strategy of Malan's Purified National party, which became intimately associated with the civil-religion and the social-emancipation movement during the thirties and early forties, thus increasingly gained the significance of a quest for Afrikaner supremacy.[38]

To summarize, it is possible to identify a whole range of nonideological components that played an important role in the formative stages of modern Afrikaner nationalism: the language and cultural movement, the special historical consciousness and civil religion, a set of nationalist political symbols, the social emancipation movement of a relatively deprived and upwardly mobile group, and a strong tradition of ethnic politics. In short, Afrikaner nationalism provides an excellent illustration of the general remarks by Carl Friedrich:

> Nationalism is typically devoid of any specific notions concerning the political and social order as such, except to insist that the order be in keeping with "national traditions." This term is usually so vague as to have no specific institutional or behavioral content, until converted into a specific ideology.... Something more than nationalism—for example, socialism—is needed. In contrast to the rival ideologies of democratic liberalism, democratic socialism and communism, nationalism has little or nothing to propose beyond the insistence upon national independence in politics, economics and culture.... It may, however, become associated with any of these rival ideologies and is in fact so associated.[39]

IDEOLOGICAL VERSIONS AND VARIANTS
OF AFRIKANER NATIONALISM

It was only in the latter half of the thirties and during World War II that significant efforts were made by various Afrikaner intellectuals and political activists to elaborate coherent political ideologies for the Afrikaner movement. Again this should be seen in a proper historical perspective. The given context of twentieth-century Afrikaner politics and political thinking had been the system of parliamentary democracy

---

"Cultural and Ethnic Politics," in R. Randall ed., *Towards Social Change: Report of the SPROCAS Social Commission* (Johannesburg, 1971), pp. 65 ff.

[38]*See* Moodie, *Afrikaner Nationalism*, pp. 186 ff.

[39]Friedrich, *Man and His Government*, p. 90.

derived from Britain. At no time, however, did this "democratic" tradition develop into positive ideological commitment to the basic tenets of liberal democracy—as witness the records of Nationalist governments on the franchise, or civil rights and rule of law issues. Socialism, on the other hand, was an almost unknown quantity. Ever since Smuts's *A Century of Wrong* in 1899 Nationalist politicians employed a strong line of anticapitalistic rhetoric, denouncing it as "imperialistic," "cosmopolitan," and "materialistic," and at times some of them evinced a (qualified) sympathetic interest in the possible relevance of socialist theory and principles.[40] The coalition with the Labour party in the twenties did not make such strange bed-fellows at all—though the content of the Labour party's brand of South African socialism is, of course, another story. The Afrikaners' very much changed attitudes toward capitalism today date largely from their increasing share in the South African economy and the strategy to conquer or "Afrikanerize" capitalism initiated by the Ekonomiese Volkskongres of 1939.[41] Still, to say the least, Nationalist governments have never been ideologically committed to the system of free enterprise and have been active in establishing large state and semistate enterprises as well as practising a substantial degree of planned state control of the economy.

The ideological activity of the thirties and the war years was mainly of two kinds. In the first place, attempts were made to produce an intellectual and indeed a philosophical, framework for the Afrikaans movement in terms of Christian Nationalism. This proved to be an elusive and hybrid construction. In part it consisted of a more intellectualized restatement of the familiar nationalist themes concerning the special historical calling of the Afrikaner people by God. This was done with the help of neo-Calvinist theology and philosophy—and accordingly much has been made ever since of the Afrikaners' "Calvinistic" lineage[42]—derived from the thought of the Dutch statesman and theo-

[40]*See*, e.g., D. Malan, "Socialism" (Lecture delivered before the Graaff-Reinet Literary Society, Graaff-Reinet, 1913); also, "Christendom en sosiale Rekonstruksie" (C.S.V., 1923), reprinted in *Pro Veritate* (15 October 1962). *See also* the attitudes expressed toward the Bolshevist Revolution in 1919 by Malan and Hertzog as quoted in Bunting, *Rise of the South African Reich*, pp. 34-5, 38; P. Meyer, *Die Stryd van die Afrikanerwerker* (Johannesburg, n.d.).

[41]D. Welsh, "Urbanization and the Solidarity of Afrikaner Nationalism," *Journal of Modern African Studies*, 7 (1969):271; *see also* Moodie, *Afrikaner Nationalism*, pp. 203-204, 207.

[42]For a critical view and analysis, *see* J. Loubser, "Calvinism, Equality and Inclusion: The Case of Afrikaner Nationalism," in S. Eisenstadt, ed., *The Protestant Ethic and Modernization: A Comparative View* (New York, 1968), pp. 367-83.

logian, Abraham Kuyper. In effect this Christian-nationalism shaded into, and was closely bound up with, a general system of neo-Calvinistic metaphysics and social philosophy developed by a school of thinkers mainly based at the University of Potchefstroom (in conjunction with their colleagues of the Vrije Universiteit of Amsterdam).[43] However, what the relation between these elaborate intellectual constructions and the mainstream of the Afrikaner political movement was or is, is far from clear. Certainly no major Nationalist political leader from Hertzog and Malan to Vorster can be called a Christian Nationalist in any sense closely related to this body of thought, nor was it ever taken up as its political program by any significant political group in the public arena.[44] In fact, with the exception of educational policy, it is not clear what the relation of Christian Nationalism to political action might be. At best it can be taken as a *post hoc* rationalized legitimation of the Afrikaner movement, but it contains few if any prescriptive principles for the political order.

In the second place, a number of young Afrikaner intellectuals and political activists experimented with elements of the authoritarian ideologies current in Europe. In an influential pamphlet N. J. Diederichs propounded a nationalistic credo couched in terms of a voluntaristic social metaphysics with obvious affinities to the intellectual roots of German romantic nationalism.[45] More specifically, semi-fascist political ideas and sentiments were espoused, ranging from expressions of anti-Semitism and a general disillusion with parliamentary democracy and party politics, to sympathetic considerations of corporative social ideals and positive adherence, to the leadership principle and the idea of the authoritarian state.[46]

It is very difficult to assess the impact, at the time, of this ideological ferment on the Afrikaner political consciousness, or to gauge its lasting influence. In fringe groups like the Greyshirts or Pirow's New Order

[43]*See* H. Stoker, F. Potgieter and J. Vorster, eds., *Koers in the die Krisis*, 3 vols (Stellenbosch, 1935, 1940, 1941); H. Stoker, *Die Stryd om die Ordes* (Potchefstroom, 1941); L. du Plessis, *Die Moderne Staat* (Stellenbosch, 1951).

[44]In the thirties and during World War II there seems to have been a close connection between the Potchefstroom-based Christian-Nationalists and the Afrikaner Broederbond, though this is of course very difficult to document.

[45]N. Diederichs, "Nasionalisme as Lewensbeskouing," (Bloemfontein, 1935). Moodie has termed this a "neo-Fichtean" social metaphysics; *see Afrikaner Nationalism*, pp. 156-159 and p. 154 m.9.

[46]*See* P. Meyer, *Demokrasie of Volkstaat* (Stellenbosch, 1942); also *Die Toekomstige Ordening van die Volksbeweging in Suid-Afrika* (Stellenbosh, 1942); O. du Plessis, *Die Nuwe Suid-Afrika: Die Revolusie van die Twintigste Eeu* (Cape Town,1942). For a general survey, *see* F. van Heerden, "Nasionaal-Sosialisme as Faktor in die Suid-Afrikaanse Politiek 1933-1948" (D. Phil. Diss., University of Orange Free State, Bloemfontein, 1972).

National-Socialist ideas were explicitly expounded. More important
perhaps, was that leading figures in the Ossewa Brandwag, the mass
movement that arose out of the great upsurge of civil religious fervor
in 1938, were also increasingly attracted to somewhat similar notions.
This was indeed one of the major issues in the traumatic schism
between the Ossewa Brandwag and the National party. After the break
with the Ossewa Brandwag in August 1941 the National party consistently came out in defense of the parliamentary system and of constitutional methods, though it had itself voiced ambiguous attacks on the
so-called British-Jewish capitalistic pseudo-democracy.[47] In the debate
on the "Republican Order" and the controversial Republican Draft
Constitution during 1941 and 1942 the leadership of the Nationalist
party steered an ambivalent and elusive course claiming that elements
of the New Order were incorporated in its own platform but avoiding
any outright support for the National Socialist ideology.[48] There were
undoubtedly serious ideological overtones to the bitter and complex
in-fighting, conciliatory moves, and realignments between the different Afrikaner factions during the war years,[49] but these are very hard
to pin down. To a certain extent this is due to the amount of ideological
confusion and ambiguity that was current. Many individuals certainly
showed a great deal of vagueness and flexibility about what crucial
political principles entailed. But a major factor undoubtedly was the
degree of political opportunism involved: German victory in the war
was expected to be the prelude to the ascendancy of Afrikaner
nationalism in South Africa, and at the time this expectation informed
the content and tone of many of the new ideological platforms. This
expediency is explicitly acknowledged as such in the major work, *Die
Stryd om die Ordes* (1941), of the neo-Calvinist philospher H. G. Stoker
where he argues for the superficial compatibility of Christian Nationalism and National Socialism: "this means that there will be a resem-
blance between our action and striving and that of National Socialism.... We are going to emphasize the valid moments in National
Socialism. We have no choice but to do this, since today Liberalism is
our major national enemy, and the plight of our people our most
urgent need. We Calvinists are going to appear as National Socialists in
our conduct. Only in appearance. For we are not National Socialists."[50]
In the aftermath of the German defeat such ideological notions,

[47]*See* van Heerden, "Nasionaal-Sosialisme ... Politiek," pp. 363 ff.
[48]*See*, e.g., *Die Republikeinse Orde* (Cape Town, 1941), containing the statement of the Federal Council of the Herenigde Nasionale Party on 10th April
1941 and two speeches of Dr. Malan given in March 1941.
[49]*See* M. Roberts and A. Trollip, *The South African Opposition, 1939-1945*
(London, 1947).
[50]Stoker, *Stryd om die Ordes*, pp. 271-2. My translation.

equally expediently, disappeared from public discussion. On the whole there does not seem sufficient reason to attribute more than a transitory and peripheral significance to these "alien" ideologies,[51] though they did form part of many an Afrikaner leader's political education.

In short, the decade before 1945 saw a heightened ideological consciousness among Afrikaner intellectuals and politicians, but this did not yet lead to the emergence of a coherent and generally accepted political ideology.

APARTHEID AS AN IDEOLOGY OF AFRIKANER NATIONALISM

It was only in the decades following on the victory of the Nationalist party in the general election of 1948 that Afrikaner nationalism became associated with a specific political ideology, that of apartheid. If the consolidation of political supremacy was an important precondition for the achievement of Afrikaner unity on the organization level (see Slabbert, p. 11), much the same holds true concerning the process of ideological unification. If we accept that "the victory of 1948 meant...that political power could not be used to give organizational consolidation to [the Afrikaners' collective] ethos" (Slabbert, p. 8), then it must also be stressed that this collective ethos was not a preexistent unified ideology, but that once in power Afrikaner nationalism for the first time became unified on an explicit ideological basis, that of apartheid. Moreover, there is a profound inner connection between the content of the ideology of apartheid and Afrikaner political supremacy. As Slabbert points out, the distinctive feature of the Afrikaners' control of political power in South Africa's plural society is that through it, they not only govern themselves, but the whole society. This is reflected in the central concern of the ideology of apartheid not with the self-definition of the Afrikaner movement, which predominated in the earlier stages, but with the structuring of race and social relations in the society as a whole, thus, as it were, with its "external" relations. Two series of questions arise from this: first, what is the relation between apartheid and the previous ideology of race relations of White South Africa, that of segregation? And, secondly, what is the ideological connection between apartheid and the earlier self-definitions or collective ethos of Afrikaner nationalism itself?

The prevailing consensus within White politics on race relations or "Native Policy" during the first half of the century was couched in terms of segregation, though within its general framework there was of

---

[51]*See* the characteristic discussion by a mainstream Afrikaner intellectual of the "alien" ideologies in C. Rautenbach, *Ons Lewensopvatting* (Pretoria, 1940); *see also* G. van Pittius, *Aktuele Politieke Vraagstrukke* (Pretoria, 1945), ch. 2.

course room for different interpretations and emphases. Though
segregation has been claimed to be specifically an Afrikaner tradition
and was very much associated with Hertzog, its intellectual and political
origins are much more varied. The roots of segregation can be traced
back to Shepstone's policies in colonial Natal[52] even more directly than
to the Boer republics; it found influential expression in the recommendations of the Lagden Report (1903 to 1905); it was first explicitly
adopted as part of its program of principles by the Labour party in
1910[53]; it was articulated and propagated by a number of English-
speaking writers such as Bell, Wybergh, Evans, Silburn, Loram, and
the early Brookes; and even the Cape liberals' attitude toward it was
much more ambiguous than is often thought.[54] In ideological terms
segregation was compounded of a number of diverse components, including a degree of territorial and residential separation, discriminatory social and economic practices such as the color bar, the assumed
superiority of European "civilization," the maintenance of indigenous
tribal structures, the necessity of White political control, the duty of
"trusteeship," and the regulated availability of Black labor for the economy, among others. A typical example is to be found in the statement
of "Native Policy" in the first program of principles of the National
party in 1914: "In our attitude towards the Natives the fundamental
principle is the supremacy of the European population in a spirit of
Christian trusteeship utterly rejecting every attempt to mix the races.
The Party further aims at providing the Native with the opportunity to
develop according to his natural talents and aptitudes."[55] There are
evident incongruities and potential conflicts between these diverse
principles and aims, but then it was very much a characteristic of segregationist thinking not to insist on ideological consistency. As a social
and political program segregation tended to take the form of a number
of piecemeal actions aimed at relatively limited goals, and it also entailed a substantial degree of laissez-faire. In mode and intent it was
largely pragmatic and orientated toward preservation of the status
quo, though with the gathering pace of social and economic change the
segregationist proposals of the Fagan Commission of 1946 to 1948 acquired rather different political implications than, say, the segregationist Land Act of 1913.

The continuities with the segregation era in the actual policy and implementation of the Nationalist government after 1948 is often very

[52]See D. Welsh, *The Roots of Segregation: Native Policy in Colonial Natal,
1845-1910* (Cape Town, 1971).
[53] See Krüger, *South African Parties and Policies*, p. 73; *see also* the speech by
Col. Creswell in ibid., p. 14.
[54]See Legassick "The Making of South African 'Native Policy', 1903-1923:
The Origins of 'Segregation' " (Unpublished paper, London, 1972).
[55]Quoted in Krüger, *South African Parties and Policies*, p. 71.

much underestimated, but on the ideological level apartheid did indeed mark a new phase. Apartheid differed from the rather eclectic ways of segregation above all in the insistence on the consistent application of a few basic principles, primarily that of separation, aimed at ensuring White survival and Afrikaner identity. It is important not to confuse this clearcut ideology with the sometimes hesitant and erratic development of official policy. The program of apartheid was indeed implemented through such legislation as that on race classification, the prohibition of mixed marriages and sexual intercourse between members of different race groups, the separate use of public facilities, group areas, and the like. The ideology also required that separation be consistently imposed in organized sport and recreation, cultural associations, educational and religious institutions, and social intercourse in general—something that was only partially attempted and never wholly achieved. Above all, according to the ideology of apartheid, the principle of separation should also apply in the political and economic sphere to the point of complete territorial separation or partition. At this point the official policy-makers balked to follow the rigid logic of consistent separation, though it was constantly invoked to justify discriminatory actions of various kinds.

The ambiguous status of a group like the Colored people could not be accommodated in such a mode of thought: every exception or compromise was an intolerable "thin end of the wedge." At the same time as insisting on consistent separation in all spheres it was possible, again at the ideological level, to replace the traditional assumptions of an inherent White superiority, or the notion of perpetual trusteeship and domination, with a generous recognition of the equality and right to self-determination of such separate(d) nations. Unlike segregation, and unlike the actual practice of *baasskap* apartheid, such an ideal of "total separation" could in principle be squared with liberal ideals, as Hoernlé already argued in 1939:

> This is segregation as an instrument of domination; segregation which joins the segregated in the same social and political structure with the dominant white group, but subjects them to the denial of important rights and keeps them at a social distance implying inferiority.... Total separation envisages an organisation of the warring sections into genuinely separate, self-contained, self-governing societies, each in principle homogeneous within itself, which can then cooperate on a footing of mutual recognition of one another's independence.[56]

Liberal or not, such a program of total separation must obviously entail a comprehensive restructuring of the social and political order. In

---

[56]R. Hoernlé, *South African Native Policy and the Liberal Spirit* (Johannesburg, 1945), pp. 168-9.

contrast to the piecemeal laissez-faire and pragmatic character of segregationist politics, the ideology of apartheid thus has a revolutionary
and totalitarian intent. Also, it is important to note that, whatever
recognition of political rights might be extended to other nations on a
theoretical basis of separation, the corollary is an absolute and unquali-
fied claim to Afrikaner (or White) political sovereignty and control
within their "own areas." In other words, while the ideologist of apartheid is prepared to recognize the eventual rights and sovereignty of
Black separate(d) states, separation is also intended to rule out any
question that Black consent may be relevant to the legitimacy of White
sovereignty and rule in the South African "heartland."

   This brings us back to the inner connection between the program of
apartheid and the maintenance of political power. In an obvious sense
the powers of government, not just formally within the realm of White
politics but in relation to society as a whole, are a necessary precondition for the realization of the ideological goals of apartheid. But
conversely these goals, the aims of total separation, serve to legitimize
present Afrikaner (or White) rule of that society; they serve to legitimize whatever coercive measures might be necessary to attain the aims
of separation itself; and they serve to legitimize whatever coercive
measures might be necessary to bolster the necessary Afrikaner (or
White) rule as such. The ideology of apartheid is thus not just a rationale for "domestic decolonization,"[57] but inherently it is equally a rationalization of the coercive order of domestic imperialism.

   The major outlines of this ideology of apartheid first emerged from
Afrikaner Nationalist circles during the forties. The intellectual roots
may go back even further, but they have not been clearly identified. In
the early forties Afrikaner intellectuals published a number of pamph-
lets on race policy,[58] and Geoff Cronje's seminal work 'n Tuiste vir die
Nageslag is reputed to have been widely used as study material by cells
of the Broederbond before its publication in 1945.[59] In 1944 the FAK
organized a Volkskongres on the race problem and in preparation for
the general election of 1948 the National party set up the Sauer
Commission to formulate its policy on apartheid. The adoption of
apartheid as a crucial plank in the National party's political platform in
1948 is widely held to have been more for its appeal as a unifying slogan

[57]See D. Worrall, "Separate Development: 1970: The Politics of Domestic
Decolonization" (Paper read at the S. A. Institute of Race Relations, Cape
Town, January 1970).
   [58]P. Coertze, F. Language, and B. van Eeden, Die Oplossing van die
Naturellevraagstuk (Stellenbosch, 1943).
   [59]G. Cronje, 'n Tuiste vir die Nageslag (Johannesburg, 1945); See also
G. Cronje, W. Nicol, and E. Groenewald, Regverdige Rasseapartheid (Stellen-
bosch, 1947).

than as an endorsement of the full ideology of apartheid. Once in power, government spokesmen repeatedly made it clear that though they supported social apartheid "total separation" was regarded as wholly impracticable and that it was not at all to be taken as official policy.[60] Verwoerd, who was supposed to be more ideologically wedded to apartheid than either Malan or Strydom, strongly denied in 1951 that it was part of official policy to grant self-government to the prospective Bantustans,[61] and he could not accept the quite moderate and realistic proposals for the social and economic development of the homelands advanced by the Tomlinson Commission in 1956. The shift, dating from 1959, in Verwoerd's position and in the official policy to "separate development" is thus not so much a new ideological departure as a movement from a relatively more segregationist policy (or baasskap apartheid) closer to the separationist ideology that had been propounded during the fifties, especially by Afrikaner intellectuals such as G. D. Scholtz and the SABRA group as well as by leading figures in the Afrikaans churches.[62] Even then Verwoerd continued to make it clear that the shift policy was not so much due to ideological conviction as to an expedient and pragmatic adjustment to changed circumstances:

> The Bantu will be able to develop into separate states. That is not what we would have liked to see. It is a form of fragmentation that we would not have liked if we were able to avoid it. In the light of the pressure being exerted on South Africa, there is however no doubt that eventually this will have to be done, thereby buying for the White man his freedom and the right to retain his domination in what is his country.[63]

Still, the sixties undoubtedly saw the most profuse use of the rhetoric of separationist ideology in official policy speeches, in particular those of

[60]See e.g., speeches in the House of Assembly by D. Malan, 12 April 1950, and by H. Verwoerd, 15 September 1958, Republic of South Africa, House of Assembly Debates, 71, col. 4250-1 and ibid., 98, col. 4060 resp.; See N. Rhoodie, Apartheid and Racial Partnership in Southern Africa (Pretoria, 1969), pp. 333 ff.

[61]Quoted in H. Wolpe, "Capitalism and Cheap-Labour Power in Africa: From Segregation to Apartheid," Economy and Society 14 (1972); 449.

[62]See G. Scholtz, Het die Afrikaanse Volk 'n Toekoms? (Johannesburg, 1954); also Volkskongres oor die Toekoms van die Bantoe (Bloemfontein, 1956). On the view that the policy of "separate development" adopted in 1959 can hardly be differentiated from the ideology of "apartheid," note that already at the FAK Kongres of 1944 it was envisaged that Africans should have "full control in their own areas" (Moodie, Power, Apartheid and Afrikaner Civil Religion, p. 263), while Eiselen in 1950 spoke of "full citizenship rights in his own areas" ("Is Separation Practicable," Journal of Racial Affairs, 1950).

[63]Quoted in M. Legassick, "Ideology and Legislation of the Post-1948 South African Government" (Unpublished paper, London, 1972). See also B. Schoeman, Van Malan tot Verwoerd (Cape Town, 1973), p. 225.

M. C. de Wet Nel. More recently the Vorster government has pushed
the political development of the homelands along, and the Transkei is
now committed to "independence" within five years, though it has
compromised on the rigid enforcement of separation in representative
sports and in selected areas of social intercourse, so that to a certain
extent the position of the fifties is being reversed.

If the efforts to develop the theory of apartheid effectively channeled off much of the ideological fervor that before 1948 was expend-
ed in articulating the cause of Afrikanerdom, the question remains
what the precise ideological connections were. Is there any substantive
link between the earlier attempts at articulating the Afrikaners' self-
definition and the content of the ideology of apartheid? There is an
obvious link insofar as the rationale for separate development often
involved a conscious analogy between the Afrikaner nationalist experience and the new "Bantu-nations." The same categories of a special
and divine calling, the right to self-preservation, the forging of an
ethnic identity, and the mobilization of national development were
freely applied.[64] A particularly striking instance of this was provided by
the formulation of the Bantu education policy in which conceptions
drawn from Christian National philosophy played a large part.[65] Still
the connection between apartheid and the Afrikaner movement is
even stronger and more basic than might be suggested by this picture
of taking categories that had first been developed in the Afrikaners'
self-definition, and then applying them to other areas and cases as well.
Something of this basic connection might appear from the use of the
very concept of "apartheid," which came to stand for the social and
political order between the different groups, for the unique calling and
identity of the Afrikaner nation itself, in a passage from P. J. Meyer in
1942: "the organic unity of Afrikanerdom, the Calvinistic basis of the
Afrikaner national life, the "apartheid" [literally, "apartness"] of the
Afrikaner national calling and national identity . . . are emphasized.[66]
The ideological "apartness" of the Afrikaner nation requires that it be
"separated from" other groups, i.e., "apartheid" in its later sense. The
mediating factor is the political power that is necessary to secure
"apartness" by enforcing separation, and thus apartheid emerges as
the political ideology of Afrikaner supremacy. Indeed, the obverse
side of insisting on the full political realization of the Afrikaners'
"identity" achieved through the language and cultural movement and
the strategy of social encapsulation in the new urban environment

[64]*See* Moodie, *Afrikaner Nationalism*, ch.13,pp.265 ff.
[65]*See* J. Shingler, "Education and Political Order in South Africa 1902-
1961," (Ph.D. Diss., Yale University, 1973).
[66]Meyer, *Toekomstige Ordening van die Volksbeweging in Suid-Afrika*, p. 8.

must, in the context of a complex plural society, be equivalent to a claim for outright sectional domination.

Since the ideology of apartheid is ostensibly aimed at ending White domination through separate development it is thus characterized by a basic and crucial ambiguity on the issue of power and domination: it is at once the ideology of Afrikaner (and White) supremacy and also provides the ideological basis for the devolution of power in a specific manner, viz., in separate political institutions or territories. The ideology's central claim is of course that it is able to reconcile these two different objectives, but, as the SPROCAS Political Report has argued, if we look to the crucial issue of the central coordination or pluralistic devolution of powers, there appears a crucial paradox between theory and practice: "Theoretically the logic of separate development requires a pluralistic devolution of power and government; in practice it embodies a supreme central integration of power and government."[67] When the SPROCAS Political Report argues that the homelands policy itself, so far from providing separate freedoms, is really "a sophisticated strategy for continued White domination"[68] then this is not merely an indictment of a failure to reach ideological objectives but a further indication of the same crucial ambiguity concerning the very content of these objectives themselves, i.e., domination or devolution.

To these ideological objectives, paradoxes, and ambiguities must now also be added the unintended consequences of the implementation of the policy and the countervailing strategies of the leaders of subject groups making use of the new political institutions and channels of communications for purposes of their own. It is arguable and has been argued at length in chapter 11 of the SPROCAS Political Report that the significant implications for political change should be sought in the dialectical interaction between the ruling and subject group constituting the actual politics of separate development, rather than in the stated objectives of the official policy or its ideological rationale.[69] If this is correct it would follow that the kind and extent of future "concessions" by the ruling group will depend not so much on the logic of their ideology as on the contingencies of the bargaining or conflict situation.

There is a second important ambiguity in the unfolding of the ideology of apartheid. We have emphasized its political and ideological links with Afrikaner nationalism, but if it is an ideology of Afrikaner supremacy, could not it equally well be said to be an ideology of White supremacy? After all, strictly speaking the premise of Afrikaner "apartness" could have entailed the enforcement of political and social

[67]Randall, ed., *South Africa's Political Alternatives*, p. 197.
[68]Ibid., p. 119.
[69]Ibid., pp. 192 ff.

separation between the other White groups as well. That this did not
happen can be interpreted in different ways: as an indication of the
growth of a wider South African nationalism instead of an exclusive
Afrikaner nationalism; as a shift from an ethnic basis of identification
to a racist one; as a pragmatic alliance and a realistic assessment of the
probable cost of outright Afrikaner domination; or as a set of unrecon-
ciled ambiguities and contrary tendencies comprising all the foregoing.

INTERPRETING THE POLITICAL SIGNIFICANCE
OF IDEOLOGICAL CHANGE

How are we to assess the significance for political change of the emergence of apartheid as a political ideology with its own internal dialectical coherence and dynamism, and with its changing relation to the
political practice of the ruling Afrikaner elite? The implicit ambiguities and central paradoxes of the ideology are such that we cannot
accept the changes of content or emphasis at face value. But then we
need some other criterion with which to determine their significance.

Kurt Danzinger has proposed a model for the analysis of ideological change in this context,[70] and it may serve as a helpful basis for
further discussion. He distinguishes between: (a) different forms or
patterns of domination, (b) different types of legitimation, within
(c) the general context of modernization. There is a complex interaction among these. Changes in legitimating ideologies are closely
related to actual changes in patterns of domination; the process of
modernization can lead to new forms of legitimation and new forms
of domination, but existing forms of domination and legitimizing
ideologies may prove to be obstacles rather than a help to economic
development.

Exceptions apart, Danzinger suggests that the general pattern of
ideological change occurs in two main dimensions. First, there is a
progressive shift from the justification of existing institutions or
forms of domination in terms of intrinsic values to their justification
in terms of instrumental utility or effectiveness. Second, the main
focus for such legitimating ideas tends to shift from cultural to
political and finally to economic institutions. In both cases the basic
transition is evidently one from particularistic to more universalistic
values, from absolute norms, divine sanctions, and sacred taboos to
more flexible and rational criteria of efficiency. It will at once be clear
that Danzinger's model is closely bound up with what, in an earlier
section, we called the modernization assumption.

[70]K. Danzinger, "Modernization and the Legitimation of Social Power," in
Adam, *South Africa*, pp. 283-99.

Danzinger now claims that this general pattern of ideological change is confirmed on both counts in the forms of legitimation prevalent among the modernizing Afrikaner elite. Before 1948 the legitimation of apartheid and Afrikaner domination was predominantly in terms of intrinsic values, such as religious sanctions and appeals to group charisma; in the fifties this became more secularized and justification of apartheid were based rather on cultural relativism; and more recently a distinctly instrumental line of defense had come in vogue, e.g., justifying White rule in terms of its greater efficiency in ensuring economic progress to the benefit of all. Danzinger does not provide much evidence for this interpretation, but suggests that research, such as content-analyses of the justifications of government policies published in the Afrikaans press, would readily bear him out. And in at least one instance this would seem to be the case: a study by Peter du Preez of Parliamentary debates in 1948, 1958, and 1968 has produced interesting evidence of, for example, a shift from racial to nationality concepts as legitimating categories, with potentially significant implications for the recognition of political rights.[71]

Nevertheless, on closer analysis, and in a wider historical perspective, Danzinger's model does not seem to hold at all well—and it is instructive to see how and why this should be so. To start with, even if we restrict ourselves for the moment just to the ideology of apartheid and to the criteria suggested by Danzinger, then the types of legitimating categories prevalent at both the earlier and the later stages would appear to be much more of a mixed bag than Danzinger claims. Thus in the germinal period of apartheid in the early forties we find that "Scriptural proof" was invoked on all sides, but the main thrust of the arguments offered by the sociologist Geoff Cronjé, and others like Eloff, was concerned with the supposed biological differences between the races and the dire consequences of racial miscegenation, for which much "scientific" evidence was adduced—a racist approach that was undoubtedly influenced by the National-Socialist tendencies then current in the Ossewa Brandwag.[72] The approach by the cultural anthropologist W. Eiselen, who was to be so influential in the SABRA group, was equally secular, though in his case it was couched rather in a vein of cultural pluralism, a paternalistic concern for the ethnic heritage of the Bantu peoples. On the other hand,

---

[71]P. du Preez, "The Construction of Alternatives in Parliamentary Debate: Psychological Theory and Political Analysis," *South African Journal of Psychology* 2 (1972): 23-40.

[72]*See* Cronje, *'n Tuiste vir die Nageslag*, chs. 1 and 2. *See also* G. Eloff, *Rasse en Rassevermenging* (Bloemfontein, 1942).

attempts to provide theological and biblical justifications for apartheid were by no means confined to the forties, but flourished well into
the second decade of apartheid. Rather than the transition from one
mode of legitimation to another, which Danzinger sees, it may simply
be the case that church leaders and social scientists each quite naturally tend to use their own peculiar mode of discourse—though it may
be significant to trace their relative prominence and influence in the
general ideological climate.

Similarly the increasing prevalence of instrumentalist legitimations
influenced by more rational criteria and universalist values may also
be harder to sustain with the historical data than Danzinger assumes.
Consider, for example, the characteristic argument advanced by
Verwoerd on the occasion of his first major public appearance at the
Volkskongres on the "poor White problem" in 1934:

> The dilemma in which we find ourselves is that in the general interest
> the welfare of the poor white must be improved, and that, also in the
> general interest, this may not be brought about in such a manner that the
> economical aspects of the coloured and native problems are rendered
> insoluble. This must be frankly recognized. If we thus venture to bring
> economic proposals entailing a discrimination in favour of the white
> worker, it must be realized that we have not merely considered what
> would be in the interest of this particular group—the poor whites—but
> of the whole country![73]

Even if he is arguing for the paramountcy of sectional interests this is
not simply proposed as an intrinsic value, but has to be legitimated in
terms of the "rational" and "universalistic" criteria applying to instrumental actions. At the same time this very purpose to represent
sectional interest as the universal interest, involving an essential
element of "false consciousness," may well be considered a typical and
basic function of ideological thinking. But how would it fit into
Danzinger's model?

The position is complicated even further if we do not primarily
focus, like Danzinger, on the period since 1948. How would the forms
of legitimation offered for segregation compare to that for apartheid
on Danzinger's criteria? The historical progression from the Afrikaner politicians influenced by the orthodoxy of Cape liberalism at
the time of union to Hertzog's era of segregation and then on to the
Nationalist ideology of apartheid must surely in important respects be
considered to show just the reverse of the pattern of ideological
change that Danzinger claims for the past quarter-century. Within

[73] H. Verwoerd,"Die Bestryding van Armoede en die Herorganisasie van
Welvaartswerk," in Dian Joubert, ed., *Toe Witmense Nog Arm Was* (Cape Town,
1972), p. 55.

such a longer historical perspective we can begin to detect the distortion caused by the modernization assumption underlying Danzinger's model. The picture he presents of the ideological change taking place through the successive forms of legitimation offered for apartheid is, in the final analysis, that of a traditionalistic and particularistic mode of thought giving way to a more modern, rational, pragmatic approach under the impact of the general process of modernization. But this ignores the crucial factor that the ideology of apartheid was advanced by an already modern and modernizing Afrikaner elite. As we have seen it may well be contrasted with the more traditionalistic aspects of the civil religion themes prevalent in the previous decades, though even that was largely an effort in revivalism in a new urban context far removed from the traditional rural community. The importance of this is that if we take the ideology of apartheid seriously as being the social and political program of a modernizing elite rather than as the legacy of outmoded legitimating categories, then it may appear that it is not at all so incompatible with continued economic development. So far from being a racist ideology that must inevitably be eroded or liberalized by the consequences of modernization, it may indeed be better analyzed as an ongoing modernizing of racial domination.

Danzinger is curiously and instructively ambivalent on the issue of coercion. He repeatedly refers to an "ideology of coercion" and associates this specifically with racial particularism. In this context ideological change toward a more instrumentalist mode of legitimation then acquires a peculiar significance. Danzinger contrasts as different patterns of domination the "rigid systems of power and privilege based on the ascribed criterion of descent" with the "more flexible institutional forms which allow for a sensitive balancing of the conflict of interests."[74] The "ideology of coercion" obviously corresponds to the former type of domination, and, it is suggested, requires it. Danzinger specifically asks what the chances are that the governing Afrikaner elite will be able to rid itself of the evil of "ideologically demanded coerciveness,"[75] and then, after outlining the pattern of ideological change he claims for the last twenty-five years, concludes: "slowly but surely the ideology of coercion becomes undermined."[76] This does indeed seem to follow from his whole model, yet in the concluding section he retracts it and substitutes a very different suggestion: the gradual substitution of more instrumentalist legitimation patterns due to the spread of the modernization process may

[74]Danzinger, "Modernization and the Legitimation of Social Power," p. 286.
[75]Ibid., p. 289.
[76]Ibid., p. 291.

have the result of strengthening rather than weakening the present system of domination: "the process of rationalization will probably continue to have its main influence on the power conflict by rendering the apparatus of domination more efficient."[77] But this would seem to suggest both that the relation between modernization, ideology and domination is much more complex than provided for in Danzinger's original model and that the criteria adopted for interpreting the significance of ideological change in this particular case are not appropriate and somehow miss the point.

IDEOLOGICAL CHANGE AND PRAGMATIC DOMINATION

If we give a central significance to the dynamics and the refinement of the coercive order of apartheid rather than to the decrease or increase in its racist quality, then a somewhat different picture of developments over the last twenty-five years emerges. We may compare Danzinger's pattern of ideological change with the very different interpretation of developments in that period given by Martin Legassick, who emphasizes the growth of a more authoritarian order dating primarily from the sixties:

> Despite its proclaimed intentions the Nationalist Government . . . [at first] moved slowly towards the implementation of its programme. Looked at in retrospect, what is remarkable is the comparative lack of large-scale social change, the comparative lack of authoritarianism in the first ten years of nationalist rule. If a considerable body of legislation was published, its enactment was delayed from year to year . . . . Many matters were the subject of Commissions of Enquiry which took several years to report . . . . In the 1960s the practice of the government became much more authoritarian. Thus it appears ironical that, having aroused on its accession widespread fears and accusations of Fascism, it should have acted so delicately at first—and that, when it in fact turned to means which could more correctly be described as Fascist, the opposition among the whites dwindled . . . . In 1963/4 there was the most serious major overhaul of urban areas/pass/influx control legislation since 1945 . . . . Ministers emphasised more confidently the migrant labour policy and its link to the mechanisation of industry . . . .[78]

It lies beyond the scope of this paper to assess the accuracy of this interpretation in its historical context. What is clear, however, is that the motive forces for any such move to a more coercive order are not so much to be found in the ideology of apartheid itself but rather in the attempts to counter the major new internal and external threats to the political order.

[77]Ibid., p. 299.
[78]Legassick, "Ideology and Legislation," p. 16.

In this connection an intriguing question is whether a more coercive order would also require a new ideological correlative, or whether one is already discernible. Certainly the ideology of apartheid in its original form no longer seems to fill the bill, and in a number of important respects it would rather seem to be at cross purposes with actual political trends. With the achievement of the ideological objectives of political separation fast approaching in the form of an independent Transkei in 1976 it is becoming increasingly questionable whether such "separate states" will serve either the security requirements of Southern Africa or provide the necessary legitimation for discriminatory practices in the vital urban centers of the Republic.

On the other hand, it also does not seem adequate merely to talk about a more "pragmatic" and flexible strategy of domination. Danzinger, for example, concludes that there is an increasing "likelihood that the *goals* of the ruling elite will be pursued by means of more flexible strategies,"[79] but leaves it unspecified what these goals are. Either they are political and ideological goals to which domination is a means, or domination becomes an end in itself, i.e., more efficient and sophisticated techniques of domination for the sake of domination. Heribert Adam likewise suggests that the decisive new feature in South Africa's version of racialism is such a means-end rationality: "This pragmatism . . . overrides the ideological implications of racial beliefs and is orientated solely toward the purpose of the system: the smooth, frictionless, and tolerable domination over cheap labour and political dependents as a prerequisite for privileges of the minority."[80] Now this may perhaps be adequate on the level of theoretical explanation, but it is very questionable that there is much explicit awareness of what the ends of "the system" are. Similarly, Frederick Johnstone has asserted that the actual goal of apartheid policies, as distinct from the ideology of apartheid, is "the pragmatic development of an economically powerful white supremacy."[81] Again this may well be true as far as it goes, but on the ideological level it seems to leave us with the lack of an ideology of "White supremacy," particularly since the ideology of separate development has increasingly substituted ethnic and national differences for racial inferiority. Whatever the prevalence of White supremacist attitudes in various fields, and despite its undoubted importance as an underlying assumption of government policy, there is simply no candidate for an

[79]Danzinger, "Modernization and the Legitimation of Social Power," p. 299.
[80]Adam, *Modernizing Racial Domination*, p. 53.
[81]Johnstone, "White Supremacy and White Prosperity," p. 126.

articulated and coherent political ideology of "White supremacy" in this sense, nor is it clear what its relation to Afrikaner nationalism would be. All this may only go to show the relatively secondary and peripheral significance of ideological change, but it may also indicate that in a transitional period we do not yet know how to identify the politically significant ideological design.

To conclude: it has been argued that Afrikaner nationalism was not primarily an ideological movement; that a number of nonideological components played a crucial role in the articulation of the Afrikaners' collective ethos; that the ideology of Christian Nationalism served as a *post hoc* rationalized legitimation of the Afrikaner movement and that the flirtation of Afrikaner intellectuals and activists with authoritarian ideologies in the thirties and forties formed part of their political education but was otherwise of transitory and peripheral significance. More specifically it is claimed that Afrikaner nationalism first found an explicit ideological basis in apartheid after coming to power in 1948; that there is an inner connection between the content of the ideology of apartheid and the maintenance of Afrikaner political supremacy in a complex plural society, and that this is also the mediating link with the earlier concern of the Afrikaners with their survival and self-definition. On the other hand it has been argued that the relation between the ideology of apartheid and the evolution of official policy has been complex and shifting; that the further career of the policy will depend not so much on its ideological logic but on the contingencies of the situation created in part by its implementation; and that a new coercive order may be in the making to which the ideology of apartheid is no longer directly relevant. In the circumstances ideological factors can hardly be expected to provide the basis for predictions about any kind of political change. At most the present transitional situation might be said to have a certain ideological fluidity that may well, within certain limits, favor more pragmatic adaptations to social and political change. To the extent that the ideology of apartheid continues to be associated with Afrikaner nationalism its significance may be found in a kind of "ideological lag" increasingly interfering with the on-going requirements of such pragmatic accommodations. In this connection the crucial questions are likely to be whether the Afrikaners will be willing or able to compromise ideological coherence and cultural identity in favor of White supremacy and economic privilege; whether they will in the long run continue to insist on exclusive political power as the precondition for all or any of these; or whether they may conceivably come to accept that Afrikaner cultural and social identity might survive in an open and pluralistic South African society without Afrikaner or White domination.

3

The Politics of
White Supremacy*

DAVID WELSH

This chapter examines political processes within the White oligarchy of South Africa. It explores the development of party politics and, with reference to the Black[1] franchise issue, seeks to explain the present deadlock in White politics.

In 1897 James Bryce wrote:

> Although the relations of the white race to the black constitute the gravest of the difficulties which confront South Africa, this difficulty is not the nearest one. More urgent, if less serious, is the other race problem—that of adjusting the rights and claims of the Dutch and the English.[2]

The validity of this observation has been repeatedly demonstrated by the development of White politics.

THE DEVELOPMENT OF THE PARTY SYSTEM
FROM 1910 TO 1948

In the making of union in 1909 and in the post-1910 period most of the key issues and major crises of the political system stemmed from this relationship. The rebellion of 1914 was a quarrel among Afrikaners on what attitude they should take toward England's war; the flag crisis of 1927 to 1928 involved the issue of South Africa's status

---

*Apart from the editors and the participants in the conference, the author would like to thank Professor T. Beard, Professor C. D. Jones, Dr. H. Giliomee, Mr. Japie Basson, Mr. Stanley Uys, and Dr. Ellen Hellmann for criticism of an earlier draft of this paper. Its shortcomings are our responsibility alone.
[1]"Black" is used instead of "non-White": it includes African, Colored, and Indian people.
[2]J. Bryce, *Impressions of South Africa*, 3rd ed. (London, 1899), p. 469.

and the imperial connection. The strains of fusion (1933 to 1934), the outbreak of war in 1939, and the constitutional crisis of the 1950s, all emanated from the division with the oligarchy.

The major political force within the oligarchy is Afrikaner nationalism, which arose as a response to British imperialism. In 1916 Tobie Muller, one of its most articulate exponents, contrasted the relative impacts on Afrikanerdom of conflict with the English and with Africans:

> Hitherto the Boers had learned only that they formed a self-conscious entity to all who were *lower* than themselves. That they formed a self-conscious entity also against other whites—their *equals*—was the big lesson they still had to learn. Against the natives white men were one, wherever they had come from. The realisation that Dutch Afrikaners had a particular and independent place among the whites was still to be born. Clashes with the natives were also mostly of a local nature and never affected our whole race simultaneously. Our entire people had first to suffer and struggle before our nation could blossom fully.[3]

At the same time, however, the two "race" problems of South Africa have been connected. An old fear of Afrikaner nationalism is that the smaller English-speaking White groups would seek Black support against Afrikanerdom to compensate for their numerical deficiency. Such considerations were an ingredient of Cape liberalism as it developed in the nineteenth century, and the converse partly explains the absence of liberalism in the English-dominated colony of Natal.[4]

For Afrikaner Nationalists the goal has been Afrikaner unity: numerical preponderance and the greater weight of the rural vote could give a united Afrikanerdom control of the political system—provided participation was limited to Whites. English hopes of tipping the demographic scales in their favor by immigration proved chimerical. By 1919 the core party of English sentiment, the Unionists, recognized that the English could not govern unaided. Their only hope of power lay in alliance with "the moderate Dutch."[5]

Until 1948 all South African governments depended upon a measure of English support, apart from a brief interval between 1929 and 1933 when the National party had a parliamentary majority of eight over the other parties. In 1924 the Nationalists gained power through a pact with the predominantly English Labour party; in 1948 they regained power in alliance with the Afrikaner party, which they absorbed in 1950. In the fifteen elections after 1910 only the 1924

[3]B. Keet and G. Tomlinson, *Tobie Muller: 'n Inspirasie vir Jong Suid-Afrika* (Cape Town, 1925), pp. 129-30. (My translation).
[4]S. Trapido, "White Conflict and Non-White Participation in the Politics of the Cape of Good Hope, 1853-1910" (Ph.D. Diss., London University, 1970).
[5]L. Blackwell, *African Occasions* (London, 1938), p. 91.

and 1948 elections resulted in decisive shifts of political power within the oligarchy. Both these shifts resulted from a substantial degree of Afrikaner unity. The Afrikaners' ability to dominate the political system when they stood together caused Smuts to remark that all South African politics was a quarrel between Afrikaners on what attitude they should take toward the English.

On color issues a substantial consensus between the major parties has existed. Until the 1920s there was general agreement that racial policy ought to be kept out of party politics. Fissures opened in this agreement in the 1924 election,[6] and in the "black peril" election of 1929 it was shattered.

The period from the mid-twenties until 1936, the era of Hertzog's segregation program, also saw a major realignment of political forces within the oligarchy and a skewing of the traditional bases of cleavage. At the heart of the program was the attack on the Cape African franchise, which had never been accepted by Afrikaner Nationalists or by a significant number of English, especially in Natal and the Transvaal. Fundamental to the franchise issue was the relationship between the White groups. Smut's offer of incorporation to Southern Rhodesia in 1922 was interpreted by Nationalists as an attempt to shore up his shaky parliamentary position by strengthening the English element.[7] The Black franchise was similarly viewed. D. F. Malan saw it as an attempt by "overseas imperialists" to use Blacks against the Nationalists.

> How did the non-European come by his vote? There is only one an-swer. Oversea Imperialist authorities, when it came to granting self government, were afraid because Afrikanerdom was in the majority and would strive for freedom. So non-Europeans were not only enfran-chised, but were set against the Afrikaners. That Imperialistic interest still exists in South Africa and still employs Natives and Coloreds "to beat down" Nationalism.[8]

On the other hand, Sir Charles Crewe, a former Unionist member of the South African Party, claimed that the bill was a thinly disguised attempt to eliminate some 14,000 pro-British voters, which would enable the Nationalists to capture thirteen Cape seats then held by the South African party.[9]

There was some truth in what both Malan and Crewe said. Most African and Colored voters had traditionally supported the Unionists

---

[6]C. O'Dowd, "The General Election of 1924," *South African Historical Journal*, 2 (1970): 68.

[7]M. Malan, *Die Nasionale Party van Suid-Afrika, 1914-1964* (Johannesburg, 1964), p. 78.

[8]G. Calpin, *There Are No South Africans* (London, 1941), p. 197.

[9]*Daily Dispatch* (East London), 19 June 1926.

and subsequently, with greater, misgivings, the South African party. Hertzog bid also for Colored votes.[10] Part of his legislative program in 1926 sought to extend limited political rights to Colored people in the North. This was an attempt to drive a wedge between African and Colored voters.[11] The proposal was not well received in northern Nationalist circles. There had been murmurings against the Colored vote for some years past among Cape Nationalists and in 1922 the Cape Congress of the party discussed a proposal that Colored voters be separately represented. But mention was made of the "improved disposition towards the National Party" that had been shown in a recent provincial council election, and the matter was dropped.[12]

In response to the alleged threat posed by the Black vote some Nationalists began to advocate the enfranchisement of White women. Hertzog was even prepared in 1928 to give the vote to "civilized" Colored women, but he would not have been able to carry this through Parliament. Many of his followers were opposed to giving the vote to women, let alone Colored women. Ultimately, however, the bait of a dilution of Black voting strength proved too much and White women were enfranchised in 1930.

With the need to acquire a two-thirds majority to alter the Cape African franchise, the position of the South African party (with 53 seats of 135 seats after the 1924 election and 61 seats of the 148 after the 1929 election) was pivotal. Smuts's difficulty arose from the heterogeneous composition of his party. The African franchise was supported mostly by Cape South African party members; it was decisive in 12 eastern Cape seats. But to many of the Natal and Transvaal members it was abhorrent. Smuts's initial response was to temporize. In 1926 he stated that the removal of Africans already on the common roll would be "a direct violation of the spirit and intention of the Constitution." He argued that the 7 members to represent Africans, proposed in the original legislation, would in fact make the African vote potentially more decisive than it had previously been.[13] He urged that the issue be considered outside party conflict by a body such as a national convention.

Hertzog initially expressed a desire to keep his colour legislation out of party politics but Smuts, although expressing appreciation,

---

[10]H. Simons and R. Simons, *Class and Colour in South Africa, 1850-1950* (Harmondsworth, 1969), pp. 247-8.

[11]According to Sir Charles Crewe, quoted in *Daily Dispatch* (East London), 23 June 1926.

[12]J. van Rooyen, *Die Nasionale Party: Sy Opkoms en Oorwinning—Kaapland se aandeel* (Cape Town, 1956).

[13]J. Smuts, *Memorandum on Government Natives and Coloured Bills* (Pretoria, 1926), p. 10.

basically did not believe this.[14] According to Heaton Nicholls, "Everyone in Parliament knew that the struggle over the Cape franchise . . . was a party political battle." Nevertheless it was agreed that party whips be taken off in the select committee proceedings and that no party leader should attempt to exert pressure over his party members on the committee.[15]

Smuts was genuinely distressed by the tenor of the 1929 election campaign.[16] Even before the election, though, the South African party had conceded vital ground. In the joint sitting of February 1929 Smuts declared his respect for existing rights, but said that this did not mean that they should be maintained forever: "We are prepared to negotiate . . . . We are not wedded to every detail of the Cape system." This debate profoundly affected the ultimate outcome of the franchise issue because the South African party leaders were persuaded that respect for existing rights did not entail Africans' continuing to vote on the common roll.[17]

By early 1930 Smuts was privately conceding that the African franchise was doomed. In May the select committee accepted by eighteen votes to eight Hertzog's proposal that the committee disapprove in principle common representation of Whites and Africans in parliament.[18] In Nicholls' judgment this vote was decisive: "Never again was there any question raised of retaining the Cape native franchise.[19]

The divisions of opinion within the South African party were serious. Probably most members from Natal and the Transvaal favored abolishing the African franchise. The sixteen Natal members (who constituted over one-quarter of the caucus and held their exclusive "Natal caucus") were a constant source of strain to the party's cohesion. Little divided them from the Nationalists on the issue of segregation, but on issues like the British connection, the status of the provinces, and compulsory bilingualism their views were polar opposites to those of the Nationalists, and an embarrassment to Smuts.[20] Hertzog was aware of these strains. His softened views on the imperial connection, which alienated many of his ardently republican colleagues, were perhaps partly due to his desire to carry his racial policy with the help of Natal votes.[21]

---

[14]J. van der Poel, ed., *Selections from the Smuts Papers* (London, 1973), 5:295.
[15]G. Heaton Nicholls, *South Africa in My Time* (London, 1961), pp. 284-5.
[16]van der Poel, *Smuts Papers*, 5:411.
[17]Nicholls, *South Africa*, pp. 281-2.
[18]Ibid., p. 288.
[19]Ibid.
[20]van der Poel, *Smuts Papers*, 5:459, 517; Nicholls, *South Africa*, p. 462.
[21]This explanation was suggested in *Round Table* 82 (March 1931): 462.

At its simplest, fusion meant a coming together in a broadly based party of Afrikaner and English, minus more extreme Nationalists on the one side and more extreme jingoes on the other. The new party, sufficiently strong to deliver the *coup de grâce* to the Cape African franchise in 1936, confirmed a truth of oligarchical politics: that when Afrikaner and English came together it was usually at the expense of the rights of the Blacks.

Uppermost in Hertzog's mind in entering into coalition negotiations was that he would probably lose the 1934 election. He told his caucus that if Smuts's offer were refused Smuts would be forced to close ranks in his party and thus would become the hostage of the Natal devolutionists and federalists. He would "therefore . . . sacrifice Afrikanerdom and the Afrikaans language to them."[22] Uppermost in Smuts's mind appears to have been the chance of breaking out of "the old racial dogfight."[23]

The negotiations for coalition nearly foundered on two issues: the status of the provinces, upon which Natal South African party members had strong feelings; and African policy, upon which the South African party was divided. Agreement was reached upon the provincial issue, but on racial policy Hertzog and Smuts had to agree to differ. Hertzog insisted upon the principle of separate representation; Smuts did not reject this outright, but insisted that no legislation on the matter be introduced so long as cooperation between the parties existed. The compromise reached amounted to an acceptance of Smuts's point of view: Hertzog's racial bills would not necessarily be proceeded with during the next Parliament.[24]

It appeared that Smuts had gone a considerable way toward accepting the principles of Hertzog's program. But Smuts made no commitment other than to make an "earnest effort" to solve the "native question" along Hertzog's lines. They agreed, said Smuts, "that we shall not unduly use the steamroller against each other," but strive to attain maximum agreement.[25] The compromise was retained in the program of the United South African National party adopted in December 1934: solution of the "native problem" should be sought as far as possible through agreement and "should be left to the free exercise of the discretion of the individual members repesenting the party in Parliament."[26]

During the coalition negotiations Hofmeyr was satisfied that Smuts "would not sell his natives to secure participation in a National

[22]C. van den Heever, *Generaal J. B. M. Hertzog* (Johannesburg, 1944), p. 593.
[23]D. Reitz, *No Outspan* (London, 1943), pp. 167-8.
[24]*Round Table* 23 (1932-33): 690.
[25]van der Poel, *Smuts Papers*, 5: 543-4.
[26]D. Krüger, ed., *South African Parties and Policies, 1910-1960* (Cape Town, 1960), p. 88.

Government."[27] Cope offers the following plausible account of Smuts's thinking:

> General Smuts had been deeply disturbed by the "Black peril" campaign of the 1929 general election. He believed that the most important political need in South Africa was "to take the native question out of the party political arena." He did not like General Hertzog's plan and he did not believe that white-black relations could be determined on a basis of segregation. But he thought that if the whole problem could be viewed dispassionately and without party political recrimination, a workable arrangement might evolve from the Hertzog plan.[28]

Both Hertzog and Smuts encountered difficulties with their followers. The more extreme wing of the Nationalists, led by Malan, entered the coalition under protest. To them the National party was a *volksbeweging*, a *volk* movement, that ought to be ideologically specific and brook no compromise with its ideals. "Bring together those who belong together," was Malan's credo; its implication was that the bringing together of those who did not belong together was immoral expediency. Malan and the Cape Nationalists, with the important support of the Broederbond, most of the Afrikaans press, and some Nationalists elsewhere hived off into opposition as the 'purified' National party. Untrammeled by fusion they became the most ardent advocates of a republic.

By comparison Smuts's problems were small. He faced criticism for not having grasped victory when it was within his reach; and some of his followers could not stomach the idea of cooperating with the Nationalists. The bone that particularly stuck in English throats was clause 2(d) of the fusion agreement, which permitted members to make propaganda for a republic. Smuts, however, was able to carry the vast majority of his English followers.

The years of fusion, 1934 to 1939, are regarded by some Whites as the halcyon days of Afrikaner-English cooperation. Fusion, however, was never complete: the United party remained an unwieldy agglomeration of diverse elements, held together by the authority of Hertzog and Smuts. Thus it lay wide open to attack, especially from the Nationalists, who could play one faction off against the others.

The Dominion party, known as the Dominionites, who won eight seats in 1938, sought to establish themselves as the party of the English interest and of the empire. Indirectly this damaged the United party: not only were some of its members sympathetic to Dominionite attitudes, but the Nationalists could portray Dominionite propaganda as

[27] A. Paton, *Hofmeyr* (Cape Town, 1964), p. 199.
[28] J. Cope, *South Africa* (London, 1965), pp. 106-7.

representing the real feelings of the English, some 80 percent of whom supported the United party compared with approximately 50 percent of Afrikaners.[29] United party Afrikaners faced allegations from the Nationalists that they had reneged on their *volk*. There was some truth in the allegations about attitudes of the English: many held views that were scornful of Afrikaner cultural progress and aspirations.

On several occasions, notably those involving the omission of the British national anthem at official occasions, fusion suffered severe strain, attacked by both the Nationalists and the Dominionites.

Racial issues provided the Nationalists with a happy hunting ground. The diversity of views in the United party meant that it spoke with several voices and rendered the government incapable of decisive action. The anti-Semitic, anti-Black propaganda of the Nationalists flourished in the fertile soil of receptive White minds. The Colored vote in the Cape was attacked, as was the government's refusal to enact futher legislation prohibiting mixed marriages in 1938. In the 1938 election the Nationalists cried "the *Kaffirs* are being spoon-fed," while the government stood "coldly and indifferently" to the interests of White small farmers, tenants, and *bywoners*.[30]

Despite the United party's inner contradictions it won a massive victory in the 1938 elections, the first electoral test of fusion. At the dissolution of Parliament the United party and the National parties held 117 and 20 seats, respectively. The Dominionites also increased their following by 3 seats. The United party's decisive parliamentary majority veiled its loss of support. The Nationalist vote was over 50 percent of the United party's. Another factor that artificially inflated the victory was that the cleavage between Hertzogites and Malanites in several constituencies enabled Smuts men to gain party nominations and then seats.

The crucial division within the oligarchy was between Hertzogites and Malanites.[31] Both appealed to Afrikaners who possess the decisive voice in the electoral system. The fragility of the United party in the face of attacks from both sides continued to inhibit its actions in passing legislative programs. In the short parliamentary session of 1938 sixty-eight bills were introduced, but twenty-seven either lapsed or were withdrawn; in the 1939 session thirty-one bills were introduced but only seventeen passed which brought further taunts from the Nationalists.[32]

The outbreak of the War in 1939 destroyed fusion and resurrected

[29]*Round Table* 27 (1937-38): 191, 405.

[30]Malan, *Nasionale Party*, p. 179.

[31]*See* Smuts's comment on his fusion partners: "they are more influenced by fear of Dr. Malan than of God," in van der Poel, *Smuts Papers*, 6: 130-1.

[32]Malan, *Nasionale Party*, pp. 184-5.

with renewed bitterness the tensions between Afrikaner Nationalists and non-nationalists. To the Nationalists South Africa's entry into the war was the ultimate confirmation of Smuts's imperialism and of Hertzog's error in 1934. However, for much of the war Afrikaner nationalism was engaged in internecine strife, which neutralized their potential thrust.[33] Reunion between Hertzogites and Malanites did not succeed; the National party faced massive opposition from the Ossewa-Brandwag and from lesser organizations.

Smuts won a resounding victory in the 1943 elections. But strong forces, which Smuts tended to underestimate, were gathering to undermine the United party. The voter alignments of the period between 1929 and coalition were reasserting themselves, resulting in an Afrikaner majority.[34] There was a cultural and religious unity underlying Afrikanerdom that, given the impetus, could be translated into political unity. Of paramount importance in the Nationalist renaissance was their capture in the 1930s and 1940s of significant opinion forming bodies. The Dutch Reformed churches provided the fundamental underpinning and a press, closely tied to the party, was also important. Equally important was the harnessing of education institutions including universities to the cause as agencies of socialization and mobilization.[35] Stellenbosch and Potchefstroom had developed as *volks* universities, and Pretoria and the University College of the Orange Free State were effectively transformed in the 1930s and 1940s. The political trend among Afrikaner students was shown when a majority broke away from the English-orientated National Union of South African Students (NUSAS) in 1933 and joined the highly nationalist Afrikaanse Nasionale Studentebond. The basic similarity of the Afrikaner universities' ethos produced an elite for the professions and for politics with a substantially homogeneous outlook, thereby creating the social tissue of *volk* unity.

In racial policy the Smuts government was rendered practically powerless by the exigencies of war, the conservatism of its supporters, and a reluctance to lose Afrikaner votes to an opposition that consistently thumped a "Black peril" drum. The United party leadership recognized the need for reform, but expediency limited action. Before the 1943 election Smuts wrote: "What will it profit this country

[33]M. Roberts and A. Trollip, *The South African Opposition, 1939-1945* (London, 1947); J. van Rooyen, *Ons Politiek van Naby* (Cape Town, 1971), ch. 16.

[34]N. Stultz, "South Africa's Apartheid Election of 1948 Reconsidered," *Plural Societies* (Winter 1972), pp. 30-1.

[35]Republic of South Africa, *Transvaal Provincial Council Debates*, 57 (1966): 47; the importance to the Nationalists of the education issue could be seen in their vigorous opposition to dual-medium education.

if justice is done to the underdog, and the whole caboodle then, including that underdog is handed over to the wrecker? To that question I see only one answer."[36]

With the growing militancy of Blacks Smuts found himself trapped in the cross fire. He was stung by a Natives' Representative Council resolution in 1946 condeming the "continuation" of a policy of Fascism." To resolve the conflict he told Hofmeyr would lead to a difficult debate in Parliament, and "we would be much weakened by what would fairly be taken as a surrender to Native dictation. I myself think our Native policy would have to be liberalized at modest pace but public opinion has to be carried with us."[37]

As far as changing the structure of South African society, the Smuts government achieved nothing. It was one thing to declare that segregation "had fallen on evil days"[38] and to introduce relatively minor piecemeal reforms; but it was an entirely different matter to contemplate structural changes that would dilute White power. But even piecemeal reforms were sufficient to tar Smuts, whose deputy was Hofmeyr, with a liberal brush in the eyes of Nationalists, and, indeed, of some of his own supporters.

The United party rested its hopes upon the retention of the "floating" Afrikaner vote: the wartime dissension among Afrikaner Nationalists made Smuts underestimate their capacity to regroup. Despite the dissension of nationalism at large the small Nationalist bloc in Parliament formed a disciplined and effective fighting group that could flay the ideologically diffuse United party with its assortment of segregationists, liberals, jingoes, *bloedsappe* (traditional Afrikaner supporters of Botha and Smuts), and unilingual cabinet ministers, all held together by the towering authority of Smuts and Hofmeyr.

The attitude of most of Smuts's followers and those of the Nationalists made it impossible for him to contemplate a significant extension of the franchise. Since 1936 the African franchise had been a closed issue. although the Nationalists clamored for the abolition of the limited communal representation of the 1936 legislation on grounds that the electoral representatives were an anti-Afrikaner force. The Asiatic Land Tenure and Indian Representation Act of 1946 did provide for limited communal representation of Asians, but Smut's primary intention was to offer a *quid pro quo* for the "ghetto" provisions also contained in the legislation. The latter provisions were acceptable to both the

[36]van der Poel, *Smuts Papers*, 6: 408; See also S. Gertrude Millin, *General Smuts*, 2 vols. (London, 1936), 2: 436-40.

[37]van der Poel, *Smuts Papers*, 7: pp. 92-3.

[38]A comment in Smuts's address to the South African Institute of Race Relations, "The Basis of Trusteeship in African Native Policy" (Johannesburg, 1942), p. 10.

major parties, but a majority of the United party caucus and the Nationalists opposed the franchise clauses. It was only Smut's authority that carried the legislation through his caucus.[39]

The Colored common roll vote remained, but since 1932, when the Cape National Party Congress had voted for its abolition, it had been a favorite target of the Nationalists.[40] The "purified" Nationalists demanded in 1936 that the legislation be widened to give separate representation to Colored voters on the same basis as to Africans. The United party remained committed to Colored voters' being on the common roll, but with some hesitation: it needed Colored votes, but this in itself incurred political risks. The Nationalists could exploit allegations of corruption in voting and registration, but, above all, it was damaging to place any reliance on a vote that was Colored and anti-Nationalist.

Ostensibly the election of 1948 was fought on the issue of apartheid, but the real issue was Afrikaner unity. Apartheid was a means to an end, a rallying cry that could swing a sufficient number of Afrikaners from the United party to the Nationalists. During the preelection years Afrikaner opposition regained some measure of unity. The election saw for the first time a major Nationalist breakthrough in urban industrial seats. On the Rand the Nationalists held only two seats but after the election the tally was eight, thanks to the mineworkers' vote.[41] Several of these victories were at the expense of the Labour party, which had shown itself unable to attract Afrikaner workers. The Nationalists were now firmly in the market for urban working-class votes, and within the party urban and rural interests would have to be reconciled.

Malan set about broadening the base of his electoral support: the Asiatic Land Tenure and Indian Representation Act was repealed in 1948 (although the Indian community had boycotted its representational aspect); in 1949 South-west Africa was given six seats, all of which were won in 1950 by Nationalists. Closely related was the abandonment of the vigorous drive for immigrants, which the United party had inaugurated after the war. Immigrants were assumed to be a source of potentially anti-Afrikaner votes, as nearly all of them came from Britain.

The determination of the Nationalists to destroy the Colored common roll vote was hardened by the results of the 1949 provincial

[39]M. Ballinger, *From Union to Apartheid: A Trek to Isolation* (Cape Town, 1969), p.130.
[40]van Rooyen, *Nasionale Party*, p. 268.
[41]L. Naude, *Dr. A. Hertzog, Die Nasionale Party en die Mynwerkers* (Pretoria, 1969), p. 239.

elections. Bredasdorp and Paarl, which the Nationalists won narrowly in 1948, were recaptured by the United party. The Nationalists were convinced that this was through the registration of new Colored voters. With a parliamentary majority of five and dependent upon nine Afrikaner party votes that were hesitant about abolishing the Colored vote, the Nationalists faced serious threats to their strength: they could lose the election through the addition of a few thousand extra Colored voters. Accordingly they decided to go to any lengths to achieve separate representation.[42] Similar considerations led to the abolition of African representation in 1959, the abolition of Colored communal representation in 1968, and the enactment of the Prohibition of Political Interference Act. This act was the culmination of a long process towards making interracial cooperation at the party level illegal.

An editorial in the most sophisticated Nationalist newspaper, *Die Burger*, in 1971 outlined the rationalization of this process:

> Political integration [i.e., any black representation in the House of Assembly] proved . . . to be the broad road to political disintegration, in the sense that it not only embittered relations between White and Brown, but between White and White to a point of near violence. The reason was that in a political system where the struggle for power was waged between two White groupings with sharply different views of the past as well as the future of South Africa the dragging in of a growing political "Brown power" [i.e., Coloured power] necessarily had to have the most serious implications. When the constitutional position allows a White party to compensate for its decline among the Whites by the registration and mobilization of Brown votes, it must expect its opponents to want to change that position at any price.

> This was indeed done in the struggle over the old Cape Coloured franchise which after a decade of turbulence was replaced by separate representation. But separate representation for a growing Brown population actually merely means that "Brown power" in the White party struggle gets shifted from the constituencies to Parliament. Instead of a decisive Brown vote in increasingly more seats, we have the possibility of a decisive bloc of Coloured representatives in Parliament. The figure of four in the Assembly, after all, could not be maintained forever. The disastrous probabilities in case of a fairly even division of seats between White parties, with the Coloured representatives as arbiters as to what party should govern, can easily be imagined by anyone.[43]

The issue remains a live one, as can be seen in continuing controversy among Nationalists over the political future of the Colored people and in the violent attacks on the United party's policy in terms

[42]*See Die Burger* (Cape Town), 17 July 1971.
[43]*Die Burger*, 15 July 1971.

of which sixteen Whites representing Blacks were to enter Parliament. To the Nationalists the fundamental issue is remaining in power and fending off their traditional foe. Of course, few White politicians would deny the greater gravity of the Black-White issue, but it remains one stage removed from the more proximate issue of Afrikaner-English relations. This latter conflict has other ramifications that impinge on the color question. In the economic sphere Nationalists have feared that *Engelse geldmag* ("English money power") would side with Black workers at the expense of Afrikaner workers. The political aspect of Nationalist anxieties have centered on English cultural institutions. Mistrust of the English churches, the lineal descendants of the hated missionaries, includes a mistrust of their educational role among the Blacks, especially Africans. Their English orientated education was an anglicizing, "de-nationalizing" force that induced Blacks, but especially Africans to look to political assimilation as the logical complement to cultural assimilation. Because of this education Africans would naturally incline to the English side, while the total cultural environment would become much more English in character to the detriment of Afrikaans culture.[44] It was not historical chance that made English the *lingua franca* of African nationalism. Such reasoning lay behind the Bantu Education Act of 1953 and the application of apartheid to the "open" universities which were producing "Black Englishmen." It accounts also for the government's hostile attitude to White students in bodies such as NUSAS, who have tried, unsuccessfully, to forge an alliance with Black students.

Another area in which fear operates is in Nationalist attitudes toward the English press. As the political commentator of *Die Burger* put it:

> The two biggest black peoples in the East, the Zulus and the Xhosas, are bombarded daily by a battery of five English language newspapers. In so far as those people can read a European language, they read English, and this will become increasingly so. And what does Soweto read? The people there obtain almost their entire image of South Africa and of the government through the coloured spectacles of the opposition press.[45]

In recent years the government's hostility has also been evoked by the substantial amount of coverage given in the English press to statements by the more outspoken "homeland" leaders.

[44]B. Nel, *Naturelle-opvoeding en-onderwys*, 2 vols. (Bloemfontein, 1942), 2:40; E. Malherbe, *Demographical and Socio-Political Forces Determining the Position of English in the South African Republic* (Johannesburg, 1966), pp. 4-6.
[45]*Die Burger*, 22 September 1973.

Guy Butler has explained much of the government's animus against focal points of the English establishment in the following terms:

> Many Nationalists believe that they could get the goodwill of the African and convince him of the rightness of apartheid, if it were not for the English press, the English universities, the English churches. Therefore . . . these sources of criticism and ideological sabotage must be rendered ineffective.[46]

THE STATE OF SOUTH AFRICAN PARTIES AFTER 1948

Successive elections from 1948 have seen the National Party consolidate its parliamentary majority to a state of electoral impregnability.

The essence of the party system lies in the fact of its resting upon immanently logical possibilities having worked themselves through, resulting in domination by Afrikaner nationalism. The National party is more than a political party; it is one arm of a *volksbeweging* that purports to comprehend all spheres of its members' lives. The party's major achievement was to draw approximately 80 percent of Afrikaner voters to its banner and to hold them, attaining the supreme goal of the republic in 1961. The hard-won *volkseenheid* made the leadership determined to keep the party together at all costs. Division meant defeat. The result was a fanatical emphasis on unity, which brooked no public dissent or criticism of policies and attitudes.

To the outsider the National party looks monolithically solid. Inside the party, however, and among para-political Nationalist oranizations absolute unanimity cannot be imposed. Provincialism has always been a factor in intraparty Nationalist politics. It is built into the party's origin as four parties, founded at different times in 1914 and 1915.[47] The serious tension between Malan and Strydom in 1948 and after was largely a manifestation of provincial rivalries. The center of gravity passed decisively to the Transvaal in 1954 when Malan retired. Malan, whose bitterness against Strydom was considerable, wanted Havenga to be his successor and told the cabinet of his intention to ask the governor-general to invite Havenga to form a government. The Transvalers objected strenuously and demanded that the parliamentary caucus should elect the leader, who should then construct his own cabinet.[48] Despite Malan this view prevailed, and

[46]Guy Butler, "The Future of English in the Republic" (Lecture given to the South African Council for English Education, Cape Town, 1962).
[47]van Rooyen, *Ons Politiek van Naby*, p. 29.
[48]Ben Schoeman, quoted in *Die Burger*, 26 May 1973.

Strydom was unanimously elected after Havenga withdrew his candidacy.[49] Malan's farewell speech to the Cape Congress of the party warned of dangers to unity: "Beware of personal rivalry inside the party. Beware of the formation of groups within the party. Beware of provincialism."[50]

Despite tensions, differences were muted in the interests of party unity and the supreme goal of the republic. The election in 1958 of Verwoerd as *hoofleier* ("chief leader") of the party, and hence prime minister, showed that there was substantial opposition to him; but again this was expressed only within the context of an unquestioning overriding loyalty to the party.

Lojale verset ("loyal opposition") is a constitutionally entrenched right within the party, and provided that members abide by the rules, they need suffer no direct sanction. From all accounts hard and frank talking occurs within the caucus and within the cabinet. Reviewing his long experience as a cabinet minister Ben Schoeman wrote: "There were indeed the usual differences—one can't agree with everything all of the time—but there were never such differences of principle that a minister felt he ought to resign. We like one another, we understand one another, even though we also differ considerably from one another." He added that voting never occurred in cabinet sessions.[51]

"Disloyal" opposition, however, is visited with serious retribution. Japie Basson, for example, was expelled from the caucus and then from the party in 1959 for opposing the abolition of African representation in Parliament. But expulsions of this kind were virtually unknown until 1969 when the *verkrampte* or Hertzogite movement reached its climax within the party. The party leadership went to extreme lengths to avoid a break, the possible scale of which was unpredictable. When the decision to move against the dissidents was made, however, action was swift and merciless: the general election was brought forward by a year because the leadership did not want to provide the Hertzogites with a platform in Parliament for a day longer than was necessary.[52]

The tight hold that Afrikaner nationalism exerts over its followers was revealed again in February 1972 when a Transvaal Nationalist provincial councillor broke away from the party. He was subjected to an immense barrage of Nationalist pressure, even from within his family. He commented: "To discard a way of life you have lived for 40 years and change everything is virtually impossible."[53]

[49]van Rooyen, *Ons Politiek van Naby*, p. 21.
[50]Ibid., p. 9.
[51]Ben Schoeman, quoted in *Rapport* (Johannesburg), 27 May 1973.
[52]Ibid.
[53]Quoted in *Sunday Times* (Johannesburg), 20 February 1972.

Restraints also apply to party members whose loyalty is beyond reproach. Thus a Nationalist member of Parliament complained in 1972 that he had been rebuked for venturing to discuss with his constituents the possibilities and implications of "fuller partnership" for the Colored people—at that time a highly sensitive issue on which opinions inside the party were seriously divided.[54]

Among para-political organizations, elements in SABRA (the South African Bureau of Racial Affairs) were heavily put down by Verwoerd in 1961 for daring to question Colored policy;[55] marginally deviant newspaper editors have also been subjected to intense pressure.[56] Individual academics and clergy, who have either completely or partially cut loose from the Nationalist fold, have paid a heavy price in terms of social and professional sanctions.

Afrikaner nationalism, in sum, has shown a strong emotional hold over its followers, and it has also displayed remarkable self-sealing qualities in the rare event of breakaways: the technique in such cases follows a consistent pattern whereby the individuals behind the breakaway are isolated and then discredited as traitors to the cause of Afrikaner unity. The fate of dissenters serves as a powerful deterrent to others who might be so tempted.

The unity of Afrikaner nationalism, however, does not rest solely or even largely upon these deterrents. In organizational terms it is directed by a group of interlocking spheres (political, journalistic, religious, cultural, economic, educational) among whose elites a substantial degree of consensus exists, the background for which is prepared by church, school, and university.[57] This is demonstrated by the relatively easy mobility that exists as among spheres (see Slabbert, p. 9).

While little evidence is available about the Broederbond its central role has probably been to coordinate the different spheres of Afrikaner nationalism, to prevent overlapping of interests, to iron out friction, and to preserve the consensus among elites. Its 6,000 members are carefully chosen from all walks of Afrikaner life to ensure that all functional interests are represented. There is no conclusive evidence to support the commonly held supposition that the Broederbond dictates to the National party, although substantial numbers of parliamentarians are members. Strydom is said to have been emphatic that the Broederbond should not interfere in the political sphere.[58] It seems likely that its role in political matters, apart from

[54] P. Marais, quoted in *Rapport*, 10 September 1972.

[55] J. Holleman, *SABRA 1961: The Great Purge* (Durban, 1961).

[56] L. Louw, ed., *Dawie, 1946-64* (Cape Town, 1965), pp. 195-206.

[57] F. van Zyl Slabbert, "Moontlikhede van Verandering," *Deurbraak* (September 1973).

[58] B. Schoeman, *van Malan tot Verwoerd* (Cape Town, 1973), p. 120.

maintaining a generally supportive ethos, is to serve as a combined sounding board and "think tank." A pressing political problem, for example, might be referred to the Broederbond for study. In turn the problem is referred to representatives of all spheres within the Broederbond. Apart from garnering useful advice such a process ensures that leading Nationalists in every sphere of society are acquainted with the policy when it finally emerges and that they can deal more readily with any Nationalist opposition.[59] In ordinary times the Broederbond seems to be highly effective at preserving unity and defusing potential conflict between spheres, but in times of acute tension within Afrikaner nationalism as a whole, the conflict has extended right into the heart of the Broederbond itself and has reduced its ability to perform its essential role.[60]

How has Afrikaner nationalism changed over the past twenty-five years?[61] Afrikanerdom has been diversified and modernized. The National party is no longer representative purely of landowning interests: it has also to reconcile within its ranks working-class, professional, commercial, industrial, and financial interests. From what meager information is available nothing suggests a marked cleavage along class lines or along urban-rural lines within the parliamentary caucus or at party congresses. Elements of class feeling have been noticed in nomination contests for parliamentary candidacies. In the 1960s the *verkrampte* group sought unsuccessfully to exploit economic inequalities among Afrikaners (which have always existed, despite the myth of traditional egalitarianism), especially in relation to the rise of the Afrikaner tycoons. But the leadership of the National party is well aware of the importance of the workers' vote and carefully cultivates the White trade unions' support, for example, when previously White jobs are opened to Blacks.

One significant change in Afrikaner nationalism derives from its position of power. The necessity to close ranks in the face of the enemy is no longer as urgently felt. The rising generation of young Afrikaners is less able to achieve the same pitch of enthusiasm for the cause. Interest in cultural organizations and in the church has declined among the youth. Apathy and "weak motivation" in politics have caused concern to party leaders. In reviewing the period since 1948 Schalk Pienaar concludes that political victory has produced in

[59] As appears to have been the case with sports policy in the early 1970s.
[60] *See* the revealing comments by D. Richard in *Dagbreek* (Johannesburg), 13 September 1970.
[61] D. Welsh, "Urbanisation and the Solidarity of Afrikaner Nationalism," *Journal of Modern African Studies* 7, (1969): 265-76; and "The Political Economy of Afrikaner Nationalism," in A. Leftwich, ed., *South Africa: Political Development and Economic Growth* (London, 1974), pp. 249-86.

Afrikaners a greater sense of security and of equality with other Whites: "having become conscious of his own power the Afrikaner, especially after the coming of the republic, has become a much more tranquil person in his attitudes to other language groups."[62]

Complementing these factors is the growing diversification of Afrikaner society: it has become less easy to ensure unity among the different spheres of Afrikaner society; and with the receding of the immediate domestic threat there has been a tendency for elements within the different spheres to bridle against the imposition of monolithic unity. This phenomenon has especially been evident among academics, students, businessmen, and journalists. However, its implications should not be exaggerated: the vigorous internal debate has been conducted within the framework of a deep-lying loyalty to the cause; the basic unity of the movement has not been impaired. *Verligte* Nationalists realize the constraints within which they must exist and they recognize that once having rejected or been cast out by Afrikanerdom their influence upon it is nil.[63] Furthermore, the relaxation of the bonds of unity could be reversed in the event of a threat (real or imagined) to Afrikaner nationalism. As the Oudtshoorn by-election in 1972 showed it remains possible for the National party to reverse minor electoral setbacks by vigorously appealing to Afrikaner emotions.[64]

One yardstick for measuring changes in Afrikaner Nationalism is provided by the Hertzogite revolt. The Hertzogites accused the National party leadership of deviating from the ideology of Afrikaner solidarity and White *baaskap*. Fundamentally their objection to new emphases in policy was the party leadership's acceptance (formally, at least) of the idea of "one White nation" based on equality of the two languages. The fact that the *verkramptes* were hounded out, branded as traitors, and destroyed electorally does suggest some movement in thinking.

In racial policy there is also evidence of changed attitudes insofar as Nationalist policy accepts that perpetual racial domination is no longer defensible. In response to world opinion to which racial discrimination has become anathema, the basis of legitimation of policy changed.[65] The decisive point at which this process was inaugurated

[62]"Die Nasionale Party 25 Jaar," Bylae tot *Rapport*, 25 May 1973.

[63]Michiel le Roux, "The New Afrikaners," in H. van der Merwe and D. Welsh, eds., *Student Perspectives on South Arica* (Cape Town, 1972); Dreyer Kruger, "Wat het dan met ons gebeur?," *Rapport*, 25 May 1973.

[64]The Nationalists alleged that the United party harbored in its ranks *Boerehaters* ("haters of the Afrikaner").

[65]P. du Preez, "The Construction of Alternatives in Parliamentary Debate: Psychological Theory and Political Analysis," *South African Journal of Psychology*

was in 1959 when Verwoerd sprang his Bantu "homelands" policy on
a startled caucus. The genius of his formula was to link White desires
for domination and local separation with a program that offered the
shadow of the traditional liberal idea of national self-determination.
Idealists could invoke the record of Afrikaner nationalism's own anti-
imperialist past. As Dawie put it: "we rejected domination of ourselves, but we have not equally rejected the domination of other
people by ourselves. . . . Colonial attitudes stand condemned, not only
in the eyes of a hostile world but before our own best Afrikaner principles."[66]

In ideological terms apartheid has changed its face, but the decisive
test is whether it has significantly liberated Blacks. The homelands
policy has not led to structural change because the maintenance of the
structure is dependent upon the network of controls and discrimination that still cover every facet of African life. Some changes have,
however, occured. For example, the expression of nakedly racist sentiments by public figures is eschewed. The effect of South Africa's isolation in the sports world has led to the adoption of a sports policy
that, notwithstanding great complexity, does make a minimal concession to racially integrated sports. Also of note is the earnest debate
on "petty" apartheid and the future of the Colored people.

On the economic front the government has been forced to abandon
any hopes of large-scale economic separation. The plan to remove
annually 5 percent of the African labor force in Western province
towns as from 1967 was abandoned not long after it had been
announced; so has any hope that 1978 would be the year in which the
flow of Africans into the "White" areas would be reversed. The
chronic shortage of skilled labor has prompted *ad hoc* raising (but not
elimination) of job reservations over a wide range. These developments underline the most serious policy problem faced by the Nationalists: the future of urban Africans, whose official status remains that
of "temporary sojourners." Increasingly the anomalousness of this
designation has become apparent to Nationalists, but so far no substantive modifications of policy have emerged. The difficulty is that
any recognition of a permanent urban African population is tanta-
mount to the abandonment of a major plank in the ideology of separate development.

For White opposition groups the most important factor has been
the dispiriting effect of the Nationalists' apparent invincibility. The

---

2 (1972): 23-40; K. Danzinger, "Modernization and the Legitimation of Social
Power," in H. Adam, ed., *South Africa: Sociological Perspectives* (London, 1971).
    [66]Louw, *Dawie*, p. 286.

optimistic hopes of some that the electorate's turning out of the Smuts government in 1948 was a temporary aberration were dashed by the 1953 election, in which the Nationalists increased their majority to thirty-one, despite a massive campaign by the United Democratic Front—an alliance of the United and Labour parties and the Torch Commando.

The experience of the United Democratic Front underlined a fundamental dilemma of White opposition forces in South Africa: they can unite in opposing the Nationalists, but they disagree among themselves upon the society's most important issue—the color question. If they come together the diffuseness of their program is vulnerable to Nationalist attack; if they separate their potential thrust is fragmented and weakened.

Given that the party system has a "built-in tendency towards illiberalism"[67] and a permanent Afrikaner majority, the United party in opposition has sought to avoid anything like a liberal tag and to emphasize its commitment to White leadership. In times of Black challenges to White supremacy, such as with the defiance campaign in 1952 to 1953 and around Sharpeville in 1960, it has emphatically come down upon the side of the established order. But within this context the United party has been ideologically diffuse. Its traditional vagueness of policy has been a reflection of its felt need to appeal both to the relatively more liberal urban vote and to the *platteland* vote. Notoriously the same policy could be given different emphases in town and country.

If before 1948 the United party's heterogeneity had been contained by the dominance of Smuts and Hofmeyr, its lack of cohesion was exposed by the relative weakness of Smuts's successor, J. G. N. Strauss. Strauss was elected leader under circumstances that offended some members of the party[68] and was finally ousted by its Union Congress in 1956, earning for himself the dubious honor of being the only leader since 1910 of a White political party to be deposed while in office.[69] His successor, de Villiers Graaff, has shown greater strength and resilience in riding out storms within the party, but he too has come under fire from Left and Right for equivocation and ambivalence.

The first major split in the United party occurred in October 1953, when four members of parliament, including the Transvaal leader,

---

[67] C. Leys, *European Politics in Southern Rhodesia* (Oxford, 1959), p. 175.

[68] Nicholls, *South Africa*, p. 436; M. Kentridge, *I Recall* (Johannesburg, 1959), p. 345.

[69] A point noted by van Rooyen, *Ons Politiek van Naby*, p. 62. It was unlikely that Strauss would have been ousted had he attended the national Congress.

Bailey Bekker, left the caucus and constituted themselves as an independent group. Shortly thereafter they were joined by three others, one of whom subsequently returned to the fold.[70] This group represented a significant part of the right-wing, which had been wooed by Malan in his efforts to secure a two-thirds majority. Their grievances were against Strauss personally and against the liberal wing of the party, which had been strengthened by an influx of new blood in 1953.[71] A liberal member, Bernard Friedman, resigned from Parliament and from the United party in June 1955, when Strauss refused to give an assurance that Colored voters would be returned to the common roll if the party were returned to power. The assurance was subsequently given, but in recent policy the principle has been abandoned.

In these times the United party remained vulnerable to the taunt that it had no coherent alternative to apartheid. Strauss appointed a committee to examine African policy in 1954, but it was unable to recommend any clear-cut new departures. More significant was the fate of a commission appointed by Graaff in 1958 to determine how best to "sell" the United party. The commission sparred with the problem, but it recognized that little could be done until agreement was reached on what policy ought to be, and its members were divided on that question. The commission's report was never tabled.

Further electoral disaster overtook the United party in 1958. It heightened frustration within the party and gave renewed impetus to the feuding between the Right and the Left. The conservatives believed that Hofmeyr had lost the 1948 election for the party and that the way to win was to angle for the (putatively) floating Afrikaner voter by emulating the Nationalists' racism. The liberals retorted that two elections had already been lost by the following this unprincipled tactic and that the time had come for the party to present an unequivocal position on the race issue.

Matters came to a head in 1959 at the National Congress of the party. Verwoerd's new vision had, as he intended, caused consternation in the United party. The conservatives saw it as a chance of turning the tables on the Nationalists and branding Verwoerd as a *kafferboetie* ("Negrophile"); the liberals saw it as an opportunity of decisively rejecting the fragmentation of South Africa and accepting the consequences of a multiracial society. In the caucus debates on the party's response to Verwoerd, polarizations became more sharply etched; every member became labeled.

---

[70] A convenient list of United party defectors is provided in Louw, *Dawie*, p. 159.

[71] Including Helen Suzman, Z. de Beer, and Jan Steytler.

Before the congress the conservatives decided to engineer a limited purge of a few of the most prominent liberals.[72] It was assumed that this would effectively silence those who remained in the party, leaving the conservatives in undisputed command and able to pursue the *platteland* vote without embarrassment. They chose the congress as their battlefield because United party congresses have traditionally been heavily overweighted in favor of more conservative *platteland* delegates, who would oppose the small band of urban liberals.

Graaff tried to avert the break: in the face of right-wing objections the party retained its undertaking to restore Colored voters to the common roll and also to extend the principle of African representation (by Whites) to the northern provinces. Graaff sought to persuade Douglas Mitchell, the right-wing party leader in Natal, not to proceed with his motion that the party oppose the purchase of further land for Africans if such land were to be appended to potentially independent Bantustans. Mitchell refused and made an inflammatory speech, which induced the congress to support the motion by a two-to-one majority.

The land issue was the proximate cause of the Progressives' breakaway. The dozen members of Parliament who left the United party included many of its ablest debaters and the cream of its intellectual resources. In a press statement they attacked the party's vacillating attempt to catch Nationalist voters with "an uncertain and watered down colour policy which in its application is insufficiently distinguishable from that of the Nationalists."[73]

Through much of the 1960s the United party enjoyed a greater measure of internal unanimity, although it experienced minor defections to the Left and the Right. The leadership surrounded itself with conservative advisors and took pains to ensure that only those who would remain loyal received nominations as candidates. The result was that a substantial proportion of the party's new blood were mediocrities.

The party also damaged itself in 1961 when it decided after hesitation to oppose a republic, arguing that its advent might have serious economic consequences. This was the response of a party that depended on English speakers for about 80 percent of its votes, but could attain power only by making headway among Afrikaner voters. Even a decision to recommend to its supporters that they vote in accordance with their personal convictions might have been better aligned with their basic strategy, but the staunchly monarchist Natal

[72]For an accurate and incisive analysis, *see* the articles by 'Adderley' (A. R. Delius) in *The Cape Times* (Cape Town), 22 and 24 September 1959.

[73]*See* the statement put out by the Progressives shortly after the break; "The Split in the United Party," mimeographed (1959).

party would not hear of it. To many Afrikaners the United party's decision came as a confirmation that it was basically the party of empire in which the old Unionist spirit still prevailed.

The broad pattern of the United party's post 1948 development has been one of lurches to the Left followed by right-wing breakaways and vice versa. With notable exceptions the party has stood by a commitment to the rule of law and civil liberties, but on critical occasions its tendency to ambivalence alienated both the Left and the Right and vocal segments of the English community including students, the clergy, and the press. An example of this was provided by the United party's involvement in the Schlebusch Commission from 1972 to 1974.[74] The issue brought to a climax the long simmering differences between the more liberal "Young Turk" elements, whose renaissance in the Transvaal had enabled them to capture control of the party there, and its conservatives, whose feelings on civil liberties were less sensitive, and who resented the gains being made by the former. The party entered the 1974 election damaged by acrimonious nomination disputes and it lost ground to both the Nationalists and the Progressives.

From its founding in 1959, the Progressives started from where the Liberal party began in 1953. Neither of these two parties could make much headway despite the presence of many able members, and in the case of the Progressives, the support of wealthy backers. White liberals and radicals who advocate the sharing of power with Blacks in a common society have had little impact on the electorate. Although the Progressive party won six new seats in the 1974 elections, their victories were in the predominantly English-speaking middle-to upper middle-class constituencies where large numbers of voters expressed their impatience at the United party's inability to resolve its internal feuds. White activists have been harassed and banned by their colleagues and in the 1970s, rejected by increasing numbers of Blacks. To appeal for a sharing of power between races in a common society runs head-on into the fundamental dynamic of politics within the oligarchy. In particular it violates the rule, which the Nationalists laid down for the conduct of politics, that 'no party or pressure group should seek Black allies in its fight against Afrikaner nationalism.

Unity of the White opposition has been impossible to achieve because of the lack of cohesion in the group that is the main source of support. English-speaking Whites have seldom been able to sink their differences and unite politically for sustained periods. Religious,

[74]A select committee, later a commission of inquiry, into certain liberal organisations. Eight students were "banned" in terms of the Suppression of Communism Act after the commission had unanimously recommended that "urgent action" be taken against them.

class, regional, and other differences and, above all, the need to make
political alliances with non-Nationalist Afrikaners have muted any
sense of group identity. "Not believing themselves to form a coherent
group with a common political goal, they have perceived no need to
define their orthodoxy."[75] The aim of seeking Afrikaner allies (rather
than Blacks, which alliance could dilute White supremacy) compels
the United party to play down its essentially English core. It means
also that in relation to the number of Afrikaner supporters a dispro-
portionate number of Afrikaners are found in leadership positions of
the party. Of the forty-one United party members of Parliament
today nearly one-quarter are Afrikaans speakers. A similar tendency
can be observed in the Progressive party. The assumption is that
dents are more likely to be made in Afrikaner nationalism if the attack
is spearheaded by Afrikaners. The effect of this is to restrain (but not
eliminate) the argument over Afrikaner-English relations in party
politics. The linguistic base of voter allegiances can be seen in the fact
that the opposition holds no seat where Afrikaner voters are in a clear
majority.

By the end of 1974 it was clear that the National party had little to
fear from the opposition parties, either as serious electoral challengers or as opportunists who would seek to embarrass the Nationalists
by right-wing criticism of any *verligte* moves. The Progressive party
and (to a lesser extent) the United party are both trying to play a constructive role in encouraging the Nationalists to move forward.

It has been argued in this chapter that the National party has
entrenched its position through its "built in" electoral majority. It has
also preserved prosperity and security among Whites. However illusory these factors may be, the majority of voters are concerned largely
with short term privileges. Poverty and unemployment among Whites
are minimal; the relative absence of class conflict within the oligarchy
can be gauged from the insignificant number of strikes by White
workers, who have benefitted from sustained economic growth and
protection against Black competition. If industrialists (of both linguistic groups) have grumbled about the shortage of skilled labor and
other restraints they have benefitted from the government's refusal
to recognize African trade unions and from other bureaucratic controls that ensure a docile labor force. The inconveniences and irrita-
tions of apartheid are, in sum, trivial in comparison with its advantages.

In view of the stake that nearly all Whites have in the existing order,
it is not surprising that beneath the vigor and bitterness of intraoli-
garchical politics there lies a wide consensus on racial issues. Intensity

[75] A. Duminy, "The Role of the English-Speaker," *New Nation* (June 1968),
p. 8.

of conflict is not necessarily a function of the distance between parties to the conflict.[76] A survey of urban White attitudes in 1969 found that 45 percent of English and 46 percent of Afrikaner respondents agreed with the government "on most points."[77] Another survey in 1969 found that 33.1 percent of a large sample of English considered Vorster to be the ideal prime minister, compared with 22.3 percent who favored Graaff.[78] A series of surveys published in *Rapport* led Schalk Pienaar to conclude that attitudes toward racial policy were not decisive in determining party allegiance, which was determined rather by habitual loyalty and by the feeling among Afrikaners that the National party was their bulwark against British pressure, and by the converse feeling among English supporters of the United party.[79] But in the event of a serious threat to White suprèmacy, it is probable that differences within the oligarchy will sink in defense of racial privileges.

CONCLUSION

This chapter has examined the evolving structure of conflict in South Africa and it has argued that the cleavage within the oligarchy was the more immediate issue in White politics until the 1950s when, under pressure of hostile international opinion and the rise of African nationalism, it was eclipsed by the race issue. However, the cleavage has not been eliminated.

The oligarchy has garrisoned itself against internal or external threat. The Nationalists have erected a formidable security apparatus by subordinating the legal system to the goal of maintaining White domination.[80] With the progressive bureaucratization of society, government has become increasingly centralized, as the decline of municipal and provincial council powers shows. (It has been estimated that of the 1.25 million economically active Whites nearly 0.5 million are employed in public services.[81])

Is the apparent deadlock an inevitable or logical consequence of the particular configuration of forces in South African society? While recognizing that "inevitable" is a dangerous concept to use of historical results, it is suggested that immanent forces have strongly propelled the South African situation into a condition of such structural

[76]L. Coser, *The Social Function of Conflict* (London, 1956).

[77]*News/Check* (Johannesburg), 17 October 1969.

[78]"The South African Political Scene," *Stats* 6 (1970): 1076-7.

[79]*Rapport*, 24 October 1971.

[80]A. Mathews, "Security Laws and Social Change in the Republic of South Africa," Adam, *South Africa*, p. 242.

[81]An estimate, cited by Mr. T. Gerdener, former minister of the interior, 18 November 1973, mimeographed.

rigidity that structural change appears to be impossible of internal generation. As Rokkan has observed of the democratization of European polities: "the decisions to extend the vote were not uniformly a response to pressures from below, they were so often the results of contests for influence at the top and of deliberate moves to broaden the bases for an integrated national power structure."[82] In the South African situation there have been contests between segments of the ruling group, but the larger segment took steps to ensure that the smaller did not seek to strengthen itself by a political alliance with the disenfranchised Black voters. Moreover, the impulse to make such an alliance was either weakly developed or strongly opposed among the smaller segment, and when after fusion in 1934 it seemed that the African vote would no longer be needed, they became willing parties to its destruction. The critical question facing the smaller, predominantly English segment has been whether the political benefits of an alliance with Blacks would be worth the cost, if the cost was the prospect of a dilution of White supremacy, which most would not pay.

It is not suggested that the motor force behind the denial of rights to others is merely an epiphenomenon of the cleavage within the oligarchy. The process, however, does have parallels with the loss of political rights sustained by southern Negroes in America in the latter part of the nineteenth century, when the thrust toward White unity and supremacy broke through the incipient interracial class solidarity of the Populist movement.

In South Africa the historic conflict between Whites has been between two major political groupings, both of which draw substantial support from all economic groups, as shown in table 3.1.

The dynamic of racial ethnic politics has rendered purely class-oriented parties superfluous: the Labour party was unable to forge a

Table 3.1 Percentage of the Total Vote by
Monthly Income Group

	Under R300	R300-R499	R500 and over
National Party	63.8	56.6	48.1
United Party	19.3	23.4	27.6

Source: *Stats* (Johannesburg, 1969).

[82]S. Rokkan, "Mass Suffrage, Secret Voting and Political Participation," in L. Coser, ed., *Political Sociology: Selected Essays* (New York, 1967), p.110.

lasting alliance between English and Afrikaans workers, and the Communist party achieved only limited success as an interracial class movement. The salience of class as a focus has been subsumed under wider ethnic and racial solidarities. All the elements of the "classic conservative coalition"[83] have been present in the making of the South African situation: mining and White farming could come together in ensuring that labor-repressive techniques were entrenched and that African influx to the towns was limited. In achieving this they could secure a favorable response from White townspeople, who feared the possible social and political consequences of such influx, and from White urban workers, who demanded protection from competition.[84]

By numbers and by the loading of the rural vote (which in extreme cases has been double the value of the urban vote), farmers attained so great an influence that no government could survive without the support of at least a substantial proportion of them. No other functional group was traditionally able to achieve a comparable influence, although in recent decades White farmers and farm workers have been numerically eclipsed by White industrial workers.[85]

The links between White workers (approximately 75 percent of the White working class are Afrikaners) and farmers have been strong, both as a result of sentiment and of a common interest in the control and allocation of Black labor. Similarly the ties between Afrikaner farmers and the rising urban Afrikaner bourgeoisie have also been strong. Non-Afrikaner entrepreneurs and workers have also benefitted from labor-repressive techniques. There have been occasions when White townspeople have complained that revenues extracted from mines, business, and industry have been squandered on subsidizing uneconomic agriculture[86] and there was resentment among employers against the implementation of the civilized labor policy in the 1920s and 1930s,[87] but in Moore's phrase, there existed between them and other White economic interests an antagonistic cooperation based upon a commitment to the existing social order.

The analysis presented in this chapter tends to confirm pessimistic views of the prospects for change in South Africa. However, with

[83]B. Moore, *Social Origins of Dictatorship and Democracy: Lord and Peasant in the Making of the Modern World* (London, 1967).

[84]W. Hancock, *Survey of British Commonwealth Affairs*, 2 vols. (London, 1940), 2: part ii, 31.

[85]Republic of South Africa, Bureau of Census and Statistics, *Union Statistics for Fifty Years* (Pretoria, 1960), table G-2.

[86]*Round Table*, 26 (1935-6): 636; ibid., 27 (1936-7): 667.

[87]F. van Biljon, *State Interference in South Africa* (London, 1938), p. 144.

the collapse of Portugal's African empire and the increasingly parlous
situation of the White minority in Rhodesia, the dangers of a blind
adherence to the status quo have become increasingly apparent to *verlig-te* Nationalists. One surmizes that they recognize the need for rapid
change on several fronts, including ridding themselves of the Rhode-
sian incubus, extricating themselves from South West Africa, accom-
modating the Colored people, eliminating "unnecessary" discrimination, and reducing the wage gap between Black and White.

On all issues involving change, including sports policy, *verligtes* have
to contend with stubborn conservative resistance. We have shown how
the different components of Afrikaner nationalism were mobilized
and coordinated in its rise to and consolidation of power. The problem now confronting the pragmatic leadership is how to persuade the
movement, now less amenable to centralized direction, to adapt to
changed circumstances and approach some kind of domestic détente.
The leadership is seriously hamstrung, if not trapped, by the legacy
which it and its predecessors built up. To move Afrikaner nationalism
forward and simultaneously preserve its hard-won unity is a delicate
and difficult task that involves carrying not only rank-and-file party
members but the interlocking network of supporting organizations as
well. Mobilization of the movement for reinforcing White supremacy
and consolidating Afrikanerdom was easier than it will be to persuade
it to "do everything in our power to move away from discrimination
based on race or colour," which the South African representative told
the Security Council of the United Nations in October 1974 is the
policy of the South African Government.

It may well be argued that *verligtheid* is a mirage, and in support of
this contention it can be demonstrated that hardly a single repressive
law has been repealed. It may equally be held that discrimination may
only be verbally substituted for by a euphemism such as "differentiation," and that *verligtes* contemplate only peripheral change, not ones
that affect the core, which is the political economy of racial domination.

One may accept these arguments: but is it not at least a possibility
that the cumulative weight of these minor changes could have a two-
way effect in conditioning White minds to prepare for more fundamental change, and to encourage Blacks to press for such change? In
other words, *verligte* measures may have a symbolic quality whose
catalytic effect is of far more significance than their actual legal or
administrative scope.

4

The Significance of Recent Changes Within the White Ruling Caste*

JEFFREY BUTLER

⌐⌐ South Africa is a plural society dominated by a minority which can be called a "caste" in the sense that ascribed inherited characteristics are the basis for group membership, power, and allocation of benefits. Membership of a group, but especially of the White group, is not left to social and economic process or to individual choice. Power in the central political institutions of the country is secured by law to the White minority. As a consequence, Whites enjoy a highly favored position in the distribution of jobs (hence of income), and of amenities, a position they have an interest in maintaining. Despite common interests, however, the White minority is divided into two major subcastes based roughly on the language of first preference; the personnel of the governing party are recruited almost exclusively from one of these subcastes. For our purposes, the White minority will be analyzed as though it were divided into two groups, "The Afrikaners" comprising 63 percent of the White population, and "the English" comprising the remaining 37 percent.[1] Such a division ignores differences in historical origin, especially in the case of Jews who are overwhelmingly English-speaking, and the development of an emerging bilingual group. These difficulties of definition are, however, insignificant for the purposes of political analysis.

An examination of change "within" groups inevitably raises problems, but there are changes that, though they clearly have their origin

*The author would like to thank Leonard Thompson, Norman Bromberger, Newell Stultz, and Denis Worrall for help in preparing this paper.
[1]It must be emphasized that both of these language groups are politically divided.

in the whole society, can nevertheless be considered in isolation. We shall examine, therefore, each of the White subcastes and the relations of the subcastes with each other. That inquiry, however, would be of little value unless it addressed itself to the significance of changes within the dominant White group for the future of relationships between the Whites and those presently excluded from power. For instance, does a mitigation of a conflict within the White caste contribute to a mitigation of conflict between the dominant and the subordinate groups? If so, does it lead in the direction of fundamental change away from the present regime of racial and coercive stratification?

Posing the question raises another: what does "fundamental" mean? A scholar who has been opposed to South African official policy for a long period is likely to be prejudiced in the direction of either questioning the existence of any change at all or of admitting the change but denying it any significance. Such views are based on a static assumption, but, as African historians have shown, such an assumption frequently arises from contempt and hostility. We are not merely identifying change as taking place by a series of great events; we are involved in a matter of judgment as to a rate of change, a process involving many discrete events. Furthermore, our notions of a legitimate rate of change are historically determined, particularly since we have lived in a period in which empires have been rapidly demolished because they lacked the will to continue ruling in the face of developing nationalist movements. In South Africa the ruling group is not notably lacking in will and has long questioned the nonracial basis of postwar policy, especially British policy, both as to the handing over of power, and, more recently, the speed with which it was accomplished. Change may be slow but it may still be "fundamental" in the sense of being incremental, cumulative and irreversible, leading ultimately to a redistribution of power and to a reduction in discrimination based on race. Such a formulation accommodates both the structure of power and its use, a distinction between the effective access, or lack of access, of the citizen to the holders of power, and the consequences of the use of that power for his "welfare."[2]

CHANGES WITHIN THE SUBCASTES
SINCE WORLD WAR II

Much recent work on the modernization of the Afrikaner community, using such variables as income, capital, and urbanization, has noted substantial social, economic, and perhaps even intellectual conver-

[2]Throughout this paper a distinction is drawn between issues of "power" and issues of "welfare."

gence between the two White communities.[3] Furthermore, change, in attitudes and life-styles rather than language, has shown Afrikaners moving toward the English, who have always been a more urbanized, secularized group.[4] In the past, Afrikaners have been fearful of anglicization, hence the denial, especially in the Transvaal, of parental choice in relation to medium of instruction, but this issue appears to be declining in importance, and the Afrikaner community may now be letting down its guard. Furthermore, it seems that rapid economic growth, social convergence, a long exercise of power, and the creation of the republic in 1961 has diminished *laager* attitudes among many Afrikaners in relation to other Whites (*see* Welsh, p. 68).[5] Although it is difficult to document, there seems to be a substantial improvement in the day to day relations of Whites with each other, especially between the heavily Afrikaner civil service and White English speakers in general.[6]

However fierce political conflict has been, there has always been considerable economic cooperation between the English and the Afrikaners, and until the recent substantial convergence in income, residence, and life-style, considerable differentiation. Between the wars, Englishmen were better educated and, on the whole, kept out of the way of Afrikaners, largely by moving up the scale.[7] Since 1933, however, there has been sustained prosperity and low unemployment of Whites. With the removal of "poor-Whiteism," almost entirely an Afrikaner phenomenon, Anglo-Afrikaner conflict on economic issues has largely disappeared. If there is serious discrimination against the English—which would hardly be surprising after twenty-six years of National party power—it has yet to appear in community relations

---

[3]D. Welsh, "Urbanisation and the Solidarity of Afrikaner Nationalism," *Journal of Modern African Studies* 7, 2 (1969) 265-76; D. Welsh, "The Political Economy of Afrikaner Nationalism," in A. Leftwich, ed., *South Africa: Economic Growth and Political Change* (London, 1974), pp. 249-85; N. Stultz, "The Politics of Security South Africa under Verwoerd, 1961-6," *Journal of Modern African Studies* 7, 1 (1969): 3-20; H. Adam, "The South African Power Elite: A Survey of Ideological Commitment," in H. Adam, ed., *South Africa: Sociological Perspectives* (London, 1971).

[4]However, Lever has written of the "cohesiveness" of the Afrikaans community. H. Lever, *The South African Voter* (Cape Town, 1972), p. 120.

[5]See *Rapport* (Johannesburg), 25 May, 1973.

[6]After a twenty-year absence from South Africa, we are astonished at the changed demeanor of Afrikaner officials in relation to Whites and to Blacks. This impression was confirmed by another scholar who returned after a slightly shorter absence.

[7]J. Butler, "Social Status, Ethnic Division, and Political Conflict in New Nations: Afrikaners and Englishmen in South Africa," in W. Bell and W. Freeman, eds., *Ethnicity and Nation Building* (Beverly Hills/London, 1974), pp. 152-3.

and politics. There is grumbling about "corruption" to be sure, but no exploitation of it as an explicitly Anglo-Afrikaner issue.[8]

In the area of political issues there has been a major change of focus. The achievement of the republic in 1961 was almost entirely symbolic in its effect; indeed, to the annoyance of extreme republicans it reenacted the South Africa Act virtually unchanged.[9] But it had an interesting result, viz., it faced National party leaders with the logical consequences of their own rhetoric. They had always argued, from the founding of the party in 1913, the impossibility of a common White nationalism before Englishmen broke their ties with the imperial power. It was hardly surprising, therefore, that National party leaders began to make wooing speeches immediately after the republic was achieved.[10] The frequent reference by Afrikaners to the English as "strangers" is now a thing of the past. Anglo-Afrikaner issues could be further exploited only if new symbols were chosen or if a move were made from the symbolic to the instrumental level, to deal in tangibles such as money for education, a deliberate policy of Afrikanerization, or serious economic discrimination.[11] There has been no such program, at least not publicly. In a by-election in 1972, the Cape leader of the National party and the party paper, *Die Burger*, conducted a virulent campaign alleging *Boerehaat* in the ranks of the official opposition, a hatred of Afrikaners, an historic resentment, quite unrelated to any current legislative or administrative issue between the parties.[12] Recent attacks on the English press by Ministers also have in part this symbolic quality, although it could be argued that the press is not threatened because it is English, but because it is generally liberal.

The achievement of the historic program has also had its effect in the cultural sphere. Slabbert (p. 15) has noted the decline of interest in activities in which history played a major part. The Voortrekker centenary celebration in 1938 inaugurated a period of intense social conflict, a manifestation of Afrikaner resentment at an English ascendancy. That conflict was immensely exacerbated by the coming of World War II. However, after a generation of Afrikaner power, this

---

[8]*See*, e.g., *Sunday Times* (Johannesburg), 3 March 1974, for a report of a speech by a United party Senator, A. Getz.

[9]B. Schoeman, *Van Malan Tot Verwoerd* (Cape Town and Pretoria, 1973), p. 186-9.

[10]Ibid., p. 197. *See also* Stultz, "Politics of Security," pp. 9-10.

[11]The flag still contains the Union Jack. S. L. Muller, a junior minister, predicted a new flag by 1971; *Beeld* (Johannesburg), 14 September 1969.

[12]This issue was revived in the general election of 1974; *see Sunday Times*, 5 May 1974.

type of conflict has totally disappeared; *boeresport* (literally, "boer games") is now a minor activity among Afrikaners and attendance at Voortrekker festivals has declined.[13]

Among the South African English changes have not been so spectacular: originally farmers they soon became predominantly an urban population, especially since the development of mining. There is a general acceptance among them of Afrikanerdom, a reconciliation to their status as a permanent minority, and a sense of depression in relation to politics.[14] Their acceptance of Afrikaner power has been aided by their alienation from British policies: Macmillan's "wind of change" speech in 1960 was a candid warning to all South African Whites. That alienation has probably been reinforced by the addition of a considerable number of refugees from former colonies—Dutch from Indonesia, Belgians from the Congo, British from East and Central Africa—resentful groups likely to support the government on the issue of retaining power in White hands. There are, therefore, few attempts to raise symbolic issues, and there is virtually no interest in the Commonwealth, which most South African English now regard with good reason as a hostile institution.[15]

There are, therefore, many pressures in the direction of reconciling the Afrikaners and the English. One should, however, be cautious in estimating the speed at which such a process can take place. Indeed, one scholar has argued recently that though Afrikaner antipathy toward the English may be declining, English antipathy toward Afrikaners may be growing, especially among the young.[16] Intermarriage, though frequent, does not produce a new social animal—an "Anglikaner"—but simply reinforces one of the existing groups. The Dutch Reformed churches retain their hold over Afrikaners, though churchgoing is declining in major urban areas; conditions of mobility make it difficult for family and church to play traditional conserving roles.[17] However, an educational system that makes possible a career

[13]It may be significant that the government, as a fuel-saving measure, cancelled the quinquennial festival of the Battle of Blood River in December 1973, not merely for a year, but for five years.

[14]M. Proudfoot, "Advice from an American," *New Nation* 12 (July-August 1973). There is heavy overseas migration of graduates from English universities; no study has been made of its extent or direction.

[15]See *The Cape Times* (Cape Town) editorial, 1 September 1969 for a nostalgic look at the Commonwealth.

[16]N. Charton, "The Afrikaners: How English-speaking and Indian South Africans See Afrikaners," mimeographed (Center for Inter-Group Studies, University of Cape Town, 1974), pp. 4, 14, 19.

[17]C. Alant, *Wat Ek van by Dominee Glo en Dink* (Pretoria, 1970), p. 92, shows the problems developing for Dutch Reformed ministers in the cities, particularly in relation to youth and to upper income groups.

from nursery to graduate school in a unilingual environment may simply replace a religious institution by a secular one. Perhaps even more important, the members of these segments of the dominant caste are free to move from city to city, suburb to suburb, and can quite clearly maintain their identities without sacrifice of material interest. The days of English dominance over the upper ranks of industry and commerce are over; an Afrikaner need not necessarily assimilate to English ways in order to get ahead.

There are other forces keeping the communities apart, as shown by social-distance measurements.[18] Major differences of value still persist, especially on such politically sensitive issues as the rule of law, freedom of the press, *habeas corpus*, and general humanitarian issues.[19] These value differences were held against the English by Albert Hertzog and his followers in 1969; the English were basically liberal, they said, and therefore, incapable of defending White power.[20] But this major attack on cooperation with the English was decisively rejected by members of the National party in the election of 1970, which seems to suggest that anti-English feeling is not so easily mobilized as it once was, and particularly, that the English were not regarded as particularly unreliable when faced with the threat of Black power.

Differences in value can be exaggerated. We ought to remember the conduct of White populations elsewhere in Africa after World War II. The French in Algeria, and Kenyan and Northern Rhodesian settlers, would not have surrendered their privileged positions without the forcible intervention of a far more powerful authority. Rhodesians have yet to be persuaded to share power with Africans. There is little reason to believe that a United party government, if elected in 1948, would not have been equally determined in its defense of White power for, as Schlemmer points out (p. 107), we are dealing with the hard facts of interest and historically determined identity. With the convergence alluded to it is difficult to find major differences of interest between the two groups. Schlemmer found a near unanimous belief in a sample of Whites in Durban in the irrelevance of the "English-Afrikaans split."[21]

Given then that processes of coalescence are operating and that Whites have major common interests, what are the implications of

---

[18]H. Lever, *Ethnic Attitudes of Johannesburg Youth*, (Johannesburg, 1968), p. 142.

[19]L. Schlemmer, *Privilege, Prejudice and Parties* (Johannesburg, 1973), pp. 10-28.

[20]*See* Hertzog's celebrated "Calvinism" speech in Republic of South Africa, *House of Assembly Debates*, 14 April 1969, cols. 3876-83.

[21]Schlemmer, *Privilege, Prejudice and Parties*, p. 26.

Q re BLACKS

recent changes in Anglo-Afrikaner relations on questions of the power and welfare of the excluded groups? The evidence is against the proposition that what changes of policy there have been are due to a groundswell of liberal opinion, especially among Afrikaners. Although there is no evidence of a major shift in traditional White attitudes in the direction of accepting a "one man one vote" constitution, the issue of power has become a central one. All parties are suggesting different ways of redistributing power without damaging the interests of its present holders. The recent victory of the Progressive party, the vigorous debate within the United party on the issue of "shared power," and the continued factionalism in the National party on the "full consequences" of separate development indicate that the virtual ending of the Anglo-Afrikaner debate on historic issues has been followed by an almost total preoccupation with the "race issue" and especially with the question of power. There is probably no causal relationship between these developments: the issues of power and welfare have been forced on to South African Whites from outside, with a consequent decline in interest in historic issues. Societies can afford bitter debates on historic issues only if they are left alone. It is not that White conciliation necessarily leads to generosity, but that serious threats to the whole structure of power force an examination of that structure, of the means by which it is sustained, and of its consequences in the daily lives of the powerless.

On the issue of welfare there is evidence of a widespread willingness to consider improvements, attested to by frequent discussions of the "wage gap," but fierce conflict once specific suggestions are made. For example, in Sea Point—an English-speaking area where the Progressive and United parties are evenly balanced—Whites showed little willingness to make available limited facilities for Black employees.[22] A similar conflict in Pretoria over public parks suggests that Afrikaners may be a little, but only a little, ahead of their English contemporaries.[23] And a poll among members of a noted athletic club in Natal as to whether the Comrades Marathon should be made multiracial gave a nearly 90 percent vote in favor of keeping it "White."[24] In the area of sports generally, there is evidence of some desire to meet the demands of overseas sporting bodies and to improve amenities for Blacks. There are no clear differences in attitude between English clubs, on the one hand, and Afrikaans clubs on the other. It

[22]*See* comment by P. Janson, Deputy Minister of Bantu Administration, on Cape Town's problems, *Rand Daily Mail* (Johannesburg), 13 February 1974.
[23]*Rand Daily Mail*, 1 February 1974; *The Star* (Johannesburg), 25 February 1974.
[24]*The Star*, 7 February 1974; for the ballot, *see* E. P. Herald, (Port Elizabeth) 22 March 1974.

seems also, however, that most bodies are far from being willing to make the concessions necessary to meet the demands being made on them from overseas.[25]

There is an acceptance in both communities of the need for change, at the moment undefined, though at the same time an implied rejection of any radical solutions.[26] The removal of Afrikaner poverty, massive residential segregation of all Whites, both combined with the perception of White-Black relations as *the* problem, may have produced a willingness to accept, though not to initiate, change, especially change at a distance, i.e., anywhere but "in our suburb." The South African White has been under attack from so many quarters for so long in a period of rapid political change that he is desperate for a "solution," a characteristic South African way of looking at politics. One of the major changes in attitude may be the development of feeling powerlessness due to a realization that segregation combined with affluence for Whites has not met the nagging demands of excluded groups for power and welfare, demands that cannot be regarded as inherently illegitimate within the framework of separate development. It may be that this feeling produces the limited freedom of maneuver to "the Left" for all White political parties that Schlemmer has noted.[27] Articulate *verligtheid* involving precise proposals is an elite phenomenon in both English and Afrikaans groups, but vociferous demands for stern maintenance of Afrikaner hegemony have been unsuccessful, attested to by the power showing of the far right Herstigte Nasionale Party (HNP) in two general elections.

ORGANIZATIONS AND POLITICS

Among South African Whites, home language remains an excellent though not infallible predictor of political loyalty, despite the existence of Afrikaans members of the United party and the Progressive

---

[25]There have, however, been some remarkable statements on the intentions of the government, e.g., Minister of Sport Piet Koornhoff has said that he wants interracial cricket at club level within three years. Koornhoff's views were repeated by Hassan Howa, the hard bargaining president of the Cricket Board of Control, a predominantly Colored and Asian body. *Evening Post* (Port Elizabeth) 22 March 1974. However, in an election speech, Minister of the Interior C. Mulder denied there would ever be "mixed sport" at any level SABC news, 28 March 1974.

[26]*Comment and Opinion* 1, nos. 6, 8 (March 1974), quoting *Die Burger*, (Cape Town), 1 March 1974, *Die Volksblad* (Bloomfontein), 4 March 1973, and *Sunday Express* (Johannesburg), 3 March 1974.

[27]Schlemmer, *Privilege, Prejudice and Parties*, **pp. 62-66.**

party, and English members of the National party. The National party receives about 70 percent of the votes of Afrikaners; the United and Progressive parties a little over 80 percent of the votes of the English. This efficient mobilization of Afrikaners is, however, a recent development, probably dating only from about 1961 when for the first time the National party gained a majority of the votes cast.[28] The 1948 election was won by an Afrikaner coalition, but since 1953 South African politics have been dominated by the National party, a single Afrikaner-based party, which steadily increased its votes and number of seats in Parliament. There was a minor reversal in 1970 when it suffered a net loss of nine seats, the first such loss since 1948. The period from 1953 to 1975 has, therefore, been the first era of persistent Afrikaner dominance in South Africa's history, and one which shows little sign of ending.

Slabbert has referred to the extensive bureaucratization of Afrikaner life, which results in the coordination of Afrikaner institutions and organizations. This coordination took place after 1948, though most of the ground work in building up the organizations had been completed by then (see Slabbert, p. 4−5, 9−10). English speakers contemplating this structure usually give a sinister and effective role to the Afrikaner Broederbond.[29] Recently there has apparently been a decline in the role of the Bond, and, on occasion, a warning from Afrikaner leaders that it should stick to its major function, the advancement of the interests of the Afrikaner, especially in economic life.[30] But such conflicts have been discreetly managed, so much so that the South African English have an inaccurate picture of Afrikaner organizations as ones in which, without discussion, loyal, dour functionaries receive and enforce the firmly given orders of the leaders of the *volk*.

The question to be asked of Slabbert is what is the implication of his argument? Is the bureaucratization of Afrikaner life the end of the road; has history, or at least one aspect of it, come to and end? The system is beginning to show some strain, which may involve for the Nationalists the beginning of a move from an ethnic party of principle based on farmers, workers, teachers, churchmen, civil servants, and small businessmen to a party of interests, still drawing the bulk of its

[28]N. Stultz and J. Butler, "The South African General Election of 1961," *Political Science Quarterly* 78, 1 (1963): 106-7.

[29]Charton, "The Afrikaners," p. 11.

[30]*See*, e.g., Schoeman's account of Strydom's views in 1955: "the Broederbond can take on projects like the founding of *Volkskas* [a bank] and *Uniewinkels* [literally, "union shop"—a chain store], or urge people not to support Indian traders, but the Broederbond should not involve itself in general policy questions or party affairs." Schoeman, *Van Malan tot Verwoerd*, p. 120.

support from Afrikaners, but now representing the whole range of actors in South African White communities, necessarily forcing it to play down its ethnic character.

The attempt to combine business and sentiment in the early days of the Afrikaner economic movement was not a success.[31] Recent developments have led to the expansion of firms that, though known to be controlled by Afrikaners, have aggressively gone into the market ethnically and racially blind, looking for customers, Black, Brown, or White, many of them English-speaking. It is historically and sociologically significant that the "new men" of Afrikaner economic life have only begun to play political roles, although some have spoken out vehemently on public issues, invariably in protest against official policy. Though conflict exists between Cape and Transvaal groups, it has yet to take organized form, either by interest groups threatening to form new political organizations, or making resources available to opposition groups. No serious conflict among Afrikaner interests has appeared, e.g., no conflict between extractive and manufacturing industries based on different attitudes toward "future affluence and mass consumption" by Blacks.[32]

The Afrikaans press has likewise changed, not merely in taking a more independent line on questions of policy, but in developing a major conflict between press groups, based in Cape Town and the Transvaal respectively.[33] Furthermore, in the late sixties, the papers of *Die Nasionale Pers*, especially *Die Burger* and *Beeld*, frequently at odds with Transvaal papers, especially *Hoofstad*, conducted a vehement campaign to identify, expose, and expel Hertzog and his conservative followers.[34] But, as in the case of business, most criticism is still from within the fold.

The part played by the churches is a complex one, because ministers play their political roles as individuals, not as officially representing their respective churches. The churches are not party churches, nor legally established. Occasionally the churches have made major general criticisms of policy, such as at the Cottesloe Conference in 1960, or major specific criticism, when one of them, the Nederduits Gereformeerde Kerk, stigmatized migrant labor as a "cancer" at the heart of South African society.[35] However serious these criticisms, no

[31]J. Sadie, "The Economic Factor in Afrikaner Society," mimeographed (Center for Inter-Group Studies, University of Cape Town, 1974), p. 9.

[32]L. Schlemmer, "Social Research in a Divided Society" (Inaugural lecture, University of Natal, Pietermaritzburg, 1973), p. 17.

[33]J. Serfontein, *Die Verkrampte Aanslag* (Cape Town and Pretoria, 1970), ch. 9.

[34]Ibid., pp. 52-3, 60-68, and ch. 9.

[35]For Cottesloe, *see* M. Horrell, ed., *A Survey of Race Relations, 1961* (Johannesburg, 1962), pp. 64-5; for the "cancer" statement of October 1966

political action followed in the form of creating or looking to other organizations for better expression of strongly held views.

One of the interesting developments of the past few years has been the failure of the right-wing HNP not merely to appeal to the electorate, but to gain the support of trade unions. Though one trade unionist, Gert Beetge, played a prominent role in HNP politics, and still protests against any relaxation of job reservation, he was not able to carry the trade union bureaucracy with him. This was probably because his grievance was an ideological and cultural one, not specifically a trade union one, though he cast it in trade union terms (see Slabbert, pp. 15–16).[36] For all the erosion of job reservation, separate development has not, apparently, hurt the White worker sufficiently to make him change his political allegiance.[37] It may be another example of change being acceptable at a distance. So long as Whites are not thrown out of work, or placed under the authority of Blacks, or even put in the position of equal status on the job, a great deal of redistribution of jobs appears to be possible. It is difficult to gain an accurate picture of change because employers, trade unions, and the government have an interest in avoiding publicity, especially in the early stages of any adjustment. Perhaps adjustments have been so limited, that there has been no need for the conservative and Afrikaner-nationalist-dominated wing of a divided trade union movement to break with the government and support either the right-wing HNP or the conservative official opposition.

The real tension within and among Afrikaner organizations is developing between those who hold cosmopolitan, secular views on the one hand and those holding inward-looking, conservative views on the other. The leadership of the National party vehemently rejected Hertzog's attempt to keep the party an exclusive *volks party*. The press joined the party leadership in looking for support outside Afrikanerdom and an editor spoke of a pluralistic Afrikanerdom in terms which Slabbert (pp. 13–14) describes as "cultural blasphemy." *Rapport* takes a strong line against censorship, especially the recent banning of André Brink's *Kennis van die Aand*, an issue which brings it into di-

---

see F. Wilson, *Migrant Labour: Report to the South African Council of Churches* (Johannesburg, 1972), pp. 264-5.

[36]Beetge was active both in trade union and in conservative circles and the founder of the Blanke Bouwerkers Vakbond (White Building Workers Union). Recently he protested anew at government relaxation of job reservation in the building industry. *See Rand Daily Mail*, 15 March 1974.

[37]This is based partly on inference from the lack of major trade union protest and partly on a preliminary report by S. Greenberg, "Trade Unionism in South Africa," mimeographed (1974).

ect conflict with powerful sections of the churches.[38] A significant conflict within National party circles may arise from the possibly growing use of the powers of the state against Afrikaners, e.g., the security police against National party right-wing dissidents in 1968 to 1970, and now the censorship of a major work by an Afrikaner.[39]

Since the late sixties conflict within Afrikanerdom has become more and more public, with the government finding itself having to use its formidable battery of powers against its own dissidents. This use of power will not call forth the almost automatic support it did when directed against those groups, usually English or Black, who could plausibly be branded as enemies of the *volk*. And within church circles—especially a group based in Potchefstroom that publishes *Woord en Daad*, "Word and Deed"—radical demands are being made for the matching of theory and practice, stated intention and performance.[40] For different reasons, many Afrikaners are adopting the same strategy as that of the homeland leaders who exploit the logic of separate development against itself. This conflict within Afrikanerdom shows no sign of abating, and recently *Rapport* even went so far as to raise the possibility of a *skeuring*, a split in the party to make possible a bold new policy.[41] These tensions are not yet apparently the basis for major changes of alignment, but a fundamental division remains between those who regard separate development as a way station on the road to a society without discrimination and those who see it as a destination.[42]

When we look at the structure of institutions in English life there is an almost total lack of bureaucratization on the Afrikaner model. The South African English have always been divided on regional, class, and ethnic lines and never developed effective organization to advance their interests. The United party, even in the days of its power, was a loose federation not noted for its efficiency or the fine articulation of its various organs.[43] Because its success depended on continued political division of Afrikanerdom, the United party was faced

[38]*See Rapport*, 24 January 1974 for a general attack on censorship and on 3 February 1974 for an attack on the banning of Brink's book; "Book Filthy Says Dominee," *E. P. Herald*, 1 February 1974.

[39]Lever, *South African Voter*, pp. 158-9, 174.

[40]*See*, e.g., the editorial in *Woord en Daad* (July, 1974), pp. 2 and 6 calling for rapid development of the homelands, questioning existing proposals for consolidation and especially the exclusion of Richards Bay from KwaZulu.

[41]*See* S. Pienaar in *Rapport*, 28 April 1974, and W. de Klerk in ibid., 16 June 1974.

[42]T. van der Walt attacked permanent discrimination at the annual conference of the Afrikaanse Nasionale Studentebond (ASB), *Sunday Times*, 7 July 1974. *See also* an article in ibid., 14 July 1974 on changes within the ASB.

[43]G. Carter, *The Politics of Inequality* (New York, 1958), pp. 285-301.

with the difficulty of producing institutions and policies that could attract and hold both Afrikaners and Englishmen. A political ethnicity would have doomed the English to permanent minority status from the beginning, just as an effective politics of religion in Northern Ireland guarantees Catholics a minority of seats.

The English have long taken their dominance of business in South Africa for granted. As the group which had arrived, they felt no need to organize on ethnic lines, as the Afrikaners had. Although the English have been able to look after their purely economic interests, they have not moved to mobilize English speakers, or to try to play a new political role. Businessmen had been important in the United party, but many have probably withdrawn steadily from the party, even from politics altogether.[44] The position of businessmen is merely symptomatic of the general position of the United party: it has lost, for the time being at any rate, the support of elites—religious, intellectual, business, and most crucially, journalistic.

The English press has been in dilemma, loyally supporting the United party in the fifties, but showing increasing impatience in the sixties, culminating in an almost total repudiation in 1973 and 1974 over the Schlebusch Commission. In 1974, *The Star* and *The Cape Times*, major daily newspapers, withdrew their support; in the election, *The Star* even went so far as to support a National party cabinet minister, Punt Janson.[45] The press tends to give Progressives (and homeland leaders) sympathetic coverage—two papers, *Daily Dispatch* and *Rand Daily Mail*, are actively Progressive—and, with a few exceptions, to support the "Young Turk" faction within the United party.

The English churches are another set of institutions whose role, like that of the Dutch Reformed churches, has become steadily more political, though without finding a secure organizational home. They are internally divided, with the clergy frequently taking a more liberal line on racial issues than the laity. Officially these churches have moved steadily to take hostile line to the policy of separate development, coming into major confrontations with the government since the early fifties.[46] The churches were in fact, through foreign

---

that the UP was nearly bankrupt, *see*, e.g., *Hoofstad* (Pretoria), 17 September 1969, but there has been a revival of fund raising, mainly by "Young Turks" in the Transvaal.

[44] The classic case of withdrawal is, of course, Harry Oppenheimer, who first withdrew from Parliament in 1958, and then transferred his support to the Progressive party on its formation. In the late sixties, it was frequently asserted

[45] For *The Star, see Sunday Times*, 17 March 1974; for *The Cape Times, see* issue of 16 March 1974.

[46] Most of the major confrontations have involved Anglican priests: Trevor Huddleston, Ambrose Reeves, Geoffrey Clayton. For recent issues involving other churches as well, *see* Horrell, *Race Relations 1972*, pp. 40-51.

born as well as through South African born leaders, challenging the government far more radically than was the official opposition, in doing so responding to the fact that the churches had far more Black than White members. It was hardly surprising, therefore, that most church leaders became alienated from the official opposition. But this development underlines the fact that among the English, as among the Afrikaners, liberalism is an elite phenomenon.

Trade unions among Whites are not organized on an explicitly ethnic basis, though some of the major unions, such as that of the mineworkers, are dominated by Afrikaner nationalists. It may be that in the past most of those trade union leaders who took a liberal line in race policy were English speakers, but the structure of White unionism is not such as to place certain unions officially on one political side, and others on another. There is therefore, no potential English, or United party, trade union base.

Such disunity and lack of political mobilization among the English is clearly to the advantage of the National party. There are 360,000 permanent residents, mostly English-speaking, who have not taken out South African citizenship, and, therefore, cannot vote, a major loss of potential support to the opposition parties.[47] The wooing of English-speaking voters by the government may be due to the perception that divisions among Englishmen are genuine and deep, and that given some conciliation, at least some English voters would support the National party. However, appeals for cooperation exposed the National party leadership to serious risk, in part causing the breakaway by the HNP of 1969. The election of 1970 showed also that, given the hope of a split among Afrikaners, Englishment were likely to return to the ethnic fold.[48] National party leaders have frequently said they would welcome a political division on some other basis than an ethnic-historical one, but they would hardly erode one basis of support without prospects of an equally stable alternative. Furthermore, they are in a dilemma as to whether to cast themselves as "liberal" or "conservative," or to abandon the old safe appeals to historic issues.[49]

There is, therefore, a real asymmetry in developments in the two major political groupings: the government combination, though show-

[47]According to *Seek*, an Anglican journal, in July, 1974, Piet Koornhoff, minister of sport, claimed that of 400,000 immigrants since 1961 only 42,000 have taken out citizenship.

[48]Lever, *South African Voter*, p. 212.

[49]For Verwoerd in 1958 on a new kind of politics, and for Vorster's similar appeal in 1969, *see* Vorster in Republic of South Africa, *House of Assembly Debates*, cols. 4495-509, 22 April 1969. Recently Vorster accused those who talked of sharing power as "hensoppers," an appeal to the bitter memories of the South African War; *Sunday Times*, 7 July 1974.

ing some signs of internal dissent, often bitter, is in no danger of breaking up, despite revolts on the "Right" and the "Left." The internalization of opposition within the National party, however, may not make it any less real. The official opposition has not resolved the conflict that broke into the open in 1959, which is now moving steadily to become a clash over ideology and leadership, with a Transvaal group challenging a Cape-based leader.

A major realignment of parties is unlikely to take place until there is a probability of a substantial break from the National party toward the Center. Such a development, however, is unlikely because the official opposition is not there to receive dissidents who wish to move to the "Left." On many issues the United party has tried, and has allowed it to appear that it is trying, to outflank the National party on the Right (*see* Slabbert, p. 14). That strategy has not been notably successful in attracting National party dissidents—it clearly has no appeal for an Afrikaner *verligte*—and seems to have been rejected by a substantial proportion of regular United party supporters. Whether the enlarged Progressive party will be attractive to dissident Afrikaners remains to be seen: if that party is to be electorally successful, the pressures on it to move to the Center will be formidable. It is more likely that White South Africans have come to accept that they live under a one-party regime, which tolerates opposition within limits. Content of policy, therefore, may well depend on the vigor of the dissidence within the National party. Up until now, many so-called *verligtes* have behaved with what Slabbert (p. 14) calls "cautious conformity." Their conduct in the future may, however, depend on the vigor of the opposition, not so much toward inducing them to leave the National party, but in increasing their determination to press for a radical implementation of policy.

DEVELOPMENT OF POLICY

If this analysis is correct, such changes as have taken place have not been such as to produce a major shift of opinion in either group of Whites, or to change the structure of South African institutional life. The hold of the National party on power seems to be secure, but this does not mean that there has been no change within it, nor, particularly, that its actions have been consistent with a clearly defined ideology. Though much legislation and administration in South Africa is concerned with welfare, i.e., with the use of power rather than its structure, separate development has as its center a proposition that power in a multiethnic society cannot be shared. For all the anomalies in South African life there has been clarity on this issue: it is the intention in the "White area" to base the authoritative law-making and law-enforcing institutions on an entirely White electorate. The question of power is, therefore, not avoidable as an examination of the development of policy shows.

As noted, the virtual elimination of the old historic Anglo-Afrikaner issues was coincidental with a move to an almost total preoccupation with racial issues, conveniently dated about 1961. At the end of the sixties there appeared a deep division in Afrikanerdom, which can be described in Mayer's terms (p. 151f) as a clash between political and cultural ethnicity. One of the major theoretical problems of separate development is its failure to define a consistent basis for the definition of a nation, a rather crucial notion for a policy that calls itself "multinational," not "multiracial." The right-wing Afrikaner rebels, in attacking the party leadership for watering the principles of Afrikanerdom, were, in fact, quite correct and consistent; South Africa can be divided into cultural nations, White and Black, but consistently only if Englishmen and Afrikaners are regarded as separate from each other, or, should that be unacceptable, if Black men are regarded as part of one nation. Only by broadening the basis of definition could a South African White nation be brought into existence. The refusal of the National party leadership to accept Hertzog's cultural and political ethnicity may, therefore, represent "some movement in thinking" (see Welsh, p. 68). If a multiethnic White nation could be accepted, why could not other groups be added? A refusal to do so would make unanswerable the accusation that policy was indeed racial.

One of the major differences between parties based on Afrikaner votes entirely, and those in which Englishmen have been the major base has been a difference over the potential political role of Blacks. Originally this difference was a regional one crossing linguistic lines, i.e., the northern provinces, Transvaal, the Orange Free State, and Natal, wanted nothing to do with the Cape liberal tradition that admitted qualified Blacks and Coloreds to the franchise, but otherwise gave them limited political influence. As the century has passed, and particularly since 1948, the major parties have divided over aspects of segregation, notably the permanence of Black urban dwellers, but not over an effective sharing of power. At first the National party pledged itself to removing Colored voters from the common roll but retained representation of Coloreds by Whites. Later it reversed itself on the latter issue, removing Colored representation in Parliament, an act quite consistent with its views on political representation.[50]

Segregation did not stop with constitutional machinery, however; certain political processes were defined by law, defining ethnic boundaries to political action. It became illegal for a political party to be

---

[50]Horrell, *Race Relations 1968*, pp. 10-13.

multiracial, or to play a part in the political life of more than one group. As the government and its press have repeatedly made clear, they will not allow White parties to appeal for Black votes, a strict, legally enforced, political nonintervention. As Slabbert argues (p. 17-18), the channels of political influence are defined by legislation and by bannings of those regarded as subversive.

The development of constitutional machinery and the legal definition of channels of political influence had a certain consistency, given the basis of definitions of the "nations." Nation and land were closely linked. The desirable state, according to a government minister, is for a people to be in a majority in its homeland, with the implication that all minorities resident there would be politically rightless aliens.[51] With the elaboration of policy, however, a major theoretical and practical problem appeared. What was to be done with the two "stepchild" groups—the Asians, who were not accepted as a part of South Africa's population until 1963, and the Coloreds, who had recently been deprived of representation in Parliament, but like the Asians had no homeland?

So far the government has refused to follow the path of consistency, though this was pressed vehemently on it by the HNP in 1971, when it demanded a homeland for Coloreds.[52] New legislative bodies with limited administrative powers were set up for each people, but the future relations between these bodies and the Parliament representing Whites only are as yet undefined. In 1969 Vorster put the solution of "the Colored problem" on to the broad shoulders of future generations; in 1974 he accepted that Coloreds and Asians were to remain part of the "White area."[53] Some kind of coordinating machinery is envisaged, but virtually nothing has been said as to its nature. The government has, however, moved to accept two groups who will be permanently in the White area and who create for policy-makers the same political problems as does the African majority in the urban areas at any one time. One major development is the increasingly repeated acknowledgement of the necessity of meeting the political aspirations

[51]The minister of Bantu administration and development, M. C. Botha, said on 3 February 1969, "according to our policy one should be in the majority in one's own homeland and in the minority in another person's land." See Republic of South Africa, House of Assembly Debates, col. 47.

[52]Horrell, Race Relations 1971, pp. 7-8. Presumably the HNP would demand a homeland for Asians too.

[53]For his statement in 1969, see Republic of South Africa, House of Assembly Debates, 4 February 1969, col. 369, for his statement in 1974, see ibid., 4 February 1974, col. 66: "they [i.e., Coloreds and Asians] do not have a homeland and . . . there will be a link between their parliament [sic] and this parliament and that will decide the issue."

of all groups, even those within the "White areas," something hardly contemplated in 1948.[54]

On the issue of development and welfare, there has been a change that can be dated roughly around 1968 with the passing of the Physical Planning Act and, subsequently, of legislation covering constitutional development that provided for separate homeland budgets.[55] The shift has been to an accelerating investment in infra-structure and further planning of "growth points" and "border areas." In the former case, there was an abandonment of Verwoerd's ban on the investment of White capital in the homelands, the principal point of disagreement between Verwoerd and the Tomlinson Commission.[56] Furthermore, Vorster has recently removed the budgetary limit on expenditures on Bantu education, a return, ironically, to the policy in Hofmeyr's budget of 1945, which has been followed by a steep rise in expenditure.[57] There has also been an acceleration in the Africanization of the civil services of the homelands and, as noted, changes in the distribution of jobs. The same mechanism of avoidance, which earlier characterized the economic relations between the English and Afrikaners, may be functioning in relation to job reservation. Within and without the homelands, consistently with policy, the whole job structure is changing.

But the major developments are still taking place in developing new structures of power; the use of power by Blacks is still limited because only limited resources and functions have been transferred. The homelands are now "self-governing" in the South African sense of that term: they enjoy limited legislative and administrative autonomy. The granting of self-government to the Transkei in 1963 did represent a new development, because for the first time the South African government discussed seriously the possibility of complete independence for

[54]*See*, e.g., Republic of South Africa, *House of Assembly Debates*, 7 February 1969, col. 359.

[55]The Physical Planning and Utilization of Resources Act, 1967; Bantu Homelands Citizenship Act, 1970; and the Bantu Homelands Constitution Act, 1971; the last act delegated power to the minister to draft and promulgate constitutions without further recourse to Parliament.

[56]M. Horrell, *The African Homelands of South Africa* (Johannesburg, 1973), pp. 79-80.

[57]Horrell, *Race Relations*, 1970, pp. 202-3. The statistics are extraordinarily difficult to interpret, but using crude budget figures there appears to be a rise from about R19m in 1959 to 1960 to R57m in 1971 to 1972, with especially rapid growth after 1966, Republic of South Africa, Department of Statistics, *South African Statistics 1972* (Pretoria, 1973), Table S5; Republic of South Africa, Department of Bantu Education, *Annual Report 1971* (Pretoria, 1973), pp. 160-1. A figure of R100m has been given for 1973 to 1974, report of news item on SABC during December 1973.

a homeland, first mooted in 1959, though nothing was said about a time table.[58] Independence is now discussed frequently, though homeland leaders tend to emphasize prior conditions that have to be met rather than to grasp independence eagerly. The creation of these authorities, however, raises a further question. In the talk of a "Commonwealth of Southern Africa" or a "power bloc," what is the nature of relationships between the members of such a bloc; indeed, how can conflicts of interest be resolved in a system of "political independence" with "economic interdependence"?[59]

This problem of relationships and overarching institutions is central. The policy of separate development has many "divide and rule" characteristics to it, especially in the denial of the existence of an African or Black nationalism, the insistence that most of the new nations be based on a single group, and, indeed, the insistence by the "imperial power" that it define the group basis of the new nationalism. If the "divide and rule" strategy were to be thoroughly applied, however, the government would insist on dealing with homeland leaders separately and on keeping them apart from each other, unless it were following some subtle policy of bringing leaders together because, according to the theory of separate development, contact produces conflict. But since homeland leaders have come into greater and greater prominence, the government has neither seriously interfered with their travels abroad, nor prevented them from holding summit meetings, nor prevented them from using platforms provided. Recently in an extension of policy, the prime minister met all homeland leaders together, and in an apparently businesslike eight-hour meeting, he participated in a discussion of important issues, initiated a joint inquiry into taxation, and provided for a further meeting to discuss the central issues of the position of urban Blacks. However, he carefully avoided any suggestion that a new system of decision-making had been instituted.[60]

The theory of politics behind this policy is oligarchical and communitarian rather than democratic and individualistic. The basic unit of politics is the nation, whether defined in terms of race in the case of the Whites, or of race and language in the case of the Blacks. (Though theoretically untidy and inconsistent, there is no reason why a dominant group should not try to make it work; dominant groups are not stopped by theory.) Nations are to be equal in status if not in power, and it is by negotiation between leaders, preferably in private with an

---

[58]Horrell, *African Homelands*, pp. 30-2.
[59]Horrell, *Race Relations, 1971*, p. 2.
[60]*Comment and Opinion* 1, no. 7 (15 March 1974); *E. P. Herald*, 7 and 8 March 1974.

agreed statement at the end for the press, that interests are to be reconciled. What has to be avoided is to have politicians pitting ethnically defined masses against each other in a single electorate, thereby raising all anxieties that come from a contemplation of the relative numbers of the various groups. Implicit, therefore, is an attempt to avoid what Chief Buthelezi called the question of "power at the center," and somehow to meet political aspirations without a common legislature that reflects proportionately all the various constituencies in the society.[61] Every group is to have a legislature and inter-relations are to be handled by some form of diplomacy. The common men must be kept apart in all but the work place, if contact there cannot be avoided, as apparently it cannot.

Much in this development of policy has close analogies with the later stages of European empires: the shift from military to administrative to political methods of government, and a move from laissez-faire economic policy where the colony had to generate most of its own capital, or was developed only if foreign capital found resources in the territory to develop, to a type of "welfare colonialism" where government becomes responsible for heavy investment without concern for profitability. It represents at least a partial abandonment of the old doctrine of "politics (or trade unions) are not for the Black man," and an abandonment of a virtually permanent trusteeship.

This survey of changes may give a clue to the nature of conflict among Whites over policy. Earlier it was a debate among Afrikaners as to their relations with the South African English and the United Kingdom, in the context of a basic agreement over retaining power in White hands; second, particularly since World War II, it has been a debate between Afrikaner-led English and most Afrikaners as to how the Blacks ought to be governed. Given a recent shift from the first to the second as the principal basis of conflict, can it be argued that the issue and the participants are about to change once more? Are Whites not moving to divide as to how political rights are to be extended to Blacks or to some of them? And having created new constitutional systems, will they be able to sustain them without transferring real power and resources to them?

IMPLICATIONS OF CHANGES IN POLICY

It has been argued above that pressure for radical implementation of separate development has come from elite groups in White society.

---

[61]G. Buthelezi, "White and Black Nationalisms, Ethnicity and the Future of the Homelands,," (The Winifred and Alfred Hoernlè Memorial Lecture) Institute of Race Relations, Johannesburg, 1974).

The South African White electorate is probably one of the most conservative in the world, because the so-called masses have such a strong interest in the *status quo*. National party leaders, however, from Verwoerd's prime ministership onward, became increasingly aware of the threats to the system, from outside as well as inside. As ministers they were better informed of those threats than either the man in the street or their own back-benchers.[62] Within the bureaucratic structure of Afrikanerdom, as early as 1949, they also came under some pressure from segments such as the Dutch Reformed churches and the press.[63] The Afrikaans press particularly, while complaining frequently of the double standards overseas, at the same time does not deny all substance to attacks on South Africa.[64] One of the most potent influences for change of attitude among Afrikaners, especially those at upper levels of income and education is the rejection of them, not merely by Communist and Afro-Asian societies, but by what they regard as the civilized communities of the West. Such pressure may not be felt so keenly by those at lower levels of income; this lack of awareness, combined with material interest, accounts for the slowness of the development of demands for fundamental reform.

Future developments may force debate into restricted channels. As Slabbert (pp. 17-18) has argued, opposition may have to take place only in those areas where the government will permit it. For example, it may resist the development of African trade unions in the White areas, not only because they could become a threat to White privilege, but because they would threaten the position of the homeland leaders, or give those leaders a base from which to intervene on behalf of homeland citizens, permanently or temporarily resident in urban areas. The government's dilemma is serious here: every African in the urban areas is a citizen of a homeland; if they are not allowed trade unions, can the homeland governments represent them? And who is to speak on their behalf on other matters of welfare?

Slabbert's point might be taken further. In conditions of a high rate of economic growth and social change, serious threats of intervention from outside, and growing disorder on the borders, a governing party is likely to show increasing intolerance of domestic opposition, especially if it harps on the crucial question of power in the "White area." It is a situation that places the White opposition groups who believe in

[62]One is struck in reading Schoeman, *Van Malan tot Verwoerd*, to see how preoccupied with external threats Verwoerd was.

[63]Carter, *Politics of Inequality*, pp. 266-81.

[64]*See*, e.g., H. Adam, *Modernizing Racial Domination* (Berkeley, 1971), p. 71, for an example of *Die Burger's* willingness to accept some foreign criticism; *see also Die Burger*, 12 March 1974 for an editorial underlining the need for a political approach to South Africa's security problem.

extending rights to Blacks in the urban areas in a difficulty, because unless they accept the policy in principle the government may severely limit their freedom of action. If opposition groups deny legitimacy to the new machinery, they may even persuade homeland leaders to refuse to cooperate. For most of the homeland leaders the problem is equally acute: what help, except personal and ideological, are liberal groups to them, especially if they come close to running foul of an all-powerful government?

Much policy in the past can be interpreted as being based on confidence: the refusal to share power implies an assumption of the possibility of ruling without it; the maintenance of an Afrikaner *heerskappy* implies an assumption of not really needing the support of White English speakers, as does the immediate cancellation of the immigrant ships in 1948. Indeed, the whole debate over Anglo-Afrikaner issues up to 1961 assumed that the White minority was sufficiently in control of the majority to be able to quarrel happily on issues of its own choosing. The threat, internal and external, was insufficient to create a White, as distinct from an Afrikaner *laager*. Policy can also be seen as based on fear: the homelands policy is an attempt to manipulate numbers in the favor of Whites; concessions in sports policy are made as a result of force applied outside, not spontaneous adjustment; the revival of sponsored immigration is due to a combination of self-confidence in maintaining Afrikaner identity even if English speakers increase in numbers, and of the realization that population growth is moving relentlessly against Whites.[65] The continued failure of policy to reverse the flow of Black population to the cities, the development of guerrilla movements immediately to the north, and, possibly, the failure of the United States to impose its will on Vietnam, North and South, may have led to a widespread dissatisfaction with purely military solutions, or rather, to a despair that the military solution is ultimately unattainable.

The probability must be faced that any move initiated by White authorities from a "coercively and racially stratified society" will be a tortuous one, with vehement denials when changes are actually made. Given the most favorable developments of attitudes within the White caste, stable political parties, and the best of intentions in rulers, their task would be a formidable one. Coercion may be used against both "Left" and "Right," because both may attack policy: the "Left" for not being radical and rapid enough; the "Right" for suggesting any sharing of power at all. The very dismantling of privilege may lead to increasing threats to order. Having created a new system of govern-

[65]*See* a major article in *Beeld* on 5 January 1969, and *The Cape Times*, 6 January 1969.

ment, the dominant group will increasingly face the problem of keeping the policy credible not only to Whites but to the homeland leaders. The greatest threat to orderly change may well lie in the fact that Vorster and homeland leaders can meet and discuss, even slowly move from a government of command by Whites to a politics of bargaining with Black leaders, with a consequent more equitable distribution of welfare, but find themselves in a situation in which they respectively represent masses whose expectations are becoming increasingly irreconcilable.

There is a sense in which the South African story is a universal one: there is no reason why South Africa should avoid the consequences of industrialization faced by other similar societies. But what are those consequences? Will South Africa become a United States at mid-nineteenth century, a Germany in the 1930s, a Britain in the 1830s, a France in 1936, a Russia in 1917, or an Israel in 1974? It can surely be argued that it will be none of these. Of all the societies named only Britain was able to create a new political system relatively peacefully. At the time of the first Reform Act in 1832, Wellington and the army were there, and the machinery of order survived. Power was slowly redistributed largely by competing oligarchies under pressure who saw, or believed they saw, an interest in extending political rights (*see* Welsh, p. 76, for a reference to Rokkan on the democratization of European polities). The dismantling of the whole structure of privilege was slow and piecemeal, yet it took place in extraordinarily advantageous circumstances, in a context of racial and linguistic homogeneity, and a common patriotism with deep roots. For a long time the rulers refused to allow the masses to mobilize their economic power. When trade unions were able to organize, they soon forged links with one of the major political parties, the Liberal party, which saw an interest in mobilizing numbers, subsequently changing the whole social basis of the party, and, incidentally, writing its own death warrant. Looking at the problem in race rather than in class terms, this is precisely what National party leaders are afraid of.

In South Africa the class and individualist basis of British society does not exist, nor will it in the future. Given the concentration of power in a racial and ethnic minority, South Africa's rulers, having made the group the basis of politics, may have seen that some groups in South African society, rather like the middle classes in Britain in the 1830s, are more conciliable than others. A real calculator of power, who could ignore much racial sentiment in the electorate, would see that Coloreds and Asians could be made defenders, if not of the *status quo*, at least of conservative, orderly reform, protecting, or conniving at existing privilege. The search by Afrikaners for allies, and not only White allies, may have begun. Security and development are now frequently linked together in speeches, and a new tone has appeared in official statements.[66]

A slowly coalescing White caste in an extremely hostile world may be facing the fact that coalescence does little to solve the problem of relations with the majority that it governs. The ending of Anglo-Afrikaner conflict removes a major distraction, but it does not produce a leadership, an ideology, and a policy capable of reconciling the interests of all the groups in South African society. In the long period of Afrikaner power there has been a steady shift from a policy of *baasskap*, a candid and explicit White supremacy, to a policy of political devolution based on groups not individuals, and with egalitarian implications. All groups are regarded as entitled to political institutions and identity; new leaders are using the institutions and gain some security from the fact that government is trying to meet outside criticism, and, therefore, cannot treat them arrogantly.

The accelerated implementation of policy involves both the creation of a new structure of power in which, however, power and welfare are still unequally shared. The modest redistribution merely creates a demand for further redistribution. If such a redistribution continues in conditions of order, it will necessarily mean a move away from the present system of racial and coercive stratification, possibly to another system in which coercion plays a smaller part but in which race is still an important divider. Peaceful devolution will depend on whether Black leaders will be able to persuade their followers in homelands and cities that change is in the desired direction and at a sufficient pace, but they will probably be able to do so only if they are given sufficient power and resources. Some redistribution of welfare could be made relatively easily within the framework of separate development, because it makes possible change at a distance, which might even delay confrontation on issues of power. Indeed, some redistribution of power may come by stealth, the result of the cumulative effects of a redistribution of welfare.

If the Afrikaner elites have realized that a hierarchical and discriminatory order, based on race and a great deal of coercion, is no longer viable, that may be the most significant recent change within the White ruling caste. But it will lead to fundamental change only if they are able to accelerate redistribution and at the same time to prevent mobilization of effective White opposition. It is beyond the competence of a mere contemporary historian to discover whether the present holders of power have the will and the capacity to do so, and whether the very

[66]*See* a speech by the minister of the interior, C. P. Mulder, in *E. P. Herald*, 25 March 1974, and frequent statements by Punt Janson on the necessity for a better deal for urban Africans. *See*, e.g., *The Star*, 14 January 1974 and *Sunday Times*, 16 February 1974.

populist character of Afrikaner society is not the major obstacle to
redistribution.

II
Changes among Africans

5

Social and Political Change
in the African Areas:
A Case Study of KwaZulu

LAWRENCE SCHLEMMER and TIM J. MUIL

INTRODUCTION

Optimistic anticipation of significant change in the collective orientations of Whites vis-à-vis Blacks in South Africa is often based on one or more of three assumptions about White political behavior: first, that an ignorant irrationality is an important basis of White attitudes; second, that sooner or later Whites will undergo some form of moral revival; third, that if it were not for certain right-wing authoritarian and group-centered ideological tendencies, among Afrikaans-speaking Whites in particular, a more just dispensation for Blacks could emerge.

However, it would probably be nearer the mark to assume that the orientations of most White South Africans, especially Afrikaners, are based on a desire to preserve a variety of material interests and to maintain historically defined group identities. Consequently, Whites hold the not unrealistic assumption that the retention of effective political power is a prerequisite for protecting their own material, cultural, and security interests.

The purpose of this apparent digression is to suggest three things: first, that major and significant opportunities for change in South Africa in the near future are not likely to arise as a result of mutations in the attitudes of a majority of Whites that arise solely within White political culture; second, that it is necessary to identify possibilities of change that may circumvent popular White racism; and third, that Black action or economically determined changes in the roles of Blacks are likely to become increasingly relevant to change in the system as a whole.

Given the well-known curbs on Black political activity, however, and the possibility that security laws and regulations will be even more rigorously enforced in the future, one is forced by a process of elimination to consider carefully the implications for change in the policy of separate development.[1]

THE CONTEXT OF THE CASE STUDY:
SOUTH AFRICA'S BANTUSTAN POLICY

The most substantial aims of the policy of separate development, in the "real-politik" sense, are to attempt to circumscribe the political aspirations of Africans and to provide a justification for withholding from them permanent political and residential rights in the so-called White areas. Such a policy would discourage mass Black political solidarity and subject Black political development in the homelands to what is expected to be the conservative influence of the traditional elites, who were given majority representation in the first constitutions for homeland government. At the same time it would reduce African population in the White areas so as to safeguard Afrikaans group identity and "White" or "Western" civilization. Thus by granting some or all of the homelands independence, South Africa's race relations problem would be redefined as a problem in international relations. Although many Whites endorse separate development in a spirit of idealism, we hold that its aims as outlined above reflect thinking in the governing political party.

In recent months, some aspects of official thinking on the policy of separate development have undergone a change: first, it is no longer forecast that the policy will eventually achieve complete race separation;[2] second, it is no longer official policy to make life as uncomfortable as possible for Africans in White areas. The deputy minister of the Department of Bantu Administration and Development has embarked on an ambitious scheme to raise private funds for the provision of more adequate social and recreational facilities in urban areas, and there appears to be a tentative policy to allow migrant workers to bring their wives with them to White areas under certain circumstances (although

---

[1]See inter alia, M. Horrell, The African Homelands of South Africa (Johannesburg, 1973); N. Rhoodie, Apartheid and Racial Partnership in Southern Africa (Pretoria, 1973); P. Randall, ed., South Africa's Political Alternatives: Report of the SPROCAS Political Commission (Johannesburg, 1973). See also the special "Bantustan" issue of Third World 2, 6 (June 1973).

[2]Financial Mail (Johannesburg), 8 June 1973, for statement by Punt Janson, deputy minister of Bantu Administration and Development.

implementation has been extremely restricted). Third, efforts to develop the economy of the homelands are being steadily increased—in particular, agriculture is receiving very earnest attention;[3] and, fourth, it has become increasingly obvious that the government is sincere in its desire to grant homelands fairly early independence and may start moving toward independence immediately, although such independence[4] may be circumscribed in the areas of external affairs, defence, customs and excise.

Obviously, if the homelands could be enlarged and develop the economic capacity to absorb and to offer employment to a majority of Africans domiciled in White areas, then they would provide a resolution to the race conflict in South Africa. However, since such development would require the ceding of so much territory that it would effectively amount to an equitable partition, one may disregard this prospect for change on grounds of the unlikelihood of its occurrence.

It can however be argued that change within or as a result of the homelands could be significant. African political mobilization and organization throughout South Africa may be facilitated. Colin Legum's assertion in this regard is taken as an hypothesis:

> Whereas the Congresses [ANC, PAC, NIC] had little effective grass-roots support in the reserves and only a precarious base in the urban areas, they [African homeland politicians] now operate legally from substantial political bases within a constitutional framework; leaders can now legally be deprived of their right to act as spokesmen for their designated constituencies only by an abrogation of the laws designed to establish Separate Development. Therefore, despite their lack of effective political power, they have been given unprecedented opportunities for political manoeuvre in their confrontation with the white establishment.[5]

[3]*See* e.g., the authoritative recent analysis by G. Maasdorp, "Economic Development Strategy: The African Homelands" (Paper presented at the Forty-fourth Annual Council Meeting of the South African Institute of Race Relations, Cape Town, 16 and 17 January 1974). *See also* T. Bell, "Bantustan Economic Development" and J. Maree: "Bantustan Economics in *Third World*, 2 (1973):30-3 and 26-9; and J. Lombard, "Problems of Regional Economic Programming in the Development of the Bantu Homelands," *South African Journal of Economics*, 39 (1971): 397.

[4]Recently the Department of Bantu Administration and Development recommended that Port St. Johns, presently a White enclave, be given to the Transkei despite years of reassurance to the contrary given to the White residents. This is seen as an attempt to satisfy the Transkei's land claims. The chief minister of the Transkei has publicly stated that he would not take independence without his land claims being granted: *Natal Mercury* (Durban), 11 February 1974. Furthermore, deputy minister of Bantu Administration and Development, Braam Raubenheimer, has held out what may be a "carrot" by stating that land claims could be negotiated after independence: *Vaderland* (Johannesburg), 18 July 1973.

[5]Legum, "Political Leadership in the Bantustans," *Third World* 2 (1973):17.

The morale and political consciousness of Africans in the homelands and in all of South Africa may thereby be improved. Furthermore, the homeland experiment could encourage middle-class, educated, and other elite Blacks to place their talents at the disposal of the rank and file. Moreover, the homeland leaders might acquire effective bargaining power and even a symbolic political "presence" in South Africa, which could influence White politics. On the economic level, the homeland experiment might secure improvement in occupational opportunity, life chances, and material security for substantial numbers of Africans in South Africa, within and outside the homelands, as opposed to a small middle-class category of persons currently deriving benefit from current policy as regards Bantu Investment Corporation business loans and the expansion of job opportunities in the homeland administration. Many or most of these possibilities might be the informal and, in some cases, unintended consequences of separate development rather than its formal goals.

It is important to emphasize that the persistence and stability of the system in South Africa does not rest solely on coercion and fear. To an important degree, what amounts to effective compliance among Blacks relates to political morale (apathy and hopelessness), status, and other cleavages within the Black community, and insufficient leadership and relevant community organization (even at a nonpolitical level).[6] No criticism of the Black community is implied by these assumptions; these features are seen as weaknesses relative to the demands of the situation but in no other sense. Significant peaceful change may depend on a process of relatively orderly, organized, and, in some way, institutionalized negotiation between Whites and Blacks emerging in the not too distant future.

KWAZULU: AN OVERVIEW OF MAJOR PROBLEMS

KwaZulu was the last territory to accept the founding act for the Bantustan, the Bantu Authorities Act. It is led by Chief Gatsha Buthelezi, a man who has been strongly influenced by the African National Congress tradition of Chief Albert Luthuli. Buthelezi is generally regarded as the most outspoken of homeland leaders and has made it quite clear that he and his people do not accept separate development willingly.

[6]A report by Nyquist based on a study in the eastern Cape reflects many of these problems. *See* T. Nyquist, *African Middle Class Elite*, mimeographed, (Institute for Social and Economic Research, Rhodes University, Grahamstown, 1970).

Poverty

A large proportion of KwaZulu territory abuts developed industrial areas in Natal. It is the most fragmented homeland, consisting at present of 48 major pieces of territory and over 100 smaller tracts of land called "Black spots."[7]

Although the main growth point in KwaZulu, Isithebe, is receiving more attention from the Bantu Investment Corporation than has been the case in the past, only 300 jobs had been created there by the end of 1973, with 900 more having been created elsewhere in KwaZulu. Nonindustrial jobs numbered about another 2,000, amounting to a total of just over 3,000,[8] or support for no more than 18,000 to 20,000 people. (The *de facto* population of KwaZulu is now near 2.25 million and new male recruits to the labor market number over 20,000 annually.) The poor prospects for the generation of industrial employment within KwaZulu, which these figures illustrate, relate particularly to its peripheral status in the economy of Natal. KwaZulu cannot compete against the core growth areas of the region because of relatively high infrastructure costs, high wage costs for skilled labor (despite overall low wages), transport costs, marketing problems, the absence of the benefits of industrial linkages and economies of agglomeration in the developed cores, and a number of other factors.[9]

In view of the difficulties in generating industrial employment, the agricultural sector assumes great importance. The picture in this regard is equally gloomy, since 58 percent of KwaZulu is mountainous and as much as 70 percent is unsuited to crop production.[10] Yields of maize seldom exceed three and one-half bags per hectare (about one-quarter to one-third of the lowest yields on White-owned farmland), and because of high density on the land, most peasants occupy land-holdings smaller than one-half the size calculated to allow cash income below subsistence levels.[11] It has been argued that the agricultural

[7]See references in note 3, as well as G. Maasdorp, "Targets of Development in Relation to Population Trends and Needs" (Paper delivered at Conference on Comprehensive Development in Zululand, Institute for Social Research, University of Natal, Durban, February 1972), publication forthcoming, Institute for Social Research, Durban; and *Natal Mercury*, 30 November 1972, 1 December 1972.

[8]*See* report on Annual Report of the Bantu Investment Corporation in *Natal Mercury*, 29 November 1973.

[9]Admittedly parts of KwaZulu penetrate into the metropolitan regions of Durban and Pietermaritzburg, but official South African government planning up to now has tended to avoid making use of the impetus for growth in these areas, presumably for political reasons.

[10]Horrell, *African Homelands*, p. 7. R. Davies et al., *A Bantu Homeland* (Durban, 1968).

[11]Horrell, *African Homelands*, pp. 84-6.

potential is much greater than present yields would suggest and could support a population of almost four times the present *de facto* population.[12] Lipton has also argued that much higher productivity could be achieved with labour—as opposed to land-intensive agriculture along the lines of Asian peasant agriculture.[13] However, because of the heightened risk element due to erratic rainfall, relatively higher opportunity costs for labor in urban migrant work,[14] overstocking of land, the absence of a peasant agricultural tradition orientated toward intensive farming as in Asia (traditional Zulu society is a warrior and pastoral society), soil erosion, marketing difficulties, and far too few agricultural extension officers,[15] improving agricultural productivity will be a long and painful process carried out in the face of mounting land densities.

KwaZulu's problems are aggravated by the fact that many thousands of Africans from White farms and "Black spots" have been resettled in KwaZulu and that about 400,000 more Africans are to be resettled there in the near future as a result of the phasing out of the labor-tenant system on White farms in Natal. These people usually qualify only for a small residential plot in a resettlement village. Rather than dispose of their cattle, they often prefer to wander round KwaZulu in the hope of begging land from a chief, resulting in a large band of homeless people wandering around the territory.[16]

Thus KwaZulu is likely to remain underdeveloped for the foreseeable future. One of the few bases of optimism is to see the economic future of the territory in the light of its role as an exporter of labor—a hard realistic view that has been expressed in government circles.[17]

Without prior consultation with KwaZulu's Executive Council, the Department of Bantu Administration and Development has proposed to consolidate the scattered territories of KwaZulu into ten pieces of land. These proposals have been adopted by Parliament. Notable features of the consolidation are that KwaZulu will have no convenient or economically useful access to the sea, that it loses certain tracts of land to open on "White" corridors between Vryheid and Richards Bay and between Pongola and the coast. Earlier excisions had removed a small reserve area just north of Richards Bay, which was considered to be "in the path of White development" (presumably KwaZulu could

---

[12]J. Grobler, "The Agricultural Potential of the Bantu Homelands," *Journal of Racial Affairs*, 23 (January 1972): 37-43.

[13]M. Lipton, "The South African Census and the Bantustan Policy," *The World Today*, 28 (June 1972): pp. 257-71.

[14]There is an average 70 percent male absenteeism rate in KwaZulu owing to various forms of migrant labor.

[15]Maasdorp, "Economic Development Strategy," pp. 14-5.

[16]Horrell, *African Homelands*, p. 17.

[17]E.g., speech by J. C. Greyling MP, Republic of South Africa, *House of Assembly Debates*, 18 May 1973, col. 6945.

have benefited from such proximity to development). In contrast to this consolidation, the KwaZulu Executive Council, perhaps only semiseriously, has claimed seventeen White towns, including Richards Bay, as part of its territory.[18]

Apart from all the obvious problems and consequences of poverty and underdevelopment two points deserve mention: first, peasants might become disaffected with homeland leaders for any strict discipline imposed in attempts to develop homeland agriculture;[19] second, blame for the circumstancces of the Zulu people is often heaped on the Zulu themselves by officials, White politicians, and others. White farmers claim it necessary to remove Zulu from the Tugela watershed because the African peasants allow excessive soil erosion to take place, ruining the Tugela catchment area. Mr. Dladla, KwaZulu's councillor for community affairs, replies that blame for the problems does not lie only with the African farmers.[20] One also finds this type of reasoning with regard to other homelands. At a conference on development in the Northern Homelands, held at the University of the North in 1973, speaker after speaker laid blame for underdevelopment on "Bantu culture."[21] There may be truth in the hypothesis that traditional African culture is not orientated toward intensive agricultural labor, but at least one author has pointed out that African farmers have responded well to market incentives in the past, before increased pressure on the land caused degeneration of peasant agriculture.[22]

[18]For a full discussion of consolidation, see Horrell, African Homelands, p. 17-28, and A. Best and B. Young, "Homeland Consolidation: The Case of Kwazulu," South African Geographer, 4 (September 1972): 63-73.

[19]In some areas of KwaZulu, like Nqutu, for example, studies have shown that the average monthly cash income (mainly remittances of migrant workers) is as little as R11.44. See Financial Mail, 15 June 1973, reporting on a study by the University of Natal Medical School and the Institute for Social Research. Buthelezi has privately expressed his fears to the first author in regard to peasant reaction to agricultural planning in KwaZulu, which must unavoidably cause discontent to many. It is worth noting that in the Transkei in 1964 many chiefs who were supporters of the governing Transkei National Independence party voted with the opposition in an attempt to suspend land rehabilitation schemes. This reflected the strong peasant reaction to these schemes. Already the KwaZulu government has experienced problems with peasants opposing betterment schemes: See Daily News (Durban), 25 July 1973. See also Financial Mail, 26 January 1973 for a statement by Buthelezi anticipating a class between traditional values and development strategy.

[20]Daily News, 6 June 1973.

[21]Report on conference at the University of North in Rapport (Johannesburg), 4 November 1973 under the heading "Skud die Bantoe nou Wakker" ("Shake Up the Bantu's Ideas"). This view has also been expressed by Deputy Minister Braam Raubenheimer with reference to KwaZulu. See Natal Mercury, 5 January 1974.

[22]C. Bundy, "The Emergence and Decline of a South African Peasantry," African Affairs, 71 (October 1972): pp. 369-88.

These two points suggest that problems of underdevelopment and poverty in KwaZulu may be self-reinforcing in some ways and cause considerable additional administrative and political problems for the homeland leaders. Apart from problems of rural discontent, one consequence is likely to be a widening discrepancy in material security between Zulu people in towns and in the rural areas with a resulting polarization of political and economic interests between these two segments of the Zulu population.

Unemployment

A related problem with a double effect is that of unemployment. Although no precise figures for unemployment in KwaZulu are available, estimates of African unemployment and underemployment in the whole country put the figure at well over 1 million.[23] McCrystal suspects that "unemployment among the Black labour force has been rising rapidly in this province [Natal]."[24] A recent tentative estimate by Maasdorp puts the figure for unemployment and underemployment in the Port Natal Bantu Administration Board area at 37 percent.[25]

High or rising unemployment in the rural homeland areas, by augmenting the labor surplus, adversely affects the bargaining strength of urban African workers. This is why rural homeland development is an essential strategy for combating race inequality in employment in the country as a whole. Buthelezi realizes this and is also faced, first hand, with the misery of unemployment. Hence he has made special pleas for overseas investments in KwaZulu, has criticized those who support the withdrawal of foreign investments from South Africa, and recently has deplored strikes by Zulu, presumably taking account of the effect of strikes on business confidence and willingness to invest.[26] Buthelezi's stance has earned him unpopularity among the urban Black intelligentsia, many of whom favor the withdrawal of foreign investment and see no harm in African labor unrest.[27]

[23]*See Financial Mail*, 2 March 1973, for estimates by Prof. Sadie and the National Development and Management Foundation.

[24]Private economic and planning consultant, L. McCrystal, "The Economic Potential of Natal" (Address to the Conference of the National Development and Management Foundation of South Africa on the Development of Natal, Durban, 7 November 1973), p. 7.

[25]*Natal Mercury*, 28 March 1974.

[26]On the withdrawal of industry, *see Natal Mercury*, 29 October 1973, *Sunday Tribune* (Durban), 7 October 1973; *Sunday Times* (Johannesburg), 18 November 1973. On strikes, *see Natal Mercury*, 26 July 1974.

[27]This impression is based on personal informal interviews and discussions with members of the urban Black intelligentsia.

The problem of unemployment has also forced the KwaZulu
government into conceding to relatively low wage rates in KwaZulu,
where the provisions of the Industrial Conciliation Act are not
applied.[28] This issue of wage differentials between homeland and
urban areas is more than likely to cause comment and perhaps even unrest among homeland workers in the future.

Shortage of Talent

One of the great disadvantages of the periphery-core relationship of
KwaZulu to Natal's industrial complexes is the lure of employment
opportunities in the city. Apart from the 70 percent male absenteeism
rate in homeland agriculture due to migrant labor, this problem also
affects the availability of professional skills. KwaZulu, with a population of over 2 million, has only some 2,400 African professional,
administrative, operating and technical personnel. Only 17 percent of
teachers above the primary school level in KwaZulu are university
graduates.[29] The director of education in KwaZulu has informed the
authors of the considerable drain of talent away from KwaZulu to the
areas of Durban and Pietermaritzburg. This process will become
aggravated as the pattern of job discrimination against Blacks in White
areas softens—apparently, an ongoing process.

A developing country requires a high degree of technical expertise
and professional talent. All over Africa and the rest of the Third
World, technical advisers from developed countries render a praise-
worthy service. However, KwaZulu is prevented from drawing on the
skills of such people, both because of official restrictons on permits for
foreigners to enter Bantu areas and also because of the stigma which
KwaZulu, as a product of Apartheid, has in the West.[30]

Development Ideology and Levels of Remuneration for Highly Placed Personnel

Related to the shortage of talent is the lower wage structure for African
professional personnel in KwaZulu. This applies to the African academic staff at the University of Zululand, to hospital services, school

[28]*Financial Mail*, 2 March 1973.
[29]R. MacMillan, "The Education of Non-Whites and the Future of Natal"
(Address to the Conference of the National Development and Management
Foundation), pp. 6-7.
[30]E.g., when the African bishop of Zululand recently invited an American
Development expert to come to KwaZulu to formulate local development
strategies, he was unable to obtain permission to enter the homeland and the
KwaZulu government could do nothing about it. Because the objectives of

teachers, agricultural officers, and to members of the KwaZulu Legislative Assembly and the Executive Council. Admirers of "African socialist" (e.g., Tanzanian) models of development might argue that the salaries of administrators, politicians, and technical personnel should not be high in a developing country. KwaZulu, obviously, is in a very different position than Tanzania, and a pocket of African socialism in a wider capitalist region would risk alienating those who feel their skills could be more adequately rewarded in White areas. In regard to his own salary and those of his executive councillors, Buthelezi has indicated quite clearly that what may be exemplary restrictions on remuneration in Tanzania or Zambia amount to a "Kaffir wage" in South Africa.[31] In this sense, the wider structure of South African society denies KwaZulu a model of development that, some would argue, is most appropriate for developing Africa.

Problems of "Social Health"

A number of social problems complicate the administration of KwaZulu. There is, for example, repeated fighting among factions in various parts of the country, particularly in the Msinga area. Thomas suggests that tendencies to factionalism are aggravated by the effect on rural settlement patterns of high population densities.[32] There is also the possibility that these rural communities are characterized by some degree of anomie, resulting from a deep and understandable sense of alienation from the formal legal system to which they are subject. However, factionalism for centuries has characterized communities in Zululand and the Transkei,, in which wide kin loyalties magnify minor disputes. To combat factionalism, Buthelezi has requested the South African police to make special arrangements to keep law and order in the Msinga area, a move that will not win him popularity.[33] He has also pointed out that faction-fighting reflects poorly on the honor and reputation of KwaZulu and the Zulu people.[34]

Facionalism exists on a small scale, as well. Buthelezi has indicated that he is aware of an unfortunate tendency among African voluntary organizations in South Africa to be troubled by internal dissent and petty squabbling, a phenomenon that is partly due to status deprivation

---

South African policy are suspect outside South Africa, homeland governments are equally suspect to many people.

[31]Buthelezi had strenuously to defend his decision to raise his salary from R4,500 to R7,000 p.a. *See* letter by Buthelezi in *Daily News,* 18 September 1973; *also Natal Mercury,* 23 May 1972.

[32]H. Thomas, "Faction Fights in Natal and Zululand" (Honours thesis, University of Natal, 1972).

[33]*Natal Mercury,* 21 May 1973.

[34]*Daily News,* 8 May 1974.

and lack of formal power among African community leaders.[35] Another problem complicating administration is a high rate of misuse of alcohol among Zulu civil servants; apparently about one-third of the staff in the KwaZulu Department of Justice, for example, has a drink problem.[36]

The Politics of Inequality

Under South Africa's regime of inequality, Black leaders do not have the same freedom as their White counterparts. Buthelezi has found reason on a number of occasions to complain publicly of too close a surveillance of his activities by the security staff of the central government.[37] He has also enumerated the following problems: a few seconded White officials make life unpleasant for Zulu civil servants who are loyal to the KwaZulu leadership;[38] some White South African government or municipal officials, outside KwaZulu government service, deliberately try to focus the frustrations of Africans on homeland leaders (e.g., "Go ask Chief Buthelezi for a job");[39] the government's Department of Information has given publicity to a KwaZulu opposition party in its monthly newsletter *Izindaba*;[40] and members of staff at the Bhekuzulu College of Chiefs are suspected of speaking contemptuously of KwaZulu leaders to students.[41] The KwaZulu executive councillor for roads and works, Chief Xolo, has accused certain South African government officials of trying to create a split between southern and northern Zulu.[42] Similar accusations, which the authors cannot verify, have been made against a few White officials by Chief Kaiser Matanzima of the Transkei and by Chief Mangope of Bophutatswana.[43]

Conflict is also formal. Buthelezi has indicated to the authors that his request for permission to develop an autonomous radio station for

[35]Buthelezi's "Address to the African Teachers' Association of South Africa," Inanda, Durban, 16 December 1971, p. 1.

[36]*See* appeal by Buthelezi reported in *Natal Mercury* and *Daily News*, 16 November 1973. *Also* statement by Executive Councillor for Justice, W. Kanye, *Daily News*, 15 May 1974.

[37]*Sunday Tribune*, 18 March 1973. *See also* statements by Buthelezi in *Natal Mercury*, 4 May 1974 and *Daily News*, 7 May 1974.

[38]*Natal Mercury*, 15 October 1973.

[39]An incident also occurred in which a South African government official ordered the demolition of the houses of some Zulu at Georgedale in the name of the KwaZulu government.

[40]*Natal Mercury*, 13 November 1973.

[41]Ibid., 26 July 1972.

[42]*Sunday Tribune*, 25 November 1973.

[43]*See Daily News*, 18 June 1973 and *Daily Dispatch* (East London), 24 September 1973.

KwaZulu was turned down after funds from abroad had been promised; that permission for a highly trained private secretary from abroad to enter the country was refused; that the South African Broadcasting Corporation's service in Zulu over Radio Bantu is felt to have been unsympathetic to Buthelezi;[44] and that Zulu announcers, reportedly, are often frustrated by "censorship" of the chief's speeches. At one time, the Department of Bantu Administration and Development attempted to impose a "protocol guide." After official rejection of proposed amendments suggested by Buthelezi, the guide has been ignored.[45] Recently, when Chief Xolo wished to attend a Lutheran Conference abroad, attempts to obtain a passport quickly failed, causing much embarrassment.[46]

Of particular note is the failure of the government to consult the KwaZulu leadership in any effective way on plans for the consolidation of KwaZulu.[47] Buthelezi has also been attempting to establish a new agricultural college but long delays by Pretoria in regard to its site have frustrated his plans.

Informal manifestations of race prejudice on the part of some White officials in KwaZulu are also disturbing. Two years ago, Buthelezi had to make a pointed comment to the effect that the commissioner general "avoid[ed] [shaking] our hands as if we had leprosy."[48] It should also be noted that apartheid is practiced in the KwaZulu government service, where separate facilities and offices are maintained. Buthelezi has remarked on the "White Bwana" attitude of many of the lower-level White officials in KwaZulu, and has criticized certain statements made by the opposition United party MP for Zululand, Radclyffe Cadman, in the South African House of Assembly.[49] It is simply not accepted by many influential Whites that Black leaders have authentic and very serious grievances, which they are quite capable of recognizing and expressing themselves.[50]

Lest these points create an unbalanced impression, it needs to be added that most of the senior White officials and directors of departments in KwaZulu are men who have generally maintained scrupulous

[44]*Natal Mercury*, 16 June 1972.
[45]*Daily News*, 5 July 1972. *See also* discussion in M. Horrell, ed., *A Survey of Race Relations 1972* (Johannesburg, 1972), pp. 176-77.
[46]*Daily News*, 15 February 1974.
[47]Ibid., 7 June 1972. Horrell, *Race Relations, 1972*, p. 172.
[48]*Natal Mercury*, 23 May 1972.
[49]*Daily News*, 4 February 1974.
[50]E.g., commentary in an Afrikaans daily newspaper suggested that the homeland leaders were victims of "enthusiastic and expert local [White] persuasion . . . [which] counselled the Black leader to put unrealistic requests to the South African Government," *Vaderland*, 18 July 1973. *See also* Horrell, *Race Relations, 1972*, p. 33.

propriety in their dealings with KwaZulu politicians and have the highest dedication to the development of the Zulu people; this view would be supported by Buthelezi. He is, however, frequently worried by the possibility of assassination, particularly in a situation where relationships within the Zulu aristocracy have become artificially disturbed. Two attempts have been made to set fire to his car, and he has received threatening letters.[51]

Buthelezi and the Black Intelligentsia

Buthelezi has said:

> Also among our officials are Blacks who cannot accept that we are their government and who are not as dedicated to the service of their people as one would expect them to be. In this group I include the smart alecks among our intellectuals who are armchair critics who delight in denigrating the KwaZulu Government over flasks of whiskey without doing anything better for their people.[52]

Buthelezi has become incensed in the past by accusations, veiled or otherwise, from certain Blacks and Whites that he is not a true leader of the African people, and that he is a "stooge" of the White government.[53] It is well-known that the Black student organization SASO (until its most recent annual congress in July 1974), the Black Peoples Congress (BPC), as well as many Black journalists reject, or have rejected, the advocacy of nonviolence by Buthelezi and his councillors.

Overview

This survey of major problems leaves one overwhelming impression: that political processes, administrative issues, and economic challenges within KwaZulu are all very much part of the political economy of South Africa as a whole. Even if KwaZulu leaders were inclined to isolate themselves, the very nature of their daily problems would force upon them the recognition that their political framework, with its opportunities and constraints, is almost totally conditioned by the characteristics of South Africa's plural society. Like the leaders of other homelands, Buthelezi could become the victim of this process. Unless he can deflect the problems facing him or at least constantly remind his people of the origin of their problem in the wider society, he could become the scapegoat for the system he set out to oppose. And he could

---

[51]Horrell, *Race Relations, 1972*, p. 79.
[52]*Natal Mercury*, 15 October 1973.
[53]*See Natal Mercury*, 13 December 1973, and *Sunday Tribune*, 23 November 1973 (an interview in which Buthelezi made particular mention of the hostile attitude of Indian intellectuals).

become a scapegoat in another way. The perceived interference from outside in KwaZulu politics as well as popular discontent make it difficult for Buthelezi to encourage opposition parties in KwaZulu (*see* below). A possible consequence, therefore, is that he will be accused of being autocratic.

PROCESS AND CHANGE

In discussing change in relation to KwaZulu, the aim is to concentrate on those processes within the ambit of the Bantustan that bear upon the overall criteria for the assessment of significant change in South Africa.

KwaZulu and the Political "Socialization" of Zulu and Africans in Urban Areas

Although other homeland leaders have become increasingly critical of government policies, Buthelezi and B. I. Dladla are still the most consistently outspoken Black politicians in South Africa of recent times. Colin Legum seems to be correct in saying that Buthelezi's public outspokenness exceeds that of the ANC and PAC leaders in the fifties and early sixties.[54]

Buthelezi makes intensive use of the political platform that his position as a homeland leader offers him; in his own words, "Politically speaking . . . [a] positive thing that has happened is, that owing to the Nationalist story that we are multi-national leaders, this has given us a measure of immunity in speaking out for our people, just in the same way as leaders of the banned African Organizations did before Sharpeville."[55] On many occasions, particularly on a recent tour of African areas outside Natal, Buthelezi has said that one of the few merits of separate development is the political platform it allows Blacks.[56]

Buthelezi is reaching more African people than many would have dreamed possible a few years ago. In Soweto he has spoken to a crowd of 10,000 and more,[57] and he and Dladla have addressed crowds of 5,000 and over in Natal.[58] A recent survey, carried out by the advertising-research firm Quadrant, asked the following question of a

[54]C. Legum, "The Principal Leaders: Who's Who," *Third World*, 2(1973): 15-16, 45.
[55]*The Times* (London), 18 May 1973.
[56]*Sunday Times News Magazine*, 13 January 1974.
[57]"Address to the People of Soweto," mimeographed, 28 October 1973, and *Natal Mercury*, 29 October 1973.
[58]*Daily News*, 24 September 1973, 22 January 1974.

representative sample of Africans in Soweto: "Which person do you admire most?" Buthelezi received highest mention of over 10 percent, which is considerable bearing in mind that the question did not focus on politicians but could refer to husbands, girlfriends, entertainers, or any individual. The proportion mentioning Buthelezi was no higher among Zulu than among other major ethnic groups.[59]

Zulu people, whether urban or rural, definitely are not estranged from their identity as members of the "Zulu Nation." Preliminary results (unpublished) of a survey of urban Africans attitudes conducted by the first author in Durban tend to confirm this. Buthelezi is a Zulu prince, and by tradition his role is that of "prime minister" to the Zulu paramount chief. He is, therefore, a traditional leader who publicly and passionately pleads the African cause and defends the imprisoned political leaders of the past.[60]

A careful assessment would be that his popularity among rank and file Zulu is unequaled in any other African leader. Most of his speeches are to Whites or to middle-class Africans. Consequently some African intellectuals say that he has not actively championed the causes of the proletariat, and many urban Blacks say in private that his popularity is waning. Laurence Gandar has said that "there are faint indications— no more than ripples on the surface—that there are some pretty radical elements around who see in Mr. Dladla the kind of Black Power strongman they would prefer."[61] Indeed, there are other Black and White individuals who feel that Buthelezi's stance is sometimes unnecessarily conciliatory. There is, however, nothing to suggest that similar views have penetrated to the rank and file; and the negative reception accorded Dladla recently by a large crowd in Umlazi suggests the contrary.[62]

Buthelezi's popularity as a leader, his position as an international celebrity, and his repeated self-identification with the African people or with the Zulu people,[63] has meant that probably his greatest significance has been in raising the morale and enhancing the pride of the African people. He is a leader of whom they can be proud and with whom they can identify.

Yet, for focusing political direction among Zulu people, more than pride and morale might be required. Buthelezi might need control of better means of mobilizing his people. Acording to the study of urban Africans' attitudes, referred to above, 60 percent of a sample of Durban

[59]Results reported, *inter alia*, in *Sunday Times*, 6 January 1974.
[60]*See*, inter alia, "Address to the People of Soweto."
[61]*Sunday Tribune*, 26 May 1974.
[62]*Natal Mercury*, 17 June 1974.
[63]We have dozens of references to this, too numerous to mention, but *see*, e.g., *Sunday Times News Magazine*, 13 January 1974.

Africans appreciate Radio Bantu, mainly for the "information it provides," while 40 percent see Radio Bantu as the propaganda organ of the Republican government. Therefore, if Radio Bantu is unsympathetic to the KwaZulu leadership, this might very well be a source of confusion for ordinary Zulu.[64]

Buthelezi has tried to serve the mass of Zulu by exhorting the middle class to identify with ordinary people.[65] The message has been clear: "The French Revolution had its Voltaires. This means that we need identifying ourselves at the very grass roots";[66] the solution to the problems of the African people lies in "self-reliance" and in "self-help."[67] There is hope for change: you "are not debarred from mass actions which will bring about social and economic changes within our community";[68] recognize the bargaining power of African labor: "Poor as we are we almost control the economy of this country."[69]

While a great number of middle-class-oriented, voluntary self-help organizations have come into existence over the past two years, middle-class Africans have yet to embrace the crucial task of adult education for community development and organization. At the present time in Durban only one African organization, the Umlazi Residents Association, has done so and from interviews conducted with its office-bearers it would seem that it is strongly opposed by the Umlazi Town Council, whose leader is also the KwaZulu Urban Envoy (see later discussion).

A much publicized new trend in Black South African political consciousness is the "black awareness" movement, which was spearheaded by a Black group in the now disbanded University Christian Movement and taken up by the SASO and the BPC. The unifying credo of these organizations is "blackness" and is directed to Colored and Indian people as well as Africans. This movement is most enthusiastically embraced by younger Black intellectuals, but it has also influenced older members of the Black middle class, among whom pride in being Black is much more evident than it was five years ago. Among rank and file Africans, however, specific connotations of

[64]It was reported that Radio Bantu referred to the KwaZulu rejection of the consolidation scheme for KwaZulu as "immature." See Natal Mercury, 16 June 1972.

[65]See, e.g., "Address to the National (Natal) Workshop for African Advancement," Durban, 15 April 1973.

[66]Ibid., p. 2. Also: "Identification at grass-roots which involves participation of the masses is crucial to our whole progress," p. 3.

[67]"Speech to the Residents of Lamontville," mimeographed, Durban, 11 August 1973.

[68]Ibid.

[69]Republic of South Africa, Government of KwaZulu, Debates of the KwaZulu Legislative Assembly (Nongoma, 1974), speech on Appropriation Bill, 1973, p. 7.

"Black consciousness" do not seem to apply. In the previously mentioned study of urban Africans' attitudes, for example, almost no
nonmiddle-class Africans revealed this type of consciousness. "Zulu
consciousness," however, was much more in evidence. Coexisting with
Black consciousness, however, among many politically self-aware
Africans is an "African consciousness," no doubt linked to the thinking
of the Pan-African Congress and of the African National Congress,
which might have become underground movements since their banning in the early sixties. There are, therefore, probably three major
nuances in the political group-consciousness of Africans in Durban—
Zulu consciousness, African consciousness, and Black (non-White)
consciousness.

Shrewdly, Buthelezi does not appear to have given undue encouragement to any of these at the cost of any other and he uses the word
"Black" ambiguously. On the one hand, he stresses the need for Zulu
unity and Zulu pride and makes frequent references to the great Zulu
kings of the past. He has accepted, in principle, the aims of the Zulu
National Congress (Inkatha KaZulu) founded in 1928 by King Solomon kaDinuzulu, and this organization and its aims have become the
basis for popular political mobilization. The first two aims of Inkatha
KaZulu are "to foster the spirit of unity among the people of the Zulu
Nation throughout South Africa, and to keep alive and foster the Zulu
Nation's traditions and a sense among the Nation of the obligations . . .
towards the other races of . . . South Africa."[70] Also, King Shaka's Day
has been declared an official holiday for KwaZulu and for the Zulu
people, and is celebrated with traditional pomp and ceremony. On the
other hand, Buthelezi has often stated that "our concern goes beyond
just Zulu ethnic politics,"[71] and his prominent stand for homeland
unity, indeed a Union of Black States, is well known.[72] In Soweto, in
paying tribute to African political leaders of the past, Buthelezi said:
"The most important thing is that they kept the African people united
and put one common goal before them."[73]

However, Buthelezi has also declared himself fully committed to a
wider Black consciousness movement and to a shared struggle by all
Blacks. Talking to Coloreds he said: "Black Identification . . . is a
positive identification as it means a unity in order to create and not a

[70]"Address to the National (Natal) Workshop for African Advancement,"
Durban, 15 April 1973, p. 3.

[71]"A Short Address to the People of Bethlehem," 24 October 1973,
mimeographed, p. 1

[72]See, e.g., Natal Mercury, 12 November 1973 and Rand Daily Mail
(Johannesburg), 7 August 1972.

[73]"Address to the People of Soweto," p. 2.

unity in order to destroy."[74] Yet he fully recognizes the objective differences in conditions and interests between Africans, on the one hand, and Indians and Coloreds on the other:

> Although discrimination is against all non-white groups, it is the Africans who are not free to sell their labour to the best labour market. Africans are the only racial group who are not allowed to enjoy normal family life . . . [and] all other racial groups can almost move freely in South Africa except Africans.[75]

Zulu pride, African unity, and Black consciousness are not necessarily incompatible and Buthelezi's stance suggests they can be complementary. Yet given the potential grass-roots appeal of tribal nationalism on the one hand,[76] and the ideological fervor with which younger adherents of Black consciousness reject anything other than a purist "Black" line, on the other, Buthelezi's "inclusive" stance, which includes the possibility of rights for "White Zulu" in KwaZulu, may be held against him. He has already spoken out against "the imposed pontification of our intellectuals"[77]—the student leaders, some of whom criticize him vehemently. Buthelezi characterizes their "confrontationist" stance as the "rattling of imaginary sabres."[78]

Political Organization

Rural/traditional. The formal political structure of the KwaZulu Legislative Assembly has a strongly tribal aristocratic base. This derives from the constitution for KwaZulu drawn up by the Republican government. The only entry into the political system for commoners is through elections or through the election of members to the few "community authorities," both together representing a minority on the Legislative Assembly.[79] After election by the Legislative Assembly, the chief executive councillor submits a list of nominees to the assembly for election as councillors. On the Executive Council there is relatively more scope for commoners, since only two councillors plus the chief

---

[74]"Address at the Official Opening of the Muslim Assembly," Athlone Trade Fair, Cape Town, 17 February 1973.

[75]*The Times*, 18 May 1973, *See also Daily News*, 14 January 1974.

[76]*See*, e.g., the interesting statement by Chief Lucas Mangope of Boputhatswana that his people would prefer union with fellow Tswana in Botswana than with other Bantustan peoples, *Daily News*, 10 September 1973.

[77]"Addresss to the National (Natal) Workshop for African Advancement," p. 3.

[78]"Speech at Lamontville."

[79]*See* details in Horrell, *African Homelands*. There will be only 55 elected members in a Legislative Assembly with a potential attendance, if all Chairmen of Tribal Authorities as well as Regional Authorities attend, of over 300.

executive councillor need to be chiefs. The present Executive Council includes three commoners, although one, W.S.P. Kanye, was an aide to the paramount chief. The other two are a former senior civil servant, J.A.W. Nxumalo, and a former business man who had achieved some prominence in local African politics in Natal and earlier on the Witwatersrand, B.I. Dladla.

With such a constitution the KwaZulu leadership cannot afford to ignore the interests of the traditional local leadership. The local chiefs still have considerable status in tribal areas,[80] which has been augmented by limited modern administrative powers. Thus, the KwaZulu leadership will probably face conflict of a type encountered in many parts of developing Africa. However, the combination of aristocratic status—Buthelezi has high traditional status—and the modern outlook of the KwaZulu leadership may be able to resolve such conflicts. There has been local resistance to agricultural planning,[81] but this does not seem to have led to any territorywide issues (unlike the case in the Transkei in which many chiefs voted against their own party on this issue), thought the new opposition party of Chief Hlengwa (Shaka's Spear) was able to capitalize on the grievances of some Zulu sugar cane growers.

In 1971 powerful and ambitious relatives of the young king first tried to prevent Buthelezi's appointment to the position of chief executive councillor. Then they tried to make the young (and possibly suggestible) king the dominant political force. Both moves created resentment since they violated custom: the king is a symbol of unity and an ultimate peacemaker. Buthelezi persuaded the Territorial Authority (since replaced by the Legislative Assembly) to pass a resolution in January 1972 that the king should be above politics. After a few more incidents, the king dissolved his Royal Council (which included some of the ambitious elements seeking to use him). The assembly passed a motion of appreciation: the council, it said, had caused "unnecessary strife" between His Majesty and his government.[82]

It seems, therefore, that Buthelezi's stature will allow his views to prevail without a collapse of support at the traditional base. Unified reaction among chiefs is unlikely because of Buthelezi's high traditional status, their own weakness due to some unpopularity among peasants, and a certain measure of control over chiefs by the KwaZulu

[80]We state this on the basis of a general knowledge of the situation in tribal areas in Southern Africa, the views of agricultural personnel and agricultural planners, local clergymen, and others.

[81]See *Daily News*, 25 July 1973.

[82]Horrell, ed., *Race Relations, 1973* (Johannesburg, 1974), p. 160. *See also* B. Mtshali, "Rough Road to Zulu Independence," *Kroniek van Afrika*, 12, 1 (1972): 30-4.

government.[83] Buthelezi's approach suggests that he will try to take the chiefs "along" with him. A tentative conclusion is that opposition movements or dissatisfied elements will have to seek alignment with urban opposition groups in order to be even marginally successful against the present KwaZulu leadership.

Urban/nontraditional. Although elected representatives are in a minority in KwaZulu politics, the urban and educated groups in the Zulu population are important since these groups provide strongest ideological support for Buthelezi in his campaign against inequality, and their skills and talents are vital for the modern development of KwaZulu. Moves to mobilize the urban population have included the resurrection of Inkatha KaZulu. Branches of this organization are being established in urban areas, and, according to Dladla in an interview, it has members from all walks of life, particularly on the Witwatersrand and in Natal.

The KwaZulu government has also appointed an envoy to the urban areas—Solomon Ngobese, a former sales representative and mayor of Umlazi, the largest homeland town abutting Durban. According to government policy, the envoy maintains communication between the homeland government and homeland citizens in urban areas and represents KwaZulu on Bantu Administrative Boards.[84] The role is, however, not tightly specified, and such an envoy could accomplish a great deal of political and community organization if adequately assisted. Dladla, as executive councillor for community affairs, has indicated in an interview that KwaZulu's thinking is to have envoys in every major urban area. Among their tasks would be coordinating workers' movements under an umbrella committee and attending to grievances. It would seem that the envoy also takes an interest in the development of Inkatha KaZulu. Thus, KwaZulu, in theory, has a comprehensive strategy for the mobilization of its urban citizens. However, the envoy would have to be a miracle-man to accomplish successfully even one of these tasks. The effective coordination of African workers, whether in trades unions or works committees, would require a small army of organizers. The daily problems of Zulu in urban areas are such as to overwhelm a reasonable staff of social workers. KwaZulu could not remotely afford the paid staff required to undertake the task of community organization in urban areas successfully. The only solution would be to mobilize volunteers, which Buthelezi has tried to do with his addresses to various middle-class organizations and groups, but with only limited success so far.

[83]*See* the excellent discussion by D. Hammond-Tooke, "Chieftainship in Transkeian Political Development," *Journal of Modern African Studies*, 2, 4 (1964): pp. 513-29.
[84]*Daily News*, 26 September 1973.

The climate appears to be improving for local voluntary effort. In Umlazi, a homeland township, the influence of KwaZulu is particularly strong, and the political atmosphere appears to be much more vital than it is in nearby KwaMashu, a township of almost equal size that has not yet been ceded to the KwaZulu administration. The KwaMashu Urban Bantu Council, however, is pressing strongly for amalgamation into KwaZulu, in itself a significant phenomenon. The number of self-help organizations in the Zulu community has shown healthy growth in the past three years, ranging from small neighborhood committees promoting literacy to more broadly based bodies, like Ubhoko, a self-help development committee under the bishop of Zululand, the Rt. Reverend Alpheus Zulu, and a proposed new official KwaZulu scheme for decentralized tutorial centers for adult education.[85] But if the Kwa-Zulu leadership is to succeed, much more voluntary mobilization is required.

Opposition parties can have the effect of facilitating the development of political interest in a population, due to the greater interplay of political ideas and the increased opportunities for leadership.[86] Two linked opposition parties have emerged recently. The first, the Zulu National party, was organized in Johannesburg by African businessmen with the support of some members of the Zulu royal family and an African former government security agent. The party circularized all chiefs, calling on them to support its program of restoring political power to the king, along the lines of the Swaziland system. The commissioner-general was criticized in the KwaZulu assembly for furnishing the addresses of chiefs.[87] The latest party, started by Chief Charles Hlengwa, at the time the speaker of the KwaZulu Legislative Assembly and chairman of a Regional Authority, is called Umkhonto Ka Shaka ("Shaka's Spear"). As a result Chief Hlengwa vacated the Speaker's Chair in the KwaZulu Assembly and was asked to resign as Chairman of his Regional Authority.

Both these parties appear to represent the same action in Zulu politics. Their members are alleged to have links with the Security Police, the government Department of Information, certain ambitious princes in the royal family, and the individual(s) who drafted a letter to Pretoria in the name of the king asking that the constitution of KwaZulu be revised. They use party names designed to rouse popular sympathy (e.g., *Zulu* National party, *Shaka's* Spear) and rabble rousing tactics (e.g., the criticism of Indians or of chiefs). Generally they press

[85]*Natal Mercury*, 3 January, 1974.
[86]Ibid., 18 May 1974.
[87]*See* discussion in *Sunday Tribune*, 26 May 1974.

for greater influence for the Zulu king.[88] The Afrikaans newspaper *Rapport* has recently suggested that Shaka's Spear reflected discontent among Zulu.[89] However, the king has strongly condemned the party in the Legislative Assembly, and cane growers, tribesmen, and residents of Umlazi have rejected it, signs of a unaminous popular rejection.[90]

These conflicts have certain unfortunate repercussions in community affairs. Recently, the Umlazi Residents' Association has been incorrectly accused of wishing to "take over" the Umlazi Town Council and of having connections with the Shaka Spear party.[91] The aims of the association at this stage appear to be along sound community organization lines. At the time of writing yet another new political group called the "Labour Party" appears to have been launched, and is also accused of having White government support, which is unlikely. If it is a viable movement it could gain the support of African trade unionists.[92]

There is some danger that the KwaZulu "project" will be weakened by the schisms and splits so characteristic of marginal politics, which Buthelezi himself has deplored.[93]

Labor Organization

The first link between KwaZulu and African labor movements in Durban occurred in November 1972, when fifteen stevedores wrote a letter to Buthelezi asking him to take up their dismissal. Neither Buthelezi nor Dladla responded in time, and the workers' disappointment was widely discussed in Durban. On another occasion, shortly afterwards, Zulu migrant workers at a large manufacturing company went on strike, and the young Zulu king attempted to negotiate on their behalf, an action criticized as inappropriate by Buthelezi, but which may have spurred on the KwaZulu leadership to consider its role in labor disputes.

In February 1973, a wave of strikes occurred in Durban, involving 60,000 African industrial workers. Buthelezi was overseas and though

[88]There are numerous press references to these features of the two parties. Only recent reports will be quoted: *Natal Mercury*, 25 April 1973; 13 November 1973; *Daily News*, 20 December 1973; 3 November 1973; 8 January 1974; 7 May 1974 (allegations by Buthelezi). *Sunday Tribune*, 25 November 1973; 26 May 1974; 12 May 1974 (admission by party official).

[89]*Rapport*, 4 November 1973.

[90]*Natal Mercury*, 10, 25, and 26 January 1974; 29 November 1973. *Daily News*, 8 January 1974; 7 May 1974 (king's condemnation).

[91]*Natal Mercury*, 7 February 1974.

[92]Ibid., 26th August, 1974; *Sunday Tribune*, 19th May, 1974.

[93]"Address to the National (Natal) Workshop for African Advancement," p. 2.

there was no direct involvement by KwaZulu in these events, the strikes established the image of the formidable potential power of African labor in the minds of the public, politicians, and employers. In over 70 percent of the individual strikes, small wage increases were granted. It has been suggested (and this is borne out by observation) that "the stature and articulate utterances of prominent Zulu leaders using separate development platforms, the inauguration of Prince Goodwill, and the celebration of Shaka Day . . . may all be inter-acting to create a new self-awareness among rank and file Zulu workers."[94]

In April the Africans at the aluminum smelter in Richards Bay went on strike for higher wages. Dladla negotiated on the workers' behalf and established high visibility for himself among the strikers and in the press, particularly by threatening to deny the plant labor, a threat he was not able to make good. However, wage increases were higher than those initially offered by management.[95]

Subsequently Dladla became even more active as a champion of the African workers' cause.[96] He warned that "we might be forced to divert our labor to where it is appreciated," claiming that it was within official policy for KwaZulu to control the labor supply to firms in White areas.[97] The Department of Bantu Administration and Development, however, rejected Dladla's right to negotiate on behalf of Zulu labor in urban areas: the envoy should simply bring grievances to the notice of the KwaZulu government, which should then negotiate at an inter-government level. Furthermore, the Natal Chamber of Industries, supported by the Federated Chamber of Industries, approached the government to put a stop to homeland ministers taking part in labor disputes in White areas.[98] Buthelezi has strongly supported Dladla's stand and warned industrialists that they were "playing with fire" in excluding KwaZulu from the affairs of urban African labor.[99]

Dladla's "visibility" among Zulu workers in Durban and Natal has steadily increased. He led a march of roughly 5,000 of some 10,000 striking workers in the Pinetown-New Germany area to a prominent textile factory and negotiated on their behalf with management, with the strong approval of the workers.[100] Dladla's details of the negotia-

---

[94]Horrell: *Race Relations, 1973*, p. 285.

[95]*See* statement by Dladla, *Natal Mercury*, 22 May 1974.

[96]He has criticized African wage rates in general and in specific sectors, as for example, Natal agriculture. *See Daily News*, 23 January 1974.

[97]When told by a large firm that labor contracts should be signed in a White area and not in homeland districts, Dladla said, "I cannot see ourselves agreeing to that . . . we want to control our labor force," Natal Agricultural Union Memo, C.20/73, p. 4. *See also Financial Mail*, 19 July 1974.

[98]*Sunday Tribune*, 2 December 1973.

[99]Ibid.

[100]*Daily News*, 22 January 1974.

tions have been disputed, but it would appear that although he persuaded the workers to return to work, he also emphasized their right to higher wages. He has also served on the Trade Union Advisory Committee established to facilitate liaison between the various African trade unions and between the trade union movement and the Kwa-Zulu government.

Both Dladla and Buthelezi have repeatedly claimed that they would prefer that African trade unions be recognized and that negotiations be conducted by them.[101] The growth, since the strikes in January 1973, of an informal African trade union movement of over 10,000 workers has added impetus to KwaZulu's demands for African unions. This new development has also apparently drawn interest away from a policy proposed by KwaZulu previously, viz., of setting up machinery to coordinate the factory Works Committees, the government-approved bodies.[102]

The KwaZulu leadership's involvement in labor matters is likely to have significant effects on the morale and determination of Zulu workers. Strikes by Zulu workers appear to be occurring with more frequency than ever before, which in turn will affect the general con-sciousness of rank and file Zulu.

KwaZulu and National Politics

Buthelezi is probably one of the three most quoted public figures in South Africa.. His outspoken statements and the publicity they have received have helped to cast serious doubt on the viability of the policy of separate development and yet have imparted a respectability to it simply by virtue of his being able to say what he does. This latter feature has not been overlooked by the government-supporting press.[103]

However, Buthelezi's aims are far broader than merely that of discrediting separate development. His public communication seems to have had the effect of helping to educate Whites, keeping the need for change constantly in the public mind, particularly through his regular bi-weekly articles in the English morning group press. Further-more, he presents the views and frustrations of Africans and other Blacks in South Africa, establishing a significant African "presence" in South African politics that has been absent since the demise of African political organizations in the early sixties. In a situation in which White perceptions of Black political leaders and Black political action are more often than not irrational, his reassurances in regard to White

[101] For Buthelezi's most recent statement, see Natal Mercury, 26 July 1974 and a call by Dladla, Daily News, 8 July 1974.
[102] See Financial Mail, 13 April 1973.
[103] Rapport, 23 December 1973.

rights in a hypothetical future may be particularly significant.[104] Both White opposition parties have sought to establish visible and regular dialogue with Buthelezi (and other homeland politicians).[105] The government has contributed to the "new politics," particularly in the "summit" between the prime minister and homeland leaders.

The KwaZulu leadership has spearheaded the achievement by homeland leaders of a transformation of separate development from a policy that could be comfortably accepted by perhaps the majority of government supporters to a policy that has become much more controversial. The implications of the policy are no longer compatible with White supremacy and White group autonomy. Separate development, as it is adapted by leaders in KwaZulu and latterly in the other homelands as well, has done more than anything else since the early sixties to reintroduce Black actors onto the South African political scene, a change in which Buthelezi played a major role.

After an exciting flurry of displays of homeland solidarity climaxed by the Umtata homeland summit,[106] Buthelezi, in a magnanimous spirit, outlined a possible "federal solution" to South Africa's race conflict.[107] The plan aims at a postponement of the issue of competition for control of a central Parliament. A federal system could emerge gradually from machinery established to reconcile the interests of the White state and the homeland territories. The thrust of his argument seems clear, viz., Whites should be reassured of maintaining control over their own affairs and over national affairs for a few generations.

Second, the plan envisages three types of state: one in which the interests of Whites would be paramount; one in which the interests of Africans would be paramount (corresponding, broadly, to the regions of the present homelands); and a third, a nonracial state. However, the White state would retain control over most of economic wealth of the country. Instead of the present system of influx control for Africans, movement from one state to another would be controlled by internal passports and a work-permit system. Hence the suggestion favors the continuation of territorial inequality and some control over the movement of African labor.

Third, the plan envisages a move to federalism. Buthelezi acknowledged that the homelands could not be dismantled and conceded their

[104]*See*, e.g., *Natal Mercury*, 5 September 1973.

[105]For the United party this was initially precipitated by the action of one venturesome party leader signing a joint declaration of principle with Buthelezi. *Sunday Times*, 6 January 1974, and *Natal Mercury*, 12 January 1974.

[106]*Sunday Times*, 18 November 1973.

[107]Hoernle Memorial Lecture, 1974, at the South African Institute of Race Relations Council Meeting, 16 January 1974, subsequently published as G. Buthelezi, *White and Black Nationalism, Ethnicity and the Future of the Homelands* (Johannesburg, 1974).

theoretical viability as a form of transition toward a federal system if several conditions were met, especially if meaningful dialogue took place and if it were understood that independence could not be foisted on a homeland to avoid such dialogue.

Buthelezi gave this address against a background of commitment by homeland leaders to a federal unity of the homelands and a joint homeland decision to press for a generous consolidation of the homelands.[108] (The South African prime minister subsequently agreed to see a deputation of homeland leaders on this issue.[109]) KwaZulu leaders offered guarantees of the rights of Whites within all of South Africa of the future;[110] and other homeland leaders offered citizenship to Whites living on territory that might be ceded to the homelands.[111] Furthermore, homeland leaders and members of the White opposition parties had earlier called for an all-race consultative council.[112]

The address attracted widespread attention in both Afrikaans and English newspapers, the newspaper *Rapport* stating bluntly that the government had to react to the initiative taken by Buthelezi.[113] Informal impressions are that senior civil servants and prominent Afrikaner academics consider that the "federal plan" has created new possibilities for the reconciliation of African and White interests. The plan appears, therefore, to have further established the existence of the homelands as a basis for political change.

PROSPECTS

Referring back to the criteria of change in the second section, political processes in KwaZulu have improved African morale and political consciousness, though the political mobilization and organization of urban Africans is still limited. It is not yet clear that middle class Africans will lead rank and file Africans;[114] Chief Buthelezi himself has privately expressed pessimism in this regard. Similarly, while the morale of urban Zulu workers has improved dramatically, and informal intervention by KwaZulu in some labor disputes has been effective, long-term bargaining power for KwaZulu in industry has yet to come. The

[108]*Sunday Times*, 18 November 1973, and *Rand Daily Mail*, 7 August 1972.

[109]*Sunday Times*, 17 February 1974.

[110]*Natal Mercury*, 5 September 1973.

[111]*See* offer by Transkei, *Natal Mercury*, 12 February 1974; 17 January 1974; *see also Daily News*, 23 January 1974.

[112]*Sunday Times*, 20 January 1974.

[113]*Rapport*, 20 January 1974.

[114]One informal additional observation of ours has been that the nascent African labor movement and other "populist" groups in Durban are not satisfied with the way and extent to which the KwaZulu urban "envoy" has addressed himself to their problems.

KwaZulu leadership cannot yet intervene in formal and enduring ways to improve the material security of Zulu in the White areas, nor can it yet effect significant changes in the material circumstances of rural life.

These shortcomings are not all due to failures of strategy. Many are inevitable in the context of the homeland policy and shortages of manpower. Buthelezi's guidance to his people, middle class and otherwise, has been appropriate to the situation. One major problem is that dynamic and innovating leadership is too concentrated. This may change after the KwaZulu elections, not yet scheduled, which should stimulate leadership talent among elected representatives.

It is, however, apparent that the unfolding consequences of the homeland policy in general, and that of KwaZulu in particular, have made a significant impact on White political debate. One must assume that this impact has not been limited to White political leadership, but, because of wide press coverage, has percolated through to voter opinions as well.

Broadly assessed, the consequences for change have been informal and somewhat insubstantial in their impact on the structures of power in South Africa. The real significance of political developments connected with the homelands may have to be sought in their future prospects and the final assessment in this analysis will, therefore, have to be speculative.

Recalling the views expressed in the first section regarding the sharp socioeconomic cleavages between rank and file Whites and Africans, it would seem that a devolution of power in South Africa is most likely to occur through an "accommodation at the top" of White and Black power hierarchies. Consultation between White and Black leaders, while achieving little in concrete concessions, has at least set a framework for political development that could lead either to real accommodation or to a means whereby Black leaders can be placated and their demands deferred or deflected. To avoid the latter it will be necessary for homeland leaders to have unity of purpose coupled with effective bargaining strength within homeland politics.

Expressed as a more concrete possibility, an established and formal Consultative Council of White and Black leaders with power to make recommendations to the republican cabinet could be a first stage in a development toward formal bilateral agreements between the homelands and the White government on the rights of Blacks in White areas; possibly later, a Federal Council with real power could follow. Although Buthelezi has this type of development in mind, it is unlikely to occur unless Black leaders control certain political resources. However, the likelihood that Mozambique and Angola will shortly be governed by Black governments unsympathetic to South Africa and that overseas pressure will mount might well augment the influence of Black leaders on security grounds. Still more bargaining power than this will probably be required.

One obvious source of bargaining power would be Black labor. Up to now KwaZulu's role in this area has been largely informal and although the recruiting of migrant labor occurs through labor bureaus within the homelands, Dladla's hint at the possibility of withholding labor as a political weapon has to be seen in the light of probable opposition from the work-hungry migrants themselves, unless it is used on a limited scale against specific employers only. At the moment labor action by Africans is sporadic and unpredictable, and about as useless to KwaZulu as it is disturbing to employers.[115] However, the formal recognition of African trade unions seems to be a not unlikely outcome of the need to maintain communication in industry and stability in the labor force. Once such bodies exist in a formal institutional context, KwaZulu could be quite entitled to coordinate their activities since they would be bodies composed of homeland citizens operating within an official ambit of KwaZulu administration—the office of the urban envoy in the KwaZulu Department of Community Affairs. Formal powers of a very substantial nature may be acquired by a homeland government in a province with a large and growing share of the country's productive capacity. South Africa's foremost industrialist, Harry Oppenheimer, has already recognized the prospects of considerable influence for the homelands in labor matters.[116]

Although KwaZulu could acquire considerable formal influence as a result of developments in the field of labor, this influence may not be decisive in altering power relations without cooperation between the homelands. Unity between the homelands will be affected by the "lure of independence," and related to this, the factor of ethnic nationalism. The attractions of independence are dramatically understood by their obvious appeal for the Transkeian leadership.[117] The possibility of the second issue—ethnic nationalism—becoming a factor hinges on the prevalence of a popular tribalism. This appears to have been one of the pressures on Mangope of Boputhatswana, for example, who has stated that his people would prefer union with the fellow Tswana people of

[115]The KwaZulu cabinet has limited Dladla's power to intervene. See *Natal Mercury*, 28 June 1974. His actions were unplanned and were probably risking a premature confrontation with employers or the Republican government or both.

[116]*Daily News*, 8 May 1974, 29 July 1974.

[117]"I do not think that in the next five years the Transkei will still be under the Republic of South Africa," said Kaiser Matanzima in October 1973 at a political rally, *Natal Mercury*, 15 October 1973. One of the Transkei's most astute politicians, Cernick Ndamse, said that the Transkei might be on the brink of independence, *Natal Mercury*, 7 February 1974.

Botswana than with other homelands.[118] The lure of independence would be strengthened by any growth of ethnic nationalism, and certain middle-class African elites could gain prestige and affluence with independence. Buthelezi, however, appears to believe that independence would severely reduce the prospects for negotiation with Pretoria. As has happened elsewhere in Africa, the popularity of leadership would decline after independence since rank and file discontent could no longer be deflected onto the "colonial" authority. At this stage, however, there does not appear to be any indication that he will be forced to mount an independence platform in KwaZulu. What could happen is that his position will be weakened by moves toward independence on the part of other homeland leaders and by the attractions of international development aid of a type reserved for independent Third World countries. It should be noted, however, that the economic position and fragmented territorial status of at least two other strategically situated homelands, Lebowa and Gazankulu, make moves toward independence by their leaders unlikely.

Another issue of importance concerns future unity within KwaZulu politics. Reference has already been made to signs of schism and division. There is also a basic ideological cleavage within the KwaZulu cabinet, which culminated in Dladla's transfer from the Department of Community Affairs to that of Justice, and more recently his resignation as Councillor, under pressure from the Cabinet and Legislative Assembly. Buthelezi is concerned with the needs of ordinary people, on the one hand, and with his responsibility in race politics at a national level, on the other. He has a very marked "welfare democracy" orientation and his concern with employment has led him to support external investment, albeit labor intensive, in KwaZulu. Dladla, on the other hand, is relatively more sympathetic to the interests of KwaZulu traders, entrepreneurs, and master farmers; he sees the number of Black tycoons as an index of development.[119] Dladla's concerns have been accompanied by an alliance with the nascent African labor movement and a highly outspoken pro-Third-World stance.

The conflict seems to be essentially between the highly critical yet tactically patient stance of Buthelezi, which also involves a concern for grass-roots development, and a more militant and flamboyant but elitist stance of Dladla. These two stances reflect the potential for a

[118]*Daily News*, 10 September 1973.

[119]These concerns can be detected in policy stances with regard to such diverse issues as the rights of ordinary township residents to grow vegetables on unused land (a threat to traders); who should run beerhalls; and the role of the Bantu Investment Corporation in the development of African commerce among others. *See Natal Mercury*, 27 September 1973; 5 and 25 June 1973; 1 June 1972; 1 June 1974; *Sunday Tribune*, 19 May 1974.

more general ideological and tactical cleavage. The latter orientation may have greatest appeal among well-educated, middle-class Africans, whose sense of relative economic and status deprivation is highest and whose "Black consciousness" is likely to make them sympathetic to allusions by Dladla that Buthelezi "dines with White liberals while his people are starving."[120] Here again, therefore, are signs that the racial tensions in the wider society exacerbate conflicts within KwaZulu.

Recently the Legislative Assembly requested the South African government to grant KwaZulu powers to control opposition parties. While clearly uneasy about the antidemocratic implications of this move, Buthelezi did not oppose it because of a fear of White support for opposition parties, fear of disunity among Zulu, and because "Black poverty is too near the bone.... The party in power may see the opposition as senseless attempts to hinder us in our attempts to better our people."[121] In view of the numerous claims of White interference in KwaZulu party politics, Buthelezi is probably right in his assessments at this stage, and the decision of the assembly, if carried out, may protect a much needed unity of purpose. However, this decision seems to be an implicit negation of the "common democracy" approach to change in South Africa.

The response of the White cabinet to proposals for joint decision-making of a federal system has been negative thus far, the usual retort being that states can enter into certain agreements in regard to economic cooperation and consultation but only on a voluntary basis after independence—an excellent way of delaying issues and of circumscribing the legitimate claim of Black leaders to power.[122] Therefore, although there are great areas of common ground between influential elements in the White opposition parties and the homeland leaders, the proposals will probably gain little response from the government at this stage. A growing weight of intellectual Nationalist opinion, however, seems to be receptive to the federalism proposals and here lies a measure of hope for a gradual change in government thinking over the next few years.

It should be realized, however, that institutionalized forms of negotiation follow rather than precede concrete and reciprocal needs for negotiation. Joint negotiation between White and Black leaders will come when the government finds it to be in its interests to negotiate. Sound proposals at this stage for a federal framework of negotiation

---

[120]*Natal Mercury*, 17 June 1974.
[121]*Sunday Tribune*, 19 May 1974.
[122]*See*, e.g., B. Vorster's speech in Parliament on 4 February 1974, inter alia, *Daily News*, 5 February 1974. *See* also his rejection of federation as proposed by Buthelezi, *Rapport*, 27 January 1974.

and accommodation may facilitate the process, but ultimately it will be the effective bargaining power of KwaZulu and other homelands in the White-controlled economy and perhaps on issues of security that will prove to be decisive factors for change in South Africa. The preceding analysis suggests that despite certain fairly strong counter-indications, such bargaining power may emerge. A powerful indirect recent boost to bargaining power is, of course, KwaZulu's position as a buffer between Frelimo-controlled Mozambique and the economic heartland of Natal. Buthelezi has already called attention to this,[123] and he will most certainly use the implications of this in his encounters with the Republican government. If nothing else, a new axis of political influence at a level of grass-roots consciousness has emerged between Lourenzo Marques, Swaziland, and Durban.

Future negotiating advantages will be greatest if KwaZulu politics maintain a high degree of internal coherence and Buthelezi and his Cabinet retain the widest possible legitimacy as African leaders in Natal. On the basis of the previous discussion the likelihood of a cleavage between the KwaZulu political establishment and middle-class-black-consciousness intelligentsia seems obvious. This political faction is extremely vulnerable to white security action, however, and has a tenuous political base. With the growing labour-movement (now involving over 30,000 African workers in unregistered Natal trade unions) and the possibility of a successful labor party on the one hand, and on the other hand a growing entrepreneural and civil-servant petit bourgeoisie with their own interests and grievances, the KwaZulu leadership will face increasingly difficult choices. Mounting peasant discontent, with increasing land densities is a further complication which raises the possibility of opposition from the rural sector. Buthelezi's latest proposals regarding requests for policy changes to be presented shortly to the South African Prime Minister tend to emphasize middle-class interests over those of African workers.[124] Buthelezi's own longer-term interests and the interests of greatest bargaining power with the White government will probably be best served if he accords peasant and worker interests highest priority and embarks on a more effective program of mobilization.

If this course is followed and if White government leadership is not driven into a defensive and negative position, significant developments could occur.

[123]*Natal Mercury*, 21 September 1974.
[124]*Natal Mercury*, 28 October 1974.

6

Class, Status, and Ethnicity as Perceived by Johannesburg Africans*

PHILIP MAYER

INTRODUCTION

As the policy of separate development or multinationalism unfolds it accentuates the gap between the Black people in the home-lands and those elsewhere in South Africa. Those in the homelands (slightly less than half),[1] who are ostensibly moving towards political independence, are predominantly tribal sub-subsistence farmers. The other half include the Black town-dwellers, who are perhaps the most "westernised" Black population in Africa, and the most highly attuned to the institutions of an advanced industrial society.

*Most of the field work for this study was financed by Witwatersrand University. Further field work and writing are being sponsored by the Human Sciences Research Council. Grateful acknowledgment is made to both institutions herewith. The opinions and conclusions of the author must not be regarded as reflecting those of either body.

Kenneth Hahlo, Sylvia Moeno and the late Rudolph Schmidt, were my principal assistants in the collection of the original material in Soweto. Mr. and Mrs. Maloantoa and Mr. Nduna helped us in checking on recent developments. Iona Mayer worked carefully through the manuscript to improve the presentation. Jeffrey Butler commented helpfully. This chapter has also been read in draft, and its general content approved, by a number of South African Black people whose judgment we value.

[1]According to the 1970 census, 46.5 percent. M. Lipton estimates that the correct figure would be even less (41 percent approximately). "The South African Census and the Bantustan Policy," *The World Today*, 28, 6 (June 1972): 261.

This chapter is concerned with Black townspeople in South Africa's largest Black urban complex—the huge satellite town of Soweto (South Western townships) outside Johannesburg, with an estimated population of 800,000. We shall try to show how Soweto people view and interpret the social universe in which they live. It seems important to know this if one wants to speculate intelligently about the next phases of change in the Republic—phases in which the position of Black townspeople will be an important, even decisive issue.

Notes on Method

The data were collected at intervals between 1965-1973. Most are derived from interviews, using loosely structured questionnaires consisting largely of open-ended questions. Each interview took upwards of an hour and filled a record of from 4-8 foolscap pages. Interviews took place either at the respondents' homes outside working hours or at their work place. They were conducted by Black and White interviewers, working sometimes singly, sometimes in pairs, in either English or the appropriate vernacular. The general approach was "anthropological" in the sense that the task was defined as discovering the concepts and views of an "unknown" population. The questionnaire was applied to an accidental quota sample of 254 people, quotas being defined in terms of various socio-economic criteria.

The ideas derived from the interviews were compared with 160 essays by high school pupils, with opinions offered in group discussions and with data obtained during fieldwork in other South African towns (Port Elizabeth, 1970; East London-Mdantsane, 1971).[2]

The Crux of the South African Dilemma

Blacks in large numbers and from many ethnic backgrounds have worked in Johannesburg since the end of the last century. In 1927 the Black population in Johannesburg (excluding those employed and housed by the mines) was estimated at 96,000, and at the end of World War II at nearly 400,000. They were mostly housed in deplorable conditions in "Native Locations," next door to White residential or business areas. After the war, and especially in the 1950s, the bulk of the African population was removed to Soweto ten miles out, to improved

[2]Fieldwork in Soweto is in progress at present (December 1974). Full documentation and theoretical analysis will be provided in a forthcoming volume. We strongly support Dr. Manganyi's wish that Black scholars may come forward and supply whatever dimensions may be overlooked by a White interpreter. N. Manganyi, *Being Black in the World* (Johannesburg, 1973) p. 8.

housing, but more control, regimentation, and isolation.[3] These town-dwelling Black people, long accustomed to wants and aspirations in Western style, remain most severely exposed to the experience of discrimination and rightlessness—the undiminished burden of differential political incorporation. For more than a decade they have been denied political expression and their intellectual spokesmen have been silenced as well.[4]

This is the crux of the South African dilemma today: for the Blacks in the "White" cities and on the White farms a policy of territorially based "decolonization" on homeland lines is not possible, and making them citizens of the rural homelands is not a realistic substitute.[5] "Millions of our people have lived in the White urban areas all their lives and have never even seen a homeland."[6] But the alternative of a common society seems at present not to be acceptable to the majority of Whites. The Whites are apprehensive partly because despite all efforts to "stem the tide"[7] there are still at least twice as many Blacks as Whites in the "White heartland" of South Africa (8 against 4 million), and the Blacks in the "White" cities exceed the Whites by about 2 million.[8]

---

[3]P. Lewis, "A City" Within a City: The Creation of Soweto (Johannesburg, 1969), provides a short history of Black housing in Johannesburg. The earlier history is ably discussed by J. Maud in City Government: The Johannesburg Experiment (Oxford, 1938).

[4]See N. Gordimer, "How to Know the African," Contrast, 3 (1967); and N. Visser, "South Africa: The Renaissance That Failed," unpublished manuscript (Rhodes University, 1973).

[5]However, Soweto's former "Mayor," Mr. Lengene, has repeatedly asked for Soweto to be declared a homeland in its own right.

[6]The World (Johannesburg), 29 March 1974.

[7]These include:

(a) Massive removals from "White" towns of "surplus" Blacks to the homelands—many to new townships specially built for them. See M. Horrell, ed., A Survey of Race Relations in South Africa, 1971 (Johannesburg, 1972), p. 168, for a list of such towns.

(b) Reclassification of Black commuter townships, previously counted as parts of neighboring White towns, as parts of the homelands. Already by 1970, reclassification of townships within a twenty-mile radius of "White towns" resulted in the reclassification of 314,000 people. See Republic of South Africa, House of Assembly Debates, (25 September 1970), col. 5013.

[8]According to the official figures for 1970, Africans in White urban areas exceeded Whites by 1,731,566. Probably the Black majority is even greater. For various reasons (including the large number of Africans who are illegally in town and have evaded enumeration), the true number of Africans in White urban areas is likely to be considerably higher than the census figure of 4,989,371. E. Hellman in Soweto: Johannesburg's African City (Johannesburg, 1971), claims underenumeration in the 1970 census of at least 17 percent. Some officials in Johannesburg give estimates of 50 percent underenumeration. See Lipton "South African Census," p. 259, n. 8.

Political and economic fears of Whites have delayed realistic long-term policy for Black town populations. Recently, however, government and *verligte* Afrikaner spokesmen have called for improved amenities for urban Africans[9] and homeland leaders have spoken of their supposed "nationals" in the White cities with a rising note of urgency.[10] After the summit meeting between the homeland leaders and the prime minister in March 1974, Professor H. Ntsanwisi, chief minister of Gazankulu, said: "The urban African will realize that he is not a forgotten factor or God's stepchild, but that he is the concern of both the homeland leaders and the Republican Government."[11]

So far, the overall situation of South African Black townspeople remains a classical case for the sociology of subordination in plural or "colonial" societies. On a different level, a social analysis of Soweto belongs with the general sociology of change in contemporary African countries, notably to the interplay between stratification and ethnic or "communal" divisions.[12] In common with other Black town populations in South Africa, the people of Soweto are becoming increasingly diversified by income and occupation, but unlike most others, they are

[9]E.g., the launching of a Recreation and Sport Fund by Mr. Punt Janson, deputy minister of Bantu administration. He has repeatedly stressed the need for making life in town pleasanter for urban Africans. "Any people who think that their lives must be made unpleasant while they are in the White areas are playing with the future of South Africa." *The Times* (London), 19 May 1973. Dr. Willem de Klerk, editor of *Die Transvaler*, has called for a revised plan for the non-Whites in the White areas. Matters that would require attention, he said, included: higher categories of work for non-Whites; their wage structure; extensions of their bargaining power; more adequate facilities to satisfy civilized and cultural needs; elimination of hurtful discrimination. *Race Relations News* (June 1974).

[10]*See* e.g., Chief Buthelezi's article "Who is Leading our Urban Blacks" *Eastern Province Herald* (Port Elizabeth), 1 April 1974.

[11]Ibid., 8 March 1974.

[12]On pluralism, see especially L. Kuper and M. Smith, eds., *Pluralism in Africa* (Berkeley, 1969). "Ultra-exploitative" is used by M. Legassick in "The Making of South African Native Policy, 1903-1923," mimeographed (University of London, 1972). On ethnic divisions and stratification *see* M. Gluckman, "Tribalism, Ruralism and Urbanism in South and Central Africa," in V. Turner, ed., *Colonialism in Africa* (Cambridge, 1971), 3:127 ff; J. Mitchell, "Race, Class and Status in South Central Africa," in A. Tuden and L. Plotnicov, eds., *Social Stratification in Africa* (New York, 1970), p. 303 ff; P. van den Berghe, "Race, Class and Ethnicity in South Africa," ibid., p. 345 ff; U. Himmelstrand, "Rank Equilibration, Tribalism and Nationalism in Nigeria," in R. Melson and H. Wolpe, eds., *Nigeria: Modernization and the Politics of Communalism* (East Lansing, 1971), p. 254 ff; Audrey C. Smock, *Ibo Politics* (Cambridge, Mass., 1971); A. Cohen, *Urban Ethnicity*, ASA Monograph No. 12, (London, 1974); various articles in the special number of *Race* (April 1972), on stratification and ethnicity, ed., W. Runciman.

polyglot, drawn from many different Black ethnic groups.[13] Two themes interweave from a Black viewpoint—the theme of White domination and that of class versus ethnicity. Where Whites tend to lean on the idea of multiple Black ethnicities, which is supportive to White domination, it appears that most urban Blacks would for most purposes place those ethicities second to class or status considerations, or they would substitute a single Black ethnicity.

Perceptions of class within the Black community are basically perceptions of status groups with varying degrees of prestige and honor. Class perceptions are sometimes extended to the field of Black-White relations too but "class" in a more Marxian sense—workers ranged against employers. Class perceptions have to compete in this context (Black-White) with the "race" concept of status ascribed by color, and the latter has more emotive power.

Some Blacks perceive themselves as being linked by common or complementary interests with some Whites, across the basic color cleavage. Some are aware of the interests that divide them from other Blacks. This combination of crosscutting links and internal oppositions provides some kind of brake on the dynamics of total Black-White confrontation. Indeed, there is not yet among urban Blacks a general sense of irreconcilable color conflict. However, the braking power is also rather uncertain. Many notions are "open-ended"—they can equally well serve a sense of cross-linkage or a sense of cleavage. For instance, the people say that most inhabitants of the townships are committed to a "Western" way of life. This commitment can be cited in support of co-operation with Whites, and rejection of a plural model, or as the basis for an anti-White Black unity.

So far, at least in the South African context, topics like race, class, and ethnicity have been discussed without systematic attention being paid to the subjective angle, the people's own perceptions. It seems a major omission,[14] as Peter Lloyd points out: "To understand behaviour of members of any one society, it is not our models . . ., based on our pre-

---

[13]According to figures supplied by the West Rand Bantu Administration Board the distribution in 1973 of ethnic groups (National Units) in Soweto and Eastern Bantu townships was as follows:

Nguni speakers	Zulu	167,309
47 percent	Xhosa	56,119
	Swazi	38,452
Sotho speakers	Tswana	90,759
40 percent	South Sotho	79,702
	North Sotho	55,422
Others	Tsonga	40,509
13 percent	Venda	24,523
	Others	8,048

[14]As an attempt to picture the interplay of class, status, ethnicity, and race

conceived ideas of what is significant, which is important, but theirs."[15] Their own interpretation of social reality is the one which will determine their choice of action, notably between peaceful accommodation or violent protest.

Degrees of "Unfreedom" of Labor[16]

There are four categories of residents of Soweto that represent different degrees of unfreedom of labor or of differential incorporation in the city in which they work.

(a) Foreign migrant workers: these are largely engaged in mining and live without families in compounds.

(b) South African migrant workers. Some of these work in the mines, some in industries: the latter live in the townships for the duration of their contract (usually one year), after which they are repatriated. Most are in lower paid and less attractive jobs,[17] and live without families in Soweto's "single quarters."

(c) The illegal residents: lodging in the houses of legal residents, illegal residents are liable to be fined and "endorsed out" when caught. They represent the main body of people prosecuted for pass offenses.[18] They live by their wits, often forced to accept cut wages from unscrupulous employers.

---

through Black South African eyes, this chapter has had little previous work to draw upon. The nearest comparable material would be in the three monographs so far available on Black South African élites: L. Kuper, *An African Bourgeoisie*, (New Haven, 1965); M. Brandel-Syrier, *Reeftown Elite* (London, 1971); T. Nyquist, *Toward a Theory of the African Upper Stratum in South Africa*, (Athens, Ohio, 1972). E. Hellman has published several excellent short studies of social change in Soweto. *See* "Social Change Among Urban Africans," in H. Adam, ed., *South Africa: Sociological Perspectives*, (Oxford, 1971), pp. 158-76. *See also* her *Soweto*; and E. Hellman and D. Goldblatt "Soweto," in *Optima*, 23,1 (March 1973): 16-21. M. Edelstein, *What Do Young Africans Think?* (Johannesburg, 1972) contains an attitude survey of African matric pupils in Soweto.

[15]P. Lloyd, *Classes, Crises, and Coups* (London, 1973), p. 15. *See also* L. Kuper, "Theories of Revolution and Race Relations," *Comparative Studies in Society and History*, 13 (January 1971): 87-107.

[16]J. Rex, *Race Relations in Sociological Theory* (London, 1970), stresses the key importance of "unfree labor."

[17]It appears that there are at present no figures available to substantiate this assumption. Through the call-in card system, employers are able to use migrants also for jobs that require steady incumbents; so far these would seem to be a small minority.

[18]Horrell, ed., *Race Relations, 1972*, p. 161. In 1971 to 1972 615,000 Blacks were prosecuted for such offenses.

(d) Legal residents: to qualify as a legal resident under section 10 of the Bantu (Urban Areas) Consolidation Act, a Black has either to have been born in Johannesburg or to have worked there for one employer for ten years consecutively or for more than one employer for fifteen years. This is the only category of Blacks legally entitled to have their family staying with them. They are not liable to be "endorsed out" if they merely change jobs, or fall out of work for a time, but only if they fall foul of the authorities. They hold the better paid jobs and benefit most from the recent improvements in the job structure and pay.[19]

This chapter focuses specifically on the last category.

Even these permanent residents remain unfree labor. They have no right of collective bargaining; they lack mobility; they have limited access to skilled work; the wage gap for comparable work by Whites is wide; and they are still stigmatized as "temporary sojourners" in the cities. Nevertheless, a sharp dichotomy between the migrants and the residents has replaced former gradual transition between them.[20] The migrants today remain a rural-oriented population by necessity. Most have no future in town and probably little inducement to participate in its social life.[21] Nearly all remit money to their families at home and keep up the links with their rural home, even with homeland politics. They have low status but could be prominent in conflict situations, since they have least to lose and many are not entirely dependent on wages. They were prominently represented among the strikers in 1973 and 1974. Those who "wait for the revolution" will put some of their money on them and on illegal residents, but as the army rather than the leadership.

The residents are the most significant category from the point of view of gradual social change, though they may also provide leadership for violent protest. They are the urban rooted core element who are evolving the norms of a new Black industrially committed society. Differentiation of occupation has progressed furthest among them and

[19]Far too little is known about the relative size of the four categories; their change in size relative to one another in recent years; their economic characteristics; their respective contributions to the high rate of crime and acts of violence in Soweto; or about their social relations with each other. One reason for our ignorance is that the contract labor system (with automatic repatriation at the end) is relatively new. *See* Republic of South Africa, "Bantu Labour Relations (Bantustan)," Government Notice No. R 74, *Government Gazette Extraordinary*, No. 2029 (29 February 1968).

[20]On the element of choice as it existed previously, *see* P. and I. Mayer, *Townsmen or Tribesmen*, (Oxford, 1974).

[21]This is brought out by G. Sack, "Black Railwaymen in a Durban Compound" (M.A. Thesis Rhodes University, forthcoming), which deals with railway single quarters near Durban.

has resulted in an elaborate status system in which the other categories are only marginally involved. The normality of the age-sex profile of the Soweto population, with its broad base of children and slight preponderance of females, indicates that residents are also the numerically predominant element.[22]

There are various types among the residents. "Ordinary working people" are mostly children or grandchildren of economically struggling rural born immigrants. They may have had four to eight years in primary school (standards 2 to 6) leaving because their parents could not afford more, or could not control them, or because of pregnancy, and seeing the small minority who went on to secondary or high school as "different," from themselves. After a period of street life, they join the ranks of the unskilled or semiskilled workers in industry or commerce, or domestic service. They speak of themselves as "poor," but also as "medium" or "middle people," because they have steady jobs and feel they can cope economically. These self-styled "middle" people then are far removed from the sociological concept of the "middle" class.

Second, there are the "better-off." These include semiskilled factory workers, drivers, policemen, teachers, sales representatives or clerks, up to professionals and businessmen. They share a general life-style—one with more Western urban middle-class amenities. In local language this is called being more "civilized." They own sitting room or bedroom suites; they can afford a more varied diet, some entertainment, sometimes a car. "Better educated" coincides largely, but not entirely, with being "better-off."

Third, there are "top" people—the bourgeoisie, the elite, or the upper stratus (as they are called respectively by Kuper, Brandel-Syrier, and Nyquist).[23] Those are a fairly small number, many of whom are concentrated in the prestigious section of Dube township. Except where they are specifically singled out, they are included in the category of the "better-off."

BLACK AND WHITE: SOWETO PEOPLE'S IMAGES
OF THE WIDER SOCIETY

The images our Soweto respondents had of their overall place in the wider South African society were framed in terms of their relations

---

[22]Or at least have been until fairly recently. For population profiles (referring to 1965), *see* Lewis, *"A City" Within a City*, pp. 49-50. F. Wilson, *Migrant Labour: Report to the South African Council of Churches* (Johannesburg, 1972), estimates the percentage of migrants in single quarters as over 40 percent of the total population of Soweto; Hellmann arrives at an estimate of 22 percent in "Social Change," p. 161.

with Whites—a stark perception of Whites being at the top and Blacks at the bottom. But this was viewed in two alternative ways. Sometimes it was put in terms of power or racial domination, sometimes in terms of capitalists versus workers. The "class" model occurred mostly among ordinary working people; the better educated respondents tended to by-pass the class model and put their answers straight into racial or power terms.

Blacks as Pariahs

The term "pariah model," is a more expressive name for the race domination or caste model.[24] It seems to convey better the sense of total deprivation experienced by people who see their Black identity as a stigmatized identity, and themselves as being despised, and effectively confined to the lowest kind of work. We are using "pariah" in a sociological sense given to it by Max Weber.[25] Weber explained the development of pariah status as often rising from the historical process of invasion and conquest, whereby conquered tribes become a guest or pariah people in the land of their birth, producing for or serving the dominant population.

A sense of Black people having been treacherously conquered by White people seemed well engraved in our respondents' consciousness. "We are oppressed in our own land and have to bow down to the will of the conqueror." As Black people see it, pariah status is made inescapable by being tied to the ascriptive criterion of color. The fact that government policy today is supposedly based on the concepts of nation or culture, rather than race, has failed to affect the reality of their experience. "The Whites are oppressing me simply because I am Black"; "a Black man is a slave whose function is to enrich the Whites."

When ordinary working people spoke along these lines, it was in moving but general terms of being denied human status, not a mere abstract concept, but the vital core of their everyday experience. Better educated respondents would list and comment on the more important institutional forms of discrimination—pass laws, job reservation, inability to own land, "petty apartheid" (which they regard as far from trivial), and lack of political expression. They used certain stock expressions that seem to be in general use in other South African towns as well. (Two illustrations out of many: Soweto, 1965: "We are keen to

[23]*See* n. 14.
[24]P. Mayer, *Urban Africans and the Bantustans* (Hoernle Memorial Lecture, Johannesburg, 1972), p. 5 ff.
[25]For a brief exposition of Weber's view of "pariah," *see* R. Bendix, *Max Weber* (New York, 1962), p. 150.

have a say and not be thought for." Mdantsane, 1971: "I can't think. The government is doing the thinking for me.")

Distinguishing between White ethnic groups, our respondents saw Afrikaners as the main human agents of their relegation to a pariah role. They combined two generalizations: Afrikaners are the government, and Afrikaners hate Blacks. "They took over the government, not because they are wise but because they are rough." "Because Chaka killed their people, they still hate all Africans." "They are the police; they arrest everybody." A more positive image of Afrikaners was confined to a very few respondents drawn from the top elite. Perhaps some have "manipulated" the "system" and have found Afrikaner officials straightforward and predictable. "Afrikaners can be very helpful friends, though only as long as the relationship is clearly defined." Some of them contrasted Afrikaner directness with English "hypocrisy."[26] Only a few isolated individuals seemed aware of a change in the Afrikaner, or drew a distinction between the better behaved "educated" Afrikaner and the "rough types." "Some of them today will say 'sorry' when they bumped into you, whereas before they used to call us 'bloody Kaffirs.'"[27]

Blacks as a Lower Class

In this, the alternative model, Black people are tracing their plight to economics, not conquest. "The reason why we are the lowest is that we don't own anything and depend on working for others." The idea of the ownership of capital and "firms" as the decisive factor in class status was carried through quite logically. Thus Coloreds were sometimes said to be no better than Africans, because they too do not "own firms" and "have to work for the Whites." Conversely, "There are some Africans who are above the Coloreds, especially those who have their own shops." Occasionally we even heard it argued that Africans rank above Afrikaners, because some Africans have shops whereas "I have never yet seen an Afrikaner with a shop." A very few informants took this to its furthest limits in claiming the employer-employee opposition as the

[26]On "hypocrisy" as part of the stereotype of the English-speaking South African, see Kuper, African Bourgeoisie, p. 397 and appendix C; for Brandel-Syrier's comments on Kuper's view, see Reeftown Elite, p. 315, n. 19.

[27]Brandel-Syrier is alone is finding among Johannesburg Blacks a greater preference (42 percent) for Afrikaners than for English (12 percent). Two comments may help to show that there is no real contradiction: her figures represent the views of fifty-five members of the elite, of whom about thirty-nine were government or municipal employees, and none were engaged in business; it is precisely from this kind of elite element that our Soweto material produced a favorable view of Afrikaners.

essential criterion cutting even across color lines; they ranked "non-White business people" next to "European business people" and above "European skilled workers."

White ethnic groups were distinguished on similar lines. "The top people are the Jews. They have money; they have businesses all over the country. The next are the English. They have experience in management and manufacturing." "The English bring us business here in South Africa"; "the Jews provide us with money and work," sometimes followed by the statement "and we must be grateful to them." The Afrikaners come last, because "they have not so much experience in business and don't own factories." Indeed some Black working people saw Afrikaners as fellow working people: "They are not so rich and not so educated. They are quite like us Black people, but all they think about is how to ill-treat us." Only a few, more educated informants were more realistic: "Afrikaners are a growing force in commerce and industries. They have made great strides in recent years."

These informants were not querying capitalist premises, not asking whether workers should be at the mercy of the owners of businesses and factories. They accepted that as legitimate. On the one hand, English and Jews were commended for their humane attitudes as employers, "English treat the African well, and we in turn respect them," (even if it was sometimes added, "they are very diplomatic in dealings with Africans"). Afrikaners, on the other hand, were often spoken of as the unilateral authority figures, whose actions are resented. "The Afrikaners work for the English and Jews as supervisors, and all they have to do is to make the African work harder." This picture of the supervisor links up with that of the Afrikaner policeman, and even the farmer, into a picture of brutal physical control. "They are cruel from nature."

Keeping the Class and Pariah Models Apart

All in all then, Black working people tended to contrapose cruel Afrikaners against "good" English. In the race domination or pariah model the Afrikaners were shown as the central villains; in the economic class model they were seen as minor villains, with the "good" English or Jew occupying the center of the scene. The crux of the matter is that the "cruel" roles of the Afrikaners are emphatically denied legitimacy, whereas the employer role of the English and Jews is not. This distinction seems to have played a critical part in preventing total Black-White polarization, for it seems to serve as a barrier against a fusion of the class and the pariah models.

While acutely aware both of their low wages (presumably paid by English and Jews) and of their pariah status in the wider system (dominated by Afrikaners), somehow Black working people do not blame their low wages on the wider system and the way it loads things in the employer's favor. Rather than query the discrepancy between White and Black wages, they would speak of their particular boss being "hard" compared with others who pay more. Many attributed their failure to obtain or to hold a reasonably paid job to their own short-comings. Such "intrapunitive" statements are in fact made in comparison with fellow Africans, who have done better than themselves, a perception of economic failure in terms of status in the townships.

In Marxist terms it would be argued that these Black workers lack proper class consciousness. If class can be seen as an "event"[28] it has not quite arrived as far as they are concerned. In the language of everyday politics they could be said to lack political awareness or even political sense.[29] They seem willing to see themselves in the role of a "normal" working class in a capitalist system and to ignore their "abnormal" position as unfree labor.

For the men and women in Soweto with steady jobs, or with residence qualifications that allow them to choose between jobs, the working life in town can have many positive, reassuring aspects. The harrowing incidents of pariah status are likely to be more sporadic and to be felt elsewhere, either at home in the townships or out in the city streets. Thus they can remain existentially separable from the everyday working life. The working life and the township life can remain, in Schütz' language, two related "sub-universes of reality."[30]

As against the workers who have forgone the development of "worker consciousness' by distinguishing English, Jews, and Afrikaners, there were those who saw Blacks and Whites in uncompromising terms of "us" versus "them," insisting that they cannot distinguish between different categories of Whites. For them all Whites are rich and all Blacks are poor. This view seems to prevail where wages are very low and reasonable jobs difficult to get, as was the case in East London-Mdantsane in 1971. There the fusion of the two sources of indignation had become widespread. "We Blacks are made poor by the

[28]E. Thompson, *The Making of the English Working Classes* (London, 1964).
[29]Similar phenomena have been noted elsewhere. W. Runciman, writing of English workers, noted that "appeals to explicit principles of overall comparison, remained as infrequent as ever . . . . The relation of grievance to hardship remained anomalous." *See Relative Deprivation and Social Justice* (London, 1966), p. 91. And M. Abrams has recently pointed to "the apparent paradox" in Britain that people are satisfied on one level, while at the same time showing disquiet about many aspects of their lives, feeling that they were entitled to a better deal and that the quality of their lives had declined. *See Social Trends*, no. 4, (London, 1973).
[30]A. Schütz, *The Problem of Social Reality*, Collected Papers I (The Hague, 1967), p. 207.

laws of South Africa." "We are oppressed by those many laws which are made just to keep us subservient." "They want me as a laborer, but don't want to give me the rights of a citizen." The fusion between political and economic dissatisfaction was more common in East London than in Grahamstown, although employment was worse in Grahams-town. There was more political awareness among the rank-and-file workers in Port Elizabeth and East London than among similar groups in provincial towns like Grahamstown or on the Rand.[31] During the Durban strikes in 1973 and in Johannesburg in 1974, it appears Africans were operating mainly within an economic model.

The better-off element in Soweto spoke less about Whites as the employer class and more about Whites as the dominant class. Since it was here that they saw the basic clash of interests, they did not identify with the working masses (except for a few politically motivated intellectuals). They visualized White discrimination as an instrument of competition rather than of "exploitation," dwelling on the better jobs and better pay received by Europeans with no higher qualifications than their own. "We (i.e., the better educated Blacks) do the same type of work as the Whites and are in a position to compare salaries." Some Black businessmen wanted to be large-scale capitalists themselves. And there were the highly educated, who unlike the ordinary people, felt qualified for decision-making positions and aspired to them. Both these groups stand to gain more directly from a change in the "system" than the working population.

SOCIAL STRATIFICATION WITHIN TOWNSHIP SOCIETY

We found in Soweto a prevalence of rather "advanced" models in which recognized social stratifications are seen as overriding "tribal" affiliations. It would be inappropriate to say of Soweto, as is said of other towns in Africa, "that kinship and other kinds of *Gemeinschaft* relationships are predominant while social class has little meaning."[32] Nor is "status crystallization" in Soweto limited to the higher strata of professionals and businessmen as in West Africa. In Soweto we are dealing with the most highly industrialised Black population in Africa. A high percentage of the ordinary workers claim to be "following Western culture"; residents of all kinds, poor and well-to-do, illiterate and well educated, share a consensus of values concerning social

---

[31]D. Carter, "The Defiance Campaign: A Comparative Analysis of the Organisation, Leadership and Participation in the Eastern Cape and The Transvaal," in the University of London, Institute of Commonwealth Studies, *Collected Papers on the Societies of Southern Africa*, 2 (London, 1972).

[32]Himmelstrand, "Rank Equilibrium," in Melson and Wolfe, eds., *Nigeria*, p. 255.

superiority and inferiority in township society that would seem to fit a functional theory of class.

The complex play of status differentiation is entirely acted out behind the impenetrable curtain of social segregation and separation of Blacks and Whites. It has not been South African policy to lift the curtain even for the highly educated Black elites in the cities. And yet the models of status differentiation that have taken hold in the townships are not without a bearing on social change in the wider South African arena. There are even some discernible lines of potential class opposition.

Successful business men who take active parts in community life, within the given framework, are accused of being stooges ultimately motivated by their material interests. The highly educated are accused of withholding their full share in community activities. Many admit to doing so, because, they say, they can perceive the futility of it all. The highly educated professionals are depicted less as leaders than as "idols" of the townships; they are symbols of Black achievement. The secondary educated are seen as incapacitating themselves by their low self-esteem and introverted bitterness, and their use of "manners" and English as distancing mechanisms to separate themselves from the ordinary people.

ETHNICITY

Many "tribal" groups are represented in Soweto, speaking mutually unintelligible languages and having different backgrounds of custom and tradition. This raises two important questions. First, whether the individual identifies primarily with his ethnic group, or "tribe," conceiving it as a clearly bounded group in opposition to other similar groups within the urban setting. This is the problem of political ethnicity—an ideological alternative to either African nationalism or nonracial South Africanism; second, whether Blacks in town continue to practice cultural ethnicity; i.e., whether they adhere to ethnic customs, norms, values, and symbols, including, of course, language. Cultural ethnicity usually supports political ethnicity, but it can stand on its own. Where it does, we have only ethnic "categories," but not ethnic "groups." The most common alternatives perceived as replacing cultural ethnicity among urban Africans are either identification with a new common Black culture or with "Western" culture.

Political Ethnicity in Town

On the evidence of various cities in independent Africa we might expect in Soweto continuing or increasing manifestations of ethnic groupings, particularly in the form of powerful tribal associations. The Department of Bantu Affairs seemed to be thinking on some such lines when in 1955 it introduced a policy of residential segregation for the major language groups in the new Johannesburg townships. However, exclusive tribal patriotism seems to have almost died in Soweto, if we consider only explicitly formulated ideologies and main institutional forms. Ideologically, it is race and class oppositions that are claimed to matter, while ethnic oppositions are denied or simply shrugged off. This was one of the most clear cut findings in the whole mass of research material.[33]

This does not tell quite the whole story, because research also indicated that ethnic categories do still have considerable resonance in daily interaction. Sometimes this can simply result from the official policy of concentrating members of ethnic groups in separate townships; e.g., associations (football clubs, choirs, and the like) recruiting their members predominately from a single ethnic group. But sometimes it reflects a voluntary preference for associates with the same ethnic or language background. Such "miniethnicity" is not infrequent among illiterates with rural backgrounds. Their leisure time friends are often not only from the same "tribe," but also "homeboys" from the same country area.[34]

Even the highly educated often *de facto* move within a circle speaking their language, but they stress that "I have never really thought about it. Ethnic grouping does not itself mean anything to me." This applies to very many people of all levels. Similarly with "tribal" endogamy. Many parents would still prefer their children to find a partner from their own language group ("I would prefer them to marry a Sotho, because they know the customs and speak the language"), but they would add significantly, "I would not force them"—a telling support for the popular claim that ethnic boundary maintenance is no longer a matter of supreme concern in Soweto.[35]

The Ideology of the Melting Pot

Many statements playing down ethnicity as a factor in group identity or individual relations obviously went beyond the objective reality. "There are so many groups. You hardly know or can be bothered about who belongs to which." Others, more in accord with reality, would say that although "tribal" divisions have not yet disappeared, their disappearance was both desirable and inevitable. Younger

[33]This emerged no less clearly from research in East London-Mdantsane. *See* Mayer, *Urban Africans.*

[34]On the concept of "incapsulation" of rural-oriented town dwellers, *see* Mayer, *Townsmen or Tribesmen.*

[35]The concept of boundary maintenance is developed by F. Barth in *Ethnic Groups and Boundaries* (London, 1969).

people remarked they would intentionally make friends from other tribes. They foretold that "in the next two generations Soweto will be a pure African national place with no Zulu, or Sotho, or Shangaan, or Xhosa, but only Africans." The preponderant ideology expressed here, that of the melting pot, is justified most consistently and emphatically by the consciousness of a common African identity, or in the language of a few years ago, by African nationalism.

Whereas in tribally homogeneous East London-Mdantsane, with its many unemployed Blacks, political consciousness seemed to focus on pass laws and job reservation, a major focus in polyglot Soweto has been the government's policy of "supporting tribalism" by introducing residential segregation on ethnic lines. The same formulae of resentment were encountered right down to the rank and file. "The motive behind this policy is to kill the spirit which was gradually growing among these different tribes—the spirit of African nationalism. If one makes the small nations to clash among themselves, they will somehow forget about the major enemy." "We are all Africans here, suffering from the same malady—the unjustice of Government."

The ideological depreciation of political ethnicity is not felt to be incompatible with singling out Shangaan and Venda for disparaging comments. "The Shangaan have funny habits. They are not clean." To the "civilized" citizens of Soweto this "distancing" does not reflect a low ranking of Shangaan as an ethnic group, but a reaction to the Shangaan display of tribal distinctiveness, and their excluding themselves from the civilized norms. It is not an expression of ethnicity, but of antiethnicity.

The Homeland Link and the Possibility of Reviving Ethnicity

Has "deethnization" in Soweto then proceeded beyond the point of no return? The government emphasizes "homeland links" and tries to propagate "national" identifications. The evidence suggests that it is too late for this kind of political ethnicity; its place is likely to be taken more and more by Black ethnicity.

Reemergence of groups based on common ethnicity is not only possible but rather common, whenever residual feelings of ethnic identity can be exploited. Pressure groups may form, using the ethnic idiom. This happened in postcolonial Africa when the departure of the White administrations offered scope for new forms of competition between groups for economic or social advantages.[36] It is happening in South Africa today.[37] In some contexts, therefore, ethnicity

---

[36]Cohen, ed., *Urban Ethnicity.*

[37]E.g., in connection with the first Ciskeian elections in February 1973, when a Rarabe-led (i.e., Xhosa) opposition movement fought the elections on

has been increasing in Soweto in recent years. However, generally speaking, the total volume of political and economic power available to Africans in the townships seem too limited for this kind of ethnic revival to become a major phenomenon.

In regard to ethnicity informants referred to the strong group consciousness of the Afrikaners and their political dominance over other Whites as well as Blacks. As we have seen, only a few traditionalists among the Blacks at present show a similar desire for boundary maintenance and group emphasis. It is unpredictable whether one day in the future, in an independent Soweto, the numerically preponderant Zulu speakers might be tempted to use ethnicity in a bid for power. So far the homelands have very little tangible to offer the urban dwellers. On the contrary, they appear to threaten a further diminution of their security in town. In East London and Mdantsane, people expressed their dread of being sent back to homelands—as they put it—"to starve."[38] The homelands are seen as places where work either is not available or is underpaid, except for the few educated who may land posts in the bureaucracy. However, urban Africans may well feel increasing sentimental or emotional concern with the homelands or their leaders. Chief Buthelezi, and other homeland politicians, are immensely popular in Soweto, especially among ordinary people.[39] Their popularity is somewhat qualified among the educated, who sympathize with Buthelezi's pragmatism and yet remain critical of the whole homeland policy. Many of them continue to support the traditional African National Congress (ANC) policy of a common, nonracial South Africa and totally reject separate development.

Urban residents who still have homeland links generally try to keep them up, because of their feelings of insecurity in town.[40] Only if or when Soweto residents, as distinct from migrants, begin to see that the homeland leaders or parties are able to wield real influence on their behalf, are they likely to give active support to organizations that are

---

tribal lines to oust the government of Chief Justice Mabandla, who is a Fingo. Cases of serious ethnic conflicts have also arisen in the ethnically mixed area north of the Reef, which has been declared Tswana. Here Tswana have been demanding that they be given trading, residential, and job preferences; Blacks of other ethnic groups resent this. *See* Lipton, "The South African Census."

[38] Mayer, *Urban Africans*.

[39] *Sunday Times* (Johannesburg), 6 January 1974, "What Black South Africans Think," quoting a market research survey based on a sample of 800 Soweto inhabitants.

[40] L. Schlemmer, "City or Rural Homeland," mimeographed (University of Natal, 1971).

developing around homeland representatives in town.[41] In any case, there is little reason why such organizations should introduce ethnic oppositions or rivalries into the urban field itself. On the contrary, the lot of the urban African may well become a major area for cooperation between the various homeland authorities, so that the homeland links, rather than "retribalizing" urban residents, might help to "Africanize" homeland policies. Defining his views on the responsibility of homeland leaders toward urban Blacks, Chief Buthelezi spoke in terms of Black solidarity as against divisive ethnicity.[42]

Here then is one of the notable differences between Black urbanism in Soweto and in many other African cities,[43] notably those in West Africa. Three reasons seem to account for this difference. First, the Soweto rank and file interpret relations with Whites in terms of economic class. In the copper belt, in the late days of colonial rule, tribalism was transcended in situations of industrial confrontations between White management and Black workers.[44] On the Rand today, all vertical divisions between Africans are conceived as undesirable, if not meaningless. "The struggle we are all facing for economic reasons is the same." Second, in the social world of the Blacks themselves, class distinctions are widely seen as more important than ethnic ones. In the copper belt of the 1950s, "tribalism" was still "the most important category of day-to-day interaction."[45] In Soweto the prestige principle has come to surpass the ethnicity principle in importance and has often supplanted it.[46] Third, the long experience of Blacks' living together has accelerated the processes of cultural integration within the townships. A strong nucleus of settled inhabitants can look back to years of ethnically intermingled living. Even for the rest situations in which tribal norms govern behavior have dwindled. The new common norms are not only designed to cope with casual encounters, but present fully developed guides to expected behavior. The common culture is seen as belonging to the same family as that of the Whites. Part of the process of cultural integration within the townships is the wide use of English and the *Tsotsi taal* or "lingo." English is claimed to be the "Black man's *lingua*

---

[41]E.g., an official KwaZulu organization, Inkatha KaZulu which is trying to build up a network of branches, including every Reef township.

[42]In his series of fortnightly articles, *Eastern Province Herald,* May 1974.

[43]Lloyd, *Classes, Crises and Coups,* p. 101. Lloyd notes the participation of the educated in ethnic and local associations.

[44]A. Epstein, *Politics in an Urban African Community* (Manchester, 1958).

[45]J. Mitchell, *The Kalela Dance,* Rhodes-Livingstone Paper no. 27, (Manchester, 1956), p. 29.

[46]*See also* A. Cohen, *Customs and Politics in Urban Africa* (London, 1969), p. 193 f, for a discussion of Ibadan.

franca," and is used freely even by those with little formal education; the *taal*, an Afrikaans-based patois, is much in vogue even by the educated who were brought up in town.

Cultural Ethnicity

Thus it should be clear that by and large Soweto today is no place to look for faithfully practiced "tribal customs" among permanent residents. Respondents would say that in their view the great mass of the permanent residents are "civilized," or "Europeanized," or "follow the Western way of life." They said it firmly and without regret or ambivalence, even if ordinary people might tend to interpret the limits of "Europeanized" a degree more generously than the higher educated, or the higher educated might attribute to the ordinary people a larger remnant of "tribal" behavior and beliefs than they would recognize themselves. "About 70 percent of our people have become Europeanized." "Places like White City, Zola, Pimville, and Orlando are behind in civilization in comparison with Rockville, a portion of Dube and Mofole, Meadowland, and Dobsonville. But they are not *tribal*, please!"

While the words "civilization" and "enlightenment" were used frequently, they meant on the whole no more than money economy and a taste for consumer goods, plus school education that teaches literacy and an awareness of other peoples and ages. "Civilized people regard themselves as leading the modern life." The "modern" life is the one suitable for an urban industrial environment. "Africans had to follow the Western way of life so as to meet the demands of the modern world." "Civilization" or the modern way of life is, as informants put it, the "nontribal way of life." It is significant that the opposition is seen as "civilized-tribal" rather than "civilized-primitive." The middle-class life-style followed by people in the fashionable section of Dube with their refrigerators, electric cookers, bathroom hot-rails, and other amenities has an unchallenged status value.[47]

While most people were able to separate the notion of "Western civilization" from that of the life-style contemporary South African Whites, they did see "civilization" as having been diffused into South Africa historically by Whites. In this light they did claim to be sharing a European civilization. We are faced, then, with a rejection of cultural ethnicity, as emphatic as that of political ethnicity, but where the rejection of political ethnicity affirms Africanism, the rejection of cultural ethnicity seems at first sight to do the reverse. No wonder that

---

[47]*See* Mitchell, *Kalela Dance*, p. 13 for the comparable phenomena in the copper belt in the fifties.

some African intellectuals feel misgivings about it. The nascent Black consciousness movement in South Africa, while supporting radical antitribalism, has called for a "consciousness of our cultural heritage."[48] Magubane argues forcefully that "A 'Europeanised' African can never . . . aspire to an independent identity."[49]

There were undeniable traces of "negative identity" when Soweto people spoke about "civilization." A common argument was expressed thus: "The Whites had civilization for centuries before us. Throughout history, Western civilization has been accepted as the correct way of life to lead and has been responsible for the reduction of brutality and barbarism. The Europeans have brought it to us, and therefore, for historical reasons, they are more advanced than us. They are still superior to us in all fields." Anxiously uncertain whether Blacks would ever be able to catch up with Whites, people would speak of "narrowing the gap." At the same time they would point out that the Whites have impeded the Africans' "becoming civilized" by withholding adequate facilities (notably educational) and keeping them down economically. This anxiety does not affect the Africans' image of the superiority of White civilization as such. It only spells out its power, and the magnitude of the task ahead; it only adds to the "existential insecurity."[50] The educated often refer to their "inferiority complexes," and it is one of the avowed aims of Black consciousness to overcome these. However, the signs of negative identification, or inferiority feelings, or "warped psychology,"[51] can be balanced by many signs of a healthy self-regard. We could say that in many respects attitudes with regard to cultural ethnicity are either "postcolonial," or else have never fully succumbed to "cultural imperialism."[52]

Whites as a Reference Group

When Soweto people speak of certain fellow Blacks as being "like Europeans," it is most likely in a critical mood, imputing arrogance, inhumanity, and ridiculous preoccupation with status and its signs. "Some people think civilization is the expensive clothes they wear.

[48]Manganyi, *Being Black*, p. 19.
[49]B. Magubane, "A Critical Look at Indices Used in the Study of Social Change in Colonial Africa," *Current Anthropology*, (October-December 1971), p. 428 f.
[50]Manganyi, *Being Black*, p. 10.
[51]Magubane, "Indices Used in the Study of Social Change," p. 428.
[52]This would also be the main impression emerging from G. Lobban's study of Soweto schoolboys, though she leans perhaps towards overoptimism. *See* G. Lobban, "The Effect of the Position of Africans in South African Society on Their Choice of Ethnic Reference and Identification Groups and Their Self-Concepts and Attitudes Toward Social Change" (B. A. Hons. Diss., University of the Witwatersrand, 1970).

The so-called Europeanized people won't talk to the one who is wearing tribal dress. Why? Because people of his or her class will say he is friendly with low classes." Speaking of the houses of the "tycoons," people will add: "Any minute you expect a European to emerge from them." The "wealthy" Africans may be actually referred to as "Whites." Quite a few better-off people feel socially isolated when they become "too European," To be accepted by ordinary working people as members of the "real elite," ideally better-off people should display *ubuntu* ("humanity") as well as motor cars or superior knowledge of English. What they found it legitimate to envy was not the White man's way of life but his privileges, his freedom, and above all, his standard of living. "I would like to remain as I am but have the comforts, money, and things of Whites." Blacks continually stressed the connection between level of income, standard of living, and "civilization." "If only the salaries and wages would be equal then we could pull up and live a civilized life."

In Soweto today, then the Whites apparently do not serve as a reference group, still less an elite, in the way they apparently did on the North Rhodesian copper belt in the 1950s,[53] except for a section of the highly educated and of the prosperous business set. A few respondents (usually highly educated) would discuss the subject explicitly as if to clear their own minds. "Africans are a subject race and as such take their norms from the Whites. They see the Whites as people with skill and knowledge. The more skill and knowledge you have, the nearer you are to the Whites."

There are also some "Uncle Toms," dwelling on the gratitude owed to Europeans for their "civilizing mission," but they are rare among the younger generation. "First the English helped us, now the Afrikaners." The holders of such views are delightful people who had had happy personal relations with White teachers, clergy, or charitable ladies; but they are all in their fifties and sixties. Younger people, without questioning the historical accuracy of such statements, regard the gratitude expressed in them as misplaced. "In recalling that the English brought us the light," they are also recalling that the urban industrial way of life was after all imported into South Africa and should therefore not be equated with the "White" way of life; that indeed White Afrikaners have had similar problems of adaptation to it as have the Blacks.[54] They also feel that present day Whites are at least somewhat ambivalent about further distribution of

[53] Mitchell, *Kalela Dance*, p. 14. *See also* P. Lloyd, *The New Elites of Tropical Africa* (Oxford, 1966).

[54] This is brought out in an illuminating way by David Welsh in M. Wilson and L. Thompson, eds., *Oxford History of South Africa* (Oxford and New York, 1971), 2:202 ff.

"light" to Blacks. "The Whites are always thinking that they have a civilizing mission, and yet prevent us from getting civilized by their own laws." For instance the emphasis on education in the mother tongue in the syllabuses of the Department of Bantu Education is seen as an attempt "to hold back the African nation."[55] At the same time Africans are fully aware that they still depend heavily on obtaining skills and knowledge from the Whites.

Except for domestic servants and some members of the top elite, Blacks have little opportunity of seeing at close quarters how White people actually live their "civilization," but they have strong inklings that they would find much to disapprove. "I don't like the way Europeans live; they don't care very much about each other. A European can live with his neighbors for months and not know who they are." Some responses to questions about Black Americans underlined the distance Soweto people felt from even the more sympathetic White South Africans, and the existential impossibility of modelling themselves unreservedly on them. "The American Negroes are Black as I am, and they have suffered more or less the same kind of oppression." Black Americans' achievements and accomplishments were seen as admirable; the problematical or seamy side of their lives seems little known or ignored. "They have freed themselves from the shackles of discrimination by their own efforts, led by their own leaders like Martin Luther King."

Ethnic Renewal?

There is, however, a sense in which cultural ethnicity seems to be making a comeback among urban Blacks. Today the value of "keeping customs" is openly appreciated by many of the better educated. Afrikaners, Jews, and Indians are quoted as successful examples of this. "Jews may be Westernized, but they still keep to their customs." The speaker may feel regretfully that it is too late for him personally. "I cannot guide anybody in his traditions. I have lost them. This is a bad thing, because along the wayside somewhere you find yourself lost. If you can, it is better to keep both [traditions and modern ways]."

Until recently traditional customs were observed more fully, but especially more openly, as one descended the educational ladder. However, the educated,[56] who appeared to be striving for complete cultural assimilation, may often have been less commited to this goal

---

[55] Hence the explosiveness of the language medium issue. *See* the insistence of homeland leaders on their right to have English taught from standard 3 not only at schools in the homelands, but also to their "citizens" in the White urban areas in, e.g., report in *Sunday Tribune* (Durban), 20 January 1974.

[56] Magubane, "Indices Used in the Study of Social Change."

than they appeared. Many educated Black townspeople have
Marrano-like quietly retained enough of the old faith to go to a great
deal of trouble to practice it *sub rosa*.[57] Our respondents blamed them
mainly for their timidity. "They do not want to be seen doing a thing
that does not belong to Western civilization, because a person may
laugh at them. They have no truth to themselves.", unlike the "simple
people" who follow the customs and traditions without wavering.
"They are like Abraham who had true faith in God. . . . He was prepared to sacrifice his only son." The present tendency among the
educated, even among intellectuals, is to be more open and tolerant in
these matters. For instance, it is very common for a goat to be slaugh-
tered at funerals and weddings in Soweto. People are fairly open with
the use of "medicines"; perhaps they are least open about witchcraft
beliefs,[58] which are referred to as "undesirable superstitions."

The whole question waits for a lead to be given by African intellectuals and trend setters. At present, as a respondent said, people
"are fumbling in darkness and don't know where they are going."
Lobola, as is well known, is widely practiced, especially so among the
better-off, and is appreciated by the women as enhancing their
dignity in a patriarchal society. In the linguistically homogeneous
African townships of the Cape it is argued that though Xhosa initiation is Xhosa and not universally African, it is still African as distinct
from European.[59] In Soweto, where there are many different African
language groups or tribes, the same argument was heard about
customs specific to any particular one of them. In this light, sentiments of African nationalism and traditionalistic tribal customs are
not felt to be mutually exclusive. Besides, many customs were claimed
to be common to all Africans: e.g., respect and hospitality, the broad
principles of lobola and clan exogamy, the practice of sacrifice, and,
of course, the all-embracing concept of "humanity" (*ubuntu*).

Soweto people, then, see themselves as settling down into a common Black identity. But they see the identity as belonging within the
family of Western (industrial-urban) cultures. In their eyes, this kind
of life-style should allow them freedom in their private lives to seek
ethnic identification or assimilation, as they choose; something that
indeed, White and other South Africans would claim as well.

[57]B. Pauw, *Christianity and Xhosa Tradition* (Cape Town, forthcoming); and
"Ancestor Beliefs and Rituals Among Urban Africans," *African Studies*, 33
(1974) : 98 f.
[58]H.J. Moller, *Stedelike Bantoe en die Kerk*, part 3, *Magie by die Stedelike Bantoe*
(Pretoria, 1973).
[59]*See* P. Mayer, "Traditional Manhood Initiation in an Industrial City: The
African View," in E. de Jager, ed., *Man: Anthropological Essays* (Cape Town,
1971), pp. 7-18, for a discussion of Xhosa manhood initiation in Port
Elizabeth.

CONCLUSIONS

What has been said here about the Black townspeople's perception of their social world relates to a period that may have been unusually fortunate and untroubled for the White authorities. The forcible repression of African political parties in the cities had been directly followed by several years of rapid economic expansion, resulting in Africans making modest economic gains. This "stick-and-carrot" sequence had apparently engendered a subdued, almost docile mood among Africans in the towns. But in 1974 the situation has changed, as if over night. Talk of the explosiveness of the South African situation is being heard again. Several factors have converged to modify both Black and White attitudes to social change: e.g., the urgent need of the economy for skilled Black labor; the crumbling of the *cordon sanitaire* of White-dominated territories to the north; suggestive demographic projections; the repoliticization of Blacks through the candid utterances of homeland leaders. Whites are asking themselves whether they can treat urban Blacks as replaceable labor units or whether Whites may not have to gain their loyalty and support.

In 1974 more Whites are more willing than ever before to make "concessions" to Black townspeople in terms of "goods and services." The Black man's right to human dignity has become a recurrent theme in Parliament, newspapers, and on public platforms. What divides Whites is the notion of "sharing power." The most likely trend for the near future seems to be to allow improved living standards and less economic discrimination, while offering little change in the substance of political domination. What can we deduce from our material about probable Black responses to this trend and about their implications for Black-White cohesion?

In South Africa there has been structural cohesion despite an absence of consensus on values, goals, and legitimacy. Cohesion, it has been argued,[60] rests on the high articulation of all parts of the system, including economic interdependence, linkages across the color cleavage, and divisions on either side of the cleavage. Let us sum up what has emerged under each of these heads.

Economic Interdependence

"As the subordinate race becomes more and more dependent for its subsistence and welfare on the economic and administrative system, manned by the dominant race, it becomes less and less inclined to

---

[60]The view is developed in Southern African context especially by M. Gluckman, C. Mitchell, and J. Rex.

destroy that system by violent protest."[61] We have seen that Soweto workers were not protesting against the industrial system as such. Their comments on management seemed to reflect their common interest in the factory continuing to exist. If the near future were to make the "unfree" nature of Black labor less conspicuous and hurtful, the workers might continue to see themselves as if they operated in the parameter of a "normal" society. They would find it easier to shut their eyes to the presence of the color caste line and would have less occasion to revert to the "revolutionary" pariah model.

Divisions Among Blacks

So far government policy has relied heavily on creating competing divisions among Blacks (which Blacks generally resent), rather than encouraging crosscutting links between Blacks and Whites (which even today Blacks generally welcome). Excluding the opposition between migrants and residents, which we have not attempted to explore, we have the following general picture:

Ethnic divisions. According to our data, the models used by government and some of its academic sympathizers have overrated the present strength of ethnicity as a political force in the urban environment—a mistake with a long ancestry in colonial administration. Nor have they always allowed sufficiently for the elementary rule that internal divisions tend to vanish vis-à-vis a common opponent. But it would, of course, be an opposite mistake not to recognize the possibilities of ethnic loyalties growing stronger as an effect of increased interethnic competition and conflict.

Insofar as town institutions (schools and the like) are to be progressively segregated, they can hardly fail to become important areas of competition for scarce resources. An ethnic revival could be encouraged by homeland establishments with vested interests or by urban leaders keen to join the bandwagon. However, Black ideologies do not seem to have been moving significantly in this direction. If anything, ethnic segregation seems rather to have backfired ideologically in stimulating people to formulate their own contrary notion of the single Black melting pot and to build it up into both a normative rejection of ethnicity and an ideological support of Black unity.

Similarly, the official endeavor to fit Black urban residents into the multinational model by stressing their homeland affiliations has not carried much conviction among Soweto residents. The indications are that it could backfire too, from the government's point of view. That

[61]J.C. Mitchell, "Race and Status in South and Central Africa," in A. Tuden and L. Plotnicov, *Social Stratification in Africa* (New York, 1970) p. 338.

is, rather than drawing the political aspirations of Black townsmen away from the "White" cities to the homelands, it might do the reverse. The single quarters for homeland-based migrants in particular could become "heat conductors" of crises over and above their normal local explosive potential.

Indeed, all the major policies meant to protect the White character of South African cities are having one important unintended consequence: they are all helping to blur the division between urban and rural Blacks. Homeland citizenship for Blacks in White cities, growing armies of contract laborers, mass deportation of urban "surplus" populations to homeland areas, the reclassification of urban workers' suburbs as homeland towns, and even border industry development seem almost custom-built for helping Blacks over the town-country divide that has been such a powerful obstacle to their political mobilization. "We can achieve black solidarity," writes Chief Buthelezi, "even through structures meant to destroy it, like ethnic legislatures and ethnic urban boards."[62] The ultimate repercussions of the decreasing social distance between urban and rural Blacks and of growing common interests between them may, by weakening the reality of their separation, be far-reaching.

Status divisions. The existing status divisions and oppositions among Soweto residents do not by themselves significantly weaken Black consensus on the paramountcy of the White-Black cleavage. They represent mainly a critique (or self-critique) of higher ranking Blacks for not living up to the standards expected of them. They may weaken Blacks to the extent of a leadership crisis, but not to the extent of seriously impairing Black solidarity. That could occur only if fairly significant sections of the township population were to be "subverted,"[63] by involving them in "alliances" across the color line and thereby creating objectively different interests among Blacks. If this were to occur the present-day status divisions would provide the blueprint for several alternative alignments. Either the present class system would be consolidated by reducing its egalitarian tendency (when the Black doctor can own his own beautiful house, all Blacks are no longer "the same"), or present oppositions could become sharpened, with possibly socialist undertones, in a resentment against Black elites joining up with the oppressor.

Crosscutting Links

Social cohesion is strengthened by cross-linking individuals in terms of a variety of associations and values, so that they do not become

[62]*Eastern Province Herald*, 1 April 1974.

[63]"Subversion" is here used in the sense suggested by F. Bailey, in *Stratagems and Spoils* (Oxford, 1969).

totally identified with one side or totally opposed to others. In Soweto, the sharp (though unrealistic) distinction drawn between the helpful English and the obnoxious Afrikaner has helped to keep the door open. Important in the development of this distinction are the happy memories of many adults of their White English-speaking school masters (in the days before Bantu education). Although since the 1960s all White-Black contact in which the White plays neither the role of employer nor of agent of state authority tend to be suspect, individual Blacks have maintained ties with individual Whites through various organizations, such as sport bodies, YWCA's, churches, the Institute of Race Relations, and others. There would be possibilities for such links to multiply, to become less exceptional and more acceptable, as a better class of jobs becomes available to the better educated Black, i.e., junior management positions in industry and commerce. Many Soweto Blacks would welcome such development (Black consciousness, as yet, would present no serious obstacle), and many Whites, especially in industry and commerce, are aware of its advantages from their point of view.

It will be interesting to observe whether a "normalization" of Black-White relations, in and outside offices, can still happen at this late hour; whether the Anglo-Afrikaner tradition of racial aloofness can still be jettisoned in an attempt to affiliate parts of the upper Black stratum to the dominant Whites. Integration in hotels and places of entertainment, of which there are already modest beginnings, would be one gesture in this direction. A member of the United party has recently suggested in Parliament that "free areas" be created "where all races could mix." He particularly mentioned restaurants, hotels, and cinemas.[64]

A partial dismantling of the formal distancing mechanisms between Blacks and Whites and especially of the apparatus of petty apartheid is a distinct possibility. Such developments, if effectively enough pursued (and this is a major "if"), would almost certainly reduce the danger of confrontation—at least for a time. They would to some extent take the sting out of the relative deprivation that the Black "intelligentsia" experiences and possibly soften their ideological position—even without the attainment of political equality. Already today some highly educated individuals are voicing optimistic interpretations of the situation: "All this bitterness is not fair. The Whites are trying their best to improve things. Tension is lessening. The young Whites in particular are always willing to help."

Crosscutting links merely in the realm of ideology, of "thinking alike," have also played their part in preventing total confrontation. Underlying Black readiness for Black-White cooperation is the old

[64]M. Streicher, as reported in *Eastern Province Herald*, 9 August 1974.

ANC ideology of a common society, which is still a powerful tradition in Soweto among men beyond their early thirties. Also, tens of thousands of Soweto inhabitants read the English language press and feel that their editorial comments often "speak for the Blacks." In this light press censorship could contribute to the weakening of social cohesion. But Black urban residents have a range of possibilities in relation to Black-White cooperation. Our material illustrates how ambiguously the notion of Black-White interdependence is reflected in the cognitive models held by Soweto people. For example, their overemphasis on the repudiation of multiple Black ethnicities in town could have meant a commitment to an ideology of a shared civilization as something more important than either Black ethnic divisions or the Black-White division. But it had this meaning only among the educated. Among the ordinary working people antiethnicity emphasized that " we Blacks are all the same; just working for the White man." One step further and the notion is transformed into a straight ideology of African unity, embracing all Blacks as against all Whites.

So too the distinction people made between the "good" English (representing achievability of status) and the "bad" Afrikaners (standing for status ascription by color) could mean a rejection of total Black-White confrontation, reflecting an ideology of interdependence. But we have seen that it only takes unemployment and low wages for that model to give away to one of total confrontation. Or in response to different stimuli, the worker-employer model would come to the fore as a socialist battle cry against the capialist system.

Calculating the Cost

However, (in the absence of consensus on values and goals) cross-cutting links and economic interdependence are conducive to the cohesion of a system only insofar as they impress on the participants the high cost to themselves of the collapse of the system or of major modifications of it, compared with the price they pay for its continuation. Many different factors enter into the way costs are reckoned and compared, including the apparent readiness of the White government for a determined use of force. It cannot be taken as certain that South African Blacks would continue to regard the cost of major change as being the higher, or as being too high, not even if linkages are multiplied, and certainly not for the mere reason that South Africa is already a highly articulated society.

We have noted that ordinary working people had developed ways of "insulating" the race or pariah model (which referred to their experience of discrimination) from the "class" model (belonging to their everyday experience as workers). To the discriminatory political aspects of the system they accorded at the most a pragmatic acceptance, i.e., they denied their legitimacy, but perceived no realistic alternative. To the "class" or economic dimension of the system on the other hand they might virtually accord normative acceptance. Many seemed to have internalized the legitimating concept that success comes to those who deserve it through "hard work" and ability. Thus, their acceptance of the status structure of location society with its middle-class aspirations shaded into a readiness to accept the economic inequalities between employers and workers, even if they recognized those inequalities as being aggravated by racial discrimination. There is then no coherent philosophy uniting the two models and pointing to total rejection of White dominance, uniting the two models in consciousness of Blacks. A similar "schizophrenic" picture has been noted among the working classes in Britain and the United States[65] but with this important difference. Whereas workers in Western countries have been observed to hold "rather confused values with surprisingly conservative bias" at the political level, largely it would seem owing to school indoctrination,[66] Black workers in Soweto tend to hold conforming values in the economic sphere and to withhold value consensus in the political field.

It is this difference that makes social cohesion more fragile in South Africa than in liberal Western democracies. The grudging pragmatic acceptance of political domination is no match emotionally or ideologically for the painful pariah experience of racial discrimination, which remains therefore (at least potentially) a dynamic force toward major change. Seen at the receiving end, the stigmata of racial discrimination go even deeper than those of class; the ascribed inferiority is the more basic indignity. Moreover, the class (worker-employer) model was stressed only among working people, whereas the pariah model was found among all sorts of residents, as well as the illegal residents and migrants who are the categories most severely affected by discriminatory regimentation. The present data then lend little support to the orthodox Marxist view on the priority of the class conflict.[67]

It seems to follow that economic concessions would not easily "buy" long-term political support, though they might further legitimize, in their own eyes, Africans' participation in the capitalist *status quo.* Second, only a fusion between the pariah and the class model would

[65]L. Free and H. Cantril, *The Political Beliefs of Americans* (New Brunswick, 1967).

[66]M. Mann, "The Social Cohesion of Liberal Democracy," *American Sociological Review* 35, 3 (June 1970): 435.

[67]For a critique of the orthodox Marxist view, *see* Kuper, "Theories of Revolution," p. 87 f; *see also* review article by L. Kuper and of H. and R. Simons, *Class and Color in South Africa, 1850-1950* (Harmondsworth, 1969) in *Race* 12, 4 (1971): 495-500; Rex, *Race Relations*; J. Rex, *Race, Colonialism, and the City,* (London 1971).

be needed to lead to bitter confrontation. So far most African trade union leaders as well as the striking workers of 1973 and 1974 have seen their business first and foremost as a struggle for bread. The government, however, regards fully fledged African trade unions as a major political risk, greater, it seems, than the risk of mediation in labor disputes by homeland officials, whereas Mr. Oppenheimer thinks industrial disputes "are best settled within industry itself, and any system which makes intervention by the political leaders of independent or semi-independent states inevitable and indeed necessary is likely to prove at once inefficient and dangerous."[68]

Soweto residents have been assessing their scope for manoeuvre rationally and realistically. Our material illustrates this on the verbal level; the recent strikes show it in action. If urban residents are to continue seeing cohesion of the South African social system as worthwhile, their stake in the system will have to be increased. They would accord legitimacy only to a system in which they have a meaningful share in the decision-making. This is a price the ruling White party is not yet prepared to pay. To this extent, change in the direction of a "democratic plural society" seems not yet to have become practical policy.

The alternative is a short-term policy, an attempt to buy time by concessions that do not affect the differential access to central political institutions: rights to own houses, scaling down of petty apartheid, endowing township boards with executive powers, giving more substance to the homeland affiliation of urban residents, and so on. It could mean the Black urban resident, while still seeing himself as "unfree," would feel significantly better off materially, compared with the homelanders who, though "free" are poverty-stricken in the country and heavily regimented in town.

Black townspeople might continue to prefer this as a *modus vivendi* compared with the trouble and agony entailed by political protest. This seems to be the basis for the hopes of most White "verligtes."

Indeed, in this sense a political moratorium for urban Blacks could "work." An upward tendency in their real income would be a *sine qua non* for its success. But we would still be left with the unanswerable question: how long the euphoria of raised material well-being could be expected to last? Only as long as it lasted would the doors remain open for peaceful "fundamental" change. And it could be abruptly ended by anything that seriously threatened the military or economic stability of the present regime.

[68] As reported in *Daily Dispatch* (East London), 30 July 1974.

7

The Political Implications for Blacks of Economic Changes Now Taking Place in South Africa*

FRANCIS WILSON

INTRODUCTION

The 64,000 dollar question with which many of the social scientists who are concerned about South Africa have been grappling in recent years revolves around the political implications of economic changes taking place there.[1] Broadly speaking those who have tackled this question may be divided into two groups: those who see the dynamo of economic growth as providing the power necessary for a peaceful transformation of the existing society to one where racial divisions and conflicts will gradually become less important; and those,

*This chapter is the fruit of a decade's discussion with numerous friends and collegues. Many of our debts are unconscious and it is not possible for us to acknowledge with any degree of accuracy the ideas absorbed from others. We are particularly conscious of what we learned while a member of the economics commission, which produced the SPROCAS report, *Power Privilege and Poverty* (Johannesburg, 1972), and from seminar discussions based on earlier drafts of this paper at the Institute of Development Studies in Sussex, the Institute for Commonwealth Studies in London and Oxford, the University of Cape Town, and the University of Natal. Like the rest of the contributors to this book, we have made substantial changes to this paper as a result of the debate at the Mt. Kisco Conference on Change in Contemporary South Africa (7 to 12 April 1974) for which it was originally written. Finally the help of Sean Archer, Jeffrey Butler, Johann Maree, Percy Selwyn and Wolfgang Thomas in writing detailed criticism of the chapter has been invaluable. Having been through this academic mill we are only too conscious of our failure, finally, to incorporate all the insights that have been gained from others.

on the other hand, who argue that there is no reason to suppose that economic growth within the framework of a coercively racist society will necessarily lead to a dismantling of the apartheid structures.

According to the first group, the demands of the expanding economy will lead to universal education for all; living standards of the poor will rise; consumers and producers will have immense power to remove racial discrimination enforced on a market place which is essentially color blind. And so, as Michael O'Dowd has put it: "About 1980, one can look for the radical constitutional reform corresponding to the second Reform Act in England and President Wilson's program in the United States ushering in the period of high liberalism corresponding to the 1870's and 1880's in England, the roaring twenties in America, La Belle Epoque in France, the present time in Japan and (probably) Italy."[2]

The other group however would argue, for example, that employers may well find it cheaper to maintain a color bar than to face the wrath of the White workers. After all, it is pointed out, the gold mining industry has managed to get by despite the "economic irrationality" of a very rigid color bar. Some indeed would go even further and argue that, far from merely surviving, the racist structures of South African society are in fact caused by the workings of the capitalist system.

Leaving aside for the moment the question as to whether or not race is more than a camouflage for more fundamental class divisions, we note simply that there is a heavy array of intellectual artillery—both liberal and Marxist—lined up on the side of those for whom the impact of economic growth in South Africa will in itself do nothing to alter the existing balance of political power between Black and White.[3]

---

[1]There is a wealth of literature on this subject. Important contributions may be found in G. Hunter, ed., *Industrialization and Race Relations* (London, 1965) and in A. Leftwich, ed., *South Africa: Economic Growth and Political Change* (London, 1974). Other important recent contributions from different viewpoints are H. Adam, *Modernising Racial Domination* (Berkeley, 1971); M. Legassick, "Development and Underdevelopment in South Africa" (unpublished Chatham House Southern Africa Group Seminar paper, March 1971); F. A. Johnstone, "White Prosperity and White Supremacy in South Africa Today," *African Affairs*, 69, 275 (April 1970): pp.124-40; H. Wolpe, Industrialisation and Race in South Africa," in S. Zubaida, ed., *Race and Racialism* (London, 1970).

[2]M. O'Dowd, "The Stages of Economic Growth and the Future of South Africa" mimeographed (n.d.) cited in the Report of the SPROCAS Political Commission, *South Africa's Political Alternatives* (Johannesburg, 1973), p. 51.

[3]Terminology is a sensitive matter in South Africa. The word Black is increasingly preferred as the inclusive term for Africans, Coloreds, and Indians. However, as this chapter is concerned exclusively with Africans, we have used the terms Africans and Black synonymously.

In preparing for this book the editors defined change as being those 'processes which may simultaneously produce structural change *away from* [our italics] the present coercively and racially stratified society.' However, it seems wise to widen the definition so that, before coming to any conclusions, one may at least examine economic changes that seem to *reinforce*, as well as those that may undermine, the existing system of apartheid.

In undertaking a re-examination of the possible implications of economic change it is important to stress the obvious, but sometimes forgotten, truth that any analysis of the future is a form of crystal-gazing by fortune tellers whose academic qualifications provide no guarantee whatsoever that they have taken into account and given due weight to all the variables that influence society. Heisenberg's uncertainty principle notwithstanding, there is a significant difference between the behavior of atoms and the conduct of men. There are, as Richard Cobb has so tellingly argued in his study of the French Revolution, no immutable laws of history. If there were, the police would surely not have been caught unawares as they seem to have been by the events of 1789. "It is not in the nature of the police," he points out, "to predict what has never happened before; their function and their habit are rather to suggest that because something has happened in a certain way over and over again, then it is likely to happen in much the same way on many more occasions in the future. . . . This is why they were better observers of behaviour than of Revolution; for they could think of politics only in terms of a certain, limited, number of objectives. . . .[4] Could one not say the same thing of social scientists? It is wise to embark upon so uncertain a sea with a due sense of the fraility of the barque in which we sail. Karl Popper has reminded us that our task is not "the prophecy of the future course of history. It is rather the discovery and explanation of the less obvious dependences within the social sphere."[5] We do not propose in this essay to undertake the exhilarating but hazardous work of making predictions about the future of South Africa. We shall try rather to chart some of the currents.

STRUCTURE OF THE BLACK POPULATION

Before attempting to analyze the actual processes of change within the economy it is necessary to have some idea of the socioeconomic structure of the Black population. There are, we would suggest, six significant divisions within this context:

[4]R. Cobb, *The Police and the People: French Popular Protest, 1789-1820* (Oxford, 1970), pp. 45-6.
[5]K. Popper, *The Open Society and its Enemies*, 5th ed. (London, 1966) 2:94.

(a) foreign migrants;
(b) indigenous migrants;
(c) urban insiders;
(d) farm workers;
(e) independent producers;

and finally that most dispossessed and powerless of classes, once termed by a South African deputy minister

(f) "surplus appendages."[6]

Let us examine briefly each of these groups in turn.

Foreign migrants are defined as those who work within the South African economy but whose homes and families are situated outside the political boundaries of the Republic. Ever since the mineral discoveries of the late nineteenth century foreign migrants have played a major role in the development of the White-controlled economy. From 1896 to 1898 for example, no less than 60 percent of the 54,000 Black workers in the gold mines of the Witwatersrand came from Mozambique. Similarly, Lesotho, before the turn of the century, provided large numbers of men not only for the mines and railways, but also as farmworkers, particularly in the Orange Free State. There is not the space to tell here the story of South Africa's dependence upon foreign migrants (to say nothing of imported slaves and indentured Indian and Chinese workers) as it has unfolded over the years. It is sufficient to note that South Africa has continued down the years to recruit labor from outside its political boundaries. Table 7.1 shows the number of Black foreign-born persons officially enumerated in South Africa since before World War II.

Table 7.1 Black Foreign Born . . . in
South Africa, 1936-1970
(in thousands)

Date	Male	Female	Total	Male-Female Ratio
1936	261	73	334	3.6:1
1946	445	111	556	4.0:1
1960	482	103	585	4.7:1
1970	443	49	492	9.0:1

Source: J.L. Sadie, *Projections of the South African Population* (Johannesburg, 1973).

[6]The phrase "surplus appendages" was used by the deputy minister of justice, mines and planning to the Junior Rapportryers, Stellenbosch and to the Rapportryers, Cape Town, *The Cape Times*, 28 June 1969.

There have been two important changes relating to foreign Blacks. First, there has been the widening, since the mid-1930s, of South Africa's labor catchment area to regions north of latitude 22° South (i.e., north of Beit Bridge). For a time this area included parts of Zambia and Tanzania. But soon after independence in the early 1960s these countries closed their borders to South African recruiters. From Malawi, however, the flow of migrants has increased rapidly. The second major change, reflected in table 7.1, is the dramatic decline in recent years of the number of foreign-born women in South Africa and the concomitant doubling in the male/female ratio from 4.7:1 in 1960, to 9.0:1 in 1970. What caused this change is not clear; presumably some women died, some went home (either voluntarily or under pressure), and some changed their birthplace for enumeration purposes. But what is certain is that the figures provide evidence of the increasing pressure exerted by the South African government to prevent foreign Black families from settling in the Republic. In general only those persons needed for purposes of employment are allowed to remain—and then only as temporary workers.

The major flow of foreign migrants is organized by the mining industry. In 1974 the total number of Blacks employed by the Chamber of Mines was 365,000, of whom 275,000 (75 percent) were foreigners. Of these 73,000 were from areas north of latitude 22°S, mainly Malawi; 102,000 from Mozambique, 78,000 from Lesotho; 15,000 from Botswana; and 5,000 from Swaziland.[7] Statistics on foreign migrants in other sectors of the economy are harder to come by, but in 1970 of the 443,000 foreign-born Black men a little over two-thirds (304,000) were employed by the mines. Most of the remaining 139,000 foreign men one suspects, were at work on White farms in the Transvaal, the Orange Free State, and parts of Natal.

The second major socioeconomic group of Blacks consist of local migrants, that is people who oscillate, generally on an annual basis, between their homes in some rural area of the Republic and their place of work. Such people are to be found in all sectors of the economy. The mining industry as a whole (including mines not affiliated to the Chamber of Mines) which in 1969 employed some 565,000 Blacks, very few of whom were allowed to live with their families near their place of work, probably draws between one-third and one-half of its Black

---

[7]Mine Labour Organizations (Wenela) Ltd., *Report of the Board of Directors for the Year Ended 31st December, 1974* (Johannesburg, 1975) p. 11. According to the minister of Bantu administration and development, the geographic sources of all foreign Blacks in South Africa in 1972 was as follows: Lesotho, 132,000; Malawi, 131,000; Mozambique, 121,000; Botswana, 32,000; Swaziland, 10,000; Rhodesia, 6,000; Zambia, 600; Angola, 200; and other African territories, 7,000. Republic of S.A., *House of Assembly Debates*, 14 June 1973, col. 1010.

workers from within the boundaries of the Republic. In agriculture (excluding the reserves) the proportion of migrants in the labor force of 918,000 men and 544,000 women (the figures are for 1969) is not known, although the number of men employed as "casual" laborers was estimated to be 314,000, approximately one-third of the total.[8] However, we do know that there are substantial flows of migrant workers from the Transkei and Ciskei to the fruit farms of the western Cape and to the sugar plantations of Natal. Some, but not all, of these flows are in response to seasonal demands. A significant development in recent years has been the establishment of recruiting organizations both by the sugar industry in Natal and by farmers in the western Cape where Black workers have been brought on annual contracts to replace the Colored laborers who, free of pass laws, are able to get jobs (though not houses) in the expanding industrial areas nearby.[9]

But the major change from 1964 to 1973, as far as indigenous migrants are concerned, related to their employment in the industrial sector. Statistics are hard to come by but investigation has shown that in industrial areas where there are no mine compounds the proportion of migrants is very substantial and seems to have increased markedly in recent years.[10] Proportions vary considerably: in Port Elizabeth some 20 percent of the economically active Black men estimated to be living within the municipal boundary are housed, as migrants, on a single basis. In Cape Town on the other hand, no less than 85 percent of the Black men are living in compounds and hostels. On most of the Witwatersrand (including Pretoria) and in Durban, migrants seem to account for approximately half the Black male labor force living legally within the municipal area. Whatever the precise figure it is clear that existence of South African migrants is central to any analysis of what may happen in the industrial areas. They form a distinct group who (if we ignore farm migrants) may perhaps best be labelled the "urban outsiders" constituting approximately half the Black male labor force living legally within the White urban areas.

In contrast to them is the third group which we may call the "urban insiders." These are the people who live with their families in the White areas within daily commuting distance of their work. By and large they form the other half of the Black urban proletariat although they include the relatively small number of the Black bourgeosie—teachers, preachers, and businessmen.[11] There are other important cleavages

[8]Republic of South Africa, Bureau of Census and Statistics, *South African Statistics, 1970* (Pretoria, 1971), p. H-46. "Casual" laborers we assume to mean "seasonal" workers.

[9]F. Wilson, *Migrant Labour: Report to the South African Council of Churches* (Johannesburg, 1972), pp. 18-19.

[10]Evidence for the assertions made in this paragraph is to be found in *ibid.*, ch. 4, pp. 29-77.

[11]Reference to "the other half" does not imply that the urban Black popula-

within the urban insider community. This paper will not examine them except to note that the tensions, for example, in Cape Town between "borners" and "non-borners",[12] or in Grahamstown,[13] may be so great as to inhibit any political solidarity amongst this group at the present time. These urban insiders live under conditions of increasing insecurity with the fearsome prospect of being sent to the Bantustans while the wage earner is turned into a migrant laborer.[14] Nevertheless there are, as we shall see, several important factors that differentiate them from the migrants. Others to be added to the group of urban insiders as thus far defined are those, particularly in Pretoria, Durban, and East London, who though working in the cities are based in the Bantustan, living in suburbs that are technically not part of the White-controlled urban areas. As yet there are no significant differences in status between those living in such places (e.g., Umlazi or Mdantsane) and those living in the other townships such as Soweto, but if the threatened policy of withdrawing such tenuous rights as may exist under section 10 of the Urban Areas Act is carried out, then the distinction between these two types of urban insider with regard to their security of tenure will be considerable. Moreover, as will be argued later, the potential power of the Bantustans may depend in large measure upon the number of urban workers commuting daily from within their borders.

The fourth group to be considered consists of farm workers and their families living on the White-owned farms which cover most of South Africa. Less is known about this group than any other in the country because the agricultural statistics are notoriously unreliable and because in-depth studies relating to the farming areas are lacking.

---

tion is split 50:50 between "insiders" and "outsiders," but rather that the economically active males in the two groups are roughly equal. The insider population as a whole also included women and children.

[12]Detailed analysis of the Black social structure in Cape Town is to be found in M. Wilson and A. Mafeje, *Langa* (Cape Town, 1963). Evidence of the acute "borner"—"non-borner" tension in the 1970s comes, in verbal communication, from Hertzog Jimba and Ben Office.

[13]T. Nyquist, *Toward a Theory of the African Upper Stratum in South Africa* (Athens, Ohio, 1972).

[14]Discussion with friends in Cape Town at the beginning of 1974 suggests that part of the borner—non-borner tension arises from the increasing insecurity felt by borners as a result of the change in urban administration from the municipality to the government appointed Peninsula Bantu Affairs Administration Board. Whether such feelings are objectively "justified" is difficult to assess, but both in Johannesburg and Cape Town reports suggest that pass laws are (in 1974) being more zealously administered than in previous months. For a discussion of ways in which an administration can, if it chooses, exert pressure to increase the insecurity of urban insiders, *see* Wilson, *Migrant Labour*, pp. 86-7.

Add to this the immobility of much of the farm population, which can lead to enormous wage differences (both in cash and kind) not only between large areas of the country but also between neighboring farms where small communities remain isolated, and one realizes how little information is available on which to base any generalizations. Nevertheless we know enough to be able to distinguish those people living permanently on White farms as a group different from the other three identified so far. These Black families are placed in a position of insecurity and total dependence upon the goodwill of their employers. A family expelled from a farm has no right to seek work in town and no claim upon a chief for land in a Bantustan. Legally such a family has no right to be anywhere at all. This fact, as we shall see later, has severe consequences for people in a society changing in response to economic forces. According to the 1970 census the number of Blacks living in White rural areas was some 3.65 million, almost one-quarter of Black South Africa, including the Bantustans.[15]

The next group of Blacks, independent producers or peasant farmers, stay all the year round in the Bantustans living off their arable land and their cattle. Such people may at some stage in their lives have been migrants and their incomes may still be supplemented by the remittances of other members of the family; nevertheless it is important to distinguish them as a group if only to point out, as Colin Bundy has so acutely done,[16] their decline. Despite their great importance as agricultural producers in the early years of industrialization their subsequent withering away has left a group that contains, it seems, relatively few people.[17]

[15]Republic of South Africa, Bureau of Census and Statistics, *Population Census, 6 May 1970* (Pretoria, 1970), p. 2. It should be noted that any attempt to quantify numbers of Blacks in different areas is severely hampered by the known inaccuracy of the official figures. For example we were informed, by somebody likely to know, that the number of Blacks working on the farms of one district in the western Cape was probably not far short of double the number actually enumerated in the 1970 census. Similarly in the urban areas the legal population of Mdantsane in 1972 was 72,000, while informed estimates of the illegal population ranged between 30,000 and 50,000. In Cape Town in 1974 the illegal Black population was thought to be almost double the official figure of 118,000.

[16]C. Bundy, "The Emergency and Decline of a South African Peasantry," *African Affairs*, 71 (October 1972): 285.

[17]There are virtually no figures available regarding land distribution in the Bantustans as a whole. In the Ciskei during the mid-1960s a Fort Hare team of researchers found that only 3.1 percent of the household heads in the Middledrift and Victoria East districts had arable holdings of 11 acres or more, where an economic unit was calculated as requiring 13.7 acres of arable land and grazing for 12 large stock units. See P. de Vos et al., *A Socio-Economic and Educational Survey of the Bantu Residing in the Victoria East, Middledrift and Zwelitsha Areas* (Fort Hare, 1971), p. 295.

Finally the sixth group, those who have been called the "surplus appendages," in reality are the wives and children and grandparents of the migrants away in the mines and in the factories. Living in the reserves, the mirror image of life in the urban compounds, their lot is almost certainly worse than that of their men away in town. With claim to little if any land (one-third of household heads in a Ciskei district have no arable land of any sort),[18] and subsisting on such remittances as workers can afford to send out of their poverty wages, these are the discarded people of apartheid, the casualties of the system.[19]

This categorization is perhaps oversimple and may mask other divisions and connections; nevertheless it will, we hope, prove helpful as we move now into an analysis of the impact of economic growth within this structural situation. In making such an analysis we wish to examine four interrelated areas where significant changes are taking place before attempting to assess the overall consequences of these changes on the existing political power structure. The four fields upon which this paper will focus are:

(a) The migratory labor system;
(b) Black worker power;
(c) Black consumer power; and
(d) The international dimension.

MIGRATORY LABOR SYSTEM

The migratory labor system in South Africa is a phenomenon so well known that it needs little description. What is important, however, is to examine the combination of political and economic forces underpinning it in order to understand just how the system is changing and why. The crux of the analysis concerning migrant labor is that South Africa is simultaneously pursuing two apparently contradictory goals. One is the goal of rapid economic growth to increase living standards—not least of those wielding political and economic power—and to reduce unemployment of a rapidly expanding population;[20] the other is the goal of separate development whereby South Africa will become a

---

[18]Ibid.

[19]C. Desmond's *The Discarded People: An Account of African Resettlement in South Africa* (Baltimore, 1971) referred specifically to all those being moved to rural settlements such as Itsoseng, Mondlo or Dimbaza. We are referring more generally to all those, whether they have been moved or not, who have been "left behind" in the Bantustans while their economically active husbands and fathers go elsewhere to earn a living.

[20]In October 1972 the minister of planning reiterated that a policy of economic growth was a fundamental goal of the present government. For the text of the relevant part of his speech to the S.A. Society for Personnel Management, *see* Wilson, *Migrant Labour*, p. 166, f.n. 29.

commonwealth of politically independent, economically viable ethnic states. The difficulty is that these two goals taken together require Blacks to be in two places at once. Economic growth in the South African context leads, as it has done everywhere in the world, to a steady pull of labor out of the rural areas into the urban centers. Consider table 7.2, which shows the official projected annual growth of employment in different sectors of the economy based on the assumption that the GNP grows each year by 5.75 percent.

Table 7.2 EDP Projections of Employment
Growth, 1972-1977

| Sector | Annual growth of employment | |
	All races	Blacks only
	(%)	(%)
Agriculture, forestry, and fishing	1.3	1.4
Mining	2.0	2.0
Electricity, gas, and water	2.8	3.2
Services	3.4	3.9
Manufacturing	4.2	5.1
Construction	4.9	5.1
Total economically active population	2.8	2.8

Source: Republic of South Africa, Department of Planning, *Economic Development Programme for the Republic of South Africa, 1972-1977* (Pretoria, 1972).

The trend is unmistakable: as the economy goes on expanding so will employment in the urban-based sectors grow faster, and agricultural employment grow more slowly, than the population as a whole.

The policy of separate development requires that these same workers be citizens of an independent homeland removed, in many cases some hundreds of miles, from the White cities. And citizenship implies some degree of residence. Indeed for apartheid planners it implied for many years a reversal of the urban flow of Black labor. There was a time when the National party government made serious efforts—by means of the Physical Planning Act and by special measures imposed particularly in the western Cape—to reduce the number of Black workers in the cities. But economic pressures proved too strong and the government had to modify its policy. Instead of laying stress upon reducing the number of Blacks in the cities the government came, during the late 1960s and early 1970s, to place more and more emphasis upon preventing nonworkers (i.e., wives and children) from moving to the cities, and upon ensuring that the new industrial workers drawn in from the countryside should not take root in the cities where they labored. The consequence of this policy has been the rapid expansion since the mid-1960s of a migrant labor system in the manufacturing sector similar to that which has existed for three generations in the gold mines.

Chart 1 may help one to understand what is happening.[21] Force 1 is the pull of labor to the cities exerted by the process of economic growth as demonstrated by the statistics in table 2. Force 2 is the push off the land, a push which in South African history was much bolstered by the political and military activities of the White conquerors greedy for more land and mining capitalists, such as Cecil Rhodes, who needed the peasants to work as laborers. In later years this rural push has been strengthened by several factors, of which population growth within the confines of the narrow boundaries of the "reserves" and the mechanization of commercial agriculture on the White farms are probably the two most important.[22] Force 3 is the pull back to the land exerted by the

Chart 1

Push-Pull Model

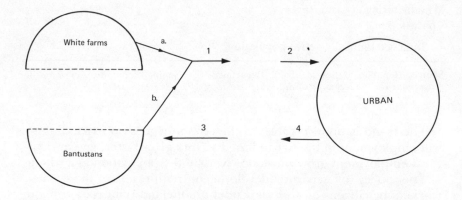

[21]This is an abbreviated but modified (after lively discussion at ICS seminars in London and Oxford) version of an earlier model in ibid., ch. 8, pp. 144-65. There is one point we wish to clarify. Migrants, for the purpose of this paper, are defined as those who oscillate, less frequently than daily, between their rural homes and their place of work. Thus defined, migrants include both those with land holdings and those who are landless. No research has been done as far as we are aware on the distribution of rural land—and how it has changed over time—held by those working in the cities.

[22]See M. Wilson and L. Thompson, eds., *Oxford History of South Africa* (New York and Oxford, 1971), 2:169-71 for discussion of the impact of agricultural mechanization. For criticism of this view see Merle Lipton, "White Farming: A Test Study of Change in South Africa," *The Journal of Commonwealth and Comparative Politics*, XII, 1 (March 1974).

social security provided by the extended family in times of unemployment, sickness, or old age. Such a rural pull seems to have existed in all parts of the world during the early stages of industrialization, but under the process of economic growth, as societies have become richer, so has social security in nonagricultural work improved in such a manner (e.g., the welfare state in Britain) that the rural areas enjoy no special advantage in this respect, and the economic force pulling men back to their rural communities fades away. In South Africa it would seem that this rural pull (Force 3) has indeed become weaker over time, although not so much because social security in the urban areas has improved dramatically as because the rural areas have become steadily more overcrowded and poorer and hence themselves unable to provide the social security that in earlier times was taken for granted.[23]

Force 4 is the push away by employers of labor from the urban areas. This is caused by a combination of economic and political factors. The economic pressure is exerted by virtue of the fact that the losses incurred by a high annual rate of turnover are outweighed by the gains to employers to be had in hiring workers who not only have a supplementary income from the land but whose families are not awkwardly present, requiring housing, water, sanitation, electricity and all the other social structure needed to support life in town. In other words there are certain situations where, by hiring oscillating migrants, employers as a whole are able to incur lower costs for their labor than they would be able to do were the families totally dependent upon the workers' earnings and were they having to meet the higher cost of urban living. However, as economies develop so the demand for skilled and semiskilled labor increases.[24] But this in turn raises the cost of turnover; for a skilled man takes time to train and cannot be replaced as easily as a man doing a completely unskilled job. And so employers find the employment of an oscillating labor force becoming more costly than hiring workers who do not have to be repatriated each year. Thus the economic gains of preventing permanent urbanization are outweighed by the losses and force 4 becomes weaker and weaker. The political dimension inherent in the desire of employers to push labor away lies in those situations in which they believe that maintenance of the oscillating pattern will facilitate control over their labor force. But the price of such control rises as workers become more skilled and employers find it increasingly in their interests to stabilize that proportion of the labor force required for more skilled jobs while maintain-

[23]Ibid., pp. 55-68. Wilson, *Migrant Labour*, pp. 98-104.

[24]Further research on the correlation between economic growth and the demand for skill is needed but the sort of trends to which we are referring have been noted, for the United States, in U.S. Department of Labor, *Manpower Report of the President, A Report on Manpower Requirements, Resources, Utilization, and Training* (Washington, 1965), p. 54.

ing, if it is politically possible, the oscillating pattern for the less skilled portion of the labor force.

However, this trend toward a weakening of the push from urban areas is considerably retarded by the existence of a color bar, whose prime purpose is to prevent Black workers moving as rapidly as they would otherwise do into the more highly skilled jobs traditionally occupied by Whites. There is thus a symbiotic relationship between migrant labor and the color bar in the sense that the existence of the color bar means that the costs of turnover of Black labor are lower than they would otherwise be were these workers in more highly skilled jobs.

This it seems, is one reason why oscillating migration has continued for eighty years in South Africa whilst in Katanga and on the Copperbelt it was phased out rapidly once the color bar began to be removed. However, even within South Africa the color bar is not a rigid, immovable, barrier. Under the demands generated by economic growth for more skilled labor, the color bar has shifted its position to a place further up the skill ladder. Its exact level is one that varies considerably between sectors and between industries. In agriculture Black managers are to be found; in mining a color bar codified at the turn of the century (when Chinese labor was indentured) has remained obstinately in place despite numerous attempts by employers to shift it. Only now—under pressure of the most severe skilled labor shortages—is the color bar in mining gradually beginning to move. But it remains far lower down the ladder than it does in manufacturing where Black workers are allowed to do jobs in a whole range of semi-skilled, and indeed in skilled capacities.[25] Despite these differences between sectors, which influence markedly the views of employers with regard to migrant labor, there is one overriding similarity concerning the color bar. This is the fact because of the political power of the White working class some sort of barrier will be maintained to ensure that Blacks will not be allowed to keep Whites out of jobs that significant numbers of individual voters still wish to fill.[26]

Coming back to the analysis of oscillating migration we see that, driven by the engine of economic growth, the forces propelling people toward the cities have, over time, become stronger and stronger, whilst

---

[25]When examining the color bar we must distinguish between its *de facto* (or unofficial) and its *de jure* (legal) position. What tends to happen in practice is that Blacks are employed in positions which whether illegal or not are not immediately publicized for fear of causing a political row. Hence the *de facto* barrier tends to be placed higher up the skill ladder than public statements might lead one to expect.
[26]The possibility of substituting Black workers for White is more complex than is suggested in this paragraph.

those moving them back to the rural areas have become weaker and weaker—albeit with some variation between sectors depending upon the precise location of the color bar. Thus where the oscillation of labor was previously maintained in large measure by the balance of these four forces, this balance has been decisively tipped in favor of the rural-to-urban flow. But this does not fit the overall political requirement that as far back as 1922 proclaimed that the Black man had no right in the towns to which he was admitted in order to minister to the needs of the White man and from which he must depart when he had ceased so to minister.[27] Thus having devoted the first half century of industrialization to finding ways of getting Blacks to go to work in the industrial centers, the Whites with political power devoted the second half of the century to finding ways of preventing Blacks from taking root as human communities in these same areas. It is within this context that we can perhaps best interpret the development of the pass-laws—particularly, but not exclusively, after 1948—as an instrument that served both to reduce the flow of people to the cities (by filtering out women, children, and men not certain of getting a job) and to push back (in terms of the annual contract) the men working in the cities to the rural areas at least once a year.

Such an instrument, however, could only be effective if backed by force. Thus, parallel to the growing imbalance between the two sets of forces analyzed in the model, there has been a sharp growth in the number of people apprehended for contravening the pass laws. Between 1936 and 1962 the proportion of Black South Africans convicted under the pass laws increased from 1.9 percent to 3.5 percent; by 1970 the proportion prosecuted had risen to 4.1 percent. In 1948 there were 176,000 convictions; by 1970 the annual rate of prosecution was well over 600,000—an average of more than one person every minute, day and night.[28]

Despite the evidence of the extent to which the migrant labor system has expanded in recent years and despite the analysis that points to its centrality within the whole apartheid structure, we are nevertheless left with a hopeful question. Is it possible that the expansion of the economy with the concomitant shifting up of the color bar will, over time, lead to firms' having to bear an increasing cost which will tip the balance in such a way that employers themselves will exert increasing

[27]Republic of South Africa, Transvaal Province, *Report of the Local Government Commission* (Pretoria, 1922), para. 267.

[28]From 1921 to 1962 pass law statistics are for convictions; thereafter they relate to prosecutions. However, the difference between the number of people prosecuted and convicted under the pass laws does not seem to be large. *See* Wilson, *Migrant Labour*, p. 233.

pressure on the politicians to phase out the migrant system and stabilize the urban labor force? It is a tempting scenario, but against it must be set two recent developments that indicate the immense sophistication of the South African political structure in adapting to economic necessity without jeopardizing the exercize of power.

The two developments are the call-in card system on the one hand, and the differential access to jobs enjoyed by urban insiders and urban outsiders, on the other. In terms of the call-in card system to which Charles Harvey drew particular attention in his recent evidence to the British Parliamentary Select Committee, firms are able to increase the possibility that contract workers who have gone back to the reserves will in fact return to the same employer.[29] Whilst there is some doubt whether the labor bureaucracy could handle effectively all the extra administration involved, it nevertheless does seem that the streamlining and centralization of the administrative machinery—by the establishment of the Bantu Affairs Administration Boards in 1972-73 and the purchase of computers—may enable most firms employing migrants to reduce substantially the turnover costs of the system by ensuring that workers wanting to come back to their same employers will be able to do so. Indeed, although there is no evidence that this is envisaged, only a small change in the rules is necessary to give employers total control by making it impossible for a man to come back to work in town unless he has first applied to the firm by which he was last employed. If what has been called the "fine tuning"[30] of the labor administration machinery is effective then the process whereby force 4 is weakened will be halted and perhaps even reversed. In other words the impact of the call-in card system could well be to reduce much of the economic pressure that might otherwise be exerted for a phasing out of the migrant oscillations.

Furthermore, there is a second development that indicates how economic pressures can be accommodated to political necessity. This is the policy—to which Jean Sinclair, Ellen Hellman and others have drawn attention[31]—of reserving the more skilled Black jobs for urban insiders by making it impossible for the urban outsiders, the migrants, to accept any but the tough, unattractive, low-paid jobs at the bottom of the economic pyramid. The consequence of the 1968 labor regulations is that if the bureaucracy can cope with the administration, the

[29]United Kingdom, Expenditure Committee (Trade and Industry Subcommittee) *Minutes of Evidence* (London, 1973), 23 May 1973, p. 321.
[30]We are indebted to Geoff Lamb for this graphic metaphor.
[31]Jean Sinclair,, "Accessories to a Crime," *South African Outlook* January-February 1973); Ellen Hellman, Review of F. Wilson's *Migrant Labour, Race Relations News* (September 1973).

costs of migrant labor could be kept from rising by virtue of the fact that the supply of urban insiders will be used to supply the demand for more skilled Blacks, while the migrants will be confined to those jobs where the costs of turnover—even in the absence of a call-in card system—are outweighed by the benefits of maintaining the oscillations.

Thus we conclude with regard to migrant labor, that the impact of economic growth by itself will not lead to a withering away of the system, but will serve to entrench it more firmly as the centerpiece of the apartheid structure and also to generate a considerable growth in the number of persons who must move like shuttles across the productive looms of the society.

This analysis has taken no account of three factors that apparently run counter to the expansion of migrant labor but whose existence does not, in our judgement, warrant a modification of the conclusion that the system is becoming more entrenched. The first factor is the creation and expansion of Bantustan-based suburbs on the distant edges of some major cities. While the existence of Mdantsane near East London, Umlazi near Durban, and Garankua and Mabopane near Pretoria may help to curb the dependence of these cities on migrants, two points are worth noting. One is that neither in Durban nor in Pretoria has there been any noticeable slowing down in the construction of what are referred to as "single-men's hostels" but which might more accurately be termed "labor batteries." Indeed such building seems to have accelerated since the mid-1960s.[32] The other point is that neither Cape Town, nor Port Elizabeth, nor Johannesburg, nor the industrial centers strung along the east and west Rand, nor many other urban growth points such as Vanderbijl Park, Vereeniging, Sasolburg, Bloemfontein, or Mossel Bay are anywhere near Bantustans from which workers could possibly commute on a daily basis. As has been noted elsewhere a society that does not pay the majority of its workers a living wage is hardly in a position to turn its entire proletariat into a jet set.[33]

The second factor that might modify our conclusion with regard to the expansion of migrant labor is the government's policy of industrial decentralization to the borders of the Bantustans combined with some effort to stimulate growth points within them. However, in the light of the work done by Trevor Bell and others[34] it seems accurate to conclude that such a policy has made almost no impact on the growth of

[32]Wilson, *Migrant Labour*, pp. 28-77. Subsequent evidence from Cape Town, Port Elizabeth and Pietermaritzburg, to name only three cities, suggests that the building of hostels is to go on apace during the mid-1970s.
[33]Ibid., p. 210.
[34]T. Bell, *Industrial Decentralisation in South Africa* (Cape Town, 1973); T. Fair "Elements Required in a Framework for Comprehensive and Inter-

employment in the existing urban areas over the past decade and that
is unlikely to be any more than a marginal aspect of the future development of the economy as a whole.

The third factor is the existence of illegal migration and the possibility that all the plans of mice and men will gang agley in the face of a
breakdown in administration as men and women surge into the cities.
It is authoritatively estimated for example that the number of Africans
actually at work on the farms of the western Cape is far higher—
perhaps double—the number enumerated in the 1970 census. Similarly it is widely known that a very large number of women (and men)
come illegally to the cities where they work and live in constant fear of
being apprehended.[35] While such "immigration sauvage" adds to the
numbers in the cities and may provide companionship for some men
it does little to alter the basic structure of the migratory system that so
brutally divides families.

However, it is impossible to make a firm prediction about the future
of the migrant system in South Africa, for economic variables are not
the only pressures at work in the society. It is possible that a combination of factors including an increasing demand for more skilled labour,
mounting pressure from overseas, greater awareness among Whites of
the evil consequences of the system, fear by employers that independent African governments may act to cut off permanently their flows of
labour to the Republic, ethnic violence within the compounds, and
protest action by African workers will cause both employers and government to take steps toward making provision for housing workers
with their families near their place of work. Examples where such
changes have been made include Rio Tinto's copper mine in Phalaborwa (1972) and de Beers' diamond mine in Kimberley (1973). In
both cases the companies concerned have moved from employing
migrants to housing all their workers on a family basis.[36] By the end of

---

dependent Development in Zululand" (paper delivered at the conference on
Comprehensive Development in Zululand, Durban, February 1972); Wilson,
Migrant Labour, pp. 205-8.

[35]*See* n. 15 regarding the number of Blacks illegally in the cities.

[36]In Kimberley, during 1973, the de Beers compound was closed and the
company began phasing out some 3,000 migrants and employing people
already living with their families in the area. Even the move to a stabilized
labor pattern is not without its ambiguities, for although no migrant lost his
job until he did not wish to renew his contract again, the consequence of the
new policy is that for Lesotho, from whence many of the diamond workers
have come for a hundred years, a valuable source of employment is now
closed. Would the policies of phasing out the migrant system in the gold mining industry imply the same thing for Mozambique and Malawi? For a discussion of the Phalaborwa changes, *see* W. Thomas, ed., *Managerial Responsibility
and African Employment in South Africa* (Johannesburg, 1973), and *also* Wilson,
Migrant Labour, pp. 11-13.

1974 it was possible to detect a hard-to-measure, but nevertheless perceptible, shift in the thinking of employers and government officials with regard to the migrant labour system. Whereas only a year or two previously the system had been unquestioningly considered a permanent feature of the South African landscape there was now an awareness that things were probably going to have to change. And this awareness was having practical results. Large employers, including the state's Iron and Steel Corporation (Iscor), were still building migrant hostels to accommodate their expanding labour force but examination of their plans showed that many of these hostels were being designed in such a way that alterations enabling these buildings to accommodate families could be made quickly and easily. However, it is still possible that changes in the different variables will not be sufficient to outweigh the political and economic advantages to Whites of the migrant system, which will thus be maintained and, because of the labor needs of an expanding economy, extended. The contradictory nature of the various pressures may, perhaps, best be seen in the fact that in his annual report for 1973 the chairman of the Anglo-American Corporation reported the successful transformation of the migrant system in the diamond mines to a pattern of stabilized labor while asserting that in the country as a whole there was "no realistic prospect of phasing the system out in the foreseeable future."[37] Similarly among government spokesmen and supporters we find contradictory ideas as to the future of Blacks—including families—in the urban areas.[38]

---

[37]*Financial Mail* (Johannesburg), 17 May 1974. It is worth emphasizing that the outbreaks of violence within the compounds, which had been so unusual and so puzzling a feature of 1974, are causing an intense questioning within the mining industry as to the viability (as far as employers are-concerned) of the migrant system.

[38]Government policy as expounded and practised by politicians responsible for Bantu Administration and Development is clearly aimed at trying to maintain Blacks in the urban areas on a temporary basis (though with better sports facilities). Other National party thinkers, however, are moving to acceptance of the facts of life and the need to examine the implications of Black urbanization. See J. van Rooyen in *Die Burger* (Cape Town), 21 August 1972. One important strand of the new thinking is that which considers the possibility of moving from a system of migrant workers to one of migrant families. In other words the possibility is being explored of government policy being adjusted in such a manner that a worker who comes to town will be allowed to bring his nuclear family with him provided a house is available either from government or employer sources but that such a worker will be considered a foreigner whether he comes from an outside country like Malawi or from inside one of the Republic's Bantustans. In other words the worker and his family will come to town on the basis of their being there temporarily while the breadwinner is at work. Africans will thus remain temporary sojourners in the white cities but the *de facto* position would change substantially.

Finally it should be pointed out that even if all Black workers became established in the cities with their families this would not in itself necessarily alter the distribution of power between Blacks and Whites. It is salutory to remember that although pass laws for "Colored" people were abolished in 1828 their subsequent urbanization and full-time presence in the cities with their families has not yet, after 150 years, had any significant impact upon their political powerlessness.

BLACK WORKER POWER

The next area to be considered in the light of the impact of economic growth is the whole field of industrial communication. A helpful way of looking at this is to consider the intriguing situations in which employers and White workers both, though for different reasons, now find themselves. To take the employers first we can begin by noting the similarities between three labour disputes that have taken place in the mining industry at almost exactly equal intervals of a quarter of a century. In 1920 eleven men were shot dead by police during the course of a strike at Village Deep gold mine in Johannesburg. African opinion was outraged. A meeting of Blacks in Cape Town viewed the methods adopted "both by the Government and the employing classes in South Africa, of settling laborers' strikes by victimization of the leaders, threatening repatriation of the strikers if they refused to return to duty before a satisfactory settlement of the dispute, and the use or display of police and semi-military force, as intimidation of the worst Prussian type . . .";[39] but there was no change in the atmosphere of industrial relations, except possibly for the worse. In 1946 a widespread strike on the mines involved, at one stage, some 74,000 Black workers. Once again violence erupted with stones on one side and bullets on the other. Nine workers were killed, more than twelve hundred injured. This time the employers backed the state's use of force with an explicit policy statement: "The introduction of trade unionism among tribal Natives at their present stage of development would lead to abuses, and irresponsible action."[40] Twenty-seven years later, in September 1973, a dispute over wages combined with very poor management-worker communication on Western Deep Levels in Carletonville led to another bullet-stone exchange between the police and workers in which, again, the workers were decidedly worsted. Eleven men were killed. Subsequently a judicial enquiry exonerated the police from blame though some criticism was voiced concerning the inadequacy of their training and readiness for riot control.

[39]F. Wilson and D. Perrot, eds., *Outlook on a Century: South Africa, 1870-1970* (Lovedale, S.A., 1973), p. 337.
[40]Republic of South Africa, Transvaal Chamber of Mines, *Tribal Natives and Trade Unionism* (Johannesburg, 1946).

At first glance, the most salient feature of these three incidents is their depressing similarity. *Kragdadigheid*, it seems, is always with us. Yet on looking more deeply into the situation the confrontation of September 1973 *may* yet emerge as significant not because of its similarity to but because of its difference from the earlier events. And the difference lies precisely in the increased uneasiness manifested by employers at the use of kragdadigheid. For there is a new dilemma facing such groups as the gold mine employers: if they do not establish effective lines of communication with their workers, then there is a danger of wild-cat strikes not only breaking out, but escalating into Sharpeville-type confrontations leading to widespread labor unrest, the flight of capital, and heavy international censure. If, on the other hand, some kind of effective consultative machinery for Blacks is set up, employers fear that workers would use this as a lever for obtaining far-reaching political concessions. Thus for employers there is no easy release.

For White workers the dilemma, though different, is equally sharp and painful. If they do not unionize Black workers, then, color bar or no color bar, they will find employers bringing in Black workers at much lower rates of pay to undercut and replace White workers. Such replacement will not occur on an obvious one-for-one basis, but will take the form of job fragmentation whereby employers will find some way of changing the structure of production so that as White workers leave or retire their places are broken up into a larger number of different jobs which are barred neither by law nor custom to Blacks. And so there is the danger, as one trade unionist explained to us, that one day the White workers may go on strike but find that everybody can do without them. If however, White workers do take steps to unionize their Black colleagues can they be sure that the latter will not take over the commanding heights of the labor movement with all sorts of dire political consequences as far as White worker privilege is concerned? Like their bosses the White workers are acutely uncomfortable. This is particularly true in those sectors, e.g., engineering, where techniques of production can be fairly easily changed and where trade union policing of employer behavior is difficult. Workers in the gold mines on the other hand are faced with much less of a problem: not only are the techniques of production difficult to alter but the industry itself—both because it is highly centralized and because of its long traditions—is relatively easy to police. There the White unions are powerful and see no need for so threatening an action as encouraging the unionization of Black workers.

But why should many employers and White unions now find themselves faced with situations that ten or twenty years ago hardly seemed to trouble them at all? What subterranean changes have been taking place in the economy to produce these new areas of concern? What we seem to be witnessing is the cumulative impact of the process of industrialization over the past generation. There is, as Jeffrey Butler has put it, "a labor shortage of a new kind—not the farmer saying he is short of labor, as he has always done, but the cost conscious industrialist who wants skill (that) *Whites* no longer supply."[41] Under the pressure of labor shortages, more and more Blacks have been moving into more highly skilled positions in the industrial, non-mining, sectors such as the motor industry.[42] These shifts in the racial composition of the productive urban labor force give rise to the possibility of various types of strike action whose spectre is coming more and more to haunt the consciousness of the White employers and government.[43] Analysis of various strikes that took place during the early 1970s in Windhoek, Durban, Johannesburg, and Carletonville may help to fill in the picture.

The Windhoek (Katatura) or Ovambo strike of December 1971 to January 1972 provides a model of well-organized mass-action aimed at the withdrawal of labor to the Bantustan base. Such a strike can—as was shown in Nambia—cripple the economy, but ultimately can be effective in wringing out real concessions only if it can be maintained for a considerable length of time. But can it? Not only must there be sufficient food in the homeland to sustain the workers and their families during the period of withdrawal but also there must be some means of preventing harsh retaliatory measures by authorities able to impose emergency regulations and a complete veil of secrecy over the activities of police and possibly other forces within the homeland. The great weakness of an Ovambo-type strike is that the focus of confrontation is removed to some distant rural area where the activities of the state in persuading the workers to change their minds can be hidden from the embarrassing and possibly restraining glare of publicity. Little evidence is available but from the snippets of information that have come through it seems accurate to conclude that the kid-gloves so much in evidence during the Durban strikes were not worn by the authorities in Ovamboland.

[41]Jeffrey Butler in written communication to the author.

[42]In research currently (1974) in progress for an M.A. thesis at the University of Cape Town on "The African Workers in the Occupational Wage Structure," D. Terrington finds, after examining twenty industries in the manufacturing and tertiary sectors, that between the mid 1950s and the early 1970s there was a strong flow of Blacks from unskilled into semiskilled jobs. This coincides with the widening (in average money wages) of the skilled-unskilled differential and the narrowing of the semiskilled-unskilled gaps, which he finds over the period.

[43]This section draws in part upon the description and analysis of L. Douwes Dekker et al. in "Case Studies in African Labour Action in South and South West Africa" (Paper prepared for the Conference on Workers and Development in Africa, Toronto, April 1973).

Does this mean then that the kind of strikes that took place in Durban during January and February 1973 are likely to be any more effective? The model here is of a seemingly spontaneous mass action which may lead to some concessions where workers grievances are very pressing (for example real wages falling because of rapid inflation), but where concessions will not in themselves do anything to alter the distribution of political power. From the state's point of view the handling of such a strike is of critical importance to avoid escalation of violence and the inflaming of world opinion. From the workers' perspective the fundamental weakness of such a strike lies precisely in its spontaneity and the absence of organizational muscle to press for any kind of political change.

Thirdly, there was the strike that took place amongst Putco bus drivers in Johannesburg in June 1972. Rejecting a pay increase of 2 percent the bus drivers went on strike. Three hundred were jailed but soon released after further action by drivers not yet in jail, and a final settlement was made whereby pay was increased by no less than one-third. The significance of this strike is that it involved urban insiders who, relatively speaking, are highly skilled. Moreover their goals, were quite specific and were confined to improving their material standard of living. Such a strike can be highly effective within its limits, but from the perspective of changing the power structure there is, as yet, no evidence that an elite group of Black workers would be willing or able to widen the terms of its struggle to include some more overtly political goals in joint action with a wider spectrum of Black workers.

Nevertheless what does emerge from analysis of the Putco strike is the possibility of different groups of skilled urban insiders taking steps to raise their wages. Such action would be likely to have two important consequences. First it will lead to a substantial increase in the Black consumer market and so raise the question of the political implications of consumer power. Secondly, it could widen the division which already exists between urban insiders and urban outsiders. In 1971 we were struck by the strength of feeling in the township of Namakrale on the outskirts of Phalaborwa expressed by urban insiders against the existence of the migrants in hostels set in the midst of their family houses. Parents, fearful for the safety of their daughters, wanted the hostels moved elsewhere. Similarly in Dube (Johannesburg) the relations between migrants from the hostel and wives of the men whose homes are nearby leads to great tension. If to these divisions we add a sharp difference in income and of life styles, the potential conflict between these two groups is likely to become more pronounced. Indeed it is salutary to recall at this point Sidney Webb's observation that "the only permanently effective Trade Union victories are won by limitation of the numbers in the particular trade, and the excluded candidates necessarily go to depress the condition of the outsiders. The

Trade Unionist can usually only raise himself on the bodies of his less fortunate comrades."[44]

Already it is said that urban insiders are against the abolition of influx control because they see such a step leading to the lowering of their own living standards. Of course there are other factors—not least the daily indignities of apartheid—which bind the two groups together, but any analysis of the impact of economic growth must note the possibility of it intensifying antagonisms in the townships.

Finally, there was the Carletonville strike in which a combination of worker dissatisfaction and poor channels of industrial communication led to an inflamed situation, resulting in the shooting of workers. But the awareness of employers, partly because of outside pressure, partly because of the rise in Black consciousness, that the use of force in this manner is becoming increasingly unacceptable and politically inflammatory means that institutional ways must be sought of responding to workers' demands in such a way that confrontation can be avoided. Such thinking has lead directly to attempts by employers in the manufacturing sector to set up some sort of institutional framework, e.g., works councils, for negotiation and bargaining. But can this be done in the mining industry where 99 percent of the Black workers are migrants, where turnover averages 100 percent per annum and where the nature and size of the compounds makes it virtually impossible for workers to be allowed to organize whilst still ensuring that they do not resort to mass action and confrontation rather than the sort of orderly negotiation far preferred by employers?

In concluding this section on the impact of economic growth on Black producer power it is not possible to do more than point to the diversity of possible developments within the urban situation. At a micro-level what happens is likely to be influenced by whether the workers are urban insiders or outsiders; whether they are skilled or unskilled, and whether they are uniethnic or multiethnic, it is probably not pure coincidence that the three major strikes involving migrants in the past fifteen years have been in Windhoek (Ovambo), Cape Town (Xhosa), and Durban (Zulu) rather than one the Witwaterstrand where migrants come from much more diverse backgrounds. At the same time there are two contrary pressures at work which make prediction entirely dependent upon one's assessment of their future relative strength. One is the ability of the authorities (employers and government) to contain and if necessary repress any worker action that is seen as a direct challenge to the exercise of power. The other is the growing

[44]We are indebted to Sean Archer for drawing our atention to this quotation from S. Webb, *English Progress Towards Social Democracy*, Fabian Tract no. 15 (1892), reprinted in E. Hobsbawm, ed., *Labour's Turning Point* (London, 1948), p. 75.

presence of skilled and semi-skilled Black workers in the mines and factories, which gives them a potential for strike action that would be quite devastating in its political effectiveness *if* it could be organized and sustained.[45]

For what it is worth our assessment of the situation is that the repressive power of the state—including a willingness to use it if White control is threatened—is greater than it has ever been and that the possibility of organizing Black labor effectively, whilst perhaps a little better than it was a decade ago, remains insignificant in comparison. The arrest (in terms of the Terrorism Act and other legislation), detention without trial for months on end, and the banning of many, though not all, of those who become actively involved in the organization of Black workers serves to remind us of the realities of power. The wave of arrests during the last quarter of 1974 of young Black leaders in the student and worker movements was by no means an isolated event but should be seen as part of "a long series of confrontations over the past few years, which resulted in the leaders being banned, house arrested and jailed."[46]

Nevertheless a question remains. Although widespread confrontation in the industrial areas leading to major political changes may be unlikely, what may be the cumulative impact at a macro-level of the myriad small changes taking place on the factory floor? This may be particularly significant when considering changes that at a micro-level may be nonthreatening, but that when accumulated do change the political options in some subtle way. For example, the rash of short strikes for better wages that took place in different parts of the country during 1974 may serve not only to raise living standards, but also to create a new mood of self-reliance among Black workers, a determination not to be messed around by Whitey. But whilst the political frustration may increase, there are as yet no signs as to how this frustration might be translated into effective political action. If living standards continue to rise and activists are either banned or directed into the running of soccer clubs and other community projects is it *inevitable* that pent-up political frustrations will burst out and change the power structure? We think not.

[45]The possibility of a spontaneous and rapid escalation of strike action following some unforeseen events such as several bad train smashes on one day involving Black commuters cannot be ruled out.

[46]"Document relating to detentions," *Programme for Social Change* (Johannesburg, November 1974). Evidence that may well prove our assessment to be wrong is the phenomenal rise of Black participation in worker organizations during 1973 and 1974. This has been particularly marked in Durban but also in the Southern Transvaal, Cape Town and elsewhere African labor is quietly becoming more organized. However, remembering the experience of the 1920s, it is too early to know whether one is witnessing a permanent change in the industrial relations scene.

A further dimension in which the political strength of Black workers must be considered relates to the interaction between the homeland leaders and the urban proletariat.[47] If organization is the prerequisite for the transformation of power from potential to actual and effective political force, is it possible that the emergence of Bantustans will provide a base from which Black labor could be mobilized? In answering this we find a distinction, which may well prove to be important, between two types of Bantustan: one whose nearest boundary is close to, if not part of, a major urban area; the other far removed from any large cities. Table 7.3 illustrates the distinction.

Table 7.3 Black Population in Bantustan
Urban Areas, 1970

Bantustan	Urban population (in thousands)	Of which (in thousands)	i.e. %	Live near
Kwazulu	236	221	94	Newcastle and within 20 miles of Durban-Pietermaritzburg axis.
Bophutatswana	125	95	76	Pretoria and Rustenburg
Ciskei	101	88	87	East London and King Williams Town
Lebowa	64	40	62	Pietersburg, Phalaborwa and Potgietersrus
Transkei	45	20	45	Umtata
Swazi	5.2	3.7	70	Nelspruit
Matshangana	4.5	–	–	–
Basotho Qwa Qwa	1.3	–	–	–
Vendaland	0.7	–	–	–

Source: Republic of South Africa, Department of Statistics, *Population Census 6th May, 1970,* Report no. 02-05-01 (Pretoria, 1970).

From this table KwaZulu, Bophutatswana, and the Ciskei emerge as the three Bantustans most likely, because of their urban commuter population, to influence the organization of the Black industrial labor force. By the same token, if Bantustan involvement in the labor move-

[47]The discussion of worker homeland interaction owes much to colleagues at the Mt. Kisco Conference on Contemporary South Africa. Table 3 was constructed after a seminar at the University of Natal and owes its origin primarily to a suggestion by Colin Webb.

ment is effective it is likely that it would be in the "homeland-oriented"[48] cities—Durban, Pretoria, East London and others listed in the above table—that such organization would first make itself felt. This is not to argue that other more distant cities such as Port Elizabeth, Cape Town or Johannesburg will not be influenced by developments within the Bantustans. Nor does it necessarily follow that those Bantustans—such as the Transkei or Basotho Qwa Qwa (Witsieshoek)—more distantly situated from any major industrial centre will be completely powerless to stimulate urban worker organization. But if it is correct to suggest that the Bantustans could provide some sort of a base on which to begin building a labor movement then it would seem that the potential power of KwaZulu or Bophutatswana is considerably greater than that of the Transkei or Vendaland. In other words, contiguity with a large city, to which it supplies labor, rather than a frontier with the wider world, may be the source of any power which a Bantustan might generate. Whether or not it will be possible for interaction between Bantustan organizers and industrial workers—migrants or urban insiders—to develop in such a way that the labor movement is strengthened is an open question. There is no way of predicting what will happen. We can only note that the difference in militancy during the early 1970s between Black workers in Durban and Cape Town is probably not unconnected with the difference in distance between these cities and the Bantustans from which their migrant workers come. At the same time, as will be argued, the net result of the creation of independent Bantustans may well be to weaken still further the political bargaining power of Black South Africans.

BLACK CONSUMER POWER

The third major area concerns the growing consumer power of the Black community. It is quite possible, as has been noted, that Black incomes in urban areas will rise substantially over the next few years. This would be in response to a combination of pressures ranging from strikes, through the moral lobby (e.g., student Wages Commissions and The Guardian campaign) to such business interests (e.g., clothing manufacturers or food chain stores) for whom the costs of higher wages are outweighed by the benefits of an increased Black consumer market. But what impact would such consumer power have? The story of the effect of opening a branch of a national chain of stores in an Orange Free State town points to one important change. Before the arrival of the new store Black customers in the town were treated like dirt; shouted at; unable to try on clothes before purchase; and generally made to feel inferior. Then the new branch opened and, treating Blacks like normal

[48]W. Thomas, "Verstedeliking van die Bantoe en stadsontwikkeling" (Unpublished paper, School of Economics, University of Cape Town, 1971).

customers, captured all the African market. Whilst such changes do much for personal self-respect they do not alter the power of the White electorate to maintain all discriminatory legislation firmly in place. The possibility does emerge however that by mobilizing their consumer power Blacks could force changes in, for example, the employment practices of large firms. Theoretically this is so, but the difficulty of organization remains. Martin Luther King and his colleagues were, despite harrassment, left free to organize in a way that is inconceivable for Black leaders in South Africa today.

There is, however, one important consequence of the changing role of Blacks as producers and consumers. This is what we might call the closing of the culture gap. It is beyond the scope of this paper to explore the cultural changes taking place in South Africa, but it is worth noting that the pressures for education exerted by labor shortages, combined with the growth of an urban culture, implies that in some senses Black and White people living in Johannesburg, for example, have far more in common than would these same Whites have with rural Xhosa from the Transkei. In itself such cultural forging together in the urban crucible does nothing to alter power relationships, but it may well alter psychological attitudes in such a way that makes the present system more difficult to sustain. Change, as Alan Paton once pointed out, will not come in South Africa until Whites lose confidence that they are destined to rule others and until Blacks gain the confidence that they have the right not to be ruled by others. It is in this context that we see the significance of the Black consciousness movement. The closing of the culture gap, which one might argue is a result of economic growth, may be a necessary though not a sufficient condition for political change.

INTERNATIONAL PERSPECTIVES

The fourth—and last—area to be discussed in this paper lies in the international arena. Some analysts would argue that any discussion of economic change in South Africa should begin rather than end with the impact of foreign investment and the role of the multinational corporation. This is indeed something which requires far more research, but the evidence so far collected by American, Swiss, British and other investigators suggests that foreign firms have tended to adapt to the attitudes and practices of the local environment rather than to influence it for change. We might well criticize such a conclusion by pointing out that without foreign investment (e.g., in the mining industry), the South African economy would be nothing like it is today. True; but that is not really the point at issue. What is at stake is the question whether it would have made any difference to the South African power structure if these investments now held by shareholders living in Europe or America had been held instead by South African citizens. The answer, surely, is "no." What needs analysis in the first instance is investment as a whole rather than that derived from a particular area. And for this paper the impact of investment has been analyzed in terms of the impact of economic growth within the existing politicoeconomic power structure. How this structure came to be what it is has not been examined here, although there is certainly need for analysis of the political impact of investment and economic growth as it has occurred in the past. As far as the future is concerned it seems reasonable to conclude that whilst foreign firms— pursued by outside pressure groups—may do something to improve their own employment practices, they are very unlikely to attempt any political action that would threaten the profitable *status quo*.[49] Even if all new investments to the country were stopped, which would be a severe political blow, it is unlikely that there would be much impact on the economy. The removal of existing investment is a fairly academic question for even if firms wanted to pull out it would not be difficult for the government of the day to prevent any large-scale withdrawal of finance from actually taking place. Meantime, the significance of the existence of massive foreign investment in South Africa lies in the fact that it is likely to bias the support of those governments whose citizens hold the investments against any activities that might seem severely to threaten these investments. To put it bluntly, in the appalling event of a major escalation of the guerrilla war in southern Africa, the western governments would be under heavy pressure to supply arms to those fighting to maintain the *status quo* rather than to those fighting to overthrow the system.

This of course is not the only possible outcome of the trend of events in southern Africa. A recent development is the rapid move towards independence of a number of countries on the periphery of the Republic, which at the beginning of 1974 were under White rule. Of these the most important is Mozambique. We would not be so bold as to attempt to assess the possible long-term political reverberations in South Africa of so recent an event. All we would do is to inject one thought that arises from an economic analysis of the situation. It is surely over-simple to assume a sort of domino-theory of de-colonialization in Southern Africa. The victory of Frelimo in Mozambique does not necessarily imply rapid change in South Africa.[50] This is because of the great

[49]A good example of outside pressure is the report of the British Parliamentary Select Committee (1974) together with its recommended code of practices, which if adopted would form an important group of these microchanges (referred to on page 191) whose macro-implications are unclear.

[50]This paragraph first drafted in 1972 well before the Portuguese coup has been rewritten in the light of events during 1974. Our argument against a domino theory of decolonisation and our assessments of Mozambique's dependence on South Africa and hence Frelimo's foreign policy constraints remain unchanged but what has altered, in the light of Malawi's ability to sustain a suspension of recruiting for months on end following the Wenela plane crash in Botswana in April 1974, is our appreciation of the capacity

dependence of the Mozambique economy on that of South Africa. Even
before the rises in wages between 1972 and 1974 in gold mines, it was
estimated that Black miners from Mozambique could earn twice as
much by coming to the Witwatersrand and the Orange Free State than
they would by finding a job at home. The remittances from 100,000 or
more men at work in the mines are a major source of income and of
foreign exchange for Mozambique. Zambia and Tanzania closed their
borders to South African recruiters but neither country sent anything
like as many migrants nor was as dependent upon their earnings. Will
a Fremolino government be able to overcome the political opposition
of all those—migrants and their families—who would presumably not
willingly forfeit the money that can be earned in South Africa? Nor are
migrant earnings the only factor. What would happen to Lourenco
Marques if the Transvaal's imports and exports were switched to
Richards· Bay and Durban, thus depriving Mozambique of all the rail
and harbor dues? Or if South African tourists were directed not to go to
Mozambique any more?[51] While a Frelimo government would obviously
move as fast as possible to extricate itself from dependence upon South
Africa, the hard fact remains that it would be a long, long haul.

The Mozambique relationship with the Republic is fundamentally
different from that of Zambia. Unfortunately for Mozambique its
Copperbelt is on the Witwatersrand. The predicament that would face a
Frelimo government regarding the closure of the South African border
derives from the fact that, for three generations, the "East Coast" has
been developed as part of the South African economy. As with the
Bantustans and the former British protectorates, most of the capital
accumulation (i.e., roads, railways, factories, and the whole infrastructure) of a modern economy resulting from the labors of those migrating
from these areas has taken place outside them in those places where
Whites are in control. How then does a Mozambique, Lesotho, or a
politically independent KwaZulu reduce its enormous economic
dependence on South Africa? In the long run, so a Mozambique
government might reason, the only way is to close the border and try to
raise living standards without becoming ever more deeply plugged into
the South African economy. But the short-term costs—and political

of Malawi (and other countries on the periphery of the Republic?) to halt
labor flows to the Republic.

[51]According to the *Financial Mail*, 21 June 1974, South Africa's contribution to the Mozambique economy in 1971 was as follows: mineworkers' remittances R50m; harbor and rail dues, R50m, exports to South Africa, R11m;
tourists R10m, making a total of R121 million or 42 percent of the total GDP.
In practice the figure is now considerably higher because much of the
miners' earnings are paid in gold at the official price, which is a little more
than one-quarter of the 1974 market price. Previously the gold was flown to
Portugal, but one early result of the coup was Mozambique's insistence in
keeping the windfall profits for herself.

difficulties—of such a step might make it impossible. Another possible option would be to retain the links in the short run and use much of the revenue from South Africa for developing, as rapidly as possible, the mineral and agricultural (especially sugar) potential of the country.

For Lesotho or an independent Bantustan the situation is much bleaker. There is, for the foreseeable future, no possibility whatever of the majority of their citizens earning their living except by migrating to the Republic. Indeed, it is arguable that a move towards political independence by a Bantustan is against the interests of those living there. For by accepting independence not only would the government of the Bantustan in question help to legitimize the existing Black-White land distribution but it would also, in effect, be conceding that its citizens had no claim to a share of the capital accumulation of the South African economy. Against this, on the other hand, must be set the possibility of independence giving Blacks a little more room to manoeuvre in their negotiations with the Pretoria government and also, perhaps, with employers.[52]

One could argue that economic dependence is not all one way: that South Africa's reliance upon Mozambique, Lesotho, or an independent Bantustan for such vast supplies of labor should enable these countries to exert some pressure on their powerful neighbor. This pressure would, of course, be even more effective if it could be coordinated amongst all the major labor supplying countries in order to wring changes out of South Africa. But would the government and people of a country like Malawi be willing to jeopardize their access to the South African labor market by participating in a general strike? For countries absorbed in nation building one can foresee action to improve the earnings and living conditions of their migrants away from home, but it is more difficult to see them threatening to withdraw these migrants in order to change the political structure particularly when such a change might well jeopardize future flows of labor. For would a Black majority South African government allow foreign workers into the country? Given the political pressure to which it would be subjected by its own voters, the answer is probably not. Cogent though this argument seemed to be early in 1974 it has been considerably weakened by Malawi's decisions to suspend recruiting pending a long investigation into an air crash in Botswana on 4 April 1974 in which seventy-five Malawian mineworkers were killed. By the end of 1974 Malawi had still given no signs of being willing to allow its citizens to go South to work

[52]*See* P. Selwyn, "Industrial Development in Peripheral Small Countries" (paper presented at Institute of Development Studies, Paper no. 14, University of Sussex, Falmer, 1973), and W. Henderson, "Independent Botswana: A Reappraisal of Foreign Policy Options," *African Affairs* 73 (January 1974):290.

and many, though not all, the gold mines were seriously embarrassed by the increasing shortage as Malawian miners went home at the end of their contract and no new men came to take their place. This fact plus Frelimo's threats to halt all Mozambique recruiting have caused the Chamber of Mines to aim at increasing the proportion of South African labor in the total force. It is not inconceivable that the mining industry could, by raising wages to compete with the manufacturing sector, by investing heavily in mechanization and by pressing for easier access to farm labor supplies, reduce its reliance on foreign labor to a fraction of what it is now.[53] Even if it could not do this the possibility remains of Malawian laborers being replaced to some extent by Africans from Rhodesia or, indeed, even from an independent Zimbabwe. Despite Malawi's success in cutting off its supply of labor to the White south in 1974 it still seems to us unlikely that all the countries on the periphery of the Republic will be willing and able to sustain a sudden and permanent end to the flow of labor to work in South Africa. Thus one is driven to conclude that unless the economies of the countries exporting labor to the Republic grow sufficiently to be able to employ at a higher wage level most of their own economically active population, or unless war, financed from outside the region, breaks out and the migrants previously available for jobs in South Africa become, instead, mobilized for military action, they will not be in a position to do much with their economic bargaining power to challenge the existing political order within South Africa.

Having considered what seem to be four of the most important areas in which the political implications of economic change need to be analyzed, it is necessary to point out that they do not cover the whole field. For example, we have not examined the possible consequences of the continuance of rapid inflation. Both in the early 1920s and half a century later, inflation seems to have been one of the proximate causes of action by Black workers. If rapid inflation persists will strike action not continue to be generated with all the "consciencization" of workers that this entails? If, on the other hand, the rate of inflation slows down will there be a concomitant dampening of the labor movement? Has the point of no-return already been reached in the sense that a whole generation of workers is experiencing, and will not give up, the possibility of direct action leading to specific change?

What, to consider another variable, are the possible economic and political consequences of population growth? Professor Sadie has

[53]There is not the space here to examine the implications for South African agriculture of such a move. Some of the possibilities include a speeding up of the phasing out of many White farmers and the growth of agribusiness, or an increase by farmers in the employment of foreigners both legal and illegal.

estimated that by the year 2020—which is closer to 1974 than the Rand Rebellion (1922) or the election of the Pact government (1924)—the number of Whites, including immigrants, will have risen from 4 million in 1970 to 9 million while Blacks will have risen from 15 million (1970) to no less than 63 million people.[54] In other words, there will be 9 million Whites trying to control a society that contains 48 million *more* Blacks (and 7 million more Colored and Asian persons) than it did in 1970. Is such a population change—with all its implications for urbanization, the creation of jobs, and the spectres of rural poverty and unemployment—possible without causing a fundamental transformation of the existing structure of political power?

The implicit assumption underlying most of this paper is that the process of economic growth is going to continue but this is not necessarily so. Readers of *The Great Crash*[55] will need no reminding that at the end of the booming twenties there were few people, least of all economists, who foresaw the spectacular crash which followed. As Robert Heilbronner has pointed out, apropos of the early 1950s, economists are very bad at foretelling what is likely to happen to some of the key variables in their trade.[56] If in South Africa the rate of growth should stop or even go into reverse, what would be the political implications? It is impossible to tell. Whites threatened with loss of their jobs in a declining economy might revert to a tighter "civilized labor" policy and dismiss Blacks in order to employ Whites at higher rates of pay. Blacks, on the other hand, having experienced working in the more highly skilled jobs and having no land to fall back on, might resist such a move very much more strongly than they did when it happened on the railways two generations previously.[57] If they did, who knows what the outcome would be?

It is impossible, it seems to us, to make any firm prediction. Our view is that the prospects of political change being generated by economic growth are exceedingly dim. But alongside the harsher facts of White power south of the Limpopoone must place such factors as the unforeseen consequences of present actions, the macro-implications of many micro-changes, and the psychological impact of decolonization outside the borders of the Republic. And we conclude that any number of plausible hypotheses can be put forward regarding the shape of the future, ranging from fundamental change by 1984, through second-

[54]J. Sadie, *Projection of the South African Population, 1970-2020* (Johannesburg, 1973).

[55]J. Galbraith, *The Great Crash, 1929* (Harmondsworth, 1961).

[56]R. Heilbronner, "The Clouded Crystal Ball," *American Economic Review* (May 1974), pp. 121-8.

[57]Wilson and Perrot, *Outlook on a Century*, p. 330.

best solutions, to an entrenched racial oligarchy living off the backs of impoverished Blacks far into the next century. All one can really do, we suggest, is try to clarify our understanding of the forces at work, to interpret some of the apparent trends, and to be ready, in the light of new facts or further insights, to modify or abandon our own particular assessment. In such a context one can only regard with considerable scepticism any analysis which suggests that a particular future is inevitable. There are so many variables at work, interacting in so many unpredictable ways, that one cannot but recall Alan Paton's sharp gibe against an earlier predictor:

> Keppel Jones, Keppel Jones
> Let me ask you in sepulchral tones;
> The night was so stark,
> The dark was so dark;
> How could you see when you threw the bones?[58]

Similarly, with due acknowledgement, one might question those who see reform just around the corner:

> O'Dowd, O'Dowd
> Let me ask you aloud;
> The light was so bright,
> The white was so white;
> Were you not dazzled with your head in the cloud?

Being wise after the event will be easy; peering uncertainly into the future is altogether a different matter.

[58]Reprinted by kind permission of the author.

8
Profile of Change: The Cumulative Significance of Changes Among Africans

J. CONGRESS MBATA

INTRODUCTION

In dealing with any aspect of the race situation in South Africa, it is necessary to divest the mind of the simplistic assumption that the country's brand of racism is the delusion of a bigoted and assertive minority and that certain minor programs are bound to dissolve the prejudices that currently dictate policy. South Africa's racism is an integral part of its total White culture: indeed, it has given the country its social structure, about which there is no ambiguity, and has facilitated a considerable measure of affluence from which flows the sense of security that the White man enjoys. In making formulations, therefore, about change—actual or potential—in South Africa, it is necessary to identify and to distinguish those factors that constitute the sometimes subtle yet persistent continuities in its history of Black-White relations. As White domination has remained the single unbroken thread in South African history,[1] it must be taken as the central point of reference in evaluating shifts in the workings of the system. Thus it is pertinent to the definition of "change" in this paper.

The pressures for change that are being exerted upon South Africa arise from a variety of different sources—economic, social, political,

---

[1]C. Mbata, "Race and Resistance in South Africa," in J. Paden and E. Soja, eds., *The African Experience* (Evanston, 1970), 2:210.

and ideological—each of which exhibits shifting patterns that render analysis difficult and prediction hazardous. Nevertheless, "change" in the South African context must be defined in terms of two processes: change can be manifested in forms that could only be characterized as "superficial." Modifications in the limitations of access for Africans to public places such as parks would fall into this category. Often, superficial change is calculated to cause the least amount of disruption of institutional structures. It may indeed if the pressures on the dominant group are sufficiently great, even result in a measure of cooptation of selected segments of the deprived group:

> When groups of the powerless succeed in organizing themselves to provoke the power structure, the response is often to coopt the moderate leaders into official structures, isolating them from their base, to repress the militant leaders, and to yield to the mass something of what they want: wage increases, city services, measured relief from police or administrative oppression. . . . These benefits are often transitory, however, and the struggle is continual and positive response reluctant.[2]

However, change must be looked upon as the removal of limitations upon the African that discriminate against his participation in all institutional spheres. Such a transformation represents "fundamental" change, which alone can be lasting and meaningful. Fundamental change requires a reordering of the power structure's priorities, and thus it could very well mean the creation of instability. Fundamental change also means the formulation of a theory of political development for the African that clearly identifies the link between political power and economic power. Thus it will mean new and radical arrangements for the redistribution of the country's wealth and resources. This is the import of the Bantustan leaders' stand on the land question. Finally, fundamental change will be seen by the people it affects to lead to development. Thus, while the creation of "homelands" constitutes change of some sort, it would be fundamental only if it were perceived by the permanent population of the "homelands" and by the urban African population and the Black rural farm population as leading to the creation of structural transformations that would liberate them from oppression and exploitation.

Development, once initiated, becomes an ongoing process;[3] but it is at the same time an overall transforming process. Development has to do with the relationship of power to the economic, social, political, and other institutional structures of society. Political power in a country like South Africa is defined and conditioned by economic

---

[2]J. Cockcroft, A. G. Frank, and Dale L. Johnson, *Dependence and Underdevelopment: Latin America's Economy* (New York, 1972), p. 292.

[3]I. Horowitz, *Three Worlds of Development: The Theory and Practice of International Stratification* (New York, 1972), p. 463.

power and the concentration of the resources of power in the hands of a dominant group. For the dominated group there may be accommodation and even selective cooptation but never development as long as these power relationships remain unaltered. Development could be marked by the release of tremendous energy and creativity for tackling social, poliical and economic problems in a society which has become convinced that its destiny lies in its own hands, and whose members would, therefore, have acquired self-confidence and a sense of dignity both personally and collectively. Dale L. Johnson has advanced a working formulation of the concept of development. He states: "Development is first of all the development of man out of conditions of exploitation, poverty, and oppression."[4] Looking more specifically at the reserves,[5] we could amplify this formulation by postulating that development is a movement toward complete self-determination for any given nation; at the same time, it is a movement toward the achievement of optimal use of the resources of the nation, such achievement being determined by the degree to which the nation enables each member of the society to meet his basic needs. The question to ask is whether the African territories see themselves moving in the direction of attaining these two ends as a result of recent changes there.

A discussion of change in South Africa inevitably involves the question not only of African responses to such changes as may be taking place, but also of the Africans' own initiatives to produce change. Since 1658, when the Khoi-Khoi fought the Dutch, charging that the latter were waging war on them with the sole purpose of taking away their land, the Africans have fought or resisted, firstly, White encroachment upon, and appropriation of, their land, and later their exclusion from the institutional arrangements of the country. Up to the 1870s they used mainly armed resistance; thereafter the resistance resolved itself into political expression. Indeed, the Black man "has never accepted his subjugation as ultimate."[6] For him therefore the struggle has never ended, even though it has become considerably circumscribed by the application of a host of

[4]"On Oppressed Classes" in Crockcroft et al., *Dependence and Underdevelopment*, p. 272.

[5]The term "reserve," although no longer frequently used, has been retained in the remainder of this paper because it is one that is most consistent with historical fact, these areas having been set aside by proclamation for African occupation. The name "Bantu Homelands" is misleading, and tends to perpetuate a historical fallacy that has been used as a rationale for limiting Africans to 13 percent of the land. It seems that some Blacks resent the word "Bantustan." The term "African territories" is used here interchangeably with the term "reserves."

[6]Mbata, "Race and Resistance," p. 227.

legal devices by the government. African voices, which even by the South African government's own standards could never be regarded as extremist, have sought to convey this message over the years. In 1920, D.D.T. Jabavu said: "The Bantu people throughout the Union of South Africa are in a state of positive discontent. . . . These feelings are largely not expressed . . . but nevertheless . . . are there, and are seething like molten volcanic lava in the breasts of these inarticulate people."[7] Using a platform provided by the government itself—the Natives Representative Council—R.V. Selope-Thema said in 1945: "We cannot turn the other cheek everytime someone hits us . . . it is the Government itself which is inciting our people to violence, and all these strikes which you see are the result of . . . the disabilities imposed on my people. . . . The time is coming when we shall have to preach 'Africa for the Africans.'"[8] The following year, in the same forum, Paul R. Mosaka was to proclaim: "You can do what you like, you can shoot us, arrest us, imprison us, but you are not going to break our spirit. We shall continue fighting for our rights until the day dawns when we shall have the right to live like human beings in the land of our birth, in the land that is ours."[9] A decade and a half later, W.F. Nkomo, addressing a conference of African women, declared: "We are not a servant race. We too have a soul that yearns for freedom and self-determination—not development that is prescribed and proscribed."[10]

A meeting of heads of governments of the reserves held on 8 November 1973 adopted a resolution viewing "any form of racial discrimination as an assault on the human dignity of black people." The meeting reached agreement on the principle of federation of their territories, and Chief Buthelezi of KwaZulu is reported to have told a gathering afterwards "that none of the architects of separate development could ever have dreamed that their policy would be used as a platform on which to build black solidarity." Paramount Chief Matanzima spoke of "the renaissance of the United Nations of 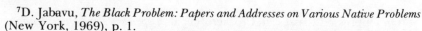 black South Africa."[11] On a previous occasion he had said, "We want solidarity of the blacks."[12]

[7]D. Jabavu, *The Black Problem: Papers and Addresses on Various Native Problems* (New York, 1969), p. 1.

[8]Union of South Africa, *Verbatim Report of the Proceedings of the Natives Representative Council (Ninth Session)*, 7-14 November 1945, pp. 129-30.

[9]Union of South Africa, *Verbatim Report of the Proceedings of the Natives Representative Council (Adjourned Meeting of the Ninth Session)*, 14-15 August 1946, p. 30.

[10]Quoted in E. Cole, *House of Bondage* (New York, 1967), p. 174.

[11]M. Horrell, ed., *A Survey of Race Relations in South Africa 1973* (Johannesburg, 1974), pp. 164-5.

[12]C. Legum, *A Republic in Trouble: South Africa, 1972-1973* (London, 1973), p. 13.

And so the struggle of the Black man in South Africa has, since the beginning of Black-White contact, oscillated between the "politics of violence and the politics of peaceful persuasion,"[13] but it has nonetheless retained clearly articulated goals. An examination of the question of change cannot ignore the variety of forms and adaptations that the militant expression of African discontent takes; for, upon the construction that the African puts on these changes rests the matter of whether they will be meaningful to South Africa as a whole. Recent utterances by Africans—some of which will be examined in this paper—suggest that as long as the White man in South Africa continues to arrogate to himself the right to define the character of change and to lay down the ground rules for development, so long will the African resist, and so long must the country continue to expect surprises in the nature and design of the mechanisms of protest that are used.

FACTORS LIMITING CHANGE

Scholars generally agree that there is little likelihood that White attitudes, in terms of which White dominance is regarded as essential for tolerable existence in the country, will suddenly change as a result of a floodlight of enlightenment or in response to what has been called a "moral revival." Explicitly or by implication many authors recognize the significance of historical continuities. The majority of White South Africans' collective inclinations are traceable to a variety of material interests; among these are possession of land and availability of exploited labor to work that land, sheltered employment, and a belief that white control implies the maintenance of stability in the economy. There is also the historical factor of group isolationism continually reinforced by posing the threat of the "Black peril." "Consequently Whites hold the . . . assumption that the retention of political power is a prerequisite for protecting their own material, cultural and security interests" (Schlemmer and Muil, p. 107). "The policy of separate development or multinationalism . . . accentuates the gap between the Black people in the homelands, and those elsewhere in South Africa. . . Town-dwelling Black people . . . remain most severely exposed to the experience of discrimination and rightlessness. . . . But the alternative of a common society seems at present not to be acceptable to the great majority of Whites" (Mayer, pp. 138–140).

Change in the radical transforming sense would conflict with the aims of the policy of separate development as borne out by the evolution of legislation and administrative practice in South Africa.

[13]Rotberg employs this apt antithesis in his introduction (p. xxvi) to R. Rotberg and A. Mazrui, eds., *Protest and Power in Black Africa* (New York, 1970).

Schlemmer and Muil set out what they have called "the most sub-stantial aims" of the policy in the "real-politik" sense. These include circumscribing "the political aspirations of Africans" by limiting them to politics in the African territories; the formulation of a rationale for exclusion of the African presence and political participation in the major areas of the country; Balkanization of the political system in order "to discourage mass black political solidarity"; the promulga-tion of the ideology of an Afrikaans group identity and a Western civilization predicated upon the assumption of a threat by the Black political and social presence in the so-called White areas (p. 108). This pattern has become institutionalized and entrenched so as not to be disturbed by superficial changes. The policy of separate development is designed, it is hoped, to create opportunity structures and mobility for Blacks within limits that are defined by the White holders of power: "The institutionalization of dependence relations are [sic] a principal mechanism of domination. Dependence is a severe limita-tion of choices available to the dominated, regulated by alternatives set ultimately by the dominant group."[14]

Writing more specifically with regard to Africans in industry, Wilson (p. 180) sees the color bar as likely to be maintained "to ensure that Blacks will not be allowed to keep Whites out of jobs that significant numbers of individual voters still wish to fill." Wilson begins his study by dividing those who have studied the implications of the economic changes taking place in South Africa into "optimists" and "pessimists." The former see the possibility of peaceful trans-formation of the society resulting from "the dynamo of economic growth." In the view of this group there will be a gradual diminution of present racial divisions and conflicts. Michael O'Dowd, who has written in this vein, thinks that "about 1980, one can look for the radical constitutional reform corresponding to the Second Reform Act in England and President Wilson's programme in the United States ushering in the period of high liberalism." Perhaps O'Dowd has not looked at Wilson's record closely enough; the contradictions in his statement would startle him, for though there was a period of high liberalism it did not involve an attack on segregation.[15] In the same way, economic growth in South Africa could lead to a selective reformism, leaving out a major social group.

Economic growth, therefore, may not be the basis for optimism. Wilson sounds a necessary warning: "Even if Black workers became established in the cities with their families this would not in itself

[14]Cockcroft et al., *Dependence and Underdevelopment*, p. 283.
[15]R. Logan, *The Betrayal of the Negro, From Rutherford B. Hayes to Woodrow Wilson* (London, 1965), pp. 360-1; and M. Steinfield, *Our Racist Presidents* (San Ramon, Calif., 1972), pp. 220-1.

necessarily alter the power structure." He finds a parallel in the history of the Colored people for whom there has never been any perceptible access to power in spite of their liberation from the pass laws in 1828 (see p. 186).

Hannah Arendt has said that "since the end of human action ... can never be reliably predicted, the means used to achieve political goals are more often than not of greater relevance to the future world than the intended goals."[16] South Africa may not be a totalitarian country today in the classical sense, but a number of mechanisms of totalitarian design are in evidence in the implementation of policies. These factors condition the struggle of the Africans and must be taken into account in any attempted projection of that struggle. In addition, they place limitations upon the nature of such changes as may occur and tend to circumscribe their possibilities.

Yet it would be entirely unwarranted pessimism to assume the position that such changes as are taking place are not worthy of scrutiny because of their superficial nature. The limited autonomy that the Transkei has achieved has enabled it, at least on paper, to loosen the throttling grip of South African policy on the education of its children. To the extent that the people of the Transkei reversed the South African trend vis-à-vis the medium of instruction in the schools, they have asserted their determination to resist efforts to tell them what to do. This is a small but significant factor in the consciousness-building process. This kind of self-assertion is capable of loosening certain bolts in the institutions imposed by the dominant group. It creates a need to make certain shifts in the power centers, however small those shifts may be, and even though they may be shifts designed to shore up the established structure. What has been said of the domestic colonial situation elsewhere applies equally well in the South African context: "The point is that raising demands for self-determination in the colony weakens the institutional mechanisms of domination through achieving concessions or by forcing the dominant to rely upon naked coercion, which may have the effect of further developing consciousness among the oppressed."[17]

SUPERFICIAL CHANGE

Economic Changes

In its report the Economic Commission of the Study Project on Christianity in Apartheid Society wrote: "Poverty exists juxtaposed

[16]H. Arendt, *On Violence* (New York, 1970), p. 4.

[17]Crockcroft et al., *Dependence and Underdevelopment*, p. 298. The authors describe Blacks, Chicanos, South African Blacks, and racial and cultural minorities as internal colonies.

with great wealth. The division follows the racial cleavages in society and poverty is made more acute by the experience of relative deprivation. The wealth of the South African economy, which now ranks with the middle income groups of nations, although generated by the labour of all its people, is not available to all the people. . . . The participation in wealth is artificially unequal."[18] This artificial situation generates stresses, and explosions occur sometimes. From October 1972 to February 1973, the deceptive calm of South Africa was shattered by a wave of industrial unrest as thousands of African and Indian workers put down tools to back their demands for better pay and improved working conditions. Rising living costs, unemployment or the threat of it, the unwillingness or inability of those who hold economic power to do anything to change conditions, these are the factors that lay at the bottom of the strikes.

The reaction of Prime Minister Vorster was surprising. He said: "Now I am looking past all party affiliations and past all employers, and experience tells me this, that employers, whoever they may be, should not only see in their workers a unit producing for them so many hours of service a day; they should also see them as human beings with souls."[19]

Among the reasons advanced to account not only for the prime minister's unexpected reaction, but also for what has been termed the government's kidglove handling of the Natal strikes, is the glare of publicity received by the latter and also South Africa's obvious efforts to maintain a favorable image abroad. The Ovambo strike of December 1971 to January 1972, while well organized, was planned to withdraw the workers to the reserve. Such a move requires the storage of sufficient food to sustain the workers and their dependents and thus prolong the period of withdrawal. Furthermore, there must be ways of preventing brutal retaliation by the authorities against the workers. One such way is the presence of news media. This was lacking in the Ovamboland case in contrast to the later case of Durban. In Durban, some concessions were won; but Wilson's criticism of the strike is its apparent spontaneity and lack of what he calls organizational muscle. Concessions in themselves do not bring about power changes; what was of concern to the government was "to avoid escalation of violence and the inflaming of world opinion" (p. 189).

Changes of a superficial nature are occurring in other areas of the economic sector. One of these areas is that of migrant labor whose origins are historical. The system was "much bolstered by the political

[18]P. Randall, ed., *Power, Privilege and Poverty: Report of the SPROCAS Economic Commission* (Johannesburg, 1972), p. 20.

[19]Republic of South Africa, *House of Assembly Debates*, 9 February 1973, col. 346.

and military activities of the White conquerors greedy for more land and the mining capitalists, such as Cecil Rhodes, who needed the peasants . . . to work as laborers." (Wilson, p. 178) It still forms the core mechanism for effecting the intended elimination of the African presence in the so-called White areas. Yet this is being offset by economic demands for labor to such an extent that African workers are being recruited back into the western Cape on a contract basis to fill the vacancies occasioned by the drainage of Colored labor, which is drifting into the industrial areas (Wilson, p. 173). The phenomenon is, of course, not new. South Africa's administrative record is a mosaic of exemptions and concessions permitting deviations from the ideological postulates that inspired the laws in the first place. The cumulative effect of these exemptions can be the establishment of an operative pattern that cannot be ignored. Africans once outside the reserves are, theoretically at least, defined as laborers; but the growth of a labor force in capacities other than those of unskilled workers has confronted successive governments with a set of problems from which there is no escape.

One emerging factor of change is the tendency that is becoming apparent in official thinking to make conditions more bearable for Africans in the urban areas. It has some relationship to recognition of the consumer power potential of the African. The change in the pattern of businessman-African customer relations that resulted from the opening of a branch of a national chain of stores in an Orange Free State town is significant. African customers for the first time in that town received equal treatment in a shop; the African market responded by gravitating to the new shop. This did not mean a change in policy structure in the country, but it did mean a change in superficial relationships in at least one town. However, the effectiveness of such changes in the long run is dependent upon the degree to which Black consumer power can be mobilized; and, as Wilson points out, the employment practices of large firms could be forced to change by such organization, but "the difficulty of such organization remains. Martin Luther King and his colleagues were left free to organize in a way that is inconceivable for Black leaders in South Africa today" (p. 194).

Another change that has occurred is the fact that the color-bar in industry "has shifted its position to a place further up the skill ladder" (Wilson, p. 180). It is, however, not affecting power and control in any fundamental way. What shifts have ocurred are regulated so that the position of the White man in the economy and in politics is not threatened. Much has been made of these shifts, but they remain superficial except insofar as they may, cumulatively, produce a whetting of the appetite for more substantial and permanent change.

future leverage

Moreover, for those who do move up the ladder it could mean the performance of key jobs that could be used as a lever to extract more concessions.

Wilson deals with a situation in which a group of "skilled urban insiders" struck and won. He foresees this kind of result leading to "a substantial increase in the Black consumer market." At the same time, it could widen the gap between the urban insiders and the migrant workers and lead to an intensification of antagonisms. In a sense, the urban insider would have some vested interest in the exclusion of the migrant workers from the urban scene (p. 189). However, the evidence that surfaces from the other investigations suggests a narrowing rather than a widening of the urban-rural gap for reasons which have a psychological orientation because of their ideological content. On the related question of illegal migration, Wilson's view is that "it does little to alter the basic structure of the migratory system that so brutally divides families" (p. 184). One thing needs to be noted, however: by its very nature this kind of migration means the existence of reserves of potentially explosive material in the so-called white areas that could feed any sudden outbreak of violence. The reverse side of the coin is that such people become chattels for unscrupulous employers to use and hold through intimidation and fear, although this merely increases the number of people who might turn on their masters in the event of a violent outbreak.

One outcome of these developments is the creation of the twin problems mentioned by Wilson as facing employers and White workers in the wake of the 1972 to 1973 strikes. For the employers there has emerged the need to set up some machinery for consultation with the Black workers if the danger of wildcat strikes is to be averted. A new provision now exists as part of the Bantu Labour Relations Regulation Amendment Act No. 70 of 1973, under which strikes or lock-outs by Africans have been legalized under certain circumstances. The stipulation is that a dispute must, in the first instance, be referred to a works or liaison committee where one exists. In the absence of such a committee, or where the committee fails to settle the dispute, the matter should be referred to the Bantu Labour Officer of the area. Thirty days must elapse after the date of such referral before a strike or lock-out can be legally embarked upon. On the other hand such machinery could be developed by the workers as a lever for obtaining far-reaching political concessions." (Wilson, p. 187) The government was faced with a similar predicament during the life of the Natives Representative Council (1936 to 1946). Abolishing the NRC did not remove the predicament.

For the White worker the question is: to unionize Blacks or not to unionize Blacks. Either way, there are dangers. If they unionize the

Blacks, the latter will sooner or later dominate the unions. If they continue their present policy of excluding Blacks, then the employers will gradually fractionate the jobs, creating new nonunion categories that they will fill with blacks, and "one day the White workers may go on strike but find that everybody can do without them" (Wilson, p. 187). This suggests that foreign investment is worth scrutiny. The foreign businessmen are not necessarily committed to South Africa's brand of racism. They are in the country primarily for money and go along with the policies as long as there is no pressure on them. With the mounting pressure back home for accountability and even withdrawal, they are likely to want to take every opportunity to demonstrate their goodwill in the situation. Job fragmentation and reallocation are the most likely directions for them to take.

The reserves have so far not produced any evidence of a potentially viable economy. Their problems are complicated, as in the case of KwaZulu, by the dumping of thousands of people who have been displaced from White farms and so-called Black spots" (Schlemmer and Muil, p. 112). The reabsorption of these people into a virtually nonexistent economy must affect the direction and development of relations, not only within the African territory itself, but also between the territory and the South African government. Looking at a different but not unrelated question, Mayer finds that people in the urban areas dread the possibility of being forced to the reserves "to starve." To them, the reserves hold no prospect of gainful work, and such employment as may exist is underpaid except for civil service positions (p. 154).

Social Changes

Notwithstanding the efforts of the government in South Africa to emphasize ethnicity, this factor appears to be unequivocally rejected by Africans even in Johannesburg's Soweto, where a number of ethnic groups are to be found (Mayer, pp. 152–158). Mayer's investigation in Soweto reveals remarkable uniformity and explicitness in the people's rejection of ethnicity. There is significance in this, not only because it belies the government's rationale for insistence upon ethnic grouping, but also because it is a step nearer fulfillment of the hopes and wishes of generations of African leaders since the Imbumba sent out its call in 1883 for Blacks to be "united on political matters."[20]

[20]T. Karis and G. Carter, eds., *From Protest to Challenge: A Documentary History of African Politics in South Africa, 1882-1964* (Stanford, 1972), 1:12. Imbumba Yama Afrika was one of the earliest African political organizations to be started in South Africa following the expansion of White power and the dispossession of the Blacks.

This conclusion is borne out in other ways. In all the urban townships investigated ethnic oppositions are firmly repudiated. Young urban Blacks are emphatic in their refusal to rank different language groups; and the residents see themselves as settling down into a common African identity. There is indeed no likelihood that development of the African territories will result in strengthening urban ethnocentrism. Mayer states "The evidence suggests that it is too late for this kind of political ethnicity. Its place is likely to be taken more and more by Black ethnicity" (p. 153).

Taken together with the call for Black solidarity by leaders of the African territories, this position becomes fraught with tremendous possibilities for relations in the country. It means that at least one ideological call is likely to be echoed around South Africa's Black world, and the cliché may yet be proved right that nothing is as strong as an idea whose time has come. Add to this the firm resolve of the young people to reject Whites in their struggle for self-determination, then indeed further concessions will have to be made or South Africa will have to be even more blatant in its use of coercion.[21] B.A. Khoapa speaks of Black withdrawal and Black awareness in terms suggesting that these have become necessary if Blacks are to regroup to continue the struggle for liberation. "Race is important. . . . It matters very much. This is what Black Consciousness is about."[22] Elsewhere he speaks of "going to the very gate of racism in order to destroy racism." Indeed, well may we ponder the words of Msimangu in Alan Paton's *Cry, The Beloved Country:* "I have one great fear in my heart, that one day when they [the Whites] are turned to loving, they will find we are turned to hating."

The idea of Black consciousness was first proclaimed by a Black group in the University Christian Movement (UCM) and later taken up by the South African Students' Organization (SASO) and the Black Peoples Congress (BPC). It is an inclusive awareness "embracing Africans, Coloreds, and Indians." This is the feature that distinguishes it from earlier manifestations of Black consciousness, which were primarily directed toward Africans. One of the earliest institutional expressions of awareness and pride in being African is found in the rise of Ethiopianism in the 1890s, with its slogan of "Africa for the

[21] The policy manifesto of SASO states: "because of their continual maintenance of an oppressive regime, Whites have defined themselves as part of the problem . . . therefore, we believe that in all matters relating to the struggle towards realising our aspirations, Whites must be excluded." Quoted in *Sechaba*, 7, 1 (January 1973): 4.

[22] B. S. Biko ed., *Black View*, SPROCAS Black Community Programmers (Durban, 1972), p. 64. B. A. Khoapa was SPROCAS Black Community Programme director until he was banned. P. Randall, ed., *A Taste of Power* (Johannesburg, 1973), p. 173.

Africans" and its motto, "Ethiopia shall stretch forth her hand to God." The current inclusiveness is new in the sense that, while there have been mergers and alliances among Africans, Coloreds, and Indians before, SASO is probably the first organization to begin with a foundation in which these elements are compounded.

The South African government has never taken kindly to any sort of rapproachement among the different population groups. Its strategy lies in creating walls separating the races and peoples and, if possible, keeping them ignorant about one another. It will tolerate ethnic consciousness, but not awareness of a more transcending nature. The government has, therefore, not been slow in retaliating against SASO. Despite this the concept of blackness seems to have taken firmer root. What gives it an even greater chance of gaining currency is the fact that it can be used to accommodate all three "awarenesses" that Schlemmer and Muil describe: ethnic pride, African unity, and all-embracing Black consciousness. These are not necessarily incompatible, as they have pointed out (p. 124). In addition, the language of Black consciousness eliminates the feelings of discomfort that arise from using such uncomplimentary terms as "Bantu," "Colored," and "non-White."

Some Africans speak of what they call "Europeanism—marked by selfishness, arrogance, and pride." This is contrasted with the attribute of *ubuntu*, the closest translation of which would be "humanness" or "greatness of soul." Mayer points out that what is true for Soweto is probably true all round, viz., that "the Whites do not serve as a reference group" (p. 158). The open articulation of this attitude is an indication of a firmer confidence in themselves and in their institutions on the part of Africans. It is this spirit that led the former editor of *The World*, M.T. Moerane, to demand that Africans be responsible for African education. He criticized the fact that African children were "taught that their forebears were savages who had been freed from ignorance by whites." He called this "indoctrination of the worst kind, not education."[23] Indeed, the South African government is going to have its hand full. Mayer points out that "A sense of black people having been treacherously conquered by white people seemed well engraved in our respondents' consciousness." These ideas have always been present among Africans; what is going to be new is the conscious reinforcement through them of the ideology of blackness as a result of disenchantment with whites. The Africans are aware that they have become pariahs in their own land because of their color: "The whites are oppressing me simply because I am black," said one of Mayer's respondents (p. 146).

[23]Legum, *Republic in Trouble*, p. 13.

This raises the question of the image that the African has of the wider South African society. Mayer's study reveals two models, both derived from the relations of the African with the dominant White group. One he calls the "pariah model" whose reference point is power or race domination under which the people see themselves as "despised, shunned, rightless, harassed, exploited, and effectively confined to the lowest kind of work for their living." The other is the "class model" in which Black-White relations are traced to economic factors. In the latter model the respondents did not seem to question the legitimacy of capitalist premises, but tended, instead, to differentiate between the Afrikaner, on the one hand, whom they associated with "brutal physical control," and the English or Jew, on the other, whose attitudes were regarded as more humane. Mayer attaches importance to this distinction as having played a part hitherto in "preventing total Black-White polarization" (p. 148).

Mayer adds, however, that there were those who saw Black and White relations uncompromisingly in terms of "us" versus "them," insisting that they cannot distinguish between different categories of Whites. It is no surprise therefore to find highly educated people repudiating elitism and supplying sophisticated political reasons for such rejection (pp. 148–149). It does mean a profound change in the people's mood. It is a far cry from the misplaced faith in the efficacy of the imperial factor that characterized the end of last century and the beginning of the present one. A wide ideological gap separates the days of "humble petitions" and "respectful deputations" from the present. Many educated men realize that there is no mobility for them unless they move with their people; and the indications seem to be that they are beginning to do just that and will move even closer to them in the future.

It must be conceded, of course, that there have always been educated Africans in the vanguard of the struggle of the Black people of South Africa. The change that has occurred today is that the educated man is being called upon to lead his people to self-determination without White influence, a task that is both easy and difficult: easy because he must turn the tables on the government by confronting it with a counterpart of its own doctrine; difficult because he must know where to stop and not become overcommitted in the wrong direction. As Khoapa put it, he must go to the gate of racism, but not further. His own people would not have him go further.

Of relevance also with regard to the matter of leadership in the urban areas and also in the reserves ultimately, especially in view of the latter's limited economic potential, is the image of the "rich." Businessmen who are seen as "playing up" to the establishment are dubbed satisfied stooges who have no commitment to change. In circumstances in which the economic conditions do not alter appreciably, as seems to be the case particularly in the reserves, the success of a few while the majority fight an endless battle to survive will only serve to strengthen this image. Schlemmer and Muil have pointed out that the prospects in agriculture in KwaZulu are gloomy, and that the future of the territory lies in exported labor.. They add that "the problems of underdevelopment and poverty in KwaZulu may be self-reinforcing in some ways, and cause additional administrative problems to homeland leaders" (pp. 112, 114). One set of minor changes is taking place: the leadership of the African territories is calling upon the elite to throw in their weight into the effort to deal with problems in the reserves; the ordinary working people in the urban areas expect commitment from the elite; and the educated elite, displaying their usual sensitivity, are responding to these calls in varying degrees. The businessman has less elbow room. His licence, and therefore his livelihood, can be affected. Yet the changes that are taking place could create an ironic situation for him. The African has tested his strike muscle and found it responsive. The African businessman has an almost 100 percent African clientele; he could be hard-hit by any decision to boycott him if the people feel that he is insensitive to their plight.

Political Changes

Frequent reference is made to the fact that the machinery of separate development has provided a platform for blacks in the reserves. Chief Buthelezi has pointed to this fact also (Schlemmer and Muil, p. 120). There is evidence that leaders in the reserves are turning it to good effect and saying things they would not be able to say under different circumstances—things for which others went to jail. Some of these have proved acutely embarrassing to the South African government but, ironically, it has found itself unable to take any action. The value of this situation is two-fold: first it reveals a significant trend among the traditional elite of the reserves to repudiate the links that have made them unquestioning conduits of government policy for more than a century. They are speaking as they have not spoken for decades, and this is recognized as a significant change. Second, it helps to beam a message to the people in the urban areas that, whatever might have been the fate of urban-centered political struggles in the past, they have not been alone in their thinking. In this sense, the struggle continues. Consistent with our proposition about the seething discontent to which Professor Jabavu referred in 1920, it would be more correct to say that these leaders have seized what appeared to them an opportune moment to take a public stance of opposition to the government.

The case of KwaMashu in Durban draws attention to another likely change that could have significant implications for the government's policy. The KwaMashu Urban Bantu Council "is pressing strongly for amalgamation into KwaZulu" (Schlemmer and Muil, p. 127). If this is achieved, then KwaMashu would become the second major reserve virtually in Durban itself; the other is Umlazi. In a strike like the Ovambo strike of 1971, the government would be hard put to it to throw a smoke screen round the focus of confrontation.

KwaMashu and Umlazi also highlight the contradictions that exist in the government's policy. What is or is not a so-called Bantu Homeland depends on how the government chooses to define each individual situation. The Africans, however, do not attach much significance to this dichotomization and, as Mayer points out, the leaders in the reserves "have begun to voice their concern about the situation of their supposed 'nationals' in the 'White' cities, with a rising note of urgency" (p. 141). Also, a number of organizations that transcend the urban-reserve boundary lines are being resurrected, particularly in Natal. Some are subpolitical cultural bodies, but all are aimed at unifying the Zulu people, and encouraging a sense of purpose and an ideology appropriate to the struggle for liberation and development (Schlemmer and Muil, pp. 123–128).[24]

An opportunity for greater politicization of the people in the reserves offers itself because of the political platform provided in those areas. We can speculate that this will be considerably reinforced, ironically as a result of the government's own program of displacing African people from the industrial areas as well as of its policy of migrant labor. We are likely to see many of the political stances normally associated with urban dwellers become common in the reserves. The effects of this will be profound both in respect to establishing grass-roots links between the industrial areas and the reserves and in respect to coordinating efforts to pressure the South African government. To appreciate the potential of this kind of situation, we need only look back to events in the late 1950s in the Zeerust area of the Transvaal, where there was an easy flowing two way stream between the reserve and the Witwatersrand.[25] Suburban African areas are likely to play a significant role in this regard.

[24]This development is reminiscent of the reemergence of the Sarekat Dagang as the Sarekat Islam (Islamic Association) in Indonesia in 1912. Its interests extended beyond its announced program and it became, for a while, an important instrument in the Indonesian struggle for liberation from the Dutch.

[25]Serious disturbances occurred in Zeerust during 1957, stemming from a number of causes including the enforcement of reference books for women. The women resisted and many of them were arrested. The husbands of many of the women worked in Johannesburg and the Witwatersrand and went home weekly or even more frequently. Johannesburg was in the throes of a strong antipass-law campaign. Horrell, *Race Relations, 1957-1958*, pp. 65-68.

In the case of KwaZulu, the involvement of the leadership in labor matters provides a further bond between the reserve and the urban people. This should go a long way toward giving the workers the necessary morale to press their demands for improved labor conditions. Schlemmer and Muil report that already "strikes by Zulu workers appear to be occurring with more frequency than ever before" (p. 130). This is likely to escalate; but, more than this, the example is likely to be followed by other areas. In addition, faced as they are with the prospect of unending poverty in their areas, the leaders in the reserves are likely also to become involved in the labor struggles of their people. Paramount Chief Matanzima's threat to resist the repatriation of his people to the Transkei unless the territory is given more land, suggests a readiness on his part to become involved in a confrontation with the South African government over the economic issues affecting his people.[26]

With the involvement of the leaders of African territories in industrial disputes, the next logical step appears to be a devolution of some of this activity on to the shoulders of their urban representatives in a far bigger sense than their narrow *rapporteur* role as envisaged by the South African government. Dladla, the executive councillor for Community Affairs in KwaZulu, has already blazed the trail. Among other things, he led a march of 5,000 African strikers and negotiated with the employers on their behalf in Pinetown, Natal. It has, of course, been pointed out that these representatives would lack the manpower resources to maintain a consistently high level of performance in this kind of role. Nevertheless, the momentum that men like Dladla have established, will need to be maintained or increased.

Power in the form of massive worker support has come into the hands of these men largely through the contradictions in the government's own policy. Tremendous potential lies in that power and, as is implied in our discussion of the absence of fundamental change, only power can produce that kind of change in South Africa. Africans can take a measure of comfort from the fact that the present KwaZulu leadership appears to have learnt something from history. A number of superficial changes have enabled the Africans to identify points of vulnerability in the White armor. They are apparently exploiting the discovery and will continue to do so with increasing determination.

CONCLUSION

Two types of change have been distinguished in this assessment: fundamental change and superficial change. There is no indication that fundamental change, the "reordering of the power structure's

---

[26]Horrell, *Race Relations, 1971*, p. 32. Legum, *Republic in Trouble*, p. 19.

priorities," is taking place at present. There is (no) suggestion of attempts to arrive at "radical arrangements for the redistribution of the country's wealth and resources." There are (no) indications of a program designed to lead to development as we have defined it. There is agreement indeed among the authors who have studied the question that there is a (disinclination) among Whites to relax their hold on "effective political power." There is (no) prospect of a self-generated change in White attitudes. Any change that is made in any area will have to be consistent with South Africa's political formulations. (Even if) the offer of independence to the African territories were realized, South Africa would be (unlikely) to surrender its prerogative of advice and consent, for the continued exercise of which the economic dependence of these territories would probably provide leverage.

On the other hand, our study of the other category of change— superficial change—leads us to speculate that the Africans, like Oliver Twist, are going to ask for more. This means that there will be no end of tension in South Africa. Struggle on the part of the African will continue, for he seeks fundamental change. The African workers in Natal struck despite knowledge—and possibly experience—of the heavy retribution that government machinery can exact in such circumstances. More strike action is surely in the offing. The resurgence of certain ideological formulations is a significant change because of the new perspectives against which these formulations are made. There is a bigger volume of effort to eliminate ethnicity "as a factor in group identity or group relations." As Mayer puts it, "the most consistently and emphatically given [reason] is the consciousness of a common African identity, or in the language of a few years ago, African nationalism" (p. 153).

It would seem therefore that one of the major strategies in the government's policy of separation is being openly repudiated in the urban areas. If this is coupled with the utterances of the leaders of the African territories about Black solidarity, then it seems that the government is being put on the defensive. Sooner or later, it will probably have to abandon its policy of sweet reasonableness toward the reserves and resume its tactics of brute force. It might be able to induce another brief lull in the struggle, but it cannot obliterate the consciousness that has been aroused. This consciousness establishes yet another link between city and reserve by stimulating concern in the African areas about the fate of the Africans in the urban areas. Mayer states: "The lot of the urban African may well become a major area for cooperation between the various homeland [sic] authorities, so that the homeland links, rather than 'retribalizing' urban residents might help to 'Africanize' homeland politics" (p. 155).

The factor of pan-Africanism (no reference is made here to the Pan-Africanist Congress of South Africa) is another item in the ideological arsenal that is building up. The African in the urban areas looks even beyond Africa and takes in the total Black experience. Mayer writes of respondents expressing "strong feelings of identification" with the Afro-American: "The American Negroes are Black as I am, and they have suffered more or less the same 'kind of oppression' . . ." (p. 159). In the reserves, while the context within which the leaders of the African territories refer to federation and African solidarity is necessarily narrow, it is inconceivable that in principle they would accept isolation from the rest of Africa. For the South African government this means contending with an ever-strengthening ideological thrust with ramifications extending far beyond the ethnic limits within which it had hoped to contain it.

When political frontiers are forced on a people, whether in the form of beacons on the ground or of provisions in the statute book, they evoke a reaction that tends in the direction of national consciousness.[27] The formation of the Union in 1910 was possible only because a compromise was reached among Whites entrenching the racial boundaries already in existence in three of the four colonies, and establishing the mechanism for the future delineation of similar boundaries in the fourth colony, the Cape. This and subsequent acts of segregation led to strong agitation "surmounting tribal and regional barriers" among Africans.[28] The policy of separate development pursued by the present government is perceived by Africans as promoting similar boundary delimitations. A wave of Black consciousness has arisen to challenge White South Africa, leaving the government uncertain as to how to react. The students repudiate any kind of legitimation by the government or by any segment of the White population. There is evidence that this stance has struck a responsive chord even in the reserves. This ideological trend is significant for its potential for supplying energy and determination.

The utterances of African leaders in the reserves indicate their strong desire to achieve unfettered self-determination for their people, and if South Africa's offers of future changes in status mean the establishment of a neocolonial relationship, then we can expect fierce reactions from these people. The major powers have tried to carve the world into respective blocs of communist and capitalist influence. But, as Irving Horowitz has pointed out, "it has been the Third World which has made the leviathans of both East and West realize that the way they had divided the world ideologically was no longer universally accept-

[27]G. McT. Kahin, *Nationalism and Revolution in Indonesia* (Ithaca and London, 1970), p. 37.

[28]P. Walshe, *The Rise of African Nationalism in South Africa: The African National Congress, 1912-1952* (Berkeley and Los Angeles, 1971), p. 20.

able."[29] South Africa will fare no better than the major "cold war" powers in retaining a cluster of ideological satellites, albeit within her borders.

While this chapter has not been concerned with external factors, it should be noted that the urge toward ideological self-assertion is likely to derive some inspiration from the recent changes in government in Portugal and the possible effect of this on developments in Mozambique. The new leaders have held talks with the liberation movements; for there could be no end to the war unless they came to terms with them. Frelimo's long association with other liberation movements of southern Africa, as well as its sponsorship by the OAU's Liberation Committee, suggests a commitment to eradicate White domination in the area. Economically, Frelimo has fostered self-reliance in those parts of Mozambique that have been under the movement's control. Malawi has had neither a commitment nor a design for self-reliance, and comparison with it is therefore not an apt one. While reading the future is a hazardous exercise, we are inclined to speculate that a liberated Mozambique will seek to become economically less dependent on South Africa, especially because in the eyes of her African people the latter has collaborated in their oppression. Also, an active independent neighbor having a long frontier with South Africa must certainly increase the likelihood of the transformation of superficial changes into fundamental ones.

[29] Horowitz, *Three Worlds of Development*, p. 479.

III
Intercaste Relations

9

The Instruments
of Domination
in South Africa

ALBIE SACHS

In studies of domination in South Africa little attention has been paid to the actual instruments of coercion. The country is frequently likened to a powder keg, but there has been little serious consideration of why the predicted explosion has not yet taken place. In the absence of real analysis of how such a manifestly divided and unequal society holds together, specious arguments are advanced to the effect that basically Africans must be happy with their lot.

This paper proceeds on the assumption that in fact anger and hatred of White domination are nearly universal among the Black population and that the majority of South Africans accords less legitimacy to its rulers than possibly any other governed group in modern society. This assumption is made neither out of hyperbole nor any sense of negative patriotism, but because the ruling class in South Africa has constituted itself into a visibly distinct section of the population and has deliberately eschewed such modes of legitimizing its rule as universalizing franchise rights or education. There is no major welfare program to ease the vast inequalities, nor is there any attempt to suggest that through talent or endeavor any individual can make his or her way to the top. The law is explicitly and manifestly unequal, and one African man in two can expect to see the inside of a prison each decade. The majority of the population does not even have a formal say in the laws under which it lives, nor is it bound by ties of kinship or historical allegiance to its rulers. Despite this the powder keg has not detonated, and clearly if ideological control is weak, physical control must be strong.

If all societies are held together by a mixture of consent and coercion, then in South Africa the element of consent must be extremely low and the element of coercion extremely high. In a country in which for historical reasons the law has come to play a prominent role in binding diverse sections of the population to a common political authority, the role of law enforcement agencies must be of special importance, yet South African lawyers have had little to say on the subject, despite the fact that their work brings them into direct daily contact with the machinery of domination. Legal scholarship has focused almost entirely on the nature of the laws, which are judged to be "good" or "bad" according to certain traditional concepts or to the rather formalistic idea of the rule of law. While it was undoubtedly an advance for lawyers in South Africa to break away from arid legal positivism toward an overtly evaluative stance—indeed it required courage to pierce technicalities and examine underlying moral issues—the new moralistic framework has tended to divert attention from the crucial problem of precisely how the law fits into the overall system of control. Most South African scholars today are aware of the extent to which their analyses are fed into current political debates, and liberal academics in particular feel impelled to deploy their arguments to resist retrogression and aid reform. Yet the widespread extent of the inequities about which they are concerned, tends to prevent their analyses from penetrating very deep. This is not to argue against a commitment to values or to accept the notion that such a thing as pure evidence somehow leads the researcher to the truth. Rather, it is to urge a deeper commitment that drives the investigator to go beyond merely documenting injustice, the existence of which is beyond dispute, toward examining more fundamental questions of how law relates to social structure. To confine inquiries to whether the laws, or the judges, or the prisoners, or the lawyers are getting "better" or "worse" is to avoid the more crucial long-term questions of how decisive the coercive apparatus is in maintaining domination and what changes are fundamental and what mere surface developments. The very investigation of the issue of bias presupposes that the desirable system of adjudication is one in which the processes of law are equally available to the possessed and the dispossessed. It virtually excludes investigation of whether even the "fairest" legal system legitimates and maintains the very dispossession and inequality without which the question of bias would be meaningless.

One of the main functions of law is to prescribe precise limits to domination so that both the rulers and the ruled may accommodate themselves more easily to it. Battles over the margins of domination tend to be dramatic, and there is a danger that by drawing all the investigator's attention, they cause sight to be lost of the essential character of the domination itself. Thus the fringe aspects of the law, such as trends in legislation, court decisions, or changes in administrative directions are studied to the exclusion of central issues, such as how domination is maintained.

This writer does not exclude his own works from these strictures. What follows is an attempt to offer some ideas and information on the question that lawyers so far have evaded and that social scientists have left to the lawyers.

By using a social science mode of presentation, this writer is not only departing from the conventions of legal analysis, but also moving away from the perspectives adopted when, in addition to being a member of the Bar, he was a political activist in South Africa. This is not to acknowledge that the techniques of contemporary social science present a more valid means of understanding than do some political analyses generally dismissed by academics as romantic. J.-J. Rousseau's *Social Contract* would not be acceptable even as an undergraduate essay today. Almost totally lacking in hard data, most of the empirical information it adduces is ludicrous. The argument, full of contradictions, does not follow a clear sequence and is not based on any systematic set of concepts. The statement "Man is born free, yet everywhere he is in chains" is a pure value judgment totally lacking in empirical verification. A random sample would show that in fact far less than 1 percent of human beings are actually held in bonds of linked metal. Yet the statement revolutionized thought for generations because the challenging perspectives it threw out corresponded to social reality in an instantly recognizable form. Similarly, Fanon's *Wretched of the Earth* would never be accepted for a doctoral dissertation, yet it contained more fresh ideas on the nature of colonialism than any piece of contemporary scholarly writing. The sound scholars of the academic world may make far fewer errors than Fanon did, but they contribute far fewer truths. The hard polemics of revolutionary theorists have frequently been seen later to have penetrated more deeply into the structural weaknesses of a society than the gentler probings of the academics.

The social survey is just one way of probing opinions and attitudes and seeking determinants of behavior. The political activist—particularly if his objective is to change the dominant institutions and norms of a society—uses entirely different sorts of evidence in relation to different sorts of questions. If he is serious the activist is also after truth. To the social scientist politics is the art of the possible; to the revolutionary it is the art of the impossible. Errors in attempting the impossible are normally punished move severely than mistakes in trying for the possible. All revolutions are impossible to the social scientist until they happen; then they become inevitable. To the activist the position is different, at least in a society that is manifestly repressive and in which there is large-scale popular anger directed at the rulers. To the activist a statement is no less of a truth because it is self-fulfilling. If the activist is convinced of a popular desire to revolt, and on the basis of this understanding he creates the means to revolt so that anger is converted into a consciousness favoring revolution, then his assessment is proved correct by virtue of its having been made. Some scholars might find this intellectually unsatisfying, but the activist is more concerned with the recreation of a particular piece of reality than with the establishment of a generalized truth.

What follows is an attempt to focus attention on the means of domination in South Africa. If the approach adopted appears unduly mechanistic in discussing instruments of control outside of the social and economic context in which they function, it is because there is a balance to be redressed. Many scholars have attempted to analyze the nature of the South African state, but none have discussed the character of the apparatus that underpins that state. If the state is to be radically restructured, that apparatus will have to be destroyed, and accordingly is worthy of some independent analysis.

DIRECT VIOLENCE

One means of maintaining control over a population is terror. Evidence of the use of direct violence by Whites against Blacks in South Africa is not hard to come by. Some of the more spectacular examples are well known, such as the firing by police into protesting crowds at Sharpeville or the more recent shooting of goldminers at Carletonville. Less well known is the fact that in the course of their routine activities White policemen kill approximately 50 Blacks each year and inflict bullet wounds on another 200. If African autobiographical literature is any guide, these figures represent the merest fraction of the total volume of violence and robust handling.

Terror can take many forms. Generations of African children have been woken after midnight by hammerings at the door and by shining police flashlights. They have seen their parents submit to the superior force of the police during pass raids and have watched processions of handcuffed men marching under guard through the streets. If documentation is required, African autobiographies demonstrate how deeply such experiences bite into the mind. It is neither surprising that the police raid should have figured as the main motif in the dreams of Africans interviewed by a social anthropologist some years back, nor that the police should generally be regarded in the townships as intimidators rather than as protectors.

It can be argued that the physical presence of an armed police force prepared to use violence freely against Blacks constitutes the chief factor in the maintenance of White domination in South Africa. Force from the police may be seen as being supplemented by violence from civilian Whites, such as farmers thrashing laborers, or White youths randomly beating Blacks in search of sport. Sharpeville, although the best known incident of its kind, was merely one in a series of characteristically South African episodes in which police fired on crowds of Blacks that were either totally unarmed or armed only with sticks and stones.

Table 9.1 is an incomplete list of some of the better known examples of police violence in the period since Union.

The figures indicate that the police have opened fire on protesting crowds on roughly thirty occasions in sixty years and killed approximately 500 Africans. The estimate is certainly on the low side, particularly because of the underrecording of shootings into rural crowds. At a rough guess a further 3,000 Africans have been killed when individual police opened fire under claim of shooting fleeing suspects or acting in self-defense. Set against these figures are the occasions when crowds killed policemen, such as at Vereeniging (4) in 1937 and Cato Manor (9) in 1960, while some policemen have been killed in individual violence each year.

These formidable totals are indicative of fairly endemic conflict. Especially significant, perhaps, is the fact that in the early part of the period under consideration White soldiers and civilians frequently took part in the shootings, whereas since World War II the police force alone has been involved.

It will be argued that however widespread racially influenced violence against Blacks might be, direct terrorization has not been the crucial mechanism of domination in modern South Africa. Although since the days of slavery and indentured labor, White farmers have exercised personal mastery and assumed the right to flog recalcitrant workers, farms today are left increasingly under Black management and physical punishments are on the decline. It is contended that basically White overlordship is exercised through the law rather than outside it. Coercive violence is mediated by the courts.

It is the pervasiveness of the court system that helps explain why lynching has been virtually unknown in South Africa. Many of the ingredients of a lynch situation would appear to have been present: a clearly identified ruling group with a strong sense of racial solidarity, extraordinarily preoccupied with sex and violence, wont to express masculinity by physical assertion against Blacks, and possessing a mythology based on smiting the forces of darkness. Yet in the past hundred years there was only one recorded case of lynching, a rural killing at Steynsdorp in the Transvaal in 1894, which led to the trial and acquittal of seven White men. Gandhi was nearly lynched on his return to Natal from India in 1896, but was saved by the Durban police chief. Africans were randomly shot down by some of the white artisan strikers in 1922, but in cold blood rather than as part of frenzied attacks involving violent and obscene rituals. One possible explanation for the absence of lynching is that it is essentially a scapegoat type of phenom-

Table 9.1 African Crowds Fired upon by Police, 1910 to 1973

Year	Place	Background	Africans killed
1917	Grahamstown	White panic over location demonstrations	2
1917	Ovamboland	"Show of force" to tribesmen	38
1920	Rand	African mine workers' strike	8
1920	Port Elizabeth	Protest over arrest of trade union leader	24
1921	Queenstown	Religious sect refusing to move	163
1923	S.W.A. (Bondelswarts)	Refusal to pay dog tax	62
1925	Bloemfontein	Punitive action in location	5
1929	Durban	Trade union office attacked	5
1930	Durban	Pass-burning demonstration	4
1930	Worcester	"Show of strength" after congress meeting	5
1933	Germiston	Protest meeting over permit raids	1
1942	Pretoria	Soldiers and police at wages protest	16
1946	Johannesburg	African mine workers' strike	9
1949	Rand	Pass and beer raids	6
1950	Witzieshoek	Rural protests	16
1950	Rand	May Day protests	18
1952	Port Elizabeth	Crowd revolt after suspect shot	9
1952	Johannesburg	Crowd revolt	3
1952	East London	Crowd revolt after police charge on prayer meeting	8
1952	Kimberley	Crowd revolt in location	14
1959	Paarl	Protest over banishment of leader	1
1959	Durban	Beerhall demonstrations	3
1959	Windhoek	Protest over location removal	11
1960	Sharpeville	Anti-pass law protest	69
1960	Langa (Cape Town)	Anti-pass law protest	2
1960	Durban	Protest over Sharpeville	3
1960	Ngqusa Hill	Protest meeting of tribesmen	11
1961	Warmbaths	Dissatisfaction with location superintendent	2
1973	Carletonville	Gold miners' strike	6

Source: Table prepared by Nancy Dick and this writer from published sources contained in the Royal Commonwealth Society Library, London.

enon used against members of minority rather than majority groups. To the extent that it is also a weapon of domination it becomes super-fluous in a society where strong law enforcement agencies act as agents of terror.

Thus any examination of coercion in South Africa must focus on institutions of government such as the army, the police force, and the legal-administrative machine and see them in the context of an economic domination that extends beyond the power of individual masters over individual servants.

THE ARMY

A second means of maintaining domination of a people is employment of the military. The point is often made that White domination was achieved by the gun and is maintained by the gun, and to some extent the South African authorities have in recent years gone out of their way to emphasize their military capacity. Yet despite centuries of armed conflict, South Africa is not a highly militarized country. Its army is small, and even after a tenfold increase in military expenditures in the past decade, its armed forces' budget has in absolute terms remained low compared with that of most other industrialized states. Only the beginnings of an industrial-military complex have emerged, and few of the relatively small number of career officers retiring each year seek important public or private positions. Organizations for former serv-icemen, which once were important pressure groups, now take their place in the ranks of the social and welfare clubs that thrive in male White society, while the formerly influential Volunteer regiments have been emasculated because of their strong British connections. Even on the platteland the commandos have become little more than rifle clubs depleted in membership by the exodus of Afrikaners to the towns; those commandos who are left are more likely to assemble in their Fords than on horseback.

Before Union the only permanent indigenous army was that formed by the Zulu under Shaka. The White settler populations were never able to maintain full-time armies. Afrikaner farmers established com-mandos consisting of mounted infantry, who wore rough clothes, elected their officers, and were mobilized according to the rhythm of the ploughing, planting, and reaping seasons. The English-speaking colonists set up Volunteer regiments modelled on those in Britain. Those Volunteers were artisans, farmers, clerks, and professional men who participated mainly in ceremonial parades, but who were on hand to give support to the imperial troops in wars of conquest against African tribes, as well as to discourage political assertiveness by Afrikaners.

In these circumstances British imperial soldiers rather than local White troops were responsible for the destruction of the tribal armies. The crucial battles were fought not in the wars of penetration of the 1830s, but in the wars of disarmament of the 1870s. Dramatic episodes, such as the Battle of the Tugela (Blood River) in the last century and Sharpeville in this century have come to be regarded as typical of the ways in which White superiority was established and maintained. These events have suggested that the decisive element has been possession of firearms, which enabled Whites to overcome weakly armed African opposition. Yet the main mode of conquest was not the slaughter of enemy soldiers in pitched battles. The *laagers* consolidated settlement, not conquest, and those massacres that took place after the 1830s were of weak retreating groups rather than of strong advancing ones. In the eastern Cape where the Xhosa farmer-soldiers put up the longest resistance to colonial domination of any indigenous group in Africa, *laagers* were not used at all in campaigns of conquest. Rather, it was the main strategy of the Imperial Army to drive the Xhosa out into open country, capture their cattle, and destroy their food supply. That the tribes offered resistance with fire-arms only complicated the process.

Thus in the decisive years White power came not so much out of a barrel of a gun as out of a barrel of pork. It was the capacity of British troops to fight throughout the year on the basis of stored food that gave them the advantage over African and Boer soldier-farmers who faced starvation if they left their farms for too long. In Natal too it was the stockpiling of supplies that eventually enabled the British to break the backs of the powerful Zulu regiments and so to pave the way for the incorporation of Africans throughout southern Africa into White-dominated economic and political structures.

The imperial Exchequer was not prepared to finance army rule in South Africa and instead supported the development of government through locally financed magistrates and police. After destroying tribal power, the imperial troops were normally concentrated into small garrisons or sent to other frontiers, rather than used as instruments of rule. Nevertheless they did provide the shield of force behind which para-military policemen and ordinary constables could operate. Magistrates proliferated in the wake of generals; if dispossession was accomplished by war, it was maintained by law.

After the destruction of Boer independence and the creation within the Empire of the self-governing Union under White control, British troops were rapidly withdrawn, and for the first time a permanent force of White South African soldiers was established. Yet its impact was to be greater on White political life than on Black, and when martial law was declared four times in the first thirty years of Union, twice it was to put down revolts of White artisans and twice to crush

Afrikaner rebellions. In the early years, soldiers were also used against Black strikers and in punitive expeditions in South West Africa (Namibia), but otherwise the Union Defense Force saw action against the foes of Britain abroad rather than against the enemies of White domination within. The police force, not the army, was used to counter internal Black opposition.

Even during the early 1960s when Black insurrection threatened, the army was used as a subsidiary of the police rather than the police as an adjunct of the army. On the whole the military threatened rather than took action. The buzzing by air force planes in 1960 of the gathering crowd at Sharpeville was generally regarded as having contributed toward the tension that culminated in the shootings. During the protests of the next four weeks soldiers and sailors were called out to seal off locations in the western Cape and to break a general strike by direct intimidation. A sailor at a roadblock fired a shot that killed an African baby being rushed to hospital, otherwise the armed forces displayed their weapons, but did not use them. In the following year when Blacks mustered forces for a general strike to coincide with the inauguration of the Republic, activity by soldiers and the air force was deliberately publicized, but the major thrust against the strike came from the police. In fact throughout this period para-military units of the police were putting down widespread revolts by African peasants in the tribal areas with little publicity. The Mobile Squads as these units were called, were a modern version of the old Mounted Rifles, which used to patrol and pacify rural areas, but now the soldier-policemen were mounted in motor cars, riot trucks, and armored cars, rather than on horseback.

During the 1960s prominence was given to massive increases in military expenditures. The sum rose from R40 million to R280 million per annum, or 17 percent of the total budget; by 1974 the figure had soared to well over R400 million. Army service for young White men was made universal and compulsory, and the size of the permanent regular force was increased. By 1970 South Africa claimed 180,000 White men under arms, but of this number only 13,500 were regulars (army, 6,000; navy 2,500; and air force, 5,000). The rest were made up of 27,000 youths undergoing compulsory training, 45,000 young men in a citizen reserve of previously trained youths, 60,000 commandos in loose militia groups based in rural rifle clubs, and 17,000 White police plus 15,000 police reserves.[1]

Short periods of call-up in the early 1960s gave rise to considerable economic inconvenience, and it may be expected that in future any prolonged call-up of the reserves will seriously affect the economy. Other countries have maintained large armies by placing vast numbers

[1]M. Horrell, *A Survey of Race Relations in South Africa*, annually, 1960-1973 (Johhanesburg, 1961-1974).

of recruits from subordinate sections of the population under the control of officers drawn from the ruling circles. Their ability to put a large army into the field and generally to militarize society has been a source of strength to the authorities, but the social divisions inside the army have been a corresponding source of weakness. In South Africa the conflict between Boer and Briton led to the exclusion of Blacks as combatants in the army, which has therefore remained dependent on a mere one-fifth of the population for its personnel. During World War II the Smuts government was able to mobilize a relatively large number of Whites despite considerable pro-Nazi sentiment amongst many Afrikaners, but the economy then, with a large reservoir of poor and semiskilled Whites to be drawn upon, was far less sophisticated than it is now. A call-up of the reserves and commandos today would place the economy under immediate strain, which would exacerbate any political crisis. This is one of the reasons why the rearmament program of the 1960s was conducted on such a large scale—the government wished to establish the posture of a strong military power without expending the manpower normally required to do so.

When the South African Army fought in Britain's wars, it could rely on Britain or Britain's allies to supply it with arms. After South Africa left the Commonwealth, however, it made itself self-sufficient in small and medium sized weapons, although it still has to import more sophisticated and expensive items such as advanced aircraft, submarines, and radar systems. The acquisition and replacement of these weapons and monitoring systems have been responsible for the great increase in military expenditures in the past dozen years, not changes in the size of the army itself. As yet the three sectors of the Defense Force do not appear to have been involved in campaigns against guerrillas in Namibia (South West Africa) and Zimbabwe (Rhodesia), though land and air troops have conducted mock counter-insurgency operations in the northern Transvaal and are also reported to have supported Portuguese troops in Angola and Mozambique.

Military strategists may ponder the practical value to White South Africa of radar systems and submarines for the type of warfare seen at present and that likely to develop in southern Africa. However, their value lies in political rather than military terms: they stand as symbols of determination to resist all forms of practical action by the United Nations. Indeed, the armament program as a whole asserts White South Africa's intention to be recognized as the dominant power in sub-Saharan Africa. Its army might be smaller than that of Nigeria, Zaire, or Ethiopia, but it projects itself as being considerably more modern, mobile, and thrustful. Possession of new weapons strengthens South Africa's claims to be an important link in the chain of worldwide anti-Communist bastions. In the meanwhile White youths are trained to annihilate the anticipated enemy, insurgent Black guerrillas. This training also contributes to the ideological molding of White South Africa by bringing English- and Afrikaans-speaking youths together in a common patriotic enterprise.

The armed forces then are preparing to play a decisive role in the maintenance of White overlordship in the future, just as in the past the British Imperial Army played a crucial role in its creation. At the moment, however, it is the police force rather than the army that has the direct responsibility for containing Black resistance.

SOUTH AFRICAN POLICE

The relative growth of the police and the corresponding decline of the army as a means of containing internal rebellion have been features of many modern states. In fact the expansion of the police and especially of the secret services can be regarded as a crucial index of modernization. South Africa in this respect has become a most advanced society. As the threat of revolt moved from the countryside to the towns, so the responsibility for countering rebellion shifted from the military to the police. Thus, whereas Afrikaner rebellion at the outbreak of World War I was located in the countryside and put down by soldiers in pitched battles, the planned rebellion of World War II was largely urban in character and was dealt with by the police with few armed confrontations. Similarly, as the thrust of African opposition shifted from the tribal areas to the towns, the controls over Africans were modified to make them more effective in an urban setting.

The growth in the power and functions of the police was only partly accomplished by an increase in its size. Table 9.2 indicates that relative to the total population of the country there was first a decline and then an increase in the personnel of the South African Police (SAP).

Table 9.2 Growth of South African Police

Year	Total South African population	Authorized police	Police per 1,000 population
1912	6,100,000	8,700	1.42
1938	10,000,000	11,100	1.11
1958	15,000,000	28,500	1.90
1972	23,300,000	34,500	1.48

Source: Figures taken from the Annual Reports of the Commissioner of the South African Police.

These figures must be treated with some caution since two supplementary forces have been created that have also exercised police powers, the so-called location police, established to help enforce location regulations, and the large corps of traffic police—both set up under municipal control. In addition a Police Reserve has been created over the past decade and one-half to provide part-time support for the police. The reserve now consists of nearly 20,000 persons, 70 percent of whom are White, whose duties range from paid full-time work on a call-up basis during emergencies to guard and support duty on a more regular basis. In 1972 slightly more than 7,000 White and 2,500 Black reservists were officially classified as active.

Official figures are presented in a way that tends to exaggerate the size of the armed forces and to understate the size of the police. Even allowing for this, the SAP is by no means as large as we might expect in relation to its special role. It is important to remember, too, that the increase in police personnel has been brought about primarily by recruiting Blacks into the force. Whereas in 1912 the ratio of Black to White policemen was roughly 1:3, by 1972 it had changed to nearly 1:1. In the intervening years Whites have risen to create a large commanding elite, while Blacks have been drawn in to fill the lower ranks. Thus from 1922 to 1972 the number of White constables increased by little more than half, while the number of White officers of the rank of lieutenant or above increased tenfold. The results of this development are indicated in table 9.3.

Table 9.3 South African Police, 1972

Position	Black	White
Officers	20 (0.1%)	4,000 (24%)
Sergeants	2,600 (17%)	4,500 (27%)
Constables	12,380 (83%)	8,100 (49%)
Total	15,000 (100%)	16,600 (100%)

Source: Figures taken from the Annual Reports of the Commissioner of the South African Police, rounded and converted into percentages.

Stratification in the police force remains as rigid as ever it was. White and Black police train at different institutes, wear different uniforms, and receive vastly different rates of pay. The differentiation is so extreme that the only item that all policemen have is a whistle. Black policemen can now rise to the rank of lieutenant (which has three ranks below and seven above) and even be placed in command of police stations, but no Black policemen of any rank can give an order to a White policeman, however much lower in rank the latter may be. Similarly Black policemen are under instructions never to arrest

White offenders, nor are Black policemen ever placed in charge of White prisoners. It is a weird experience for a White political detainee held because of his antiracist activities to emerge from prolonged solitary confinement to hear a Black constable ordered to fetch a bucket of water for the *baas*.

As a general rule all uniformed White police carry revolvers, whereas no Black policemen do. White police are also trained to handle rifles and sten-guns, which are kept securely under White control. (Similarly guns for hunting and personal defense are given under license to White civilians but never to Blacks.) The small number of Blacks promoted to the rank of lieutenant has in fact been issued pistols, but as a general rule Black policemen have no training in the use of or access to arms.

There has been one major shift in connection with guns for Blacks, which has considerable symbolic significance and may turn out to have far-reaching practical implications as well. Since February 1972 Black policemen have been trained for antiguerrilla activities and placed under White control on the borders. The 1973 annual report of the commissioner for the SAP carries on its cover a photograph of Black and White policemen on patrol in the bush carrying sten-guns. In an unconsciously ironical echo of sentiments expressed by leaders of insurrectionary movements such as Mandela and Fischer, the head of the SAP recently declared that "in the struggle the police did not see themselves as black or white."

Since the wars of Black disarmament a century ago no government has dared openly to put guns into the hands of Blacks, whether they were soldiers sent to the front against Germany or policemen sent to capture lawbreakers in South Africa. At the moment the remoteness of the borders from the homes of the Black police and the absence of areas under permanent guerrilla control to which they could defect render the arming of these police relatively safe for the authorities. Should the areas of conflict spread, however, the consequences might be different; reliable information from the Portuguese colonies and from Zimbabwe on the activities of Black soldiers might provide some useful pointers.

Important though the virtual White monopoly of firepower might be, it should not be allowed to overshadow what is perhaps the major source of White dominance inside the police force itself, control of its organization and technology. One consequence of industrialization in South Africa has been the technical modernization of the police force. At the turn of the century bicycle and foot patrols were supplemented by horse and even camel patrols. Today the force rides around in 750 riot vehicles and armored cars, 250 heavy trucks, 2,500 patrol vans, 3,000 cars, and a various assortment of motorcycles, dog cars, and hearses making up a total of over 7,000 vehicles (good orders for multi-national motor manufacturers here). It also owns two aircraft, three helicopters, and nearly two dozon motor patrol boats.[2] These vehicles and crafts are almost exclusively under the control of Whites, as is the system of communications whereby they are directed. Similarly the national telegraph, telephone, and radio systems—police as well as civilian—are run almost exclusively by Whites. It is significant too that at police headquarters in Pretoria there are 1,300 Whites compared to only 160 Blacks and that the Security Police and Special Guard Unit are staffed exclusively by Whites.

The power structure of the police force, then, reflects and reinforces the power structure of the society at large. Even in the Transkei the latest figures show that there are fifty White but only two Black commissioned officers, while all major police stations throughout the country as well as regional and national commands are firmly in White hands. A few of the smaller police stations have been handed over entirely to the Transkei police, a body that may be regarded as operating in the interstices rather than outside of the SAP, but like other institutions in the Transkei their dependence on Pretoria is merely mediated by the Transkei government, whose scope is particularly limited in the field of law enforcement.

The Whites in the police force are overwhelmingly Afrikaans speakers. Ninety percent of White recruits give Afrikaans as their first language. They form a relatively homogeneous social group whose allegiances tend to be to the Nationalist party. The generation of police who during World War II were loyal to Smuts has now retired. The SAP is no longer a haven for former soldiers or for Whites from poor families faced with unemployment, since improved salary scales and prospects of rapid promotion have enhanced the status of the force in the White community. The Security Police has in particular over the past decade achieved for the force as a whole a measure of glamor formerly lacking. Most Afrikaans- and many English speaking Whites have been considerably impressed by its successes, without being concerned about the methods it uses to achieve them.

More than anything else the growth of the Security Police can be regarded as marking the emergence of the SAP into the modern age. In its early years the force merely required certain members of the Criminal Investigation Department to keep their eyes on what were regarded as subversive groups. It was only toward the end of the 1920s that a "special branch" of the SAP was established at headquarters to deal with "Communist and other agitators, unscrupulous persons who issued propaganda to ignorant and peaceable natives."[3]

[2]Annual Report of the Commissioner of the South African Police, 1973.
[3]*Report of the Commissioner of Police for 1928-1929*, U.G. 13/1930.

The special branch remained small until World War II when it played a key role in collaboration with Military Intelligence in keeping pro-German sabotage and insurrectionary movements under control. Among the persons interned during this period were the present prime minister, B. J. Vorster, and the present overlord of security, H. J. van den Bergh, whose close friendship while in internment was to lay the foundation for each achieving top positions in the state twenty years later.

After the war the special branch once more turned its attention to what the police reports referred to as "Communist and other agitators." It initiated a number of prosecutions for sedition and treason during the 1940s and 1950s, but these failed so ignominiously and Black opposition groups survived with such manifest vitality that the special branch became something of a laughing stock among those it attempted to suppress. During this period it consisted of only about 100 members in groups scattered throughout the country, whose information was correlated at headquarters. The whole section was eventually renamed the Security Branch and in 1960 its head was called director of security and appointed to a special committee of officers who advised the commissioner of police. It was only when Vorster became minister of justice in 1961 that the Security Branch achieved a dominant position inside the SAP and a leading position in South African political life generally. One of his first moves was to place van den Bergh at the head of the Security Police, which was rapidly built up and given increased powers, including the right to detain suspects in solitary confinement for successive periods of ninety days. Where police raids, telephone-tapping, the placing of informers, and the issuing of hundreds of banning orders had failed, the "ninety-day law" succeeded. Solitary confinement was both a form of duress in itself and an opportunity to apply further duress. Teams of interrogators broke the resistance of captives and obtained important information from them. Some members of radical opposition groups were so crushed by prolonged periods of total police control that they agreed to give evidence against former colleagues.

Formerly political detainees had been subject to harassment and abuse, but because like all persons in custody they were entitled to be brought before a court within two days, and unlike many other prisoners they were aware of their rights and in a position to assert them, they were rarely subjected to violence. Now the immediate sanctions against the application to political suspects of the violence used against other suspects fell away. At least nineteen detainees have died while in the hands of the Security Police, and there is extensive evidence that electric shock torture, beatings, and sleep deprivation have been used on a large scale and with authorization from on high. Some critics of torture seek to buttress their opposition by saying that it is a totally unreliable method of obtaining information. Unfortunately South African experience does not bear this out. Whatever the position may be where torture is designed to get confessions in public of heretical beliefs or diabolical practices, when it comes to eliciting information about real opposition it is only too useful. Destruction of the will by violence or by interference with the senses or bodily functions has proved decisive not only in degrading opponents, but also in obtaining crucial information that has then been checked against intelligence gained in routine fashion. This permits the police at a time of their choosing to use the mechanisms of judicial trial followed by imprisonment (or execution) for the ultimate disposal of the detainees. Direct terrorization and violence in the privacy of interrogation rooms are thus combined in peculiarly South African fashion with the punctillio and etiquette of public forensic proceedings.

Although it has been argued that the use of torture against political suspects was the decisive means of breaking the centers of Black insurrection in the 1960s, it was clearly part of a wider program of information-gathering. The network of police informers was rapidly expanded both as to size and range so that it not only supplied intelligence but gave rise to fear and suspicion throughout all Black communities, as well as in sectors of the White churches, press, and universities. Clearly, too, the Security Police have increased the amount of technical equipment for monitoring conversations, intercepting mail, and recording the movements of suspects.

Finally, the police still make extensive use of the kinds of control first employed in the 1950s. Banning orders on individuals or organizations were then the major though rather ineffective means used to repress radical opposition; now they have become far more effective as subsidiary aids to detention and imprisonment. Petty harassment at the local level, which formerly could be shrugged off, has now become far more menacing because of the threat of indefinite detention and torture.

Resistance leaders have been isolated by imprisonment, banning orders, and exile, and the clandestine activities of organizations such as the African National Congress make far less public impact today than did their open campaigns of earlier years. Some commentators have gone so far as to speak of the subject people of South Africa being totally atomized by these controls and deprived of all effective leadership. A corollary of this approach is that when some form of mass Black activity does take place, such as the recent Natal strikes, it is described as spontaneous. In this writer's view, the description "spontaneous" in relation to political action simply means that the patterns of leadership and channels of communication do not correspond to any mode known to the social scientist using the term.

Furthermore, underground activity by its very nature does not lend itself to analysis by outsiders. It is virtually only when resistance workers are captured and put on trial that their work gets publicly reported, and anyone who has been involved in such trials knows that it is rare for either the police or the accused to be completely candid during them.

In constitutional terms what has happened since Union is that statutory powers for the police have replaced material law as the main means of counteracting actual or threatened rebellion. Martial law was technically illegal while it lasted, but the courts voluntarily abdicated their right to interfere until the emergency was over, when an indemnity statute granted retroactive validity to the acts of the military. Now powers are granted in advance and permanently by statute to the police to take preemptive action to frustrate rebellion, and even when a state of emergency is declared, as happened after Sharpeville in 1960, it is the police rather than the military who act on behalf of the authorities.

Paradoxically the failure of the Security Police to protect Verwoerd from assassination led to Vorster's becoming prime minister and to van den Bergh's becoming the leading policeman in the country and opened the way to the further erosion of military power by the police. The Security Police developed two major arms. The first arm was operational and was responsible for apprehending and interrogating suspects. The information it gained, as well as information it received from intelligence agents and informers, was collated and interpreted by the second arm, which subsequently became known as the Bureau of State Security (BOSS). This latter section expanded into the foreign affairs field, which led to friction with military intelligence. Eventually BOSS was formally institutionalized as head of all intelligence relating to the security of the state and to the capacities of actual or potential enemies. At its head was van den Bergh, who for some years had been titled security adviser to the prime minister and was now restyled secretary for state intelligence. Military intelligence was totally subordinated to BOSS and to van den Bergh, a clear example of the extent to which the police function was seen as predominant in the total picture of state security, or, to adapt a saying from elsewhere, politics was placed in command.

THE LEGAL-ADMINISTRATIVE MACHINE

Domination in South Africa cannot be understood simply in terms of the use or threatened use of direct violence by Whites against Blacks. The monopoly that Whites have of the possession of firearms is clearly of great importance, as is the fact that only Whites receive combat training. Similarly White control of the police and of the wide network of informers has special significance. Yet if domination were dependent merely on the exercise of superior force, we would expect many more confrontations involving large-scale loss of life on the pattern of Sharpeville. What happens in the years between such killings? Is it that the memory of past shootings and the threat of future massacres is enough to keep the Black population in line? It is suggested that the crucial instrument of control is in fact the legal-administrative apparatus that grinds on extensively and unspectacularly throughout the years, serving simultaneously the needs of the economy and the needs of security. Here too in most vivid form we see domination in South Africa being exercised through the law rather than outside of it.

Judicial statistics, rightly treated with reserve when used as an index of the volume of actual lawbreaking in any society, are more reliable, however, as indicators of what kinds of rule-breaking lead to official punishment. In this respect much is to be gleaned from the annual figures for different categories of prosecutions in South Africa. Striking is the large volume of prosecutions for what may for convenience be called race statute offenses, that is, contraventions of statutes that penalize Blacks as such for infringements of various specified restrictions. The pass laws are the best known example, but the ambit is considerably wider and appears to have been subjected to remarkably little study.

Three interrelated points should be made at the outset. First, these laws and the machinery for their implementation are not the creation of Afrikaner Nationalists, nor are they relics from the Boer republics or the old slave society at the Cape. On the contrary, the system was first established in the Cape Colony, then utilized in harsher form in the Transvaal after the Anglo-Boer War, and finally extended throughout the country after Union. Second, far from these laws being inconsistent with growing industrialization, they have been closely associated with it and have tended ·to become more rigid as the economy advanced. These two points need underlining, not to score debating points about historic responsibility for the present state of affairs, but to emphasize how deeply rooted the present system of controls is and how relatively untouched it has been by current discussions about modernizing or softening apartheid.

Third, it is fallacious to assume that the segregatory laws have arisen because of ethnic and cultural diversity, or that they are destined to fall away as soon as the cultural gap between Blacks and Whites is reduced. On the contrary, the more alike the peoples of southern Africa have become, the more the law has been used to divide them. Segregation has proceeded out of integration. The creation of a common society on the basis of a single economy laid the foundation for the establishment of modern state controls. When different ethnic groups lived in different areas and were involved in different economies, legal segregation in the form of state-enforced separation was unnecessary. Viewed in this way, segregation in South Africa is essentially an urban rather than a rural phenomenon and a feature of industrial society rather than of the older rural communities. Equally, conflict has arisen out of similarities of interest and values rather than out of differences. Thus the various peoples have fought primarily over cattle, land, wages, jobs, the vote, and political power, and the contestants have tended to be precisely those members of the different groups who have had the most in common. This is illustrated by the extent to which members of the elitist legal profession such as Gandhi, Smuts, Hertzog, Seme, Bunting, Pirow, Swart, Vorster, Mandela, and Tambo have played prominent roles in national and class struggles.

The major source of information on trends in prosecutions of lawbreakers is the annual report issued by the commissioner of South African Police. In the early years after Union the figures in this report were given separately for each province and for each of the various sections of the police. Collation of the figures immediately after Union reveals that the Transvaal had the highest rate of prosecutions for race statute offenses (45 percent of 120,000 prosecutions), followed by Natal (40 percent out of 50,000 prosecutions), then by the Cape (estimated 14 percent out of 56,000 prosecutions). The figures for South Africa as a whole show that race statute prosecutions accounted for roughly one-third of the total of a little over one-quarter million prosecutions.[4] In the decades that followed, the total figures for prosecutions of all kinds soared, partly because of a general increase in the number of common law offenses detected, partly because of new offenses being created such as those concerned with motor traffic, but largely because of a great increase in the number of persons charged with infringements of race statutes. Thus by the late 1960s the total number of prosecutions had risen ninefold, while the total number of race statute prosecutions had risen elevenfold, that is from 33 to 44 percent of all prosecutions. Table 4 shows that during the period when South Africa developed from having a farm- and mining-based economy into a powerful industrial state with extensive secondary industry, the number of race statute prosecutions rose spectacularly. Furthermore, the total kept rising irrespective of what party was in power. The upward progression reached its peak during the boom years of the late 1960s, illustrating how a capitalist economy unrestricted by welfare programs could be efficiently served by a regimented labor force.

[4]Figures collated by this writer from the Annual Report of the Commissioner of the South African Police, 1912. Percentages calculated by this writer.

For purposes of comparison we may point out that race statute
offenses in 1967 accounted for 44 percent of all prosecutions,
motoring offenses for 18 percent, drunkenness and drugs for 5
percent, assault for 5 percent, and common theft for 3 percent.[5]

Table 9.4 Increase in Race Statute Prosecutions, 1913-1972

Year	Total population (in millions)	Total prosecutions	Race statute prosecutions	Col. 3 as a % of col. 2
1913	6.0	267,000	89,000	33
1927	7.7	503,000	188,000	37
1947	11.4	1,020,000	418,000	41
1967	19.4	2,300,000	1,043,000	44
1972	23.3	2,700,000	900,000	33

Source: Figures taken from the Annual Reports of the Commissioner of the South African
Police, rounded and converted into percentages.

The figures for 1972, when Africans were being prosecuted under
these special laws at the rate of 2,500 per day as compared with 250
per day in 1913, show a 10 percent decline. While this does have some
significance, it by no means amounts to a dismantling of the apartheid
apparatus. To understand the latest trends we must break down the
global figures into their constituent groups.

It is convenient to divide the race statute prosecutions into five
main groups: those concerned with liquor, masters and servants,
taxes, pass and trespass laws. The liquor laws formerly penalized
possession by Africans of any form of liquor, now they prohibit
brewing and possession of so-called Bantu liquor (a lucrative municipal monopoly). The masters and servants laws apply in practice
exclusively to Black servants indentured to White masters, mostly on
the land. The tax laws penalize failure by Africans to produce on
demand annual receipts for poll tax. The pass laws refer to documents of identity and permits relating to work and residence, now
contained in one book to be produced on demand. The term "pass
laws" is used here in a wide sense to include curfew laws and location
regulations, which cover such crimes as failure to pay rent on due
date. The trespass laws are directed at Africans found without
permission on land or premises owned by Whites.

Fluctuations in the totals for these specific groups of race statutes
are given in table 9.5.

[5]Calculations made by this writer from figures in the Annual Reports of the
Commissioner of the South African Police.

Table 9.5 Prosecutions under Different Groups of Race Statutes

Year	Liquor	Masters and servants	Poll tax	Pass	Trespass
1928	33,000	43,000	60,000	44,000	10,000
1968	26,000	23,000	243,000	670,000	166,000
1972	31,000	20,000	60,000	612,000	171,000

Source: Annual Reports of the Commissioner of the South African Police.

The figures for the liquor laws may be misleading since the number of prosecutions in fact rose beyond the 200,000 mark in the 1950s and only plummeted in the year after Sharpeville, when prohibition of the sale of so-called European liquor to Blacks was lifted. The scrapping of the restrictive liquor laws deserves some attention, since it has to be considered as a possible precursor of the abolition of other apartheid laws as South Africa is modernized. The liquor laws were originally sponsored by liberals as part of a worldwide temperance campaign, the objective of which was to save Blacks from the ravages of brandy just as it was to save the workers of Europe and America from the evils of gin. In traditional African society intoxicants such as beer and marijuana (*dagga*) were frequently used and were associated with ceremonies that contributed considerably to social solidarity. However, in the context of colonialism it became convenient to regard Africans as being peculiarly susceptible to the effects of liquor and to attribute the social dislocation and misery that was consequent on dispossession and the destruction of tribal society to individual weakness of Africans in the face of drink. Temperance theory was then allied to racial theory, and the argument was developed (or rather regarded as self-evident) that to allow Blacks access to liquor was to encourage them to overthrow the thin layer of control they were said to possess and to release their alleged primitive and child-like passions. In fact even less than disease, liquor knew no color bar. Alcoholism ravaged Whites as it did Blacks, and the implementation of the liquor prohibitions, involving as they did massive arrests and midnight raids, caused far more hardship than the abuse of drink they were designed to suppress. It is highly unlikely, however, that these factors would have carried much weight in themselves, even in the period of post-Sharpeville shock when the authorities were questioning which parts of the apartheid edifice were of granite and which were of chalk. What proved decisive was not the complaints of Africans nor the appraisals of sociologists, such as they were, but the pressure for change from within the administration. Senior police-men had long complained about the problems caused to the force by the liquor laws. Whole police stations were being corrupted by liquor traffickers, with consequent loss of disciplinary control. Moreover liquor raids in the locations aroused a peculiarly intense anger from residents, which frequently put the lives of policemen at risk. Another strong source of support for reform came from the wine farmers' lobby, which had long campaigned for the ending of prohibition. Thus the Sharpeville crisis may have precipitated an inquiry into whether the laws should be retained, but powerful administrative and economic factors have been decisive in ending them.

The decline in prosecutions under the old and cumbersome master and servants laws has been gradual over the years, reflecting the steady reduction in the importance of indentured farm labor. (The mines still rely heavily on contract labor but have their own system of sanctions and controls that operates outside of the state penal system.) Had other race statutes not existed for purposes of statistical compari-son, it might have seemed remarkable that in a highly industrialized society as many as 20,000 persons per year could be prosecuted for what the official statistics refer to as "desertion, disobedience, being unfit for work due to liquor, etc., negligence and noncompliance with service contracts." As it is, other statutory controls are invoked on such a large scale that the masters and servants laws are overshad-owed by them.

The most dramatic change in the figures for the past four years has been the sudden fall in the number of prosecutions under the poll tax laws. The poll tax, originally a means of getting Africans to finance the machinery of their own control, subsequently played an impor-tant role in impelling Africans into a money economy by requiring them to sell either their crops or their labor for cash. Today, however, the poll tax is a relatively minor source of revenue compared with income tax and excise on goods, and the migrant labor system is so securely based on rural poverty that it needs no extra reinforcement. In addition the tax can now be collected by getting employers to make deductions from pay packets, a much more efficient system than relying on random checks in the streets for defaulters. It seems, then, that the poll tax laws are not being repealed, but are being enforced increasingly in nonpenal ways. Even though their actual contribution to the total annual budget is now a tiny one, it is unlikely that they will be abolished, since they help to perpetuate the notion that Africans have separate citizenship from the Whites, while at the same time appearing to demonstrate that it is White taxpayers who subsidize virtually all expenditure on Blacks.

The recent decline in prosecutions under the pass laws has been small, amounting to only 10 percent over four years. Nevertheless the previous steep upward climb in the figures appears to have been halted. Had the momentum of the early sixties been maintained there would by now have been as many as a million prosecutions each year under these statutes alone. A detailed breakdown of the published statistics suggests that whereas there has been a tightening up of control in the locations, there has been some attempt to reduce the number of Africans brought to court because they could not produce appropriate documents on demand. It appears that the police now institute more inquiries than formerly, either themselves or through Aid Centers established for this purpose. If the violator has the necessary permission or qualification to be where he is or to do what he does, he will not be prosecuted, even though he may not have produced his document on demand or it may not be up to date. If, however, he does not have the legal right to be in a particular area, or take up particular employment, or live in a particular house, the law will be enforced with all its vigor. Thus the pass laws are not being abolished. Rather their enforcement is being rationalized to reduce some gratuitous indignities without altering basic objectives. Employers gain from the new approach in that it happens less frequently that Africans lawfully in employment fail to arrive at work simply because they had been found the previous night without their documents on them. Another beneficial change from the employers' viewpoint has been an amendment to the law that enables workers living in an urban conglomerate to take employment anywhere in that conglomerate and not only in the administrative unit in which their place of residence falls. This change has been consistent with the government's move finally to take over from local authorities all control of Africans living in urban areas. What has emerged is a highly centralized system of directing the movement of labor through a network of labor bureaus. Max Weber once wrote that exact calculation—the foundation of capitalism—was only possible on a basis of free labor. South African experience suggests that this thesis requires modification, since capitalism appears to have thrived there on the basis of directed rather than free labor and by virtue of the maintenance rather than the total destruction of traditional rural ties. What appears to have happened is that traditional structures that might have kept Africans out of the White-dominated economy have been destroyed, whereas those that have reduced the cost of their labor have been maintained.

The one group of prosecutions that has risen in the recent period falls under the trespass laws. These laws are directed at two distinct groups of Africans. The first group consists of Africans allegedly "squatting" on White-owned land, i.e., living on small plots, usually in rural areas, where they reside neither in official locatiions nor as full-time employees of the landowners. The elimination of squatting drives more Africans into full-time employment and also results in the extension of controls over the former squatters. The second group consists of Africans who without authorization visit or stay with friends or kinfolk who live on the premises of their White employers. Thus a White who objects to the presence on his property of Africans not employed by him calls in the police to eject and prosecute the trespassers. Here the security aspect is dominant. Although prosecutions of squatters might decline as their numbers are reduced, it seems unlikely that there will be much diminution in the prosecution of trespassers. By definition these prosecutions do not inconvenience Whites, since they are normally instituted only at the instigation of discontented Whites.

Thus a large group of apartheid laws still serve the economy and play a crucial role in the maintenance of domination. At face value the penalties for breach of these laws are not severe, especially when compared with penalties imposed for common law offenses or for transgression of the security laws. Normally a fine equivalent to about two weeks' wages will be imposed. However these fines are frequently coupled with removal orders, in terms of which the convicted person may be taken under escort to the one area where he is said by the court to be legally entitled to live. Moreover the persons most at risk under the pass laws are precisely those whose economic position is likely to be desperate—wives of semimigrant workers seeking to live with their husbands, children who have just reached the age of sixteen, the elderly and infirm who are unable to find work, widows unable to pay location rents, and so on.

The court system is not unduly clogged up by the great multitude of prosecutions under the race statutes, since they are tried in special courts before special magistrates (Bantu commissioners). Cases, grouped together for administrative convenience, are heard on successive days. Each trial lasts only a few minutes, since most accused plead guilty and the evidence usually consists of a short statement by a policeman or an official in charge of records. Lawyers rarely act on behalf of the accused, and the court interpreters play a skilled role in hurrying cases through. Fines help to defray costs so that administrative controls are imposed by means of penal sanctions on a vast scale and in a manner that is speedy and cheap for the authorities.

The administrative records used as the basis of the prosecutions in these trials perform a special function in the total system of domination. Individual Africans may be totally unknown to the persons seeking to impose controls on them, but through the system of documentation their identity can be quickly established as well as their status as employees, work seekers, residents, and dependents. A worker who falls foul of an employer risks far more than losing his job. He may be endorsed out of an area in which he has lived and worked for years to an area of total poverty and unemployment. A person who comes into conflict with a policeman of an official will have his records investigated, and if any irregularity appears he too may suffer severe consequences. The Security Police have ready access to files that automatically record all movements of work or residence of the whole African population.

It is the economic dependence of Africans that makes them so vulnerable to the legal-administrative machine. Whites own all the mines, almost all industry, and most of the developed agricultural land. Africans are overwhelmingly indigent and dependent on employment from Whites for their livelihood. In this situation the everyday life of Africans becomes conditional on documents being in order and officials not being displeased. Controls restrict the independence of all Africans, whether they be ordinary workers, capitalist entrepreneurs, or socialist organizers. The laws, the courts, the prisons, the documents, the police, and the bureaucrats—these are the primary agents of domination. They ensure that the authorities keep track of individuals and control over communities. Africans living in locations are subject personally to control by the superintendent, and collectively to control by the police, and if necessary, the army. The locations lying outside the cities can be isolated from each other and sealed off from supplies of food, water, and gasoline. Africans may mobilize in the townships, but they cannot threaten White property or security from there. It is significant that the only time White South Africa has been seriously shaken in recent years has been when Africans have marched to the centers of cities, viz., after Sharpeville in 1960 and during the Natal strikes last year. The authorities have avoided the procedure of armed confrontation since it could have led to crowd revolts that might have spilt over into the commercial and residential centers of town and given rise to extensive damage to White property. These considerations have long applied in South Africa. International interest in the country may have heightened the concern of the authorities to avoid physical confrontations, but it is White self-interest that created this concern.

CONCLUSIONS

In discussing change in South Africa one should recognize that whatever constitutional and legal rearrangements there might have been in recent years, the Whites maintain tight control not only of the economy of the country but of the instruments of state coercion as well. The reduction in the number of signs of apartheid and the granting of formal self-government to the Bantustans may have some political importance, but these developments have done nothing either to redistribute resources or to place the instruments of power into different hands. The law enforcement agencies actually operating in the so-called Homelands are virtually indistinguishable from those in the rest of the country, and it is significant that the only African police who bear arms today are those operating in integrated para-military units on the borders of South Africa or in other countries, and not members of the small and powerless Bantustan forces.

Modernization of South Africa has meant modernization of both the economy and the instruments of control. A stronger economy—in the hands of the Whites—has intensified Black economic dependence; similarly, greater efficiency in the agencies of domination has increased Black political repression. As far as changes in the implementation of apartheid laws are concerned, a useful distinction can be drawn between those laws that may be regarded as instrumental and those that may be regarded as symbolical. Instrumental laws are those that directly serve the economy and maintain security, including pass, trespass, and security laws. Symbolical laws are those that emphasize race distinction as an end in itself, including the so-called petty apartheid regulations, job demarcation provisions, and laws forbidding interracial sex. The hypothesis may be advanced that whereas the instrumental laws will continue to be enforced with vigor, the symbolical laws may, on an uneven basis, gradually be allowed to lose their force.

A second more far-reaching possibility that should be considered is that race factors will gradually come to play a less significant role in South Africa and that law enforcement will lose much of its overtly racist character. In this writer's view this is a most remote possibility, but on the assumption that modernization really will lead to "deracialization" of South African society, it is suggested that this would not reduce conflict, but merely shift it from an apparently racial basis to a class basis. Writers on South Africa have understandably focused on the race factor, since this gives the country its distinctive character. Yet preoccupation with race has tended to obscure the features South Africa has in common with other countries. There is no reason to assume that merely because race plays such a prominent role in the definition of its social groups, South Africa is somehow exempted from the social forces found in all other industrialized societies. The gap existing between owners of capital and the great majority of workers is a vast one, which would not be eliminated by the repeal of apartheid laws. The contending groups might be defined differently, but in essence they would be the same.

Thus there is no reason to believe that modernization of South Africa, if by that is meant partial or total relaxation of racial controls, will in any way reduce actual or potential social conflict. The police, the army, and the legal-administrative machine would continue to act as repressive agencies, performing functions different in form but similar in function to those performed today. The police would continue to be the primary agency of repression, protecting the peace and wealth of the prosperous few by means of the common law and special statutes, while the army would be in reserve to cope with crisis situations. The legal-administrative machine, appropriately revamped, would still be the means of keeping the poor in their place at the local level. Only a radical redistribution of wealth and of political power could lead to any real transformation of the coercive apparatus in South Africa.

10
South African Indians:
The Wavering Minority

KOGILA A. MOODLEY

The Indians of the diaspora, though motivated to leave their ancestral homeland by similar circumstances, were scattered in very different milieus. Their varying patterns of adjustment to new environments provide telling insights into social behavior under different circumstances. In Africa alone, the major areas of Indian settlement in East Africa, Central Africa, and South Africa have attracted different types of immigrants as well as engendered varying reactions. East and Central African Indian communities comprised mostly trading groups, while their South African counterpart consisted initially of an indentured community with a very small portion of independent traders. To a greater extent than other Indian settlements in Africa, with the exception of Rhodesia, South African Indians found themselves in an increasingly White-dominated, race-stratified society to which they have evolved several unique political responses.

Three comprehensive accounts by historians record in detail the major events that have marked the life of South African Indians.[1] In similar vein, two well-known social scientists have described the cultural perseverance as well as the changes in customs and traditions of three generations of Indians abroad.[2] Attention has also been focused on the economic situation of Indians.[3]

[1] G. Calpin, *Indians in South Africa* (Pietermaritzburg, 1949); M. Palmer, *The History of the Indians in Natal* (Cape Town, 1957); B. Pachai, *The International Aspects of the South African Indian Question, 1860-1971* (Cape Town, 1971): *see also* R. Huttenback, *Gandhi in South Africa: British Imperialism and the Indian Question, 1860-1914* (Ithaca, 1971).

[2] H. Kuper, *Indian People in Natal* (Pietermaritzburg, 1960); F. Meer, *Portrait of Indian South Africans* (Durban, 1969). For articles with a more political focus, *see also:* H. Kuper, "Strangers in Plural Societies: Asians in South Africa and Uganda," in L. Kuper and M. Smith, eds., *Pluralism in Africa* (Berkeley, 1969); F. Meer, "Indian People: Current Trends and Policies," in SPROCAS, ed.,

While these studies provide useful material and empirical data, their disciplinary focus often renders them inadequate for our purpose. That specific aspects of the Indian community are treated more or less in isolation from the total South African structure is highlighted by the absence of any study of what is perhaps the most important issue, the political behavior of the Indians.

In this chapter an attempt is made to supplement the existing literature by analyzing the political behavior of Indians in interaction with other racial groups. While the focus is on the contemporary South African scene, the historical perspective is taken into account by relating present political behavior to its previous forms. Thus the political strategies adopted by the group at various stages are explored, as is its political role insofar as it is likely to engender change in the total societal context. The adequacy of the concept "community development" to describe the present Indian position is assessed in the light of the changes accruing from the destruction of community through racial legislation. Finally, contrary to the predominant focus on changes in culture, ethnicity, and identity, this study investigates the extent to which class differences have replaced ethnic identity or coincide with it.

SOCIOPOLITICAL GROUP CHARACTERISTICS

Indians in South Africa, like the Coloreds, constitute an intermediate caste in the sociopolitical sense in that they have neither the numerical power of the African population, nor the political power of the White minority. Indians account for 2.9 percent of the total population.[4]

Though the Indian and Colored castes are economically and legally approximately at the same level of discrimination by the Whites and relative privilege vis-à-vis the Africans, several important differences between these two groups exist, among which the most decisive is the sociocultural cohesiveness of the Indians as compared with the virtual anomie of the Coloreds. This is reflected in a vast discrepancy between the two groups in crime rates, illegitimate births, alcoholism, and other indicators of social integration.

For a Colored person the likelihood of coming into conflict with the law is ten times greater than for an Indian. One in every 126 Coloreds

South Africa's Minorities (Johannesburg, 1971); and "An Indian's Views on Apartheid" in N. Rhoodie, ed., *South African Dialogue* (Johannesburg, 1972.)

[3]C. Woods, *The Indian Community in Natal* (London, 1954); A. Muller, *Minority Interests: The Political Economy of the Coloured and Indian Communities in South Africa* (Johannesburg, 1968).

[4]Republic of South Africa, Bureau of Census and Statistics, *Bulletin of Statistics,* (Pretoria, 1972).

is in prison on any day of the year as compared with only 1 in every 1,250 Asians.[5] Similarly, there was no Indian among the 393 persons shot at and killed or wounded by the police in 1972.[6]

Distinct cultural traditions, and not only a slightly better economic status, seem responsible for a three times lower infant mortality rate among Indians than among Coloreds (40 of 1,000 live births among Indians, 130 of 1,000 live births among Coloreds) as well as a relatively higher life expectancy (59.3 years for Asian males, 48.8 years for Colored males).[7] But no other figure demonstrates more clearly the deterioration of traditional institutions among a marginal group than the 43 percent rate of illegitimate births among Coloreds as compared with the 7 percent rate among Asians.[8] Other figures in the realm of health standards and educational advancements reveal similar discrepancies between Indians and Coloreds.

This relative cohesiveness of the Indian Community is remarkable in light of the fact that in religious and linguistic terms the Indians constitute the most highly diversified group in South Africa, comprising Hindus, Moslems, Christians of various denominations, Zoroastrians, and Agnostics. The older generation speaks Tamil, Telegu, Hindi, and Gujerati, although most speak English to varying degrees. Approximately 70 percent are Hindu and 20 percent are Muslim, with either Urdu or Gujerati as their mother tongue.

HISTORICAL BACKGROUND

The Indian presence in South Africa dates back to 1860 when the colonial government of India at the invitation of its Natal counterpart, which claimed indigenous labor was "unreliable," sent out laborers to work on the sugar plantations.[9] Such Indian laborers were contracted to serve a five-year period of indenture, after which they could reindenture themselves or take up any other type of employment. After ten years, they were to be given the option either of returning to India, passage paid, or of becoming permanent settlers in Natal with a grant of Crown land of equal value. Most Indians who came to South Africa under these conditions opted to settle. The early settlers engaged mainly in agricultural activity and were soon supplying Durban's fruit and vegetable requirements. Other former inden-

[5]M. Horrell, ed., *A Survey of Race Relations, 1973* (Johannesburg, 1974), p. 70.
[6]Ibid., p. 74.
[7]M. Horrell, ed., *A Survey of Race Relations, 1972* (Johannesburg, 1973), p. 64.
[8]Ibid., p. 65. No figures are available for Africans, which can be estimated to be even higher.
[9]For further discussion of this point, *see* Palmer, *Indians in Natal*, pp. 10-13.

tured workers moved into the coal mines, railways, and general services.[10]

Subsequently another wave of immigrants, the so-called free or passenger Indians, began to arrive in South Africa, mostly through Mauritius, to engage in trade. Like the White settlers, they found a profitable existence in Natal's expanding economy, and in the opportunities for trade in the Transvaal, hence changing the image of the Indian from dependent laborer to potential competitor.

The antagonism that soon began to arise between the White settlers and Indians led to a series of discriminatory measures. In 1893 the parliamentary franchise was officially withdrawn from Indians in Natal, though only a few hundred were entitled to it. Then a poll tax of three pounds per annum was levied on males above sixteen and females above 12 years of age who refused to reindenture themselves or return to India. In 1913 the Indian Immigration Act prohibited the entry of new immigrants, apart from the wives or children of established settlers. In 1923 the insertion of anti-Asiatic clauses in title deeds was legalized; and in 1924 the municipal franchise was withdrawn in Durban. This struggle between politically dominant Whites and Indians trying to establish themselves generated considerable ill-feelings.[11] When Indians attempted to gain security through the purchase of land or businesses, anti-Asiatic clauses hampered them. When they tried to acquire the necessary skills to advance in industry, political and economic color bars were increasingly institutionalized. Despite various agreements between the colonial governments of India and Natal to the contrary, these trends continued until 1948 when the Afrikaner Nationalist party came into power. Initially it only reiterated the anti-Indian sentiments of the preceding era and continued to favor repatriation as the solution to a problem that it defined as one of an "unassimilable minority," although it had long since become evident that the South African Indians' response to repeated discriminatory acts was not to repatriate themselves but to stay and contend with them.

However, in dealing with its "foreign" minorities the Nationalist government had to take into account the changed world situation, particularly the universal disgust with racial ideologies after the Nazi defeat and the emerging protest against continued colonial subjugation, accentuated by India's independence in 1947.[12] India was at the

[10]Ibid., pp. 41-2.
[11]M. Webb, "The Indian in South Africa: Toward a Solution of Conflict," in *Race Relations*, 11, 1 (1944), p. 2.

[12]The legalistic approach of the Indian government to its former nationals abroad was noticed again recently when the Ugandan Indians were expelled. India was conspicuous by its silence on the matter.

forefront of the struggle for decolonization and played a leading role at the United Nations. The case of South African Indians was frequently brought to the fore there. At the same time, the Nationalist government in South Africa, having experienced the failure of repatriation schemes, was in the predicament of finding a suitable justification for the differential treatment of South African Indians. Furthermore, the emerging ideology of apartheid needed elaboration and legitimation if it were to be credible. This legitimation, which stressed as the basis for a stable society the persistence and mainte-nance of the very "unassimilability" for which Indians had been criti-cized over the preceding two decades, marked a new approach in the form of a policy of separate development. In May 1961 an official statement to the effect that Indians "must be accepted as the country's permanent responsibility . . . and that they be accordingly entitled to the benefits inherent in such citizenship" heralded this new policy.[13]

Consequently the government established the Department of In-dian Affairs to cope with the specialized tasks of a race bureaucracy; a nominated Indian Council that the government regarded as being "representative" or at least "responsible" for Indians and therefore worth consulting; and Local Affairs Committees (LAC) to introduce a semblance of Indian electoral participation in local government, defined as essentially consultative in nature. Despite these seeming advances, the position of the Indian community has remained sub-stantially unchanged to the present day. Indians continue to be restricted in the trading sphere; they are residentially segregated after having been moved from developed urban areas to developing periurban areas under the Group Areas Act; they are restricted in their interprovincial movement[14] and are entirely prohibited from living in the Orange Free State; and above all Indians are subject to inferior segregated facilities, like other subordinate groups, in regard to education, health, public transport, restaurants, theaters and other public and civic amenities, while being provided with only symbolic political machinery to redress grievances.

Although many of these restrictions do not apply to the Coloreds, and are surpassed only by the discrimination against Africans, South African Indians outstrip both these two groups economically, as shown in Table 10.1.

[13]Republic of South Africa, *Report of the Department of Indian Affairs, August 1961—December, 1970,* (Pretoria, 1971), p. 2.
[14]Travel permits were issued to 21,003 Indians in 1972 (*Daily News,* (Durban), 16 February 1973). On 20 June 1973 the minister of Indian affairs gave Indians "greater freedom" to travel between provinces; i.e., they may now visit specified provinces for up to thirty days for bonafide reasons without a permit (*Rand Daily Mail,* 21 June 1973).

Table 10.1 Income by Racial Group

Group	Percentage of total population	Percentage of estimated income (1968)
Whites	17.5	73.4
Coloreds	9.4	5.4
Asiatics	2.9	2.4
Africans	70.2	19.8

Source: H. Adam, *Modernizing Racial Domination* (Berkeley, 1971), p. 7.

Of the two intermediate castes, Indians have the larger middle class: 2.6 percent of Indians earn R2,000 and above, as compared with 1.2 percent of Coloreds.[15] However, despite the relatively higher percentage of the Indian middle class vis-à-vis other Blacks, there is also still considerable poverty in the community. Indian household incomes are generally lower than those of Coloreds due to the lower percentage of Indians with independent incomes. In the 1970 census, 53.7 percent of Whites, 64.4 percent of Coloreds, but 70.7 percent of Indians were reported without any income.[16] In the past, this has been largely attributed to the reluctance of the Indian woman to enter the labor force—a trend now on the decline. In 1960 only 4.9 percent of Indian women were economically active, whereas in 1970 the figure has more than doubled to 10.8 percent with the accelerated entry of Indian women into manufacturing jobs.[17] This merely highlights social changes within the group at large. Communal life, the extended family, and the family business have been the fundamental building blocks upon which Indians were able to accumulate initial capital. However, the trend is now toward the nuclear family and stronger emphasis on individualism, including women's emancipation. These developments reflect those of transitional societies moving from traditional means of production to industrialization. Similar changes have affected the traditional, relatively undiversified occupational structure of the Indian community. There is now a high concentration of Indians in manufacturing, commerce, and services, compared with other groups, as illustrated by table 10.2.

[15]Republic of South Africa, Bureau of Census and Statistics, *Population Census, 6 May 1970*, as quoted in *Race Relations News*, 35, 5 (May 1973).

[16]Ibid. African figures were not yet released.

[17]Republic of South Africa, *Report of the Department of Indian Affairs, July 1971—July 1972* (Pretoria, 1973), p. 15.

Table 10.2 Breakdown of South African Population by Employment

Economic Sector	Indians	Coloreds	Whites
Manufacturing	10.3%	8.4%	7.5%
Commerce	8.2%	3.8%	7.3%
Services	3.8%	8.0%	8.7%

NOTE: Unfortunately, no percentage figures for the economically active portion of the population groups are available. These would further demonstrate the overrepresentation of Indians in certain jobs.

Source: M. Horrell, *Survey of Race Relations, 1972* (Johannesburg, 1973), p. 248.

Despite these changes, Indians in South Africa have maintained their cultural identity fairly intact. As a group, they have frequently been accused of being separatist and exclusivist. In Africa, generally, this has been interpreted by Europeans as proof of their "unassimilability," and by Africans as their being racist and discriminatory against the indigenous population. Indeed, there is ample evidence of this exclusivism: distinctive clothing; scores of voluntary associations that are confined to Indians; little social mixing with other groups except at the professional level; and, above all, few marriages between Indians and Africans or Coloreds, although there is no prohibitive legislation in this respect.[18] Even the few Indian-White marriages contracted abroad are in general frowned upon in the Indian community. It is not surprising that Indians are the lowest offenders under the Immorality Act.[19] For the majority these tendencies can be partly explained by the influence of traditional Hindu culture. Most South African Indians originate from India in which rural values predominated. Immigration had begun before traditional Indian society had been disturbed by modern political events and ideas, and even then traditional rural values were upheld and glorified. As a means of surviving in a hostile environment, South African Indians

[18]There are more Colored-Indian marriages than there are African-Indian marriages, the latter being virtually nonexistent. As a result of a rare African-Indian union in a rural community, representations were known to be made by some Indians to the government, requesting legislation similar to that of the Immorality Act to prevent such marriages. Whatever sexual contact does exist between Indians and Africans usually takes place between Moslem Indian men and African women.

[19]From March to December 1971 only 12 Indians were convicted of offenses under the Immorality Act, as against 201 Africans, 90 Coloreds and 262 Whites. (Horrell, *Race Relations, 1972*, p. 65.

clung to traditional cultural tenets and found solace in their history and philosophy. Furthermore, given their distance from India and stringent legislation preventing contacts through further immigration, even for purposes of marriage, there was a virtual freezing of Indian culture in South Africa at the level of the late nineteenth century. Though the average working-class Indian has little knowledge of the sacred scripts and intellectual tenets of his culture and religion, and the Indian elite know it only as a broad philosophy, there exists a general conformity to cultural and religious norms and practices for all life-cycle rituals as well as to a more diffused notion with regard to every day behavior.

The basic predicament of Indians in South Africa has been how to respond to a schizophrenic milieu. Though the rewards to be gained from their labor were coveted, their continued presence was not. They were sought after and given the option of remaining, yet when they chose to exercise that option a barrage of legalized obstacles rapidly emerged. For most of the first generation of immigrants their best years had been spent in the country of their adoption. They had developed bonds among themselves, and new expectations in a strange land; they had compromised their traditional caste exclusiveness by mixing with noncaste members and had in some senses become "impure" in the eyes of their fellow countrymen. They were trapped in a situation in which there was no going back and little hope in staying.

EARLY POLITICAL RESPONSES

Indian political responses to a situation generating increasingly repressive measures took various forms. Beginning with a relatively individualistic, legalistic, and nonconfrontational approach, Indians gradually turned from exclusivism to more universal, collective actions. In so doing, the demands of all underprivileged groups were for a while linked, until politico-legal conditions generated increasingly greater obstacles to Black unity, reducing it to theoretical levels only.

Before any organized political action, individual Indian laborers had protested against work conditions when they became intolerable. There were instances of small-scale strikes on estates. Individual traders resorted to the law courts to protest cases of illegal discrimination. One such lawsuit of a wealthy Indian trader brought to South Africa Mohandas Gandhi, a young Indian, English-trained barrister on a year's contract. This was the beginning of organized Indian political expression in South Africa, later to have its impact on the independence movement in India itself. A year after his arrival

Gandhi was instrumental in forming the Natal Indian Congress (NIC), initially as a reaction to a bill threatening disenfranchisement of Indians there. A petition with 10,000 signatures was submitted, the basis for protest being essentially legalistic. Gandhi believed strongly that equality was a fundamental human right and that treaty obligations were sufficient to bind South Africa to extend equal citizenship rights to all Indians. As a Gujerati-speaking Indian of respectable caste background with an overseas education, Gandhi was highly respected among the traders. The sobriety of his approach to authority appealed to them and he rapidly became a spokesman for Indian interests, at that stage especially the traders' interests.

South Africa provided the context within which Gandhi's ideas of nonviolence were to develop into a political instrument. The first passive resistance campaign was directed against the Transvaal Immigrants Restriction Act, which required residents to submit to educational tests and restricted their movement to the Tranvaal from Natal. Though applicable to all Indians, the initial impact of this law was felt mostly by traders, who supported Gandhi's campaign solidly.

The second passive resistance campaign, which ended in 1913, was motivated by broader issues, though still related exclusively to the position of the Indian. It focused on the excessive poll tax demanded of the indentured who decided to remain in South Africa after termination of their initial contracts and laws that made marriages solemnized under traditional Indian rites illegal. Since these concerns cut across the interests of both the indentured and the traders, a temporary unity developed between them. The campaign was successful insofar as it led to the Smuts-Gandhi agreement and the passing of the Indian Relief Act. The poll tax was abolished and Indian marriages according to traditional rites were formally recognized.

The former indentured had previously distanced themselves from Gandhi's approach, disagreeing with his compromising approach to authority, his persistent respect for the so-called standards of the British Empire,[20] and his tendency to appeal to a "change of heart" by involving them in the Anglo-Boer War.[21] He was considered as a

----

[20]When the queen's Diamond Jubilee approached, Gandhi was still sufficiently enamored of the British Empire to write a warm message of felicitation: "We are proud to think that we are your subjects, the more so as we know that the peace we enjoy in India, and the confidence of security of life and prosperity which enables us to venture abroad, are due to that position." Quoted in Huttenback, *Gandhi in South Africa*, p. 82.

[21]Despite his disappointments, Gandhi urged Indians to join the army and fight for Britain during World War I. He organized an Indian ambulance corps comprising 800 free and 300 indentured members, who placed their services at the disposal of the Natal government. Ibid., pp. 82 and 123.

colonial with a British education that he continued to take seriously. By contrast, the former indentured had been radicalized by harsh experience of discriminatory conditions and knew the extent of British exploitation.

In 1914 Gandhi returned to India, having initiated a new technique of political response, *Satyagraha*. His gradually widening circles of concern never quite succeeded in including the plight of the African,[22] although he had worked with White liberals. However, the political strategy he formulated was to be meaningful in the early years of organized African resistance.

The post-World-War I trade depression, which led to increased White unemployment, accentuated the hostility of Whites toward Indians. Increased restrictions against Indians were suggested in the Areas Reservation Bill of 1925, whose main objective was to implement residential segregation.

To quiet the tide of White antagonism, Indians, in their pathetic powerlessness, began to accede to various White maneuvers. For instance, while at this stage no law existed to prevent Indians from acquiring or occupying property anywhere in the province of Natal, leaders of the NIC, at the instigation of European authorities, began voluntarily to dissuade Indians from acquiring property in, and thereby "penetrating" White areas.[23] Compliance was virtually forced on the grounds that otherwise compulsory segregation, which Indian leaders hoped to forestall, would result.[24] The psychological impact of a situation forcing such actions must have been profound and widespread indeed, if Indians felt that they should voluntarily withdraw from exercising their legal rights and virtually make themselves inconspicuous so as to be left in peace.

Previously, Indians had constituted themselves into various provincial associations: the Cape British Indian Council, the Transvaal British Indian Association, and the Natal Indian Congress. Accelerated restrictions had the effect of temporarily unifying these bodies in 1923 into the South African Indian Congress (SAIC). This enabled the community to express its demands in the international forum with one voice. The outcome was a meeting between representatives of India and South Africa that produced the Cape Town Agreement of

[22]M. Gandhi, *Collected Works III* (Delhi, 1958) p. 245.

[23]The extent of "penetration" had in fact been exaggerated out of all proportion as evidenced in a memorandum of the Natal Indian Congress to the Durban City Council. It was pointed out that the value of property held by Indians in the old Borough was 4 million pounds, as compared with a European holding of 35 million pounds. Indians owned 1,783 sites as against 12,782 owned by Europeans. Pachai, *South African Indian Question*, p. 167.

[24]Calpin, *Indians in South Africa*, pp. 128-30.

1927, containing many promises of change. The South African government agreed not to proceed with the Areas Reservation Bill, and the Indian government offered to assist with repatriation of those who so desired.

This era of Indian dissension was dominated by a particular approach, motivated by what can be described as a "trader mentality." It was based on a minimal awareness of rights and a maximal focus on methods of gaining and maintaining the goodwill of those in power. Characterized by negotiations, deputations, petitions, conferences, and discussions, the underlying strategy was one of gradualism, bargaining, and compromise. These methods were to be abruptly confronted by the next generation of Indian leaders with a very different political maneuvering, which was to have implications for the community's increased self-confidence.

CONFRONTATION INSTEAD OF PERSUASION

The Cape Town Agreement of 1927 raised some hopes among Indians. It accelerated the availability of educational opportunities, which were fully utilized. At the same time Indians began to finance their own schools and to form welfare, cultural, and religious organizations to fulfill their needs in a society where few if any such facilities were provided for them. The demands of Indians of this time differed considerably from those of the preceding generation. They were keen users of any possible educational opportunity, and almost every young person aspired to complete secondary education. Many parents scrounged together what money they could to send their children to Britain for professional education, since they saw in it the only security for the future. It was from among those who studied abroad, who experienced more equalitarian treatment in a different society, that the future political leaders were to emerge. Even those who had studied within the country had experienced more egalitarian contact with English schoolmasters, White missionaries, and other philanthropic figures than the former generation. The impact of these contacts was an overall politicization of the younger middle-class generation. Simultaneously many young workers with different needs and expectations found the ideas of trade unionism and socialism to have increasing relevance to their situation.

The new leadership, comprising young Indian professionals and the intelligentsia, pursued a more radical political course than the old commercial and entrepreneurial elite, seeking common cause with workers of all deprived groups. Numerous small strikes, though not always successful in realizing their aims, helped to consolidate morale among workers against discrimination on the basis of color. In no other context was the meaning of worker exploitation so abundantly clear as in South Africa. The constant coincidence of race and deprivation was more vivid and visible than class struggle could ever be in a racially homogeneous society. Hence Indian workers felt the justness of their cause spoke for itself.

Furthermore, the inequity within the Indian community itself became increasingly evident, exposing the link between the policies of Indian organizations and the class background and interests of their leadership. The nonconfrontational approaches, which had never produced effective results, were gradually replaced with candid views for direct resistance to authority. Open, clear demands based on what were considered to be fundamental human rights were seen as preferable to humiliating and vague pleas for mercy.

The dialectical impact of colonial education was further evident in the perspectives of the young radicals. Instead of becoming "adjusted" Indian Englishmen, they returned more self-confident in their Indian background. Consequently, they tended to be more nationalistic than the compromising older commercial elite had been.

Evidence of these divergent viewpoints emerged during World War II. The SAIC, in its customary pursuit of expediency, passed a resolution pledging loyalty to the British cause. By contrast, the young nationalists refused to associate themselves with a war they considered to be in the interests of British imperialism. Subsequently, they constituted themselves as an opposition group, called the Anti-Segregation Council, within the NIC. They increasingly viewed their local struggle in international terms, identifying with the independence movement in India. The Anti-Segregation Council also introduced to the political arena worker support, which previously had been ignored. More significantly, for the first time in South African Indian political history the aspirations of Africans were incorporated into programs, and Africans shared the same platform. Their joint demands were universal suffrage on a common nonracial roll, equality in employment and status, freedom of movement, and removal of all existing restrictive and discriminatory legislation.

This strategy contrasted too strongly with the bargaining tactics and gradualism of the older activists, who split and formed the Natal Indian Organization (NIO) in 1947. They criticized the NIC for unnecessarily alienating White support, for being Communist-inspired, and for heading on a collision course damaging to existing Indian economic prospects. For the first time the impact of a long-existing undercurrent of differing interests never before articulated within the seemingly homogeneous community became clearly expressed in public policy and strategies. The NIO was comprised of a majority of Gujerati-speaking Muslims, originally of passenger status with substantial commercial interests.[25] The NIC appealed for the most part to workers, with its leadership composed of sympathetic professionals. Articulation of different interest groups in organizational terms also served as a more active rallying point, thereby increasing public participation.

In March 1946 the NIC organized the third passive resistance campaign, which was directed against the Ghetto Act of 1946. Without achieving many demands, the NIC succeeded in mobilizing thousands of Indians for a political and cultural revival period. Indian morale was exceptionally high at this time, being linked with optimism about India's impending independence.

Despite the impressive community mobilization of the passive resistance campaigns, Indians recognized their powerlessness as a minority. Greater linkages with the recently formed African National Congress (ANC) became the crucial issue if change was to be effectively coerced.

While the fourth passive resistance campaign (1952) gained motive power from the specific discrimination of the Group Areas Act of 1950, it aimed at unjust legislation in general; its theme was "Defiance of Unjust Laws."[26] The protest was multiracial in character, the result of a formal alliance with the ANC. Indeed, solidarity between Africans and Indians was evidenced two years later when 8,557 people were arrested for participating in the campaign; they were mostly Africans.[27]

The 1952 campaign aroused much international comment and once again drew attention to the plight of the subordinated peoples of South Africa, though the focus still tended to be on the position of Indians. These developments lent some strength to the domestic struggle. In 1955 the Congress of the People, held in Johannesburg and attended by a multiracial gathering of 2,884 delegates, adopted the Freedom Charter.[28] Its impact was soon felt in a number of arrests terminating in the trial of a multiracial group for high treason in 1956. In 1960 the ANC was banned, and subsequently the entire NIC executive, though not the organization, shared this fate.

This virtually marked the temporary end of unified Black political activity. While it must be conceded that the NIC at the end of the forties and in the early fifties made strides from its traditional, exclusivist predecessors, the need for two separate congresses on racial lines has never been clear. At that stage, it would seem to have still

[25]At the 1948 conference of the Natal Indian Organization of 189 members, 148 were Gujerati Muslims. Meer, "An Indian's Views on Apartheid," p. 441.

[26]For detailed discussion of the 1952 campaign, see L. Kuper, Passive Resistance in South Africa (New Haven, 1960).

[27]Pachai, South African Indian Question, p. 242.

[28]Ibid., p. 252.

been possible for both racial groups to work together, especially since their political aim was an integrated South African society.

THE IMPACT OF NATIONALIST LEGISLATION

Since the beginning of Nationalist rule in 1948, Indian life has been altered by several changes in the nature of the politico-social environment. The Group Areas Act of 1950 was the most severe piece of legislation to affect Indians as they were the only subordinate group with substantial property holdings at the time.[29] Considerable financial loss was incurred by Indian property owners in developed areas. By the end of 1971, 38,561 families had become disqualified to remain in their homes, and a total of 4,546 Indian traders were declared disqualified occupants throughout the country.[30] Expropriation took place under government-dictated terms, frequently resulting in compensation far below market value.[31] The injustice was heightened by the profits made on the subsequent resale of these properties by the Department of Community Development.[32] Dispossessed homeowners had to pay inflated prices for accommodations in newly declared Indian areas, the amount of which was far too small for the demand. This artificial land shortage for Indian home development continues to be a major complaint of a rising Indian middle class. On the other hand, tenants who had to be evicted and were unable to gain accommodation in large new monotonous housing complexes, such as Chatsworth in the Durban area, were forced to become dwellers of transit camps, often of "sub-sub-economic" standards.

From the perspective of "community development" these changes ironically enough seem to have been more efficient at community destruction, eroding the traditional South African Indian way of life. The members of the extended family generally had lived either together in a single household or within convenient commuting distance from one another. Frequent visits to relatives were part of daily life. As the most self-sufficient of the subordinate groups,

[29]It was estimated that up to 1,763 Indians were dispossessed of 6,638 acres of their original landholdings of 10,323 acres of rateable land in the Durban municipality. Figures reported by J. N. Singh, in an affidavit in Supreme Court of South Africa, Transvaal Provincial Division, in the matter between P. N. Bhoola and the State, 1963.

[30]Horrell, *Race Relations, 1972*, pp. 128 and 133.

[31]The discrepancy between municipal valuation and actual compensation is illustrated in the following examples. In 1964, Indian-owned property with a municipal valuation of R11,200 was compensated with R5,000; another valued at R960 was compensated with R50. M. Horrell, *A Survey of Race Relations in South Africa* (Johannesburg, 1969), p. 223.

[32]Examples of this are two Indian properties in Durban, bought by the

Indians financed either totally or partly over 80 percent of their own schools and organized a proliferation of associations, usually in the city's central area, to cope with their needs. Being an essentially urban people, their homes were within reach of shops and places of entertainment. These living arrangments had made material deprivation somewhat bearable: transport costs were relatively low; the nuclear family could rely on the extended family for child care; and the paucity of public conveniences in the city for Indians was alleviated by central settlement patterns. Furthermore, telephones were usually available and a car was not a necessity. In this way poorer groups were compensated by geographical proximity and better public amenities for the private advantages of wealthier sections in suburbia. With the passage of the Group Areas Act, for the first time in the history of the Indian community extended families had to split and resettle according to individual financial means. Thereby, class differences became greatly accentuated; kinship bonds could no longer hide individual poverty as well as accumulated wealth in the same family.

This haphazard resettlement resulted in large-scale social disorganization, hitherto unknown in the Indian community. Though still considerably lower than other racial groups, the common indicators for degrees of social anomie, such as rates of divorce, illegitimate births, and crime showed a marked increase within the community itself. This picture stands sharply in contrast to the situation in older areas of Indian settlement, with their heterogeneous composition of residents from various economic and racial groups, with their temples, mosques, and other communal facilities. The extent of the impact of this single piece of legislation is summed up in a public wedding invitation, a form very seldom used by Indians: "Mr. and Mrs. . . . of . . . wish to extend a cordial invitation to friends and relatives with whom they have lost contact due to displacement under the Group Areas Act, on the occasion of the marriage of . . . . "[33]

In the South African context, Africans, Coloreds, and Indians should be living within convenient distance from the city's center, instead of the contrary arrangement envisioned by residential segregation.

Department of Community Development for R20,000 and R11,000 respectively and resold within fifteen months for R47,000 and R67,000 respectively. This means a percentage increase of 135 percent and 509 percent respectively. SPROCAS Economic Commission, *Power, Privilege and Poverty* (Johannesburg, 1972), p. 82.

[33] Indians traditionally deliver wedding invitations personally from home to home, not relying on an impersonal postal service, to ensure a good turn-out at the wedding. *The Leader* (Durban) 20 July 1973.

The belated official recognition of Indians as South Africans, in 1961, also introduced a new era in Indian political life.[34] Having been deprived of the parliamentary franchise in Natal in 1896, and the municipal franchise in 1924, Indians were now offered a limited involvement in local and national affairs.

The Department of Indian Affairs, established in 1961 to serve as a central channel through which the Indian community could express its needs, took over the functions originally performed by the Directorate of Immigration and Asiatic Affairs, and subsequently by the Department of the Interior's Asiatic Division.[35] The minister at the head of the Department of Indian Affairs works in consultation with the South African Indian Council, which the government established in March 1968 to bypass such critical political organizations as the NIC.

Unlike the Coloured Representative Council, which is partly elected and partly nominated, or the various Bantustan authorities, which have some executive powers as well, the South African Indian Council was to be fully appointed and to have no authority to make decisions independently. Twenty-five members were nominated by the minister for a period of three years on a provincial basis. A chairman was elected from among the members. The executive committee comprised five members of the council, four of whom were elected by council members and a fifth, the chairman, was appointed by the minister.[36]

The council's specific function had been outlined at its first meeting in Cape Town in March 1964. It was to serve as a consultative body to assist the relevant government bodies, in preparation for the day when it would be an elected body to cope with such Indian affairs as might then be delegated to it. The promise of graduation to elected status, at first as a partially elected body and only subsequently to be fully elected, could however only be fulfilled when Indian resettlement had reached a more advanced stage, making it possible to

[34]In May 1961, the minister of the interior announced in the House of Assembly: "In the past the Asiatics were justified in feeling they were being regarded as a foreign group and did not belong here. . . . But gradually people came to realise . . . that the Indians in this country were our permanent responsibility. They are here and . . . the vast majority of them are South African citizens. . . . As such they are also entitled to the necessary attention and the necessary assistance." (*Daily News*, 25 November 1961).

[35]This includes control of welfare services, granting and payment of pensions, issuing of identity cards, travel documents, educational services, and other related matters. It specifically excludes, however, issues of landholding and job reservation, though it serves as a link with those departments. (*Report of the Department of Indian Affairs*, August 1961—December 1970, p. 3.)

[36]Ibid., p. 18.

establish electoral districts and a voters' roll. Accordingly, local affairs and consultative committees have been established on a partially elected basis and are the responsibility of the various provinces. However, the real reason why the promised Indian election had not taken place by 1974 was the government's calculation that such a free expression of Indian sentiment would result in the rejection of apartheid candidates, as had occurred in the first election to the Coloured Representative Council in 1969. A comment, frequently heard informally from Afrikaner politicians was: "We do not wish to make the same mistake with the Indians as we did with the Coloureds."

The response of Indians to these changes varied. Four basic positions can be delineated. At the one extreme is that of total acceptance, as epitomized by the South African Indian Council, which not only accepts but collaborates with the government, believing in the sincerity of its intentions and the values of its programs of separate and equal development. Many representatives of this attitude fear an African takeover, which they consider as totally detrimental to Indian interests. They prefer to view themselves as allies of the Whites in a common struggle to keep "unpredictable" African demands under control. Second, there are those who accept government policy and government-appointed bodies on the basis of expediency and use these channels discriminately. They argue that such policy contains the seeds of its own destruction and should be exploited for this potential. Third, there is a sizable group who have little faith in either the government or its Indian collaborators. They see themselves as being powerless and don't want to "become involved in politics." They point to the infiltration of the Security Police in all aspects of organizational life and are intimidated to the extent of apathy by the government's police machinery. Finally, there are those who feel considerable antagonism toward the South African Indian Council as an exploitative body, accomplishing nothing and having no authority from the community to act as its representative. Any changes that do occur they attribute to the government, not its stooges in the Council. They reject on principle ethnically exclusive political activity in government-created institutions aimed at splitting a potentially united Black front. This is the position of the Indian members of the South African Students Organization (SASO) and the Black Peoples Convention (BPC) as well as of a substantial section of former political activists now forced into the role of reluctant spectators.

In brief, while government-appointed bodies such as the South African Indian Council and Local Affairs Committees are tolerated by some, they are neither respected nor supported by most Indians. In fact they are more hated than the government and frequently are scapegoats for it.

In defense of their positions, council members have argued that although they do not entirely accept their admittedly limited roles, they participate in such a body in the interest of the community for want of better alternatives. One council member expresses his view thus: given the failure of earlier militant measures there is one way of establishing dialogue through the use of a strategy, which can be considered a far more effective way of persuasion. Face to face contact or even polite confrontation with authorities is felt more likely to remove mistrust and suspicion among Whites. Above all, it is said, only such an approach can be considered realistic in view of the fact that the White man is in power, and Indians are a voteless people.[37]

The late chairman of the executive council, A. M. Rajab, on the other hand argued that though he believed in a democratically elected council such a council was not necessarily better than or as effective as a "carefully selected hand-picked one." He considered his council to be a more effective, responsible, forceful, and objective body than any previous organization. Furthermore, in defense of the government, he stressed the need for patience, since "the area of race relations is usually slow of improvement" and it was "not the government per se, but the white electorate that resists change."[38] Along these lines, unlike the Coloured Representative Council, its Indian equivalent condoned and justified the government's policy in crisis situations. While for instance Colored students received the support of the Coloured Representative Council in their strike against their university administration, a year earlier in the summer of 1973 in a similar situation the Indian Council virtually acknowledged White generosity in providing Indians with a university.[39]

This syndrome of behavior,[40] which distinguishes the style and calibre of the Indian Council from that of Buthelezi, or the Colored Representative Council, may perhaps only be explained in terms of the Indian community's position as the most powerless of all the subordinate South African groups, with neither the numerical basis of African strength, nor the claim to partial Afrikaner ancestry of the Coloreds. The Indian Council is not likely ever to abolish itself or

---

[37]*The Graphic* (Durban), 16 July 1971. Letter to Editor, signed M. B. Naidoo.

[38]Public address in Lenasia, 26 March 1972 by A. M. Rajab.

[39]H. Joosub, "The Future of the Indian Community," in Rhoodie, *South African Dialogue*, p. 433.

[40]One noticeable exception to this pattern is an outburst on the part of an executive council member, who is also an educationalist. Y. S. Chinnasamy publicly called for a change in the racial composition of the faculty at the Indian university, which is 70 percent White, for the removal of Broederbonders in positions of authority, and for improvement in the quality of education. (*The Graphic*, 27 April 1973.)

openly to challenge the basic tenets of government policy, as the
Colored Representative Council did so spectacularly in 1974.

The establishment of the Department of Indian Affairs was a step
in elaborating the racial bureaucracy that is the fabric of South Africa.
Many new positions were created for Indians. Employment of Indians increased from 27.5 percent of the total bureaucratic establishment in 1961 to 75.7 percent in 1970.[41] This number includes
inspectors of education, educational planners, subject inspectors,
social workers, and a wide range of clerical staff. However, all positions occupied by Indians within the Department of Indian Affairs
are subject to a superstructure of positions occupied by Whites. In
addition there is an information-yielding network of Indian and
White Security Police. The sugar coating in the takeover of Indian education by the Department of Indian Affairs was in the increased
salaries offered to Indians, although the gap between White and
Indian salaries has not decreased significantly, and Whites are frequently paid an unofficial "inconvenience allowance" for working with
Indians.

Related to the establishment of the Department of Indian Affairs
are opportunities for greater diversification of Indian economic
activity, more manufacturing outlets, the establishment of Indian
banks, and companies developing Indian townships. Frequently,
there is a connection between members of the Indian council and
these entrepreneurial activities.[42]

These signs of "prosperity" and "progress" are countered by the
experience of other members of the population who feel the department's effects in an overall bureaucraticization and negative politicization of life. The department's bureaucratic tentacles are felt especially strongly in the schools. School administration under the
Department of Indian Affairs differs qualitatively from that under its
predecessor, the Natal Provincial Administration, despite the provision of better physical facilities. Teachers complain about the overemphasis of bureaucratic requirements, enforced by frequent "in-
spections," at the expense of innovative teaching. This is reflected in
the sharp decline in the number of Indians entering the teaching
profession, despite high salaries, and the number of qualified teachers leaving the profession to go into other areas of employment.

[41]In absolute numbers there were 28 Indians employed in 1961 and 466 in
1970. (*Report of the Department of Indian Affairs, 1961-1970*), p. 12.

[42]A recent court case brought to the fore the role of Mr. Desai, an SAIC
member and director of companies, developing Indian townships on land
declared for Indian occupation. Other SAIC members are also known to be
managing directors of newly opened Indian banks, or own prime Indian
property in areas just declared Indian.

"Service conditions" and the general restrictiveness of the profession are frequently cited as the main reasons for seeking other employment.[43]

Furthermore, many teachers speak of the general "politicization" of the profession under the Department of Indian Affairs, even though they are explicitly required to "refrain from politics." The very institutions are political in that they represent a political perspective that teachers and students cannot escape. Teachers and principals are not allowed to invite any guest speaker to address a school without the permission of the Department of Indian Affairs; no surveys or research projects may be conducted without the department's approval; and teaching personnel may not speak to the press without the department's consent. Hence teachers may not operate freely and creatively within the profession. Dissatisfaction was frequently articulated by teachers at the Annual Conference of the South African Indian Teachers' Association in 1973. It was evident that the effect of politicization was contrary to that intended by the authorities. A similar process has taken place at the government-run University of Durban-Westville, where both students and the Indian faculty, who comprise 25 percent of the total faculty, share similar experiences with lower level teachers.[44]

Government authorities, seeking legitimation for their policies, frequently speak of the acceptance of their efforts by the Indian people, in support of which they point to attendance figures at school open days and various university occasions. However, parents have no choice to behave otherwise, given the lack of alternatives. Perhaps the greatest indictment against government-controlled segregated education is that some of its chief Indian supporters and a sizable number of the Indian elite, who appear tacitly to support the government's efforts, send their own children abroad to study.

Whenever the opportunity arises to express dissent with government policies in the form of nonparticipation, it is seized. For example, in 1973 Indians successfully boycotted Local Affairs Committee elections in the Chatsworth-Merebank area of South Durban and in the North Durban area by refusing to return voter registration forms because they could not have direct representation on the City

[43]Only about one-third of the Indian graduate teachers are working in their profession. *See* Address of the President of the South African Indian Teachers' Association, Annual Conference 1973. *Daily News,* 11 July 1973.

[44]For a further discussion of this issue, *see* K. Adam, "Dialectic of Higher Education for the Colonised," in H. Adam, ed., *South Africa: Sociological Perspectives* (London, 1972).

Council.[45] Similarly the Ratepayers Association of Asherville, a community with a heavy concentration of professional as well as working-class people, boycotted the North Durban Indian Affairs Committee elections, condemning such committees as "meaningless bodies" having "no real power." Others objected to them because they were for Indians only. "We want direct representation . . . and want to vote as residents, not as Indians."[46]

REVIVAL OF POLITICAL ORGANIZATIONS

The New Natal Indian Congress

After the successive bannings of its entire executive in 1960 and a decade of resigned adjustment to stronger forces, the Natal Indian Congress emerged publicly again in October 1971. Its first meeting was well attended by students and young professionals of divergent viewpoints, seeking to devise an alternative forum of political expression to that of government-appointed bodies. A new generation was prepared to give it another try by testing the government's ideology. In addition, changed political constellations of the previous decade called for a rethinking of accepted policy. Among these three main issues came to the fore (1) the attitude to Black consciousness; (2) open membership of the NIC to all racial groups; and (3) the NIC's policy on the Indian council.

(1) Black consciousness was summed up by the NIC as being "a reaction to White oppression" seeking "to redefine the Black man in fresh terms" and rejecting "all established White values." The NIC rejected Black education in favor of a "broad, universal, enlightened and objective education." After an intense debate a slight majority perceived in Black consciousness a genuine danger of potential Black racism. Furthermore, it was considered insufficient as a political program.[47] (2) With regard to membership, the majority in the NIC maintained its position of 1894, viz., to keep membership exclusively Indian on the grounds that there were too many legal and tactical obstacles to the creation of a multiracial body. The exclusive group appeal would allow for more effective mobilizing of Indians toward the goal of a common society. Fear of being unsuccessful in achieving multiracial membership and of losing Indian support seemed to dictate the NIC's "temporary" racial character. (3) On the question of

[45]*Daily News*, 6 June 1973 and *The Graphic*, 26 January 1973.
[46]*The Graphic*, 26 January 1973.
[47]F. Meer, "Natal Indian Congress," in *Reality*, 4, 3 (July 1972):5. For further clarification of the ideology of Black consciousness in South Africa, *see* H. Adam, "The Rise of Black Consciousness in South Africa," *Race*, 15, 2 (October 1973).

collaboration with the Indian council, it was argued that a decision endorsing collaboration should be postponed until 1974, when council elections were due; in the meantime as a creation of apartheid for the entrenchment of economic and political power of the ruling class it should be rejected in principle.[48]

The NIC annual conference of 1973, by contrast with the 1971 revival gathering, was poorly attended. A strong minority still favored abandoning the organization's exclusive character in favor of a common association of apartheid opponents. A second controversy concerned a proposal to encourage members to seek positions on the Local Affairs Committees and in the Indian council to subvert these bodies from within. Subsequent discussion left the former issue in abeyance and accepted the latter perspective as a potentially effective political move. The noticeable differences in enthusiasm between the 1971 and 1973 conferences may well be explained in terms of the political crossroads at which Indians find themselves, and the ensuing indecision of organizations faced with the choice between pragmatism and principle, or an innovative combination of both.

Black Consciousness

A body that appears to be gaining increasing though not substantial support among Indian students and young professionals is the South African Students Organization. It was the prime mover in introducing the term "Black" to replace "non-White" to refer to Africans, Coloreds, and Indians in South Africa. The latter is now used by SASO sympathizers as a derogatory label for Blacks who align themselves with Whites socially and politically. Black people are defined as "those who are by law or tradition, politically, economically and socially discriminated against as a group in South African society, identifying themselves as a unit in the struggle toward the realization of their aspirations."[49] Central to this thinking is the idea of Black consciousness, an American import, which is described as a way of life through which a self-definition of essentially Black values takes place. It is viewed as a sign of awareness on the part of Blacks of their potential economic and political power, giving rise to group solidarity. This involves the exclusion of Whites, as the SASO believes that "a truly open society can only be achieved by blacks."[50]

Although Indians are prohibited by official university regulations from being members of the SASO, some work informally in con-

---

[48]Meer, "Natal Indian Congress," p. 6.
[49]*Policy Manifesto* of SASO 2nd General Students Council, Durban, July 1971.
[50]B. Khoapa, ed., *Black Review, 1972,* (Durban, 1973), pp. 41-2.

junction with it; others are the prominent members in the leadership of the SASO and the subsequent Black Peoples Convention.
Nevertheless, the SASO's failure to attract much Indian support so
far has been attributed to various factors, typically highlighting
Indian indecision:

(a) The militant rhetoric of SASO exponents is said to undermine
    confidence in the organization as a vehicle to fight for a nonracist
    society.
(b) An overemphasis on Black domination at the expense of Black
    consciousness raises Indian fears of being dominated by a new set
    of masters. Most Indians, therefore, see their ultimate security in
    a racially integrated, liberal-bourgeois South Africa.[51]
(c) Whereas in the United States Black consciousness created among
    Blacks a search for their history and a return to their cultural
    roots, in South Africa, given the diversity of the subordinated
    groups, an African-dominated cultural and political unity could
    easily amount to a denial of specific Indian history and tradition.
    While this may be temporarily necessary to close the ranks of sub-
    ordinates and to counteract the White policy of fragmentation by
    creating Black consciousness, its shortcoming lies in its tendency
    to glaze over instead of accepting essentially different politico-
    historical identities.

These factors, coupled with the traditional Indian exclusiveness,
not only vis-à-vis non-Indians but within the group itself, does not
make the ideas of Black consciousness very appealing to most Indians.

Fringe Groups

Marginal attempts at forming political parties were launched by
several individuals. It is worthwhile briefly to investigate these splinter groups of a political subculture not because of their impact or
success, which is nonexistent or negligible, but because they signal
dissatisfaction with existing constitutions. Like sects splitting off from
religious denominations, marginal political expressions could indicate
potentially significant trends and, at the least, highlight nonconform-
ist ideological perceptions, often too rapidly dismissed as patholog-
ical.

In October 1971 G. M. Singh announced interest in forming a
party for the working man, which, not to antagonize White employers, would be less militant than the congress. It was to have an exclusively Indian membership and would neither integrate with Coloreds

[51]Meer, "An Indian's Views on Apartheid," p. 455.

and Africans nor work with them, since the government would be intolerant of a militant and integrated body. The "Peoples Democratic party" as it was called, would be nonviolent and would put up candidates when the Indian council became an elected body. However, three months later the plan was shelved until the council's future became known.[52]

Similarly, preparing for the promised future elections of the council, and working within the government framework, a Chatsworth resident and member of the Southern Durban Indian Local Affairs Committee named Rajbansi initiated the People's party. It endorsed the council and separate development as the only workable policy for South Africa, called for "Indostans" (separate geographical areas under Indian control, equivalent to Bantustans), and an equitable application of government policy. While cooperation with leaders of other races was favored, racial integration was rejected. Cooperation with the government was to be on a totally equalitarian basis. It was intended to be a workers' party, fighting for improved conditions, opposing group areas, the mass removal of people, and petty apartheid.[53]

A year later, in July 1973, these ideas reemerged in a very different form. The Indian press revealed that an underground group based on the concept of the Afrikaner Broederbond had been formed that aimed at taking control of Indian political and civic affairs and controlling the seats in the council if elections were held. The organization was said to have a closely knit membership of twenty-seven, including businessmen, a former trade unionist, factory workers, an attorney, and a doctor; its financial strength was described as "close to a quarter million rand." The motivation for its formation seemed to be that certain Indian organizations were under the control of a few, who had "vested interests" and "had to be replaced by others who had the man-in-the-street at heart."[54] Though many of these statements were based on rumors and probably resulted from the imagination of journalists, they were discussed seriously and raised considerable concern. A member of the council reported that the Indobond "excluded Moslems and Gujerati-Hindus from its secret order. . . . we feel it is a highly dangerous state of affairs and will ask the government to crush it."[55] The leader of the Bond however denied sectarianism but retorted that "the only people afraid of the Bond are the Indian exploiters, who we are determined to destroy."[56]

[52]*The Graphic*, 15 September 1971 and 28 January 1971.
[53]Ibid., 4 February 1972.
[54]Ibid., 27 July 1973.
[55]*Rand Daily Mail*, 31 July 1973.
[56]*The Graphic*, 10 August 1973.

These splinter groups as well as the major Indian political organizations of the seventies reveal increasingly the widening class differences among Indians. The closing of the chasm between the council and the NIC as reflected in the most recent NIC policy statement is symptomatic of this. On the other hand, the formation of a workers' party and demonstrated identification of the enemy as Indian exploiters suggests a high degree of political introversion.

Voluntary Associations

In contrast to the approach of the political organizations stands the role of various voluntary associations. Established on the basis of specific homogeneous interests, they have undergone a change of function: away from their previous socializing roles to a more direct, confrontational, and instrumental strategy in the pursuit of their members' interests. No longer is aid for adjustment in a strange or hostile environment the prime purpose of these associations, but representation and struggle for specific interests. In this sense voluntary associations form an integral part of Indian political behavior, although these groups do not consider themselves political organizations. However, in the extremely regulated and politicized South African context even the most apolitical organizations, such as sport clubs, are bound to encounter political conflicts in which they have to take a stand, often against their explicit intentions.

A voluntary organization with a substantial backing is the Southern Durban Civic Federation, which represents the various ratepayers' associations in the city's southern sector—an area housing the Indian lower economic strata. The first conference of this organization in 1971 used as its major theme the relationship between politics and Indian civic life. It was a marked change in approach from previous ratepayers' associations, which viewed politics as being somehow outside their realm. The conference stressed that ratepayers could no longer function in isolation if their complaints were to be heard and their interests were to be met. It pointed out that the quality of their lives—where and how they lived and their political rights—were dependent on the political pressure they as a group could exercise.[57]

Despite the iniquitous experience of discrimination and unsatisfactory facilities, there is little public mass involvement of residents in any form of political articulation of grievances, which seems to end with their expression by the leaders. In view of the fact that Indians generally have a tradition of participation in voluntary associations, this relatively low involvement is astonishing, but can be explained in various ways:

[57]The Ratepayer (Durban), 5 June 1971.

(a) The haphazard resettlement of people with no regard for livable heterogeneous groupings and no amenities to bring them together atomized and alienated former community members from each other. Suspicion of one another, noninvolvement in community affairs, and general withdrawal behavior resulted from the destruction of established settlement patterns.

(b) Abstract alternative possibilities have little credibility in a situation without expectations that life can become progressively better.

(c) Fear of police reprisals and repercussions on family and job security are very real indeed, despite assurances by the Ratepayers Association that political involvement is "our right . . . our duty . . . and it is legal."[58]

However, while there is a lack of sustained political involvement on the part of most Indians, in contrast to the past, there are ready responses to such specific issues as proposals to increase bus fares and to stop the bus service altogether in favor of the use of trains. On both issues residents quickly constituted bodies to articulate their dissent and they turned up in their thousands.

Sporting associations also have assumed some political importance in South Africa. The role of Indians in the administration of multiracial sports associations has been noticeable. Hassan Howa, the president of the multiracial South African Cricket Board of Control, for instance, has been instrumental in exposing and exploiting the discrepancy between the legal situation and government policy on the question of multiracial sports. Despite warnings by the minister of sport that the government would not tolerate a flouting of its policies through the establishment of a multiracial cricket club, the Aurora Cricket Club in Pietermaritzburg went ahead with the election of an Indian captain and chairman and a White vice captain, thereby forcing upon the government a confrontation that it would have preferred to avoid.[59] Similarly, the South African Soccer Federation was successful in influencing the Federation of International Football Associations to withdraw its previous special dispensation to stage international soccer tournaments in South Africa.[60] These instances have demonstrated the power of subordinate groups to influence the participation of the dominant group in international sports. That many Black sports administrators, among them Hassan Howa and Morgan Naidoo, have been refused passports to attend sporting events abroad is a measure of the impact of their policies.

[58]Ibid.
[59]*The Natal Mercury,* 30 June 1973.
[60]*Sunday Times* (Johannesburg), 11 February 1973.

INTERSUBORDINATE GROUP RELATIONS

Underlying Indian-African relations, especially among the older generation of Indians, is the trauma of the 1948 Durban communal riots, in which more than 100 people, mostly Indians, were killed. The riots articulated antagonisms that then existed between Indians and Africans. For Africans the prevalent image of the Indian was that of a cheeky trader, not unlike Indians in East Africa, despite their different economic position. While Indians in Uganda, for instance, dominated the agricultural sphere,[61] the Indian in South Africa, where workers outnumber traders, sweeps the streets of Durban. Nevertheless, Indians in South Africa are still scapegoats for Africans at the grass-roots level. Various goodwill gestures have been made by the Indian leadership to change this negative image. Donations to African schools, scholarships for African students, invitations to African leaders to act as patrons of Indian organizations have had little effect. Above all, contact has remained at the level of formal gestures, unlikely to bring about the mutual identification of the two subordinate castes. Occasional socializing at the elite level has only clouded the underlying mutual suspicion.

In a society in which the privileged group is so visible, this lack of common cause and identification on the part of subordinates is astonishing. Among the various explanations for it the South African setting deserves the greatest attention. People are identified as members of racial groups rather than as individuals with common interests, contacts, and associations. Apartheid in its differential application to the various races engenders different responses and thereby divides the subordinate strata. Not the least, there is a cultural arrogance on the part of Indians, which in the South African context has been heightened to an intense cultural narcissism as an escape from subordination and insecurity. Common political goals to end White supremacy at the leadership level have hardly found an emotional equivalent of mutual concern and identification among the Indian and African masses. Furthermore, although Indians resent the discrimination by Whites, they also fear potential African domination, as illustrated by the arbitrary treatment of Indians in East Africa. Given the ambivalence of Africans toward Indians, on the whole South African Indians see the present situation as more tolerable than an uncertain future under African domination.

Indian-Colored relations are characterized by similar discords. Coloreds are seen by Indians as displaying great arrogance toward

---

[61]H. Patel, *Indians in Uganda and Rhodesia: Some Comparative Perspectives on a Minority in Africa,* Studies in Race and Nations, 5, 1, (1973-74):11.

them as a so-called non-Western people with an outmoded culture. On the other hand, Indians stereotype Coloreds as a community lacking an integrated cultural tradition, living by the day, without much care for other concerns in life. However, these attitudes have to be seen in the context of far less contact and mutual suspicion between the two middle-groups than between Indians and Africans.

With the exception of a frustrated Colored intelligentsia and certain Colored leaders, who now see the assurance of a better future only through a total identification with all other Blacks, the majority of this group, despite its increasing rejection of Whites, has so far not identified with the African cause. According to the surveys by Edelstein, for instance, only a small minority of Coloreds preferred the label Black.[62] However, even the Afrikaner press has begun to notice with concern the changing mood among the Colored youth and intelligentsia:

> The open way in which the well-known Coloured leaders identified themselves with the "Blackpower" movement has now reared its head very clearly for the first time. Warning voices have in the past been raised that we must not reject the Coloured people as allies.
>
> That a man like Mr. Adam Small can describe himself in virtually so many words as "Black" is an indication of how far the Coloured man has been pushed in the direction of the Black man.[63]

By contrast, given the precarious position of the Indian minority, a clear choice to join either side would seem to be unwelcome. In the unlikely event that Whites would ever shed their deep-seated prejudices toward Indians and agree to a merger, Indians would immediately make themselves a target for the wrath of the African majority. However, were Indians to join fully with other subordinate groups in the Black-White struggle, they would be even more vulnerable in their own view. What has been sought throughout by Indian activity is not radical change as such, only some concessions to make life more tolerable.

COMMUNITY HOMOGENEITY OR CLASS STRATIFICATION

It has been argued earlier that the concept "community" is no longer entirely appropriate to describe the social organization of South African Indians in view of their ethnic diversity, size, and increasingly secondary character of human relationships. These tendencies have been accelerated and accentuated by the Nationalist government's policies in two ways: the impact of the Group Areas Act has solidified

[62]Horrell, *Race Relations, 1973,* p. 20.
[63]*Vaderland,* (Johannesburg) 9 July 1973.

into relatively class homogeneous settlement patterns, thereby clarifying emerging intracommunal class distinctions; the designation of an elitist Indian council, comprised of the Indian economic upper strata, defined by the government as "leaders," despite the status inconsistency they themselves experience as powerless "non-Whites," is far removed from the interest of workers. This official alliance with the Indian bourgeoisie further undermined the former appeals to the sense of community and heightened the awareness of more significant intracommunal distinctions.

Indians generally have responded to this new situation with three ambiguous and contradictory attitudes, which are often not held simultaneously, but are activated according to the situation and issue involved. There is a higher degree of "political introversion"; that is, instead of focusing directly on the real source of oppression, the frustrations of group members are increasingly directed against the Indian Council, which is blamed for the exploitation of the existing inequality. Given their tenuous group security, Indians still emphasize cultural superiority in their quest for identity and use it as a bulwark against political domination, as well as a psychological substitute for economic success. While its positive effects can be seen in the high level of the group's self-confidence, it also results in the reification of identity and militates against political effectiveness. Cultural narcissism prevents real intersubordinate alliances. Contradicting political introversion and cultural narcissism are newer interest-based alliances among the three subordinate groups. However these cross-ethnic ties need as their activating incentive either a highly developed political consciousness, as reflected in the Indian membership of the SASO, or direct, concrete advantages. Thus during the strikes in 1972 Indian workers sometimes joined Africans in the demand for higher wages, frequently against Indian employers. Such a breach of ethnic group solidarity would have been inconceivable during the early phases of the Indian struggle. At another level, symbolic contact also continues between the new Indian and African administrative elites, although this has differing implications and is generally in the interests of maintaining a slightly modified *status quo*.

While common bases of class interest that cut across ethnic lines theoretically can easily be isolated and strengthened, the administrative aspects and the differential application of separate development to the various groups succeed now, more than ever before, in differentiating the problem of one group from another.

At the same time, heightened intragroup class distinctions, and the feeling experienced by many Indians of being exploited by their own group members, have tended to accentuate the decline of the relevance of sentimental community affiliation. Instead, interests determine action in concrete situations. To what extent such interests will continue to predominate is, however, dependent on the nature of the assurances and the type of security that the more sizable African subordinate group offers the wavering Indian minority, as well as the kind of concession to Indians that the ruling group is willing to grant to prevent a threatening subordinate alliance.

11
Major Patterns
of Group Interaction
in South African Society*

MICHAEL SAVAGE

INTRODUCTION

Although historians have recently stated "the central theme in South African history is the interaction between peoples of diverse origins, languages, technologies, ideologies and social systems, meeting on South African soil," scant attention has been paid to such interaction by social scientists.[1] Most work in these disciplines has been focused on the internal arrangements or attitudes of one group in the population and on movements around and within the selected group, rather than on the relationships of that group to other groups or to the wider society. Indeed, the political framework of contemporary South Africa, with its emphasis on group separation, has helped to obscure the obvious fact that no group in the society exists in isolation from other groups, while the polarities of the society also have adversely influenced the pattern of social research into the sensitive area of group interaction. The result is that outside of the work of historians, there has been more examination of group separation than of group interdependence and interrelationships between groups. Yet a study of the types and consequences of interaction between the different groups in the South African population would provide one key to an understanding of the social structure and of the forces that may help change or transform that society.[2]

*The author wishes to acknowledge the help and assistance of Peter Randall in preparing both the framework and the content of this chapter.
[1]M. Wilson and L. Thompson, eds., *Oxford History of South Africa* (Oxford, 1969), 1:v.

280

   This paper will survey the significant patterns of group interaction occurring across those lines of class, color, ethnicity, and politics that so clearly demarcate the major groups in South African society. While its primary focus will be the present, it must be recognized that existing patterns of group interaction are largely the outcome of a past series of often highly structured and intricate conflicts between such groups. Three centuries of Black-White contact in South Africa have produced the existing imbalance of power between these groups, resulting in the subordination of the Black population and the inequitable distribution of economic and political resources. However to focus exclusively on this imbalance and its historical origins is to emphasize the power of the White regime, or even the static nature of White rule, at the expense of examining the subtle and divergent changes that are taking place within and between the groups in the population.

   While it is important to analyze what accounts for the endurance and relative stability of the present pattern of inequalities, it is equally important to examine whether these very inequalities in South African society provide a potential source of political and social change. Empirical evidence exists to show that they do and to indicate that the social system is subject to permutations. This flexibility in White domination obviously is reflected and contained in the patterns of contact and interaction between the major groups in the society. Thus, for instance, changes in the positioning of the occupational color bar, in petty apartheid laws, in the context of Black-White political interaction, all provide testimony to the flexibility of White domination. Such changes however raise the central question of whether they contain within them any significant threat to White hegemony, or whether they are merely surface movements illustrating dynamism without change, that is, alterations being made that do not threaten the structural bases of existing economic and political inequalities.

   Two major positions can be outlined in terms of attempting to assess the cumulative effect on the social structure of changes in patterns of group interaction. One position views the central problems of South Africa as arising from the irreconcilability of economic rationality and institutional or personal racism. It is believed thus that "economic rationality urges the polity forward beyond its ideology"[3] and that consequently "the dissolution of colour injustice has been continuously assisted by competitive capitalism."[4] According to this

---

[2]For purposes of this paper "interaction" is defined "as any process in which the action of one entity causes an action by, or change in, another entity." H. Fairchild, *Dictionary of Sociology* (New York, 1964). Also, the term "Black" will be used in this paper to refer to Africans, Indians, and Colored people.

[3]R. Horwitz, *The Political Economy of South Africa* (London, 1967), p. 427.

[4]W. Hutt, *The Economics of the Colour Bar* (London, 1964), p. 180.

conventional position slow evolutionary changes, under the pressure of economic growth and the requirements of an industrial society, are gradually undermining apartheid and racial discrimination. The proponents of this viewpoint would consider, for instance, the abolition of several so-called petty apartheid laws as a significant alteration indicative of an evolutionary movement toward the abolition of the racial bases of inequality. The second, or revisionist, position views South African society as a "labor repressive" one in which the lines of economic exploitation largely coincide with the color line between Blacks and Whites.[5] The majority of the changes in patterns of group interaction that have occurred are thus viewed as being part of an effort to modernize and rationalize the basis of economic exploitation to preserve the dominant position of Whites. Economic growth is therefore viewed as inevitably bringing changes in both the practice and ideology of apartheid, but these changes are seen as being implemented to strengthen the structural bases of existing inequalities.

The analysis and argument that follows is based on a rejection of the "conventional" viewpoint. Instead the hypothesis is advanced that the major changes in patterns of intergroup contact constitute attempts by the state to legitimize itself, to rationalize the system of domination, to formalize behavior, and to police it in situations of interethnic contact.

However no assumption is made that the system in which group contacts are embedded is a monolithic entity, infinitely capable of rationally neutralizing internal pressures for change. South African society must be seen as being both static and dynamic, and the contradictions between these two features raise the possibility that the pragmatic changes, made in the effort to preserve White domination, themselves could generate forces contributing to the ending of such domination. In other words, while attempts are being made to "modernize racial domination" and to entrench existing patterns of political and economic inequality, these very attempts have unintended consequences that may contribute toward undermining racial domination.

For instance, an unwritten "iron law" that no Black should be placed in a position of authority over a White conditions all contact across the castelike lines dividing South African society. The very few exceptions to this law, occurring mainly in churches, in voluntary organizations, in isolated businesses, serve only to emphasize its widespread appli-

[5]S. Trapido, "South Africa in a Comparative Study of Industrialization," *Journal of Development Studies,* 7, 3 (April 1971). Also on the "revisionist" perspective, *see* F. Johnstone, "White Supremacy and White Prosperity in South Africa," *African Affairs,* 275 (April 1970), and A. Asheron, "Race and Politics in South Africa," *New Left Review,* 53 (January 1969).

cation. However, as this law has been taken out of the context of crude *baasskap* and transferred to the institutions and organizations of the apartheid state, the basis of the attempted legitimization of it, as well as the basis on which it is implemented, has had to be changed. The ideology of domination now stresses ethnic identity rather than White domination, and a series of ethnically exclusive institutions has been created to replace many common institutions led by Whites. These very changes though pose new problems: for the focus on ethnic identity has helped stimulate a racial awareness and a Black consciousness movement, while racially exclusive bodies (e.g., Bantu-stans' assemblies, Representative Councils, the SASO) have come to provide platforms for some Black political leaders and for involving considerable numbers of Blacks in organized political activity. Conse-quently, modernizing the iron law of intergroup contact to ensure that Blacks and Whites remain contiguous but remote could help generate new challenges to it.

This leads to the hypothesis that where once segregation was solely a technique of domination, it has called forth a countervailing separation that is now being used as one strategy for liberation. Thus while the government has forced political and social activity, as far as possible, into officially sanctioned channels and imposed its form of segregation across a wide spectrum of organizational life, this segre-gation has developed some momentum of its own that cannot necessarily be controlled by Whites. In short, government policies are being exploited to provide a channel of political confrontation between Blacks and Whites and to create some sense of group soli-darity among Blacks, which is an essential precondition for any effective challenge to the power structure.

While the changes introduced to modernize White domination may have unintended consequences, it is doubtful whether without mass Black political action such consequences do more than facilitate limited challenges to the power structure. What above all needs to be emphasized, as Adam has done so effectively, is the pragmatic nature of White rule and the flexibility of the regime in its efforts to control change.[6]

This can be seen specifically in the area of interracial contact, where to maintain itself the system has introduced controlled changes to ensure that Black-White contact remains within "permissible" bound-aries. The government pragmatically has set about formalizing inter-racial behavior, through creating an extensive system of punishments and rewards to control the degree and type of contact between Blacks and Whites. However it has also allowed a series of pragmatic adjust-

[6]H. Adam, *Modernizing Racial Domination* (Berkeley, 1971).

ments to be made to existing laws by permitting, to use Sachs' word, those laws that are "symbolical" of White domination and serve no real purpose in maintaining White control, to decline in significance (*see* p.248). The formalization of interracial behavior and the adjustments being made to the petty apartheid laws have helped produce at present a surface calm in race relations, but the basic issues of potential conflict have not been altered. It may even be, as both Adam and Sachs have tentatively suggested, that the White oligarchy is capable of continuing changes to the point where they deracialize society in favor of producing a class stratification system, if this would help entrench their supremacy. However even such a deracialization would not in itself constitute a radical change.

Meanwhile can the polarization between the rulers and the ruled, for which there is growing empirical evidence, destroy White domination of South African society?

As it is difficult to consider these hypotheses and processes over the whole spectrum of interethnic contact and to impose some order on this problem, it appears best to investigate first interaction in the broad political arena, secondly interaction at the organizational and institutional level, and finally interaction at the personal or individual level.

THE POLITICAL FRAMEWORK OF BLACK-WHITE INTERACTION

The fundamental feature of South African society is the domination of Whites over Blacks. In maintaining this domination clear distinctions have been drawn, by the privileged White minority, between themselves and the African, Colored, and Indian populations. The imposition of these distinctions, dividing the population, forms one of the major techniques by which White domination is perpetuated.

Despite these distinctions the major groups in the population remain interdependent, occupy a common society, and operate within common economic and political structures. The more industrialization has drawn ethnic groups in South Africa together—geographically, economically, culturally—the more White rulers have attempted to impose their distinctions between ethnic groups and maintain a social distance between them. The growth of industrialization has been closely associated with the growth of segregatory and discriminatory legislation for the machinery of apartheid is precisely the machinery by which the forces of integration that are stimulated by industrialization and urbanization are attempted to be controlled and even reversed to maintain racial domination.

The White oligarchy in drawing clear distinctions between Blacks and Whites has erected a castelike line, formally built around a battery of legislation, to control the degree and type of interracial contact. Informally the line is both policed and maintained, or where "missing" it is filled in by the forces of customary segregation. Thus while no law imposes segregation in shops, in most jobs, and in many public facilities, custom creates a climate in which *de facto* segregation is imposed to prevent egalitarian contact.[7]

Nevertheless interracial contact probably increases daily. The expanding economy, in which Blacks and Whites work in close physical proximity with one another and the growing urbanization of all groups in the population are among the many factors forcing Blacks and Whites into situations of contact. Indeed, it is ironical that the machinery of the apartheid state itself helps cause integration. For to carry out the policy of segregation a web of government departments with officials who are mainly White are placed in ever-increasing contact with the Black population.

Obviously the type and degree of contact across castelike lines is largely conditioned by the framework of the political economy. Here the Whites' near monopoly of economic and political power enables them to institutionalize in a politico-legal framework their definition of the situation and to dictate the parameters of contact that are acceptable to them. These parameters however have had to be changed to accord with altering economic and political realities (e.g., the growing need for more skilled labor or the need to seek international legitimacy for White rule), and consequently far from contact situations being rigidly frozen by prescribed rules into set patterns, they are inherently flexible and capable of those changes that do not threaten White rule. Thus in the formal realm of political interaction the policy of separate development is continuously involved in the delicate balancing act of trying, on the one hand, to ensure that society remains broadly unified in an economic and political sense while attempting, on the other hand, to ensure that the significant groups remain culturally and socially differentiated from one another.

Ideologically, the primary stated objective of the policy is to assist Black groups "to develop along their own lines, in their own areas, to independent nationhood." This clearly implies that the White government views itself as a colonial power whose aim is to grant self-determination and independence to the colonies within South Africa,[8] a fact that has drawn unwelcome attention from the United

[7]Section 31 of the Shops and Offices Act merely empowers the state president to make regulations concerning such facilities, but no regulations for elevators have been made and few regulations for toilets in office buildings have been made.

[8]J. Dugard, "The United Nations, Decolonization, and International Terrorism," mimeographed (University of Cape Town, 1973).

Nations Committee on Decolonization to government policies. As the Indian and Colored populations have no territorial base outside of White areas, it is widely presumed that the government's ultimate intention for them is that they should remain in White areas, politically under the White Parliament, but with some limited powers of political decision-making.

Contrary to the expectations of many, there appears to be a grudging acceptance by Africans of government-created political institutions, particularly among those domiciled in the homelands. This can be deduced, for example, from the increased support in successive elections for Chief Kaiser Matanzima, or from Chief Gatsha Buthelezi's decision to accept the leadership of KwaZulu. However, caution must be exercised in interpreting the nature of this support. Mantanzima's support, for example, is drawn both from a small traditional elite who have a vested interest in the continuance of the system and from an electorate whose support for him has increased as he has more vigorously articulated African demands for more land and greater political and economic power. While Buthelezi, who opinion polls among Africans, even among urban Africans, indicate is the most popular Black leader, has made it clear that he does not subscribe to the policy of separate development and that he is only involved with it because he sees no other way open for meaningful political activity within the existing society.[9]

The application of the Bantustan policy appears to be obtaining its chief support among Blacks to the extent that it clarifies some of the major issues in contemporary South Africa and offers a platform from which to attack apartheid. The platform, although an extremely circumscribed one, has been exploited by Bantustan leaders to come openly into political conflict with the central government. The dynamics of contact and conflict between the government and Bantustan leaders have several major consequences for Black political activity.

First, the conflict has propelled homeland leaders into taking more radical political positions vis-à-vis the government. Thus, while initially Matanzima was reluctant to criticize the government and White domination, he now openly attacks both. Similarly, other Bantustan leaders have launched attacks on government policy, apartheid, the educational system, economic inequalities, and discrimination in the economy among other items. In short, political interaction with the White government appears to have made the transparency of the connection between White political power and Black subjugation

[9]G. Buthelezi, "Kwa Zulu Development," in S. Biko, ed., *Black Viewpoint* (Durban, 1972), pp. 49-56.

clearer to Black leaders, with inevitable politicizing and even radicalizing consequences.

Second, government interaction with Bantustan leaders has unified these leaders on critical issues, so that they now believe that group solidarity is an essential precondition for any resistance to White policies and pressures. Thus, in November 1973 six Bantustan leaders met in Umtata to frame a program of minimum "demands" that they would make of the government and to lay the foundation for creating "one Black nation, not weak tribal groupings divided along ethnic lines." This meeting resulted in formal talks being held with the prime minister in March 1974. In this way, Black solidarity is challenging the old colonial strategy of divide and rule, which was a major motivation behind Bantustan policy.

Third, the experience of Black homeland leaders has led them to raise in the public arena issues that Whites do not want to discuss. These issues fundamentally concern questions of the reallocation of resources and of the forms of Black-White political contact. In short, the homelands are providing a base for Black leaders to launch a struggle for at least partial reentry into the sphere of "White" and national politics and to inject into national discussions the ideas of redistribution of resources and of a sharing of political power in some form of a common society.[10] Such issues, ironically, are precisely the ones the government wished to keep off the political agenda by its Bantustan policy.

Fourth, political interaction between Black and White leaders in regard to the Bantustans has stimulated the growth of political awareness among the Black population living outside these homelands and helped foster some few organizational links between Bantustan bodies and other Black organizations. Of particular significance is the intervention of the KwaZulu government in recent labor disputes in Natal, which has established legitimate association between Black political leaders and Black workers. Thus, political segregation along ethnic lines is acting as a "collective bond" heightening consciousness of identity and, by so doing, stimulating the growth of other Black organizations.

While these are the unintended consequences of the government's Bantustan policy, there are also many intended consequences that work toward retarding significant political change. For instance, the fostering of tribal institutions serves to retard the growth of modern political values; the overall divide-and-rule strategy creates divisions in the ranks of homeland leaders; the unfulfilled promises contained in the Bantustan program may well foster a mood of increasing

[10]For a summary of the bargaining on one such issue, see Rand Daily Mail, 28 February 1974.

political powerlessness and apathy among the Black population; and, the growing number of Blacks with some vested interest in the system helps to stabilize government institutions.

In regard to the other formal political machinery institutionalizing Black-White political contact (e.g., the Colored Representative Council, the South African Indian Council, and the Urban Bantu Councils), the tight control that is exerted over these bodies by White officials has prevented them from developing as independent a political momentum as homeland bodies. The former remain to a much greater extent puppet organizations that do not have the broad support of the population they are meant to serve. Indeed, it would appear that the government's policy toward them relies far more heavily on coercion and control than it does on erecting a negotiating machinery through which it attempts to legitimate its rule and institutionalize political conflict.

While government-created bodies have weakly and partly filled the gap caused by the crushing of mass African and Indian political movements, Black political organizational activity nevertheless still occurs outside these channels. A significant feature of such Black activity is that it is founded on a new strategy—a "separatist" one, aimed essentially at the creation of a Black institutional network to counter White domination and to foster Black organizational development across those ethnic and tribal divisions that apartheid seeks to perpetuate. Thus, such organizations as the Black Peoples Convention, the Black Community Programs and the SASO have emerged vehemently to oppose the "Buthelezi Strategy" and to stimulate the growth of Black political consciousness. The response of the government to these organizations has been systematically to harass or destroy them, banning their leadership and members, and by so doing forcibly to demonstrate its strategy of containing all Black-White political interaction in the channels it has created and hopes to control.

Achievement of Black solidarity has not only been thwarted by government efforts but also by the tensions that exist among African, Colored, and Indian groups, tensions that are stimulated by the fact that the system tends to favor Coloreds and Indians relative to Africans. The very fact that many members of the Colored and Indian communities see themselves as occupying an upper subordinate stratum and as having greater occupational mobility and security and a firm status in the urban areas, has meant that they are reluctant to risk losing their "higher" status through too energetic attempts to improve it.[11] This is particularly so when there remains open the

---

[11] For a perceptive analysis of this process, see H. Dickie-Clarke, *The Marginal Situation: A Sociological Study of a Coloured Group* (London, 1966).

possibility that Whites, to maintain themselves in power, may permit or seek integration with Coloreds and Indians to create a common alliance against Africans.[12]

The calls for Black solidarity thus have not been mirrored by any significant increase of formal political interaction between Africans, Coloreds, or Indians. Clearly within each upper subordinate community a process is occurring that divides the community, with some members desiring peaceful cooperation with the government to obtain concessions and others rejecting this approach and aligning themselves with the forces of Black solidarity. However, symbolic interaction between Black political leaders at the top has certainly increased, but the nature of the society with its pyramidal arrangement of subordinate strata discourages the emergence of that active unity among Blacks that would potentially threaten White hegemony.

The flexibility of White domination in the realm of political interaction with Blacks, a flexibility demonstrated in the creation of new political subsystems and in the responses to challenges from them, demonstrates the pragmatic nature of White rule. The rulers, by creating political subsystems, have attempted to institutionalize political conflict and, if necessary, it would appear that they would be prepared to absorb the Colored and Indian communities into the White community, if such a pragmatic move would preserve their domination. Thus, on the one hand, there is intransigence by Whites to those Black political activities that attempt to unify the Black community and that occur outside government-created political channels, while, on the other hand, there are some accommodations to Black political demands and aspirations that represent no real threat to White domination. Essentially, however, these pragmatic adjustments are in themselves marginal changes that, although significant, do not represent a weakening of the power structure of White supremacy.

PATTERNS OF INSTITUTIONAL
AND ORGANIZATIONAL INTERACTION

Social institutions, and the organizational life surrounding them, are the building blocks of any society, patterning human conduct into forms deemed desirable by society. The maintenance of these patterns of conduct relies not merely on coercion, but also on the processes of voluntary compliance, socialization, and ideological control.

The first, axiomatic point to be made is that the patterns of group interaction in social institutions are profoundly affected by the political system in which the institutions are embedded. In South African society the major institutions experience a state of tension between the

[12]*See* M. Whisson, "Organizations Available for Change," P. Randall, ed., *Towards Social Change* (Johannesburg, 1971), p. 94.

need to coordinate and provide an integrative setting for the activities of individuals and the need to preserve and even reinforce the cultural diversity and social segmentation on which society rests.[13] Thus the various groups in the population meet in the economy where they have been welded into economic interdependence and cooperation, yet the economy, through its power structure and distribution of rewards, functions to preserve the larger pattern of power distribution and to reinforce the social cleavages of the society. Similarly, educational institutions are torn between the need to teach individuals the knowledge and common skills required in the society and the need to reinforce the cultural and social cleavages of the society. These tensions in institutional life help to explain the basic patterns of social inequality.

In view of the basic inequalities of South African society, the process of group interaction raises certain common problems within institutional life. The first the the question of the extent to which Blacks should be either included in or excluded from the organizational life of institutions. Within the political system the protagonists of separate development claim to have an answer to this problem. However, the very implementation of the policy creates new problems of interaction, requiring the establishment of new mechanisms to meet them. A further example of this problem is provided in the economic system. Here the intention has been to contain the problem of Black participation in the economy by denying Blacks direct access to bargaining situations, offering as a substitute the system of works and liaison committees.

The second problem that institutions face regarding group interaction arises from their relationship with the central government. Simply expressed, the problem concerns the degree to which prevailing apartheid patterns should be imposed on those institutions that are not close to the center of political power. While the segregationist strategy is to generalize apartheid measures across the whole system of institutions, this strategy is not easily applied to some forms of religious, cultural, educational, and economic organizations. The predicament for the government is how to deal with the organizations, such as the National Union of South African Students (NUSAS), that have insisted on holding non-racial conferences, those professional societies that remain integrated, and those churches and ecumenical bodies that engage in multiracial activity. Conversely, the problem for many organizations is how to respond to the demands and constraints of separate development. The Trade Union Council of South Africa

[13]This argument is made in regard to education by H. Dickie-Clarke, "The Dilemma of Education in Plural Societies," in H. Adam, ed., *South Africa: Sociological Perspectives* (Johannesburg, 1971).

(TUCSA) must decide whether to be representative of all workers or representative of only White workers; and employers must decide the degree of rigidity with which segregationist practices should be imposed in the work place.

The third major problem that has to be confronted involves, for the participants in the institutional setting, a decision as to the degree and type of contact that they should establish across ethnic lines, while for those in society in general, a determination of what should be the permissible bounds of interracial association.

The problem of interracial contact is well illustrated in the sphere of work. Socially Blacks and Whites scarcely meet, but at work they are forced into situations in which they have to communicate, collaborate, and engage in joint activities. This raises immediate problems for the individuals involved. Hahlo, in one of the few studies of Black-White interaction in the work place, argues that interaction across the color line confronts workers with the problem of whether to be friendly, impersonal, or antagonistic in their daily relationships.[14] At the lower occupational levels the problem was partly resolved by developing a master-servant relationship into a paternalistic joking relationship, whereas at the higher occupational levels a "sponsor-client" relationship developed that was based on a privileged friendship involving mutual rights and responsibilities that cut across social boundaries. Significantly, Hahlo reports that Blacks who entered into sponsor relationships were often beaten up by fellow Blacks, while the White "sponsors" were regarded by fellow Whites as sell-outs. In short, social pressures operate against establishing any relationship at work that is viewed as an anomaly within the societal setting.

It is in the economy that initial responses to these three problems are made and that many basic patterns of interracial contact are most clearly seen. It is also in the economy that many of these patterns are first formulated in response to changing political and economic circumstances. This can be seen at present in regard to the growing skilled labor shortage.

To counteract the already critical shortage of skilled and semiskilled labor the occupational bar has been allowed to move upward at an accelerating pace. The movement of the color bar is no new factor, for Blacks continually have filtered through to semiskilled and even some skilled positions, but at present a far more pragmatic attitude toward its movement has been adopted by both the government and White unions. What is not generally recognized is that the maintenance and movement of the color bar are not essentially due to any legislative changes. For despite the battery of labor legislation safeguarding

[14]K. Hahlo, "A European-African Worker Relationship in South Africa," *Race,* 2, 2 (July 1969): 13-34.

White jobs from Black competition, the major force positioning and upholding the color bar has been White customary segregation. White unions and employers fear that either White workers or the government will act against them if they allow Black job mobility. Legislatively there exist at present only twenty-seven job reservation determinations, of which ten have been officially suspended, and over 1,000 exemptions to the remaining seventeen have been granted by the minister of labor.[15] Job reservation covers only some 3 percent of White jobs and it is widely flouted: for instance, a snap inspection in 1972 of 2,501 building sites in Johannesburg revealed that there were job reservation contraventions in 63 percent of them.

The framework in which Black occupational mobility occurs ensures that it does not overtly challenge the status of Whites. The three guiding principles of Black mobility are that it can occur only if it does not create job insecurity for Whites, if it does not result in a Black being placed in a position of authority over a White, and if it does not threaten the status of White workers. Five processes to handle this mobility under these principles have emerged:

(a) White workers are given occupational mobility and higher pay before Black workers fill their positions at lower pay.
(b) Whites are moved into supervisory or inspectional positions while their previous jobs are fragmented and usually retitled, before being made available to Blacks at lower pay.
(c) White workers who resign from jobs are not replaced and their positions are later surreptitiously filled by Blacks (this occurs particularly in areas of the service sector of the economy not covered by Union or Industrial Council agreements).
(d) State employment is offered to White workers who are unable to improve their position and who fear loss of status or employment if Black mobility were to occur; thus many Whites who would resist such mobility are "removed" into the semipublic or public sectors of the economy.
(e) An avenue of mobility has been opened in the homelands and "border areas" for Black workers and political ideology is used to justify Black occupational advance in these geographical areas.

These processes help to ensure, in the words of the prime minister, that as long as Black mobility occurs in "an orderly fashion and with the concurrence of [White] Trade Unions"[16] the government will not oppose it. In this way the gap between White and Black labor is maintained and the status of the White worker is safeguarded. Despite claims to the contrary it is how to preserve the status of the White

[15]Personal communication from Robert Kraft, Research Officer, TUCSA.
[16]*Financial Mail* (Johannesburg), 26 October 1973.

worker and not how to prevent his physical contact with Black workers that is a major force retarding Black upward mobility.

In one sense the raising of the color bar is an important change in that it improves the job security of certain Black workers (as Adam points out (p. 322), semiskilled workers are not as easy to dismiss as migrants who can be easily replaced), raising their standard of living and increasing their potential bargaining power. However, the economic pyramid still has an exclusively White top and a Black base, and the movement of the color bar neither has affected substantially (if at all) the income gap, nor has it affected the overall distribution of decision-making power between Blacks and Whites.

One of the major changes in the economy has been the growing use of *de facto* strikes by African workers. In many cases these strikes have achieved certain limited objectives, thereby demonstrating the potential power of Black labor to effect demands. This has inevitably raised White fears that labor organization and action amongst Blacks will lead to an "involvement in politics." As Kane-Berman has pointed out this fear rests

> on a false distinction between politics and economic or labour relations issues. The weak bargaining power of the African proletariat, its lack of trade union rights, its low wages, and its poverty are direct results of the fact that it has no vote. Poverty is but one aspect of a more complex picture, which includes migratory labor, pass laws and high unemployment. All these issues which some people might regard as political rather than economic contribute to low wages and will be seen in that light sooner or later. Denied the vote and therefore normal political channels, Africans are likely to voice demands concerning these issues through trade unions.[17]

While we have seen that Whites adopt pragmatic responses to those pressures that do not threaten the fundamentals of their domination, it remains to be seen whether trade union organizations for Africans represent one of these areas. Pragmatic responses are, however, clearly adopted in most areas of institutional life in relation to those practices that contribute little to the maintenance of the existing system of political control.

Sachs (p. 248) has argued that it is precisely those laws that are symbolic of White domination, laws dealing with segregation of public amenities, job classification, and interracial sexual contact, that are seen as being "petty" and allowed to decline in significance; while laws that are instrumental in perpetuating White control will be maintained and rigorously enforced. Similarly, van den Berghe sees the "micro-

---

[17]J. Kane-Berman, "African Workers Are On Their Own," *Race Relations News* (Johannesburg), May 1974, p. 4.

segregation" of public amenities and facilities as being a luxury aspect of apartheid, functioning mainly to provide emotional gratification to Whites and to symbolize to them the racial hierarchy. Consequently such segregation can be abolished without threatening White rule, or meso- and macro-apartheid that is concerned with geographical and political separation.[18]

The willingness of the rulers to scrap or not to enforce those laws that contribute little to the maintenance of their continued domination can be argued to indicate that they are shedding a commitment to segregation in favor of increasing their commitment to controlled change. Thus those laws that are seen as being "the ugly side" of separate development, as giving rise to grievances that exacerbate daily contacts between Blacks and Whites and as stimulating some avoidable hostility toward Whites, are no longer being rigidly enforced (or not enforced at all) as the attempt is made by Whites to demonstrate to a skeptical outside world that they practice "enlightened coexistence" with Blacks.

Exactly what segregatory practices will be dropped by Whites will probably depend on the ideological lag between the electorate (many of whom still believe in old-style segregation) and the government, which is attempting to implement apartheid pragmatically.

All these influences ramify through the voluntary organizational structure of the society (churches, welfare organizations, educational groups, recreational bodies) at a much more individual level as well as operate through the formal institutions of government. Thus the total institutional and organizational structure acts as a filter to bring the patterns of interaction and conflict in the overall society down to a personal level.

CONTACT AT THE PERSONAL LEVEL

Central to the ideology of apartheid lies the hypothesis that contact between people of different racial and ethnic origins generates friction, which ultimately is followed by overt conflict and the growth of racial antipathies. This hypothesis has found expression continuously in White South African political and social life and has been used extensively in justifying segregation at both the national and local level as well as at the level of personal relationships.

The few academic studies in South Africa concerned with Black-White interaction at the personal level do not lend much support to the "contact-friction" hypothesis. Van den Berghe, for instance, found in an attitudinal study that people who claim to have had much contact with Africans are less anti-African than those who claim to have had

[18]P. van den Berghe, "Racial Segregation in South Africa: Degrees and Kinds," H. Adam, ed., *South Africa*, pp. 37-49.

less contact.[19] No evidence though is given by van den Berghe to prove that his subjects had the contact with Africans that they claim to have had, or that their favorable attitudes found expression in overt behavior. More important in this regard are the limited number of studies of actual behavior at points of contact, such as those carried out by Russell and by Watson. These studies also do not suggest that there is any inevitability of contact leading to friction.

Russell studied a residential area in Durban where, before the application of the Group Areas Act, Colored, Indian, and White citizens held freehold property and lived side by side.[20] Russell's findings are particularly interesting in that they show that despite all the pressures of the wider community to keep friendly relations to a minimum contact led to interaction and interaction led to friendly relationships being established between Blacks and Whites. However, any spiralling of this sequence, in terms of breaking down prejudice or developing embryonic community organizations was inhibited by constant reinforcement of the strict norms for segregation in the community. Consequently, there was a carry-over into the neighborhood of White superiority, which revealed itself in an arrogance on the part of Whites that they could make demands and that their demands would be met. In this way the relationships reflected the wider pattern of race relations, in which the Black is the server, the helper, the loser, while the White gains from the relationship and is politically powerful enough to dictate its course. Watson also found, in an area of Cape Town that had both Colored and White residents, that contrary to apartheid dogmas relations between residents were generally cordial.[21] However, here too the general structure and prejudices of White society were reflected in these relationships.

These and other findings suggest that the conventional White view of ruthless struggle at points of contact is not accurate. This is particularly significant in view of the fact that the Whites studied by Russell and by Watson, on the whole, were either poorer, or older, or of lower status than most other Whites and thus belonged to groups that could be expected to be highly prejudiced and not well disposed to establishing any relationship with Blacks outside the dominant master-servant one.

In situations of contact then it is the conditions under which contact occurs that are crucial in determining its outcome. Simple contact in

[19]P. van den Berghe, "Race Attitudes in Durban, South Africa," *Journal of Social Psychology*, 57 (1962): 55-72.

[20]M. Russell, *A Study of a South African Interracial Neighbourhood*. Monograph no. 3, Institute for Social Research (Durban, 1961).

[21]G. Watson, *Passing for White: A Study of Racial Assimilation in a South African School* (London, 1970).

itself does not lessen prejudice or intergroup hostility; indeed, at times it may exacerbate it by raising the level of awareness of heterogeneity and thereby producing "perceptual points for alarm." Allport points out that it is only when two groups that are in contact possess equal status in the situation, seek common goals, are cooperatively dependent on each other, and interact with the positive support of authorities, laws, and customs that it is likely that they will share values and beliefs and develop harmonious relations.[22] However, even then the acceptance generated by contact is typically limited to the particular situation that created it. In short, the simple contact-friction hypothesis cannot easily be accepted.

The structure of the wider society in South Africa ensures that there are strong boundary-maintaining mechanisms between groups that make it difficult for most, if not all, of these preconditions for successful contact to exist. When Blacks and Whites have contact the great imbalance of power and differential access to political and economic resources of the parties immediately underpins whatever relationship exists, while laws and community norms set a framework for the relationship itself that emphasizes whatever differences exist between the individuals involved. From the start contact between Blacks and Whites is predisposed to a variety of severe structural strains that serve to maintain the political and social identity of those engaged in contact at the individual level and thereby help to stabilize the sociopolitical order.

Thus in general, Blacks and Whites are contiguous yet utterly remote. The bulk of their contact occurs within a framework of a master-servant relationship that is at times either mitigated by an element of paternalism or harshened by capricious racist conduct of Whites. Despite this a note of cautious optimism can be introduced. The work of Russell, Watson, and Hahlo leads us to infer that with the removal of existing racist programs, individuals would be likely to develop a consciousness of class, rather than of color. If correct, this could mean that were a nonsegregationist state to be established, many individuals would be quick to recognize and act upon the interests that unite them.

However, the system of segregation has been entrenched, and White political attention has become focused on the two immediate problems of how to maintain it and how to forestall any significant changes in it. Characteristically, this has immediately involved the attempt to legitimate the structure of the society in the eyes of its members, so that they embrace the White conception of what is regarded as appropriate behavior vis-à-vis one another and do not attempt to alter this conception.

[22]G. Allport, *The Nature of Prejudice* (New York, 1954), ch. 16.

Specifically this has involved, and continues to involve, a process of formalization of behavior. In this, the law is being used at an increasing pace as an instrument of domination to promote an extensive system of punishments and rewards that reinforce the social order that governs the framework of interpersonal relations. An analysis of statutes has shown that since 1909 some 200 laws have been passed that seek to regulate relations between the races or that are applicable to the behavior of specific racial groups.[23] The number of these laws has progressively multiplied as crude *baasskap* has declined. In the pre-Nationalist period of 1908 to 1948, 49 such laws had been passed; then in the period from 1948 to 1960, 53 such laws were passed; and in the period of 1961 to 1971, 98 such laws have been passed. This legislative attempt to formalize behavior, as Kuper has argued, has extended the number of situations in which racial classifications form a mandatory guide to conduct and has led to such classifications increasingly being woven into the perceptions of individuals so that they are led to apply social definitions to a widening range of situations.[24]

The consequences of this are difficult to determine. In one sense, race relations, in Adam's words, "appear to have assumed the form of a relatively smoothly functioning, correct business relationship despite increased institutionalized separation."[25] Opinion surveys have reported recently that Blacks have experienced an improvement in their relationship with Whites. Thus a survey in 1973 in Soweto concluded, "The feeling is that more communication is taking place, that the White man is more approachable than before. General courtesy and manners have improved and slowly discrimination is becoming less."[26] However, the same survey reports that only one-third of those interviewed believed race relations to be improving, while one-quarter thought they were deteriorating, and the remainder saw no real change either way. It would appear that the formalization of race relations has introduced some surface changes in their daily manifestations that are often appreciated by Blacks, while the roots of Black discontent with their position remains unchanged. This in itself was illustrated in the survey cited. While it was being conducted, the shooting of eleven Black miners in Carletonville took place. In one day the proportion of those who thought race relations were improving dropped from 33 to 23 percent, while those who thought they were deteriorating increased from 23 to 33 percent. It could be concluded from this that any feelings on the part of Blacks of improvements in race relations occurring are

[23]Quoted in P. Randall, ed., *Towards Social Change*, p. 29.
[24]L. Kuper, "The Heightening of Racial Tension," *Race*, 2, 1 (November, 1960).
[25]Adam, *Modernizing Racial Domination*, p. 81.
[26]Report of Quadrand International Survey in Soweto in *Sunday Times* (Johannesburg), 6 January 1974.

fragilely superimposed upon the political and economic realities of their daily lives.

If increased formalization of situations in which interethnic contact occurs has produced a superficial improvement in race relations, it appears that it has done so by removing most elements of ambiguity from situations of personal contact, through providing individuals with a clear definition of their role and of prescribed behavior. In this way the likelihood of Blacks experiencing capricious treatment at the hands of Whites is lessened and consequently race relations are seen as being "improved." It is impossible to know whether this process is at work but it appears that it may well be. The impact that the state has on such agencies of socialization as schools and the mass media enables it to influence considerably the political socialization of individuals and to imbue them with an official definition of their identity and group membership. Such a definition carries with it clear implications for how individuals should behave in interethnic contact and what behavior they should expect from others. It may, therefore, lower the expectations of many Blacks of what is considered appropriate behavior from Whites and condition them to the behavior that is experienced. Furthermore, the interaction of legislation and socialization work toward ensuring that alternative patterns of race relations are not presented and only limited types of political information are available to Blacks. This may well inculcate feelings of inevitability about existing patterns of interethnic contact and, even at times, of identification with such patterns among sections of the Black population. It can be argued that these and other factors combine to help rigidify and stabilize situations of interethnic contact and, in this way, to "improve" race relations by giving them a surface calm.

Recently associated with the formal regulation of contact between ethnic groups has been a segregationist attack on many potential growth points for personal contact between members of different groups and interracial cultural cooperation. The segregationist attack, in its long march through the major institutions of the society, has only recently devoted considerable attention to the regulation of individual points of interracial cultural cooperation. Thus, where active cooperation was until recently easily possible between Blacks and Whites in such fields as social work, art, and drama, now most voluntary organizations have been compelled to segregate their activities and committees on ethnic lines. Social work agencies, for instance, are no longer registered by the state or allowed to appeal to the public for money unless they impose segregation upon themselves. Similarly, many individuals who have attempted to establish personal contacts with Blacks outside the framework set by community norms have experienced harassment from government agents and fellow Whites, having had their cars burned or their lives threatened on the telephone, or being officially punished in some way. Such developments serve to weaken any impulse to engage in contact outside officially sanctioned channels.

While helping to stabilize the existing system, the formalization of patterns of interethnic contact has also introduced new conflicts among Whites about how far to carry this formalization and how best to legitimize it in the eyes of the Blacks. These conflicts are particularly manifested in the debate over so-called petty apartheid. In 1961 Verwoerd stated that "When separation had been carried far enough, discrimination must be eliminated." The distinction between these two concepts has been used, particularly by Afrikaner intellectuals, to question the necessity of continuing practices "which are no longer necessary in the bigger framework of separate development" and "which endanger human relationships" and "the whole scheme of things to come."[27] Thus, recently, such cities as Johannesburg, Pietermaritzburg, and Pretoria have taken steps to remove some forms of customary segregation in public amenities under their supervision or control (in terms of the Separate Amenities Act of 1953). These acts have brought warnings from the prime minister that the process should not be carried too far, and have also reopened the intricate debate among Whites on petty apartheid.[28] How Blacks view this debate and any changes in segregationist practice is not known, but it is doubtful whether it basically modifies their position.

An important change related to the debate over petty apartheid is the movement that has occurred in the government's sports policy, mainly as a result of international pressures. The new policy is based on the Nationalist's political conception of South Africa as a "multinational" country, rather than a multiracial one. As applied to sports "multinationalism" permits each "nation" to participate separately in international or "open" sporting events, while continuing to impose apartheid at the local level.[29] Thus it becomes possible for South African "nations" each to play against international teams that themselves could be multiracial. However, in international events South Africa itself never becomes represented as a single nation by one team.

This complex policy, which is aimed at enabling South Africa to continue to take part in international sporting events on an apartheid basis, has opened up a division in Black sporting bodies between those

[27]Quoted by D. Richard, "Petty Apartheid: The Tip of the Iceberg?" in N. Rhoodie, ed., *South African Dialogue* (Johannesburg, 1972) pp. 104-5.

[28]Richard, "Petty Apartheid," pp. 100-10.

[29]An outdated but good survey of the sports policy can be found in J. Kane-Berman, "Multi-nationalism versus Non-racialism," SAIRR mimeographed paper RR 55/72 (Johannesburg, 1972).

who believe a policy of gradualism will eventually bring about integrated sports and those who hold to a policy of nonracialism and thus
noncooperation with the practice of "multinational" sports. Non-racial
sporting bodies continue to act as an irritant to the government, by
rejecting its sport policy and thus by contributing to the maintenance of
international pressure on it. This pressure is of significance, for it is
difficult not to conclude that the government has been forced to make
the limited concessions embodied in "multinationalism" by the threat
of isolation and expulsion of South Africa from certain international
sporting events. In line with this new sports policy the government
continues to take stringent action to prevent multiracial sports being
played at the local and club level, recently instituting action against the
non-racial Aurora cricket team under a new proclamation that appears
to extend the Group Areas Act especially to prevent such sport taking
place.[30]

Two implications of the changes in official sporting policy are
important. First, the changes demonstrate that Whites are prepared to
alter some, but not all, of their patterns of interracial behavior under
pressure when they see it to be in their interests to do so. Second, the
power of lower participants in the society to effect national decision-
making has been demonstrated, and it is likely that their power (reinforced in this instance by international connections) will be used to
wrest further concessions from the government in the sporting arena.
However, the extent to which events in the sporting world will have
more than a "demonstration effect" and will actually stimulate other
Black voluntary organizations to seek international support and adopt
pressure tactics remains to be seen.

Changes in interracial situations that have recently taken place do
not speak to the major grievances of Blacks. Edelstein, for instance, in a
recent survey indicates that these grievances among Africans in
Johannesburg, in order of their importance, were inadequacy of
political rights, influx control, and inadequate and unequal income;
and among Coloreds they were unequal pay for equal work, job
reservation, and inadequate educational opportunities. It is probably
true that the same types and ordering of grievances would be expressed by the Black population at large.[31]

Most of the recent changes sketched out above do not appear to
affect the basic issue in these grievances, the pattern of the distribution
of power and wealth. What the changes have done is to bring about a
surface calm in situations of personal interracial contact, a calm that

[30]M. Horrell, *A Survey of Race Relations in South Africa, 1973* (Johannesburg,
1974), p. 113.
[31]M. Edelstein, "What Do Young Africans Think?" (Ph.D. Diss., Pretoria
University, 1972) reported in *The Star* (Johannesburg), 8 September 1973.

fundamentally rests on the power of the state to formalize behavior and police it. Furthermore, such changes as have occurred demonstrate that the political economy has been receptive to modifications that help stabilize it and adjust it to new economic and geographical patterns. Meanwhile, as Whites make a cautious series of adaptations, there is growing evidence that Blacks, particularly those who are younger and more educated, no longer see personal relationships with Whites as a significant area of concern.

CONCLUSION

The major theme that has emerged from this analysis is the flexibility of White rule in adapting to changing conditions. This flexibility has enabled it to engage in a series of essentially marginal changes that do not affect the basic inequalities in South African society, but that help to "rationalize" the system of domination, so that this domination can be more easily perpetuated and reproduced under conditions of growing industrialization. In the process of engaging in pragmatic changes the rulers have spotlighted those areas of the apparatus of domination they consider to be unchangeable. It has become clear that the government will not allow political dissent or opposition to exist outside the channels that it has created. Consequently, it has engaged in a systematic attempt to force Black and White political action into government channels and to harass and suppress those organizations attempting to bring about change outside this framework. Similarly, it has erected a battery of legislation to formalize the mechanisms governing social and economic interaction between Blacks and Whites so as to preserve the "iron law" that no Black should be placed in a position of authority over a White.

However, the very series of pragmatic concessions that eventually may even extend as far as deracializing the society have not reduced the potential for fundamental political and social conflict between Blacks and Whites. Ironically, many of the pragmatic changes may well have increased the potential for such conflict. Thus, for instance, the creation of political subsystems has given some Black leaders "a taste of power" and has provided a limited organizational rallying point for Black political action. Likewise such changes in the economic sphere as the occupational advancement of Blacks and the de facto recognition of strikes have increased the strategic power of Blacks in the economy. These and other changes have led subordinate group members to experience, or sense, some limited improvement in their condition and to heighten their expectations about the possibility of further improvements. This greater strategic power of Blacks, coupled with their rising expectations, has increased the likelihood of mass Black political action

conflicting with the White power structure over demands for significant change.

Nevertheless, for the present, it would appear that such conflicts can be contained. The powers of the state to fragment the organizational life of the Black population, to police intergroup boundaries, and to impose significant social and political divisions within ethnic groups are important factors helping to maintain existing patterns of intergroup relations. It would appear that increasingly the very machinery of apartheid, which conditions and controls contact across the castelike lines of South African society, is fostering a political consciousness amongst Blacks that separation can be used as a strategy to create an organizational base from which to challenge and to change the structural bases of existing inequalities.

12
Internal Constellations and Potentials for Change

HERIBERT ADAM

A survey of the internal forces that are working to alter or maintain the existing arrangement of power and privilege in South Africa can best begin by distinguishing four means of White control as well as actual or potential Black challenges to them. (1) *Coercive control*, as discussed by Sachs, encompasses the machinery of law enforcement through direct sanctions or threats of sanctions by state agents. Its most severe weapon is the physical destruction or confinement of opponents. While all governments ultimately rely on this deterrent in a crisis, modern states, including South Africa, favor (2) *ideological control* of the subject population as more expedient, feasible, and ethical, since it is based on voluntary collaboration, persuasion, and belief in the legitimacy of state power. Control over the minds and attitudes of people is nowadays mainly achieved through the major public socialization agencies, such as mass media, educational institutions, and churches. At a higher level, both coercive and ideological control can be seen as usually perpetuating but also sometimes undermining the existing arrangements of (3) *political control* with which it is closely interwoven in nondemocratic systems. The differential access of competing interests to the crucial political power centers, the way in which political decision-making has institutionalized participation or exclusion of important interest groups largely determines the legitimacy of domination and hence the degree and nature of conflict or consensus in a society. From a Marxist perspective at least, all three means of control are considered to secure the most salient realm of domination, (4) *economic power*. In this sense, specific economic relations have to be viewed as another means of control as well as its most important end. The sterile debate over how economic forces will affect the political set-up frequently overlooks their common purpose.

All four means of domination are of course interrelated and, therefore, much more should be said about their dialectical relationship and their relative importance in specific historical circumstances. However, they are introduced here merely as analytical tools to isolate trends and explore unique South African phenomena in more detail. They also have to be assessed in the context of external factors, since South Africa has ceased to function as an isolated fortress. But if in the age of multinational corporations and the corresponding internationalization of revolutionary commitments it is still meaningful to distinguish between internal and external forces of change, then domestic developments would clearly seem to have the more decisive bearing on the South African situation. On the scale of historical causes, subtle changes in the local scene weigh far more than the often schematic view of activists in exile is able to detect.

Given the inevitable strictures of space, a review of the chapters by Savage, Sachs, and Moodley will be undertaken within the outlined framework, instead of criticizing each contribution separately. Reference is made to these chapters as well as to other contributions, whenever it seems relevant to the survey of internal forces, operating for and against maintenance of the castelike system.

The three chapters have in fact only a few common threads. Savage reviews theoretically well-known patterns of ethnic interaction and attitudes. Sachs concentrates on the changing instruments of coercion with little or no attention to other methods of control. Moodley, above all interested in paradoxical ethnic exclusivism and reactions to discriminatory legislation, confines her analysis mainly to the relatively privileged and culturally distinctive Indian subgroup. More comparisons with the political activity of the other two subordinate castes, particularly the similarly placed Coloreds, could have clarified the relationship between cultural identity and political opposition under authoritarian conditions. It seems worthwhile to further explore the hypothesis that cultural identity rather than marginality or atomization of individuals is a prerequisite for risk-taking in political resistance.

Sachs, explicitly, Moodley and Savage, more implicitly, seem to agree on one important development: deracialization toward class stratification is taking place, if not *de jure* then *de facto*. As no other trend has more implications for this survey, this proposition will be examined in the light of further empirical evidence, in the discussion of the changing economic control, which concludes this analysis.

COERCIVE CONTROL

Among the many insights that Sachs and other analysts of the coercive South African system of domination have stressed is the salience of an unspectacular legal-bureaucratic machinery for the maintenance of that country's unique order. However, what is seldom questioned (and also unanswered by Sachs) is why "White overlordship is exercised through the law rather than outside it." That South African law enforcement agencies are strong and therefore make terror and illegal violence superfluous is only a partial explanation of a remarkable legalism that sometimes goes so far as to pay compensation to the Black victims of police assaults.[1] No modern authoritarian system has allowed its courts to interpret, mediate, or cancel state coercion so frequently as has South Africa, though this freedom is declining annually with the passage of more sophisticated laws restricting judicial autonomy. Superficial observers often attribute the South African legalism to the British tradition of fair play or contrast the so-called rule of law in a "civilized" society with the "anarchy" of Black Africa. In fact South Africa's legalism, the insistence that proper procedures be followed even where provisions amount to a travesty of generally recognized norms, is almost a necessity in a settler state in which the appearance of legality is essential for the minority's domination. Only by soliciting a certain amount of acquiescence and even loyalty on the part of the subject population, based on the belief in the "rightfulness" of White rule, can the ruling minority hope to function without straining its scarce manpower with permanent police tasks. Therefore, political opposition has to be criminalized rather than merely suppressed. What the doubtful comparison with totalitarian systems elsewhere frequently overlooks is that repression in South Africa is calculable and predictable. As such, it stands in contrast to the kind of arbitrary and "irrational terror" that students of fascism and Stalinism have described as "the most universal characteristic"[2] or "the vital nerve of the totalitarianism system."[3] Although the consequences for the victim of both systems hardly differ, a cogent distinction made by Ahrendt is that "dictatorial terror" of the South African kind—as opposed to "totalitarian terror"—is confined to the authentic opponents of the system.[4]

[1] From 1971 to 1972 compensation payments to all population groups were made in twelve cases of unlawful arrest and thirty-four cases of assault by the police; several cases were settled out of court through *ex-gratia* payments. In 1972, 79 White and 126 Black policemen were convicted of crimes of violence. *See* M. Horrell, *A Survey of Race Relations in South Africa, 1973* (Johannesburg, 1974), pp. 74-5.

[2] Z. Brzezinski, *The Permanent Purge* (Cambridge, Mass., 1956), p. 27.

[3] C. Friedrich and Z. Brzezinski, *Totalitarian Dictatorship and Autocracy* (New York, 1963), p. 132.

[4] H. Ahrendt, *The Origins of Totalitarianism* (New York, 1951).

This makes a decisive difference from the perspective of potential political activists. By strictly abiding by the imposed political restrictions, the Blacks in South Africa, in contrast to the Jews of German-occupied Europe or the even more arbitrary and numerous victims of Stalinism for whom no laws existed at all, can manage to avoid direct state violence. "To stay out of trouble" with the authorities has undoubtedly now become the overriding motivation of Blacks in South Africa, if ever it has been otherwise.

Sachs rightly draws attention to the paradox of the high proportion of persons affected by the array of racial legislation and the relative absence of direct coercion. This emphasis on the most common enforcement of the caste order, however, tends to neglect the specific ways with which the state deals with an important subcategory of victims: those who are not merely recipients of institutionalized force, but who respond to it with active political opposition. A closer analysis of the instruments of coercion used against political activists reveals more about the unique South African system of dominance than enumerating shootings or the strength of the police.

Just as surprising as the fact that the police force "is by no means as large as we might expect in relation to its special role" (*see* Sachs, p. 234) is the relatively small number of political prisoners in the country. As of January 1972, 464 persons (430 Africans, 11 Coloreds, 14 Indians, 9 Whites) were serving jail sentences under the various security laws. Given a population of 18 million Blacks and bearing in mind the thousands of political detainees in other totalitarian regimes, this is hardly a comparable figure. Indeed, "subsidiary aids to detention and imprisonment" (Sachs, p. 238) now function as effective means of controlling active dissent.

The array of the specific controls practiced against political activists indicates the streamlining that the system has undergone, as compared with the practice of the relatively simple and frequent arrests of dissidents. But even if all these provisions are taken into account, the total number of persons directly affected remains comparatively small—not more than 1,000 inside South Africa, including the 171 Blacks and 21 Whites banned as of July 1973. This state of affairs would appear to result not from a growing consensus or lessening frustration among South African subordinates, but from the state's effectiveness in destroying the organizational shelter of political opponents. The state has succeeded in atomizing political activism and thereby in destroying an organizational atmosphere of mutual reinforcement that seems a prerequisite for risk-taking. Political opposition, though as audible as ever, is now reduced to ineffectual acts of individual dissent, which require much more courage to carry out than collective action.

It is worthwhile to explore this in some detail with reference to the material that Moodley has provided. She does not answer the question of why Indians organized and protested against all odds in the past, but fail to do so in a similar vein now when certain structural conditions would seem even more favorable. There is obviously no lack of potential political leaders among this subordinate group, which has a far higher proportion of university-educated professionals than any of the other Black castes.[5] If the sociological concept of status inconsistency has any political implications we would expect it in this group with a wealthy and educated middle class. Among the political activists who were singled out in the sixties for sanctions it is this stratum that is almost solely represented among the banned and jailed, though there were a few workers as well. No theories about traditional conservatism and vested interests of a relatively privileged intelligensia and professional class would fit the South African case.

The prosecutions of the early sixties have had a lasting impact. The state crushed opposing organizations and destroyed some of the most able activists psychologically, even if they could not be broken into collaboration. No sensitive person can stand unaffected by ten years of social excommunication during a banning order, let alone a period of monotonous stone-breaking at Robben Island. But perhaps of more profound consequence for the greater number of potential activists are the intimidating effects of family and social pressure in the absence of the countervailing support of prestigious political organizations. To take on single-handedly a powerful state apparatus almost presupposes a "social insanity." It is the psychological climate, rather than organizational effectiveness, that makes political resistance within the protective framework of mutual support so much easier as compared with the efforts of individuals.

The attitude to avoid potential risks and troubles under any circumstances is also fostered by increasing class stratification within all the

---

[5]The Bureau of Census and Statistics gives the percentage of the total population who had passed standard X (matric) as follows: Whites, 22.8; Coloreds, 0.9; and Indians, 3.3. No figures for Africans are available, but they can be assumed to be much lower. The enrollment figures at South African universities in 1973 break down as follows: Whites, 90,201; Coloreds, 3,105; Asians, 5,017; and Africans, 7,348. Two obvious points need to be stressed here: the Indian group is one-quarter as numerous as the Colored group and one-thirtieth as numerous as the African group. Yet it has twice as many students as the Colored group and almost as many as the African. Second, the differential access to higher educational opportunities between Whites and Blacks is far greater than the economic inequality of different wage scales. In fact, far superior educational opportunities for Whites seem to ensure this group's socio-economic dominance and better life chances even in a future legally non-racial society in which deep psychological and environmental barriers to higher education for competing Blacks will still have to be overcome. For figures on university enrollment see Horrell, *Race Relations, 1973*, p. 332.

ethnic subgroups, as Moodley stresses for the Indians. Worlds separate
the houseowner in Reservoir Hills from the poor Indian in Chatsworth. Not only do different strata within an oppressed ethnic group
increasingly perceive their situation in different terms, but their
interests are objectively different. By allowing for individual economic
advancement, although restricted by the overall caste arrangements,
the system has provided escapes from political frustrations. It has
succeeded in what could be called the "privatization of politics":
political action outside apartheid institutions has become a matter of
individual risk, better to be forgotten in favor of improving a specific
microcosm. Political action can be expected on limited issues by subgroups—teachers, ratepayers, textile workers, or bus passengers—but
hardly any more as total ethnic groups rising for comprehensive
demands of Africans, Indians, or Coloreds.

Regarding future developments in the sphere of coercive control,
there is no evidence that the government will relax its firm grip on all
extraparliamentary dissent and opposition outside apartheid institutions. On the contrary, as the recent reading of the Riotous Assemblies
Act and increased bannings and investigations of antiapartheid organizations indicate, there is likely to be a further tightening of control.
Correspondingly, there is little evidence that any internal opposition
group has found ways to circumvent or undermine the efficiency of
state coercion. Afrikanderdom even feels confident to shed historical
traumas and to give up its arms monopoly in light of an outside threat.[6]
If the Rhodesian and the Portuguese examples are any indication, the
government will take little risk in arming respectively indoctrinated
Black antiguerrilla fighters, but by doing so will greatly strengthen its
military capacity.

The relatively easy success of coercive control would not have been
achieved without corresponding ideological manipulation, political
rearrangements, and economic outlets to which we will turn in the
remainder of this chapter.

IDEOLOGICAL CONTROL

It is frequently maintained that to focus on African attitudes as the
critical factor in revolution is to ignore the lack of opportunities for
revolution and the Africans' material incapacity to wage it. Apart from

[6]Asked whether he thought greater use should be made of Blacks in the
Defense Force, the chief of the army, M. Malan, replied: "Yes, we have our
Coloured Corps; who are doing very well." See Sunday Express (Johannesburg),
8 July 1973. Vaderland (Johannesburg), 11 March 1974 suggests: "We must ask
ourselves in all seriousness whether we should not also begin to make the
homelanders, our allies, better able to defend themselves militarily."

the fact that motivation and capability are inseparable, such an emphasis often leads to unquestioned assumptions, for instance about general "Black combativeness," that have little empirical basis. However, wishful thinking would seem to be the deception to which revolutionary commitment can now least afford to fall victim as has so often happened in the past. Kuper stresses an often neglected point by insisting that "the perceptions of the structure of the society may be at least as significant in the revolutionary process as the 'objective reality' and they may be quite varied in their relationship to that reality."[7] Therefore an analysis of the "ideological struggle" and of empirically discernible attitudes must form an essential part of the investigation of any potential for change. The forces of the *status quo* themselves attest to this by their elaborate measures for indoctrination and restrictions of alternative visions.

Media, educational institutions, and churches are the three most formidable public agencies in shaping perceptions of reality. As far as the press is concerned few changes are discernible, though some Afrikaner papers are now self-critical of formerly sacred practices. While the ever-present threat to muzzle the English language press seems to have been abandoned for the time being, its general line, though still highly critical of the government tactics, adheres to patriotic standards for the national good, as defined by White interests.[8] Though often annoyed by the frank criticism of the English language press, the government finds the free-speech labels so useful for its international image that it now distributes throughout the world free of charge an airmail weekly reprint of the major editorials in the South African press, including the outspoken *Rand Daily Mail*. South Africa seems to be the first authoritarian regime in history which not only feels no need to silence such criticism within the overall framework of "responsible" White standards but displays proudly its "repressive tolerance." An alternative Black press remains a utopia that would have to overcome the dual obstacles of finance and government interference. Censorship still removes from the local market important alternative sources of information in the form of some 13,000 banned books, including almost all African writing with political implications; it cuts or prohibits films, plays, and even poetic dreams. Though the wisdom of this "negative indoctrination" is strongly debated among the affected Whites, it includes for the first time Afrikaans novels as well.

While some optimists expect that television, which is to be introduced in 1976, will mark the breakthrough from South Africa's

[7]L. Kuper, "Theories of Revolution and Race Relations," *Comparative Studies in Society and History,* 13 (1971): 87-107.
[8]For a recent analysis, *see* E. Potter, *The Press as Opposition: The Political Role of South African Newspapers* (London 1974).

cultural isolation, it is much more likely that it will be as firmly in the grip of the Broederbond as the South African Broadcasting Corporation. In fact, by substituting locally produced films for foreign canned programs as much as possible, television can be expected to function as a powerful instrument of indoctrination in the hands of government supporters.

Ideological control of the lower educational institutions is maintained by "Christian Nationalism" for the Whites and "Bantu Education" for the Africans. The complete material dependence of teachers on supervising inspectors ensures overall conformity to rigid disciplinary rules and severe sanctions for violations. So intimidated are many Black teachers by now that they will not even discuss anything related to politics. The only important defeat for Afrikaner educational policy has been the insistence by several Bantustans on the use of English as a medium of instruction instead of what they see as the restricting vernacular that Pretoria wanted to prescribe.

However, a different challenge to the ideological tenets of White domination originated, predictably, at the very centers of higher tribal indoctrination, the five Black universities. In recent years these have been the venues of repeated student unrest, articulating unprecedented assertions of Black nationalism and solidarity, frequently countered by the dismissal of the majority of the student body and the temporary closure of the institutions. Where the sanctions were not quite as severe, as for instance at the Durban Westville College, the campus has been described "as in a state of cold war."[9] Though desired by the rectors as instruments of manipulation, Student Representative Councils are boycotted or do not exist and there are minimal academic rights for students and staff alike. It was mainly these paternalistic restrictions on ordinary freedoms by Afrikaner administrators, not dissatisfaction with the otherwise reasonable facilities and material conditions, that precipitated the frictions.[10] As institutional nerve centers for a humiliated intelligentsia, the Black universities only reflect more clearly the prevalent frustrations of the minority-dominated society at large. Where the frictions became too serious and tended to spread into the surrounding communities, such as at the Colored institution in Bellville in 1973, the government visibly had to step down from a formerly intransigent position. Above all, the demand for community control of the institution was conceded in the form of the appointment of a Colored rector and more Colored faculty

[9]*The Leader* (Durban), 22 February 1974.
[10]For further details, *see* K. Adam, "The Dialectics of Higher Education for the Colonized," in: H. Adam, ed., *South Africa: Sociological Perspectives* (London, 1971), and L. Meyer, *Oppression or Opportunity: Inside the Black Universities in South Africa* (Waltham, Mass., 1973).

members. It is likely that this example will also be followed gradually by the other institutions, although the ratio of White to Black faculty has undergone almost no change since the inception of the separate universities in 1960. A large-scale replacement of the predominantly Afrikaner faculty at the "tribal universities," according to the apartheid ideology, confronts the vested interests of members of this group who frequently moved into academia from lower paid positions in the civil service. Under these pressures by some of its most loyal members, the Afrikaner establishment is unlikely to relinquish more than symbolic control of its own creations in the near future. The Bantu Laws Amendment Act specifically removes university education from the list of matters that can be controlled by the legislative assemblies of the Bantustans. Some homeland leaders had criticized Afrikaner dominance of the institutions and suggested that foreign faculty members should be invited to teach in the so-called homelands. Increased solidarity between students and the Black staff as well as increased friction between White and Black staff, such as publicized at the University of the North, can be expected as long as the tribal universities are under White control. However, it seems unlikely that this line-up will continue once the institutions have a Black rector and a majority Black faculty, who then will come under much more student pressure to renounce their relative privileges and support more radical demands for Black liberation in general. At some of the institutions, particularly the Indian one, many students already express their dissatisfaction with instructors of their own group for being more authoritarian and conformist than some of the White teachers. The *status-quo* indoctrination at all Black universities would certainly not be automatically jeopardized by a future replacement of White faculty and administrators by equally conservative Black educators; in fact the overall system would have much to benefit from this change to self-policing as it did in other areas of nominal Black authority.

To maintain the ideological control of Black higher education as well as the vested interest of its present Afrikaner staff the option of closing down the showpieces of apartheid permanently is not open to the government. In addition, Black students would then have to be readmitted to the traditional liberal-oriented "open universities," since higher education can no longer be denied to the colonized, especially if they are increasingly needed to staff a modern economy and their own administrations. It is interesting to note that Afrikaner universities have for the first time agreed to admit a few Black graduate students under certain conditions, which reiterates that it is not segregation itself, but Afrikaner control through educational segregation that is the real issue.

The Black Consciousness Movement, which has been analyzed in

detail elsewhere,[11] has also hit the traditionally White-dominated
Christian churches, among them strongly hierarchical institutions such
as the Catholic church.[12] Although theoretically integrated organizations, the churches, too, are impelled to split along racial lines by
basically prejudiced White parishioners, a conservative hierarchy, and
an increasingly frustrated Black laity. Black priests complain about
discriminatory salaries and appointments. In this situation "Black
theology" finds a receptive ground inside and outside the traditional
institutions. The tremendous growth of separatist African churches in
southern Africa underlines these trends.

But the most salient factor to have affected intergroup perceptions
in recent years has undoubtedly been a relaxation of *baasskap* traditions. In this area of ideological control the system, moving toward a
modernized multiracialism, can most easily make concessions in outdated practices. Symbolic apartheid laws, as Sachs calls them, that is,
the regulations of petty apartheid that have no essential or "instrumental" function in maintaining crucial power relationships, are
increasingly being discarded. White officials are told to respect the
dignity of Blacks, White salesgirls now treat their Black customers with
ostensible politeness, and even the enforced segregation under municipal authority in parks and libraries has been conspicuously abandoned, stopping short only of integrated swimming pools and toilets.
Several multiracial sports events have also added to the tokenism of
considerable symbolic value.

While these gestures do not alter the structure of the castelike
system, they have great psychological impact in shaping optimistic
perceptions of improving race relations. More than ever, Africans in
Soweto now think that things have changed for the better according to
opinion surveys.[13] Without too much difficulty the South African
system could bring itself further in line with external ideological trends
by abandoning old-style racial segregation and manifest symbolic
discrimination and instead by emphasizing more acceptable criteria of
stratification, such as differential life-style, culture, wealth, and education. Thus it will probably not be too long before restaurants and
entertainment facilities are integrated, the costly segregated transport
system abolished, and even the Immorality Act formally scrapped.

[11]H. Adam, "The Rise of Black Consciousness in South Africa," *Race*, 15, 2
(October 1973): 149-66.
[12]For a rare empirical study, *see* K. Jubber, "Integrated Organization in a
Segregated Country. The Case of the Southern African Council of Priests"
(Paper presented at the Fourth Congress of the Association for Sociology in
Southern Africa, Roma, Lesotho, July 1973).
[13]*See* "What Black South Africans Think," Report on a Market Research
Survey by Quadrant International SA, on the basis of a sample of 800 persons
in Soweto, *Sunday Times* (Johannesburg), 6 January 1974.

Above all, more gestures to placate the international audience, such as the inclusion of an African, Colored, and Indian "delegate" in the South African representation at the United Nations, can be expected from public relations experts in the Department of Information, eager to convey the image of an embattled national family in which all members stand side by side to fight the onslaught by intruding "terrorists."

With large-scale residential segregation as an almost irreversible fact, for a long time even after a hypothetical revolution the points of interracial contact would be greatly reduced outside the economic sphere. The segregated system functions on its own and hardly needs the legally enforced symbols of White dominance. It is not only what Savage (p. 299) calls the "formalization of patterns of interethnic contact" but, above all, the gradual abolition of interracial contact altogether that now seems to shape attitudes more than any intentional indoctrination. In this vacuum of mutual ignorance and suspicion official definitions of what is "proper" can flourish. At the same time the norms of the ruling minority, which are imposed on the subjugated majority as universally valid, no longer resemble the stereotypes of racism or even paternalistic condescension. With the increased practice of racial segregation, its justifying ideology has been equally deracialized and substituted by "cultural pluralism." Savage (p. 299) quotes Verwoerd as predicting: "When separation had been carried far enough, discrimination must be eliminated." The separate development doctrine has been largely successful in clouding the fact that the White-dictated separation constitutes discrimination with far deeper implications than the now discarded *baasskap* behavior. The African, Colored, and Indian, confined to his own group in all meaningful contacts and encouraged to be proud of this parochialism masked as "cultural identity," gradually begins to accept as natural and inevitable this overwhelming reality. Here at least, he is not exposed to the hazards of interethnic competition and the latent anxiety of unpredictable contacts with strangers. Savage (p. 298) perceptively points to the psychological rewards of prescribed and formalized interaction: insofar as the rules remove ambiguity, "the likelihood of Blacks experiencing capricious treatment at the hands of Whites" is diminished and interethnic contact is stabilized. From this the impression results that race relations have improved. In reality they have been increasingly substituted by mere intragroup contact. The African, travelling among fellow Africans from his distant township, or the Indian in his exclusive suburb, serviced by Indian dealers and officials, has hardly anything to do with Whites any more. The Blacks in South Africa, even more than the Whites, now prefer to keep to themselves socially, and only the few White liberals at the few phony interracial gatherings grieve about integration in which they would have had the dominant role anyway.

With the disappearance of the hope of shared institutions and a more equitable distribution of the economic rewards, the expectations of Blacks have become geared to the opportunities within their own group. It should not be underestimated that these opportunities do exist in an expanding, industrialized system, in which the ruling section is simply unable to provide all the manpower for administering, educating, or policing its various components. By offering outlets for individual advancement and the fulfillment of limited material aspirations—though at a discriminatory scale, compared with the privileges of the Whites—the majority of the politically rightless is nevertheless sufficiently motivated to try the narrow roads open instead of breaking down the barriers to the highways.

It is this racially ordered reality, rather than the specific agencies of mind control, that is responsible for a depoliticized consciousness, often inconceivable to the outside observer. Blacks and Whites no longer need to be specifically socialized for their differential expectations and roles, but just exposed to a social structure so powerful that it commands adherence almost by itself.

POLITICAL CONTROL

While coercive and ideological control refer to the way in which given laws and policy goals are implemented, political control refers to the preceding process of how laws are defined and different policies are articulated. In this realm, inevitably and even within the fossilized constellation of South Africa, much is in flux: pressures are meeting counterpressures and manifold interaction is taking place at the intergroup level. This review will exclude the sphere of intragroup politics, particularly the most important processes of policy formation within the ruling White elite. Elsewhere, attention has been drawn to the increasing heterogeneity, urbanization, secularization, and class stratification within Afrikanerdom, all of which deeply affect the perception of ruling interests as well as strategies to safeguard them. It is also not necessary here to reanalyze the sphere of White party politics in which even the periodic election noises and their results seem as predictable as the change of seasons, despite overpublicized shifts and rifts between the two powerless opposition parties. Instead Black-White political interaction as well as important underlying issues of Black politics will be examined.

The new important figures, as far as the institutionalized political interplay between Blacks and Whites within the country is concerned, are undoubtedly the Bantustan officials, particularly their chief ministers. Portrayed by apartheid opponents abroad as conservative sellouts, government stooges, or ignorant traditionalists, they in fact fit none of these labels. Nor are they necessarily pushed by an imagined militancy of African peasants to adopt an increasingly antigovernment line. What they do have in common is their search for legitimacy and popular support among their own constituency. In this respect they have made gains since their start, and it is simply untrue that they keep their office only because of the support of government-nominated members of their assembly (as, for instance, in the Coloured Representative Council). In the six Bantustans that have held elections, chief ministers of five (Vendaland is the only exception) are supported by the majority of elected members. The chiefs in the assemblies by no means form a monolithic block and many support parties whose objectives are at variance with those of the White central government. Furthermore, only three of the six elected Bantustan leaders are in fact chiefs.

Thus far Bantustan leaders have made little headway among the urban Africans. Only 5 percent of eligible voters are estimated to have voted in some elections in Soweto. The "urban insiders," as Wilson calls them, do not wish to be linked to an imposed and fictional citizenship that might, in their view, be used to deprive them of their remaining fragile rights as articulated in section 10 of the Urban Areas Act.[14] With their limited appeal to the most advanced and powerful section of their constituency, Bantustan leaders are hampered in their quest for more recognition and power. Many of their recent policies can be seen as a conscious attempt to win over the urban constituency to strengthen their base with the most important pressure group. The Bantustan leader who has succeeded most in this effort is undoubtedly Gatsha Buthelezi. He draws increasingly larger crowds in urban areas and has become the widely accepted champion of a new era of African politics. According to the market research survey quoted earlier, Buthelezi tops the list of the most admired persons among Soweto inhabitants and his "appeal is not restricted to the Zulus but is widespread among all ethnic groups" (*see* note 13).

The Bantustan spokesmen do not have real power, politically, economically, or militarily, and are unlikely to acquire these capacities to any relative degree even if they are granted full political independence, as the Transkei now is likely to receive. In this respect, Savage, together with many White opponents, seems to overestimate the challenge that the Bantustan leaders pose to the central government. The frequently quoted "unintended consequences of the government's Bantustan policy" (p. 287) are rhetorical only and even carefully

----

[14]This section is the only remaining legal guarantee for an African to live in a "White" area, provided he has worked ten years continuously for one employer or fifteen years continuously for several employers, or has been born in the area.

calculated by more sophisticated apartheid engineers. Their favored paper itself makes this clear:

> We think too much emphasis is placed on the so-called "outbursts." What we should remember is that these people are prepared to operate within the system which has been created for them. It is not necessarily disastrous that they use it to obtain the best possible deal for their people. The fact is that they use it, and in doing so help it to succeed.[15]

Rather than a growing political polarization between Blacks and Whites, this perspective would seem to indicate a growing institutionalization of Black-White political conflict, with the Whites still calling the tune in a disharmonious orchestra.

Nevertheless, once established as the necessary political superstructures of a precapitalist social system, which the state was interested in sustaining as cost supplements in the production of cheap migrant labor, the new Bantustan institutions developed their own dynamic by creating a new psychological atmosphere in the country. By allowing for the airing of grievances and popular feelings, they functioned as mouthpieces as well as instigators of demands formerly suppressed. The power of a Buthelezi lies in his very powerlessness, as he himself was the first to recognize realistically. Symbolic challenges to White domination that have by now acquired institutional protection and therefore cannot be silenced as easily as before have created new visions, hope, and confidence. It will later be argued that the surprising strikes of 1973 cannot be understood without taking proper account (among many contributing factors) of the new awareness of African rights, demonstrated by Bantustan demands on a political level. With the decade-long intimidation and resignation overcome, more of the exploited were ready (and, of course, forced by impoverishment) to do something themselves about their misery.[16]

To be sure, Bantustan leaders are not socialist revolutionaries. They owe their overrated publicity partly to the business-oriented English language press, which supports the new Black opposition for its own reasons. At the same time their balanced pronouncements and shrewd methods have revealed dimensions of political alternatives hitherto unknown or suppressed in South Africa. These have included the rejection of government-sponsored ethnicity and political fragmentation in favor of close African collaboration, demands for additional African-controlled land in which members of all racial groups would enjoy the same rights including property ownership, and a federal concept of widely decentralized political power, as well as a concern

[15] *Rapport* (Johannesburg), 23 December 1973.
[16] Even Afrikaners now admit "there is a growing awareness of the power, the claims and the rights of the Black man from ordinary worker to homeland leader." *See Vaderland*, 28 December 1973.

about the fate of South African exiles and political prisoners with whom some of the Bantustan leaders have openly expressed solidarity. Regardless of much of the rhetoric and personal politicking involved, it is decisive that the government can no longer suppress the voices of its creations. Not only is Pretoria forced to respond somehow to prudently articulated demands, but even more important is the impact of these demands on the general political climate.

Contrary to government intentions that each tribal and racial group concern itself only with its own politics, there are regular public, and many more private, intergroup contacts at various levels. Meetings of Bantustan leaders with each other as well as with all three White party leaders have now become commonplace, although the government initially sought to restrict such activity through a "protocol guide" for Bantustan officials. The invitation to African spokesmen to address the annual congresses of the two opposition parties in 1973 and even staunch Afrikaner audiences at Stellenbosch, and the enthusiastic reception awarded them, indicate a growing desire on the part of the more enlightened White elite to arrest potential racial polarization and to come to some political consensus with their traditional, though in the South African context also radical, African counterparts. It can be assumed that these tendencies will grow into more institutionalized interracial arrangements, which, of course, will face their real test not in polite mutual consultations but in a crisis situation, for instance during a general strike.

So far there have been few occasions when common issues drew together public spokesmen of all three subordinate sections outside the realm of specific interest groups. In July 1973, however, for the first time since the suppression of the Congress alliance a decade earlier, African, Colored, and Indian spokesmen of varying political view points shared the same platform in a "Black consciousness" demonstration in Cape Town in support of the striking students of the Colored university. But while the contact at the elite level among the three Black groups is increasingly sought on the basis of a new awareness of a common destiny, a still vast social distance among the ordinary people hardly corresponds to the calls for unity from above.[17] If a broad and undogmatic Black consciousness movement is ever able to achieve

---

[17]While there are no attitude surveys comprising members of all racial groups since P. van den Berghe's (1962) and T. Pettigrew's (1960) studies of Durban students, the survey by M. Edelstein, *What Do Young Africans Think?* (Johannesburg, 1972), again underlines the prevailing distance of Soweto pupils to Indians and to a much lesser extent to Coloreds. Edelstein's second survey on the attitudes of 500 Johannesburg middle-class Coloreds confirms the social distance of this section to Africans, though equally to Afrikaners, who are much more rejected now than they were five or ten years ago.

unity, an emphasis on common political rather than cultural bonds among the subordinate groups would seem a prerequisite.

While on the formal political level of the new public spokesmen there is little interaction between Africans and Coloreds or between Colored and Indian representatives, there are renewed close ties between prominent Africans and Indians. This has been facilitated by both geographical proximity in Natal and a conscious desire by leading Indians, as Moodley points out, not to repeat the historical mistakes of their East African counterparts. Thus, for instance, Indians recently collected funds for the building of new schools in Zululand and ceremoniously handed them over to Buthelezi, who introduced his entire cabinet at the occasion. The ritual was in some ways typical for the new political-cultural atmosphere in Natal: the Durban Muslim Brigade provided a "guard of honor" for the "dignitaries," Chief Buthelezi was garlanded, Mrs. Albert Luthuli said prayers, Indian and Zulu dancers displayed their art before the "Durban adult choir," and a "Vote of Thanks" concluded the program. Many persons present at this show had also applauded some months earlier at the inauguration of the ostentatious Indian university in Westville, when Vorster was garlanded with similar pomp. Rather than "wavering" between Africans and Whites about which they should lean more heavily on, as Moodley suggests, the true minority in-between pays allegiance to both powerful antagonists.

More than the gestures of mutual deference of respective elites, however, it would seem that the situation at the work place will turn out to be the decisive factor for the relationship among the subordinates. Given the privileged position of Coloreds and Indians in terms of wages and status, there is a likelihood that many will seek individual advancement rather than collective solidarity with the African proletariat, as the privileged white-collar strata has in Europe. On the other hand, there is evidence that in a crisis situation such as the 1973 Durban strikes Indians showed and would show a high measure of solidarity with African workers, even though many may have been motivated by fear. Seventy-six percent of Indian respondents answered affirmatively to the question: "If African workers of a factory go on strike, do you think that Indian workers at the factory should join them?"[18] A similar attitude can be expected of Coloreds. What hampers solidarity and causes great resentment among Africans is the widespread practice by White employers of differential promotion of Coloreds and Indians over African workers, who hardly ever reach a supervisory position over an Indian. Indeed, discriminatory job mobility among Blacks has greatly contributed to the causes of the Natal strikes.

[18]G. Mare, "Attitudes to the Durban Strikes," unpublished manuscript (Durban, 1974).

At the same time, what has been speculated about the behavior of relatively privileged Colored and Indian intermediary castes, is likely to apply much more to a gradually arising petty bourgeoisie within all three subordinate groups, including the African *abaphakamileyo* (the "high ones").[19] It is primarily this group that government policy has recently been trying to accommodate through relatively unnoticed changes, which are likely to be similar in their psychological impact to the abolition of petty apartheid.

Contrary to earlier Nationalist party policy, which aimed at keeping the townships as bleak as possible, there is now official and private effort to improve the amenities for the "urban insiders." Recent decisions have allowed employers to house key African workers instead of providing them with single-quarter accommodations. New by-laws compel property developers to provide restaurant facilities for Blacks in "white areas," until now consistently vetoed by the government. In recognition of the increasing mobility of a Black middle class, motels are provided for the first time. It can be expected that the services for Blacks (schools, cinemas, shops, and the like) will improve under a gradual transfer of the communal administration to the township boards.

It may not be too far off when one central concern of a rising urban African middle class will be alleviated, viz., ownership rights in the townships. It would be entirely consistent with the present system to allow the right to own the house but to withhold title deeds to the land, or grant long-term leases on it to the houseowner. Not only United party city councillors, but also more pragmatic members of the Afrikaner establishment, have come to recognize the conservative value of a property-owning urban African stratum, particularly in the light of increased external pressure. In this vein, a director of the Afrikaanse Handelsinstituut, D. Greyling, reminded the readers of *Die Vaderland* in a frank discussion of the role of urban Africans that "the right to own a house of one's own fosters self-respect and the desire to hold to one's own and to fight for it. Ownership rights and national pride are the binding factors in a multinational country which has to fight terrorism inside and outside the country."[20] The author referred to "the more enlightened vision [of the businessmen] than the politician who must protect the interests of self-seeking pressure-groups," and seemed to reflect a growing uneasiness among industrialists about the attitudes and living conditions of their most valuable work force.

Whether such changes in the urban microcosm are sufficient to arrest more radical demands for Black equality remains to be seen and

[19]T. Nyquist, *Toward a Theory of the African Upper Stratum in South Africa,* Papers in International Studies, African Series (Athens, Ohio, 1972).
[20]*Vaderland,* 28 October 1973.

depends on the economic interracial constellation to which our attention must now turn.

ECONOMIC POWER

If we do not view South African racialism as an end in itself, because Whites are prejudiced or fearful, then we can see that one of the main purposes of the grand apartheid scheme is the preservation of tribal African society for a specific economic function: "By caring for the very young and very old, the sick, the migrant labourers in periods of 'rest,' by educating the young, etc., the Reserve families relieve the capitalist sector and its state from the need to expand resources on these necessary functions."[21] Only because of its economic basis in a precapitalist reserve economy and a tribal social system could the migrant labor force be remunerated below its normal level of reproduction. A vast amount of legislation, both of a restrictive nature, regarding the mobility of Africans, and of a positive nature, concerning "Bantu development" in the reserves, is aimed essentially at sustaining this symbiotic relationship between a modern capitalist and a precapitalist sector. In this sense, South Africa is not "simultaneously pursuing two apparently contradicting goals," viz., the "goal of rapid economic growth" and the "goal of separate development," as Wilson states (p. 176), but each complements the other, guaranteeing economically cheap, politically powerless, and psychologically docile African laborers. However, owing to a number of new factors, not the least the increasing impoverishment of the reserves, this system is breaking down and the Bantustans provide a declining fraction of the overall subsistence of migrant workers. This is accompanied by other recent trends in the labor market, most of which are perceptively analyzed in Wilson's chapter.

Before we focus on the actions and attitudes on the industrial front, these central structural factors and objective contradictions will be briefly summarized and projected into the future, based on the assumption of a continuing private-profit-oriented, expanding economy in South Africa, mediated by increased state interference.[22]

---

[21]H. Wolpe, "Capitalism and Cheap Labour Power in South Africa: from Segregation to Apartheid," *Economy and Society*, 1, November 1972: 425-56.

[22]As in most other capitalist economies, increased state interference takes place both through direct legislation and executive actions as well as through public economic activity. In 1973 the state was responsible for 26 percent of total fixed investment, compared with only 15 percent twelve years ago. As a direct employer, the state absorbs 19 percent of the economically active White population in the public service. *See The Star* (Johannesburg), Weekly Edition, 23 February 1974, p. 19.

The shortage of skilled White labor is likely to increase unless alleviated by considerably stepped-up immigration, which is unlikely notwithstanding recessions in Western Europe. Hence, more Blacks will occupy skilled positions despite a legal color bar, which is already being circumvented or simply disregarded as long as White workers are unaffected or are compensated. In a rapidly expanding economy such as that of South Africa there is little objective justification for the historic fear that White workers could be replaced by cheaper Blacks. Both can easily be absorbed by the economy, though absorption would still take place in a differential fashion.

A prerequisite for the use of more skilled Blacks is training. Once an employer has invested in his workers he is interested in a low turnover and a stable labor force. The migrant labor system is incompatible with this interest, even if streamlined by a call-in card system under which the contract worker would have to return to the same employer. It is likely that migrant workers will increasingly be channeled into low paid unskilled jobs, while a new "labor aristocracy" from the permanent urban African population will be absorbed into the skilled positions. The important decision by the Chamber of Mines to step up local recruiting in the light of potential labor boycotts by neighboring states will only be successful if wage and working conditions on the mines are substantially improved. However, by absorbing a substantial number of local surplus-labor the mines are strengthening the bargaining position of the African labor force in other branches as well.

At this technological stage of industrial development, individual productivity becomes a decisive cost factor. A certain amount of identification with the job is a prerequisite for a proper functioning of a skilled worker. The employer would be interested in fostering such a necessary work ethos, not only through an acceptable wage structure but generally by harmonious industrial relations and better management. Life in the townships, including political dissatisfaction with discriminatory racial legislation, would have a direct adverse effect on the individual performance at the work place. Greater employer pressure to improve the local microcosm of the African labor aristocracy can therefore be expected, as well as the provision of other rights and services to which workers elsewhere have long been accustomed.

As evidence we can point to the most immediate response of South African employers to the recent unexpected strikes that precipitated a critical look at their nineteenth-century management techniques. Training programs along the American model and with American personnel are now being seriously pursued and a new glossy journal with the significant title *People and Profits* gives a taste of the scope for channeling and manipulating grievances through sophisticated management techniques. One of its editors, the national director of the Institute of Personnel Management, preaches as a new philosophy: "All our research confirms that whereas poor wages breed discontent, it takes more than money to motivate workers to high productivity."[23] Similar lessons are recognized by employers' organizations, such as the South African Federated Chamber of Industries, whose journal recommends: "The provision of adequate fringe benefits makes good sense to the employer who is anxious to reduce his labor turnover and build a solid and stable core of satisfied workers. Social security fringe benefits may be described as a sound investment in human capital, particularly insofar as the non-White worker is concerned."[24]

These trends increase the bargaining power of the urban Afican, as a producer as well as a consumer. More than before, the system will be dependent on the voluntary collaboration of Blacks. In a strike, skilled workers cannot be as easily dismissed as migrants[25]; a consumer boycott by a better paid working class would have a greater impact than the determination of starving people, who have to spend most of their income on food anyway.

While these changes would seem inevitable in the long run, their pace, their specific form, and their direction will largely depend on conscious action by those who are at the receiving end of the present arrangement. It was only after the lowest paid African workers struck in Natal that their wages were increased on an average by 20 percent. It is therefore to this front of industrial action our analysis has to turn to reach some conclusions about short-term prospects.

It has often been pointed out that the "fundamental weakness" of the spontaneous strike "lies precisely in its spontaneity and the absence of organizational muscle to press for any kind of political change" (*see* Wilson, p. 189). The same had been said about the illegality of a strike, which has proved to be no obstacle to its taking place. But the question of African trade unions or any other form of organization is central for achieving more than short-term success.

Most industrialists, White trade unionists, and the government view independent African unions as a severe threat for different reasons. However, they face the predicament that unorganized frustrated strikers represent an even greater menace to their interests than organized laborers, and that labor disputes in an institutional vacuum

[23]D. Jackson, "South Africa's Labour Problems: Towards a Solution" (Paper read at *Strikes: The lessons from Natal.,* a symposium on how to avoid and deal with strikes, organized by the South African Institute of Personnel Management, Pietermaritzburg, 1973), p. 47.

[24]*Federated Chamber of Industries Viewpoint* (Johannesburg), October 1973, p. 2.

[25]Several editorials in the English language press reflect this new situation, perhaps best crystallized in a comment of the *Natal Mercury,* 7 March 1974: "It is an unwise management that cannot see that the tactic of 'sacking the trouble-makers and getting in a new lot' has had its day."

can get completely "out of hand" without "lines of communication open." The Afrikaanse Handelsinstituut, which represents the smaller Afrikaner entrepreneurs with newly acquired capital, recommends, therefore, in the traditional paternalistic fashion, that "compulsory contact points be enforced between employer and African employee."[26] The newly revived Works Committees on the factory level are supposed to achieve this. The official rationale behind them is that until the African has "reached a stage to negotiate his own affairs, the Department of Labour must remain his guardian."[27] The British section of South African capital and part of the White union movement would prefer to see the inclusion of Africans "under the disciplines and the protection of the ordinary, multiracial trade unions."[28] They are confident that these could not be taken over by its new members "to cripple industry."

All shades of White interest are strongly opposed to a new phenomenon that has found little attention so far. The missing organizational muscle could well be provided by the Bantustan governments, which could hardly be stopped from engaging in the welfare of their citizens "at home" and "abroad." In their quest for acceptance and legitimacy among the urban Africans, they could take the lead in a crisis situation. Mayer has pointed to the possibility that instead of the urban Africans being tribalized, the "homelands" could be Africanized. Buthelezi, as the African spokesman of the area most affected, has readily accepted this role as potential union organizer. "Some people circulated stories during the strikes, that I was behind the strikes. This of course was not true [he was in the United States during the early strikes in February 1973], but even if it was true, I would not have been in the least ashamed of it. I wish there was a legal way in which I could organise my people to exercise labour bargaining rights."[29] Perhaps more significant to the future solution of irresolvable labor disputes was the direct involvement of one of Buthelezi's ministers, as well as the relief of some Natal undertakings to have finally found a negotiating partner, accepted and called for by the workers themselves. Commenting on an African strike in Pinetown in January 1974, an editorial warned ominously:

> But it was more than a confrontation between workers and employers. It was between the workers' government and the management. A Kwazulu Cabinet Minister was right there in the forefront. You can see what is going to happen. Given Bantustan autonomy, African labor disputes

[26]*The Star,* Weekly Edition, 19 May 1973.
[27]Ibid.
[28]Ibid, 23 January 1974.
[29]Jackson, "South Africa's Labour Problems," p. 3.

will be international incidents, with the African governments in a powerful position to cripple industry by withholding labour.[30]

The eventual recognition of Black unions and the failure of the
Works Committees are however already anticipated. The *Financial
Times* states that "most companies will admit that the Works Committee
System is unlikely to be a long-term solution and the more far-sighted
businessmen acknowledge, if only in private, that Black unions will
have to come one day."[31] From the perspective of these industrialists
the crucial question will be whether such an organized Black labor
movement can be brought under the tutelage of some conservative
leadership to guarantee restraint in wage demands. From the view of
the political revolutionary it would seem more decisive whether Black
unions, like their counterparts, in most of the rest of the capitalist
world, will confine themselves to bread-and-butter issues and a policy
of gradual reformist measures regarding the life chances of members,
or whether an explicit political strategy will be adopted, aiming at a
change in the institutional arrangements through which the accumulated wealth can be redistributed. The hopes for the latter should not
be stated too high. There is already a widespread belief that African
unions should stick to their particular private concerns and not act as a
political threat. In this vein, the general secretary of the African
Transport and Allied Workers' Union, which has a great number of
members from the Public Utility Transport Corporation strikers,
believes: "We are not for disrupting anything, just for improving the
labour situation. We do not concern ourselves with politics, but only
with bread-and-butter issues. We leave politics to the politicians. Trade
unions to be successful, must keep out of politics."[32] We might doubt
whether such publicized tranquilizers represent the real view of the
speaker, and, above all, whether they will not be swept aside inevitably
in a crunch. But over-optimistic revolutionary speculations should not
ignore the significant finding by Mayer that legitimacy is emphatically
denied only to the "cruel" roles of Afrikaners as supervisors, but not to
the employer roles of the English and Jewish industrialists. Mayer
seems justified to attach great importance to this perception in
preventing total Black-White confrontation, despite the Natal strikes.
If there exists, indeed, a widespread readiness to exclude cross-racial
reference and to blame low wages not on the wider system but on a
particularly greedy boss or company, then improvements within the

[30]*The Star*, 23 January 1974.

[31]*Financial Times* (London), Survey on South Africa, 22 January 1974; The
Natal Mercury, 7 March 1974, comments similarly: "There is no assurance that
trade unions will prevent Black workers from striking. But if that is what they
are doing anyway, and illegally at that, what is there to lose?

[32]*Sunday Times* (Johannesburg), 24 February 1974.

overall discriminatory structure can promise short-term successes in containing tensions. It is not surprising that the government itself fosters such an apolitical consciousness by expressing sympathy with the strikes against individual employers, who are seen as jeopardizing the whole for private gains. In doing so the South African racial oligarchy seems to prove again its scope and flexibility in the face of pressure to make concessions within the overall framework of continuing White dominance.

CONCLUSION

Rather than a relaxation of coercive power against political opponents outside the approved institutional framework, all evidence points to a tightening control of extraparliamentary dissent by Blacks and Whites alike. In addition, ideological control by the ruling oligarchy ensures conformity in nonpolitical spheres. Nevertheless, many significant changes in the political climate and the economic realm show a profound impact on Black-White relationships in South Africa. The emergence of outspoken Bantustan leaders, ideas of Black consciousness, and, above all, spontaneous strikes, though all without tangible result for the overall power structure as yet, have nevertheless created the impression that things are finally moving. The government has responded to these expectations by scrapping some noninstrumental symbols of White dominance and by making provisions, for the first time, for the aspirations of urban Africans.

The effects of these trends seem to aim at a new three-fold socio-economic stratification among South African Blacks in addition to ethnic fragmentation and residential segregation: stratification within the African, Colored, and Indian subgroups according to wealth and education; stratification between the privileged urban Africans with access to skilled jobs, and temporary migrant workers in urban areas, confined to unskilled labor; and stratification among the three subordinate race groups with job and wage discrimination against Africans whenever Coloreds and Indians are available.

Future developments will largely depend on the constellation in the labor market and whether Blacks will be able to create solidarity and organizational cohesiveness among their various subgroups or whether they will continue to be weakened by the traditional White divide and rule policy. Any prognosis ought not to underestimate the sophisticated nature of White rule, which can combine the rewards of an advanced economy, the efficiency of a modern bureaucracy, and the zeal of a privileged caste to be flexible where it counts little, but adamant where the overall system is threatened.

Unlike the European colonialists in Africa, including the Portuguese, South African Whites constitute settlers on their own with no dependence on a specific metropole. Rather like the Israelis, they can be expected not to give in, but to resist threats to what they consider the essential conditions for survival. Therefore, the impact of political independence in the former Portuguese territories on Afrikaner morale should not be overestimated. Their self-confidence to face successfully a potential military challenge on South African soil is unbroken, and for the time being no self-delusion. At the same time, the events in Mozambique have strengthened the *verligte* factions in the National Party who argued for an internationally defensible policy of non-interference, combined with economic offensiveness and flexibility on the Rhodesian front and the South West African issue. The Portuguese withdrawal has also brought into public focus the predicament of Christian-liberal apartheid opponents who began to debate whether an unjust state ought to be defended against outside attacks. But above all, Frelimo triumph has boosted the morale of politically conscious Africans, with obvious signs of anxiety among many middle-class Indians. That the Whites have to accommodate expectations of their opponents is certain; that they will be substantially defeated by their might is unlikely. The safest prediction one can venture in light of the total internal and external constellation is that the outdated racial hierarchy in South Africa will be gradually undermined by an evolving class structure, in line with Western societies, in which a small elite of the subordinate strata increasingly participates in the economic rewards and political status of the system. Such a deracialization in favor of class stratification within an overall capitalist economy does not constitute radical change from a revolutionary, socialist perspective, but it does mean an improvement, compared with the previous subordination; just as the neocolonial, political independence of an indigenous bourgeoisie in Africa represents a certain progress, compared with traditional colonialism. Real liberation of the oppressed and impoverished masses has still to come, in Black Africa not less than in the White South. Only those with a dogmatic, theological belief in their cause can offer a timetable. To take full account of a complex, contradictory reality distinguishes social science from wishful thinking.

IV
External Factors

13

The Effects on South Africa of Changes in Contiguous Territories*

CHRISTIAN P. POTHOLM

Concerned over the fragmented nature of the study of southern African politics and the treating of the units in this area as if they were discrete and totally independent entities, many scholars have recently turned to an analysis of the region as an integrated subsystem.[1] Whether looking at economic activities or transaction flows, military cooperation or intergovernmental relations, these authors have stressed the regional interaction of its units and stressed its distinctiveness as a subsystem operative in international relations.[2] And, as might be expected, most have generally focused on both the centrality of the Republic of South Africa and its critical importance for the maintenance of the subsystem.

This chapter seeks to provide a somewhat different perspective for it is intended to explore those influences that are now being, or may in the future be, exerted on the Republic by events in the contiguous

*The author is indebted to the many persons who read earlier drafts of this paper: Jane Titcomb, Richard Morgan, John Donovan, D. Scott Palmer, Kirk Emmert, Richard Weisfelder, Richard Dale, John Grotpieter, Olin Robison, Robert Small, and John Rensenbrink.

[1]L. Bowman, "The Subordinate State System of Southern Africa," *International Studies Quarterly* 12, 3 (1968): 231-61; C. Potholm and R. Dale, eds., *Southern Africa in Perspective: Essays in Regional Politics* (New York, 1972); and T. Shaw, "Southern Africa: Dependence, Interdependence and Independence in a Regional Subsystem" (Paper delivered at the Workshop on Southern Africa, Dalhousie University, August 1973).

[2]In fact, the Dalhousie conference itself, organized by Kenneth Heard and Timothy Shaw, is an indication of the extent to which the subsystem concept has taken on a life of its own. *See also* K. Grundy, *Confrontation and Accommodation in Southern Africa: The Limits of Independence* (Los Angeles, 1973).

states and territories. For these purposes Angola, Mozambique, Rhodesia (Zimbabwe), Malawi, Lesotho, Swaziland, Botswana, Zambia, and the Malagasy Republic are included under the generic heading "contiguous," even though they do not all strictly speaking form integral parts of the subsystem.[3] While other chapters in this section, notably those of Nolutshungu and Gervasi, provide overarching analyses of other influences on southern Africa, we have attempted to limit observations to factors in the contiguous areas.

Because of the plethora of events currently taking place in these nine areas and the need to organize the data into manageable form, we have separated the forces and influences into six categories: demographic, economic/investment, infrastructural/communications, military/para-military, intergovernmental/diplomatic, and philosophical/ideological.[4] These are not of course discrete analytical compartments. They often overlap and are usually mutually interacting, but separating them should enable the reader to capture the essence of the present situation and more accurately to summarize the cumulative effect the events they contain are likely to have on the future of the Republic of South Africa.

DEMOGRAPHIC

Several aspects of the present demographic situation in southern Africa are important in assaying the future of the area. The first of these is the question of refugees.[5] Following the turbulent events of the late 1950s and early 1960s, numerous refugees fled South Africa for the former High Commission Territories. Due to the permeable nature of their frontiers and the opposition to refugee political and economic activity (especially in Swaziland and Lesotho), many refugees then left these territories for Tanzania and Zambia. As a result of the recent fighting in Mozambique, Angola, and, to a lesser extent, Namibia, other refugees have fled to these countries, although some have also settled in Botswana. While the refugees represent something of a pressure group within their host countries, especially in terms of

[3]Bowman, Potholm, and Dale include Zambia but exclude the Malagasy Republic; Grundy includes both plus Tanzania and Zaïre. Certainly if we wished a case could also be made for the psychological "contiguity" of Guinea-Bissau.

[4]As Sheridan Johns and Lawrence Schlemmer have suggested, there may be additional influences subsumed under "culture" or "life-style" that can be perceived as spilling over into a number of the categories.

[5]R. Dale has explored this matter in some analytical detail in "Refugees from South Africa to Botswana: The External Ramifications of Internal Security Policy" (Paper delivered at the annual meeting of the American Political Science Association, September 1973).

providing often vocal support for the various exile groups, they do not now exert much direct influence on the Republic. While it is possible to project a larger role for them should their numbers increase substantially, at the present time their discernible impact is small.

More recently, White refugees have been fleeing from Mozambique to South Africa as the forces of FRELIMO have begun to assert their authority over the southern portion of the country. It remains to be seen whether these refugees will have any substantial impact on South Africa itself, but it seems quite likely that both their flight and the circumstances surrounding that flight will bolster the resolve of White South Africans to maintain the *status quo*.

A second category is labor migration. It is estimated that between 800,000 and 1.5 million nonindigenous Africans are present in South Africa at any given time.[6] Those on contract vary from contiguous state to contiguous state (ranging from 6,200 from Rhodesia to over 130,000 from Lesotho and Malawi).[7] Molteno has vigorously challenged the notion that these workers by finding employment, learning skills, and remitting paychecks substantially help their home countries.[8] And, while we must conclude that the labor-exporting countries are highly dependent on South Africa for a major portion of their national income, it also seems clear that the migrant labor issue is an area in which the contiguous states exert considerable, albeit indirect, influence on South Africa. This is one category of interaction that could affect the future of South African power in the region. For one thing, these migrant workers, however economically inefficient, represent important bargaining chips, which Pretoria uses in bilateral relations. Also, because they are far less likely to become politically mobilized while in the Republic and more susceptible to negative sanctions such as repatriation, migrant laborers are more valuable politically to a government seeking to maintain industrial peace. Working together the migrant labor-exporting countries could use their dependence and that of the Republic in diplomatically interesting ways. For example, if the three former High Commission Territories and Malawi were to act in concert, several important South African industries, such as gold and coal producers, would be substantially affected. Interestingly enough, with the exception of some Malawian labor to Rhodesia and Mozambiquean labor to Swaziland, the major demographic patterns tend to be bilateral between the contiguous states and South Africa rather than among the contiguous states.

[6]*Sechaba*, 7, (May 1973): 3 sets the higher figure, while the African Institute puts the figure at more than 800,000 with 441,148 present on a strictly contract basis during 1972. *See South African Digest* 22 June 1973, p. 3.

[7]*South African Digest* 22 June 1973, p. 3.

[8]R. Molteno, *African Labor and South Africa* (London, 1971), pp. 14-16.

There continues to be considerable ambiguity about the role labor migration will play, in either systemic alteration or maintenance. For example, the coming to power of Frelimo in Mozambique may lead to a cutoff of contract labor from that country, thereby putting economic hardship and diplomatic pressure on the Republic. Conversely, a Frelimo government, seeking to consolidate its control over all of Mozambique and unable in the early stages of its rule to provide alternative employment for the more than 100,000 migrant workers, might well avoid a direct confrontation with South Africa over its racial policies.

Summarizing these two demographic factors, we conclude that refugee resettlement and labor migration do not currently appear to be destabilizing influences on the subsystem and that any increase in impact on policy-making within the Republic of South Africa lies in the future, not the present.

ECONOMIC/INVESTMENT

Economic trends within the region indicate the extent to which the Southern Africa subsystem is becoming increasingly integrated.[9] As economic development continues and the major investment projects in Angola, Botswana, and Mozambique proceed apace, it would appear that the contiguous states are becoming more dependent on South Africa. At the same time, the scene is not without considerable ambiguity, if we take a longer view.

Certainly, the availability of capital and skilled manpower, technical assistance, and economic planning guidance give South Africa an attractive aid package to offer the surrounding, poorer nations, and the Republic has not been averse to using that package for diplomatic advantage. For example, during 1970 at the height of the dialogue strategy, South Africa and the government of Philibert Tsiranana concluded an agreement calling for economic cooperation between the two countries and for the development of a tourist industry in Malagasy. With the coming to power of General Gabriel Ramanantsea many of the projects were terminated, including the development of Nossi-Be Island, and in June 1972 the South African government

[9]For background on this phenomenon, *see* P. Robson, "Economic Integration in Southern Africa," *Journal of Modern African Studies* 5, 4 (1967): 469-90; P. Smit and E. van der Merwe, "Economic Cooperation in Southern Africa," *Journal of Geography;* and E. Rhoodie, "Southern Africa: Towards a New Commonwealth," in Potholm and Dale, eds., *Southern Africa in Perspective,* pp. 276-97. The importance of South Africa varies considerably from country to country. For example, while South Africa is second in importance as a trading partner with Mozambique, its share of the Angolan market is less than 4 percent. *See Commerce and Industry* (May 1972), pp. 339-41.

announced the suspension of the agreement. These developments clearly underscore the fragility of South Africa's outward movement beyond the confines of those subsystem units that it clearly dominates.

Within the core of the subsystem, however, there continues to be further economic integration. This is particularly true in the case of the three former High Commission Territories. Despite their attempts to diversify the sources of both their aid and their export markets, Swaziland, Botswana, and Lesotho find themselves more intrinsically bound up with the Republic than ever before. The new customs agreement that went into force on 1 March 1970 sharply revised upward the annual portion of the customs revenues due each territory. The previous agreement was based on the ratio of total customs duties collected by each territory to the total customs revenue for the entire area during 1906 to 1908.

As a result of the new arrangement, Swaziland's yearly revenues jumped by over 100 percent and those of Lesotho by 500 percent. Ironically, these new revenues only increase the territories' dependence on the Republic, since British grants-in-aid are no longer necessary to balance their budgets and the British have been able to scale down the level of their aid.

While dependence on South Africa varies from territory to territory, it is generally considerable. Lesotho takes nearly 80 percent of its imports from South Africa and sends over 60 percent of its exports to the Republic. In addition, the South African government will provide the major financing for Lesotho's Maliba-Matso water development project. In the case of Swaziland, South Africa continues to provide 80 percent of the country's imports, although Japan, Great Britain, and the United States take a major portion of its exports. In the case of Botswana, it is interesting to note that despite the government's more independent diplomatic stance, its level of economic dependence remains considerable. In fact, knowledgeable observers have concluded that the recent economic boom in the country has increased, not decreased, its reliance on South Africa.[10]

The exploitation and development of the mineral resources in Botswana seem to offer the hope that Botswana, now one of the poorest countries in the world, can improve its economic situation. Projects involving nickel, copper, coal, and diamonds have attracted major amounts of venture capital from the United Nations, United States, Great Britain, Canada, Germany, and South Africa. It is anticipated that the total investment package will exceed $150 million.

[10]S. Johns, "Botswana's Strategy for Development: An Assessment of Dependence in the Southern African Context" (Paper delivered at the Conference on Dependence and Development in Africa, Carleton University, February 1973).

The importance of Anglo-American investments, the major private investment source, to the development of Botswana's mineral riches underscores the insights of Huntington in his examination of transnational organizations.[11] The Anglo-American Corporation, like its American and European counterparts, is able to move personnel and resources from one portion of its holdings to another across national frontiers, and, seeking access rather than territorial holdings, provides impetus for development of a transnational society subsystem. Huntington suggests an index of development by which, generally speaking, the more developed the country economically, the higher its price of access. In this regard, it is instructive that the government of Botswana's share of the proposed project is distinctly a minority one, 20 percent. Huntington also suggests that while such corporations both seek and initially reinforce the *status quo*, in the long run, by creating new demands, new life-styles, and new ideas, their activities are destabilizing. Because of the dychronic and dysrhythmic impact of investment, the transnational corporations are sowing the seeds of future social and political upheaval at the very time they are creating new linkages among the units in which they operate.

Not subscribing entirely to the Huntington hypothesis, we can project the possible future impact on South African foreign policy as economic development proceeds throughout the subsystem. In the case of Botswana, while the near term brings greater dependence on South Africa, it is by no means clear that the long term will continue this pattern, and there are situations, particularly in the former Portuguese territories, in which increasing economic integration leads to diplomatic and political interdependence, which from the South African point of view may be dysfunctional indeed. For example, the $350 million project at Cabora Bassa in Mozambique and the $200 million hydroelectric facility at Kunene, together with the South African-sponsored pipeline to transport natural gas from Mozambique, all involve substantial investment by South African firms and all anticipate South Africa taking major portions of the energy generated from these projects.

Thus South Africa is involved in the fate of the former Portuguese territories and, as a result of these projects, military and political events far from the Republic have potentially more resounding implications than they would have had a decade ago. At this stage the extent to which these projects will become hostages to, or important influences upon, South Africa's foreign policy is a matter for speculation. The increasing economic integration of the region is not without considerable importance for the future diplomatic posture of the Republic and

[11]S. Huntington, "Transnational Organizations in World Politics," *World Politics* 25, 3 (April 1973): 333-68.

may have as yet unseen consequences for its domestic scene. It also makes South Africa more vulnerable to situations over which it has little control, such as the coup in Portugal of 25 April 1974.

What, for example, will be the leverage enjoyed by an independent Mozambique over South Africa with regard to these investments? So long as Mozambique seemed likely to remain under Portuguese control well into the future, the celebrated Cabora Bassa dam appeared to promote the economic integration of the region and hence its stability. Depending on South Africa's power needs for the coming decade, however, and the independent government's willingness to use power generation in instrumental ways (it was never intended, for example, that the electricity generated by Cabora Bassa dam could or would be used solely by Mozambique), increasing pressure to modify its internal racial policies could be brought to bear on South Africa.

INFRASTRUCTURAL/COMMUNICATIONS

The communications and transportation infrastructures of southern Africa are currently heavily dependent on South Africa. Despite the efforts of the governments of the contiguous states, this dependence is likely to continue into the indefinite future.

In Lesotho, for example, the government is seeking to construct a new international airport near Maseru to develop direct service to Zambia and Botswana. At the present time, air service runs through the Republic and flights to and from Lesotho must stop at South African facilities to fly over South Africa. Telex and telephone lines to the rest of the world run through South Africa and the only railroad to the capital is South African. While a new airport might give the government some options with regard to refugees from South Africa and some degree of psychic independence, it seems highly unlikely that this proposed change will alter Lesotho's overwhelming infrastructural dependence on South Africa.

Botswana too is attempting to alter the infrastructural patterns of southern Africa. Except for a narrow water belt where Botswana abuts Zambia, the country is surrounded by South Africa (including Namibia) and Rhodesia. Most of its population lives within fifty miles of the Republic and the country's only rail line runs from Rhodesia and through South Africa, as do most of its telecommunication links with the rest of the world. Botswana is attempting to reduce this level of dependence. Of major symbolic importance for the country is the proposed tarred highway that will link Gaberones and the southern portion of Botswana with Livingstone in Zambia by means of the Kazangula ferry. Ever since its inception, the project has been strenuously opposed by South Africa. Nevertheless, with American, British,

World Bank, and Swedish assistance, the tarring and extension of the road continues and the completion date is set for mid-1975.

The completion of the road and the options it will provide for Botswana could alter the infrastructural patterns of that portion of the subsystem and, in time, reorient some of Botswana's trade toward Zambia and the emerging eastern African subsystem. As indicated, the Rhodesian railroad runs through Botswana and, together with Rhodesian rail lines that connect with their Mozambiquean counterparts, represents that country's access to the sea. Were Botswana able to reduce its dependence on the railroad, especially that portion that runs through South Africa, it could take advantage of Rhodesian dependence by threatening or actually nationalizing that portion of the Rhodesian rail line that goes through Botswana. This helps to explain Rhodesian interest in linking up directly with South Africa through the Beit bridge route. Although expensive, this extension would reduce Rhodesian dependence on Botswana and a potentially hostile government.[12]

We could well argue that despite the recent flurry of interest in Botswana and emphasis on the psychological importance of its links to the north, there is little to indicate that the events surrounding the northern road will be of more than transitory and superficial importance to the Republic.

In the case of Swaziland recent events suggest that South Africa continues to stand astride most of that country's links with the outside world. All its international telephone traffic goes through Johannesburg, mail and telecommunications go through Pretoria. Most of its road net, bus lines, and cable car system terminate in South Africa. Together they carry nearly 80 percent of Swaziland's imports. Since the completion of the Swaziland-Mozambique railroad in 1964 and weekly air flights to Lourenço Marques that began in 1973, some observers have speculated that Mozambique could loom large in Swaziland's diplomatic and political future,[13] and because of the importance of the port of Lourenço Marques for the South African rail traffic to and from the Rand, this could be important for South Africa as well.

The Swazis, long accustomed to the stability of the region and the political and economic insulation provided by the White regimes in South Africa, Rhodesia, and Mozambique may well find themselves on the horns of a dilemma, forced to choose between supporting the new

[12]Ironically, from 1971 to 1972 the Batswana found themselves lobbying privately to get the United States to sell new rolling stock to Rhodesia despite existing sanctions, since Botswana was so dependent on the Rhodesian railroad for its trade with South Africa.

[13]C. Potholm, "Swaziland," in Potholm and Dale, eds., *Southern Africa in Perspective*, pp. 141-53.

Black government in Mozambique (thereby facing South African economic reprisals) and the systemic *status quo* (thereby facing Mozambiquean threats to cut off Swaziland's access to the port of Lourenço Marques). For its part the South African Railway Board indicated in 1973 that a proposed link between the Swaziland railroad and South Africa was not feasible at that time.[14]

Only in the case of Malawi is there presently major South African dependency. The refueling and landing rights that South Africa enjoys at Lilongwe, together with South African privileges at Sal Island in the Cape Verde Islands, enable South African aircraft to fly to Europe despite the opposition of many African states. While the Republic could probably develop a set of alternatives, these are desirable links to maintain. However, they do represent situations in contiguous territories that might affect South Africa's transportation and telecommunication lines in the future.

MILITARY/PARA-MILITARY

South Africa has made strenuous efforts over the past decade to increase its military capability and has been highly successful in this endeavor.[15] Moreover, recent indications are that South Africa has developed capacity to manufacture most if not all of its defensive armaments.[16] And, although he indicates that there are numerous important constraints on South African behavior in this regard, Spence suggests that South Africa has the capability of developing an independent nuclear deterrent.[17] Recent reports suggest that South Africa is indeed moving toward acquiring an increased nuclear capability.

Despite its enormous military strength and its demonstrated ability to crush would-be revolutionaries within its borders, South Africa remains vulnerable to the evolving situations in the contiguous states of Angola, Mozambique, and Rhodesia (Zimbabwe). Portuguese decol-

[14]*Times of Swaziland* (Mbabane), 71, 3 (19 January 1973): 1.

[15]T. Shaw, "South Africa's Military Capability and the Future of Race Relations," in A. Mazrui and H. Patel, eds., *Africa in World Politics: The Next Thirty Years* (New York, 1973), pp. 58-9; J. Spence and E. Thomas, *South Africa's Defense: The Problem of Internal Control*, Security Studies Paper #8 (Los Angeles, 1968); J. Spence, "Southern Africa: The Military and Political Framework," in J. Spence, ed., *The Strategic Significance of Southern Africa* (London, 1971), pp. 22-32; and C. Petersen, "The Military Balance in Southern Africa," in Potholm and Dale, eds., *Southern Africa in Perspective*, pp. 298-317.

[16]*Africa Research Bulletin* (1-31 January 1973), p. 2725.

[17]J. Spence, "Nuclear Weapons and South Africa," in J. Larus and R. Lawrence, eds., *Nuclear Proliferation: Stage II* (forthcoming).

onization, whether rapid, as in the case of Mozambique, or more drawn out, as in the case of Angola, will surely pose grave threats to South Africa's military situation, both by further exposing Rhodesia's defense lines and by providing possible sanctuaries for anti-South African guerrillas.

Recent events in Rhodesia, in which South Africa is most directly involved, underscore its potential vulnerability. South African police and para-military forces operate on a daily basis in Rhodesia and there are signs that the South Africans have recently stepped up their commitment. During July 1973, for example, it was reported that South African Super Frelon helicopters were openly in action in support of Rhodesian-South African military units.[18] It seems clear that the longevity of the Smith regime and the failure of settlement talks between Rhodesia and Great Britain have reinforced the South African decision to keep Rhodesia afloat. By sending police and para-military units to aid in counterinsurgency operations, the South African government has a visible and important symbolic commitment to the Smith regime.

It is in this regard that the recent military events in Rhodesia loom large. As long as the various African exile groups were riddled with dissension and prone to fighting among themselves, there was little chance they would pose a significant threat to either the Rhodesian government or the white-dominated subsystem of southern Africa. The feuding between the Zimbabwe African Peoples Union (ZAPU), the Zimbabwe African National Union (ZANU), and the more recent Front for the Liberation of Zimbabwe (FROLIZI) has been well documented elsewhere.[19] Recently, however, there were signs that this factionalism could be diminishing. On 17 March 1973, representatives of ZANU and ZAPU signed an agreement under Organization of African Unity auspices that would set up a joint military command and a unified political council.

In addition, there was the outbreak of new fighting near the Chiweshe tribal homeland near the Matusadonha mountains. Although there are various claims as to who was responsible for the upsurge in attacks on European settlers in the area,[20] the movement of

[18]*The Washington Post,* 11 July 1973.

[19]K. Grundy, *Guerrilla Struggle in Africa* (New York, 1971), pp. 107-15; and R. Gibson, *African Liberation Movements* (London, 1972), pp. 158-84. For a dispassionate survey of the situation, *see* A. Wilkinson, *Insurgency in Rhodesia, 1957-1973: An Account and Assessment,* Alelph: Papers #100 (London, 1973).

[20]*The San Francisco Chronicle* reported on 15 May 1973 that most of the recent fighting was done by FROLIZI and ZANU, while Peter Niesewand gave primary credit to ZANU and ZAPU. *See* P. Niesewand, "What Smith Really Faces," *Africa Report,* 18, 2 (March-April 1972): 16-20. Winter Lemba gave credit to ZANU. *See* W. Lemba, "Liberation Rivalry Buried," *Africa Report,* 18, 3 (May-June 1973): 15.

guerrilla forces through Mozambique and into Rhodesia from the flank of the Rhodesian-South African defensive line in the Zambezi Valley suggests that the war could be entering a new strategic phase. Much of course depends on the insurgents' ability to sustain operations, but if this can be done, it would stretch Rhodesian defense forces to such an extent that South Africa might have to step up its own commitment to the Smith regime.

The decolonization of Mozambique may substantially increase the military pressure on Rhodesia and by extension, on the Republic. For several years before the 1974 coup, it appeared that the major African liberation movement, the Mozambiquean Liberation Front (FRELIMO), was on the defensive. Following the assassination of its leader, Dr. Eduardo Mondlane, in 1969, FRELIMO experienced severe internal difficulties and major defections to the Portuguese.

Taking advantage of the situation, the Portuguese launched a series of major counter-offensives that disrupted FRELIMO's control over much of Cabo Delgado Province and pushed many of the insurgents back across the border into Tanzania. Yet FRELIMO proved to be resilient, opening a new front in the province of Tete, site of the Cabora Bassa dam, and by early 1973 the nationalists had opened up two new fronts in the area of Manica and Sofala, circumventing the Portuguese defensive positions to the north and outflanking the Rhodesia-South Africa forces in the Zambezi area. During this period South African government officials continually expressed concern over the deterioration of the military situation in Mozambique and offered additional aid to the Portuguese.[21]

A FRELIMO government in power may initially pause to consolidate its control over the entire country, but sooner or later it seems highly likely such a government will increase the military pressure on South Africa as well as Rhodesia, if only by providing a sanctuary for the exile movements in territory abutting the Republic.

While the political and military situation in Namibia falls outside the purview of this paper, recent events in Angola also suggest that South Africa may be forced to reassess its commitment to help defend the entire subsystem. There, despite ten years of fighting, the guerrillas have not defeated the Portuguese and the Portuguese in turn have not been able to eliminate the guerrilla bands of the Angolan National Liberation Front (FLNA), the Popular Movement for the Liberation of Angola (MPLA), and the National Union for the Total Independence of Angola (UNITA), despite their history of disunity and fratricide.[22]

[21]South Africa, Rhodesia, and Portugal did share intelligence data and some equipment. See A. Venter, *Portugal's War in Guinea-Bissau* (Pasadena, Calif., 1973).

[22]R. Chilcote, *Portuguese Africa* (Englewood Cliffs, 1965); J. Marcum, *The*

Therefore, unlike the situation in Guinea-Bissau and Mozambique, no single African movement has emerged as the clear heir to the Portuguese colonial government in Angola. Decolonization is likely to be slower there than in the other areas, and the make-up of the eventual independence government is far more difficult to predict. But in the long run the Angolan-Namibian border is likely to be an increasingly difficult defensive area for the Republic.

Thus, over the next few years South Africa could find itself in a military situation in which it is faced with direct military efforts on its northern and eastern borders. Previous South African strategy had assumed that with modest South African input Portugal and Rhodesia could keep their respective insurgents in check. If Portuguese decolonization proceeds effectively in Mozambique and Angola, and if the guerrillas are able to sustain major escalation efforts in Rhodesia, South Africa will be faced with a most unpleasant dilemma: drastically to increase its commitment to Rhodesia or to see the military situation there deteriorate further. Certainly the present level of force of the opposition does not seriously challenge South African hegemony in the area, but we could extrapolate an increase in guerrilla strength that would threaten the present position of the Republic.

Also, it should be noted that, as Johns and others have observed, the very existence of exile movements and the presence of armed guerrillas, however weak and remote from the South African heartland, do alter the political context within South Africa.[23] It is difficult to imagine, for example, such Black leaders as Kaiser Matanzima and Gatsha Buthelezi having the same room to maneuver if there were not less desirable alternatives from the South African point of view. In the last analysis, this may ultimately be the most important contribution that the exile movements will make to South Africa's political future.

Although the full import of the Bantustans for the future of South Africa is covered in the chapters of Schlemmer and Muil, Wilson, and Mbata, our own opinion is that they will function as political insulation for the Republic. Like the "dolos,"[24] the eight-sided concrete anchor

---

Angolan Revolution (Cambridge, Mass., 1969); D. Wheeler and R. Pélissier, *Angola* (New York, 1971); D. Abshire and M. Samuels, eds., *Portuguese Africa* (New York, 1969); MPLA, *Revolution in Angola* (London, 1972); Gibson, *African Liberation Movements*, pp. 197-242; Grundy, *Guerrilla Struggle*, pp. 91-107; and D. Barnett and R. Harvey, eds., *The Revolution in Angola: MPLA, Life Histories and Documents* (New York, 1972).

[23]S. Johns, "Opposition in Southern Africa: Segments, Linkages, and Cohesion" (Paper delivered at the Workshop on Southern Africa, Dalhousie University, August 1973).

[24]The name is taken from the Afrikaans *doloose*, knuckle bones of the sheep or goat, which South African children pretend are imaginary oxen.

blocks that the South Africans invented to stave off the onslaughts of the sea, the Bantustans may well provide a surprisingly substantial buffer to moderate the forces of change within the Republic.

INTERGOVERNMENTAL/DIPLOMATIC

It is precisely this stand that we wish to explore further under a different heading. The mere existence of Lesotho, Botswana, and Swaziland as *de jure* independent states and the normalcy of their relationship with South Africa (however dependent that relationship) seem to suggest the style of future relationships between the Republic and the emerging Bantustans. In the middle 1960s many observers and political actors in the High Commission Territories were concerned that, as time went on, their status vis-à-vis South Africa would approximate that of Bantustans. These fears have not been borne out by events.

Moreover, South Africa's outward policy, despite its present moribund state and the setbacks it suffered with overthrow of Dr. Kofi Busia in Ghana and President Tsiranana of the Malagasy Republic, has interjected a new dynamic into the diplomacy of the subsystem. The exchange of diplomatic representatives with Malawi and the various state visits and South Africa's professed adherence to a good neighbor policy have had an important feedback on the Republic's relations with Lesotho, Swaziland, and Botswana. These diplomatic currents, when taken together with the increasing implementation of the Bantustan program within South Africa, have produced a sharp departure from South Africa's decades-old efforts to incorporate the former High Commission Territories.

The Bantustans represent at once important bargaining chips for South Africa in its relations with the independent Black states south of the Zambezi and, more germane for the purposes of this study, they have offered the possibility of considerable feedback that could have consequences for the Republic in the years to come. For example, there are currently some 450,000 Swazi living in the Republic, most of them in the Transvaal. Although there has been little public sentiment in Swaziland for a "gathering in" of these Swazi, it seems clear that South Africa and the present regime in Swaziland see some mutual benefit in discussing the possibility of transferring at least some of the South African Swazi to the jurisdiction of Swaziland. Late in 1972 the deputy minister of Bantu development, J. J. Raubenheimer, indicated that there might be future homelands for the Swazi that could then affiliate with Swaziland.[25] This announcement followed an October 1972 meeting between commissioner general for the Swazi, P. H.

[25]*Times of Swaziland* (Mbabane), 70, 47 (24 November 1972): 1,

Forlage, and the Swazi council of the Nsikzai region authority near Plaston.

The South African government has not issued a public statement about the possibility of the Swazi Bantustan being incorporated into Swaziland, but it is of significance that the proposed homeland is being consolidated into a single area that abuts Swaziland's northwestern corner. More importantly, the Swazi homeland is one of the smallest Bantustans and Braam Raubenheimer, the assistant deputy minister of Bantu development, while calling such speculation "premature," did indicate the importance of the Bantustans having significant infrastructure for independence.[26]

The relationship between Swaziland and South Africa is a complicated one, containing strong undercurrents of complementarity.[27] Although the Swazi government is opposed to apartheid, there are subjects of substantial agreement with the Republic, most notably in the areas of economic integration, the avoidance of guerrilla warfare in southern Africa, and keeping South African refugees in Swaziland out of politics. At the same time, we have to be careful not to misperceive the kind and amount of direction that Pretoria is able to give to the Swazi government. As some observers have noted, Swaziland, like many other African countries, needs to take a regional approach to its governmental planning,[28] and since the Republic looms so large in Swaziland's economic and military picture, it is not surprising that the Swazi take the South African position into account on many issues.

At the same time, South Africa cannot have been displeased with the royal coup in Swaziland, and there is some evidence that South Africa either initiated diplomatic inquiries about or proved most receptive to Swazi interests in acquiring South African arms for its new army.[29] There is additional evidence that King Sobhuza had been planning his moves for some time. Late in January he told a gathering of the Emabutfo that one duty of young men was to deal with any trouble that might threaten the peace of the nation. He also indicated that they would be called upon in the near future.[30] The South African government also looked with favor on the subsequent banning of political parties in Swaziland, including the Ngwane National Liberatory Congress (NNLC) of Dr. Ambrose Zwane, and the suspension of the 1968 constitution. We can well argue that the subsequent detention of the

[26]Ibid., 71, 18 (4 May 1973): 1.
[27]C. Potholm, *Swaziland: The Dynamics of Political Modernization* (Los Angeles, 1972).
[28]J. Lea, "Underlying Determinants of Housing Location: A Case Study from Swaziland," *Journal of Modern African Studies*, 11, 2 (1973): 211-25.
[29]*The Star* (Johannesburg), 24 March 1973.
[30]*Times of Swaziland* (Mbabane), 71, 5 (2 February 1973): 1.

NNLC leadership,[31] including Dr. Zwane and T. B. Ngwenya, was hardly to the Swaziland government's credit, but South Africa's pleasure at this turn of events does not in our opinion constitute, in and by itself, influence.

Sobhuza's action strengthened the hand of the conservative elements within the Imbokodvo National Movement and the pro-South African elements within the government. Indicating that the present constitution was divisive because it "permitted the importation into our country of highly undesirable political practices alien to, and incompatible with the way of life in our society and designed to disrupt and destroy our own peaceful and constructive and essentially democratic methods of political activities," Sobhuza suggested that a new constitution would be drawn up that would more fully reflect the realities of Swazi national life.[32] As far back as the government of Prime Minister Verwoerd, South Africa has indicated that the multiracial constitutions based on one man-one vote ran counter to its interests. Therefore, it will be most interesting to watch further constitutional activities in Swaziland and their possible relationship to the acquisition of additional Swazis and land from the Republic. From the South African point of view, there is thus substantive ambiguity in the warm reception accorded Gatsha Buthelezi's visit to Swaziland in February 1974.

As will be seen in the next section, there are certain core values that the Swazi, the Batswana, and the Basotho are not prepared to sacrifice. Thus while South Africa has additional advantages in working out *quid pro quos* for the additional population and land that could affiliate with these states, and while we could argue that South Africa by this process simply absolves itself of responsibility for those persons, the possibility of affiliation through federation with Bantustans such as Kwa-Zulu and the Transkei does offer those who would challenge the *status quo* in southern Africa some substantial opportunities previously not available to them.

In fact, contemporary events in Lesotho and Botswana indicate that the leaderships in these two contiguous states are prepared, at least on the verbal plane, to oppose South Africa. Lesotho's prime minister, Chief Jonathan, has recently expressed his opposition to dialogue and his new government of "national reconciliation," with its somewhat broader base of support, has moved away from the early, closer collaboration with South Africa.

---

[31]Ibid., 71, 18 (4 May 1973): 1 and 18 reported that the detentions resulted from the NNLC leadership's alleged attempts to continue political activities despite the ban, more specifically on 12 April 1973.

[32]King Sobhuza II, "Proclamation to All My Subjects—Citizens of Swaziland," (mimeographed, Lobamba, 1973), p. 1.

In recent months and particularly after the kidnapping of Fanele Mbale in 1973, Lesotho's delegation to the United Nations has been noticeably cooler toward the Republic.[33] While economic dependence and military vulnerability continue to be overriding influences propelling Lesotho into continuing docility, recent diplomatic/intergovernmental relations have been strained compared with previous years. For its part, Botswana has refused to exchange ambassadors with South Africa, has rejected dialogue, and does not accept direct grants-in-aid from South Africa.

These trends suggest that if the Bantustans indeed attain full independence and the former High Commission Territories remain independent, there are significant possibilities for African cooperation within southern Africa—cooperation that, on the economic and diplomatic fronts at least, could offer some challenge to South African hegemony in the future. At the present time this is mere speculation, but both Kaiser Matanzima and Gatsha Buthelezi have expressed the desire to link the Transkei and KwaZulu with other African units in southern Africa.[34]

Perhaps the most significant change in the southern African diplomatic context on the horizon today is the independence of Mozambique. Whatever the final composition of the new Mozambiquean government and its short and intermediate range goals, the very existence of a Black government, which attained power through revolutionary struggle, is bound to present South Africa with a harsh new set of diplomatic considerations. What if the Bantustans wish to federate with an independent Mozambique? What if the government of Mozambique offers aid, economic or military, to the Bantustans? If the new government is willing to have diplomatic relations with the Republic, what will be its price for such an arrangement? Can the government of South Africa co-exist with a militant, Black government whose socialist internal policies are anathema to South Africa? Will the South African electorate, which has accepted cooperation and diplomatic interchange with docile and supportive Black regimes, be willing to give the present government room to maneuver with the new forces holding sway in Mozambique?

[33]For the most celebrated instance of South African penetration into Lesotho, see J. Butler, "South Africa and the High Commission Territories: The Ganyile Case, 1961," in G. Carter, ed., Politics in Africa: Seven Cases (New York, 1966), pp. 245-83. A similar case occurred in 1973 when the South African police crossed into Lesotho and departed with Fanele Mbale. In the recent history of Swaziland, there have been a variety of similar incidents when refugees from the Republic have either been abducted or have disappeared under mysterious circumstances. See Potholm, Swaziland, pp. 144-5.

[34]For a fuller examination of some of these themes, see M. Lipton, "Independent Bantustans," International Affairs 45, 1 (January 1972): 1-19;

PHILOSOPHICAL/IDEOLOGICAL

There are currently a number of distinctly countervailing philosophical and ideological currents operative in southern Africa. These have to do with fundamental assessments about the nature of human collectivities that the various entities have made and with the nature of the power diffusion within them. Four states (Lesotho, Botswana, Swaziland, and Malawi) have governments that stress nonracist societies and economic and political systems based, at least in theory, on nonracial criteria for advancement; three entities (South Africa, Namibia, and Rhodesia) have pronounced philosophies of racial separation and exclusivity; while until recently two (Angola and Mozambique) have stressed a type of multiracial society in which the cultural values of the one racial group, the Europeans, are held to be superior, but upon adopting these values, one can be accepted as a social and political equal.

We do not have attitudinal surveys to enable us to say with assurance how widely the core values are held in these various societies. Nor are we able to assert definitely the extent to which these generalized philosophies are realized by the governments in question. Nevertheless, it would seem that the self-perceptions of the governments and the societies themselves are of considerable importance in helping us to understand what is taking place in southern Africa. However, although the following observations are both preliminary and tentative, what impressionistic evidence we have seems to support them.

In the first place, over the last decade the Portuguese and the South African governments, however much they may have been committed to the *status quo* in southern Africa, avoided forming an open and formal military alliance. While the South Africans had certain military reservations about a formal alliance, the Portuguese seemed to be most troubled by the psychological and philosophical aspects of such an alliance. And, since the Rhodesians were moving toward the South African core values rather than toward a nonracist society, the Portuguese were also reluctant to support the Smith government without reservation.

With the decolonization of Mozambique and Angola, it remains to be seen to what extent the values embodied in the ideal that the Portuguese professed of an non-racial society will be actualized by the independence government, whose own stated values are non-racial but whose movements have generally not included Whites in any significant numbers.

---

and C. Hill, "Botswana and the Bantustans" (Paper delivered at the Workshop on Southern Africa, Dalhousie University, August 1973).

For South Africa, a viable non-racial society in Mozambique might appear to provide a challenge by example. Much, of course, depends upon the outcome of powerful societal forces only recently released. If there are continuing racial clashes within the country, with concomitant flights by Europeans, especially those from Beira and Lourenço Marques, then White South Africans would probably be bolstered in their belief that a non-racial society rule by a Black government is not viable, thereby reinforcing their resolve to maintain their segregated society at all costs. On the other hand, a stable non-racial society functioning so close to the South African heartland might, in incremental ways at least, influence some White South Africans to reassess their own racial attitudes.

Botswana, Swaziland, and Lesotho have all made firm commitments to the development of nonracist societies. Regardless of the levels of their dependency on South Africa, all three governments have stated categorically their opposition to apartheid, indeed to the very core values on which South Africa is based. It has been argued that the very existence of these Black-run states, committed as they are to nonracist societies, would serve as an example to White South Africa to moderate its racial views. There is little evidence to suggest that such a process of psychological interaction has taken or is taking place.

On the other hand, these African states have exhibited great reluctance to jeopardize their independent standing in the African and world communities, and their very independence can be seen as a culmination of a struggle to avoid European domination that stretches back over a century. As was suggested in the previous section, we consider that the very existence of these states offers both direction and psychological succor for those African leaders in the Bantustans who would, insofar as the narrow perimeters of South African policy will permit, seek to move toward *de jure* and *de facto* independence. The persistence of racial domination and segregation in South Africa and its increasing implementation in Rhodesia have, in systemic terms at least, to be balanced with countervailing commitments on the part of the Portuguese (at least in theory), and very definitely on the part of such states as Botswana.[35] In other words, the implementation of the Bantustan program, when taken in conjunction with the variety of core values currently operative in southern Africa, suggests that future repercussions for South Africa, now only dimly perceived by both

[35]S. Khama, *Botswana: A Developing Democracy in Southern Africa* (Uppsala, 1970); R. Dale, *Botswana and Its Southern Neighbor: The Patterns of Linkage and the Options in Statecraft*, International Studies, Africa Series, #6 (Athens, Ohio, 1970) and *The Racial Component of Botswana's Policy, Studies in Race Relations*, 2, 4 (1970-71): 1-29; and E. Munger, *Bechuanaland: Pan-African Outpost or Bantu Homeland* (London, 1965), p. 86.

actors and observers alike, could alter the texture and ethos of the region.

CONCLUSION

Elsewhere we have suggested that there are a number of possible scenarios for South Africa, based in part on what happens within the Republic but also contingent upon what happens elsewhere.[36] More recently, we have been concerned with the type of subsystem evolving in the region and with its physical and psychological limits of growth. Our conclusions are that the subsystem has probably reached its limit of growth and that the evolving fragmentation of the area will lead to some systemic retrenchment in the years ahead.[37] In short, South Africa appears to retain its ability to maintain itself and hold sway over some of the contiguous states despite the potentially serious threats to its position.

Some have argued that the systemic approach to southern Africa is not "productive" because it "legitimizes" the subsystem by ignoring or underplaying extrasystemic forces that could substantially alter its nature and especially its heartland, South Africa.[38] Full consideration of these concerns lies outside the scope of this chapter and will be more fully treated in those that follow, especially that of Thompson, but it seems appropriate to suggest that further analysis of the future of the region should focus on a number of previously undertreated themes.

The first of these has to do with the increasing implementation of the Bantustan program in South Africa and the emergence of new leaders within its context. Will these leaders be able to escape the stigma of too close cooperation with Pretoria and yet avoid curtailment of their activities? Will they be able to build bridges to other Black elites, not only within the subsystem but beyond? To date they have not been overly critical of the various exile movements and this may suggest the possibility of future interaction. At the very least, the continuing existence of South African exile movements, whatever their long-term opportunities to actually overthrow the system, aids and abets these leaders by providing them with room for maneuver vis-à-vis the South African authorities.

The second theme that needs a good deal of further study and the generation of hard data is the continuing dissonance between the

[36]C. Potholm, "Toward the Millennium" in Potholm and Dale, eds., *Southern Africa in Perspective*, pp. 321-31 and "After Many a Summer? The Possibilities of Political Change in South Africa," *World Politics* 24, 4 (July 1972): 613-38.

[37]C. Potholm, "The Limits of Systemic Growth: Southern Africa Today" (Paper delivered at the Workshop on Southern Africa, Dalhousie University, August 1973).

[38]Zdenek Cervenka and Ake Magnusson of the Scandinavian Institute of African Studies, Uppsala, Sweden, are leading exponents of this position, as are Sean Gervasi and Sam Nolutshungu, whose chapters follow.

economic and military dependency of the former High Commission Territories and their independence with regard to the core values of their societies. As long as Rhodesia, Mozambique, and Angola remained under White control, these core values could not have much impact on South Africa, but with any or all of these three territories under like-minded governments, the cumulative impact on the Republic could be considerable.

The possible pulling away of Angola and Mozambique from the subsystem is not without precedent. Zambia has made substantial progress in its policy to reorient trade and transaction flows away from the subsystem and its long-term gravitation pull may have substantial impact on Botswana and Malawi.[39] In the longer run South African influence over the area may be undercut as much by these developments as by the more dramatic and transitory political events that so often capture our attention.

Finally, there is the question of the capability of the South African system to cope with these changes. Quite apart from the rightness or wrongness of its core values and its dominance over those people in the area who are not white, the South African political system is, in purely systemic terms, strong indeed. It emerged from the internal turmoil of the 1950s and early 1960s stronger than it had been before. It reacted to international opposition and the more recent energy crisis with resourcefulness and power. It remains, in terms of its military and economic power, the most prominent and strongest unit in the region and seems, at this point at least, well able to sustain at least a truncated version of the subsystem.

These aspects, like so many others, need our continuing analysis for in southern Africa, at least, there are no surprise-free scenarios.[40]

[39]D. Anglin, "Zambia's Disengagement From Southern Africa: A Transaction Analysis" (Paper delivered at the Canadian Association of African Studies, February 1973), and his more recent, "Reorientation of Zambia's External Relations—Disengagement from Southern Africa and Integration with East Africa: A Transaction Analysis" (Paper delivered at the Workshop on Southern Africa, Dalhousie University, August 1973). *See also* J. Leech, "Zambia Seeks a Route to Fuller Independence," *Issue* 2, 4 (Winter 1972): pp. 6–11.

[40]C. Potholm, "The Scenarios Revisited: A Framework for Speculation" (Paper delivered at Princeton University, March 1974).

14

The Politics of "Accelerated Economic Growth"

SEAN GERVASI

INTRODUCTION

In recent years the debate over the future of southern Africa has taken a new turn. For a long time there seemed to be two alternatives: the system of White supremacy would survive or southern Africa would see a profound upheaval. Most observers believed that the White redoubt was impregnable, that nothing could challenge the superior power of South Africa, Portugal, and Rhodesia. Others argued that the liberation movements would eventually defeat the White powers and carry out a revolution. These were the main arguments in the decade after Sharpeville. Everything seemed to turn on whether the liberation movements could mount a serious military challenge to White power.

The liberation movements have now proved that they are mounting such a challenge. They have defeated Portugal in Africa and brought about the collapse of Portuguese fascism. No one can doubt that their military power will grow. The White fortress has begun to crumble, and at some point there will be a major upheaval.

It has been clear for a number of years that the White regimes could not stand for ever. The collapse of Portuguese power was seen as a distinct possibility as early as 1970. Nonetheless, Western governments refused to see what was obvious to many. Warnings sank into the sand in which ministers buried their heads. And at the very moment that the storm began to break they began to find hope in a third alternative. Suddenly we are told that the dilemma of choosing between upheaval and stability could be avoided. From 1970 influential people began to talk of "peaceful change." Government officials, scholars, and other observers began to say that the problems of racism, colonialism, and exploitation in southern Africa will only be resolved through "evolutionary means."

The essential argument given for this third alternative is a simple one: the White powers have begun to realize that modern economies cannot function efficiently when freedoms are restricted. They are already moving toward a significant liberalization of the present political systems. Moreover, the natural trend of economic forces can produce over time many of the benefits that the liberation movements have set out to secure for the oppressed majority. These forces have already begun to create a new prosperity for many Africans. Thus a combination of economic and political trends can be expected to produce the "revolution" that the vast majority seeks. While this conclusion is often stated implicitly, some proponents of this view make the point quite explicitly. They argue that the trends in question are on the point of producing radical changes in the distribution of power and wealth.[1]

However, it should be noted that everything turns on economics, on the view we take of the process of economic growth. Part of the argument is directly economic. Economic growth, the expansion of job opportunities, rises in African wages, all will in themselves bring far-reaching changes in the lives of Africans. Poverty, it is implied, will be significantly reduced, if not eliminated. The rest of the argument is indirectly economic. Political liberalization will have to come. For apartheid, forced labor, and racism are all obstacles to efficiency and expansion. Those with power want to eliminate them, if only gradually. Apartheid and colonialism are, in this view, "irrational."

The main proposition that is put forward, then, is that capitalist economies tend naturally in the course of their expansion to eliminate poverty and reduce inequality. One aim of this paper is to subject this proposition to careful analysis to determine whether it is based upon a sound description of the mechanics of capitalist expansion.

In assessing the validity, however, of this new theory of social change, we must question more than economics, for the ideas now being put forward about "progress through evolutionary means" in southern Africa derive their real meaning from their use as political instruments. Individuals, interest groups, and governments are using them in an attempt to influence the debate over whether to support the liberation struggle on the subcontinent.

This has now become a burning issue, for southern Africa is in the midst of a crisis. A new stage in the struggle for the elimination of colonialism and apartheid has been reached: the White powers have suffered a serious military defeat in the buffer states of Angola and Mozambique; the situation in Rhodesia (Zimbabwe) is becoming increasingly difficult. The liberation movements have become a

[1]The point is in fact made in some of the contributions to this book.

credible force in African politics, and many informed observers believe that an eventual military confrontation between the White powers and the liberation forces must come. In this situation uncommitted nations must decide where they stand, whether they will support the White powers or the liberation movements. The choice, for many nations, is not an easy one, and governments that are not compelled to act out of a need to protect vital interests are likely to try to avoid making it.

In the context of crisis the new theory has some striking political implications. The first is that the liberation movements, by creating "instability and chaos," may be doing far more harm than good. For were they to work within the framework of "the system," they could achieve their ends without violence. In consequence, their armed struggle must be seen as tragic and wasteful. The second implication is that those committed to the African cause should seek to preserve stability in the area. By doing so they would be helping to preserve the framework within which constructive change can take place. Finally, there is the implication that we should help the existing governments in southern Africa to speed liberalization and economic growth. Thus the political meaning of the theory of peaceful change is that the *status quo* should be preserved.

Furthermore, in many Western countries "discussion" of the new theory has now taken on the dimensions of a massive campaign, with arguments being put forward that were scarcely mentioned a decade ago. When the liberation movements were only entering the stage of armed struggle, no one thought to urge "liberalization" and "accelerated economic growth" on the White powers. Now, however, these arguments are much discussed in the media. Reporters are sent to Africa to write about the "change of mood" that is taking place in countries where much of the population is forced to live on the margins of starvation. Foreign ministries circulate brochures about the "revolution" in wages and job opportunities for African workers in South Africa. We cannot escape the impression that this is an orchestrated campaign, that important interest groups and governments are somehow trying to change the image of apartheid and colonialism.

Thus the debate has taken several new turns. A new view of the possibilities of change in southern Africa is being put forward, which offers uncommitted countries an "easy way" out of the dilemma of having to choose sides in the gathering crisis. Furthermore, it is clear that powerful interests are devoting a great deal of time and money to publicizing the case for "gradualist" solutions in southern Africa.

New questions therefore inevitably arise. How did this new theory of social change evolve? What were its origins? Were they political or academic? Is this new theory as applied to southern Africa essentially an ideological one? Is it an optimistic distortion of reality designed to further certain ends? If so, what ends? These questions need to be examined if we are truly to understand the new thesis, what it is intended to do and why. The second aim of this chapter, therefore, is to place the theory in proper perspective. It is as important to understand how theories are used as it is to know whether they are true. In the present crisis we might almost say that it does not matter so much whether the current notions about peaceful change are true. What matters is whether people believe them to be true.

SOUTHERN AFRICA AND THE WESTERN BLOC

Southern Africa has recently become the focus of serious concern in the chancelleries of the major Western powers. This is an entirely new development. The subcontinent was until very recently a peripheral area in world politics, important only to Great Britain. Southern Africa, furthermore, was quite stable, and British interests were secure. The situation has changed in two ways. First, spectacular economic interpenetration throughout the capitalist world during the last twenty-five years has produced a high degree of interdependence— economic, technological, military, political, and cultural—among countries, and southern Africa has been integrated into this new system. The major Western powers now have important, indeed vital, joint interests in the area.[2] Second, these interests are far from secure. Africa has been polarized, and the polarization is increasing. There is a war going on across the whole northern perimeter of the subcontinent. The forces supporting liberation in the South have proved far more powerful than most Western observers expected them to be. There is everywhere a sense that the continent is moving toward a major crisis.

It will be useful to review briefly both the extent of Western interests and the military situation in the area.

There is, first, an obvious political interest. Southern Africa has been part of the Western sphere of interest since the period of British colonial expansion. The foundation of Western influence in the area is the system of political power that now prevails there. The erosion or loss of Western influence in southern Africa would have many and far-reaching consequences for Western countries, which are therefore bound to wish to preserve the present political system, the present distribution of power between Africans and Whites.

[2]The importance of Western interests in southern Africa is discussed at length in S. Gervasi, L. Bowman, and E. Frey-Wouters, *Portugal, the NATO Powers and Southern Africa* (New York, forthcoming).

There is also a less obvious political interest. South Africa is the most powerful industrial state in Africa. An upheaval on the subcontinent could easily, in the present circumstances, produce a regime hostile to Western interests. Such a regime, resting on a powerful industrial base, would exert great influence throughout the African continent. The world economic system is increasingly unstable. The conflicts of interest between the rich and the poor countries already threaten to undermine the neocolonial relations of the last twenty-five years. A powerful South Africa hostile to Western interests might be seen as a threat to Western interests throughout Africa.

The major Western powers have important investments in the region; direct investments alone now probably exceeds $15 billion.[3] British investments in southern Africa are very large, yielding large revenues for important companies and foreign exchange for the balance of payments. Britain would be in some economic difficulty without its southern African investments, and its allies cannot afford to ignore this fact. Furthermore, investments in the region are expanding very rapidly. South Africa and Angola in particular have become magnets for United States, European, and Japanese funds.

Trade with southern Africa is also important to the Western powers. Again, Britain has the most important trade with the region, but exports to the region are growing rapidly in every industrial country. Furthermore, most Western countries have positive trade balances with southern Africa.[4] By 1972 four Western countries alone—Britain, the United States, West Germany, and France—were exporting goods worth $3,500 million to the area.[5]

In the last decade many Western countries have become heavy importers of raw materials, especially of minerals. The Michaelis Report, presented to the European Economic Commission in late 1972, indicated that in the future the European community will be critically dependent upon South Africa for supplies of strategic raw materials.[6] Other countries in southern Africa also export large quantities of important materials, in particular, nonferrous metals. Their dependence upon such supplies gives the major Western powers an important stake in the region that they did not have before.

---

[3]This is a rough estimate. In 1971 South Africa alone had some $10 billion in foreign liabilities. *See* South Africa Reserve Bank, *Quarterly Bulletin* 108 (June 1973). For an estimate of foreign investment in Rhodesia, Angola, Mozambique, Zambia and Malawi, *see* R. Murray and C. Stoneman, "Private Overseas Investment in Southern and Central Africa," mimeographed (London, 1970).

[4]*See Directions of Trade Annual, 1968-1972.*

[5]Ibid.

[6]H. Michaelis, *Memorandum uber eine Europaische Rohstoffsversorgungspolitik* (Brussels, September 1972).

South Africa, furthermore, has the only industrial base in Africa—a fact of increasing importance to the multinational corporations, which use it to export goods to various parts of Africa, and even to the Mediterranean, and benefit from exceedingly low labor costs. For this reason alone, countries like Great Britain and the United States have new and important interests in the area.

Finally, the Western countries have an important military-strategic interest in the area. Europe is now highly dependent upon shipments of oil from the Persian Gulf. Even with the Suez Canal open most of this oil will have to come around the Cape. A great deal of other trade passes around the Cape in both directions. Naval strategists believe that the littoral countries, and especially South Africa, must be either friendly or neutral if the Western countries are to keep this vital lane of trade and communications open.[7]

The security of these Western interests in southern Africa obviously turns on the military situation, a situation that has changed significantly in the last fourteen years. In 1960 the system of White rule was almost undisputed. There was considerable political agitation in various parts of southern Africa, but the white regimes had determined to resist the tide of African nationalism. They had begun to dig in; their police and military power was already massive; they could not have been dislodged by arms at that time. The African nationalist movements were simply too weak, and at the time they were given almost no chance of gaining ascendancy in the forseeable future.

Today the situation is very different. The conflict has exploded, and the whole of Africa is being shaken by it. There have been a number of important changes in the military situation.

Portugal has now been forced to leave Africa. Mozambique is on its way to independence. A settlement is likely to be reached in Angola soon. South Africa and Rhodesia have lost a powerful ally.[8]

This defeat was suffered despite a massive military mobilization by the White powers. In South Africa the military budget has increased more than fourfold in the last decade.[9] Portugal was until recently spending nearly half its national budget on the war in Africa.

South Africa and Rhodesia have been spending very large amounts of money, much of it abroad, to obtain the military equipment they

---

[7]The argument was set out in full in the North Atlantic Assembly, Military Committee, *Report on the Soviet Maritime Threat* (November 1972).

[8]*See* Ch. 5 of Gervasi, et al., *Portugal, the NATO Powers and Southern Africa.* The collapse of Portuguese military power in Mozambique has now created a major military-strategic problem for South Africa on this border.

[9]United Nations, Unit on Apartheid, B. Ahmad, *South Africa's Military Establishment* (New York, December 1972), p. 3. South Africa's defense estimates for 1961 to 1962 were R72 million. By 1971 to 1972 the figure had risen to R316 million.

require. Between 1960 and 1969, South Africa spend nearly one billion dollars on the purchase of military equipment.

Strategically, South Africa and Rhodesia have suffered a major blow. The outer defense ring of the White redoubt has been smashed. The liberation of Mozambique has brought the war to the border of the Transvaal. It will also lead inevitably to greater pressure on Rhodesia.

The liberation movements have begun to wage war within Rhodesia (Zimbabwe) itself. The Rhodesian Whites are unlikely to remain in control beyond 1976 or 1977.

Despite some reverses the liberation forces have been able continually to increase the tempo of their activities. This is the decisive factor in guerrilla warfare. The achievements of the liberation movements suggest that, barring outside intervention, they will eventually defeat South Africa.[10]

It was evident some years ago that the forces that have since produced these changes were then on the move. The facts were perfectly clear to military analysts in the Western countries, and they were deeply concerned about the matter. By the late 1960s they had begun to follow the situation closely and to consider their options in the event of a major threat to the stability of the region. Thus, at the very moment that the Western countries became aware of their stake in southern Africa, they found that their interests there were threatened. Southern Africa was no longer a region to be taken for granted, it had assumed a new importance in conditions that demanded action.

THE STRATEGY OF CONTAINMENT

It is necessary now to shift the focus of analysis. The changing military balance in southern Africa was beginning to cause real concern in the late 1960s in a number of Western countries. At that point the logic of interests began to assert itself, and the major Western powers began to devise a strategy for confronting the situation. Britain, the United States and other powers are not opposed to change in southern Africa, but they are opposed to change which they cannot control. In 1968 and 1969 they became exceedingly worried about the prospect of an upheaval in the region that they considered to have "deteriorated" quite suddenly. They could not, as they saw it, stand idly by while the liberation movements dismantled, piece by piece, the whole structure of White power in the industrial heartland

---

[10]This had happened even before the collapse of the Portuguese military effort in Africa. The *Frelimo* campaign in Tete Province in Mozambique from 1971 probably marked the decisive turning point in the battle for the "buffer states."

of Africa. As the facts of the situation became known, then, they began to reconsider their traditional policies toward southern Africa, to abandon the "anticolonial" positions that they had once taken, and to move toward closer relations with the White regimes. They began, in fact, to move toward intervention in the liberation struggle.

The major Western powers adopted a classic indirect strategy as they could not allow themselves to be implicated in a direct attack on the liberation movements. They could, however, try to turn the balance of forces against them. And having substantial resources and power, they could use these in southern Africa to influence events. As leaders of the Western bloc, the United States and Britain decided on three lines of action to confront the crisis. First, they determined to force the pace of change in every part of the subcontinent, with or without the cooperation of the White powers. They embarked upon a concerted effort to move those powers in the direction of certain obvious and needed reforms. Second, they resolved to strengthen the White powers so that they would be better able to meet the military challenge posed by the liberation movements. This obviously had to be done very discreetly. Finally, they began to prepare the way for more direct and substantial military assistance to the White regimes. This was essentially contingency planning. It nonetheless reflected a definite commitment to go to the assistance of the White regimes in the event of a major crisis.[11]

At the time of writing, this summary analysis of the emergence of a Western strategy for southern Africa seems speculative to some. It is not. Some of the most important relevant documents will have been published by the time this book is published, and those who follow events in southern Africa will know precisely what kinds of preparations were made in Western chancelleries in anticipation of the present crisis. It will be realized that the major Western powers set a deliberate course at the turn of the decade, that they began to intervene extensively in southern Africa affairs in the belief that they could somehow prevent the collapse of the system of White supremacy.

For the moment, however, public sources will suffice. The *New York Times* has published an important account of a major shift in policy that took place under the first administration of President Richard Nixon. This account is far from complete, but it tells us a good deal

---

[11]A commitment of this kind was proposed openly in the *Soviet Maritime Threat*. It appears to be implicit in the recent decision by the Defense Planning Committee of NATO to begin contingency planning for "crisis situations" in southern Africa. See *De Volkskraant* (Amsterdam), 14 May 1974; the *Sunday Times* (London), 19 May 1974; and the *Observer* (London), 19 May 1974. See also ch. 9 of Gervasi et al., *Portugal, the NATO Powers and Southern Africa*.

about the movement of the major Western powers toward intervention. It is known, furthermore, that the shift in United States policy followed a similar shift in other countries.

According to the *Times* account President Nixon, within a few months after assuming office, requested that the National Security Council undertake a major review of policy toward southern Africa. There was evidently considerable dissatisfaction with the policy of previous administrations, which expressed mild disapproval of the White regimes in the area. Instead, President Nixon decided actively to seek improved relations with South Africa, Portugal, and Rhodesia. The *New York Times* reported:

> The Nixon Administration is quietly pursuing a policy of deliberately expanded contacts and communication with the white governments of southern Africa. . . . In practical terms, the policy has resulted in a number of concrete developments, ranging from major new economic undertakings, such as the recent Azores agreement with Portugal, to the authorization of previously forbidden sales of jet aircraft to Portugal and South Africa.[12]

The National Security Council evidently placed three basic options before the president. All these options, in fact, were choices that favored the White regimes. The possibility of assisting the liberation movements in the struggle for independence was never given serious consideration. The only real question, it appears, was how far the United States would actually go toward assisting the White regimes. The first option, for instance, known as the "Acheson" option, after the late former secretary of state, suggested "treating the white powers as any other nation," that is, without regard to their racial policies. Indeed, this option, supported by the Department of Defense and opposed by the Department of State, classed the White powers as "friendly countries," eligible for military aid in case of "attack." The second option was to move toward "selective involvement" with the White regimes. It was intended to be a policy of more active diplomatic, political, economic, and military assistance to the White regimes and was in fact the policy adopted. The third option was to continue the policy of the previous Democratic administrations, in essence, a policy of "watchful waiting." Although it would have allowed the continued development of economic ties and the maintenance of normal diplomatic relations, official assistance would have been kept to a minimum. However, the White regimes had already benefited, and would have continued to benefit, from such a policy.

[12]*New York Times*, 2 April 1972.

The deliberations of the National Security Council and the analyses of its staff led to the preparation of a study, which was ready by August 1969 when government officials met to discuss the matter with the president. It was decided that option 2 was the best policy for the United States at that time, and the decision was formalized in a National Security Decision Memorandum of February 1970. Thus the United States embarked on a mission to "maintain the balance of power" in a part of the world that few Americans knew anything at all about. It is interesting to note that the policy of "selective involve-ment" with the White regimes that President Nixon decided on was referred to as the "tarbaby" option, for those who criticized it—and they were primarily in the Department of State—believed that "Wash-ington would find it impossible to let go even if the policy proved a failure."[13]

Confirmation of the accuracy of this account is to be found in other public sources. In a speech on "Our Options in Southern Africa" at the end of 1970, Assistant Secretary of State for African Affairs David Newsom appears to have summarized the proceedings in the National Security Council.[14] He described southern Africa as a "problem con-stantly before the world and the United Nations," adding that "it has within it the seeds of violent explosion which could make it an even greater dilemma for us and for the world." He then considered the various approaches to this problem that might be taken by concerned nations. The first, he stated, was acceptance of South Africa—and presumably other White regimes—as it was. Some of those who believed in this policy, he indicated, thought that "we should put our chips on it [South Africa] in the global struggle." However, Newsom belived that this approach was inconsistent with efforts to "solve the problem of prejudice." The second option was support for the libera-tion movements. This was, however, the "road to violence." And Newsom said that "even a sympathetic observer finds it difficult to see this path as being either right or effective." The third approach was isolation. This meant the breaking of diplomatic relations and the withdrawal of investments from the area. Newsom took the view that this policy might not be workable as there was no assurance that any-one "would respond constructively to the pressure of total isolation."

Newsom indicated that there was really only one solution for the problem of southern Africa that the United States could countenance. This was a policy of communication. He was not entirely clear about how this policy would work, but the general idea was that it would help to "break down the barriers between countries." This policy did

[13]Ibid.
[14]D. Newsom, "Our Options in Southern Africa," (Washington, 1970), mimeographed.

not mean, according to the assistant secretary, an acceptance of the White regimes. (He spoke of South Africa in particular.) It did not mean departing from the arms embargo or remaining silent about the evils of apartheid. It did mean that "each side knows better what the other is talking about. It could mean that greater hope would be given to both whites and blacks in South Africa who seek another way."[15] Newsom did not give further details about what the "other way" might be. But he clearly seemed to be addressing himself to those who might be inclined to support the liberation movements. He was asking, at the very moment that the liberation movements were beginning to press the White regimes militarily, that the world hold back, that it not give them the support that many thought they deserved.

Clearly, the options set out by Newsom in his speech were the same ones that, according to the *New York Times*, the National Security Council had already considered during its policy review. And the option that he regarded as the most promising line for United States policy was the very one that President Nixon had chosen at the end of that review. All indications are that the Ford Administration plans to continue this policy. There have, indeed, been many signs of an accelerated effort to build closer relations with South Africa in particular.

ECONOMIC GROWTH AND SOCIAL CHANGE

The main thrust of the new United States policy, and of that of other Western governments, is to promote peaceful change in southern Africa. The purpose of military and economic aid to the White powers, which was the second line of action in Western strategy, is to buy time. If the White regimes were strengthened, the argument goes, they would have more time to implement reforms and speed economic growth. In an important sense, then, the plausibility of the whole policy rests upon economics. Or so it seems.

Press accounts make it clear that the theory of peaceful change played a central role in the deliberations of the National Security Council. According to the *New York Times*, the theory was the basis for the formulation of option 2—and at least one variation of it. The *Times* reporter stated that,

> The National Security Council Staff, represented by Roger Morris, a specialist on Africa, plumped for a variation of "tarbaby" that would combine partial relaxation towards South Africa with cooler language at the United Nations and elsewhere.
> The conceptual basis for this approach was an idea known as "the green bay tree theory," first outlined in an article in the British weekly, *The Economist*, in 1968. The theory holds that like the hardy green bay

[15]Ibid.

tree, which flourishes in a hostile environment, the black majority in South Africa will ultimately break the barriers of apartheid because of the blacks' vital role in the expansion of the country's booming economy.[16]

Therefore the National Security Council staff, and many others, must have considered the new theory to be true, or at the very least, reasonably plausible.

What, however, does the new theory say precisely? What is it? For the moment let us consider the argument only as it applies to the system of apartheid in South Africa. The theory presumably applies by extension to other areas of southern Africa.

The basic argument, as has been noted, is that economic growth will somehow cause the breakdown of the whole system of White supremacy. Economic growth, in other words, transforms the social system, it changes the distribution of power in society. The plausibility of this argument depends on a rather narrow definition of apartheid. It tends to identify apartheid and colonialism with poverty. And the real argument is that economic growth will significantly reduce or even eliminate poverty.

There are essentially two versions of the argument. The first, which we shall call the "weak" version, is that economic growth will bring a general rise in incomes. The relative position of every group in society will remain the same; distribution of income will not change. But the rising level of absolute incomes eventually will raise even the poorest groups above the level of poverty. Economic growth, in other words, eventually produces a qualitative improvement in the material conditions of life for the poor; it raises them out of poverty.

The "strong" version of the argument holds that economic progress will produce two results. It will lead to a greater flexibility in the economy by creating higher incomes overall. This will create "space" for a certain redistribution of income in favor of the poor, for, with higher incomes, redistribution will involve less sacrifice for Whites. At the same time growth will produce changes in the occupational structure, and non-Whites will have opportunities to acquire new skills and higher pay. Malherbe states the strong version succinctly: "What is needed rather is to create a much larger national cake in which case fairer slices could be distributed on the basis of higher contributions."[17]

That is really the essence of the matter. The "theory" does not go further than that. There is no reasoned, articulated argument. There are simply two rather general propositions, one about economic

[16]*New York Times*, 2 April 1972.
[17]E. Malherbe, *Bantu Manpower and Education* (Johannesburg, 1969), p. 32.

growth and the other about income distribution. And the proposition about inequality is only about possibilities; it is not about necessary consequences.

The "theory" of peaceful change does not really address itself to the problem. An explanation worthy of the term should indicate how economic growth causes the breakdown of a system of institutions, which is what apartheid is. The argument that growth will change the situation by reducing poverty is interesting, for the system of discrimination and control might be easier to bear if everyone could live above the poverty line. But the argument is entirely irrelevant. Poverty and apartheid are not the same thing. Poverty is one consequence of the way the system functions; it is by no means the organizing principle of the system.

South Africa is a racist society. But what is the source of this racism? It is the form of economic and social organization that is the matrix of daily life. The basis of apartheid was, and remains, a degree of arbitrary violence that is no longer accepted in most civilized societies.

In the beginning the territory known as South Africa was taken by force. The Africans populations were subdued by force and were made to do the work required by simpler settler communities. Thus a tradition that has governed the relations between Whites and Africans for the whole of South African history was established. This tradition is the foundation not only of White supremacy, but also of white prosperity. This becomes clear when one sees that both depend upon a vast system of forced labor. This is arbitrary violence in its most modern form—a system, built expressly by legislation, that leaves Africans nothing in life but the necessity of doing the White man's work.

Apartheid and colonialism are systems of power; and they can, to an important degree, adapt to changing circumstances. Apartheid in particular has shown itself to be remarkbly adaptable over the last two and one-half decades. South Africa experienced very rapid economic growth during this time, yet apartheid survived. Growth led to extensive changes in population distribution and occupational structure, but the laws that define the system were changed to preserve White supremacy in the new circumstances. As industrialization proceeded, apartheid was extended to the industrial sector and to urban areas. There is no reason to believe that those who have power in South Africa cannot continue to do what they have always done. Economic growth does not in itself change the distribution of power, and power determines the distribution of income, wealth, and opportunities as well as the degree of freedom that individuals can exercise. Apartheid today is in many ways stronger than it has ever been. This does not mean that it is secure; but the system remains powerful.[18]

It is important to stress the role of power. Power derives from the positions that people occupy in the system. The fact that South Africa is, in effect, a vast labor camp thus becomes very important, for Africans remain powerless in that system. It is only if we confront such realities that the obstacles to change in South Africa can be seen for what they are. The prosperity of South Africa, and therefore the profitability of most foreign investments, rests upon the forced labor system. Many of the solutions that are now being argued for the problems of southern Africa, and particularly for South Africa, do not take into account either the existence of a forced labor system or the difficulties that dismantling it would present to entrenched interests. The only solution that the African population will accept will be one that eliminates the system of forced labor. This would have the most far-reaching consequences for the life of South Africa, entailing not merely an abandonment of discriminatory legislation, but a revolution on the land, the ending of White economic privilege, a social upheaval, and the abolition of a totalitarian state.

Let us examine a typical statement of the theory of peaceful change against this background. In 1968, Sir Alec Douglas-Home, a former prime minister of Britain and foreign secretary from 1970 to 1974 in the Heath government, wrote an article in the *Sunday Times* of London in which he made the conventional points. In arguing the case for peaceful change in southern Africa, Sir Alec's emphasis was on the situation in South Africa.

Sir Alec emphasized the importance of economic change as the vehicle of progress. "Prodigious work" was being done to improve the "standards of life" of the African majority. Economic growth and industrial reform, he argued, were likely to solve South Africa's "racial tensions." The sum of the argument was that "the problem" could be solved within the framework of existing institutions. Sir Alec did not note that the South Africa of which he spoke was the same country in which a minority had tried for years to make the system of White supremacy unchallengeable. He did not deal with the obvious objections to his thesis. He simply asserted that the path he suggested was the one that "reasoning" people would see as the best way ahead. It was the alternative to change inspired by "doctrine," and it would avoid "violence." Sir Alec ended his article with the following summary:

> South Africa is a great country. On the one hand are all the signs pointing to expansion and economic prosperity. On the other there are the historic fears of one or other ethnic group for its neighbor. To create

[18]*See* F. Johnstone, "White Prosperity and White Supremacy in South Africa," *African Affairs*, 69, 275 (April 1970). *See also* S. Gervasi, *Industrialization, Foreign Capital and Forced Labour in South Africa* (New York, 1970), ch. 2.

a harmonious and complete nation, she needs time to solve her daunting problem, and friends who can help her to use that time well.[19]

This seems as bland a formulation as we could expect to find anywhere. It skirts around the deep problems of reconstruction to which the ending of apartheid would lead. Yet many observers continue to take this simplistic view of the matter: economic change is the engine of progress.

ECONOMIC GROWTH AND POVERTY

Nonetheless, the theory does try to say something. It suggests that growth will lift Africans out of poverty. Although a much more modest proposition than the claim to fundamental social change, it is important nevertheless.

If economic growth could lift the mass of the population out of poverty in a relatively short time that would be a significant achievement. It would not be a revolution, as many middle-income American Blacks will testify, but it would be substantial and important progress. The question is whether we can really expect economic growth to produce such results in contemporary southern Africa. To assess this we must return to our original proposition. Do capitalist economies tend naturally in the course of their expansion to eliminate poverty and reduce inequality?

What precisely do we mean by "poverty"? In essence "poverty" must mean the lack of basic necessities to sustain life or to lead a decent life. Most people in southern Africa live at or below the margin of subsistence. They have little or nothing because they live on very poor land or because they work for low wages in the White areas. They can neither produce nor purchase what they need. And the economy does not produce what they need since there is not sufficient profit for producers in turning out large quantities of the requisite goods for the mass of the African population.

Indeed, poverty is so extensive in southern Africa that it could be eliminated only by a massive effort aimed at increasing the quantities of basic necessities produced. This would entail reducing or holding back the production of other kinds of goods.

One of the principal obstacles, in a capitalist economy, to the elimination of poverty is poverty itself. The problem is a circular one. General poverty means that a large section of the population has little or no effective demand for many commodities. People lack many things. But this only means that there is need; there is not enough purchasing power to buy the goods that are needed. Consequently,

[19]*Sunday Times* (London), 24 March 1968.

there is very little incentive for corporations to produce the things that are needed. Most production is therefore for the wealthy urban market or for foreign buyers.

Let us see what happens in such an economy, in a very poor economy, as income and output grow. It is important here to distinguish between the two. In the first place, the rules that determine the distribution of income remain the same. The "black box" that produces the distribution of income is not tampered with. Shares remain the same. Therefore, at every new and higher level of income, the existing distribution of income will be reproduced. As incomes grow overall, then, families in the highest income groups will receive very considerable additions to their incomes in absolute terms. Families in the poorest sections of the population will receive fairly small additions to their incomes in absolute terms. Thus the gap between the rich and the poor widens.

Real resources will be directed, in the course of growth, to the most profitable new uses that producers can find for them. The very small increases in the incomes of the poor will not be enough to cause a massive switch by producers to the production of far larger amounts of basic commodities. To do this producers would also have to overcome a number of bottlenecks that already exist as a consequence of the unbalanced structure of production. The incomes of the wealthy, on the other hand, do present important new opportunities for profit. The wealthy are likely, in the typical country in the region, to be receiving anywhere from 65 to 85 percent of the total income in the country. And a very substantial portion of their incomes is likely to be "free" or "discretionary." The rise in their absolute incomes means that the rich have increasingly larger amounts of such free income. This group will therefore be likely to extend its consumption.

The tendency, therefore, will be for real resources to move continuously into the production of more goods and new goods for the relatively wealthy sections of the population, including the overseas market, with which the real spending power lies. It is by catering to the demands of this group that profits are to be made. Thus the kinds of production that will receive priority and will dominate economic growth are those that are linked to high-income consumption patterns or that have rapidly expanding foreign markets. Production of basic necessities may increase, but it is not likely to do much more than keep pace with the growth of population. It may not even do that.

In a country with a highly unequal distribution of income the pattern of growth thus tends to be uneven. The system continuously reproduces an uneven distribution of income, which generates an uneven distribution of consumption. Inequality produces inequality. A large part of the resources that become available for growth are "trapped" by the spending power of the wealthy. The poor are thus left in poverty. Resources are bid away from them; they cannot draw resources out of other kinds of production. Thus at every new and higher level of production the pattern of output and consumption is likely to reflect the degree of inequality prevailing in society. This will remain true as long as the distribution of income continues to remain unequal.

A trend toward greater equality in income distribution would hold out some hope for the elimination of poverty in the course of economic growth. The shift towards greater equality, of course, would have to be substantial. Although data are scarce, those available indicate that economic growth typically tends to produce increasing inequality in a poor market economy. For instance, Weisskoff, in a study of distribution trends in Puerto Rico, Argentina, and Mexico, concluded that, "It appears that the particular mechanism of the growth process in these countries has led to increasing inequality, despite the efforts by respective governments to modify and lessen the stresses generally associated with Western industrialization."[20] The data used in the study were supported by an analysis that isolates the factors probably responsible for the trend. The use of inappropriate technologies, for instance, holds back the growth of jobs, and that in turn causes a slower growth in low-income groups. A number of similar factors tend to hold back the growth of income among wage earners and the poor in almost every underdeveloped country. All these factors are present in southern Africa.

Southern Africa, of course, has its own unique problems. However, these do not affect the general conclusion about trends in distribution. If anything, the peculiar conditions of the subcontinent would tend to increase the trend toward greater inequality in the course of growth. The tight control of educational and other opportunities, for instance, tends to restrict the possibility of Africans moving up the occupational hierarchy. And such restriction, again, tends to hold back the growth of income among the poorer groups. There may be some tendency now toward slightly higher incomes among small groups of urban Africans, but the overall trend in distribution is likely to be toward greater inequality.

POLITICS AND THE PROSPECT FOR CHANGE

We can only conclude that the theory of peaceful change cannot be taken seriously. In the first place, it is not a theory of social change at all. It deals with one aspect of social change only, and at that it deals

[20]R. Weisskof, "Income Distribution and Economic Growth in Puerto Rico, Argentina and Mexico," *Review of Income and Wealth* (December 1970).

with the outward sign, or result, of change rather than with the process itself. There is no attempt to analyze the social forces at work in the southern African setting, nor is there any proper definition of what social change would mean. The theory deals in superficialities. It does not come to grips with the main problem of explaining how change could transform the system. The theory lacks clear definitions, premises and logic. In short, it is empty. It is not a "theory" in any proper sense of the word, but only a set of slogans, the purpose of which is to make an impression and to avoid the need for reasoning.

Second, the assertions made about social change, to the extent that there are any, are probably quite wrong. The main conclusion of the "theory," or perhaps the main "theorem," is that growth can eliminate poverty. This may be possible, in some capitalist economies, if there are deliberate attempts to reduce inequalities of income distribution in the growth process. It is not possible if the economy is characterized by a highly unequal distribution of income and if that distribution never changes for the better. Therefore, even in its own very limited terms, the "green bay tree theory" is refuted by the facts of historical experience. One of the great "laws" of economics has been thought to be Pareto's theorem that distribution remain the same over time. If this is so, then in a very poor economy poverty cannot be eliminated by growth.

In short, the theory of peaceful change just does not stand up. And those who hope that significant social change will come in southern Africa by "evolutionary means" seem to be lost in a wilderness of confusion, vagueness, and wishful thinking.

This is precisely the clue to the real nature of the theory in question. It is a political theory in almost every respect. That is, it is an idea that developed out of the need to persuade the world that it should refrain from supporting the liberation movements in the gathering crisis. The theory was born out of politics and has its only real meaning in relation to politics. This conclusion is suggested by a number of considerations:

No one seriously suggested, before the late 1960s, that the aims of the African majority in southern Africa could be attained through "evolutionary change." The idea of radical change, of a significant change in the lives of the majority, was simply not on the agenda.

There has never been a closely reasoned analysis among academic or nonacademic social scientists of the main issues raised by the new theory. Nor has there been any serious empirical investigation of the meaning of "radical" or "significant" change.

The new theory emerged at a moment of gathering crisis in southern African affairs, that is, during the late 1960s. It was the minority regimes, and the major Western powers, that were in "crisis" at that time.

It was introduced by politicians who had an interest in persuading public opinion of its truth. These politicians were the leaders in the major Western countries of a campaign to assist the minority regimes in their growing difficulties in holding off the liberation movements.

In the past few years the theory has been at the center of a world-wide attempt by conservative interest groups, including certain governments, to mobilize support for the White regimes. As has been noted, this is now a massive campaign, that appears to be carefully orchestrated.

Seen against the background of intellectual confusion and super-ficiality described, these facts suggest that the theory is a classic example of ideology. It is an optimistic distortion of reality designed to lull us into unthinking acceptance of whatever is said. This is not to say that it is a fully conscious and deliberate distortion. There may be those who do misrepresent the facts quite deliberately. However, this is not the way ideologies develop and evolve. They evolve as part of a generally automatic attempt to avoid a confrontation with unpleasant-ness and contradictions, and this appears to be as true of states as it is of individuals. What we are talking about here, then, is "false con-sciousness." The theory of peaceful change as applied to southern Africa in the present situation must stand as a classic example of this kind of self-deluding behavior on the part of the nations, groups, and individuals that have been so caught up with it.

This is not to say that "accelerated economic growth" will bring no benefits at all to the African population of southern Africa. Some will no doubt benefit, but they will be in the minority. The natural trend of market forces will be to reproduce and extend inequalities. Eco-nomic growth will not eliminate poverty. It may alleviate it to some extent; some people may rise above the poverty line; they may be in the majority in certain limited areas. The conditions of life for the majority will remain essentially unchanged; they will still be locked into a system that offers them very little in life. Others, and in particular the White population, will reap most of the benefits of growth. Some of these will accrue as well to foreigners, who receive raw materials or investment incomes. In short, accelerated economic growth will mean change without change, change within the system. There will be progress of a sort, but it will be limited.

It is often argued that those who seek to promote accelerated growth are the real revolutionaries in southern Africa. The liberation movements, we are told, will produce "violence and chaos" from which Africa might never recover. The strategy of peaceful change. however, holds the promise of a truly better life, at least for some. It can bring change by "evolutionary means."

This argument can now be seen for what it is. The kinds of changes proposed for southern Africa by outside powers are necessarily more or less marginal ones. The hidden assumption in the strategy of accelerated growth is that power is to remain in the hands of the White minority. Improvements and changes are to be sought; but they are to take place within the system. This sets the most stringent limits to the possibilities of change. All change must be consistent with the basic nature of the White-dominated system. There is no question, in other words, of "destroying the white way of life."[21] The real aim of those who promote the idea of peaceful change is to make the system as liberal and humane as possible; but precisely to preserve it. This may not be the conscious motive of all those who support the new theory of gradualist change. But it is certainly the purpose of those who originated it.

Thus the real objective is not so much to promote change as to forestall revolution. The major Western powers seek to ensure stability above all things. And they are now promoting change to prevent instability. President Nixon stated the philosophy behind this approach in his report to the Congress on United States foreign policy in 1970:

> We cannot expect U.S. military forces to cope with the entire spectrum of threats facing allies or potential allies throughout the world. This is particularly true of "wars of national liberation." Experience has shown that the best means of dealing with insurgencies is to pre-empt them through economic development and social reform and to control them with police, paramilitary and military action by the threatened government."[22]

Thus the new strategy for accelerated growth is not at all what it seems. It is certainly not a strategy for "progress" for the majority of Africans in southern Africa. It is much more in the nature of a "counterinsurgency" operation.

[21]A United States Foreign Service Officer wrote not long ago that "Basic to the problem of race in southern Africa is the necessity to show and convince whites that majority rule need not mean destruction of the white way of life or chaos in southern Africa." See C. Pappas, An Issue in Black and White: Insurgency in Southern Africa (Maxwell Air Force Base, Alabama, 1970), pp. 87-8.

[22]R. Nixon, "United Nations Foreign Policy for the 1970s, a New Strategy for Peace," (Washington D.C., 1970), p. 127.

15

The Impact of External Opposition on South African Politics

SAM C. NOLUTSHUNGU

INTRODUCTION

Since the end of World War II, South Africa has been subjected to continuous external criticism of her apartheid policies. As the decolonization of Africa gathered pace in the late 1950s and early 1960s this opposition mounted and became more militant. The Union, soon to become the Republic, was excluded, at the insistence of African and Asian states, from a wide range of intergovernmental agencies and conferences; it was isolated in the United Nations and became the object of an economic boycott by the vast majority of African states and by many Asian states.[1] They hoped that the boycott could be widened into universal economic sanctions, backed by the United Nations, against South Africa.[2] Pressure groups secured South Africa's exclusion from such major sporting events as the Olympic Games. Even those countries that opposed action against South Africa were wary of open amity with the Republic, adjuring state visits and

[1] This movement gained particular momentum from events within South Africa itself, especially the Sharpeville massacre, as well as from the general radicalization of world politics as a result of decolonization and nationalist movements, on the one hand, and the context of ideological competition which was a part of the Cold War, on the other.

[2] This view became orthodoxy among radicals, though often for different reasons. *See*, among others, P. van den Berghe, *South Africa: A Study in Conflict* (Middletown, 1965); L. Kuper, *An African Bourgeoisie* (New Haven, 1965); C. Legum, *South Africa: Crisis for the West* (London, 1964); and R. Segal, ed., *Sanctions Against South Africa* (Harmondsworth, 1964), all of which advocated sanctions.

some limiting arms trade with the Republic. Agitation for the complete isolation of South Africa continued throughout the 1960s, though with less prospect of success as the years passed.

Toward the end of the decade with increasingly open collaboration on arms between South Africa and France, West Germany, and Britain, and with firmer statements by the United States and Britain of their opposition to change by revolutionary means in South Africa, it began to appear that the ostracism of South Africa had collapsed. Some African states began to advocate "dialogue" with South Africa in place of economic boycotts and support for revolutionary campaigns. South Africa's ability to support with impunity Rhodesia's successful resistance to economic sanctions made the prospect of sanctions being applied universally against South Africa itself appear wholly chimerical. On the other hand, the expansion of the South African economy and the country's strategic location attracted even more Western investment and trade. Western governments became anxious to reverse even in Africa itself the policy of boycotting South Africa, a goal that by the middle and later 1960s they seemed likely to achieve. The shift in policy of some African regimes was attributable to the fact that, while the prospect of easy victory in South Africa had receded, distinct opportunities of financial and economic advantage were being offered to them by white South Africa. In general the African regimes favoring dialogue were conservative and feared the "danger of Communism" in Africa, which revolutionary struggles seemed to portend. Those who sought dialogue inevitably called into question the efficacy of the external pressure that was being brought to bear on the Republic.[3]

South Africa's position in Africa seemed, however, quite secure and gave rise to exaggerated estimates of its role as the "power house" or center of a regional system. The interdependence of southern African territories was often stressed and there was a widespread belief in the power and possibilities of a booming South African capitalist economy, now inspired by a "modernizing" ideology, and armed, above all, armed to the teeth. And so it seemed to Western and White South African analysts that African decolonization might after all have ended to the north of the Zambezi (the anomolous former High Commission Territories notwithstanding) and that there was indeed a "White Africa" that was governed by its own special laws as—to use the expressive "scientific" terminology characteristic of such assessments—a "subsystem."[4]

[3]See S. Nolutshungu, *South Africa in Africa: A Study in Ideology and Foreign Policy* (Manchester, 1974).

[4]See, e.g., J. Lombard, J. Stadler, and P. van der Merwe, *The Concept of Economic Cooperation in Southern Africa* (Pretoria, 1969); E. Rhoodie, *The Third*

Nothing, however, is quite conclusive in the art of temporal government. The military coup of April 1974 that has brought to an end a half-century of fascist rule in Portugal has once more thrown open the whole issue of colonialism in Africa and of racism, which is closely associated with it. The vulnerability of South Africa to the continental forces of decolonization and nationalism has once more been brought vividly into focus, now dramatized by the drastic deterioration of its security situation. South Africa invested much—politically and otherwise—in the continuation of Portuguese fascist rule in the colonies neighboring it.[5] In the attempts that the Portuguese are now making to maintain as much influence and to preserve as much of the wealth of their colonies as possible by other means than the rude imperialism of the past, South African and Portuguese views and interests diverge and even conflict. And, increasingly, South Africa is being thrown into a deeper isolation in which the wasting asset of White Rhodesian friendship becomes of limited diplomatic, economic, or even strategic use.[6]

As the geopolitics of South Africa changes as a result of the declining commitment of its most regional partner (on the assumption of whose continued resilience the South African defense system was largely based), the prospect now emerges of increasing guerrilla warfare against South Africa itself.[7] As the prospect of South Africa's being drawn into armed conflict increases the scope for external intervention broadens.

In the light of these developments it is not premature to raise the question of this paper (and to attempt to construct a framework of ideas for the answering of it), viz.: what have been the effects of pressure on political development and conflict in South Africa in the last decade and one-half or so?

Africa (Cape Town, 1968); also ch. 16 of J. Barber's *South Africa's Foreign Policy, 1945-1970* (London, 1973) actually titled, "The southern African Bloc." Even G. Arrighi and J. Saul nearly succumbed to this view in their "Nationalism and Revolution in Sub-Saharan Africa" in G. Arrighi and J. Saul, *Essays on the Political Economy of Africa* (New York, 1973). For a work that explicitly uses the notion of "subsystem" but with considerable skepticism as to its value or the durability of the "southern African subsystem," *see* K. Grundy, *Confrontation and Accommodation in Southern Africa* (Berkeley, 1973).

[5] The Cabora Bassa dam project, for example, would have been inconceivable without South African encouragement and participation.

[6] There is, however, resistance to South Africa's abandoning Rhodesia— apart from the fact that South Africa already has police fighting guerrillas there. *See* S. Nolutshungu, "The Implications of the Rhodesian Settlement Proposals for South Africa," in S. Wilmer, ed., *Zimbabwe Now* (London, 1973).

[7] Instead of having relatively secure buffer states South Africa now finds its long frontier exposed on several sides, placing the task of preventing infiltration on its own armed forces—and that probably with neighbours no longer as helpful as the later fascist regime in Portugal.

The focus of this contribution is on the impact of foreign pressures on government and politics, and more specifically, the state, and the emergent and potential social alignments in political conflict. Discussion, therefore, centers on the characteristics and behavior of the state in major areas of national life as well as on the reactions to, and the general results of, such state action in the wider political society.[8] This treatment is influenced by structure-functionalist notions, and social scientists will no doubt detect the instances in which these ideas have been used. In general, however, we have been informed by a sense of fundamental societal conflict that is essentially alien to structure-functionalism and that we believe to be basically Marxist. In thus using structure-functionalist ideas in a discussion based upon basically Marxist concepts, we are not motivated by either an irresolute eclecticism or a desire to synthesize the two approaches. It has of course been argued, notably by van den Berghe,[9] that such a synthesis is not only possible but also desirable, although it is also a fact that in practice a comprehensive theoretical synthesis has never been successfully undertaken. The differences between the two approaches as basic theories of society are well known and do not require elaboration here. It is, however, worth noting that van den Berghe argued not for a synthesis between Marxism and Functionalism—both embodying substantive claims to factual knowledge as well as methodologies—but for the combination of the idea of "function" with that of "dialectic" as a heuristic device.[10] There are of course many "dialectical" approaches that are not only non-Marxist, but are also profoundly anti-Marxist.[11] Moreover, there is all the difference in the world between partial adoption of a theoretical method as a heuristic device, or, put more bluntly, a methodological dodge, and adopting it as a basically, scientifically truthful account of how things "really are" or "really work." That is perhaps the greatest problem in the way of a synthesis.

[8]Some of the aspects of these developments have been dealt with elsewhere in this volume, especially those relating to military and other coercive responses of the state to its political crises, and reference to them in this chapter will be briefer than their relevance and importance warrant. Occasionally, however, the demands of logical completeness have to take precedence over economy; there is consequently some, hopefully constructive, overlap with earlier chapters.

[9]P. van den Berghe, "Dialectic and Functionalism: Toward a Theoretical Synthesis," *American Sociological Review*, 28, 5 (October 1963). *See also* his *South Africa*.

[10]Ibid.

[11]*See* L. Althusser, *For Marx*, B. Brewster, trans., (London, 1969), and of course, Marx himself, in "Afterword to the second German edition," in *Capital* (London, 1971), 1:22-9.

The justification, then, for the approach adopted here is different. First, there are areas in which the two approaches manifestly do not conflict and may even be supplementary to each other; second, structure-functionalism is singularly useful in analyzing certain aspects of societies including political institutions and organizations. However it is practically useless in a discussion of conflicts relating to the very idea of society (in any particular place and time) when what is wanted is not some idea of how the societal system is structured and "functions" but how the antisocietal forces located within and outside it behave to constitute or destroy that system and its overall structural and functional characteristics. In this area ideas of a Marxian kind seem, in our view, to have the advantage.[12]

Finally, the empirical discussion is informed by the presumption that the main forces for change are within South Africa itself and that the foreign pressures—particularly at their present level—are more likely only to contribute to these essentially internal determinations than themselves decide the course of political conflict in South Africa.[13]

DOMESTIC POLITICAL CONFLICT

External opposition to South Africa's apartheid regime has come at a time when the effects of gradual changes in the structure of the economy have begun to be felt and to have political consequences. The main structural changes of the rapid economic expansion of the 1960s were those associated with the emergence of manufacturing as the major growth sector in the economy and with mining and construction and agriculture declining in terms of their relative contributions to the gross domestic product.[14] Associated with this has been increased concentration of economic activity in all sectors of private business with the result that the small farmer and businessman have been under threat of absorption or extinction by larger competitors with better access to capital and skills. Another important feature of economic growth has been the growth of local capitalism associated, for example, with a growth in gross domestic investment that was sufficient to ensure that, although during the first four years of the

[12]After all, Marxism is nothing if not the theory of fundamental and revolutionary social change *par excellence*. Put otherwise, revolution has been for over a century the business of Marxists; they ought to know something about it. The changes that have generally been demanded of South Africa especially by its Black citizens are nothing short of revolutionary.

[13]This very much presumed for empirical purposes. As a point of theory it would, of course, require considerable qualification.

[14]*See* S. Nolutshungu, "Issues of the Afrikaner 'Enlightenment'," *African Affairs*, 70, 278 (January 1971).

1960s South Africa was a net exporter of capital (due mainly to adverse speculative stock exchange dealings stimulated by the domestic political situation), it could, with some help in the form of International Monetary Fund loans, find the capital required to sustain a high rate of further expansion throughout the decade. Within the field of capital accumulation, also, concentration has been evident not only in mergers among enterprises or the much belabored interlocking directorates, but also in the growth of large institutional investment activity relative to personal investment (the "decline of the small man," again).[15] These changes have had their impact on society and politics and have adduced differing, often contending, political reactions. The split in the National party was largely a product of these developments. These economic transformations not only created the basis of political and ideological controversy, but also affected the character of the state itself in subtle but important ways.[16] To understand the impact of external pressure on the alignment of forces of political conflict within South Africa it is important to understand the political situation created by these changes.

The State and Capitalism

Since 1960 there has been a rapid accretion of power of the state in various directions, ranging from its ability and readiness to intervene extensively in the economy to its practically unlimited discretionary powers over citizens. Although apparently separate, these developments were, however, closely related. First, the economy required for its stability that government ensure not only a "stable" industrial order but also a "stable" political order. This in itself provides the main basis of state intervention in the economy. On the other hand, political order depends in no small way upon the existing economic order being maintained, and this provides a major motive for the state to seek to increase its control of economic affairs in a period of political crisis. Second, there is a particular need felt in conditions of rapid change, for state support of investors through laws as well as with capital. Afrikaner capital has depended considerably on Afrikaner political power and patronage for its growth.

[15]See J. du Plessis, "Investment and Balance of Payments of South Africa," *South African Journal of Economics*, 33, 4 (December 1965).

[16]The Herenigde Nasionale Party sought to defend among others the small Afrikaner capitalists and to mobilize their support, as can be seen from the columns of its organs, notably *Die Afrikaner* (Pretoria), throughout 1970 to 1971, for example. *See* S. Nolutshungu, "Party System, Cleavage Structure and Electoral Performance," *African Review*, 2, 4 (1972). The controversy during the 1970 election campaigns over Land Bank loans dramatized the political issue of the state's role in private concentration.

Third, economic growth itself spawns both a growth "psychology"[17] and ideology. The former refers to the irrational need felt during periods of rapid growth for further expansion and the material expectations that arise on the part of populations, which can only be met through such growth. The ideology of growth relates to the more or less systematic belief that a given political and economic order, especially one that is stratified, crucially depends on growth and can indeed resolve conflicts arising from inequality by means of further growth; the ideology of growth includes the prior commitment to such a system as well as the subsequent conscious dependence on growth as a condition of political order.[18] These tendencies in themselves would have given impetus to interventionism in what was, in any case, never a laissez-faire economy;[19] but the fact that the period of economic expansion in South Africa was also one in which planning had become orthodoxy throughout the rest of the capitalist world intensified these propensities. The result of these factors is that there is now a much closer, more explicit identification of state interests with the daily performance of the economy.

The National party was never a party of laissez-faire. Although it did not fervently seek direct control through ownership of all the commanding heights of the economy, it early established a clear pattern of political patronage through regulative interventions in industry and agriculture in favor of those White groups with which it was identified. This has remained the pattern. Intervention ranges from job reservation to the suppression of African trade unions; from the regulation of domestic trade in favor of Whites to similar political use of external tariffs.[20] But, above all, such interventionism finds its most distinctive expression in the regimentation of the African labor supply through taxation, pass laws, and the creation of land scarcity by legal restrictions. These measures were not singularly invented by National party governments: they always were, in varying degrees, the basic economic features of the political system that emerged from the union of 1910—itself the product of a colonial order of dispossession and systematic exploitation. The Nationalist government can, however, be credited with insisting more than any of its predecessors on the maintenance of this system and of a more comprehensive,

[17]*See* du Plessis, "Investments and Balance of Payments."

[18]H. Laski identified this view with European liberalism in its more capitalist-idological aspects. *See The Rise of European Liberalism* (London, 1936), p. 243 ff.

[19]R. Horwitz, *The Political Economy of South Africa* (London, 1967).

[20]On external tariffs, *see* M. Kooy and H. Robertson, "The South African Board of Trade and Industries, the South African Customs Tariff and the Development of South African Industries," *South African Journal of Economics,* 34, 3 (September 1966).

authoritarian, and doctrinaire policy on all these matters, and especially in regard to labor.

The governmental interventions through which African labor is kept low paid and largely poorly skilled result from demands from pressure groups in the White polity that span the entire White community. While this solidarity of White interests against Blacks has, as is well known, not always been automatic, and differences of class interest have often led to conflicts among Whites, yet it has been maintained, and White farmers, workers, and capitalists still have an overriding community of economic and political interests in White rule in South Africa.[21]

However, the differences in class interest in the economy and in politics do provide a clue to the nature of the mutations in the character of the state in a period of economic expansion as well as political crisis. For what has happened is that the traditional role of the National party as the representative of the White workers and the lower middle class (constituted of Afrikaners) has been submerged in a wider role in which it has become more responsive to the interests of big business as well. This was due, in part, to the fact that a substantial section of the Afrikaner elite has become major capitalists; but it was also due, in part, to the fact that the political crisis dramatized the identity of interest, against certain challengers, between, on the one hand, the party and the majority of its membership and, on the other, what they had previously regarded as international monopoly capitalism and an ally of "British-Jewish imperialism." The end of formal imperialism in most of Africa and the growing militant opposition to White minority rule in southern Africa created a situation in which the contradictions within the White community diminished considerably in political importance as they came to be understood, ideologically as well as practically, for what they really were—minor, and largely negotiable differences so long as the existing overall system of exploitation could be maintained. However, all contradictions are essentially antagonistic.[22] The relevant problem here is that under

[21]For extensive bibliographies of South African political economy, *see* F. Wilson, *Labour in the South African Gold Mines 1911-1969* (Cambridge, 1972); and H. Simons and R. Simons, *Class and Colour in South Africa, 1850-1950* (Harmondsworth, 1969).

[22]This complicated theoretical concept of "contradiction" is so important in revolutionary thought that it is essential to state clearly what is intended here. We dissent from the view expressed in Mao Tse-tung, *Selected Works* (Peking, 1967), 1:311-47, at least as it is popularly understood, though not from its subtler theoretical presentation in Althusser, *For Marx*, pp. 101 ff., which is in fact similar to the view expressed here. If we reserve the term "contradiction," as we should, for fundamental incompatibilies, rather than apply it to any differences of ideological opinion or paradoxes; if, in other words, we use the term as Marx did and Hegel did—then it is clear that there can be no strictly

certain conditions any contradiction may be nondefinitive while in another situation it may be decisive for system survival. Consequently, although we take the view that, in general, disputes among Whites were fairly easily subordinated to the more immediate and definitive conflict with Blacks, we shall later give consideration to the conditions in which, and the modalities whereby, these contradictions could be not only "intensified" but also become relevant in a crucial way to the liberation of Black people.[23] To return to present themes, the change in the relation of the state to capitalism in South Africa can be seen to represent the integration (at the ideological and material levels) of Afrikaner capital into international capitalism.[24] This involved the deradicalization of the National party as a movement-regime and its increasing bureaucratization; and, in specifically functionalist terms, the integration of the economic and political systems.

The growth of state power, and the shifts in the scope and directions of its application, have been the result of two distinguishable sets of influences—economic growth and structural change on one hand, and growing political opposition to the apartheid regime, on the other. To both sets of factors external pressure has been of obvious importance, and both have, in turn, affected the extent and effectiveness of external pressure. Economic growth was threatened by the agitation for economic sanctions against the regime and as a result various White economic interest groups in South Africa felt motivated to prevent boycotts and rallied behind the government's foreign policies. Because, however, the economy was booming, South Africa was able to attract foreign investment, trade, and immigrants, and

---

nonantagonistic contradiction. Contradiction is itself antagonism. In Marx the term has, in addition, a distinctive historical and social scientific specificity. It relates to the fundamental contradiction of capitalist production. A Marxist use of this term is thus distinguished from all others by this: that all contradictions in society, to be properly called such, must be definitely relatable to contradiction between the forces of production and the relations of production. It is of course the theoretical and historical complexity of this relatability that has given rise to Mao's famous formulation, which, correctly theorized, is also intimately related to Lenin's theory of imperialism (and thus to any coherent rendering of Marxism in the light of the twentieth-century experience), as Althusser very rightly points out in both *For Marx* already cited, and *Lenin and Philosophy and other Essays* (London, 1971).

[23]This is an important distinction since "contradictions" tend to be "intensified" all over the place without the oppressive regimes changing in any recognizable way in the expected directions.

[24]H. Wolpe, "Class, Race and the Occupational Structure" and S. Trapido, "South Africa in a Comparative Study of Industrialisation," both in University of London, Institute of Commonwealth Studies, *Collected Seminar Papers on the Societies of Southern Africa in the 19th and 20th centuries,* 2 (London, 1972).

even to expand the flows from Western European countries with which it had had very little dealings in the past.[25]

Domestic political opposition was encouraged by the difficulties the government was experiencing abroad, to which the African nationalists and other radicals also contributed by petitioning well-disposed governments, promotional groups, and even intergovernmental organizations. South Africa's neighbors, especially Botswana, Lesotho, Swaziland, and Rhodesia, became important, first, as havens for political refugees from South Africa and, later, as possible transit bases for guerrilla attacks on South Africa itself.

The inensity of the African states' hostility to apartheid promoted overestimates, in South Africa and elsewhere, of their potential to wage war, which, in turn, was catalytic to quite important changes. It led to the development of the defense forces' capability, primarily with an external orientation, and to preoccupation with arms procurement from both Western sources and domestic manufacture. Both were exploited. State expenditure in this regard naturally acted as a stimulus to the economy, but the importance of the decision to develop a military capacity that was, in regional terms, both offensive and defensive, was, however, greater than this. It altogether altered the image of the armed forces and increased their prestige in Afrikaner perceptions, with the result that further expansion of the armed forces became irresistible. What the full effects of these changes will be on domestic politics is uncertain, but there seems no doubt that the deployment of military personnel in neighboring countries creates scope for considerably more military influence on foreign policy than before. At the same time, as the strength of the armed forces continues to be increased beyond strictly defense needs, a certain amount of role-seeking behavior by the military can be expected. The South African Navy's expansion, for instance, keeps alive the idea of a South African naval role in Western global strategies and may have encouraged the notion that South Africa should share with Western powers in the development of Diego Suarez in Malagasy as a naval base in an area that Pretoria increasingly regards as being within its naval defense perimeter.[26] An important conse-

[25]The unwillingness of Western interests to disengage from South Africa is the main obstacle to effective international action against apartheid. *See also,* for a general survey of Western economic involvement in South Africa, R. First, J. Steele, and C. Gurney, *The South African Connection: Western Investment in Apartheid* (London, 1972).

[26]*See* Nolutshungu, *South Africa in Africa,* 2. Note, however, that the expansion of the South African navy has been limited in relation to both the growth of the other services and the extravagant claims often made for South Africa's role in protecting Western shipping in the Indian Ocean against a growing Soviet naval presence.

quence of the expansion of South African military power is the range of options South Africa now has in the event of political-revolutionary activity being stepped up within its territory—or even in neighboring states. It could among other things follow the logic of the doctrine of "hot-pursuit" to its conclusion of "preemptive hot-pursuit." The reach of the South African Air Force across a wide area of southern Africa integrates the neighboring territories ever more closely into the conflict situation within South Africa. The disparity of military power between South Africa and its Black neighbors, on one hand, and the increasing calls on South Africa for assistance from Rhodesia, on the other, create a new political opportunity and a new order of motivation in which defense and strategic doctrines become increasingly more assertive and the predisposition of policy-makers toward intervention is enhanced.[27] And in addition, the dispersal of South African personnel to the armed services of various southern Africa countries enhances the probability that South Africa may be drawn deeper into conflicts in the area.[28]

Conventional military power carries prestige that now weighs fairly heavily in the councils of the powers contemplating intervention and is even more likely to be decisive with Western powers, which claim to adopt "realist" policies toward southern Africa.[29] South Africa has also become a major consumer of military technology as well as of war materials. In arms sales and procurement may be discerned another

[27]The argument about opportunity here is similar in some ways to that used by D. Landes, "Some Thoughts on the Nature of Economic Imperialism," *Journal of Economic History*, 21, 4 (December 1961), except for the very important emphasis we place on the effect of opportunity on motivation which differs from Landes's theory that the motives are "human nature." We also hold that the most powerful sets of motives are likely to be some expectation, illusory or justified, of material gain, combined with some notion of strategic (in the military sense) necessity.

[28]Changes in the Portuguese colonial empire following the coup in Portugal increase the urgency of all these pressures, while it seems that the inevitable deterioration of South Africa's security situation may militate against extensive expansion as envisaged in the mid-1960s, in favor of intensive intervention in the areas of White settlement in Rhodesia and possibly in Angola and Mozambique. These options may however be more abstract than real, as events and the inherent logic of expansionism may adduce contradictory and, almost certainly, maladaptive responses.

[29]Practically all the major powers intervene in the South African situation. Western powers do so by various means, some governmental (diplomatic support, sale of arms), and others nongovernmental (private sector investments and trade). Recently the (British) Trades Union Congress has also intervened in ways that are complementary and supportive of the aims of the governments and private companies of the NATO countries. The issue being contemplated is therefore not whether intervention should take place, but what specific objectives are to be sought by what modes of intervention.

important response to external pressure: South Africa's decision to build its own arms industry. Apart from the obvious advantages of enabling South Africa to evade some of the boycotts, this development opens up new scope for interventionary action in the peripheral area. South Africa can now be arms supplier to well-disposed African regimes, e.g., Malawi.

The tendency to expand outwards in response to the pressures with which the regime was faced in the 1960s was confirmed and reinforced by the domestic economic changes that, in their own right, made highly desirable the development of extensive South African links with the subcontinent to create opportunities for South African investors, and, most important, to find markets for South Africa's expanding manufacturing produce.[30] Such an outward movement presupposes substantial state activity in fields in which it was previously dormant and in roles which were previously minor though acknowledged: e.g., that of facilitating the expansion of South African economic dominance in southern Africa. Thus, here, as in many cases in international history, expansionism contributes to étatism and bureaucratization at home and thereby contributes to the evolution of the state.[31]

Defense was by far the greatest growth department in the period, its percentage share of the budget rising from 6.16 percent in the tax year 1958 to 1959 to 21.01 percent in 1964 to 1973 and declining to 13.13 percent in 1970 to 1971. Much of the expansion of state activity has been in the foreign policy "sector" or "subsystem" of government, as can be seen from the share of budgetary expenditure taken by departments that have much to do with foreign relations. Foreign Affairs also increased although much less markedly, while police and justice shares actually declined. The overall budget was increasing by an average annual rate of 10.05 percent (sd 4.74 percent) from 1958 to 1972. Immigration was set up as an item or subdepartment in 1960 to 1961 and showed an upward increase until 1967 to 1968 and thereafter stabilized at the mean figure of 0.36 percent. Table 15.1 gives a brief summary of the movement of these budget shares. These figures themselves, which illustrate the increased attention to areas which do depend on foreign attitudes and policies to apartheid, demonstrate the salience of foreign pressures in the South African conflict.

---

[30]The theoretical view to which we incline is that of A. Emmanuel in his *Unequal Exchange: A Study of the Imperialism of Trade* (New York, 1972), which implies that all imperialisms are basically imperialisms of trade.

[31]Liberals schooled in the classical tradition (which is now practically lost) fully appreciated this, as did e.g., the very representative L. Hobhouse in his *Democracy and Reaction* (London, 1904).

Table 15.1 Annual Percentage Increase of Budgeted Expenditure of Select Departments

Year	Foreign affairs	Information	Immigration	Tourism	Defense	Police	Justice	Total
1959-60	3.39	35.43	–	–	8.89	7.41	7.39	5.57
1960-61	2.79	-7.95	–	–	9.41	6.69	0.86	9.11
1961-62	10.02	53.66	1279.15	–	64.12	6.07	9.03	10.24
1962-63	6.78	61.74	38.97	81.85	67.29	6.26	5.31	10.68
1963-64	16.33	17.75	17.06	31.71	1.59	12.43	8.41	6.58
1964-65	7.21	14.39	25.73	22.76	89.14	12.91	10.49	22.93
1965-66	17.19	0.16	43.45	7.29	-0.26	8.82	4.76	7.82
1966-67	13.28	5.02	-0.56	17.95	11.53	4.15	7.24	12.90
1967-68	-7.88	5.35	8.47	7.08	4.53	14.05	7.51	9.50
1968-69	16.33	18.02	-12.54	–	5.10	7.74	10.00	7.47
1970-71	–	–	–	–	–	–	–	–
1971-72	12.15	17.03	5.17	4.47	23.10	10.75	11.85	-7.72

Source: Republic of South Africa, *Estimates of Expenditure to be Defrayed From Revenue for Year Ending March* (Pretoria, 1960-72).

In summary, the external pressures to which the Republic was subjected were catalytic to the development and realization of growth forces in the state and the economy. Whether these changes contribute materially to the viability of the state in the conflict in which it is involved cannot however be automatically inferred from the fact that they were meant to do so. It is by considering the character of domestic conflict under the impact of external pressure that we can approximate an answer to that question. It is to that task we now turn.

POLITICAL CONFLICT AND THE
RANGE OF POLITICAL OPTIONS

If external pressure has contributed to changes in the character and the role of the state, what has been its impact on political conflict and its social character?

Revolutionary minded analysts tend to focus their hopes for change in South Africa exclusively on responses of Blacks to the political situation. This is legitimate as a rejection of the alternative view, which regards attitudes of Whites as the main determinants of change in South Africa.[32] However, the history of revolution teaches that changes in the ruling class or elite also make a decisive difference to the occurrence, and the course, of revolutions. It is, therefore, important to understand the character of the forces at work within the White community, not in the hope, probably vain, of concessions from that quarter, but to understand the limits of White solidarity, and, by implication, of White power. We shall, accordingly, consider in turn the effects of external pressure both on White and on Black political activity.

Political conflict among Whites was dramatized by the split in the National party in the 1960s between the so-called *verkramp* and *verlig* Afrikaners. These divisions have been amply discussed elsewhere and it is not the intention here to repeat what is by now fully familiar.[33] It is, however, desirable to note their implications for the development of conflicts and alignments in the emergent political conditions. If nothing else the split indicated that political adjustments on the part of the Afrikaner elite, aimed at meeting, among other things, the requirements of outsiders, would meet with vigorous

---

[32]As Denoon and others have reminded us, Blacks have often had the historical initiative. D. Denoon with B. Nyeko and the advice of J. Webster, *Southern Africa since 1800* (New York, 1973), pp. 230-33. *See also* T. Hodgkin, "Some African and Third World Theories of Imperialism," in R. Owen and B. Sutcliffe, eds., *Studies in the Theory of Imperialism* (London, 1972), p. 115.

[33]*See*, e.g., H. Serfontein, *Die Verkrampte Aanslag* (Cape Town, 1970); and Nolutshungu, "Afrikaner 'Enlightenment'," and works there cited.

opposition. The importance of the disputes, however, lies in the patterns of political mobilization for which dissidents opted, as these were revealing of the social character of political conflict among Whites, as well as of the political consciousness of Afrikaners.

The Herstigte Nasionale party (HNP), which emerged as the ruling party's main right-wing, Afrikaner, challenger, focused its attention on the less well-to-do Afrikaners and projected a nationalist, populist, image. It sought to appeal to both the working class and the middle class (mainly, the lower middle class) and also to the poor. Such a broad appeal was understandable since in a competitive elective system single-class appeals usually have a low pay-off in electoral terms. The wider identification also reflected, however, the fact that the discontented were not particularly the White workers, although some of them did join the HNP, but the lower middle class. In a period of rapid economic growth White workers had, with a few exceptions, done very well in terms of wage increases, work conditions, and security from Black competition, while, as has already been suggested, many in typically lower middle-class positions suffered economic status deterioration (as much in relation to industrial workers as to the groups above them), as a result of concentration and of the differential responses of incomes to economic change in traditional middle-class occupations (farming, small business, and many government services), and industrial situations.[34] These political and economic factors are closely related to a third one, which is both political and economic: the fragmentation of the lower classes, especially the working class, in modern, growing, capitalist economies. The relations of various sections of the working class to the means of production objectively differ, but these differences are overvalued subjectively.[35] The full explanation of this is probably psychological, but it also has much to do with the reality of personal upward mobility for suffi-

[34]A similar process has been at work in the older capitalist states in relation to "small men" and white-collar workers, and several professions.

[35]In advanced capitalist countries this is often reflected in the strident arguments of better paid workers who wish to maintain substantial pay differentials among workers themselves, and in the phenomenon of working class racism whereby White workers assert a claim to a higher status and greater entitlements than their Black colleagues. Of course, a worker's concern over the deterioration of his status vis-à-vis lower placed comrades usually reflects concern over the worsening of that worker's position in the overall class hierarchy. This may signify that such sensitivities on the part of workers are only partially a manifestation of "false consciousness," as Marxists put it, and are thus indeed an "epiphenomenon of the class struggle." Kuper observed much status consciousness among Durban Africans; see his African Burgeoisie. Similar observations have also been made in Latin America: see A. MacEwen, "Differentiation Among the Urban Poor: An Argentine Study," in E. de Kadt and G. Williams, eds., Sociology and Development (London, 1974).

ciently large sections of this class to provide a real challenge to the objectivity (within the lifetime of a generation or so) of the claim to an overriding class identity.[36] This results in the working class adopting the social outlook of the petty bourgeois rather than the proletariat, emphasizing personal opportunity, and tending to require nothing more than that the political system be used by whatever means—including racialism and quasi-socialist practices—to tip the balance of opportunity in favor of greater mobility for those lower middle and upper working classes. This is precisely what the HNP called for with its recondite political rhetoric. Since, in so much of the capitalist world, it has been hard for the working class to realize that proletarian consciousness that Marx anticipated, it is not to be wondered at that this, the most privileged of all working classes, should be no less content—political and economic conditions remaining as favorable as they are—to make its peace with the rulers of what Godimer has called the "late bourgeois world."[37]

External factors have contributed to the disputes among Afrikaners primarily because it was in its foreign policy adjustments (admitting Black diplomats and giving aid to Black states) that change of government attitudes were most dramatic. Its decision to allow, upon certain conditions, foreign Black sportsmen to complete against White South Africans within the Republic was singled out by the HNP as the most symbolic "sell-out" on the part of the Vorster government. This "concession" was, of course, in direct response to external pressure. However, domestic economic change contributed considerably to the political conflicts in the National party since the HNP represents, among many other things, the discontents of those who feel that they have lost out in increasing class and status differentiations among Afrikaners that are directly attributable to economic change. The HNP revolt has, thus far, been small in terms of its support and ambiguous in its subjective class identification. Yet its very vagueness in class definitions, which masks its objectively lower middle-class nature (in terms of leadership and policies),[38] casts light on the range of radical options in White politics. It suggests that, within the White polity, the "Super Right" is likely to continue to hold the radical initiative.[39]

[36]Personal mobility in this regard functions very much like growth, with which it is closely associated. This suggests that breakdowns of the capitalist system are as much a determinant of working-class consciousness as the final collapse and successful revolutions against such a system are dependent on working-class consciousness.

[37]N. Gordimer, *The Late Bourgeois World*, (New York, 1966).

[38]This amplifies the view we expressed in "Party System," p. 461.

[39]This usage is suggested by W. Tordoff's and A. Mazrui's "The Left and Super-Left in Tanzania," *Journal of Modern African Studies*, 10, 3, (October

Whether the competition between the Right, represented by the National party, and the Super-Right, to which the HNP and others belong, will grow in importance to affect the ability of the overall system to survive, it is difficult to say. However, it is quite possible to envisage conditions in which the consensus among various White occupational groups and classes would break down. We can envisage a realization crisis—in Marxist parlance—arising if it became no longer practically possible to maintain the alliance and pay-off patterns now obtaining.[40] If this meant that substantial sections of the White lower middle and working classes substantially lost their privileges vis-à-vis Blacks and became increasingly insecure, then, it is conceivable, the Super-Right could form the nucleus of a neofascist movement with a considerably greater following than the present HNP. It depends, however, on "stress," (or "crises") either internally generated or exogenous, whether the intra-White conflicts would remain capable even of pragmatic, negotiated settlement, since being contradictions, they would be incapable of reconciliation within the system. What the consequences for revolution would be of such division among the Whites would depend on the overall circumstances obtaining at the time. It is barely possible that the neofascist movement could be reintegrated in a National party, which would itself have become neofascist, and that this would merely strengthen the state to act arbitrarily in regard both to lower-class Whites and to Blacks generally, making, for example, adjustments in favor of a more "rational," "universalist" system of racial and economic domination at the expense of the particularist claims of lower middle-class Afrikanerdom. It might, in such circumstances, be possible for the Afrikaner ruling class to divorce itself from the rest of its group in ideology and in practice, resulting in the replacement of apartheid with economic domination through a less explicitly racist institutional framework. Were such adjustments seen to hasten the collapse of White domination, then conflict of this kind among Whites would be discovered to be directly relevant to the problem of Black liberation.

1972). It is a felicitous expression that will, however, not abide all interrogation.

[40]Specifically such conditions would exist if, for example, further economic growth becomes impossible without substantially undermining the privileges of White workers; or if the White lower middle class is exposed to extensive economic competition from Blacks (as well as to the other pressures of economic change to which reference has been made); or if international crises (e.g., the collapse of settler rule in Angola and Mozambique) make imperative substantial concessions by the ruling elite either as a means of buying time in South Africa itself or of gaining acceptability on the continent (which would be less safe strategically and, equally important for the entrepreneurial classes, in economic terms).

The circumstances considered here are extreme and seem, at present, remote. Nevertheless right-wing criticism of the government, by its electoral mobilization, limits the extent to which the government can proceed with concessions to external opponents, and, generally, it reinforces the conservative character of the political system.

On the rest of the White political parties—the United party (UP), the Progressives and the Liberals—the impact of external pressure has been less dramatic. South Africa's leaving the Commonwealth put an end to imperial loyalty as a conservative rallying cry among English speakers, while the external threats to the regime, coupled with intense domestic opposition by Blacks, forced the UP to look for a national image that could appear less liberalistic to the White electorate. This was also a consequence of that earlier polarization of political positions within the UP, which had resulted in the breakaway first of the Liberals, and, later, of the Progressive party. The Progressives, in common with the UP, have identified themselves with the government's opposition to sanctions and overseas boycotts against South Africa, although they have urged upon the government a much more conciliatory attitude toward even those African states that are most militant in their opposition to apartheid. At the same time their toleration in South Africa is very much due to external pressure. The Liberal party has been extinguished, but it does not appear that the fortunes of this party were influenced by external pressure as much as by the government's apprehension of political dangers within the state. If external pressure has made any contribution in this area, then, it has been in dramatizing the need, from the point of view of apartheid, of tightening control over domestic affairs, to which, of course, the Liberals and others have fallen victim.

One area of government policy on which external pressure has had some impact is that of the White administration's relations with Blacks. Although the government has continued to detain, imprison and restrict Black opponents, indeed, even much more than before, it has responded to external criticism. Its decision to develop the Bantustans[41] politically, as well as its attempts to discipline relations between its personnel and Africans (to avoid unnecessary friction), the eventual concession to Blacks of the right to strike (under very limited conditions), and the comparative restraint manifested by the South African police in the series of strikes from 1971 to 1973 (although not in the disputes at the City Deep Level Mine in September 1973) were all influenced by the need to present a favorable

[41]Sometimes these are euphemistically, but quite absurdly, referred to as "the African homelands." "Native reserves" would be a better analytical term as it brings out the colonial essence of this "new" dispensation.

external image. Verwoerd's use of the Bantustans as a propaganda instrument aimed at external critics continued after him, and the Bantustan system became an ideological model of Black and White "cooperation" to be applied to the wider continental relationships envisaged under the outward looking policy. The holding of multi-racial sports events and the occasional infractions of social apartheid—as during visits by African diplomats—are also undertaken in this spirit. Similarly, the encouragement given to some private capital accumulation by individual Africans and the scope given to conspicuous expenditure within those urban "White" areas from which many Africans are daily being ejected, are due both to the need to win over some of the better-educated and more well-to-do Africans and the desire to hold up to the world an image of African well-being under apartheid. From the point of view of conflict, however, it is interesting to note that attempts are consciously being made to accommodate the pattern of class formation among Africans into the overall pattern of White domination and political control. Judging from the perspective of previous nationalist and bourgeois revolutions it seems unlikely that this can forever forestall a nationalist revolution. Indeed, the partial improvement of the position of the "African bourgeoisie" could itself be a stimulus for greater assertiveness on the part of that class. What is, however, likely is that if a distinct awareness of a class interest emerges among the African bourgeoisie, although it may not be considered coterminous with the interests of the present state, it will enter into profound conflict with the interests and aspirations of other progressive and revolutionary forces in South African society. And only time will tell whether, when the great convulsions come, those who have vested interests in South Africa now may not discover in some of these Africans their surest allies against total revolution, allies through whom they might yet salvage something of the old in the new order. It is for this and similar reasons that the creation of collaborative institutional roles, more or less coupled to class formation among Africans within the system of dominance, must be seen to be among the most important features in the development of the apartheid state in response to both domestic and external challenges. Certainly, the Bantustan system has had the effect of opening up, in more definite form than before, a stratum in the African population that can have a different relation to the system of domination from the rest of the population—at both the economic and political levels. The tribal "polities" produce their own self-perpetuating oligarchies and under them a welter of interest groups oriented to the Bantustan pattern of patronage. Civil service appointments, Development Corporation loans, and other business suppot are included in the range of items that the tribal oligarchies can allocate. The view has been expressed with considerable conviction that this system carries the seeds of the destruction of apartheid as, apparently, the concession of limited autonomy to tribal polities and their responding anti-White ideologies constitute contradictions in the apartheid system. It is difficult to find evidence in support of the view that the "Black consciousness" of the tribal oligarchs is revolutionary and there is little good argument in support of the "contradictions" theory used here.[42] Indeed, this notion of "internal contradictions" used by liberal determinists is most misleading, as it incorporates a "time-bomb" element commendable—if at all—more by its arresting theatricality than by its basis in clear social theory and analysis. For example, it focuses on African attitudes as the critical factor in revolution, which Bantustans will develop, while it totally ignores the fact that it is not, and has for long not been, Africans' attitudes to revolution that have been wanting but their material capacity and opportunities for revolution. This is well attested even by profoundly antirevolutionary analysts.[43]

With regard to international relations specifically, it should be noted that Bantustan leaders are very much influenced by the reactions of foreign governments to them and to the South African government, while their prestige within South Africa is enhanced by their overseas travels and meetings with Western heads of government. More materially, the decision of the Vorster government to allow some foreign investment in the Bantustans opens up another area in which foreign actors can support apartheid and is therefore very closely related to the idea of external pressure. In fact, all the major Bantustan leaders have spoken against boycotts of South Africa, on the familiar argument, to which they are now supposed to impart especial authority, that it is the Blacks who would suffer most from sanctions.

On African political and other protest action against apartheid, external pressure on South Africa has also had some influence. Not only have African nationalist organizations operating underground within South Africa received external support, but groups that have

[42] H. Adam, *Modernizing Racial Domination* (Berkeley, 1971), ch. 6.

[43] E.g., E. Feit, *Urban Revolt in South Africa, 1960-1964* (Evanston, Ill., 1971). It is, of course, the case that "the two go together" but it is a mistake to think that Africans have ever been unaware that they are oppressed or unconcerned or not desirous of freedom (and revolutionary change). Were organisational and other opportunities for bringing about such a change to emerge, then their awareness would be alive and oppression would be discovered to be even more intolerable. But then attitudes would be not a determinant but an aspect of revolution, and then, in a deeper, truer, sense "the two would go together." To say that this will be determined by the discomfiture of the Bantustan oligarchs and the South African government as the "inadequacy" of the system "becomes apparent"—was it not always so?—is to adopt a frivolously simple view of social change.

emerged since the banning of these organizations have derived considerable encouragement from such support. In this regard should be mentioned also the ideological support from pan-Africanist and Black Power movements elsewhere, elements of the ideologies of which bodies like the South African Students' Organization have, to some degree, assimilated. There is evidence also that the Namibians, who went on strike in 1971, thereby spurring on to strike action many other workers in South Africa as well,[44] were influenced by the difficulties South Africa was encountering in the United Nations and with the South West Africa People's Organization.[45] Foreign pressure boosts the morale of those who oppose the system, for, it is clear, Africans might be less confident of ultimate victory if the rest of the world saw apartheid and its ways as perfectly normal.

It is, however, in the support for revolutionary activity in South Africa through guerrilla infiltrations (intended to lead, eventually, to the arming of a substantial section of the population) that pressure makes its greatest impact on African political positions. It has separated out those who are ready and willing to resort to violence from those, within the nationalist movement, who are not. This has merely confirmed a process that had begun before the period of wars of liberation in southern Africa; yet it has contributed significantly to it. Moreover, the different characteristics of donors to liberation movements have sharpened the ideological differences within the nationalist movement as well as radicalized these organizations in exile. The result is that to conceive of nationalism or national liberation in regard to South Africa in a socially undifferentiated way has become increasingly meaningless and may become even more so as differences in interests and locations in the system of dominance become more distinctly structured and therefore are more in conflict. To be sure, the main reasons for these differentiations are endogenous to the South African political economy; it is our argument, merely, that external pressures have contributed to their expression in specific political alignments among Africans. Whether the process of African liberation, the outcome of which is, in any case, assured, will become easier or more difficult as a result seems almost impossible to say. However, new conflict configurations become possible, with their distinctive patterns of escalation, and in the clarification of alignments may well emerge mutual dependencies between government and

[44]It does appear that there is a spread effect—demonstration effect or empathy diffusion—in protest behavior under these conditions of repression, even when there is no direct organisational link between protestors. Supporting cases would include the women's demonstrations in Natal in the late 1950s, Poqo, and more recently the demonstrations against the Home-Smith Settlement proposals for Rhodesia.

[45]*Observer* (London), 13 February 1972.

some African interests that, in times of intenser confrontation, may be points of weakness and vulnerability as surely as divisions among Africans have made collaboration, and the relatively easy suppression of mass action thus far, possible.[46]

Thus far discussion has focused almost exclusively on development themes—changes in the structures and processes of conflict and politics deeper and more permanent than daily shifts in policy. There is, however, a view that small reforms and small inhibitions of government policy in response to external criticism may either cumulatively contribute to total African liberation, or may be, in their own right, worthwhile and important. Thus it is reasoned that if a company raises the pay of its African workers by a positive amount that is something to be thankful for. It is a view that has to be taken into account. One area in which external criticism has extracted concessions is that of sports, when the Vorster government overturned the policy of Verwoerd of not admitting, in any conditions, mixed teams or Black sportsmen to South Africa. Another area that has been important and controversial is that of South Africa's diplomacy in Africa. South Africa is drawn toward Africa by both strategy and the need for outlets for its manufacturing produce. (As expansion continues this may become increasingly important as a pressure on policy-makers.) As a result of these and other considerations Pretoria has sought to establish friendly relations with African states, which, in turn, has meant according Black diplomats accredited to the Republic, or stopping over on visits, the same treatment due to their White colleagues. In providing, for example, for the education of the Malawian representative's daughter in a White school the government is made to infringe its own policy of social apartheid. As the government increasingly needs Black collaborators these anomalies may be expected to occur with greater frequency as will Bantustan chiefs' receiving red-carpet treatment. The argument that is usually derived from this is that the ideological justifications of apartheid will be undermined and, in some more or less mysterious way, apartheid itself will collapse. We believe this to be mistaken for one fundamental reason: it attaches inordinate importance to the symbolism of racial domination and little understanding to the material conditions of race rule

---

[46]For example it might be easier to start revolutionary action by attacking the Bantustan oligarchs, there gaining ground and only later spreading to the main citadels. Urban "guerrilla warfare" in places like Soweto could also be a stage in revolutionary mobilization—the relatively privileged Blacks forming a preliminary target? Certainly it is a wellknown fact that revolutions gain a great deal of their support by successfully harassing this sort of range of functionaries whose power and privilege are more immediately felt by the masses and because their less social distance is more intensely resented.

(which, of course, are the main components in the racist ideology properly understood). But there are other reasons of a contingent rather than theoretical kind. First, apartheid has coexisted with infractions of racial segregation policy from the beginning of the Union—especially at the level of interactions between "elites" in the various ethnic and racial segments of society (this is quite apart from the sexual and other interpersonal rather than intersocial exchanges). Second, in the emerging situation there is every likelihood that "intermingling" can be so regimented that it will occur only among those occupying higher social positions, while racial segregation will continue at the lower occupational echelons.[47]

The policy "concessions" of the South African government diminish even further in political significance when it is considered that no regime has ever liquidated itself by piecemeal concessions. Racial domination is intrinsic to the regime in South Africa and it is difficult to conceive of it being eliminated, more or less inadvertently, by an accretion of governmental concessions. What, in any case, would the final concession be in exchange for?[48]

There is probably some force in the argument that the South African government's policy concessions to external pressure in the industrial field may increase the bargaining power of Black workers and thereby their power to overthrow the system. It is not possible to examine this argument in detail here but there is a sense in which, say, a shortage of skilled labor (through termination of White migration to South Africa) could result in Africans doing jobs that would make strike action, although hazardous for them, immensely injurious economically to the White community. In fact, large-scale shortages of

[47]This would create the cognitive dissonance that some writers believe is a contributor to ideological change. See K. Boulding, *Conflict and Defence: A General Theory* (New York, 1963), ch. 14. However, it seems to us that, in this case, the resulting cognitive dissonance with which White racists, surveying these conditions, would be burdened would be more tolerable than the live political alternatives open to them (e.g., further ideological revision). Should that cease to be so then the presumption must surely be that for the majority of Whites, right-wing radicalism will be at least as alluring as, if not more compelling than, liberality. It does appear that in politics publics can tolerate a great deal of cognitive incongruity, i.e., conflicting images can peacefully coexist for long periods.

[48]We are concerned here with only those concessions that are more or less "voluntary" acts of policy whereby the South African government would reform itself piecemeal without being coerced, but in response, maybe, to the "suasive force" of external opinion. This distinction is ultimately untenable, since it is as easy to argue that all concessions are in some sense voluntary as it is to say that they are all determined despite their apparent voluntary nature. The central fact is that common to both nominal kinds of concessions is the context of the conflict in which the government is involved. We maintain the popular distinction, however, for expositional and epideictic purposes.

manpower could make a profound difference to the industrial situation in South Africa, and so, of course, could shortages in investment capital, trading outlets, and imported industrial inputs—if pressure ever were extended or intensified to such a point. In such a case, however, it would not be a matter of making "concessions" in the voluntarist sense of that phrase, but of being confronted with a novel alignment of productive forces and relations, which would make present modes of operation not merely inexpedient or even undesirable, but socially impossible.

The present importance of "concessions" must be sought elsewhere: in the encouragement they give to further pressure by the proof they give that not even White South Africa is impervious to privation, whether at the level of affections[49] or at the functional level of economic and security requirements. What is most interesting about South Africa's "concessions" is that they seem to depend very much on the government's widening scope for initiative and the increasing difference in life-styles and interests between Afrikaners in the ruling class and the rest of their congeners. And this brings us back to the wider developmental forces with which we began and the interrelations of which have been one of our main objects of study.

Integrative Summary: The Impact of
External Pressure on Domestic Politics

It has been the task of this paper to identify the impact of external pressure on changes in South African politics at two distinct but closely related levels: that of governmental institutions and institutional spheres related to the foreign policy issue area and that of the conflict alignments that are emerging as a result of changes in the conditions of the people of South Africa. At both levels of analysis there can be described an intricate intermingling of external influences with domestic developments in which, it has been suggested as a general presumptive point, external pressures act as secondary causes and as catalysts for essentially internally determined changes. It is our hope that the preceding discussion has indicated that such a presumption is not vitiated by empirical investigation while, on the contrary, it does assist the intellectual oganisation and interpretation in a convincing and practical way of what has happened in South Africa in the period of external pressure.

---

[49]D. Brutus in *Letters to Martha* (London, 1968), has expressed this well in the lines celebrating his part in South Africa's exclusion from the Olympic Games: "Nowhere else does apartheid exact so bitter a price/nowhere else does the world so demonstrate its disgust/in nothing else are the deprivers so deprived."

What has happened in South Africa within the development areas examined seems to be this: the physical capacities and the social characteristics of the state have changed, and closely associated with this, social differentiation within ethnic and racial segments of society has occurred, creating the potentiality for the greater elaboration of existing and new political alignments and behaviors as the conflict unfolds. We have elsewhere argued[50] more fully that the economic and political circumstances that brought this about produced appropriate ideological changes within the inner core of the White political elite in favor of emphasis on power, state interest, and more explicitly materialistic concerns, to the disadvantage of the more recondite identitive aspects[51] of Afrikaner-Nationalist ideology. This is in itself a consequence of the social changes described and of the diminishing hold on the state of the less privileged Afrikaners.

Social change and the ideological revisions that express it make possible greater freedom of action on the part of the government in regard to its constituents and it may be expected that the government will become less doctrinaire and more flexible, within the framework of White racial domination, to respond as it deems fit to the dangers and challenges confronting White rule. Such freedom of action presupposes, however, a basis of state power as nearly unshakeable in all spheres as possible and that includes, of necessity, the retention of the existing processes of repression.[52] Flexibility, when seen in this light, has, therefore, more in common with arbitrary étatism than with liberty. Thus, although a "modern" or "liberal" aspect may from time to time attach itself to government policy, this can only be an illusion arising from the essentially unpredictable, arbitrary character of realpolitik, especially when compared with the more familiar, more coherent, particularist (and therefore socially specific) aspects of Afrikaner nationalism, which it now increasingly threatens to supercede.[53] Thus, while some "concessions" may continue to occur, especially in regard to what is often referred to as "petty apartheid," the overall political system becomes, with every passing year, more completely authoritarian, and more étatist in its basic characteristics.

---

[50]Nolutshungu, *South Africa in Africa,* and "The Pan African Policy of the Government of South Africa," University of London, *Collected Seminar Papers,* vol. 2.

[51]*See* D. Apter, "Ideology and Discontent" in D. Apter, ed., *Ideology and Discontent* (London, 1967).

[52]This can be seen from the progression of laws in the 1960s from the original Suppression of Communism Act (which now almost seems benign), through the "Sabotage" Act to the Terrorism Act. The law creating the Bureau of State Security was also a morsel from the harvest of "modernization" and "liberalization."

[53]"Coherence" in this sense should not be confused with "consistency."

In pointing this out we do not claim to have discovered anything new. Other writers have also noted these tendencies.[54] What we have tried to contribute in this examination of the impact of external opposition is an institutional and political-sociological definition of étatism that is developmental in its main focus and at the same integrally related to foreign policy—or statecraft—the *locus classicus* of state interest.[55]

To discover the full implications for action that may be contained in the foregoing analysis—beyond the conclusion that external pressure is of some, admittedly limited, value to oppositional forces—would require detailed tactical and strategic arguments that, mercifully, it is not our present assignment to excogitate. The present study would, however, be incomplete without some examination of external pressure itself, its dynamics, and its limits. It is to that task that we devote the rest of the discussion.

THE CHARACTER AND LIMITS OF EXTERNAL PRESSURE

The effectiveness of pressure against apartheid will depend on the quality of the pressure applied: its intensity and its universality as an international measure. This is self-evident. For the completeness of this account of pressure, the paragraphs that follow attempt to give, very briefly, a picture of the forces on which the extensiveness and intensity of measures against South Africa may depend.

International opposition to apartheid has always involved a wide diversity of political groups and governments, favoring different approaches to the resolution of the problem of racial domination in South Africa. Indeed, some of the positions that are said to be in opposition to apartheid are indistinguishable from collaboration with it (consider, e.g., the policies of the Britain and the United States), while others seem to include apartheid, almost as a merely incidental detail, in broadly sweeping revolutionary visions of the world. Within this multiplicity of private and public attitudes and strategies for change are distinguishable, however, the broad polarities of revolutionary radicalism and antirevolutionary reformism.[56] Characteristically associated with both, and with the intermediate positions—and

[54]*See* J. Barber, *South Africa's Foreign Policy, 1945-1970* (London, 1973); and J. Barratt, "The Outward Movement in South Africa's Foreign Relations," *South African Institute of International Affairs Newsletter*, 3 (August 1969) and "Dialogue in Africa: A New Approach," *South African International*, 2, 2 (October, 1971), both cited by Barber, although neither writer does more than assert that realpolitik is now an important influence on foreign policy.

[55]*See* Nolutshungu, *South Africa in Africa.*

[56]Those who oppose apartheid include active opponents as well as supporters of revolutionary change. To note this polarity is of course not to deny that many people's views are not well defined and often lie somewhere between these opposites.

there are intermediate positions—are distinctive groupings of governments as well as popular organizations and publics. The radical position favoring the complete overthrow of the existing political system in South Africa has been upheld by African, Asian, and Caribbean states with the support of the Communist countries. The anti-revolutionists willing to exert themselves only in favor of minor adjustments within the framework of White rule have been represented mainly by the United States, Britain, France, West Germany and other Western European states—with the exception of Sweden, which has favored radical solutions.

The pressure against South Africa owed its origin as much to the active opposition within South Africa to apartheid as it did to the moral repulsiveness of that system of racial rule. Events within South Africa, which seemed to indicate that the system was near breakdown, gave considerable encouragement to external pressure, providing purchase to those who believed that apartheid was not only wrong, but bound to fail. In the middle and later 1960s mass political activity by Africans in South Africa was severely suppressed, and that sense of imminent victory and of a population in revolt which had earlier captured liberal imaginations the world over seemed to recede. This has probably to some extent contributed to a declining sense of urgency in the world about South Africa, and at the same time, seen against the military and economic advances of the White government, called into question the efficacy of the measures earlier proposed against South Africa, viz., the boycotts and systematic support of insurgents.[57]

It would however be a mistake to focus upon the domestic African response as the main factor in the formation of world attitudes. For one thing, it was not so much the opposition within South Africa to apartheid, but the worldwide revolt against colonialism in the postwar period, especially, that not only encouraged hopes and militancy on the part of South African blacks themselves, but also dramatized the worldwide rejection of the imperialist order then passing, of which South Africa was both a remnant and a potent symbol. It was the political pressure of the emergent states, whose radical fervor and historical right seemed in the 1950s and early 1960s irresistible, that turned apartheid from a purely domestic South African concern into an international issue of some magnitude. It was the radicalism of their nationalisms that made Asians and Africans recognize some identity, and manifest solidarity, with Black South Africans. It was the dissociative situation[58] of decolonization that disposed all of them, in

[57]See J. Mayall, *Africa: The Cold War and After* (London, 1971), ch. 7.

[58]For the genesis of this concept, *see* P. Nettl and J. Robertson, *International Systems and the Modernisation of Societies* (London, 1967) pp. 63-127. The

varying degree, to call into question, not only their own immediate past, but the whole spectrum of cognate world political relationships.

Differences soon became manifest among the emergent states in their attitudes toward colonialism and racialism with which it is so closely associated, and those differences were to become more pronounced as many of the governments of the states succumbed to what Fanon calls the "pitfalls of national consciousness,"[59] turning inward and deradicalizing or simply dismantling the movements by which they had come to power. The struggle against South Africa became more intractable and more complex as it emerged that the pattern of emancipation experienced in most of colonial Africa would not be followed there. African regimes that are now no longer revolutionary, or even radical, are apprehensive of the radicalization of the continent that might result from a revolution in South Africa. Their reticence on this issue is linked with that general retreat from earlier radical positions that they sounded on the morrow of their own independence, in the very hour of their success.[60]

It has been argued also that the influence of the African and Asian states on this, as on other issues, has declined as a result of the end of the Cold War, it being assumed that during the Cold War, because of the competition between the United States and the Soviet Union for global influence, such states could maximize their advantages by playing the one off against the other. This argument is, however, doubtful. Many governments in Africa, especially those that now question the idea of militancy against South Africa, were always unambiguously pro-Western. Moreover, even during the Cold War the extent to which Western powers were prepared to go against South Africa was extremely limited. Finally, the credibility of the tactics attributed to Black states soon declined as it appeared that too many of them were unwilling to upset their special relationships with Western countries, including their former imperial metropoles.[61] The African governments were, after all, limited by their own domestic politics and the characteristics of their societies. The external behavior of these states may in future be expected to undergo dramatic alteration as these domestic circumstances themselves change. In the wider international context it seems at least as plausible to argue that the behavior of non-African powers toward southern Africa, the intensity of the pressures they are prepared to bring to bear against White minority rule there, depend in a deep sense on what is happening on

---

decolonization movement gained considerably from the fact that the dominant powers after World War II were opposed to old-style colonialism.

[59]F. Fanon, *The Wretched of the Earth*, (New York, 1966).

[60]*See* Nolutshungu, *South Africa in Africa, passim.*

[61]*See* D. Austin, *Britain and South Africa* (London, 1966).

the rest of the continent of Africa, as it is credible to suppose that, with the end of the Cold War, Africa shrank to size in the world context and with it the antiapartheid issue.

There is greater plausibility in the argument that with the end of the Cold War and, especially, of late, with the competitive attempts of the Soviet Union and Communist China to establish detente with the West, truly meaningful Communist support for insurgency in areas in which the West is sensitive may not be as readily available as it might have been before. It is also likely that such contests as will continue to be fought between the major Communist powers and the West will be, for the near future, in Asia rather than in Africa, unless events within Africa force a change.[62] However, this may affect the possibility of Western intervention, insofar as Western powers may be less ill-disposed toward radical nationalist movements.

It has been argued from a revolutionary point of view that changes in a radical direction are not likely in the near future because of the weakness of progressive forces in Africa and the late "rationalization" of neocolonial domination there.[63] This argument looks only to radicalism in the Marxist tradition and ignores the possibility of right-wing radicalization now already occurring in a number of countries and the effect that it might have on the development, or consolidation where they exist, of socialist revolutionary forces.[64] Besides, Zambia indicates that an African state can for nonsocialist reasons still be radically nationalist, especially when the residues of the colonial period continue to be confronted as obstacles in domestic life as well as being apprehended as real military dangers. The failure of the "dialogue" movement and the repudiation of the "prodialogue" leaders after successful coups against some of them indicate that even from purely nationalist considerations most African elites will be motivated to continue to reject unremittingly the apartheid state and what it represents. The end of the Cold War, and consequent lack of eagerness on the part of African governments not to create difficulties for the West or foreclose apparent openings to Communist influence (real or imaginary), may make this more likely.[65] South Africa is so related historically to that colonial experience of Black states against which every impulse for self-improvement, freedom, and justice is, and will continue to be, in revolt that it cannot avoid,

[62]See A. Buchan, "The New Climate of World Politics," The Listener 90, 2329 (15 November 1973).

[63]This is basically the argument in Arrighi and Saul, "Nationalism and Revolution."

[64]Amin-type regimes may, paradoxically, by polarizing domestic politics hasten the development of insurgent movements with radical left-wing ideologies.

[65]Tsirainna's policy in Malagasy fell victim to this movement.

except in a few, very temporary, and obviously anomalous situations, being caught in that historical tide of the rejection of colonialism and White domination on the one hand, of Black assertion and regeneration on the other. In short, the liberation of southern Africa is indissolubly interfused with this wider issue of Black progress, the African revolution itself.

Africa is, however, not isolated; neither in its revolution generally nor on the question of the freedom of South Africa. Many organizations and groups in non-African countries, and not least in the countries most closely collaborating with South Africa, play an immense part in pressuring popular opinion and governments. Promotional groups operating in these countries probably have no small impact on Africans themselves. It does appear also that opposition to collaboration with South Africa has become a symbolic political position in the domestic politics of Western as well as African states. This probably signifies the integration at the ideological level of antiapartheid and anticolonial feeling into the political lives of these states—a matter that limits the freedom of governments to collaborate with Pretoria.

It is, of course, the case that the major Western powers not only refrain from imposing pressures against apartheid, but also actively collaborate in the defense of apartheid in a number of ways, including economics, politics and strategy.[66] Such collaboration, like the pressures brought to bear on South Africa, will depend on the development of revolutionary forces in Africa as well as in these states. As the struggle intensifies the notion may become irresistible that from the point of view of the liberation of Africa, the Western powers may themselves have to be regarded as appropriate objects of revolutionary transformation. Beyond the limited question of the freedom of South Africa, the idea of international pressure points to larger problems in the wider international system, from which that liberation will no longer if it ever was, be capable of meaningful separation in practice as well as theory.

CONCLUSION

External pressure was originally conceived by many as a prelude to international sanctions against South Africa that would in a fairly short time bring that regime down. The hope of sanctions has receded—and in the light of Rhodesia's experience since its unilateral declaration of independence, seems even less credible than before. Accordingly the isolation of South Africa now only makes sense as a

[66]*See*, e.g., First et al., *South African Connection;* and Barber, *South Africa's Foreign Policy.*

long-term tactic that is seen to contribute in small, often ambiguous ways to the wider processes of transformation in southern Africa. It is from that perspective that we have sought to identify the conse-quences and the characteristics of international opposition to South Africa. If by this accounting the impact of pressure is small indeed, it seems to us that this can only be because earlier expectations were too sanguine, based on concepts of political change that were perhaps too naive, and not because the idea of international action is itself empty or poor.

16
White Over Black in South Africa: What of the Future?*

LEONARD THOMPSON

INTRODUCTION

✳ (Prediction) in human affairs is an extremely precarious undertaking. The variables are so many, their relationships so complex, and the injection of fresh factors so frequent that prediction is the function of the diviner rather than the scholar—if by prediction we mean forecasting specific events with specific results in a specific timetable.

In *Modernizing Racial Domination*, which was published in 1971, Heribert Adam showed that several of the prophecies Pierre van den Berghe had made in 1965 were false, though Adam did not highlight van den Berghe's rashest assertion of all—that "conditions will have become favorable for these [revolutionary] developments within five years at most."[1] Moreover several of the counter-assertions that Adam included in his book are themselves now looking suspect. For example, Adam was sufficiently impressed by the diplomatic offensive that South Africa was conducting at the beginning of the present decade to declare that more and more independent African countries would soon "settle for peaceful co-existence" with the Republic,[2] whereas in 1974 South Africa's outward policy is in disarray.

---

*I am grateful to Jeffrey Butler, David Robinson, and Stanley Greenberg for helpful comments on drafts of this chapter.

[1]P. van den Berghe, *South Africa: A Study in Conflict* (Middletown, 1965), p. 263.

[2]H. Adam, *Modernizing Racial Domination: The Dynamics of South African Politics* (Berkeley, 1971), p. 121; *See also* Adam's item 8 on pp. 121-2.

Nevertheless, a social scientist worth his salt understands contemporary processes in terms of his own discipline better than a layman and the authors of the previous chapters—social scientists of several disciplines—jointly possess an exceptional understanding of contemporary South Africa. Moreover change is always in large measure a product of the past. Consequently, the contributors to this book may claim to be exceptionally well equipped to assess the consequences of the processes of change that are presently discernible in South Africa.

Unfortunately, however, understanding does not produce unanimity, because subjective factors inevitably affect judgment. Even if several specialists have all reflected long and hard about South African problems and tried their best to come to "objective" conclusions about what is happening and what is likely to happen, they cannot be expected to agree. This book shows very clearly that the perceptions of a scholar are affected not only by the approach of his discipline but also by his domicile, his citizenship, and his past or present status and affiliations in South African society. Scholars domiciled in South Africa fall within the scope of the Republic's laws, which prescribe horrendous penalties for expressing ideas that are commonplace elsewhere; whereas many scholars domiciled outside South Africa live in milieux where it is customary to disparage people who have the responsibility for coping with the situation from within. A White person lacks the knowledge that comes from experience of life in the subordinate strata of South African society, and conversely with a Black person. Above all, it is difficult to keep one's rational faculties and one's moral sensibilities in separate compartments—to prevent one's judgment as to what will happen from being influenced by one's convictions as to what should happen. Wishful thinking and ominous forebodings are the greatest distorting factors in any attempt to peer into the future.

Consequently, for subjective as well as objective reasons, it would be foolhardy to attempt to distill from the previous chapters one or more specific scenarios, replete with timetables, for the future of South Africa. Who, a year or two ago, would have predicted that in 1974 the price of gold would soar above $190 an ounce, or that the Caetano regime would be overthrown in Lisbon and its successor would rapidly transfer power to the African liberation movement in Guinea-Bissau and start a similar process in Mozambique and Angola? Nevertheless we hope that this chapter, concluding a book in which diverse authors have analyzed a series of particular aspects of the South African situation, may provoke thought about how the multidimensional jigsaw puzzle fits together and what it augurs for the future of South Africa. What is the resultant of the external forces now operating upon South Africa? How, cumulatively, are they affecting the structure of South African society?

In the first chapter in this section, Potholm analyses the changes that have recently been taking place in the relations between the Republic and the other territories in southern Africa. Malagasy and Zambia have recently gone a long way toward reorienting their trade away from the Republic, and even Botswana, Lesotho, and Swaziland are acting more independently than they were a few years ago. In addition, whereas until recently the Republic was buttressed by White regimes in Angola and Mozambique as well as Rhodesia, the Portuguese territories are now in the process of decolonization, which places White Rhodesia, too, in jeopardy. Moreover, as Potholm demonstrates, the differences between the core values that prevail in the Republic and Rhodesia and those that prevail in the other territories are becoming accentuated rather than diminished. Nevertheless, Potholm concludes that the Republic is capable of adapting to these changes in its neighborhood without itself undergoing fundamental change.

It is possible that Potholm's conclusions are somewhat weakened by his association with the systems-analysis approach to southern Africa that has recently become fashionable among American political scientists. To apply this organizing principle to southern Africa is to presuppose a degree of stability that has not existed among the territories of the region since the Republic left the Commonwealth and the British African Empire began to dissolve. No two analysts have agreed upon a list of the territories that comprise the subsystem and individual analysts have had to alter their lists to keep pace with events, or to propound intricate formulas of differential relationships to validate the applicability of the concept to southern Africa.[3] Potholm himself starts his chapter by including Zambia and Malagasy "under the generic heading 'contiguous,'" but in later passages he omits them from his analysis. A model with an inherently static bias is not a wholly satisfactory device for explaining contemporary interterritorial relations in southern Africa.

Sean Gervasi's chapter focuses on the purpose and effect of the southern African policies of the Western powers, especially the United States and the Great Britain. Not only does he demonstrate that the Western involvement in the South African economy is large, increasing, and exceptionally profitable, but he also contends that Western governments consider they have a vital interest in preserving their access to raw materials located in South Africa and their control over the sea route around the Cape of Good Hope. For these reasons, he

---

[3] K. Grundy, *Confrontation and Accommodation in Southern Africa: The Limits of Independence* (Berkeley, 1973), pp. 303-23.

maintains, conservative public and private authorities in the West, alarmed at the successes of the liberation movements in the territories to the north of the Republic, have been pursuing a strategy of containment aimed at forestalling revolution. This strategy includes discreet aid to the White regime and preparations for assistance to it in the event of military conflict spreading to the Republic. It also includes a reform component, but the reforms envisaged are marginal and are not intended to undermine the structure of South African society. The strategy is made to seem humane and progressive by being presented to the public as promoting peaceful, evolutionary change through accelerated economic growth. In fact, however, Gervasi concludes, there are no grounds for expecting that accelerated economic growth will promote a redistribution of power or wealth.

Sam Nolutshungu agrees with Gervasi and takes his argument further. He regards Western pressures upon South Africa as "antirevolutionary reformism" (as distinct from "revolutionary radicalism," which he associates with Communist and Third World pressures), and he correlates the effects of such Western pressures with a class analysis of South African society. From this he deduces that since members of the Afrikaner elite are now major capitalists with international affiliations, the National party is quite willing to promote reforms of the sort desired by Western governments. Such reforms include concessions to the Black bourgeoisie (including the Bantustan politicians), who, he claims, are thereby becoming separated from the Black workers and peasants—the potential revolutionaries—and turned into collaborators.

The Gervasi-Nolutshungu propositions verge on a conspiracy theory, in which the conspirator is "international capitalism," including the major Western governments, the South African government, the Afrikaner elite, and the Black South African bourgeoisie. This theory requires careful examination.

Are we to believe that the major Western governments are irrevocably committed to policies that amount to "antirevolutionary reformism"? In terms of motives, there is no doubt that many Westerners desire modifications in South Africa because they consider that that is the best way of ensuring a continuous flow of high profits and scarce raw materials to the West. But others advocate reforms for quite different purposes: to alleviate the daily sufferings of Black South Africans and also to start a process that may snowball and culminate in a radical redistribution of power and wealth.

In terms of effects, the theory is a-historical because it ignores the fact that the consequences of actions differ—and often differ profoundly—from the motives of actors. Even reforms sponsored with the "antirevolutionary" motives that Gervasi and Nolutshungu ascribe to the West may in fact generate fundamental change in the

distribution of power and wealth in South Africa. Radical changes
elsewhere have usually been preceded by reforms that were intended
to stabilize regimes. Reforms initiated by established authorities have
been the preludes not only to the major shifts of power in modern
Europe, but also to the decolonization of Francophonic tropical
Africa, and there is no reason to believe that South Africa should be
an exception.

The Gervasi-Nolutshungu theory also implies that nation-states
and multinational corporations are static and monolithic institutions.
For example, Gervasi's demonstration that the Western powers have
vital interests in South Africa does not necessarily mean that Western
governments and corporations will support the White regime indef-
initely and at all costs. There are at least three objections to that logic.
First, the internal political processes in Western countries are extremely complex, and, even if Gervasi is correct in his exposition of
the motives of the Heath and Nixon administrations, both have now
collapsed and their successors or their successors' successors may
become more responsive to domestic antiapartheid lobbies than they
were. Second, the debacles in Suez, Algeria, and Vietnam have produced domestic constraints that would make it very difficult for any
British, American, or French government to intervene militarily in
South Africa to prop up a racist regime threatened by popular upris-
ings. Third, recent events have shown that the external deterrents to
Western support for the White regime may become strengthened by
pressures from Arab oil producers, or from combinations of Third
World producers of other raw materials. So, even if we take the most
cynical view of the motives of Western governments and multinational corporations, the time may be approaching when they will
deem it expedient to hedge their bets in South Africa in the hope that,
if fundamental changes do take place, they will be able to do business
with the new regime.

THE GUERRILLA THREAT

Despite their failure to oust the Portuguese in the 1960s, the guerrilla
movements in the Portuguese African territories generated substantial power in the early 1970s. By the end of 1973 the African Party for
the Independence of Guinea and the Cape Verde Islands (PAIGC)
controlled one-third of Guinea-Bissau and was recognized as the
legitimate government by the Organization of African Unity (OAU)
and over seventy members of the United Nations. In the early part of
1974 the Popular Movement for the Liberation of Angola (MPLA)
was maintaining a presence in northern and eastern Angola and it
and the Zaire-based National Front for the Liberation of Angola
(FNLA) were developing serious thrusts into the Cabinda enclave

north of the lower Congo, important for its off-shore oil fields. More immediately threatening to South Africa were the operations of the Front for the Liberation of Mozambique (FRELIMO) in Mozambique where, infiltrating southwards from its long-established bridge-heads in the northern provinces, it was making a series of attacks on three major railroads: Beira-Malawi, Beira-Umtali, and Tete-Cabora Bassa.

These events precipitated a crisis in Portugal, a small and relatively underdeveloped European country that had been spending about 40 percent of its national budget and 5 percent of its gross national product, and straining the loyalty of its young men, in efforts to sup-press the rebellions. In February 1974 General Antonio de Spinola, a highly respected deputy chief of the General Staff and former governor-general of Guinea-Bissau, published a book in which he declared that no military victory was possible in Portuguese Africa and pleaded for a political solution with self-determination for the colonial peoples. In March junior officers circulated an underground document asserting that a political solution must "safeguard national honor and dignity as well as all the legitimate interests of the Portu-guese settled in Africa," but should also "make allowances for the irre-versible and undeniable reality of the deepest aspirations of African peoples to govern themselves."[4] In April these officers overthrew the Caetano government and installed a coalition cabinet, including Socialist and Communists. The new government immediately began to negotiate with the leaders of the guerrilla movements in the three territories, evidently in the hope of transferring power to the PAIGC in Guinea-Bissau but of transforming Angola and Mozambique into semiautonomous states with a loose and subordinate relationship to Portugal. However, the coup opened up a wider range of possibilities and the situation soon developed even more rapidly than it had in French tropical Africa, where French efforts to maintain the sub-stance of power by concessions in 1956 and 1958 led to independence in 1960.

Initially, some observers expected that organized groups of White settlers and Black collaborators might seize power in Lourenço Marques and hold onto as much territory as possible, counting on South African military assistance. In that event the Pretoria govern-ment would have been faced with a difficult decision. Hawks would have argued that South Africa should intervene to acquire control over at least the southern part of Mozambique, for Lourenço Marques is the closest port to the Witwatersrand and it has been coveted by South Africans for over a century. On the other hand, doves would

[4]*Le Monde,* cited in *The Guardian* (Manchester and London) weekly edition, 23 March 1974.

have reasoned that intervention would discredit South Africa's claim to be a nonaggressive state.

In fact, the White settlers offered only partial and ineffective resistance when FRELIMO representatives began to participate in the government of Mozambique, and during May 1974 the prime ministers of South Africa and Rhodesia issued a joint declaration that all they wanted was "good" and "stable" government in neighboring territories and that they were not concerned about the possibility of their being Black governments. However, although FRELIMO will probably become the ruling organization in an independent Mozambique during 1975 and it has a strong revolutionary socialist orientation, its policy towards South Africa will be constrained by economic factors. Mozambique is a poor country. It derives a large part of its meager wealth from the earnings of its men on the Witwatersrand gold mines, and for the foreseeable future South Africa will be the only possible major consumer of power from the Cabora Bassa dam which is scheduled to begin production in 1975.[5]

In Rhodesia 260 thousand White settlers are trying to maintain control over more than 5 million Africans in a territory as large as California. Great Britain regards Rhodesia as a rebellious colony; no foreign government recognizes it; and the United Nations has imposed general economic sanctions against it. That the regime has survived as long as it has since its unilateral declaration of independence (UDI) in 1965 is due primarily to South Africa, which has ignored the sanctions, contributed military aid in the guise of police, and provided moral support; and secondarily to Portugal, which has permitted it to trade through Beira and Lourenço Marques. Although sanctions have not toppled the regime, they have caused a serious shortage of goods and foreign exchange; there is a crucial dearth of white manpower; and morale is brittle. In the second half of 1973 the number of White emigrants actually exceeded the number of White immigrants; and since December 1972 well-armed and well-trained guerrillas, operating from bases in Mozambique, Tanzania, and Zambia have been conducting small-scale but effective operations inside Rhodesia.

To maintain itself the government has resorted to increasingly desperate measures, most of them derived from South African precedents: arbitrary arrests and detentions; executions; forced removals of entire populations; group punishments on villages; and expulsions of foreign journalists and university teachers. In 1972 Rhodesia's main effort to gain British recognition was found by the

[5]R. First, "Southern Africa after Spinola" and G. Bender, "Portugal and her Colonies join the Twentieth Century: Causes and Initial Implications of the Military Coup," *Ufahamu*, 4, 3 (Winter 1974), pp. 88-108 and 121-62.

Friday re ANC page 407 but no mention here. Confusion with line 33?

WHITE OVER BLACK: WHAT OF THE FUTURE?   407

Pearce Commission to be unacceptable to the people of Rhodesia as a whole. The government's subsequent attempts to make a deal with Bishop Muzorewa's African National Council to the satisfaction of Great Britain came to nothing during the tenure of the Heath administration, which was well disposed to such an outcome. With the Labour party confirmed in office in a general election in October 1974, Rhodesia's chances of winning British recognition without fundamental change dwindled to vanishing point.

Even before the Portuguese coup, the Salisbury regime was hard pressed—politically, economically, and militarily.[6] Now, if FRELIMO succeeds in consolidating its power throughout Mozambique, the prospects of White Rhodesia will plummet catastrophically. The territory will have become nearly surrounded by Black-controlled states and all its trade routes will be under Black control, except southwards across its 150 mile border with the Republic to distant South African ports.

In 1973 Dr. Connie Mulder, South African minister of the interior and of information, said that South Africa preferred the front line against terrorism to be the Zambezi rather than the Limpopo and Prime Minister Vorster declared that "we know what to do if our neighbour's house is on fire."[7] Nevertheless, the Rhodesian situation is under constant and anxious review in Pretoria, and the South African government may soon have to decide whether to become more fully engaged in the defense of the Zambezi line or to sacrifice White Rhodesia. No doubt there are strong demands for full military commitment, for many White South Africans have relatives in Rhodesia or have invested heavily in the territory. But there are also powerful counter-arguments that weigh heavily with the Pretoria politicians. The Smith government has not been very skilful, and it has made some of its most momentous decisions without consulting Pretoria—including the decisions to seize UDI in 1965 and to close the Zambian border in 1973. South Africa has made thorough preparations to hold the Limpopo line, which is more defensible than the Zambezi. And, by astute diplomacy and economic incentives South Africa will hope to moderate the policies of an African regime in Zimbabwe as well as in Angola and Mozambique.

As the dust settles on the changes sparked off by the Portuguese coup, the guerrilla threat to South Africa will become more serious. Indeed, if the White regime in Rhodesia collapses, South Africa (with Namibia) will face potentially hostile neighbors along a frontier stretching two thousand miles across the continent from the Cunene

[6]K. Good, "Settler Colonialism in Rhodesia," *African Affairs*, 73, **290** (January 1974), pp. 10-36.

[7]*Africa Research Bulletin* 11, 8 (August 1973), p. 2961.

River to Delagoa Bay, and Botswana as well as Malawi will be able to reduce its dependence on the Republic, as Zambia has already done.

In these circumstances South Africa will probably have to yield at least the northern part of Namibia, where the African population has cultural and historical links with the population of southern Angola and has been held down with increasing difficulty by subservient African chiefs. Elsewhere, however, although it has been argued that guerrilla activity on the Maoist model will be the harbinger of revolution in South Africa,[8] the Republic will probably be able to contain any such activity for some time to come, provided that that is the only threat it has to cope with. Regimes that have been overthrown by guerrilla forces were either colonies, such as Algeria and the Portuguese territories, in which the guerrillas' task was to convince a metropolitan government that it was in its interests to withdraw, or weak and corrupt political systems in preindustrial countries, such as Batista's Cuba and Chiang Kai-shek's China. South Africa is neither of these. In resisting "terrorists" its government has the ardent support of 4 million Whites who consider their very survival is at stake. South Africa has a far more powerful industrial base and far more formidable military equipment than any government that has been overthrown by guerrilla forces. It has the capacity to produce atomic weapons; the terrain in the vicinity of its borders is treeless or sparsely wooded savanna, which affords guerrillas scant opportunity for concealment. Moreover, the South African revolutionaries in exile are divided into rival factions; the capacity of Black African states to launch military expeditions against the Republic is limited by domestic economic and political weaknesses, interstate rivalries, and serious logistic problems; and neither the Soviet Union nor the People's Republic of China seems prepared to make a major commitment in southern Africa in the near future. Consequently, although guerrilla groups launched across South Africa's land frontiers may become a continual irritant to the regime, they do not seem likely to be able to overthrow it.[9]

The rulers of the major states in central Africa—President Kaunda of Zambia, President Nyerere of Tanzania, and President Mobutu of Zaire—are experienced and realistic politicians. Insofar as they are able to exert diplomatic pressure and coordinate the strategy of the liberation movement as a whole, they are likely for the foreseeable future to concentrate on assisting FRELIMO to consolidate its hold

[8]M. Legassick, "Guerrilla Warfare in Southern Africa," in W. Cartey and Martin Kilson, eds., *The African Reader: Independent Africa* (New York, 1970), pp. 381-400.
[9]S. Johns, "Obstacles to Guerrilla Warfare: A South African Case Study," *Journal of Modern African Studies,* 11, 2 (June 1973), pp. 267-303.

over Mozambique, on consummating the transfer of power to a predominantly African government in Angola, and on promoting fundamental changes in Rhodesia and Namibia. These goals will not necessarily be achieved smoothly or rapidly. Moreover, as the transition
proceeds the new governments will be preoccupied with grave
internal political and economic problems and in no condition to
precipitate physical confrontations with the Republic. The South
African government, in turn, while continuing to perfect its military
defenses and to try to improve its reputation with the outside world,
will be obliged to make serious efforts to establish normal working
relationships with the new governments as they come into existence in
neighboring territories. Consequently, if fundamental changes are to
take place in South Africa itself in the near future, they will probably
be generated primarily by pressures inside the Republic.

BLACK POWER IN THE BANTUSTANS AND
THE SOUTH AFRICAN CITIES

What, then, are the effects, actual and potential, of foreign influences
upon domestic affairs in South Africa? Foreign criticisms have
already had a profound influence on morale in the Republic. Despite
its tight control over the educational system, the radio services, and
the form of the political institutions, the government has not succeeded in insulating South Africans from the knowledge that world
opinion virtually unanimously condemns the theory and practice of
racial discrimination. Although many White South Africans discount
this knowledge by accepting the official propaganda line that the
policy of separate development will eliminate racial discrimination
and that poverty, instability, and injustice are just as endemic in other
societies, influential Whites in numerous occupations are deeply concerned. Many industrialists, trade unionists, sportsmen, clergymen,
intellectuals, journalists, authors, and artists have overseas affiliations
and the politicians themselves are by no means isolationist, but
anxious to obtain Western approval. Moreover, many of the Black
leaders and potential leaders who have emerged within the government's own separatist institutions—Bantustan politicians and university and high school students—are overtly rejecting government
propaganda. There seems to be no way in which the regime can stop
Black consciousness from penetrating deeply into Black South African society, for the workers and peasants are well aware that their
conditions are unjust.

It is much more difficult to assess the on-going effects of foreign
involvement in the South African economy. The evidence is overwhelmingly strong that in the past the managements of foreign subsidiaries, with very few exceptions, have complied not only with South

African law but also with South African custom in the wage rates, job allocations, and fringe benefits they have provided for their Black workers.[10] Until recently, Western criticism of the performance of foreign corporations in South Africa was confined to relatively small groups of zealots closely associated with South African exile groups. Now, however, the antiapartheid lobbies are influencing larger segments of the populations of Great Britain and the United States. During the last few years the *Guardian's* exposures of the employment practices of British subsidiaries and revelations of the practices of American subsidiaries by the Diggs Committee (the Subcommittee on Africa of the Foreign Affairs Committee of the United States House of Representatives) have reached a wider public, with the result that Western corporations can no longer expect the behavior of their South African subsidiaries to be ignored.[11] These pressures may increase. In the United States, for example, it is conceivable that the 11 percent of the population who are of African descent will use the government's South African policy as a bargaining counter in domestic politics.[12]

Black South African organizations in exile and also many Westerners who are repelled by the injustices in South African society, including the World Council of Churches, have called for complete "withdrawal" or "disengagement" from South Africa. This proposal has the persuasive quality of ideological purity; but it is not realistic. The involvements of Great Britain, and even of the United States, France, West Germany, and Japan are probably too important to their national interests to be abandoned. Even if the government of one such country decided to "withdraw," it would be extremely difficult to enforce the decision on its citizens, and insofar as it managed to do so other companies, foreign or South African, would merely acquire the relinquished assets and operate them. Indeed, the prospects of general withdrawal are nebulous, for there are always governments and corporations that find ways of seizing profitable openings, as the French did when others were respecting the United Nations' embargo on the supply of arms to South Africa.[13]

Since withdrawal is unrealistic, the crucial questions are narrower ones: what are, and what are likely to be, the effects of reforms, actual

[10]R. First, J. Steele, and C. Gurney, *The South African Connection: Western Investment in Apartheid* (London, 1972).

[11]For example, *see* J. Simon, "Yale's First Year as a 'Socially Responsible' Stockholder," *Yale Alumni Magazine* (February 1974), pp. 17-23.

[12]C. Keto, "Black American Involvement in South African Race Issues," *Issue*, 3, 1 (Spring 1973), pp. 6-11.

[13]To say that withdrawal is not likely to occur is not to deny that it may be tactically advantageous for antiapartheid pressure groups to call for withdrawal.

and potential, on South African society? Are Gervasi and Nolutshungu correct in assuming that any conceivable reforms would merely strengthen the regime and prolong the system of White political and economic domination?

It is necessary to distinguish, as Sachs and other contributors to this volume have done, between reforms that have no direct bearing upon the power structure and reforms that create new sources of power. The so-called petty apartheid laws are in the former category. For example, White domination is not directly affected if Blacks are allowed to use the same transport facilities as Whites or to participate in selected sports events with Whites, or if foreign Black diplomats are given special treatment. It is the White monopoly of political and economic power that is fundamental to the system.

In 1959 Verwoerd initiated the Bantustan policy with conservative objectives: to defuse foreign criticism and to divert African political activity from the center and fragment it along ethnic lines. Fifteen years later, as Schlemmer's chapter demonstrates, the effects of this "reform" are highly ambiguous. On the one hand, the Pretoria government still exerts a great deal of control over the Bantustan authorities, and even if the territories acquire formal political independence, their freedom of action will be severely limited by their continued economic dependence on the Republic. On the other hand, some of the Bantustan politicians are skilfully exploiting the possibilities that are available to them. They have won the right to substitute an international language—English—for their different vernacular languages as the principal medium of instruction in the African schools and colleges, and they are developing a degree of cooperation with one another that was not foreseen by Verwoerd. That is to say, a political program that was intended by its White creator to be a stabilizing factor has developed its own dynamics, which are already posing serious problems for the regime. Nolutshungu is surely incorrect in dismissing all the Bantustan politicians as "tribal oligarchs" and implying that as conflict develops they will all prove to be collaborators with the White regime.

Before 1973 no comparable reforms had been made in the industrial sector. Nevertheless, important changes had been taking place in the structure of the labor force. The White population of South Africa is deeply committed to continuous economic growth, but three factors have been making it impossible even to sustain the existing level of productivity on the basis of a labor force rigidly divided between permanent White skilled workers and migrant Black unskilled workers. First, the White proportion of the total population of South Africa is declining. It decreased from 21.4 percent in 1911 to 17.2 percent in 1973, and an Afrikaner economist has estimated that it will fall to 14 percent by the end of the century and to 11 percent by

A.D. 2020.[14] Second, more and more Whites are being drawn away from the productive sectors of the economy into the burgeoning bureaucracies. By 1973 over 360,000 Whites were employed in the central, provincial, and local administrations and the Railways, Harbours and Airways Administration.[15] Subsequently, moreover, the decolonization of Angola and Mozambique has placed still higher demands on the limited pool of White manpower for military service in the frontier areas. Third, the tendency of developments in modern industrial technology is to require that an ever-higher proportion of the labor force shall possess skills that at the minimum can only be acquired by permanent and secure employment. Consequently, by 1973 the government had to cease treating the African population as an indifferentiated mass of interchangeable migrant laborers with homes in the reserves and was obliged to permit industrialists to employ an increasing number of Africans on tasks requiring skill and experience.

The 1973 strikes of African workers highlighted these developments and placed the Whites on the horns of a dilemma. To continue totally to exclude Africans from the industrial decision-making process is to incur the risk of further disturbances that are extremely difficult to foresee and suppress and that cause bad publicity overseas; whereas to allow it may be to give African workers the means to erect an organizational structure with immense power potential. Currently, this dilemma is causing vigorous debate among Whites. Sections of management and White labor are pressing for the admission of Black workers into recognized trade unions; government and other sections of management and White labor are opposing it. The government handled the 1973 strikes with a caution it had not previously displayed in similar circumstances and it subsequently provided for the creation of African works and liaison committees. In their present form these committees allow for African participation in communication with management but not in bargaining, and they are no more significant than the first steps in the "homelands" policy were in the early 1960s. But this concession, too, may prove to be a vital step in a cumulative process that will escalate beyond the intentions of its generators. Committees necessitate organization, and organization is a means to power.[16]

---

[14]M. Horrell, ed., *A Survey of Race Relations in South Africa, 1973* (Johannesburg, 1974), p. 49.

[15]Ibid., pp. 251-8.

[16]The reports of SPROCAS (The Study Project on Christianity in Apartheid Society), ed. P. Randall, highlight the crucial importance of Black industrial organization: e.g., *Power, Privilege and Poverty: Report of the SPROCAS Economics Commission* (Johannesburg, 1972), pp. 60-70.

Of course the government intends that any concessions it makes shall not shake the established order. As Wilson suggests, part of its strategy may be to confine the benefits of reform to the group he aptly calls "urban insiders" (Mayer's "urban core") at the expense of the "urban outsiders," who are intended to remain migrant, insecure, and unskilled, in the hope of driving a new wedge within African society by creating an upper segment of the working class with a stake in the status quo.

Nolutshungu apparently expects that this device will work—that African skilled workers, given privileges relative to the migrant workers, will become a stabilizing force for the regime. On the other hand, Mayer's researches in Soweto, a large African township on the Witwatersrand, show that already among the urban core internal class cleavages, though strong, are moderated by a consciousness of an overriding identity of interests with all who fall on the subordinate side of the major divide in South African society. It is surely premature to deduce from a Marxist analysis that the Black skilled workers (and likewise the Bantustan politicians) will collectively serve the interests of the Whites. No doubt many will do so. But since it is precisely the more privileged Africans who have rising expectations and it is these expectations that are blocked by the overriding color bar, some are likely to respond to the demands of the African masses, among whom conquest and systematic exploitation have instilled a vast reservoir of resentment.

As Adam has demonstrated elsewhere, the South African regime has a remarkable talent for controlling the direction of change.[17] However, its means are not limitless. Greater power is now being accumulated by Black rural authorities and urban workers than Africans have possessed in South Africa at any time since they were conquered in the nineteenth century. While it is difficult at this stage to perceive by what precise mechanisms Black power will escalate, it is also difficult to see any way in which the process of escalation can be reversed.

If this analysis is sound—if South Africa has entered into a period of internal instability pointing toward fundamental change—the use that Western public and private authorities now make of their leverage there can prove to be extremely important. It can affect, the tempo of change, the process of change, and the future alignment of a reconstructed South Africa. If they continue to act conservatively, as adumbrated by Gervasi and Nolutshungu, by the time South African Blacks have broken down the barriers of apartheid their leaders will have become completely alienated from the West. Such alienation already exists among many Black intellectuals. However, there is no

[17]This is the central theme of *Modernizing Racial Domination*.

No reason to assume, with Gervasi and Nolutshungu, that Western authorities are either so racist or so inflexible they are incapable of realizing the opponents of apartheid have a cause that will triumph in the long run. Taking a longer view of their own interests, industrialists, for example, can apply fair employment practices in their South African subsidiaries—providing their Black workers with superior training and with job assignments, wages, and fringe benefits commensurate with their talents; and governments, which have apparently been caught unprepared by the onset of Portuguese decolonization, might deem it expedient to establish contacts with leaders of the South African liberation groups as well as with the Bantustan politicians. By aligning itself with the dynamic forces in South Africa, when fundamental changes do take place, the West will find that the successor regime will be as pragmatic in its external policies as the Black regimes in tropical Africa are now.

Selected Bibliography
of Publications
Since 1970

This list is supplementary to the one in Heribert Adam, ed., *South Africa: Sociological Perspectives* (London: Oxford University Press, 1971), pp. 301-32. Adam's bibliography includes items dated 1960 to 1970 inclusive; this bibliography consists of items dated 1970 to 1974 inclusive (but without duplicating any entries in Adam's book).

The bibliography is selective. It is limited to items dealing with contemporary South Africa; moreover, many relevant articles with fewer than ten pages have been omitted. Books containing chapters by several authors have been listed only once if all or most of the chapters deal with South Africa; otherwise, a relevant chapter is listed seperately.

To update this bibliography, the reader is referred in the first instance to the quarterly journal *African Affairs,* each number of which includes a select bibliography of recent books and articles.

Adam, Heribert, ed. *South Africa: Sociological Perspectives.* London: Oxford University Press, 1971.

———. "The Rise of Black Consciousness in South Africa." *Race* 15, 2 (October 1973): 149-65.

———. "The South African Power-Elite: A Survey of Ideological Commitment." *Canadian Journal of Political Science* 4, 1 (March 1971): 79-96.

Alant, C. J. *Wat Ek van my Dominee Glo en Dink.* Pretoria: N. G. Kerk-Boekhandel, 1970.

Alverson, Hoyt. "Africans in South African Industry: The Human Dimension." Paper delivered to African Studies Seminar, University of Witwatersrand, December 1971.

Amelunxen, Clemens. "The Rule of Law in Multi-National South Africa." *Plural Societies* 1, 1 (December 1970): 53-68.

Anglin, D. G. "Confrontation in Southern Africa: Zambia and Portugal." *International Journal* 25, 3 (Summer 1970): 497-517.

———. *The International Arms Traffic in Sub-Saharan Africa.* Ottawa: School of International Affairs, Carleton University, Occasional Papers, no. 12, 1971.

Anon. "South Africa: A United White Front?" *Africa Confidential* 14, 13 (22 June 1973): 4-6.

———. "South Africa's Coloureds: Genuine New Deal?" *Africa Confidential* 14, 6 (6 March 1973): 4-6.

Archer, Sean. "Perverse Growth and Income Distribution in South Africa." Unpublished seminar paper, Institute of Development Studies, University of Sussez, February 1973.

Ashley, M. J. "The Education of White Elites in South Africa." _Comparative Education_ 7, 1 (August 1971): 32-45.

SAIRR Auerbach, F. E. _Education, 1961-1971: A Balance Sheet._ Johannesburg: South African Institute of Race Relations, 1972.

Barber, James P. _South Africa's Foreign Policy, 1945-1970._ London: Oxford University Press, 1973.

Barker, Paula Stapleton, ed. _Issue_ 3, 4 (Winter 1973). (Papers and proceedings from panels at the 1972 annual meeting of the African Studies Association.)

Baron, Barnett F. "Southern African Student Exiles in the United States," _Journal of Modern African Studies_ 10, 1 (May 1972): 73-91.

Barratt, John. "Dialogue in Africa: A New Approach." _South Africa International_ 2, 2 (October 1971): 99-109.

Bell, J. B. "The Future of Guerilla-Revolution in Southern Africa." Paper presented to African Studies Association, Denver, 3-6 November 1971. Mimeographed.

Bell, Trevor. _Industrial Decentralisation in South Africa._ Cape Town: Oxford University Press, 1973.

Berger, Allan. "Mass Population Removals." _Third World_ 2, 6 (June 1973): 36-7.

Bernstein, Hilda Watts. _South Africa: Political Trials and the Use of Torture._ London: Christian Action, 1972.

Best, Alan C. G. and Young, Bruce S. "Homeland Consolidation: The Case of Kwa Zulu." _South African Geographer_ 4 (September 1972): 63-73.

Biko, Steve. "SASO—A Hope for Black People at Large." _Aspect_ (March 1971): 3.

———. "Black Consciousness and the Quest for True Humanity." _Reality_ 4, 1 (March 1972): 4-8.

———, ed. _Black Viewpoint._ Durban: SPROCAS, Black Community Programmes, 1972.

Birley, Sir Robert. _The African Worker in South Africa._ Leeds: University Press, 1971.

Blashill, John. "The Proper Role of U.S. Corporations in South Africa." _Fortune_ 86, 1 (July 1972): 48-53, 89-91.

Boisselier, X. "La Politique Aurefère de l'Afrique du Sud et ses Incidences sur le Système Monetaire International." _Economie Appliquée_ 23, 4 (1970/4): 735-86.

Boot, J. J. G. "Apartheid: Pro and Contra." _Plural Societies_ (Summer 1972), 51-72.

Booth, Richard. _The Armed Forces of African States._ London: Institute for Strategic Studies, 1970.

Bowman, Larry W. _Politics in Rhodesia: White Power in an African State._ Cambridge, Mass.: Harvard University Press, 1973.

———. "South Africa's Outward Strategy: A Foreign Policy Dilemma." Papers in International Studies, _Africa Series_, no. 13. Athens, Ohio: Center for International Studies, 1972.

———. "South Africa's Southern Strategy and Its Implications for the United States." _International Affairs_ 47, 1 (January 1971): 19-30.

Brandel-Syrier, Mia. _Reeftown Elite: A Study of Social Mobility in a Modern African Community on the Reef._ London: Routledge and Kegan Paul, 1971.

Bransky, D. M. "Consideration of Marx's Concept of Money and Its Application to the Reproduction of Money-Material." B. Phil. thesis, York University, 1973.

Braverman, R. E. "Apartheid, Industrialization and the Trade Unions." *African Communist* 50 (1972): 38-53.

Breytenbach, W. J. "The Multi-National Population Structure of South Africa." *Plural Societies* 2, 1 (Spring 1971): 53-68.

British Council of Churches and Conference of British Missionary Societies. *Violence in South Africa: A Christian Assessment*. London: SCM Press, 1970.

Budlender, Geoff. "Universities and Social Change." Cape Town: University of Cape Town S.R.C., 1972. Mimeographed.

Buitendag, J. J., and Van Der Merwe, H. W. "Occupational Mobility of Afrikaners: The impact of urbanization and South African Politics." Paper delivered to Seventh World Congress of Sociology, Varna, Bulgaria, 1970.

Bundy, Colin. "The Emergence and Decline of a South African Peasantry." *African Affairs* 71, 285 (October 1972): 369-88.

Bunting, B. *Education for Apartheid*. London: Christian Action, 1971.

Buthelezi, Chief M. Gatsha. *White and Black Nationalism, Ethnicity and the Future of the Homelands*. Johannesburg: South African Institute of Race Relations, 1974.   *SAIRR*

Buthelezi, Manas. "Black Christians Must Liberate Whites." *Reality* 5, 3 (July 1973): 3-6.

Butler, Jeffrey. "Social Status, Ethnic Division, and Political Conflict in New Nations: Afrikaners and Englishmen in South Africa" in *Ethnicity and Nation-Building*. Edited by Wendell Bell and Walter E. Freeman. Beverly Hills/London: Sage Publications, 1974.

Carlson, Joel. *No Neutral Ground*. New York: Crowell, 1973.

Carlson, Joel et al. "Round Table: The Dilemma of Foreign Investment in South Africa." *American Journal of International Law* (September 1971): 293-322.

Carter, Gwendolen M. "Challenges to Minority Rule Southern Africa." *International Journal* 25, 3 (Summer 1970): 486-96.

Cassese, Antonio. "L'azione delle Nazioni Unite contro l'apartheid." *La Comunità Internazionale* 25 (August-October 1970): 619-45.

Červenka, Zdenek. *Land-Locked Countries of Africa*. Uppsala: Scandinavian Institute of African Studies, 1973.

Charton, Nancy C. J. "Ethnicity and Its Significance for Local Government and Constitutional Planning in the Republic of South Africa." *Studies in Comparative Local Government* (Winter 1972): 44-52.

————. "The Afrikaners: How English-Speaking and Indian South Africans See Afrikaners." Center for Inter-Group Studies, University of Cape Town, 1974. Mimeographed.

Chipembere, Henry B. Masauko. "Malawi's Growing Links with South Africa—A Necessity or a Virtue?" *Africa Today* 18, 2 (1971): 27-47.

Christie, Michael J. *The Simonstown Agreements*. London: Africa Bureau, 1970.

Cilliers, S. P. *Appeal to Reason*. Stellenbosch: University Publishers and Booksellers, 1971.

————. *Coloured People: Education and Status*. Johannesburg: South African Institute of Race Relations, 1971.   *SAIRR*

Cockram, Gail-Maryse. *Vorster's Foreign Policy*. Pretoria: Academica, 1970.

Curtis, N. "South Africa: The Politics of Fragmentation." *Foreign Affairs* 50, 2 (January 1972): 283-96.

Dale, Richard. *Botswana and Its Southern Neighbor: Patterns of Linkage and The Options of Statecraft.* Papers in International Studies, *Africa Series,* no. 6. Athens, Ohio: Center for International Studies, 1970.

————. "Refugees from South Africa Botswana: The External Ramifications of Internal Security Policy." Paper delivered at the annual meeting of the American Political Science Association, September 1973.

Daniel, John. "NUSAS 1963-73: Ten Years of Conflict." *South African Outlook* 104, 1232 (January 1974): 10-13, 17.

Davis, R. Hunt. *Bantu Education and the Education of Africans in South Africa.* Papers in International Studies, *Africa Series,* no. 14. Athens, Ohio: Center for International Studies, 1972.

Davis, Michael I. "Infringements of the Rule of Law in South Africa." *International Commission of Jurists Review* 7 (December 1971): 22-32.

Delius, Anthony. "Southern Africa Faces the Modern World." *African Affairs* 72, 289 (October 1973): 430-7.

Denoon, Donald, with Nyeko, Balam, and the advice of Webster, J. B. *Southern Africa Since 1800.* New York: Praeger, 1973.

Desmond, Cosmas. *The Discarded People: An Account of African Resettlement in South Africa.* Baltimore: Penguin Books, 1971.

De Villiers, Dawid. *The Case for South Africa.* London: Tom Stacey, 1970.

De Vos, P. J., et al. *A Socio-Economic and Educational Survey of the Bantu Residing in the Victoria East, Middledrift and Zwelitsha Areas.* Fort Hare, 1971.

Diggs, Charles C. "Action Manifesto." *Issue* 2, 1 (Spring 1972): 52-60.

Douwes Dekker, L., et al. "Case Studies in African Labour Action in South and South West Africa." Paper delivered at the conference on "Workers, Unions and Development in Africa," University of Toronto, April 1973.

Douwes Dekker, L., and Watts, H. L. "Certain Attitudes of White Industrial Employers in Durban Towards the Indian Worker in Contrast to the African Worker." *Humanitas* (Pretoria) 2, 2 (1973): 109-23.

Doxey, Margaret. "International Sanctions: A Framework for Analysis with Special Reference to the U.N. and Southern Africa." *International Organization* 26 (Summer 1972): 527-50.

Dubb, A. A., Melamed, L., and Majodina, M. "African Attitudes in Town: The Search for Precision." *African Studies* 32, 2 (1973): 85-97.

Dugard, John. *The South-West Africa/Namibia Dispute.* Berkeley: University of California Press, 1973.

————. "The United Nations, Decolonization and International Terrorism." Cape Town: University of Cape Town, Arts Students Symposium, 1973. Mimeographed.

Duggan, William B. *A Socioeconomic Profile of South Africa.* New York: Praeger, 1973.

Duncan, Sheena. "The Plight of the Urban African." Johannesburg: South African Institute of Race Relations, Topical Talks no. 23, 1970.

Du Preez, Peter. "The Construction of Alternatives in Parliamentary Debate: Psychological Theory and Political Analysis." *South African Journal of Psychology* 2 (1972): 23-40.

Durant, J. J. F. *Swartman, Stad en Toekoms.* Johannesburg: Tafelberg-Uitgewers, 1970.

Du Toit, Brian M. "Afrikaners, Nationalists and Apartheid." *Journal of Modern African Studies* 8, 4 (December 1970): 531-51.

————. *People of the Valley.* Cape Town: Balkema, 1974.

Edelstein, Melville L. *What Do Young Africans Think?* Johannesburg: South *SAIRR*
African Institute of Race Relations, 1972.

————. "What the Coloureds Think?" *The Star* (Johannesburg), 8 September
1973.

El-Ayouty, Yassin. "Legitimization of National Liberation: The United
Nations and Southern Africa." *Issue* 2, 4 (Winter 1972): 36-45.

Emmanuel, A. *Unequal Exchange: A Study of the Imperialism of Trade.* New
York: Monthly Review, 1972.

Enloe, Cynthia. *Ethnic Conflict and Political Development.* Boston: Little, Brown
and Co., 1973.

Fanou, T. B. "Capital Accumulation and the State in South Africa." Paper
read at Conference for Strategies for Economic Develoment: Africa and
Latin America, Dakar, 1972.

Farah, Abdulrahim A. "Southern Africa: A Challenge to the United
Nations." *Issue* 2, 2 (Summer 1972): 14-24.

Feit, Edward. *The Urban Revolt in South Africa, 1960-1964: A Case Study.*
Evanston: Northwestern University Press, 1971.

First, Ruth, Steele, Jonathan, and Gurney, Christobel. *The South African
Connection: Western Investment in Apartheid.* London: Temple Smith, 1972.

Gerber, Louis. *Friends and Influence: The Diplomacy of Private Enterprise.* Cape ✳
Town: Purnell, 1973.

Gervasi, Sean. *Industrialization, Foreign Capital and Forced Labour in South
Africa.* New York: United Nations, 1970.

————. *Poverty, Apartheid and Economic Growth.* United Nations Unit on
Apartheid, Document 30/71, July 1971.

————. "South Africa's Economic Expansionism." *Sechaba* 5, 6 (June 1971):
15-21.

Gibson, Richard. *African Liberation Movements.* London: Oxford University
Press, 1972.

Gluckman, Max. "Tribalism, Ruralism and Urbanism in South and Central
Africa." *Colonialism in Africa*, 3. Edited by V. Turner. Cambridge:
Cambridge University Press, 1971.

Goguel, A.-M. "L'apartheid jusqu'à quand?" *Esprit* (January 1972): 89-112.

Goldblatt, I. *History of South West Africa from the Beginning of the Nineteenth
Century.* Cape Town: Juta, 1971.

Good, Kenneth. "South African Settler Colonialism: A Present-day Summa-
tion." *East African Journal* 9, 11 (n.d.): 4-13.

————. "Settler Colonialism in Rhodesia." *African Affairs* 73, 290 (January
1974): 10-36.

Good, Robert C. *UDI: The International Politics of the Rhodesian Rebellion.*
Princeton: Princeton University Press, 1973.

Gordimer, Nadine. "Apartheid in the Primary Homelands." *Index* 1, 3/4
(1972): 25/30.

————. " White Proctorship and Black Disinvolvement." *Reality* 3, 5 (November 1971): 14-16.

Great Britain. *Legal Obligations of Her Majesty's Government Arising Out of the
Simonstown Agreements.* Cmd. 4589, London: HMSO, 1971.

————. House of Commons. *Wages and Conditions of African Workers Employed
by British Firms in South Africa.* 3 vols. London: HMSO, 1973.

Greenstein, Lewis J. "Slave and Citizen: The South African Case." *Race* 15, 1
(July 1973): 25-46.

, H. Gann & Peter Duignan (eds.), Colonialism in Africa, 1870-1960 (Cambridge U. Press)
— lst volume in 1969. It is projected in 4 volumes

Grice, D. C. "The Approaching Crisis—Land and Population in the Transvaal and Natal." Presidential address. Johannesburg: South African Institute of Race Relations, 1973.

Grobler, J. H. "The Agricultural Potential of the Bantu Homelands." *Tydskrif vir Rasse-Aangeleenthede* 23, 1 (January 1972): 37-43.

Groth, S. "The Condemnation of Apartheid by the Churches in South West Africa." *International Review of Missions* (April 1972): 183-95.

Gruhn, Isebill V. *British Arms Sales to South Africa: The Limits of African Diplomacy.* Denver: University Center of International Race Relations, Race and Nations Monograph Series, 3, no. 3, 1972.

Grundy, Kenneth W. *Confrontation and Accommodation in Southern Africa: The Limits of Independence.* Berkeley: University of California Press, 1973.

———. *Guerilla Struggle in Africa: An Analysis and Preview.* New York: Grossman, 1971.

Guelke, Adrian. "Africa as a Market for South African Goods." *Journal of Modern African Studies* 12, 1 (March 1974): 69-88.

Gutteridge, William F. "Africa's Armies and the Fortress of Southern Africa." *Commonwealth* 13, 5 (October 1970): 179-84.

Gwala, Mafika Pascal, ed. *Black Review 1973.* Durban: Black Community Programmes, 1974.

Haasbroek, D. J. P. "The Interpretation of Race Attitudes by South African Historians." *Humanitas* (Pretoria) 2, 1 (1973): 47-52.

Hain, Peter. *Don't Play with Apartheid.* London: Allen and Unwin, 1971.

Hart, Gillian. *African Entrepreneurship.* Occasional Paper no. 16. Grahamstown: Institute for Social and Economic Research, Rhodes University, 1972.

Harvey, Charles, "British Investment in South Africa." *Journal of Southern African Studies* 1, 1 (October 1974); 52-73.

Heard, Kenneth A. *General Elections in South Africa 1943-70.* London: Oxford University Press, 1974.

Hellman, Ellen. *Soweto: Johannesburg's African City.* Johannesburg: 1971.

Hellmann, Ellen, and Goldblatt, D. "Soweto." *Optima* 23, 1 (March 1973): 14-35.

Henderson, Willie. "Independent Botswana: A Reappraisal of Foreign Policy Options." *African Affairs* 73, 290 (January 1974): 37-49.

Hepple, Alex. *South Africa: Workers Under Apartheid.* London: Christian Action, 1971.

Higgins, E. "The Religious Functionary in Multi-Racial South Africa: Some Calvinist and Catholic Role Profiles." *Social Compass* 19 (1972): 29-47.

Higgins, Rosalyn. "The Advisory Opinion on Namibia." *International and Comparative Law Quarterly* 21, 2 (April 1972): 270-86.

Hirschmann, David. "Pressures on Apartheid." *Foreign Affairs* 52, 1 (October 1973): 168-79.

Hoagland, Jim. *South Africa: Civilizations in Conflict.* Boston: Houghton Mifflin; London: Allen and Unwin, 1972.

Horrell, Muriel. *The Education of the Coloured Community in South Africa, 1652-1970.* Johannesburg: South African Institute of Race Relations, 1970.

———. *Action, Reaction and Counter-Action: A Brief Review of Non-White Political Movements.* 3rd. ed. Johannesburg: South African Institute of Race Relations, 1971.

———. *The African Homelands of South Africa.* Johannesburg: South African Institute of Race Relations, 1973.

————. *South Africa: Basic Facts and Figures*. Johannesburg: South African Institute of Race Relations, 1973.

————, ed. *A Survey of Race Relations in South Africa*. Johannesburg: South African Institute of Race Relations, annually.

Horwitz, Ralph. "South Africa: The Background to Sanctions." *Political Quarterly* 42 (April-June 1971): 165-76.

Hubbard, M. *African Poverty in Cape Town, 1960-1970*. Johannesburg: South African Institute of Race Relations, 1971.

Huber, Bettina. "Images of the Future Among the White South African Elite." Ph.D. dissertation, Yale University, 1973.

Hutson, Major-General Henry P.W. *Majority Rule—Why? Co-operation Not Confrontation in Southern Africa*. London: Johnson, 1973.

Huttenback, Robert A. *Gandhi in South Africa: British Imperialism and the Indian Question, 1860-1914*. Ithaca: Cornell University Press, 1971.

Hynning, Cliford J. "The Future of South West Africa (Namibia)" *American Journal of International Law* 65, 4 (September 1971): 144-68.

Hyam, Ronald. *The Failure of South African Expansion, 1908-1948*. London: Macmillan, 1972.

Institute for Strategic Studies. *The Military Balance, 1971-72*. London: The Institute, 1971.

International Labour Organization. *The ILO and Aprtheid*. Geneva: ILO, 1971.

Ireland, Ralph R. "Education for What? A Comparison of the Education of Black South Africans and Black Americans." *Journal of Negro Education* 41, 3 (Summer 1972): 227-40.

————. "Transkei." *Plural Societies* 3, 1 (Spring 1972): 39-58.

Jackson, D. A. "South Africa's Labour Problems: Towards a Solution." In *Strikes—The Lessons from Natal*, a symposium on 14 March 1973 on how to avoid and deal with strikes, organized by the Institute of Personnal Management. Pietermaritzburg: The Natal Witness (Printer), 1973.

Jeeves, Alan H. "African Protest in Southern Africa." *International Journal* 28, 3 (Summer 1973): 511-24.

————. "The Problem of South Africa." *International Journal* 26, 2 (Spring 1971): 418-32.

Jinadu, L. Adele. "South West Africa: A Study in the 'Sacred Trust' Thesis." *African Studies Review* 14, 3 (December 1971): 369-88.

Joffe, Frank. "Recent Trends in South African Politics: A Survey of Election Results, 1966-1972." M.A. thesis, University of Essex, 1972.

Johns, Sheridan. "The Thrust of Pretoria's African Policy of Dialogue." *South Atlantic Quarterly* (Spring 1973) 179-97.

————. "Obstacles to Guerilla Warfare: A South African Case Study." *Journal of Modern African Studies* 11, 2 (June 1973): 267-303.

Joosub, H. E. "Race Relations: An Indian Point of View." *New Nation* 7, 1 (October 1973): 3-5.

Jubber, Ken. "Integrated Organization in a Segregated Country: The Case of the Southern African Council of Priests." Paper presented at Fourth Congress of Association for Sociology in Southern Africa, Roma, Lesotho, July 1973.

Kane-Berman, John. "The Rich Get Richer: Foreign Investment in South Africa." *Reality* 4, 3 (July 1972): 10-13.

————. "Sport: Multi-nationalism versus Non-racialism." Johannesburg: South African Institute of Race Relations, 1972. Mimeographed.

Kapungu, Leonard T. *The United Nations and Economic Sanctions Against*

Rhodesia. Lexington: Lexington Books, 1973.

Karis, Thomas, and Carter, Gwendolen M. *From Protest to Challenge: A Documentary History of African Politics in South Africa, 1882-1964*. 3 vols. Stanford: Hoover Institution, 1972-1974.

Kennan, George. "Hazardous Courses in Southern Africa." *Foreign Affairs* 49, 2 (January 1971): 218-36.

Keto, Clement Tsehloane. "Black American Involvement in South Africa's Race Issue." *Issue* 3, 1 (Spring 1973): 6-11.

Kettle, M., and Moss, R. P., eds. *Southern African Studies: Report of a Symposium Held at the School of Oriental and African Studies, 1969*. Birmingham: ASA (UK), 1970.

Khaketla, B. M. *Lesotho 1970: An African Coup Under the Microscope*. Berkeley: University of California Press, 1972.

Khoapa, Bennie, ed. *Black Review, 1972*. Johannesburg: Black Community Programmes, 1973.

Kleinschmidt, H., ed. *White Liberation*. Johannesburg: SPROCAS, 1972.

Kooy, Marcelle. "The Contract Labour System and the Ovambo Crisis of 1971 in South West Africa." *African Studies Review* 16, 1 (April 1973): 83-105.

Kornegay, F. A. *The Balance of Power in South Africa III: Selected Survey of Foreign Investment 1959-1972. Current Reading List Series* 9, 1. Washington, D.C.: African Bibliographic Center, 1972.

Kuper, Leo. "Class and Colour in South Africa: Some Problems in Marxism and Pluralism." *Race* 12, 4 (April 1971): 495-500.

―――. "Race, Class, and Power: Some Comments on Revolutionary Change." *Comparative Studies in Society and History* 14, 4 (September 1972): 400-21.

―――. "Theories of Revolution and Race Relations." *Comparative Studies in Society and History* 13 (January 1971): 87-107.

La Guma, Alex. *Apartheid: A Collection of Writings on South African Racism by South Africans*. New York: International Publishers; London: Lawrence and Wishart, 1971.

Lawrie, Gordon. "Britain's Obligations under the Simonstown Agreements." *International Affairs* 47, 4 (October 1971): 708-28.

Lazar, Leonard. *Namibia*. London: Africa Bureau, 1972.

Leftwich, Adrian, ed. *South Africa: Economic Growth and Political Change*. London: Allison and Busby, 1974.

Legassick, Martin. "Development and Underdevelopment in South Africa." Unpublished seminar paper for the Southern African group, Royal Institute of International Affairs, Chatham House, London, 1970.

―――. "Guerrilla Warfare in Southern Africa." in *The African Reader: Independent Africa*. Edited by W. Cartey and M. Kilson. New York: Vintage Books, 1970.

―――.. "The Making of South African 'Native Policy'. 1903-1923: The Origins of 'Segregation'." Unpublished paper, Institute of Commonwealth Studies, University of London, 1972.

―――. "The Dynamics of Modernization in South Africa." *Journal of African History* 13, 1 (1972): 145-50.

―――. "South Africa: Capital Accumulation and Violence." *Economy and Society* 3,3 (August 1974): 253-91.

―――. "Legislation, Ideology and Economy in Post-1948 South Africa." *Journal of Southern African Studies*, 1, 1 (October 1974): 5-35.

————. "South Africa: Forced Labour, Industrialization and Racial Discrimination." In *The Political Economy of Africa*. Edited by R. Harris. Boston: Schenkman, 1974.

————. "Class and Nationalism in South African Protest: The South African Communist Party and the Black Republic." In Occidental Papers, Program of Eastern African Studies, Syracuse University: Syracuse, forthcoming.

Legum, Colin. *The United Nations and Southern Africa*. Falmer: Institute for the Study of International Organisation, 1970.

————. *A Republic in Trouble: South Africa, 1972-1973*. London: Rex Collings, 1973.

Legum, Colin, and Legum, Margaret. "South Africa in the Contemporary World." *Issue* 3, 3 (Fall 1973): 17-27.

Leistner, Gerhard. *Economic and Social Forces Affecting the Urbanization of the Bantu Population of South Africa*. Occasional Paper no. 32. Pretoria: Africa Institute, 1972.

Le May, Godfrey H. L. *Black and White in South Africa: The Politics of Survival*. London: MacDonald; New York: American Heritage, 1971.

Lemba, Winter. "Liberation Rivalry Buried." *Africa Report* 18, 3 (May-June 1973): 15.

Lerumo, A. *Fifty Fighting Years: The Communist Party of South Africa, 1921-1971*. London: Inkululeko Publications, 1971.

Lever, Henry. "Anomie, Authoritarianism and Ethnocentrism in South Africa." In *Papers from the First Congress of the Association for Sociologists in Southern Africa*. Durban: University of Natal, 1973.

————. "Changes in Ethnic Attitudes in South Africa." *Sociology and Social Research* 56, 2 (January 1972): 202-10.

————. "Factors Underlying Change in the South African General Election of 1970." *British Journal of Sociology* 23, 2 (1972): 236-44.

————. *The South African Voter*. Cape Town: Juta, 1972.

Lewsen, Phyllis. "The Cape Liberal Tradition: Myth or Reality?" *Race* 13, 1 (July 1971): 65-80.

Limp, Walter. *Anatomie de l'Apartheid*. Paris: Casterman, 1972.

Lipton, Merle. "The South African Census and the Bantustan Policy." *World Today* 28, 6 (June 1972): 257-71.

————. "Independent Bantustans?" *International Affairs* 48, 1 (January 1972): 1-19.

Lobban, G. "The Effect of the Position of Africans in South African Society on Their Choice of Ethnic Reference and Identification Groups and Their Self-Concepts and Attitudes Towards Social Change." B.A. thesis, University of Witwatersrand, Johannesburg, 1970.

Lombard, J. A. "Problems of Regional Economic Programming in the Development of the Bantu Homelands." *South African Journal of Economics* 39, 4 (December 1971): 388-401.

Loubser, Jan. "The Modern Afrikaner." *South African Outlook* (June-July 1972): 93-8.

Loudon, J. B. *White Farmers and Black Labour-tenants*. Leiden: Afrika Studie-centrum, 1970.

Lourdes, J. G., ed. *What About South Africa?*. Mexico: Comp. Periodistica, 1971.

Louw, N. P. van Wyk. *Vernuwing in die Prosa*. Cape Town: Human and Rousseau, 1970.

Maasdorp, G. G. "Targets of Development in Relation to Population Trends and Needs." Paper delivered at a conference on comprehensive development in Zululand, Intitute for Social Research, University of Natal, Durban, February 1972.

McRae, Hamish, ed. "South Africa: a Survey." *Banker* 121 (September 1971): 1029-97.

Maccrone, I. D. *The Price of Apartheid: Presidential Address.* Johannesburg: South African Institute of Race Relations, 1970.

Madavo, C. E. "Government Policy and Economic Dualism in South Africa." *Canadian Journal of African Studies* 5, 1 (1971): 19-32.

Magubane, Ben. "African Opposition in South Africa." *Africa Review* 2, 3 (1972): 433-47.

———. "The South African Problem as a View of Imperialism." *Journal of Black Studies* 3, 1 (September 1972): 75-94.

———. "A Critical Look at Indices Used in the Study of Social Change in Colonial Africa." *Current Anthropology* 12, 4-5 (October-December 1971): 419-45.

Manganyi, N. Chabani. *Being Black in the World.* Johannesburg: SPROCAS/Ravan Press, 1973.

Manning, Charles A. W. *The United Nations and South West Africa.* London: South African Society, 1970.

Marcum, John A. "Southern Africa: Problems and U.S. Alternatives." *Intercom* 70 (September 1972): 6-20.

Maree, Johan. "Bantustan Economics." *Third World* 2, 6 (June 1973): 26-30.

———. "Problems of Definition and Measurement of the Underutilisation of Labour in the Traditional Rural Sector of An Economy with Migrant Labour." M.A. thesis, University of Sussex, 1972.

Marks, Shula. "Liberalism, Social Realities, and South African History." *Journal of Commonwealth Political Studies* 10, 3 (November 1972): 243-9.

Marquard, Leo. *A Federation of Southern Africa.* New York and London: Oxford University Press, 1971.

———. "Black Consciousness." *Reality* 5, 4 (September 1973): 10.

Matajo, R. E. "A New Weapon to Smash Trade Union Apartheid." *African Communist* 55 (1973): 57-68.

Mathews, Anthony S. *Law, Order and Liberty in South Africa.* Cape Town: Juta; Berkeley: University of California Press, 1972.

Matthews, Robert O. "Refugees and Stability in Africa." *International Organization* 26, 1 (1972): 62-83.

Maud, Ruan. "Racialism in Rag Time: The Psychology of Capitulation in South Africa." *Universities Quarterly* 27, 4 (Autumn 1973): 407-19.

Mayall, James. *Africa: The Cold War and After.* London: Elek Books, 1971.

Mayer, Philip. " 'Traditional' Manhood Initiation in an Industrial City: The African View." In *Man: Anthropoligical Essays.* Edited by E. de Jager. Cape Town: C. Struik, 1971.

———. *Urban Africans and the Bantustans: Hoernlé Memorial Lecture 1972.* Johannesburg: South African Institute of Race Relations, 1972.

Mbata, J. Congress. "Race and Resistance in South Africa." In *The African Experience.* Edited by John N. Paden and Edward W. Soja. Evanston: Northwestern University Press, vol. I, 1970.

Mechanic, David. "Apartheid Medicine." *Society* 10, 31 (March-April 1973): 36-44.

Meer, Fatima M. "The Natal Indian Congress 1972." *Reality* 4, 3 (July 1972): 5-6.

Melamed, Leslie, "The Relationship Between Actions and Attitudes in a South African Setting." *South African Journal of Psychology* 1 (1970): 19-23.

Mitchison, Naomi H. *A Life for Africa: The Story of Bram Fischer.* London: Merlin Press, 1973.

Mokgatle, Naboth. *The Autobiography of an Unknown South African.* London: Hurst; Berkeley: University of California Press, 1971.

Möller, N. J. *Stedelike Bantoe en die Kerk.* Pretoria: 1972.

Molteno, Robert. *Africa and South Africa: the implications of South Africa's 'outward looking' policy.* London: The Africa Bureau, 1971.

————. *African Labour and South Africa.* London: Africa Bureau, 1971.

————. "South Africa's forward policy in Africa." *Round Table* (July 1971): 329-45.

Moody, T. Dunbar. *The Rise of Afrikaner Nationalism.* Berkeley: University of California Press, 1974.

Morris, Michael. *Terrorism: The First Full Account in Detail of Terrorism and Insurgency in Southern Africa.* Cape Town: Timmins, 1971.

Morrison, Rodney J. "Apartheid and International Monetary Reform." *Review of Politics* 32, 3 (July 1970): 338-46.

Motlhabi, Mogethi, ed. *Essays on Black Theology.* Johannesburg: University Christian Movement, 1972.

Msimang, H. S. *H. Selby Msimang Looks Back.* Johannesburg: South African Institute of Race Relations, 1971.

Mtshali, B. V. "Rough Roads to Zulu Independence?" *Kroniek van Afrika* 12, 1 (1972): 30-34.

Naidoo, L. V. "The Problem of Social Integration in South Africa." Paper read at East Africa Social Science Council Annual Conference, Makerere, Uganda, December 1971.

Nielsen, Peter. *The Blackman's Place in South Africa.* Westport, Conn.: Negro Universities Press, 1970.

Niesewand, Peter. "What Smith Really Faces." *Africa Report* 18, 2 (March-April 1973): 16-20.

Nkosi, Z. "Elections in South Africa." *African Communist* **42 (1970): 69-85.**

Nolutshungu, Sam C. "The Implications of the Rhodesian Settlement Proposals for South Africa." In *Zimbabwe Now.* Edited by S. E. Wilmer. London: Rex Collings, 1973.

————. "Issues of the Afrikaner 'Enlightenment'." *African Affairs* 70, 278 (January 1971): 23-36.

————. "Party System, Cleavage Structure and Electoral Performance: The South African General Election of 1970." *African Review* 2, 4 (1972): 449-65.

————. *South Africa in Africa: A Study in Ideology and Foreign Policy.* Manchester: Manchester University Press, 1974.

Nyquist, T. E. *Toward a Theory of the African Upper Stratum in South Africa.* Papers in International Studies, Africa Series, no. 15. Athens, Ohio: Center for International Studies, 1972.

Orpen, Christopher. "Authoritarianism and Racial Attitudes Among English-Speaking South Africans." *Journal of Social Psychology* 84, 2 (1971): 301-2.

————. "The Effect of Cultural Factors on the Relationship Between Prejudice and Personality." *Journal of Psychology* 78, 1 (1971): 73-9.

————. "Internal-External Control and Brown Militancy." *Sociology and Social Research* 56, 4 (1972): 466-70.

Orpen, C., and Morse, S. J., eds. *Contemporary South Africa: Social Psychological Perspectives.* Cape Town: Juta, forthcoming.

Osieke, Ebere. "Sale of Arms to South Africa: Legal Obligations of Her Majesty's Government." *Indian Journal of International Law* 11, 2 (April 1971): 187-204.

Pachai, Bridglal. *The International Aspects of the South African Indian Question, 1860-1971*. Cape Town: C. Struik, 1971.

Pahad, E. "The Development of Indian Political Movements in South Africa 1924-46." Ph.D. dissertation. University of Sussex, 1972.

Palmer, Vernon U., and Poulter, S. M. *The Legal System of Lesotho*. Charlottesville, Va.: The Michie Company, 1972.

Park, Stephen, and Lake, Anthony. "Business as Usual: Transactions Violating Rhodesian Sanctions." *Issue* 3, 2 (Summer 1973): 7-17.

Paton, Alan. "Black Consciousness." *Reality* 4, 1 (March 1972): 9-10.

Pauw, Berthold A. *Christianity and Xhosa Tradition*. Cape Town: forthcoming.

Peele, S., and Morse, S. J. "Ethnic Voting and Political Change in South Africa." Unpublished manuscript, 1973.

Petersen, Paul. "The Social Basis of Nationalist Party Power." *Sechaba* 6, 7 (July 1972): 2-11.

Pierson-Mathy, Paulette. "L'action des Nations Unies contre l'apartheid." *Revue Belge de Droit International* 6, 1 (1970): 203-45.

Pillay, P. D. "White Power in Southern Africa." *African Quarterly* 10, 1 (April-June 1970): 32-9.

Potholm, Christian. "After Many a Summer? The Possibilities of Political Change in South Africa." *World Politics* 24, 4 (July 1972): 613-38.

————. *Swaziland: The Dynamics of Political Modernization*. Berkeley: University of California Press, 1972.

————. "The International Transfer of Insurgency Techniques: Sub-Saharan Pathologies." *Plural Societies* (Autumn 1972): 3-21.

————. "South Africa: The White Laager." *Current History* 64, 379 (1973): 102-5, 130, 133.

Potholm, Christian, and Dale, Richard, eds. *Southern Africa in Perspective: Essays in Regional Politics*. New York: Free Press, 1972.

Potter, Elaine, *The Press as Opposition: The Political Role of South African Newspapers*. London: Chatto and Windus, 1974.

Proudfoot, Merrill. "Verligte Action: Advice from an American." *New Nation* 6, 12 (July-August 1973): cover, 3-4.

Randall, Peter, ed. *Anatomy of Apartheid*. Johannesburg: SPROCAS, 1970.

————, ed. *Directions of Change in South African Politics*. Johannesburg: SPROCAS, 1971.

————, ed. *Education Beyond Apartheid*. Johannesburg: SPROCAS, 1971.

————, ed. *Some Implications of Inequality*. Johannesburg: SPROCAS, 1971.

————, ed. *South Africa's Minorities*. Johannesburg: SPROCAS, 1971.

————, ed. *Towards Social Change*. Johannesburg: SPROCAS, 1971.

————, ed. *Power, Privilege and Poverty*. Johannesburg: SPROCAS, 1972.

————, ed. *Apartheid and the Church*. Johannesburg: SPROCAS, 1972.

————, ed. *Law, Justice and Society*. Johannesburg: SPROCAS, 1972.

————, ed. *South Africa's Political Alternatives*. Johannesburg: SPROCAS, 1973.

————, ed. *A Taste of Power*. Johannesburg: SPROCAS, 1973.

Rex, John. "The Plural Society: The South African Case." *Race* 12, 4 (April 1971): 401-13.

————. *Race, Colonialism, and the City*. London and Boston: Routledge and Kegan Paul, 1973.

————. *Race Relations in Sociological Theory*. London: Weidenfeld and Nicolson, 1970.

Rhoodie, N. J. "The Coloured Policy of South Africa." *African Affairs* 72, 286 (1973): 46-56.

——, ed. *South African Dialogue: Contrasts in South African Thinking on Basic Race Issues.* Johannesburg: McGraw-Hill, 1972.

Rive, Richard. *Emergency.* New York: Macmillan, 1970.

Robertson, Janet. *Liberalism in South Africa: 1948-1963.* Oxford: Clarendon Press, 1971.

Rogers, Barbara. *South Africa's Stake in Britain.* London: Africa Bureau, 1971.

——. *South Africa: The "Bantu Homelands."* London: Christian Action, 1972.

Rose, Brian, and Tunmer, R., eds. *Documents in South African Education.* Johannesburg: Donker, 1973.

Roux, Marianne, and St. Ledger, Milly. *Grahamstown: Fingo Village.* Johannesburg: South African Institute of Race Relations, 1972. ✱ SAIRR

Royal United Services Institute for Defence Studies. *The Security of the Southern Oceans—Southern Africa the Key: Report of a Seminar, 16 February 1972.* London: The Institute, 1972.

Rutman, Gilbert L. "Some Economic Costs of Separate Development in Africa." *Co-existence* 8, 1 (January 1971): 53-63.

Sachs, Albie. *Justice in South Africa.* Berkeley: University of California Press; London: Heinemann, 1973.

Sadie, J. L. "The Economic Factor in Afrikaner Society." Center for Inter-Group Studies, University of Cape Town, 1974. Mimeographed.

——. "An Economic Commission for Southern Africa." *South Africa International* 1, 4 (April 1971): 161-75.

——. "Population and Economic Development in South Africa." *South African Journal of Economics* 39, 3 (September 1971): 205-22.

——. *Projection of the South African Population, 1970-2020.* Johannesburg: Industrial Development Corporation, 1973.

Sadie, Thys. *Apartheid voor die Regterstoel.* Durban: Die E.S.P.-Instituut, 1970.

St. Ledger, F. Y. "Attitudes of Black and White Journalists in South Africa." *Communications in Africa* 1, 5 (March 1974): 1-25.

Schlemmer, Lawrence. "City of Rural 'Homeland': A Study of Patterns of Identification Among Africans in South Africa's Divided Society." *Social Forces* 51, 2 (December 1972): 154-64.

——. "Employment Opportunity and Race in South Africa RR42/72." Johannesburg: South African Institute of Race Relations, 1972. Mimeographed.

——. "White Attitudes to the Bantustans." *Third World* 2, 6 (June 1973): 41-4.

——. "Social Research in a Divided Society." Inaugural Lecture. Pietermaritzburg: University of Natal Press, 1973.

——. *Privilege, Prejudice and Parties: A Study of Patterns of Political Motivation Among White Voters in Durban.* Johannesburg: South African Institute of Race Relations, 1973. SAIRR

Schoeman, B. *Van Malan Tot Verwoerd.* Cape Town: Dagbreekpers, 1973.

Selby, John, *A Short History of South Africa.* London: Allen and Unwin, 1973.

Selwyn, Percy. "Industrial Development in Peripheral Small Counries." Institute of Development Studies Discussion Paper, no. 14, University of Sussex, 1973.

Serfontein, Jan Hendrik Philippus. *Die Verkrampte Aanslag.* Cape Town: Human and Rousseau, 1970.

Shamuyarira, Nathan M. *Essays on the Liberation of South Africa.* University of Dar es Salaam Studies in Political Science no. 3. Dar es Salaam: Tanzania Publishing House, 1971.

————. "The Lusaka Manifesto on Southern Africa." *African Review* 1, 1 (March 1971): 66-78.

Shaw, Timothy M. "South Africa's Military Capability and the Future of Race Relations." In *Africa in World Affairs: The Next Thirty Years.* Edited by Ali A. Mazrui and Hasu H. Patel. New York: Third Press, 1973.

Shepherd, George W. "Changing South Africa: The New Debate." *Africa Today* 19, 4 (Fall 1972): 78-82.

Shingler, John. "Education and Political Order in South Africa 1902-1961." Ph.D dissertation, Yale University, 1973.

Sibeko, Alexander. "Students Fight for Freedom." *African Communist* 51 (1972): 73-87.

Slabbert, F. Van Zyl. "Moontlikhede van Verandering." *Deurbraak* (September 1973).

Slonim, Solomon. *South West Africa and the United Nations: An International Mandate in Dispute.* Baltimore: John Hopkins University Press, 1973.

Smith, Timothy H. *The American Corporation in South Africa: An Analysis.* New York: Council for Christian Social Action, 1972.

South African Institute of Race Relations. *Education for progress with special reference to the needs of the coloured community.* Johannesburg: South African Institute of Race Relations, 1971.

————. *The Future of the Homelands: Papers Given at the 44th Annual Council Meeting of the South African Institute of Race Relations.* Johannesburg: South African Institute of Race Relations, 1974.

South African Students Organizaton. "Frank Talk: Lets Talk About Bantustans." *SASO Newsletter* (October-November 1972): 18-21.

Spence, Jack E. "Nuclear Weapons and South Africa." in *Nuclear Proliferation: Stage II.* Edited by Joel Larus and Robert M. Lawrence. Forthcoming.

————. *The Strategic Significance of Southern Africa.* London: Royal United Service Institution, 1970.

SPROCAS 2. *"A People Company": Report of an Investigation into Standard Telephones and Cables (S.A.) Ltd., an Associate of I.T.T.* Johannesburg: SPROCAS, 1973.

Stadler, Alf. "Industrialization and White Politics in South Africa During the Twentieth Century." Paper delivered to African Studies Seminar, University of Witwatersrand, May 1974.

Steinhart, Edward I. "White Student Protests in South Africa: The Privileged Fight for Their Rights." *Africa Today* 19, 3 (Summer 1972) 39-54.

Stokes, R. G. "The Afrikaner Entrepreneur: Social Origins, Psychological Dispositions, and Values." Ph.D. dissertation, Duke University, 1971.

Stone, John. *Colonist or Uitlander?: A Study of the British Immigrant in South Africa.* Oxford: Clarendon Press, 1973.

Stultz, Newell M. "South African Cabinets and Ministers: Some Empirical Findings." *South Africa International* 3, 1 (July 1972).

————. "South Africa's 'Apartheid' Election of 1948 Reconsidered." *Plural Societies* (Winter 1972): 25-38.

————. "Who Goes to Parliament?" *South Africa International* 4, 1 (July 1973): 1-15.

Suzman, L. J., ed. *The Rights and Responsibilities of Universities in Contemporary Society.* Johannesburg: University of the Witwatersrand, 1974.

Synge, Richard. "Transkei: Industrial Colonialism." *Africa* (London) 4 (October 1971): 18-19.

Themba, Can. *The Will to Die.* New York: Humanities Press, 1972.

Thomas, H. J. "Faction Fights in Natal and Zululand." B.A. Thesis. Natal University, 1972.

Thomas, W. H., ed. *Labour Perspectives on South Africa.* Cape Town: David Philip, 1974.

Tinker, Hugh. "The Politics of Racialism: South Africa's Indians." *Journal of African History* 14, 3 (1973): 523-7.

Trapido, Stanley. "South Africa in a Comparative Study of Industrialization." *Journal of Development Studies* 7, 3 (April 1971): 309-20.

————. "White Conflict and Non-White Participation in the Politics of the Cape of Good Hope." Ph.D. dissertation, University of London, 1970.

Troup, Freda. *South Africa: An Historical Introduction.* London: Methuen, 1972.

Tucker, Robert C. "Apartheid Labor Laws in the Republic of South Africa: Socio-Historical Parallels with U.S. Labor Customs." *Renaissance Two* 1 (1971): 41-50.

Turner, Richard. *The Eye of the Needle: An Essay on Participatory Democracy.* Johannesburg: SPROCAS, 1972.

————. "Black Consciousness and White Liberals." *Reality* 4, 3 (July 1972): 20-22.

Turok, Ben. "South Africa: The Violent Alternative." In *The Socialist Register 1972.* Edited by Ralph Miliband and John Savile. London: The Merlin Press, 1972.

Umozurike, U. O. "International Law and Self-Determination in Namibia." *Journal of Modern African Studies* 8, 4 (December 1970): 585-603.

UNESCO. *Apartheid: Its Effect on Education, Science, Culture and Information.* Rev. ed. Paris: UNESCO, 1972.

Unger, Manfred. *Die Entwicklung der Bantu in der Republik Südafrika im Rahmen der Politik der getrennten Entwicklung.* Würzburg: 1970.

United Nations Unit On Apartheid. *Repressive Legislaton of the Republic of South Africa* (ST/PSCA/SER.A/7). New York: United Nations, 1969.

————. *Apartheid in Practice* (ST/PSCA/SER.A/9). New York: United Nations, 1969.

————. *Industrialization, Foreign Capital and Forced Labour in South Africa* (ST/PSCA/SER.A/10). New York: United Nations, 1970.

————. *Foreign Investment in the Republic of South Africa* (ST/PSCA/SER.A/11). New York: United Nations, 1970.

————. *Maltreatment and Torture of Prisoners in South Africa* (ST/PSCA/SER.A/13). New York: United Nations, 1973.

United States, House of Representatives (Subcommittee on Africa of the Committee of Foreign Affairs). *Implementation of the U.S. Arms Embargo (Against Portugal and South Africa, and Related Issues).* Washington, D.C.: U.S. Government Printing Office, 1973.

————. United States Business Involvement in Southern Africa. 3 vols. Washington, D.C.: U.S. Government Printing Office, 1972-1973.

University of London, Institute of Commonwealth Studies. *Collected Seminar Papers on the Societies of Southern Africa in the Nineteenth and Twentieth Centuries* 1, n.d.; 2, 1971: 3, 1973.

Unterhalter, Beryl. "A Content Analysis of the Essays of Black and White South African High School Pupils." *Race* 13, 3 (January 1973): 311-29.

Van den Berghe, P. "Class and Ethnicity in South Africa." In *Social Stratification in Africa.* Edited by Arthur Tuden and L. Plotnicov. New York: Free Press, 1970.

Van der Horst, Sheila T. *Progress and Retrogression in South Africa—Presidential Address.* Johannesburg: South African Institute of Race Relations, 1971.

Van der Merwe, H. W., and Welsh, D. J., eds. *Student Perspectives on South Africa.* Cape Town: David Philip, 1972.

Van der Merwe, H. W., and Kivedo, B. D. "Coloured-White Contacts and Attitudes: Some Tentative Comments on Contact Patterns and Their Implications for Race Relations." Paper presented at Fourth Congress of Association of Sociologists of Southern Africa, Roma, Lesotho, July 1973.

Van der Merwe, H. W., Ashley, M. J., Charton, N., and Huber, B. *White South African Elites: A Study of Incumbents of Top Positions in the Republic of South Africa.* Cape Town: Juta, 1974.

Van der Meulen, J. W. "Zuid-Afrika aan de vooravond van veranderingen." *Internationale Spectator* 25, (22 May 1971): 992-1004.

Van der Poel, Jean, ed. *Selections from the Smuts Papers,* vols. 5-7. Cambridge: Cambridge University Press, 1973.

Van der Post, Laurens. *A Story Like the Wind.* New York: William Morrow, 1972.

Van Heerden, F. J. "Nasional-Sosialisme as Faktor in die Suid-Afrikaanse Politiek 1933-1948." Ph.D. dissertation, University of the Orange Free State, 1972.

Van Jaarsveld, F. A. *Afrikaner Quo Vadis?* Johannesburg: Voortrekkerpers, 1971.

————. *Van Van Riebeeck Tot Verwoerd: 'n Inleiding tot die Geskiedenis van die Republiek van Suid-Afrika.* Johannesburg: Voortrekkerpers, 1971.

Van Rooyen, Jan J. *Ons Politiek van Naby.* Cape Town, 1971.

Van Wyk, F. J. "Black Consciousness—The Institute's Position as I See It. RR 120/72." Johannesburg: South African Institute of Race Relations, 1972. Mimeographed.

Verwoerd, H. F. "Die Bestryding van Armoede en die Herorganisasie van Welvaartswerk." In *Toe Witmense Nog Arm Was.* Edited by D. Joubert. Cape Town, 1972.

Visser, N. W. "South Africa: The Renaissance That Failed." Unpublished manuscript, Rhodes University, 1973.

Von Maltitz, A. A. "South African Minerals and Their Importance to World Industry." *South Africa International* 1, 4 (April 1971): 221-8.

Vosloo, Ben, and Lever, Jeffrey. "Student Outlook at Stellenbosch." *New Nation* 4 (February 1971).

Walshe, Peter. *African Nationalism in South Africa.* Johannesburg: SPROCAS, 1974.

————. *The Rise of African Nationalism in South Africa: The African National Congress 1912-1952.* Berkeley: University of California Press, 1971.

Watson, Graham. *Passing for White: A Study of Racial Assimilation in a South African School.* London: Tavistock, 1970.

Watts, H., Lett, H., and Agar Hamilton, J. "Border Port: A Study of East London, South Africa, with Special Reference to the White Population." Grahamstown: Rhodes University Institute of Social and Economic Research Occasional Paper no. 13, 1970.

Webster, Eddie. "Black Consciousness." *Dissent* 5, 1 (March-April 1974): 1-4.

Welsh, David. "The Cultural Dimension of Apartheid." *African Affairs* 71, 282 (January 1972): 35-53.

————. *The Roots of Segregation: Native Policy in Colonial Natal, 1845-1910.* Cape Town: Oxford, 1971.

————. "Truth in a Hot Climate." *Reality* 4, 6 (January 1973): 19-20.

West, Martin E. *Divided Community: A Study of Social Groups and Racial Attitudes in a South African Town.* Cape Town: A.A. Balkema, 1971.

Whisson, Michael G. *Domestic Servants: A Microcosm of the 'Race Problem' in the District of Simonstown.* Johannesburg: South African Institute of Race Relations, 1972.

————. *The Fairest Cape? An Account of the Coloured People in the District of Simonstown.* Johannesburg: South African Institute of Race Relations, 1972.

Whisson, Michael G., and Van Der Merwe, H. W., eds. *Coloured Citizenship in South Africa.* Cape Town: Abe Bailey Institute of Interracial Studies, 1972.

Wilson, Francis. "Labour Problems in South Africa." *Rhodesian Journal of Economics* 6, 4 (December 1972): 46-8.

————. *Labour in the South African Gold Mines, 1911-1969.* Cambridge: Cambridge University Press, 1972.

————. *Migrant Labour: Report to the South African Council of Churches.* Johannesburg: South African Council of Churches and SPROCAS, 1972.

Wilson, Francis, and Perrot, Dominique, eds. *Outlook on a Century: South Africa, 1870-1970.* Lovedale, S.A.: Lovedale Press and SPROCAS, 1973.

Wilson, Monica, and Thompson, Leonard, eds. *Oxford History of South Africa.* Vol. 2. Oxford: Clarendon Press; New York: Oxford University Press, 1971.

Wilson, William J. *Power, Racism, and Privilege.* New York: Macmillan, 1973.

Witton, Ron. "Australia and Apartheid: The Ties That Bind." *Australian Quarterly* 45, 2 (June 1973): 18-31.

Woldring, Klaas. "The Prospect of Federalisation in Southern Africa." *Kroniek van Afrika* 13, 2 (1973): 133-57.

Wolpe, Harold. "Industrialism and Race in South Africa." In *Race and Racialism.* Edited by S. Zubaida. London: Tavistock, 1970.

————. "Capitalism and Cheap Labour Power in South Africa: From Segregation to Apartheid." *Economy and Society* 1, 4 (November 1972): 425-56.

Worrall, Denis, ed. *South Africa: Government and Politics.* Pretoria: Van Schaik, 1971.

Young, Bruce. "Development in Zululand." *Journal of Modern African Studies* 10, 2 (July 1972): 300-4.

Zulu, A. H. "The Dilemma of the Black South African." Cape Town: University of Cape Town, 1972. Mimeographed.

Index

De Klerk, Dr. Willem, 12-13, 14, 141 n.
Delagoa Bay, 408
De la Rey, Gen. Jacobus, 6
Demographic change, in southern Africa
    region, 330-32
  migrant labor, 331-32
  refugee movement, 330-31
Development and welfare policy, recent
    changes in, 96-97
De Wet Nel, M. C., 6, 41-42
Diamonds, in Botswana, 333
Diederichs, N. J., 35
Diego Suarez, 378
Diggs Committee, 410
Diplomatic policy, South African, 390-91
"Divide and rule" strategy, 97-98
Dladla, B. I., 113, 120-121, 125, 126,
    128-30, 135-36, 217
Dobsonville, 156
Domination of Africans, means of
  by army, 229-33
  by direct violence, 226-29
  by legal-administrative machinery, 239-
    47
  by police, 233-39
Dominion party, 57-58
Douglas-Home, Sir Alec, 362-63
Dube, 156, 189
Du Preez, Peter, 45
Durban, ix, 85, 115, 121, 122, 128, 137,
    173, 184, 183, 188, 190, 193, 215,
    216, 227, 228, 252-53, 269-70,
    276, 295, 318
Durban Westville College, 269, 310
Dutch Reformed churches, 12, 59, 84, 99
Dutch refugees, 84

East Africa, refugees from 84
East London-Mdantsane, 139, 149-50,
    153, 154, 174, 183, 193, 228
Economic change
  growth of GNP, 177
  migratory labor system, 176-86
  political implications of, for Africans,
    168-200
    Black consumer power, 193-94
    Black worker power, 186-93
    international perspectives, 194-200
    rural-to-urban population transfers,
    177
  superficial, analyzed as, 207-11
Economic cooperation, between White
    subcastes, 82
Economic growth, 206-7
  British support for, 362-63
  and poverty, 363-65
  refutation of, 365-68
  theory of, 360-62
  thesis of reduced inequality and greater

    liberalism through, 349-68
  Western bloc commitment to, 367-68
Economic relations, between South Africa
    and neighboring countries, 332-35
Economist, 359
Economy, structure-functionalist analysis
    of, 373-82
Edelstein, Melville, 277, 300
Education, 42, 63, 97, 159, 310. *See also*
  Bantu education
  ideological control by, 310
  of Indian population, government pol-
    icy toward, 268-69
  KwaZulu, 115
Educational institutions, and Afrikaner
    unity, 7
Eiselen, W., 45
Ekonomiese Vokskongres (1939), 32, 34
Elections
  and shifts in political power, 52-53
  1924, 52, 53, 54
  1929 ("black peril" election), 53, 54,
    55, 57
  1934, 56
  1938, 58
  1943, 6, 8, 59
  1948, 5, 8, 53, 70, 87
    apartheid issue in, 37, 61
  1949, 62
  1953, 70
  1970, 85, 93
  1972, 68, 83
  1973 (Ciskeian), 153 n.-54 n.
  1974, x, 17, 73
Elites, modernizing, Afrikaners as, 26-27
Eloff, G., 45
Employment
  projection of, 1972-77, 177
  of racial groups, by economic sector,
    256
Enloe, Cynthia, 27
English language, African use of, 155-56
English population, 79, 83-84
  domination of business by, 91-92
  as issue in Afrikaner politics, 51-78
  view of, by Africans in Soweto, 148
English press, 92
  Nationalist hostility toward, 63-64
Ethiopia, 232
Ethiopianism, 212
Ethnic division, among Africans, govern-
    mental misreading of, 162-63
Ethnicity, in African population of Sowe-
    to, 142 n., 151-60, 211-12
  cultural, 156-57
  ideology of melting pot, 152-53
Ethnogenesis, and Afrikaner unity, 5-6
Ethos, Afrikaner, 20
Étatism, 392-94

INDEX

439

view of, by Africans in Soweto, 148
Johannesburg, ix, 150, 183, 186, 188,
    189, 193, 194, 228, 262, 299, 336
Johannesburg Africans, perceptions and
    self-perceptions of, in Soweto, 138-
    67
  attitude toward Afrikaners, 147
  attitude toward Colored population,
    147
  attitude toward English population,
    148
  attitude toward Jewish population, 148
  class perceptions of, 142
  ethnicity
    cultural, 156-57, 159-60
    homeland links, 153-56
    negative identity, 157
    political, 151-52
    Whites as reference group, 157-59
  image in relation to wider society
    lower-class model, 147-48, 148-50,
      165-66, 204
    pariah model, 146-47, 148-50
    power and class bases of, 146
  lack of homeland for, 139-40
  relocation of, 139-40
  social stratification of, 150-51
Johns, S., 340
Johnson, Dale L., 203
Johnstone, Frederick, 49
Jonathan, Chief Leabua, 343

KaDinuzulu, King Solomon, 123
Kane-Berman, J., 293
Kanye, W. S. P., 125
Katanga, 180
Kaunda, Kenneth, 408
Kazangula, 335
Khoapa, B. A., 212, 214
Khoi-Khoi, 203
Kimberley, 228
King, Martin Luther, Jr., 159, 194
Ko-ordinerende Raad van Suid-Afrikaan-
    se Vakbonde, 7
Kotzé, D. J., 13
Kruger, Paul, 6, 8
Krugerism, 31
Kunene, 334
Kuper, L., 297, 309
Kuyper, Abraham, 34-35
KwaMashu, 127, 215-16
KwaZulu Bantustan, 107-37, 196, 217,
    286, 287, 343, 344
  agricultural sector in, 111-13
  apartheid practiced in, 118
  factionalism in, 116-17
  labor organization in, 128-30
  major problems of, 110-20
    politics of inequality of central gov-

ernment, 117-19
    poverty, 111-14
    social, 116-17
    talent shortage, 115
    unemployment, 114-15
    wage levels, 115-16
  political organization, 124-28
    rural/traditional, 124-126
    urban/nontraditional, 126-28
  political processes, 120-32
  political socialization in, 120-24
  population of, 111, 192, 193
KwaZulu Executive Council, 112, 113,
    116, 124-25
KwaZulu Legislative Assembly, 116, 124-
    25

Labor
  attracted to cities by economic growth,
    178-81
  job mobility and racial interaction, 291-
    94
  migrant, 176-86
  political use of African, 134
  skilled and semiskilled, increased de-
    mand for, 179-80, 291-94
  unfree, 143-45
  urban, and unemployment in home-
    lands, 114-15
Labor movement, 89-90, 167, 186-93
  and economic change, 186-93
  legislation regulating, 210-11
  in KwaZulu Bantustan, 128-30
Labor unions
  African, 224-25
  African membership in White unions,
    187, 412
  English, 92
  KwaZulu, 128-30
Labour party, 61, 77
  in KwaZulu Bantustan, 128
  pact with National party, 52
  position on segregation, 38
  role in United Democratic Front, 70
Lagden Report, 38
Land Act (1913), 38
Landes, David, 379 n.
Langa, 228
Language, as predictor of political loyalty,
    87
Lebowa homeland, 135, 192
Legal residents, 144-45
Legassick, Martin, 48
Legum, Colin, 109, 120
Lenin, V. I., xiv
Lesotho, xiii, 171, 172, 196, 197, 378, 402
  dependence upon South Africa, 333,
    335
  intergovernmental relations with South